MUTUAL
FUND
INVESTOR'S
GUIDE 2001

MUTUAL FUND
INVESTOR'S
GUIDE 2001

KIRK KAZANJIAN

NEW YORK INSTITUTE OF FINANCE

NEW YORK • TORONTO • SYDNEY • TOKYO • SINGAPORE

ISSN 1531-4545

Printed in the United States of America

10 9 8 7 6 5 4 3 2 1

This publication is designed to provide accurate and authoritative information in regard to the subject matter covered. It is sold with the understanding that the publisher is not engaged in rendering legal, accounting, or other professional service. If legal advice or other expert assistance is required, the services of a competent professional person should be sought.

> *. . . From the Declaration of Principles jointly adopted by a Committee of the American Bar Association and a Committee of Publishers and Associations.*

Although the information and data in this book was obtained from sources believed to be reliable, neither the author, publishers, nor Value Line assumes the responsibility for its accuracy. Under no circumstances does the information in this book represent a recommendation to buy or sell stocks or funds.

All charts and data are copyrighted by Value Line Publishing, Inc.

ISBN 0-7352-0156-0

 NEW YORK INSTITUTE OF FINANCE

An Imprint of Prentice Hall Press
Paramus, NJ 07652

On the World Wide Web at http://www.phdirect.com

NYIF and NEW YORK INSTITUTE OF FINANCE are trademarks of Executive Tax Reports, Inc., used under license by Prentice Hall Direct, Inc.

To my mom and dad,
with love and admiration.

CONTENTS

Chapter 3

Index Funds—Better Than Active Management?   30

Chapter 4

Shopping at the Fund Supermarkets   39

Chapter 5

100 Powerhouse Performers for 2001   46

Chapter 6

Putting Your Portfolio Together   250

Chapter 7

The 25 Best Internet Sites for Mutual Fund Investors   267

Chapter 8

Value Line Performance Data for Some 9,000 Funds   276

FOREWORD

My task is . . . by the power of the written word . . . to make you see.

Joseph Conrad, 1897

I started this foreword with a quote from the great author and teller of sea tales, Joseph Conrad, for two reasons: One is purely selfish—he's my favorite author. The other is because Conrad, as a writer, makes the world of the sailor come alive. He helps the reader understand what it must have been like to sail across the ocean on clear days and in deadly squalls. His vivid descriptions of people, places, and things make the reader "see" what is at the heart of his characters. You aren't just told that a character acted in some way, you understand *why* the character did it. A subtle difference to some, a distinction between mediocrity and greatness to others.

While they seem quite different, I believe Kirk Kazanjian does the same thing in the *Mutual Fund Investor's Guide 2001*. Kirk does not simply throw out a bunch of numbers or give you bland, meaningless prospectus descriptions. Instead, he helps you understand the essence of mutual fund investing. Kirk quickly and succinctly makes you see what a fund is all about. You instantly know if a particular fund is right for you. But, there is more.

This book, though predominantly about mutual funds, starts out by giving you a framework with which to steer your entire portfolio. A compass, if you will allow my analogy, to guide you across the investment ocean.

And what a trip you will have! By reading this book, you will receive training by a seasoned captain. You will have his notes and Value Line's charts to follow. All that is left is for you to find the treasure that resides on the other side of the ocean in the wonderful world of mutual funds.

Do not, however, expect smooth sailing the whole way. No trip of this magnitude ever ends without some adventure. For instance, we've had several steep stock market corrections over the years. But the market has always eventually recovered and moved on to higher ground. Those investors lacking the discipline Kirk describes risk succumbing to fear and losing their course in these rough waters. Let Kirk guide you through the market's gyrations as you sail your way to investment prosperity.

Reuben Gregg Brewer
Manager of Mutual Fund Research
Value Line, Inc.

INTRODUCTION

Welcome to the *Mutual Fund Investor's Guide 2001*. This annually updated book contains everything you need for making smart decisions about investing in funds, whether you're a seasoned pro or just starting out. You'll find plenty of helpful advice for putting together a winning investment plan, including specific recommendations, model portfolios, and comprehensive performance data from the *Value Line Mutual Fund Survey*. (This information isn't found in any other book on the market today.) Plus, you'll discover 25 must-see Internet sites for investors loaded with information you can access absolutely free. It's like having the services of a trusted investment adviser at your fingertips all year long. You'll also find profiles of 100 of the most promising funds for virtually every investment objective for 2001. I call them my "Powerhouse Performers." Each one is written up in a research report that includes historical graphs and a multitude of performance data. I can tell you that when it comes to funds, there are plenty of dogs out there. Fortunately, I have done all the homework for you to uncover some real gems.

Without question, mutual funds are *the* investment of choice among today's smart consumers. In fact, figures from the Investment Company Institute, the fund industry trade association, show that one in three Americans now own shares in at least one fund. Many books have been written on the subject of fund investing, but none contain the kind of specific and timely information found in this *Guide*. It will give you all the tools you need to build a comfortable financial future for yourself and your family. By the time you have finished reading this book, you will know:

- Precisely how mutual funds work
- What to look for when choosing them
- Which specific funds should do best in the year ahead

- How to construct your own personal portfolio plan
- Ways to make even more money using your computer.

Exhaustive performance data are given for some 9,000 stock and bond funds, along with a glossary of commonly used investment terms that all fund investors should know. You'll want to refer to this valuable information again and again.

HOW TO USE THIS BOOK

▬▬ If you're brand new to fund investing, you'll want to start with Chapter 1 and work your way through the book from the beginning. Along the way, you'll learn all about how funds work, determine whether you are better off in index or actively managed funds, discover the many ways to buy and sell funds, and get all of the tools you need to put together a winning investment plan. If, on the other hand, you are a more advanced fund investor, you might want to skip around a bit. Perhaps you can start off by reading the keys to finding great funds in Chapter 2. Then you can turn to Chapter 4, to learn about the only free lunch you'll find on Wall Street. (Hint: It's available only to fund investors.) After that, you can look through the "100 Powerhouse Performers" in Chapter 5, to uncover new ideas for your portfolio in the new millennium, and be sure to check out my list of the best Internet sites for fund investors in Chapter 7. Finally, everyone should spend some time going through the exhaustive list of Value Line data in Chapter 8. This wealth of information, found in no other book, will give you historical performance information on virtually every fund imaginable. That way you can compare what you own now with the many other choices available out there.

Don't forget, I update this book each year, complete with new fund recommendations, model portfolios, Internet sites, fund manager interviews, performance data, and much more. Be on the lookout for *Mutual Fund Investor's Guide 2002* at a bookstore near you!

For now let's get started on the road to developing a mutual fund investment plan for the coming year that you can profit from for decades to come.

MUTUAL
FUND
INVESTOR'S
GUIDE 2001

1

MUTUAL FUNDS—
TODAY'S INVESTMENT
OF CHOICE

Access to the world's leading investment luminaries used to be reserved exclusively for the chosen few—those wealthy individuals with $1 million-plus portfolios. Even plain vanilla index funds were off limits to all but the largest institutions. Anyone else who wanted to participate in the fortunes of the stock market had to rely on tips from a commission-based broker, who was likely schooled in salesmanship, not investing. The only alternative was to put money in a bank, where it earned a comparatively inferior rate of interest.

How times have changed! Now, someone with just $1,000 to invest can tap into the same expertise that is available to a corporate CEO with a $20 million portfolio. This is made possible through arguably the greatest invention ever created for individual investors—mutual funds. Virtually every noted Wall Street money pro now either runs a fund of his or her own or is involved in the management of one. Therefore, it's possible for almost everyone to hire the leading brainpower in the business for a very small fee. In fact, owning funds is much cheaper and rewarding than buying stocks for most investors.

THE EXPLOSION OF MUTUAL FUNDS:
A BRIEF HISTORY

≡ Investors around the world have been pouring money into funds at a record pace since 1995, but these investment vehicles have been around much longer. The mutual fund industry traces its roots back to 1868, when the Foreign and Colonial Government Trust ("the Trust") was formed in London. This British investment company, which issued a fixed number of shares, spread its portfolio across a number of different stocks. The Trust resembled today's closed-end funds: the daily price was determined by supply and demand, instead of by the actual underlying net asset value of the securities. (Closed-end funds trade on one of the stock exchanges and must be purchased and sold through a broker.)

The first open-end fund—the kind we will be focusing on in this book—was launched in 1924, when the Massachusetts Investors Trust opened for business. It began with a $50,000 portfolio containing 45 stocks. In an open-end fund, new shares are continuously offered to the public. Shares can be sold at any time, and their prices are based on the current net asset value of the portfolio's underlying holdings. It's pretty simple to calculate a fund's net asset value. Simply add up the value of every security in the portfolio, based on the closing market price, and divide that result by the number of outstanding shares. In other words, if you have a portfolio worth $100 and you own a total of 100 shares, the net asset value per share is $1.

TOUGH BEGINNINGS

The mutual fund industry got off to a rocky start in the United States. The 1929 stock market crash, and the resulting Great Depression, scared many investors away from equities in general. These events also caused Congress to enact a series of laws regulating the securities and financial markets, in an effort to protect investors. The Securities Act of 1933, for example, required every fund sponsor to issue a prospectus describing how the portfolio would be invested. The most important law for fund investors is the Investment Company Act of 1940, which mandates that funds be priced based on the day's closing market value. It also prohibits transactions between a fund and its manager, sets up a statutory system of independent fund directors, requires funds to redeem shares upon demand, and sets out a series of rules that must be followed in the area of bookkeeping.

WHAT IS NET ASSET VALUE?

$$\text{Net Asset Value} = \frac{\text{Total Assets} - \text{Liabilities}}{\text{Number of Shares Outstanding}}$$

Mutual funds began to catch on with the American public during the 1940s and 1950s. In 1940, there were fewer than 80 funds, and their total assets were around $500 million. Two decades later, there were 160 funds with collective assets of $17 billion. Almost all of these early funds had a front-end sales load and were peddled exclusively through stockbrokers. The "load" averaged around 8 percent and served as a commission taken right off the top to compensate the broker. If you invested $100 in a fund with an 8 percent load, $8 immediately went into the broker's pocket, effectively putting only $92 to work. Even behemoth Fidelity Investments, which was formed in the 1930s, distributed its funds through brokers. That policy was changed after the brutal 1973–1974 bear market, which once again soured the public's appetite for mutual funds. In an effort to create new business, Ned Johnson, Fidelity's founder, came up with a unique idea. He introduced the first money market fund with a check-writing feature. These investments were touted as safe vehicles that offered investors easy access to their money. To keep the fund's yield as high as possible, Johnson decided to try selling it directly to the public by advertising a toll-free number in the newspapers. The strategy was so successful that he soon converted many of his stock and bond funds to "no-loads" and began offering them through this channel as well.

According to Lipper Analytical Services, there are now some 12,000 mutual funds in the United States alone—including all share classes. That's more than the number of available individual stocks. These funds' combined assets are more than $6 trillion. This amount is even more staggering when we realize that less than one decade ago, total fund assets stood at a mere $1 trillion. Throughout the mid-1990s, money from individual investors flowed into funds at a feverish pace. Most of this cash landed in stock funds, which showered investors with incredible returns, thanks to a roaring bull market. Without question, this constant stream of new money fueled the market's rise. As of mid-2000, 59 percent of total fund assets were in stocks, 17 percent were in bonds, and 24 percent were in money market funds. What's more, it's estimated that one in two Americans invests in mutual funds.

FUNDS ARE HOT

One reason funds have become so popular is that we are now being forced to invest. A generation ago, a recent graduate would go to work for a large company that promised to pay a sizable monthly pension after

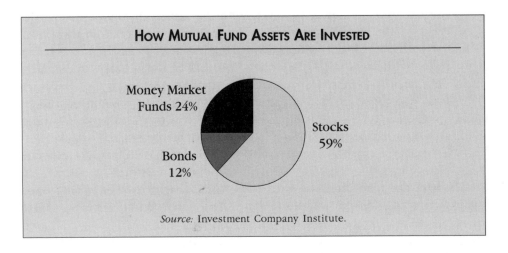

HOW MUTUAL FUND ASSETS ARE INVESTED

Money Market Funds 24%

Bonds 12%

Stocks 59%

Source: Investment Company Institute.

retirement. That pension, combined with a Social Security check, would surely provide enough income to live comfortably in the sunset years, or so people thought. For better or worse, things are much different now. Most companies, especially smaller ones, don't even have pensions. Instead, employees may be offered a chance to contribute to a retirement program such as a 401(k) or SEP-IRA, in which workers have a certain percentage of their income deducted and usually placed into a portfolio of funds. It's up to each employee to figure out how that money is invested, be it in stocks, bonds, or money market instruments. Therefore, millions of everyday folks have had to bone up on investing, since they are required to make these integral decisions about how to save for their financial future. The other changing dynamic is that most younger Americans don't believe Social Security will be around when they need it, despite the federal government's assurances. Therefore, in addition to contributing to employer-sponsored retirement plans, wise individuals are setting up investment portfolios on their own, both regular and IRAs (individual retirement accounts), to make sure they are taken care of financially when they ultimately decide to leave the workforce. The *really* smart ones invest their money through carefully selected mutual funds.

WHY YOU SHOULD INVEST IN FUNDS

There are a number of reasons why funds make so much sense for most investors. I'll begin with a few of the obvious ones: diversification, low costs, professional management, ease of buying and selling, convenience, and a mix of asset classes.

Diversification

One of the first rules of investing is: Don't put all of your eggs in one basket. That's especially true with the stock market. In today's volatile trading environment, a small disappointment from even a blue-chip company can cause its stock to get hammered severely. What's more, a constant sector rotation is going on in the market. Financial stocks may do well this quarter, but technology companies may find favor with investors in the next quarter, followed by the pharmaceuticals, and so on. If you own a well-rounded list of stocks, you increase the odds that at least a portion of your portfolio will always be in the right place at the right time. Having a large list of holdings also reduces your "specific stock risk"—the danger that a company you own will see its share price get sliced as a result of some unforeseen bad news. When you buy into a stock fund, you instantly tap into a portfolio that likely owns shares in dozens of different companies. Even the most concentrated funds usually contain at least 20 names. The same is true for bond and money market funds, which can spread their portfolios across a broad range of companies and maturities to smooth out volatility and increase overall returns. Unless you have at least a six-figure amount to invest, it would be cost-prohibitive to buy a basket of individual securities on your own. The commissions alone would kill you. When you invest in a fund, you instantly benefit from the economies of scale enjoyed by spreading these costs among a large base of shareholders. And even with a six-figure portfolio, most investors are still better off in funds. After all, when you go it alone, you're competing with the pros.

Low Costs

Every mutual fund, whether it has a sales load or not, comes with underlying management fees. These charges, expressed in the form of expense ratios, can be found near the front of every prospectus. The average expense ratio for stock funds is around 1.40 percent; for fixed-income portfolios, it is under 1 percent. If you have $1,000 in a stock fund with an expense ratio of 1.40 percent, you would pay the fund $14 a year for managing your money. The fund never sends you a bill for this charge. Instead, the fee is automatically deducted from the net asset value each day. Just think: for $14 a year (give or take a few bucks, depending on the particular fund you choose and the amount you invest), you can hire a highly educated investment expert, backed up by a team of equally smart research analysts, to make buy-and-sell decisions on your behalf.

Incidentally, I recommend that you always stick with no-load funds, especially if you're making your own investment decisions. In the pages that follow, you will be given an enormous amount of information you can use to put together a winning fund portfolio, including Chapter 5's list of 2001's "100 Powerhouse Performers." These funds were selected after doing an exhaustive amount of proprietary research. You'll notice that every one of these funds is offered on a no-load basis. You won't pay a penny to buy or sell them, so every cent of your investment dollar can work for you.

PROFESSIONAL MANAGEMENT

When you buy shares in a fund, you truly gain access to some of the sharpest minds on Wall Street. A few decades ago, this simply wasn't possible unless an investor placed a ton of money into an individually managed account. The expertise is similar, by the way, whether we're talking about actively managed funds (run by a human) or passive funds (index funds or similar offerings run solely by a computer). After all, it takes a high degree of intelligence to program a computer to properly replicate a given index in the first place. Over the past few years, I have been struck by the number of people who are convinced that they could do just as well, if not better, by choosing individual stocks on their own rather than using funds. This belief has been exacerbated by the abnormally high returns offered by index funds in the late 1990's, which led to a media storm of bashing active managers. If your attitude is "These highly paid fund managers can't beat the market, so I might as well do the stock picking on my own," think about what you're saying. You're contending that you have more brilliance and savvy than experts who spend 16 hours a day researching and watching the market. In an occasional streak of good luck, you might pick a stock that doubles or triples in a short period of time. But, as market veterans often warn, "Don't confuse brains with a bull market." When you make individual stock selections on your own, you are competing against pros who have much more experience and clout than you do.

MUTUAL FUND FEES AND EXPENSES

Two types of costs are involved in running a fund: (1) shareholder transaction expenses and (2) annual operating expenses.

1. **Shareholder transaction expenses** are fees charged directly to the investor for purchases, redemptions, or exchanges. For the most part, these expenses apply only to load funds. However, some no-load funds charge fees for early redemption, to discourage short-term trading. The following expenses can be expected:

   - *Front-end sales load.* This fee, charged at the time of purchase, compensates financial professionals for selling the fund to you. By law, this fee may not exceed 8.5 percent of the initial investment.

   - *Deferred sales charge.* Also called a "back-end load," this fee is charged at the time you sell shares in a fund. It is normally used as an alternative to a front-end load. In many funds, the deferred sales charge is reduced or eliminated over time.

   - *Redemption fee.* This is another type of back-end charge imposed for redeeming shares. It can be expressed as either a dollar amount or a percentage of the redemption price. It is occasionally imposed by no-load funds as a way of deterring short-term trading.

   - *Exchange fee.* This charge is imposed on shareholders when transferring money from one fund to another within the same family.

2. **Annual operating expenses** are the normal costs involved in operating a fund (i.e., for research, management, and equipment). Unlike transaction fees, these expenses are deducted directly from fund assets on a daily basis, instead of being billed to the investor. They are expressed as a percentage of the total net worth of the investment.

   - *Management fees.* This is what the fund's investment adviser charges for running the fund. Management fees are typically between 0.5 percent and 1 percent of assets, and ideally are reduced as the asset base increases.

   - *12b-1 fees.* This expense, named for the SEC rule that created it, is being charged by an increasing number of funds. It is used to pay for marketing, advertising, or sales costs. By law, 12b-1 fees cannot exceed 0.75 percent of net assets.

   - *Other expenses.* These include special charges for transfer agency and for accounting costs that are not included in any of the above expenses.

EASE OF BUYING AND SELLING

Mutual fund shares are highly liquid. With a single phone call, you can buy or sell as many shares as you want, and get a check for your proceeds in as little time as one day (especially if you place your transaction through a discount broker). All shares are either purchased or redeemed at their net asset value at the close of business on the day you place your order. It's true that most individual stocks and bonds are equally liquid, but you have to pay a commission when you convert these other instruments into cash. When you buy no-load funds, there is no fee on the way in or out.

CONVENIENCE

Mutual funds provide a clear element of convenience. Chances are you have a day job that doesn't involve selecting and monitoring investments. Maybe you're retired and spend your days improving your golf score or enjoying the great outdoors. In either case, you probably don't have a lot of time to research new investment ideas, follow the market, and continually analyze every one of your holdings. Investing truly is a full-time job, and an array of recordkeeping is involved when purchasing individual securities. When you buy a fund, the fund family or discount broker reduces your work to a minimum by doing most of this recordkeeping for you. Then, at tax-filing time, you only have to deal with a single 1099 form that gives you all the information you need to keep Uncle Sam satisfied. Most funds will gladly reinvest your dividends and capital gains distributions automatically, allowing you to profit from the magic of compounding. Often, you can get a money market fund from your discount broker or fund company as well with check-writing privileges and the ability to make exchanges from one fund to another.

MIX OF ASSET CLASSES

Finally, funds allow you to easily target specific asset classes, which is increasingly important in the current market environment. Here's what I mean: In a broad sense, you have various types of securities—stocks, bonds, and cash—available for investment. But there are subcategories within each of these classes. On the equity side, for example, you have small caps, mid caps, large caps, and international securities. Informed investors have exposure to all of these areas in their portfolios. In fact,

---

WHAT'S A MARKET CAP?

A stock's market capitalization is calculated by multiplying the number of outstanding shares by the price per share. For example, a stock trading for $1 with 10 million shares outstanding would have a market capitalization, or market cap, of $10 million. Stocks are categorized into four primary classes and have the following general guidelines:

1. **Micro-Cap.** Stocks with market capitalizations of $0 to $500 million.
2. **Small-Cap.** Stocks with market capitalizations of $500 million to $1.5 billion.
3. **Mid-Cap.** Stocks with market capitalizations of $1.5 billion to $5 billion.
4. **Large-Cap.** Stocks with market capitalizations of $5 billion or more.

---

research has shown that having the right asset-class mix is even more important than security selection in determining long-term investment performance. It's virtually impossible to target specific asset classes like this through individual security selection. We'll delve deeper into the subject of asset allocation, and the categories that should be represented in your portfolio, in Chapter 6.

THE DRAWBACKS

Nothing in life is perfect, and that includes mutual funds. As wonderful as they are, funds do have a few shortfalls. For example, despite being closely regulated, funds still aren't held to high standards for disclosure. They don't have to tell you how much fund managers make, and only twice a year must they give you a list of the securities they own. Similarly, because you are hiring a manager to make all of your investment decisions, you have no say as to which stocks or bonds you own. (Some people hate letting go of that control.) Furthermore, although diversification is designed to give you smooth and respectable returns over the long haul, it prevents you from scoring any phenomenal home runs. If you own only one stock and it goes up 1,000 percent, you will become rich. But if you have a portfolio of 200 names and that same stock goes up 1,000 percent, it won't have much of an impact. Keep in mind that stocks have the same chance of falling 100 percent as they do of rising 1,000 percent. This is why diversification makes so much sense. Even with modest returns of 8 to 10 percent a year, if you start early, save religiously, and use excellent funds, I'm confident you will wind up with more money than you know what to do with.

The *biggest* disadvantage to owning funds rather than individual securities relates to taxes. By law, funds must pay out a majority of their built-in investment profits to shareholders at the end of each year. These profits are distributed in the form of dividends and capital gains. When you own individual securities, you don't have to pay taxes on any capital gains until you redeem your shares. With funds, you may incur a tax liability even if you hold on. This drawback has received a great deal of attention since Congress lowered the maximum rate for long-term gains to 20 percent. With funds, you don't always know in advance what percentage of your gains will be counted as long- or short-term, because some portfolio managers trade more frequently than others.

I look at the whole issue of taxation in two ways. First, there are steps you can take to reduce your tax liability. One remedy is to buy tax-efficient funds. You can find out how tax-efficient a fund is by examining its past distribution record. Generally speaking, funds with low turnover rates are more tax-efficient than those which do a lot of trading. A fund's annual turnover rate can be found in the prospectus. Low-turnover funds generally hold on to their positions longer, allowing the gains to be carried on for years. Funds don't have to distribute gains to you until they have been realized, so low turnover usually, but not always, translates into greater tax efficiency. You can also buy index funds, which are inherently tax-efficient because they rarely do any trading among positions.

Second, you will eventually have to pay taxes on your gains anyway. Holding on and building them up only delays the inevitable. You get to add any fund distributions to the cost basis of your shares, which will reduce your capital gains liability when you finally sell out. So, although I would rather not share my profits with the IRS until I absolutely have to, I don't think the potential tax consequences should prevent investors from getting involved with funds. Taxes are a major issue in roaring bull markets, but, even then, they can be kept under control with proper planning and good fund selection.

Some Notes on Taxes

Gains are typically paid out at the end of each calendar year, so you should avoid purchasing shares of a fund in December, until it has paid out its annual distribution. Otherwise, you will be taxed on the entire gain, even though you might have owned the fund for only a few weeks. Also, statistics show that 70 percent of all fund assets are in tax-deferred retirement accounts anyway. (You don't have to worry about taxes until you make withdrawals from such accounts.) Therefore, in most cases, the one major argument against fund ownership doesn't even apply. For more information on the taxation of mutual funds, request Publications 550 (Investment Income and Expenses), 551 (Basis of Assets), and 564 (Mutual Fund Distributions) from the Internal Revenue Service. To get them, call (800) TAX-FORM, or visit www.irs.gov.

MAKING YOUR INITIAL INVESTMENT

≡ In Chapter 2, I will give you guidance on selecting individual funds. For now, let's assume you already have your list of fund choices from Chapter 5 and are ready to make an investment. Where do you go from here? Your first step is to order a prospectus, annual report, and application from the fund. Simply dial the toll-free number listed for the fund in Chapters 5 and 8, and ask for the information you need. Once you have the prospectus and report in hand, be sure to look them over, paying close attention to what really matters. For example, in the prospectus, you'll want to find out what the fund's expense ratio is. (See the box for more on the various fees and expenses charged by funds.) You'll also want to learn about the manager's background, how long he or she has been at the fund, the types of investments he or she is allowed to buy, and the minimum amount required for initial and subsequent investments. Prospectuses are typically thick documents, full of incomprehensible legalese. Fortunately, the Securities and Exchange Commission (SEC) passed a "plain English" rule in 1998, requiring fund companies to use, whenever possible, common words, short sentences, and tables or bullet lists for complex material. They also must refrain from using highly technical legal jargon and multiple negatives.

Next, look through the annual report and read the list of specific securities in the portfolio. Examine whether the fund is properly diversified

UNDERSTANDING THE EXPENSE RATIO

The following table is similar to an outline of a fund's various expenses, found in every fund prospectus:

Annual Portfolio Operating Expenses:

Management and Administrative Expenses	0.50%
Investment Advisory Expenses	0.25%
12b-1 Marketing Fees	0.25%
Other Expenses	None
Total Operating Expenses (Expense Ratio)	**1.00%**

The operating expenses for each fund will be different. In this example, the fund's total expense ratio is 1%, or $10 per $1,000 of assets.

and whether it owns the kinds of investments you would expect it to. For example, if it's a small-cap fund and you find IBM among its list of holdings, you know something is wrong. By the same token, if it's supposed to be a large-cap, blue-chip fund, and you've never heard of any of the holdings, that should also trigger an alarm. This caution also applies if you are trying to determine how to invest your 401(k) money. You are normally given a list of at least a dozen funds to choose from. Demand a prospectus and report for each one, so you can make an informed decision about where to put your money.

After you have this information and can determine whether a particular fund is right for you (more help with this is on the way), you are then ready to make an investment. You can do it the traditional way: fill out the application that comes with your material, and mail a check directly to the fund. Or, you can purchase your shares through one of the major discount brokers, including Charles Schwab, Jack White & Co., Fidelity Investments, and Waterhouse Securities. I highly recommend the latter method, especially if the funds you are considering are part of the broker's no-load, no-transaction-fee (NTF) programs. Chapter 4, which is devoted to these virtual fund supermarkets, will show you how to use them most effectively.

HOW TO READ THE NEWSPAPER FUND TABLES

Mutual Funds

Name	NAV	Net Chg	YTD % Ret
WonderFund	7.24	−.03	+2.3
BestFund	10.04	+.13	+5.8
TechFund	8.54	−.01	+7.8
BondFund	3.32	+.22	+1.5

1. This is the name of the fund. In some papers, the listing begins with the name of the fund family in bold, with each individual fund printed below it.

2. This is the fund's net asset value (NAV).

3. This is the difference between the closing NAV price today versus yesterday.

4. This is the fund's year-to-date total return, expressed as a percentage.

KEEPING TRACK OF YOUR HOLDINGS

After buying your funds, you'll want to keep track of how they perform on a regular basis. Notice I said *regular,* not *daily.* I would argue that once a quarter will suffice. What you are looking for is how your funds compare to their peers. In other words, *don't* judge a bond fund next to the S&P 500. *Do* compare a small-cap fund to the Russell 2000 index, which is the benchmark for small-cap stocks. Find out whether your funds are keeping up with the averages. Ideally, your funds should be running ahead of them. If not, you must find out why. Is the manager just having a bad quarter? Is the fund overconcentrated in a lagging sector? Has the fund's manager changed? Have assets bloated the portfolio to the point where the fund is no longer nimble? Once you've answered these questions, you can determine whether to hang on or move on. I don't recommend selling a fund unless it has underperformed for at least 18 months. I've chosen this particular time line for two reasons: (1) you will be able to take advantage of the maximum 20 percent capital gain rule when you sell out, and (2) more important, all managers underperform at one point or another. Funds are designed to be a long-term investment. What's 18 months when your time horizon might be 20, 30, or even 40 years or more? Giving a good manager 18 months to get back into shape is often a wise investment decision.

2
FINDING THE FUND THAT'S RIGHT FOR YOU

Given that there are thousands of stock, bond, and money market funds currently available, finding the true gems in this enormous mix is a daunting task. After all, funds now outnumber stocks on all of the major exchanges combined. Not to worry. This chapter will give you some guidelines to help you narrow down the field of choices and make smart decisions about which funds are best for you.

This chapter offers several tips to keep in mind when you are scouring the field of contenders. These are the principles I adhere to with my own portfolio, and they were the basis for my Powerhouse Performers selections. I have broken down the characteristics to look for in each asset class—namely, stocks, bonds, and money market funds. Traits you *must* find in stock funds don't necessarily apply for bond funds, and vice versa.

ALWAYS REMEMBER: GO NO-LOAD

═══ The overriding rule you should adhere to, regardless of which type of fund you buy, is: *Always* stick with no-loads. There is no reason, in my opinion, to ever pay a sales commission to purchase or sell a fund you have selected on your own. I have nothing against the folks who peddle load funds. They're entitled to make a living. But that commission comes out of your pocket and goes into theirs. If you're making the selections on your own, there is no reason to pay them. Besides, research by several independent organizations shows that load funds as a group actually perform *worse* than their no-load counterparts. When you buy a load fund, not only is some of your principal immediately wiped away, but you risk poor performance to boot.

15

Without question, there are some fantastic load funds. Among my good friends are several pristine managers who run only funds that carry sales charges. Nevertheless, for every terrific load fund they might show me, I can almost always point to an equally fine no-load alternative.

So, repeat after me: "I will *never* pay a load to buy or sell a fund that I have selected on my own." By following this rule, you may cut in half the total number of funds you have to sift through. See how much easier I've already made the job of analyzing funds—and we haven't even delved into the good stuff yet!

STOCK FUND SELECTION

Let's begin with the process of finding equity funds. This is the asset class that requires the most analytical work on your part, because there are so many variables to consider. Remember, a mutual fund is nothing more than one large portfolio with the collective assets (stocks and other securities) of hundreds or even thousands of shareholders. You are paying for the manager's expertise in selecting the right investments for the portfolio. Therefore, the first thing to keep in mind when hunting for a stock fund is that *the manager is everything*.

PROVEN MANAGEMENT

In my opinion, you want a manager with a proven track record of beating his or her peers for at least five years—the longer the better. The manager doesn't necessarily have to be at a particular fund for five years. Some of the best investments available are new funds run by experienced managers who have a long history of outperformance. Tom Marsico is a good example. His Marsico Focus Fund, one my "100 Powerhouse Performers," has been around only since the beginning of 1998. However, Marsico spent almost a decade running the Janus Twenty fund, and he racked up a tremendous record. While I can't go back five years to see how Marsico Focus Fund has performed, I can evaluate manager Tom Marsico's record for a much longer period.

Some people fall into the trap of buying funds after reading an ad or article, without checking whether the manager who posted the touted numbers is still in place. In many cases, the manager has moved on. Make sure the manager of a fund you are considering has at least a five-year track record.

If necessary, call and ask the fund. If you're told the manager has been at the fund for a shorter period of time, ask which fund he or she managed before that. If the answer is "only private accounts," demand to see the manager's performance record going back as far as possible. If you're told the manager just got out of school, move on to another selection.

A Record of Outperformance

A famous line appears in every fund advertisement and prospectus: "Past performance is no guarantee of future results." This is absolutely true. Just

FUND MANAGERS: AN UP-CLOSE LOOK

What exactly happens to your hard-earned money after you send it to your favorite fund? To whom are you entrusting your financial future, and what do these folks do with your money? Beyond that, what does it take to become a fund manager? Brains, good looks, financial savvy, luck, good genes, an Ivy League education, or all of the above?

First, when most funds get your money, they place it with a custodian, like a bank, for safekeeping. Then the fund manager uses it to buy additional securities for the portfolio, based on the rules of the prospectus. (In other words, if it's a stock portfolio, the manager will buy stocks. If it's a fixed-income fund, bonds will most likely be added.)

The background of each fund manager is quite different. Some received degrees from prestigious universities, earned MBAs, and have a family pedigree of investment genius. Others are high school graduates who happened to be in the right place at the right time. I have found that no one trait tells you up front whether a fund manager is going to be a brilliant stock picker, but it is certainly encouraging to come across someone with good educational credentials and a pristine performance record to boot.

Also, the most successful managers remain true to their discipline. In other words, if they use value techniques, they never stray into growth stocks just because value happens to be temporarily out of favor. And, perhaps most importantly, great managers have a real passion for what they do.

because a manager has been beating the market for the past five years doesn't mean he or she will continue to do so during the next five. But past performance is the only indicator of what the future might hold. It tells you what kind of ability a manager has. If the record shows his or her fund continually lags the market, there is no reason to believe that pattern will change anytime soon. On the other hand, if you find a manager who hits the lights out year after year, you know something is going right. Performance in sports is similar. If a certain player can be relied on for continually scoring, you expect that level of play during every game. Steady performance sets other standards as well. If you're a good driver with a track record of avoiding accidents, your insurance company will reduce the amount of your premium. If you're applying for a loan and have a clean credit report, you'll probably be approved. The lender will check your previous credit history to evaluate whether you're a good risk for the future. So, despite what the SEC-mandated warning tells us, a manager's past performance is our only indication of the future results we can expect. The returns from each fund vary, but we can determine that the manager has a demonstrated trend of outperformance.

When I started telling you how to evaluate managers, I said to make sure they had a record of besting *their peers*. I didn't say besting *the S&P 500 index,* which is the benchmark most media sources and investment advisers refer to. The S&P 500 is a market-weighted index composed primarily of large-cap stocks. Broad market conditions affect all stocks (i.e., when one index goes up, the rest usually follow), but, during certain periods, small-caps and mid-caps can perform much differently than their large-cap brethren. Consider what's been going on with U.S. stocks since 1995. Large-cap stocks, as a group, have far outshined small-caps. Therefore, if you compared a small-cap fund to the S&P 500, you might conclude that the manager fell asleep at the wheel. Instead, you must stack like against like. Large-cap funds should be evaluated next to the S&P 500, which is an appropriate benchmark. Small-cap funds, however, are better compared to the Russell 2000. You also need to check how funds compare to their peers in the same category. Lipper Analytical maintains "category" indexes that are published regularly in the mutual fund section of *The Wall Street Journal.* For a quick feel for how a fund has stacked up against its peers, look at its overall Value Line rank, included as part of the performance data in Chapter 8. This number takes both performance and risk into consideration. On a scale of 1 through 5, look for a fund ranked 1 or 2. A higher number may mean something is wrong. (The

Value Line rank is based on performance over a five-year period, so make sure the manager who achieved it is still at the helm. If not, every performance statistic available, including Value Line's, is worthless as a predictor for how the fund might do in the future.)

Reasonable Expense Ratio

Up to this point, we have talked exclusively about evaluating actively managed funds. Let's review the parameters for selecting stock index funds. Because these investments are run by a computer, issues concerning management and performance are less important. After all, an index fund, by definition, can't beat its benchmark. Therefore, a key factor to look for in an index fund is its expense ratio. The lower, the better. The two Vanguard index funds in my "100 Powerhouse Performers" have expense ratios that are among the lowest in the industry. As a result, they have managed to slightly outperform the competition. All other things being equal, a low expense ratio is the most important thing to consider when searching for index funds.

Now let's turn to actively managed funds. I prefer low expense ratios here too, but I'm willing to pay a bit more for performance. If a manager makes money for me, I'm not going to quibble over the expense ratio. Plenty of funds have low expense ratios and horrible track records. I don't want to own any of them! On the other hand, there are funds with above-average costs that whip the socks off the competition. My general rule is: Look for stock funds with expense ratios of less than 1.5 percent. If we're talking about large-cap U.S. stocks, that number should be even lower. When the topic is international equity funds, the expense ratio often reaches toward 2 percent, because of the added cost of researching foreign securities. The lower, the better; but don't avoid a quality manager because of expenses alone.

Low Turnover

Earlier, we discussed how low turnover often helps to reduce year-end capital gains distributions and keeps your tax liability down. But there's another reason to favor low-turnover funds. Each time a manager buys or sells a stock in the portfolio, a trading commission must be paid, and that fee is *not* reflected in the fund's expense ratio. Excessive trading can shave several percentage points off a fund's annual performance.

I have also found that low-turnover funds tend to do better over time because buy-and-hold investors usually make more money in stocks than do frequent traders. If you don't believe me, just ask a guy named Warren Buffett. Although it has stumbled recently, one of the most successful funds in history is the Sequoia Fund, which has a mere 4 percent annual turnover. Sequoia manager Bill Ruane adheres to Buffett's teachings in running the portfolio, and the fund's largest holding is Buffett's Berkshire Hathaway. Unfortunately, Sequoia has long been closed to new investors, which is why it's not one of my "100 Powerhouse Performers." Contrast Sequoia with one of the worst performing funds over the past five years, American Heritage, which checks in with an annualized return of −12.13 percent (compared to +24.08 percent for the S&P 500). American Heritage manager Heiko Theime turns over his portfolio 1,100 percent a year. This doesn't mean all high-turnover funds are bad, but less frequent trading seems to be a huge advantage.

MANAGEABLE ASSET BASE

Is it possible for a mutual fund portfolio to grow too large? That's a debatable question that still hasn't been decisively answered. There are plenty of tiny funds (in terms of asset size) that have been dismal performers for years. At the same time, a number of very large funds offer excellent returns. At some point, size does seem to become an issue for funds, especially those investing in small-cap stocks. Several reasons can be offered. To begin with, the more money a fund attracts, the more stocks a manager normally has to buy. Each time another name is added, the performance punch provided by the biggest winners is diluted. As a portfolio grows in size, the research efforts get severely squeezed. I don't know any managers who can get to intimately know hundreds of different companies, while staying on top of every new development. It isn't humanly possible.

An even greater problem for small-cap funds is liquidity. Many companies in this universe have market capitalizations (market price multiplied by the number of shares outstanding) of less than $100 million. Diversified funds, by law, cannot have an ownership position of more than 5 percent in any one company, so a $1 billion small-cap fund will have to own a large number of names to meet this requirement. In addition, small-cap stocks tend to be less liquid than their larger counterparts. If a fund manager holds a significant position in any one company, it may be difficult for the fund to get out without severely lowering the share price—if buyers can even be found. Fidelity Investments, the fund giant, apparently concurs that, at some point, fund size is an issue. In 1997, the company closed its $100 billion flagship Magellan Fund to new investors, after years of subpar performance. Then, in 1998, Fidelity shut the doors to its Contrafund and Low-Priced Stock funds, which also began to experience floundering returns after reaching assets of $30 billion and $10 billion, respectively.

My belief is that large-cap funds start to lose their ability to be effective after hitting around $5 billion in assets. However, for small-cap funds, that cutoff amount is much less. I grow uncomfortable when a small-cap fund gets larger than $500 million. I put it on close watch after it hits the $1 billion mark, and I almost always sell it by the time it gets up to $2 billion. I am convinced that small-cap funds with assets greater than $1 billion, and certainly above $2 billion, can provide shareholders with little more than average performance at best, because of the severe limitations placed on the manager. Almost every small-cap fund I have analyzed that is larger than $2 billion has been forced to change its focus from small-cap companies to either mid-cap or large-cap companies, which defeats the purpose of buying the fund in the first place.

Below small-caps is a relatively new category called micro-caps. In terms of market capitalization, these are the tiniest stocks available to investors. Some of these companies could have capitalizations as low as $10 million. I would avoid any micro-cap fund larger than $300 million in assets; the smaller the better. As for mid-cap funds, I think the $2 billion mark is about as high as I would want a fund in this category to go because, again, there are liquidity issues.

Tax-Efficiency

I won't cover the whole issue of mutual funds and taxes again, other than to remind you that funds distribute taxable gains at the end of each year. You should favor funds that try to keep distributions to an absolute minimum when investing for a taxable account. In retirement plans, this isn't an issue because all distributions are tax-deferred anyway. Low-turnover funds generally have the highest tax efficiency.

Affordable Investment Requirement

The final item to check, when evaluating stock funds, is the minimum investment amount needed to open an account. Although the average fund requires around $2,500, some let you in for as little as $100, and others make you pony up at least $1 million. You should also check the fund's minimum amount for additional contributions, especially if you want to set up a dollar-cost averaging program. Dollar-cost averaging calls for adding a set amount of money to your favorite funds on a regular basis, which enables you to take advantage of market fluctuations. I'll tell you more about this technique in Chapter 6, when we discuss how to structure your personal portfolio.

THE QUANTITATIVE VARIABLES

≡ In addition to these more fundamental characteristics, I also take a look at a slew of quantitative statistics for each fund. This analysis can be quite complex, and well beyond the means of most individual investors. The two numbers you should pay attention to are *alpha* and *beta*. To get these figures, you'll need to use one of the more advanced fund screening tools on the market today, such as the Value Line Mutual Fund Survey. (Note that beta is provided for each of the "Powerhouse 100" funds in this book.)

In essence, alpha tells you how much value the manager has added to performance, outside of just being in the market. In other words, when the overall market goes up, so do most stock funds. Alpha tells you how much of a fund's return was due to market forces versus stock picking brilliance on the part of the manager. The higher the alpha relative to the market, the better.

Beta gives you an idea of how volatile a fund is compared to the general market. For instance, the S&P 500 has a beta of 1. A fund with a beta below 1 is less volatile than the S&P, while a fund with a higher beta will tend to be much riskier. Therefore, you should expect funds with high betas to go up more than the market in rising periods, and down more when stocks fall.

As an individual investor, beta will likely prove to be a much more useful number. If you want to temper the volatility of your portfolio, look for funds with a low beta. Similarly, if you're considering a fund with stellar returns but an extremely high beta, you should expect some wild and bumpy rides over time. In a perfect world, every fund you buy would have a rare combination of high performance with a low relative beta. And if the same funds had high alphas too, you'd really be on to something!

BOND FUNDS

▤ What should you look for when choosing a bond or fixed-income fund? Think of buying bonds as being the same as lending money to a company or a government. As a lender, you are paid a set interest rate, usually between 3 and 8 percent today, depending on the credit quality of the issuer. Short-term bonds are safer and fluctuate less, but they come with a lower yield. Long-term bonds pay more but are highly volatile, especially in times of rising interest rates. Bonds are most suitable for investors seeking to generate income in their portfolios. They can also serve as an added form of diversification, if you want to move away from stocks. When evaluating bond funds, look for low expense ratios, credit quality, and favorable maturities.

LOW EXPENSE RATIOS

Choosing bonds for a portfolio doesn't take nearly as much analysis as is required for stocks. Therefore, you should expect to pay the manager of a bond fund less than a manager who picks stocks. As a result, all other things being equal, favor bond funds with the lowest expense ratios. Yields today are relatively low to begin with, and high management fees can quickly eat up your overall returns. If you're investing in short-term Treasuries, for example, the portfolio might be expected to throw off 6 percent a year in dividends and appreciation. If you're paying 1 percent of that for expenses, your return instantly drops to 5 percent. Look for bond funds with annual expenses below 0.5 percent and never pay higher than 1 percent of assets. Depending on your needs, you might also consider buying bonds directly from a discount broker, especially if you plan to hold on through maturity. In that way, you'll avoid paying management fees altogether. (The one exception, which I am about to get to, is high-yield or "junk" bonds. Because these are so risky, I think you're better off buying them through a fund.)

CREDIT QUALITY

It's pretty much a given that the higher the yield offered by a bond fund, the lower the credit quality of the securities in the portfolio. This stands to reason; high-risk companies are forced to pay a premium to borrow money. If you're determined to invest in high-yield bonds, the best way to do it is through a fund. Diversify widely in this area of the market, especially if it looks like the economy could be slowing down or even heading into a recession. Before getting in, understand that if you buy a portfolio of low credit quality, you can expect a heightened degree of volatility, similar to what you would get from a typical stock fund.

FAVORABLE MATURITIES

Bond funds have an inverse relationship to interest rates. As rates rise, bond prices fall. The opposite is also true. If this doesn't make sense at first glance, let me illustrate why this relationship exists. If you buy a bond today at par, or $1,000, offering a 6 percent yield, and tomorrow interest rates rise to 6.2 percent, I'm certainly not going to pay you $1,000 to buy that 6 percent bond. The value of the bond must fall, to compensate for the higher rate I can get on new issues. If I give you only $950 for that $1,000 bond, the 6 percent yield is suddenly worth more: I'm earning 6 percent annually on $950, which translates into an effective yield of 6.3 percent. The point here is: The longer the maturity on a bond or bond fund, the more interest rate risk you take. If you'll need your money in less than two years, by all means buy only short-term bond funds. In today's low-interest-rate environment, where the chances are that rates will go up before they go down much more, I think it makes sense to favor short-term and intermediate-term maturities, even if you have a long investment horizon. In addition to short-term bond and Treasury funds, you might also consider Ginnie Maes (GNMAs, or Government National Mortgage Association bonds), which are mortgage-backed securities with intermediate-term maturities.

MONEY MARKET FUNDS

▄▄▄ With bank certificates of deposit and savings passbooks offering such paltry interest rates these days, you would be wise to consider putting your liquid cash into a carefully selected money market fund. Almost every major fund family, broker, and bank has at least one to choose from. You can select from regular taxable funds, U.S. government funds (which are often exempt from state taxes), and municipal funds (which may be exempt from both state and federal taxes but offer a much lower yield). Money market portfolios are comprised primarily of short-term bonds and other cash-equivalent instruments, and are designed to offer higher returns while maintaining a steady per-share net asset value of $1. Current yields range from around 2 percent for municipal funds to 5.5 percent for taxable accounts. Unlike traditional bank accounts these funds are not insured by the government, but they have historically been just as safe.

QUALITY COMPANIES

How do you choose a money market fund? For one thing, because money market deposits aren't insured, invest in funds sponsored by companies of integrity. You probably can't go wrong with any of the major brokers or recognized fund families. The reason that's important is this: Only twice in recent memory have credit defaults threatened to push a money market fund's net asset value below the magic $1 level. In both cases, the fund management company stepped in and made up the difference, preventing this from happening. Big firms know that letting their money market funds dip under $1 would do irreparable harm; clients would fear for the safety of the entire organization. Therefore, they simply won't let it happen.

HIGH YIELD

Do some research to find the fund with the highest yield. Because there isn't much wiggle room with the securities in a portfolio, funds with the lowest operating expenses almost always have the highest yields. Funds at the top of the yield list often waive some or all of their management fees to attract new assets. It's up to you to keep an eye on the date when those fees kick back in, so you can move to another fund if the yield becomes less competitive. You can find the highest yielding funds on a regular basis in publications like *The Wall Street Journal* or *Barron's,* and by visiting the

IBC Financial Data Internet site at www.ibcdata.com (a profile of the IBC site is given in Chapter 7).

CONVENIENCE

Because money market funds are generally used as short-term parking places, you want those that give you easy access. Most funds offer some kind of check-writing feature, but look at the rules for this very closely. A few funds cap the number of checks you can write each month; others impose a minimum amount ($500 or more) on each check. Some funds offer ATM card access to your account and other perks that make them more like regular bank checking accounts. You'll normally find that the more perks you are offered, the lower the yield. But that's not always the case, so be sure to shop around.

SELL STRATEGY

Up to this point, the sole focus of this chapter has been on what to look for when deciding to *buy* a fund. It's equally important to know when to *sell*. Here are several good reasons for getting rid of one fund and replacing it with another.

- **A new manager arrives.** If the manager of a fund you own moves on, you should too, unless he or she is replaced by someone whose track record you admire just as much.

- **A better fund comes along.** If you stumble across a fund that's even more attractive than the one you currently own, it might make sense to switch, especially if the new fund is run by a seasoned manager.

- **You need the money.** This is a no-brainer reason. If you're saving money for a long-term goal such as retirement, you will have to sell your fund when your day of need ultimately arrives.

- **Expenses are too high.** Occasionally, funds will actually *raise* the expense ratio, usually for a nonsensical reason. If that happens with your fund, get out.

- **You spot underperformance.** Every manager goes through bad periods. I think it's reasonable to give managers 18 months to get their acts together. If they are still underperforming their peers and comparative benchmarks after that, they probably should get the boot.

- **Tax efficiency is missing.** If you're investing your money in a taxable account and the year-end distributions are unreasonably high, it might be wise to switch into a more tax-efficient fund.

- **Asset allocation is skewed.** We'll get into asset allocation in Chapter 6. Suffice it to say, if the particular fund you own no longer fits your desired asset mix, it's time to move on. (In other words, if you need to reduce your overall exposure to stocks, you may have to trade a stock fund for a bond fund to get things into balance.)

- **Style drifts occur.** If you bought a small-cap fund that has grown so large it now concentrates on mid-cap stocks, you may want to replace it with a true small-cap offering. Alternatively, if a manager who used to concentrate on value stocks suddenly turns into a growth investor, see the move as a red flag that something's wrong.

- **The fund has become too big.** As a general rule, funds with comparatively tiny asset bases have the potential to perform better than larger ones. This is especially true in the small-cap area. You should consider selling micro-cap funds if assets grow much past $500 million, small-caps after $1 billion, mid-caps after $2 billion, and *any* fund bigger than $5 billion. There are always exceptions to this rule, but these are good guidelines.

- **You own too many funds.** If you have a tendency to fall in love with funds, you might want to do some housecleaning. No matter how much money you have to invest, you probably don't need to own more than 10 to 15 funds. If you're above that limit, consider cutting back.

THE SEVEN DEADLY SINS OF MUTUAL FUND INVESTING

1. BUYING LAST YEAR'S HOT PERFORMER

Many investors falsely believe that buying the fund that did best during the previous year is a smart move. They figure the manager will continue to post the same incredible numbers, and they don't want to miss the ride. The sad truth is: Time and time again, one year's winner turns into the next year's dog. Among the many reasons for this reversal, "star managers" tend to get inundated with new cash, which can disrupt the portfolio and hurt existing shareholders.

2. TIMING THE MARKET

This is clearly a loser's game. I personally know many of the top names on Wall Street, and can tell you that *no one* is able to *consistently* forecast the direction of the market. That's why it pays to stick with your strategy and stay fully invested at all times. In the 1980s, the annual return on stocks in the S&P 500 index was 17.6 percent. During that period, if you were in cash on the top ten trading days, your return dropped to 12.6 percent. Had you been on the sidelines for the 20 best days, you earned only 9.3 percent. And if you missed the 30 biggest advancing sessions, your return plummeted to 6.5 percent. Especially when it comes to stocks, not being fully invested is costly. It would be great to avoid major market declines and bear markets. Unfortunately, this cannot be done with any degree of accuracy.

3. BLINDLY FOLLOWING THE STARS

Based on all of the fund advertising that's out there today, you might think a fund with four or five stars from a rating service like Morningstar is a surefire winner. The truth is, even the president of Morningstar will tell you that the company's rating system is far from perfect, and that picking a fund solely because of the number of stars it has been given is a loser's game. The Morningstar system is based on risk-adjusted past performance, which has very little predictive value. The manager who earned the stars may no longer be there. Think in terms of buying *managers,* not *funds,* and never rely exclusively on a simplistic rating system for advice, especially without doing further research on your own. You might build a lousy portfolio by buying only five-star funds.

4. PURCHASING FUNDS, NOT MANAGERS

Looking at a fund's track record is not enough. Some of the best-performing funds are those that have been around for just a few years but are spearheaded by veteran managers who have outstanding long-term records. New funds run by seasoned talent are some of my favorites. I am always on the lookout for them. Good managers tend to get a lot of money sent their way, which can bloat their portfolios and hamper performance. When these luminaries launch a new fund, they're able to start with a clean slate. Take advantage of their talents while the fund is still small and nimble.

5. FALLING FOR THE MEDIA'S "FUND DARLING OF THE MONTH"

Members of the media are extremely short-term oriented. I should know. I used to be a television news reporter. The truth is, the mainstream press usually won't feature a fund until it is poised to underperform. Here's why: They wait until a fund builds a hot short-term performance record, then they do a big write-up on it. Fresh money flows in, and the portfolio manager gets overwhelmed with new cash and underwhelmed with places to put it. As a result, performance usually plummets. It can take years for that situation to reverse itself.

6. FOCUSING ON QUANTITY INSTEAD OF QUALITY

It's a common belief that by simply owning eight or ten different funds, an investor is properly diversified. Unfortunately, that kind of portfolio may not be diversified at all. The reason: Funds with similar investment objectives often hold the same stocks. For example, suppose you own ten different aggressive growth funds. Your diversification is very limited because you are exposed to only one area of the market. Without question, asset allocation decisions are a critical starting point for constructing a well-rounded investment plan.

7. TAKING YOUR EYE OFF THE BALL

Investors often think they can buy a great fund and never look at it again. There are many flaws with that kind of logic. The fund industry is constantly changing, and you need to keep up with it. The manager running a fund when you bought it may move on and be replaced by a lesser practitioner. That's one of several good reasons to get out. Or, as we've already discussed, funds may grow too large for their own good. Some managers lose their focus or change their investment strategy, which often leads to abysmal results. You should always keep an eye on your fund and be ready to pull the trigger if necessary.

3

INDEX FUNDS—
BETTER THAN
ACTIVE MANAGEMENT?

Once considered inferior investments suitable only for those who didn't know any better, index funds are now among the darlings of the mutual fund industry. Index funds used to be publicly berated by mainstream money managers and stock brokerage houses alike. In fact, for almost two decades, the Vanguard Group was the only major fund company that even offered index funds to the public.

How things have changed! Index funds began to find big-time favor with both Main Street and Wall Street beginning in 1995. That's when investors started to realize what had been true all along: Index funds tend to outperform actively managed funds some 70 percent of the time. From 1996–1998, the percentage of outperformance, as measured by the Standard & Poor's 500 index, was closer to 90 percent.

Once this fact became evident a few years ago, index funds got hotter than ever. They were soon touted on the covers of one personal finance magazine after another. Even the mainstream magazines—such as *Time, Newsweek,* and *Esquire*—began to tell how wonderful index funds were. And, in a startling development, major actively managed fund sponsors, including Fidelity, T. Rowe Price, and Dean Witter, began to roll out and tout index fund offerings of their own. To show you how much favor index funds have found among investors, Vanguard's Index 500 Portfolio is now the second largest fund in the country, just behind the giant Fidelity Magellan.

WHAT ARE INDEX FUNDS ANYWAY?

▬▬ Many people are talking about them, but I'll bet that most investors have no idea what index funds are, nor do they understand exactly how they work. They may know that their fund is tied to a benchmark like the Standard & Poor's 500 index (S&P 500, for short). But what does that mean? I'll explain in a moment.

First, it's important to realize that index funds are referred to in the industry as "passively managed" investments. In other words, they are based solely on computer models set up to replicate a given index. And there are plenty of indexes to choose from. On the stock side, some choices are: the S&P 500; Dow Jones Industrial Average; Russell 2000; Wilshire 4500; Wilshire 5000; Morgan Stanley International; and Europe, Australasia, and Far East (EAFE) index. The list goes on and on. (Incidentally, the vast majority of stock funds today are tied to the S&P 500.) Fixed-income investors also have several indexes to choose from, most notably the Lehman Brothers Aggregate Bond index.

An index fund is comprised of either a complete or a representative sample of the stocks or bonds found in the underlying index. For example, the ideal S&P 500 fund would hold proper weightings of each of the 500 funds found in the index.

A LOOK INSIDE THE INDEXES

You're probably wondering which stocks are found within the various indexes. As I mentioned, there are many different benchmarks. What follows are brief descriptions of the major indexes.

S&P 500

By far the most common index used in the fund industry, the S&P 500 holds a basket of 500 stocks. It is designed to mirror the large-capitalization sector of the U.S. equity market. The S&P 500 represents about 70 percent of the value of the entire market. But it's not necessarily composed of the 500 largest companies. Instead, an eight-member panel selected by Standard & Poor's is responsible for hand-picking which companies are listed in the index, and the list does change from time to time. The committee makes its selections based on market value, company financial conditions, and trading liquidity; it isn't looking for the next hot stock. The goal is to have the index properly represent the country's leading industries. At last check, the S&P 500 was comprised of about 380 industrial, 70 financial, 40 utility, and 10 transportation issues. The S&P 500 is a market-weighted index: the higher a company's market valuation, the more emphasis it is given in the index. Therefore, the stocks of the biggest companies are weighted more heavily and drive a large portion of the index's performance. Among the companies with the most substantial weightings in the S&P 500 are:

General Electric	(4.2 percent)
Intel	(3.6 percent)
Cisco Systems	(3.5 percent)
Microsoft	(3.4 percent)
Pfizer	(2.4 percent)
Exxon Mobil	(2.2 percent)
Wal-Mart Stores	(2.0 percent)
Oracle	(1.9 percent)
Citigroup	(1.6 percent)
Nortel Networks	(1.6 percent)

The largest 60 stocks make up about half of the value of the index. Therefore, if these 60 stocks were all down 20 percent for the year, and the remaining 440 were up 20 percent, the S&P 500 would merely break even.

DOW JONES INDUSTRIAL AVERAGE

The Dow Jones Industrial Average (DJIA, or "The Dow"), by contrast, is a price-weighted index. This means that the higher the share price of a stock in the index, the greater the influence it has. Accordingly, a big change in a single company can give a false reading for how the overall market is behaving. The Dow is the most often quoted index in the media today. It was born in 1884, when a journalist named Charles Dow compiled a list of 11 companies and tracked their performance. Two years later, he increased the number of stocks to 12 and began publishing their performance in the pages of a publication he called *The Wall Street Journal*. He wanted readers to get a better feel for what was going on in the stock market. Back then, most of the DJIA's representative companies were in the railroad industry. By 1916, the number of stocks in the DJIA had grown to 20, before leaping to 30 (the current number) in 1928. The 30 stocks listed have changed over the years, either to align with the economy or in response to acquisitions and other events that make previous choices all but irrelevant. As just one example, the DJIA now includes a number of technology companies, reflecting our evolution from a manufacturing-based to a technology-based economy.

RUSSELL 2000

This index is made up of the stocks of small, unseasoned U.S. companies. It is generally considered the best indicator of how the NASDAQ market, and small-cap stocks in general, are doing. NASDAQ stands for National Association of Securities Dealers Automated Quotation System. (You can see why they just call it NASDAQ.) This index is weighted by market value and represents domestic companies that are traded over-the-counter.

WILSHIRE 5000

Despite its name, the Wilshire 5000 tracks more than 6,000 publicly traded securities. It is therefore the most accurate measure of the health of the overall market, and the most diversified index available. Roughly 70 percent of the stocks in the Wilshire 5000 are large caps; the remaining 30 percent are mid- and small-caps. This benchmark's cousin, the Wilshire 4500, tracks 4,500 stocks that are not part of the S&P 500.

A BRIEF HISTORY OF INDEX FUNDS

The formation of index funds can be traced back to July 1971, when Wells Fargo Bank launched a $6 million fund to manage the pension assets of luggage-maker Samsonite. This fund held an equal amount of every company listed on the New York Stock Exchange. Two years later, Wells Fargo began the first index fund tied to the S&P 500. Both funds were the creation of William Fouse, a jazz saxophonist-turned-banker from West Virginia. Fouse initially developed this electronically driven strategy for picking stocks while working at the Pittsburgh-based Mellon Bank in the late 1960s. But when he suggested that Mellon should start a fund run entirely by computer, without analysis by a human manager, he was asked to leave. Ironically, Fouse has since returned to Mellon, which now runs a number of index funds of its own.

As retail investors, you and I, and millions of others, were given our first chance to invest in index funds in 1976, when Vanguard launched the First Index Investment Trust, which was tied to the S&P 500. This fund was originally sold exclusively through brokers and carried a hefty 6 percent load. One year later, at the urging of Vanguard founder John Bogle, the fund became a no-load. Because of the Trust's limited assets in the beginning, the initial portfolio contained only 280 stocks—the 200 largest, plus 80 selected by various optimization models designed to roughly match the remaining companies in the index.

Bogle's timing couldn't have been worse. After outperforming nearly 70 percent of all equity funds from 1972 to 1976, index funds *underperformed* 75 percent of active managers from 1977 to 1979. "This sort of reversal in form, which seems to plague all new fund concepts, is hardly surprising," Bogle says in retrospect. By 1982, the Trust had $100 million in assets, but only because it merged with another fund. Fortunately for Vanguard, this was right at the start of a boom in the stock market that has continued to this day. Index funds soon bounced back to the top of the rankings. By 1990, there were 43 registered index funds, including two from Fidelity, which, before, touted nothing but the advantages of active management.

Still, index funds never quite caught on with the public until around 1995. By then, they had racked up a string of stellar returns. From 1994 to 1996, index funds tied to the S&P 500 outpaced 91 percent of all actively managed offerings. As usual, money followed performance. When this fact was noticed by the media, one story after another began proclaiming how index funds were the next best thing to nirvana. Suddenly, Vanguard's Bogle was a hero, even though he had been preaching the merits of indexing for several decades. And, as index funds rose in notoriety, so did the number of available funds. Today, there are dozens of index funds, tracking virtually every benchmark you can think of, including one just for socially-conscious investors.

Index fund investing is predicated on two beliefs: (1) the market is too efficient to beat, and (2) investors can do no better than the market because they *are* the market. This idea was further popularized in a 1973 book, *A Random Walk Down Wall Street,* by Princeton University Professor Burton S. Malkiel, who has long been a strong advocate of index funds.

WHY BUY INDEX FUNDS?

Will the dazzling returns provided by index funds continue in the future? Millions of investors are betting it will, but the odds are against them. Traditionally, "hot" investment fads don't last forever. There is already evidence that the brilliant outperformance enjoyed by index funds of late is starting to fade. But index funds will always remain excellent investments.

There are several reasons why you might want to include index funds in your portfolio. For one thing, most index funds operate at bare-bones expenses. Vanguard's Index 500 charges just .20 percent of assets. The USAA index fund charges slightly less, at .18 percent. That's some 1 percent less than you would pay to own the average actively managed stock fund. The reason index funds are cheaper is simple—a computer runs the show. Fund companies don't have to pay computers the seven-figure salaries that good human managers pull down. As a result, index funds normally are given a huge 1 percent head start right at the beginning.

Second, index funds are generally highly tax-efficient. I mentioned earlier that funds have to distribute all of their capital gains and dividends to shareholders at the end of each year. If your money is not in a tax-deferred account, this can add a significant bite to your tax bill. Index funds, on the other hand, rarely experience any gains because their portfolio turnover is so low. (Managers sell a stock only when they must meet redemptions or make necessary adjustments to stay in line with the index.) Therefore, if you are looking to keep your year-end distributions to an absolute minimum, index funds make a lot of sense.

Third, I have long emphasized the importance of "choosing *managers,* not *funds*." (I talked about this in the previous chapter.) Unfortunately, fund managers change jobs with the speed of a Texas tornado these days. With an index fund, the manager is not as important because the fund is run entirely by a computer. Therefore, if you want to buy and hold and forget about your investments until you're ready to touch the money years down the line, index funds may be right for you.

Because you aren't paying for management expertise, a low expense ratio should be your number-one concern when selecting an index fund. All other things being equal, go with the fund that offers the lowest expenses for the benchmark you are trying to track. Index funds from the Vanguard Group are often very cost-efficient, although several other companies have been lowering their expenses to become more competitive. And *never* pay a sales load to buy an index fund. A number of these "deals" are out there, so beware.

The Downside of Index Funds

We've talked about the good features. Now it's only fair that we discuss some of the arguments *against* owning funds. For one thing, by definition, you will never be able to outperform the index you are tracking. By contrast, actively managed funds always have a shot at earning more. Granted, a lot of lousy managed funds will severely underperform these passively managed indexes. I've already told you that just choosing the "100 Powerhouse Performers" for this book, from a list of more than 12,000 candidates, was quite a task. However, a number of brilliant stock pickers consistently manage to outperform the indexes. If you're willing to do the work to find them (this book will be an enormous help in that pursuit), I am confident that, over time, you can outperform index funds by a respectable margin. (Even a percentage or two, in the long term, can add significantly to your net worth.)

What's more, index funds have taken in hundreds of millions of dollars in the past few years alone. If their winning streak comes to an end, investors are likely to begin fleeing these investments in favor of actively managed funds. Unfortunately, investors (both novices and professionals) have very short attention spans and time horizons. The long term, for them, means "as long as the fund is performing as well as it was when I bought it." Once the personal finance magazines and newspapers start writing that "index funds are no longer the great investments we once told you they were"—and I expect they eventually will—index fund investors are likely to run for the exits. That, of course, would severely hurt the prices of the stocks in the indexes, while creating significant capital gains distributions for shareholders who stick with these funds.

ENHANCED INDEX FUNDS

Some fund families have come up with a compromise between the active and passive approaches. They have introduced so-called "enhanced index" funds. In essence, such funds mirror most aspects of the index but try to do something different in an effort to produce market-beating returns. (Remember, true index funds can never outperform their benchmark.) The most common technique used by such funds is complicated and exotic: they buy futures contracts as a way of arbitraging the index. "An S&P 500 enhanced index fund might, for example, invest in the S&P 500 stocks and then switch the portfolio into S&P 500 futures contracts when those contracts are undervalued relative to the stocks," notes a study prepared by Ibbotson Associates, a fund consulting group in Chicago. The study is entitled "Are Enhanced Index Mutual Funds Worthy of Their Name?" Its conclusion? "No, most of them are not worthy." As the Ibbotson study also points out, an enhanced index fund is really actively managed. If you're not replicating the stated benchmark exactly, you're not really running an index fund. As for returns, Ibbotson found that a majority of the enhanced funds it examined *underperformed* their respective indexes—in some cases, by a considerable margin.

FINAL THOUGHTS ABOUT INDEXING

Is indexing right for you? That, of course, is a personal decision only you can make. By now, you should have a good feel for what indexing is, how it works, what kinds of stocks are in the various indexes, and the pros and cons of this approach. Before I end this chapter, let me leave you with some additional thoughts.

For starters, I believe that index funds, particularly those tied to the U.S. market, will remain admirable performers in the future. This belief, in large part, is based on my conviction that the U.S. stock market will continue to rise over time, and those willing to take the risk of investing in equities will be richly rewarded. As a result, I have no problem with your holding an S&P 500 index fund as a core position in your portfolio. It's a fine substitute for almost any large-cap mutual fund you will come across, and it has produced an average annualized return of 16.3 percent since 1978. That's impressive by any measure. For small-cap and foreign investing, however, I think you are better off with actively managed funds. History backs me up on this. Over the past 10 years, more than half of all diversified international stock funds have whipped the performance of the Morgan Stanley Capital International Europe, Australasia, Far East (EAFE) index. And U.S. small-caps are much less efficient than their large-cap brethren, making it possible for active managers to shoot the lights out with selected issues.

If you want a truly passive approach that will allow you to participate in the rise of the market without doing any research to uncover the most promising funds available, indexing may be right for you. Should you opt to go this route, however, I would offer a suggestion: If you're going to buy only one fund, I strongly encourage you to purchase one that tracks the Wilshire 5000, instead of the S&P 500. In that way, you'll get exposure to all areas of the market, not just large-cap stocks. The Wilshire 5000 is also much more diversified because the biggest companies are not weighted as heavily. The best funds in this category are Vanguard Total Stock Market, and the Wilshire 5000 Portfolio. Both are among my "100 Powerhouse Performers." As I note in the profile for these funds in Chapter 5, either could be the sole holding for the U.S. equity portion of your portfolio, especially if you have a relatively modest amount of money to invest.

I truly believe that, with a little work on your part and with the help of this book, you can beat the indexes by investing in outstanding funds run by the best stock pickers in the business. A study compiled by a financial consulting firm, Evaluation Associates, affirms this. It found that the S&P 500, the index against which most funds are measured, beat less than half of all actively managed large-cap funds during rolling five-year periods from 1981 to 1996. So, while it makes good sense to consider putting a core position of your portfolio in an index fund, to ensure that you'll never significantly underperform the market, I am convinced that a more active approach to investing is not only more fun but can also produce greater results over the long haul.

4

SHOPPING AT THE FUND SUPERMARKETS

We learn early that there's no such thing as a free lunch. But when it comes to buying mutual funds, America's leading discount brokers are trying to break this perennial rule.

You already know that one way to purchase shares in a fund is by calling the fund directly, ordering a prospectus and application, completing the necessary paperwork, and sending it all back to the fund with your initial investment to get the ball rolling. When you decide to redeem your shares, you once again have to phone the fund and then wait for your check to arrive. If you want to switch from one fund to another in a different family, you have to order the prospectus and application for the new fund, request a redemption from your old one, fill out a new set of paperwork, cash the check your old fund sends you, and write out a check for the new fund. This is not only a hassle, but valuable time is being consumed. Because transferring from one fund to another can take days or weeks, you risk missing out on gains in the market during the interim.

Now, however, this way of doing business with your favorite funds is becoming a thing of the past. Top discount brokers, including Charles Schwab, Fidelity, and TD Waterhouse, have created what I call virtual "no-load, no-transaction-fee supermarkets." Their programs enable you to buy and sell hundreds of funds in a single account without paying a penny in commissions. The programs are convenient, cost-effective, and, arguably, the most important new development for fund investors in recent memory.

THE START OF SOMETHING BIG

In 1984, San Diego (California) discount broker Jack White & Co. was the first to start selling no-load funds to clients. Rival Charles Schwab quickly did the same. Each offered about 150 funds that could be traded for a minimal transaction fee, similar to the commission charged on stocks.

Both brokers threw in a variety of services that were never before available to those dealing with no-loads—for example, statement consolidation and the ability to purchase shares without having to mail in an order form. However, initial public reaction to the concept, even with the small fee, was disappointing. Schwab soon realized that the transaction fee was a stumbling block, since people could still invest free by calling the funds directly. It was apparent that, for many clients, the convenience factor alone wasn't enough to overcome the $30 to $50 transaction fee they were being charged.

In 1990, Charles Schwab himself began working on a plan to get the fund companies to pay the transaction fee on behalf of his clients. He knew that in selling funds he was on to something big, but he understood that investors wouldn't welcome the idea until he completely got rid of the commission. What's now known as Schwab's OneSource program was born in 1992. Just as he had transformed the way people bought stocks 17 years earlier, Schwab dramatically changed the distribution channel for no-load funds with the birth of this program.

ONE-STOP SHOPPING

From the start, OneSource allowed clients to purchase and sell shares from a handful of large fund companies free of charge. How? By charging the participating fund companies anywhere from $.25 to $.35 for every $100 in assets that Schwab brought in. This was considered to be a marketing and distribution fee. Because the funds saved the cost of performing these functions on their own, Schwab argued that it was a good deal for them. Initially, the idea ran into resistance. Many fund families approached it with a "wait-and-see" attitude. They wanted to see how the competition reacted before taking the plunge themselves.

Jack White & Co. (which has since merged with TD Waterhouse) soon introduced a similar program, although founder and president Jack White had some doubts that it would ever take off. He knew many fund managers personally, and figured they would resist paying to be part of a program that made it so easy for investors to buy and sell their shares.

Fund companies, as a rule, hate traders and market timers because frequent buying and selling disrupts the normal flow of funds. Just to meet redemptions, managers may have to sell positions they like, thus hurting other shareholders.

As it turned out, the concept caught on and spread like wildfire. One fund family after another started courting Schwab and Jack White to sign up. Before long, fund behemoth Fidelity Investments joined the party with a fund supermarket of its own and was closely followed by almost all of the other major discount brokers, including Muriel Siebert and Waterhouse Securities.

WIDE AVAILABILITY

Today, no-load, no-transaction-fee (NTF) programs have amassed some $200 billion in assets. Almost all of the major no-load fund families participate, as do a number of smaller boutique funds that were formerly available only to high-net-worth institutional investors.

Noticeably absent from the current list of available offerings are funds from giants T. Rowe Price and Vanguard, which maintain that the cost of participation is simply too high. (Funds from these families can still be purchased from the brokers, although a small commission is charged for each transaction.) Even full-service brokers like Merrill Lynch and Smith Barney, once famous for bad-mouthing no-loads, are joining the NTF fund bandwagon to stem the flow of lost assets, as are some of the fund families themselves.

THE WAVE OF THE FUTURE

Some industry analysts predict that funds and brokers that refuse to join these programs will struggle to survive as NTF supermarkets become more popular. Many of the participating funds already get more than half of their assets from them. In fact, most start-up money managers are designing their new funds specifically around the supermarkets, to make sure they can get in right away.

THE ADVANTAGES

It seems inevitable that NTF supermarkets would gain such widespread acceptance. After all, with one phone call, clients can buy and sell hundreds of high-quality funds from dozens of different families, and all of their holdings are consolidated on one monthly statement. In addition, the brokers keep track of pertinent tax information, leaving clients to contend with only one 1099 form at the end of the year. Other advantages include fee-free IRAs and SEP retirement plans, which are perfect for small business owners; no-cost reinvestment of dividends and capital gains; around-the-clock account access by phone and computer; free check writing; and, in some cases, the ability to trade on margin.

THE DRAWBACKS

There are a few drawbacks. When you buy shares through an NTF supermarket, the fund companies won't know you exist. Your investment gets lumped into one omnibus account registered in the name of your broker, so don't expect to get much promotional mail touting your fund companies' new products and services. Your annual reports and other information will likely arrive a few days later than normal, because everything must be sent through each discount broker's third-party mailing center.

In addition, most brokers have short-term trading rules, which require payment of a transaction fee if a fund position is sold before a given time period (usually, six months). The rules are designed to discourage frequent switching around. That's probably a good thing; such regular trading usually leads to lower returns anyway. But all in all, the downside is relatively minor.

GETTING STARTED

How can you take advantage of this first free lunch on Wall Street? Begin by opening an account with the broker of your choice. It usually takes at least $5,000 to get started, and the extra perks start to kick in at around the $10,000 level.

Which broker is best for you is a very personal decision. Your choice depends on your own needs and preferences. Let's say you want to do most of your trading online. Every broker offers a computerized trading program and/or Internet site, but Schwab and Fidelity currently have the most sophisticated products. If you desire personal face-to-face service, Schwab, Fidelity, and TD Waterhouse have branch offices located across the country. (Keep in mind that it's possible to conduct all of your business over the phone or by computer, so not having a branch office is no big deal.) TD Waterhouse offers the most funds, but Fidelity and Schwab aren't far behind.

You may want to look at some of the smaller details. For example, Fidelity has by far the best-looking and most comprehensive monthly account statements. TD Waterhouse and Fidelity are the only brokers that don't charge for using the ATM debit card that comes with your money market account. (Everyone else charges up to $2 per ATM transaction.)

YOUR ONE-STOP BANK, TOO

When you open a brokerage account, you establish an entire cash management program that not only links all of your funds and other investments (including stocks and bonds), but also gives you easy access to an interest-bearing money market account. All of your available cash is automatically swept into this account at the end of each day. You can then write as many checks as your account balance allows, or use a debit card to get cash from automated teller machines (ATMs) around the world. For all intents and purposes, you could make this your primary checking account, and would be well advised to do so. You'll earn a much higher rate of interest than you'll ever get at your local bank, and this option makes it easy for you to invest in your favorite funds on a regular basis.

The beauty of these programs is that they cost you nothing, and the fact that you're getting a lot of free services should be an important consideration. At Fidelity, for example, your account is charged a $12 annual fee for each fund that has a balance below $2,500. If you can't keep your balance that high, look elsewhere. On the other hand, Fidelity waives IRA and Self-Employed Retirement Plan (SEP) fees for balances above $2,500. Schwab requires a minimum $10,000 balance for this waiver. TD Waterhouse doesn't charge for IRAs, regardless of your balance.

CHOOSING YOUR BROKER

Here's the best plan of action for deciding which broker is right for you: Call or visit each one and ask for more information and an application. (You'll find a list of names, toll-free numbers, and Internet addresses in the box on page 44.) Then, on paper, map out the products and services you are seeking. Next, determine which broker(s) offer most of

10 REASONS TO BUY YOUR MUTUAL FUNDS THROUGH THE NTF FUND SUPERMARKETS

1. Purchase hundreds of top-performing no-load funds from more than 90 different families without paying any commissions or transaction costs.

2. Have all of your investment holdings (stocks, bonds, cash, and funds) consolidated on one easy-to-read monthly statement.

3. Gain entry into exclusive funds once available only to high-net-worth institutional investors.

4. Get 24-hour-a-day access to your portfolio holdings and values by phone and computer, allowing you to keep constant tabs on your investments.

5. Buy into funds with minimum investment requirements of up to $1 million for as little as $1,000.

6. Receive a fee-free retirement account (IRA, SEP, Keogh, etc.) for yourself and your employees, while choosing from a plethora of no-load funds to build your wealth.

7. Enjoy same-day order execution of your fund transactions, and avoid having to rely on mail delivery and signature guarantees to redeem shares.

8. Let your discount broker keep track of all fund gains and losses, making tax time a breeze.

9. Get a free high-interest-bearing checking account linked directly to your investment portfolio.

10. Keep more money in your pocket by avoiding "loaded" funds, and benefit from the many services provided by America's top discount brokers.

NTF DISCOUNT BROKERS

Broker	Telephone	Internet Address
Charles Schwab & Co.	(800) 845-1714	www.schwab.com
Fidelity Investments	(800) 544-9697	www.fidelity.com
Muriel Siebert & Co.	(800) 872-0711	www.msiebert.com
TD Waterhouse	(800) 934-4443	www.waterhouse.com

the things on your list. Some of the more popular features include free IRAs and SEPs, large availability of NTF funds, strong computerized trading programs, and all-in-one asset management accounts. I also recommend checking out each broker's Internet site. If you plan to use your computer to keep track of your investments, see what each broker offers via online technology.

Regardless of which broker you ultimately choose, you're sure to find NTF supermarkets a convenient and less expensive way to buy no-load funds in the future. As for the free lunch, the fund families are picking up the tab so eat and enjoy. Deals like this don't come along very often.

5

100 POWERHOUSE
PERFORMERS FOR 2001

I have given you the tools you need to effectively select your own funds, but there are some 12,000 names to sift through and analyze, and the number keeps growing each day. I'm assuming you bought this book to make your investment life easier, and that's exactly what I'm going to do in this chapter. I have performed exhaustive research to uncover the 100 most attractive no-load stock and fixed-income funds for the year ahead. All have brilliant track records and are spearheaded by seasoned managers with a proven talent for picking winning investments. I call these funds my "Powerhouse Performers." Every Powerhouse Performer is profiled in a two-page report that starts with the fund's name, objective, and manager.

Within each group, the funds are arranged alphabetically by the first word of their name. Entries 1 through 91 represent the equity side; entries 92 through 100 represent the fixed-income side.

I have described each fund's style as precisely as possible, based on the manager's most recent portfolio composition. Style refers to the kinds of securities a fund holds. This information tells you whether a given fund will add an element of diversity to your portfolio. Having exposure to many different styles will help you to weather the market's constant fluctuations and sector rotations. You can find definitions for each of these investment styles in the Glossary in the back of the book.

Generally speaking, growth fund managers look for companies experiencing rapid earnings and/or sales growth. Shares in these companies often trade at a premium to the overall stock market. Value fund managers hunt for bargains, often buying slower growing or troubled businesses that are available at depressed prices.

Each Powerhouse Performer's report contains a brief overview of the fund, a description of how the manager invests the portfolio, and why the fund made my list. The accompanying tables show various returns and rankings. You'll find each fund's annualized return over the past one-, three-, and five-year periods (through June 30, 2000) where applicable.

Next come the fund's overall and risk rankings, according to Value Line. The overall ranking takes into account how a given fund has performed compared to its peers. Ranking is on a scale of 1 through 5, with 1 being best. The risk ranking gives you a feel for how volatile the portfolio is. On a scale of 1 through 5, 5 is the riskiest.

Also included are a handful of useful statistics, including the fund's annual turnover rate, expense ratio, 12b-1 fee, maximum sales load, and three-year beta coefficient. Beta is a measure of a fund's volatility in relation to its benchmark index (usually the S&P 500, for stocks). The S&P 500 has a beta of 1. Funds with a beta lower than 1 fluctuate less than the overall market; funds with a beta above 1 are more volatile. If you are conservative and seek to temper your market risk, you need to favor funds with low betas.

For each fund, I give the minimum investment requirements for both regular and IRA accounts, the toll-free telephone number, and the Internet address (where applicable). You can use this information to get a prospectus and/or more information, such as a listing of which discount brokers (if any) carry the fund through their NTF supermarket.

On the second page of every report are two graphs (courtesy of Value Line). The first graph shows the return on a $10,000 investment in the fund over a period of years compared to its benchmark index. The second graph is a measure of individual annual performance, illustrating, year by year, what kind of returns the fund has generated since its inception or since 1978, whichever is longer. (For some of the newer funds, this information is not available.) Finally, there is a box showing the fund's most recent top 10 portfolio holdings.

In Chapter 6, I will help you put together a portfolio tailored to your individual needs, drawing from my lineup of Powerhouse Performers. For now, let's take a look at some of the most deserving candidates for your investment consideration in 2001.

THE 100 POWERHOUSE PERFORMERS FOR 2000

ALLEGHANY MONTAG & CALDWELL GROWTH

OBJECTIVE:	*Large-Cap Growth*	
MANAGER:	*Ronald E. Canakaris*	*1*

FUND OVERVIEW:

Alleghany Montag & Caldwell Growth manager Ronald Canakaris seeks to generate long-term capital appreciation by investing in a relatively concentrated portfolio of equities. He buys companies that he believes are undervalued based on both current earning power and ability to generate strong earnings growth over the next 12 to 18 months. Many of the names in the portfolio are established brands with long histories.

"We continue to be quite positive on the outlook for the shares of high-quality growth companies," Canakaris says. "Because we expect more moderate growth in the U.S. economy and corporate profits in the future, the superior and consistent earnings growth rates of these companies should become increasingly attractive." Many of his companies do business around the world, which Canakaris feels gives them a tremendous advantage. "With the U.S. economy already operating at a high level of activity, the multinational consumer, healthcare, and technology companies in the fund are particularly well positioned to benefit from the greater growth opportunities that exist in global markets," he adds.

ANNUALIZED RETURNS		PORTFOLIO STATISTICS	
1-Year	7.80%	Beta	0.98
3-Year	19.48%	Turnover	32.00%
5-Year	25.03%	12-Month Yield	0.00%
Overall Rank	3	12b-1 Fee	0.25%
Risk Rank	3	Expense Ratio	1.12%

MINIMUM INVESTMENT		CONTACT INFORMATION
Regular	$2,500	*Alleghany Montag & Caldwell Growth*
IRA	$500	*Fund*
		Telephone: (800) 992-8151
		www.alleghanyfunds.com

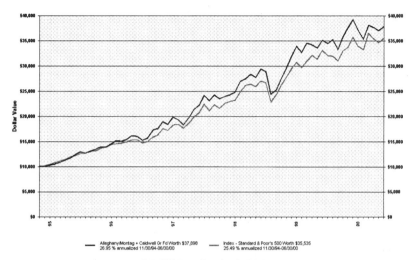

GROWTH OF $10,000

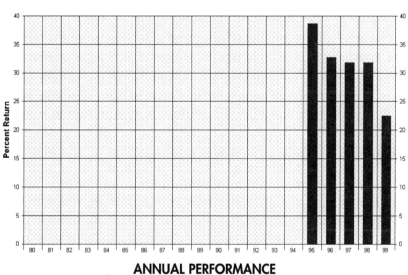

ANNUAL PERFORMANCE

TOP 10 HOLDINGS	
Johnson & Johnson	Procter & Gamble
McDonald's	Coca-Cola
Pfizer	MCI Worldcom
Bristol-Myers Squibb	Home Depot
Gillette	General Electric

BERKSHIRE FOCUS FUND

OBJECTIVE:	*Large-Cap Growth*	*2*
MANAGER:	*Malcolm Fobes III*	

FUND OVERVIEW:

Make no mistake about it: Berkshire Focus is a technology sector fund in drag. As of the most recent report, Berkshire manager Malcolm Fobes had nearly 100 percent of the portfolio invested in tech stocks. That's really no surprise, since Berkshire's offices are in the Silicon Valley, and Fobes readily admits he favors technology stocks. Even the so-called "financial services" holdings in the fund are online brokerage concerns. This concentration, in large part, explains this relatively young fund's incredible performance.

By prospectus, Fobes always keeps at least 25 percent of the fund in the tech sector, but has the freedom to go in all the way if he wants. In building his portfolio, he attempts to identify areas and industries that should benefit from future trends that he's uncovered doing a "top down" analysis of the economic landscape. From here, he finds those companies with franchise durability, sustainable revenue and earnings growth, pricing power, and strong balance sheets. Count on great volatility, but the potential for huge gains in this fund, especially if technology stocks continue to do well in the future.

ANNUALIZED RETURNS		PORTFOLIO STATISTICS	
1-year	144.50%	**Beta**	N/A
3-year	N/A	**Turnover**	13.00%
5-year	N/A	**12-Month Yield**	0.16%
Overall Rank	N/A	**12b-1 Fee**	0.00%
Risk Rank	N/A	**Expense Ratio**	1.00%
MINIMUM INVESTMENT		**CONTACT INFORMATION**	
Regular	$5,000	*Berkshire Focus Fund*	
IRA	$2,000	*Telephone: (877) 526-0707*	
		www.berkshirefunds.com	

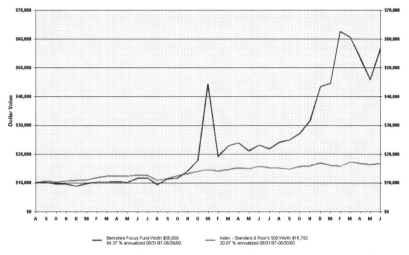

GROWTH OF $10,000

Berkshire Focus Fund Worth $56,600
84.37 % annualized 08/31/97-06/30/00

Index - Standard & Poor's 500 Worth $16,792
20.07 % annualized 08/31/97-06/30/00

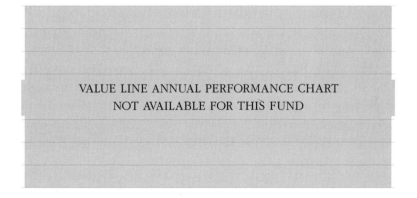

VALUE LINE ANNUAL PERFORMANCE CHART
NOT AVAILABLE FOR THIS FUND

ANNUAL PERFORMANCE

TOP 10 HOLDINGS	
Cisco Systems	Exodus Communications
EMC Corporation	Yahoo!
America Online	Qualcomm
PMC-Sierra	Nokia Corp. ADR
JDS Uniphase	Sun Microsystems

DREYFUS APPRECIATION

OBJECTIVE:	*Large-Cap Growth*	*3*
MANAGER:	*Fayez Sarofim*	

FUND OVERVIEW:

Since taking over management of Dreyfus Appreciation in 1990, manager Fayez Sarofim has turned this fund into a growth-oriented portfolio full of large-cap global names. Sarofim is no rookie to the investment scene. He founded his firm, Fayez Sarofim & Co., in 1958. It serves as the fund's subadviser and manages some $33.4 billion in assets. Sarofim and his comanager, Russell Hawkins, are convinced that overseas exposure by dominant blue-chip companies will give them an impressive earnings boost over the long run. That's why they are banking on such stocks. Because the top 20 names in the portfolio often account for 60 percent of assets, this can be a more volatile fund than others in the category.

Dreyfus Appreciation's emphasis is on U.S.-based companies that are easily recognized and get at least 35 to 40 percent of their income from international markets. Visibility of earnings is also important. Sarofim will occasionally buy American Depositary Receipts (ADRs) when he feels purchasing them is appropriate. The visibility of a company's future earnings growth is an important consideration, because Sarofim tends to stick with a buy-and-hold strategy.

ANNUALIZED RETURNS		PORTFOLIO STATISTICS	
1-Year	6.60%	Beta	0.92
3-Year	16.51%	Turnover	11.77%
5-Year	22.64%	12-Month Yield	0.49%
Overall Rank	2	12b-1 Fee	0.25%
Risk Rank	3	Expense Ratio	0.88%
MINIMUM INVESTMENT		**CONTACT INFORMATION**	
Regular	$2,500	*Dreyfus Appreciation Fund*	
IRA	$750	*Telephone: (800) 782-6620*	
		www.dreyfus.com	

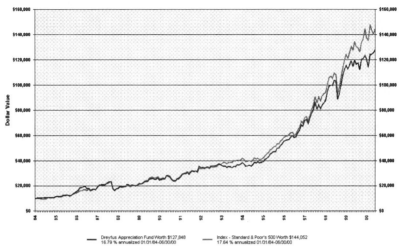

Dreyfus Appreciation Fund Worth $127,848
16.79 % annualized 01/31/84-06/30/00

Index - Standard & Poor's 500 Worth $144,052
17.64 % annualized 01/31/84-06/30/00

GROWTH OF $10,000

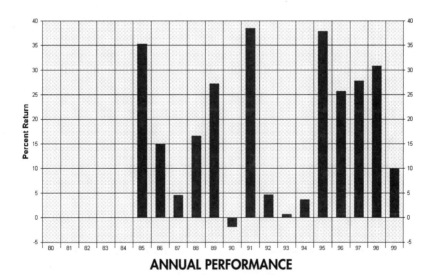

ANNUAL PERFORMANCE

TOP 10 HOLDINGS	
Pfizer	Citigroup
Intel	Microsoft
Cisco Systems	Johnson & Johnson
Merck & Co.	Coca-Cola
General Electric	ExxonMobil

DREYFUS DISCIPLINED STOCK

OBJECTIVE:	*Large-Cap Growth*	
MANAGER:	*Bert Mullins*	*4*

FUND OVERVIEW:

Dreyfus Disciplined Stock manager Bert Mullins says his goal is to beat the S&P 500 with less volatility. So far, he's managed to achieve this objective. Mullins gathers information from a diverse group of sources to construct computerized valuation models that rank stocks as being either over- or undervalued. The models measure such things as actual and estimated earnings changes, along with price-to-book, price-to-earnings, and return-on-equity ratios. There are 15 different screens in all. The computer then categorizes stocks in various industries according to relative attractiveness. That's when Mullins sends his analysts out to do additional fundamental research. They determine which companies are truly most attractive, and, conversely, which should be sold.

How can Mullins run a portfolio that's less volatile than the S&P 500? By doing good security selection and making sure the fund isn't over-weighted in any one sector or industry. To keep his computer models up-to-date, the screening criteria get updated every two weeks. Mullins remains fully invested most of the time, although he's allowed to keep up to 20 percent in cash if necessary.

ANNUALIZED RETURNS		PORTFOLIO STATISTICS	
1-Year	7.50%	Beta	1.03
3-Year	18.80%	Turnover	28.05%
5-Year	23.25%	12-Month Yield	0.10%
Overall Rank	3	12b-1 Fee	0.10%
Risk Rank	3	Expense Ratio	0.50%
MINIMUM INVESTMENT		**CONTACT INFORMATION**	
Regular	$2,500	*Dreyfus Disciplined Stock Fund*	
IRA	$750	*Telephone: (800) 782-6620*	
		www.dreyfus.com	

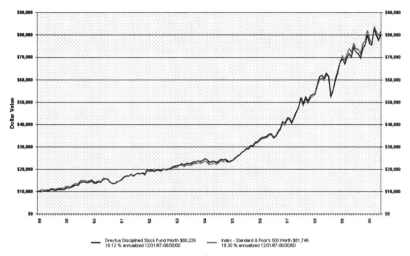

GROWTH OF $10,000

Dreyfus Disciplined Stock Fund Worth $80,229
18.12 % annualized 12/31/87-06/30/00

Index - Standard & Poor's 500 Worth $81,746
18.30 % annualized 12/31/87-06/30/00

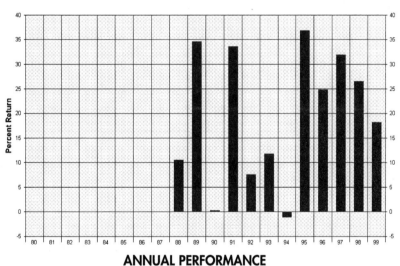

ANNUAL PERFORMANCE

TOP 10 HOLDINGS

General Electric	Oracle Corp.
Microsoft	Warner-Lambert
Wal-Mart	Intel
Cisco Systems	Sun Microsystems
ExxonMobil	Tyco International

GABELLI GROWTH

OBJECTIVE:	*Large-Cap Growth*	**5**
MANAGER:	*Howard Ward*	

FUND OVERVIEW:

Gabelli Growth manager Howard Ward invests in a diversified portfolio of large, seasoned, well-managed companies that he believes have favorable earnings dynamics and price appreciation potential. His companies normally boast above-average or expanding market shares, high profit margins, and respectable returns on equity. Ward does a lot of hands-on research. He especially likes businesses with a demonstrated competitive advantage that benefit from one or more secular trends, such as the technology revolution, aging of the population, and globalization. He also focuses on valuation, hoping to buy these growers at attractive prices.

The fund's largest weightings are in the financial services, drug, technology, newspaper, and broadcasting sectors. "Virtually all of our companies occupy leading positions in their fields," Ward explains. "We should do well when large growth company stocks do well, and less well when they periodically stall." Ward is a strong advocate of diversification, but he doesn't believe in being spread out more than necessary. He expects to keep his portfolio at around 50 to 70 names, to prevent his best ideas from being unfairly diluted.

ANNUALIZED RETURNS		PORTFOLIO STATISTICS	
1-Year	33.80%	Beta	1.09
3-Year	33.64%	Turnover	52.00%
5-Year	31.44%	12-Month Yield	0.00%
Overall Rank	1	12b-1 Fee	0.25%
Risk Rank	3	Expense Ratio	1.37%
MINIMUM INVESTMENT		**CONTACT INFORMATION**	
Regular	$1,000	*Gabelli Growth Fund*	
IRA	$1,000	*Telephone: (800) 422-3554*	
		www.gabelli.com	

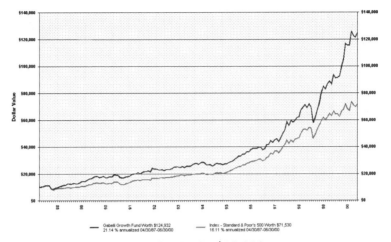

GROWTH OF $10,000

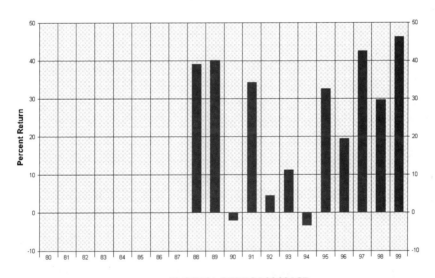

ANNUAL PERFORMANCE

TOP 10 HOLDINGS	
Home Depot	Marsh & McLennan
Texas Instruments	Time Warner
Cisco Systems	State Street Corp.
EMC	Sun Microsystems
Warner-Lambert	Media One Group

HARBOR CAPITAL APPRECIATION

OBJECTIVE:	*Large-Cap Growth*	**6**
MANAGER:	*Spiros Segalas*	

FUND OVERVIEW:

Harbor Capital Appreciation is one of the more aggressive large-cap growth funds you will come across. Although Spiros Segalas fills his portfolio with blue-chip household names, he's not afraid to trade around his positions with frequency and will concentrate in specific sectors if he thinks that's the best course of action. Segalas is an admitted momentum player. If one of his companies fails to achieve or exceed his expected earnings target, he'll get rid of it, although he doesn't try to time the market itself.

Segalas's bottom-up management style seeks out growth at a reasonable price. He prefers companies with market capitalizations of at least $1 billion and with track records of superior sales growth, high returns on equity, and solid balance sheets. Earnings numbers are also critical, and he is constantly reevaluating his expectations.

Harbor Capital Appreciation has been a stellar performer since Segalas took over in 1990. It has an extremely low expense ratio for a fund of this nature. Clearly, you can expect it to be volatile. But if you can stand these more frequent fluctuations, you will likely be rewarded.

ANNUALIZED RETURNS		PORTFOLIO STATISTICS	
1-Year	29.20%	**Beta**	1.18
3-Year	32.24%	**Turnover**	68.14%
5-Year	28.71%	**12-Month Yield**	0.00%
Overall Rank	1	**12b-1 Fee**	0.00%
Risk Rank	4	**Expense Ratio**	0.66%
MINIMUM INVESTMENT		CONTACT INFORMATION	
Regular	$2,000	*Harbor Capital Appreciation*	
IRA	$500	*Telephone: (800) 422-1050*	
		www.harborfund.com	

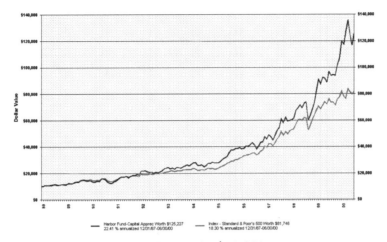

Harbor Fund-Capital Apprec Worth $125,227
22.41 % annualized 12/31/87-06/30/00

Index - Standard & Poor's 500 Worth $81,746
18.30 % annualized 12/31/87-06/30/00

GROWTH OF $10,000

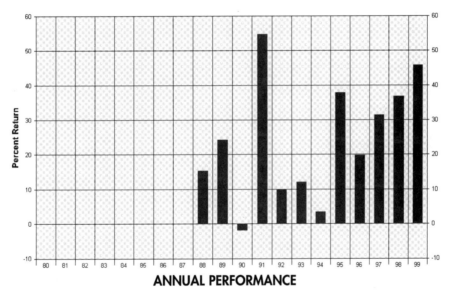

ANNUAL PERFORMANCE

TOP 10 HOLDINGS

MCI Worldcom	American International Group
Microsoft	Home Depot
General Electric	Cisco Systems
Citigroup	Texas Instruments
CBS Corp.	Intel

MANAGERS CAPITAL APPRECIATION

OBJECTIVE:	*Large-Cap Growth*
MANAGER:	*Kevin Riley and Joseph McNay*

7

FUND OVERVIEW:

Running the Managers Capital Appreciation Fund is a team effort that brings together two fine money managers: Kevin Riley from Roxbury Capital Management, and Joseph McNay at Essex Investment Management. Each get about half of the assets and can invest this money as they see fit. It's been a winning formula since the two began working together a couple of years ago.

Riley and his colleagues at Roxbury focus on companies with strong competitive positions and sustainable growth in both earnings and cash flow. They begin by using quantitative screens to find candidates with high returns on invested capital, healthy balance sheets and positive cash flow. From here, they visit with management to see whether the story makes fundamental sense.

McNay also believes that a company's earnings growth and profitability will drive its future performance. Thus, he looks for names with accelerating, sustainable earnings growth, with dominant products or services and a strong management team. He calls these companies "franchise opportunities." The blended approach creates a portfolio of about 50 to 60 industry leaders.

ANNUALIZED RETURNS		PORTFOLIO STATISTICS	
1-year	60.00%	Beta	1.28
3-year	50.75%	Turnover	200.00%
5-year	35.60%	12-Month Yield	0.00%
Overall Rank	2	12b-1 Fee	0.00%
Risk Rank	5	Expense Ratio	1.26%
MINIMUM INVESTMENT		CONTACT INFORMATION	
Regular	$2,000	*Managers Capital Appreciation*	
IRA	$500	*Telephone: (800) 835-3879*	
		www.managersfunds.com	

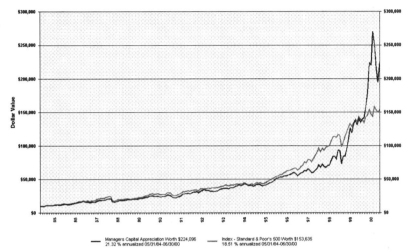

GROWTH OF $10,000

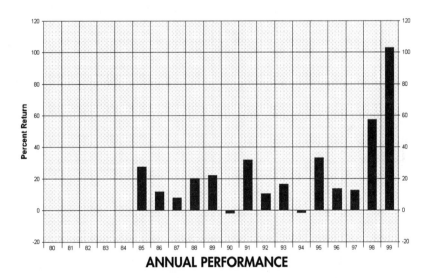

ANNUAL PERFORMANCE

TOP 10 HOLDINGS

Viacom C1. B	Voicestream Wireless
Nokia Corp. ADR	Costco
AT&T—Liberty Media	General Motors C1. H
Qwest Communications	Echostar Communications
Home Depot	Gap

MARSICO FOCUS

OBJECTIVE:	*Large-Cap Growth*	
MANAGER:	*Tom Marsico*	

FUND OVERVIEW:

Tom Marsico built a stellar record at the Janus Twenty fund, steering it to a 22.38 percent annualized return from January 31, 1988 to August 7, 1997. (That compared favorably to an 18.20 percent return for the S&P 500.) He left Janus in late 1997 to start his own shop, and he launched Marsico Focus at the beginning of 1998. The portfolio looks almost identical to the old Janus Twenty, only better because he is working with a smaller asset base. Marsico Focus holds this proven manager's 20 to 30 favorite stocks. This added concentration increases both the fund's potential risks and rewards.

Marsico considers this to be a global portfolio, meaning he can invest in both U.S. and foreign securities. He prides himself in being an out-of-the-box thinker who looks for variables that aren't obvious from examining conventional financial analyses. He spends a lot of time talking with the management, suppliers, customers, competitors, and critics of the companies he owns. Among the characteristics he looks for in his high-growth, large-cap businesses are: an element of change, a strong franchise, products with a global reach, and the potential to benefit from a positive emerging social or economic theme.

ANNUALIZED RETURNS		PORTFOLIO STATISTICS	
1-Year	23.90%	Beta	N/A
3-Year	N/A	Turnover	173.00%
5-Year	N/A	12-Month Yield	0.00%
Overall Rank	N/A	12b-1 Fee	0.25%
Risk Rank	N/A	Expense Ratio	1.31%
MINIMUM INVESTMENT		**CONTACT INFORMATION**	
Regular	$2,500	*Marsico Focus Fund*	
IRA	$1,000	*Telephone: (888) 860-8686*	
		www.marsicofunds.com	

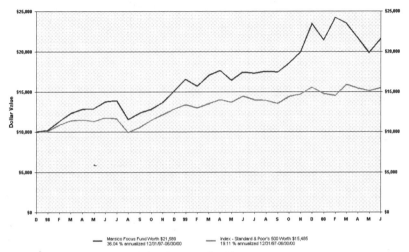

GROWTH OF $10,000

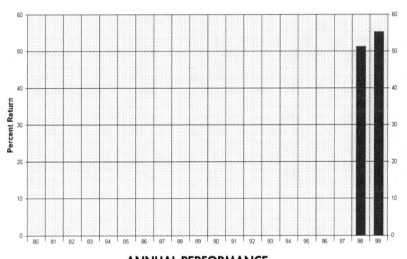

ANNUAL PERFORMANCE

TOP 10 HOLDINGS

EMC	Federal National Mortgage
Genentech	Home Depot
Cisco Systems	3Com
Corning	Oracle Corporation
Sony Corp. ADR	Time Warner

NORTHEAST INVESTORS GROWTH

OBJECTIVE:	*Large-Cap Growth*	*9*
MANAGER:	*William Oates*	

FUND OVERVIEW:

William Oates puts his money where his mouth is—literally. He's the largest shareholder of his Northeast Investors Growth Fund. So, unlike many of his peers, his interests are strongly aligned with those of his shareholders. Oates seeks long-term growth, but is also interested in a company's ability to generate future income. While he favors large-cap stocks, he is known for eclectically sprinkling the portfolio with small, lesser-known names as he uncovers promising opportunities.

Oates targets companies with an earnings growth rate that is twice that of the overall economy. He also wants to see dividends growing at two times inflation. And while not a pure value manager, he focuses on stocks with low prices relative to earnings potential, net worth, or book value. What's more, he's not allowed to keep more than 25 percent of the total portfolio in any one industry, furthering the fund's overall diversification.

Another unique positive is that Oates makes himself personally available to answer shareholder questions about Northeast Investors Growth. That's something most fund managers today aren't willing to do.

ANNUALIZED RETURNS		PORTFOLIO STATISTICS	
1-Year	17.60%	Beta	1.15
3-Year	25.42%	Turnover	31.39%
5-Year	27.48%	12-Month Yield	0.00%
Overall Rank	2	12b-1 Fee	0.00%
Risk Rank	3	Expense Ratio	0.84%
MINIMUM INVESTMENT		**CONTACT INFORMATION**	
Regular	$1,000	*Northeast Investors Growth*	
IRA	$500	*Telephone: (800) 225-6704*	
		www.northeastinvestors.com	

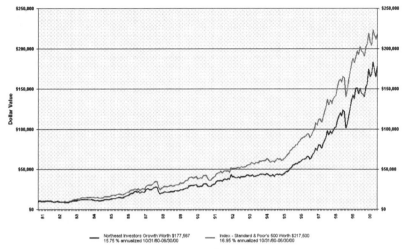

Northeast Investors Growth Worth $177,567
15.75 % annualized 10/31/80–06/30/00

Index - Standard & Poor's 500 Worth $217,500
16.95 % annualized 10/31/80–06/30/00

GROWTH OF $10,000

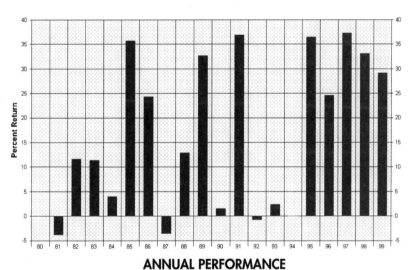

ANNUAL PERFORMANCE

TOP 10 HOLDINGS

America Online	Wal-Mart Stores
EMC Corp.	Cisco Systems
Time Warner	Yahoo!
Microsoft	America Online
General Electric	Intel

PAPP AMERICA ABROAD

OBJECTIVE:	*Large-Cap Growth*	*10*
MANAGER:	*L. Roy Papp and Rosellen Papp*	

FUND OVERVIEW:

Roy Papp knows there's a world of opportunity out there for investors. He's seen much of it with his own eyes, having traveled around the globe throughout his life. But he's too scared to trust any of his own money to one of the foreign stock exchanges. That's why he started a fund designed to profit from global growth through buying domestically domiciled companies. Papp America Abroad invests primarily in U.S. multinationals, most of which do more than half of their business overseas. Among the many dangers of investing directly in foreign soil, Papp cites currency risk, varying accounting standards, higher transaction costs, political instability, and the loss of SEC protection. He also notes that U.S. companies tend to be more technologically advanced and competitive than their international counterparts, which means their profit potential is greater.

In addition to the international business component, Papp's ideal company is an industry leader—better yet, a monopoly. It is also growing at a rate of 20 to 25 percent a year, and trades at or near a market multiple at the time of initial purchase.

ANNUALIZED RETURNS		PORTFOLIO STATISTICS	
1-Year	24.60%	Beta	1.08
3-Year	18.28%	Turnover	8.87%
5-Year	24.69%	12-Month Yield	0.00%
Overall Rank	2	12b-1 Fee	0.00%
Risk Rank	3	Expense Ratio	1.09%
MINIMUM INVESTMENT		**CONTACT INFORMATION**	
Regular	$5,000	*Papp America Abroad Fund*	
IRA	$1,000	*Telephone: (800) 421-4004*	
		www.roypapp.com	

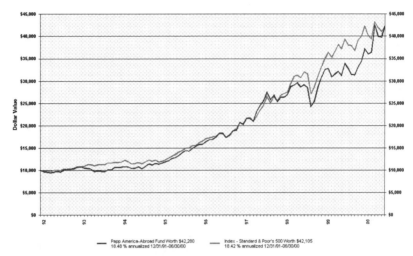

Papp America-Abroad Fund Worth $42,280
18.48 % annualized 12/31/91-06/30/00

Index - Standard & Poor's 500 Worth $42,105
18.42 % annualized 12/31/91-06/30/00

GROWTH OF $10,000

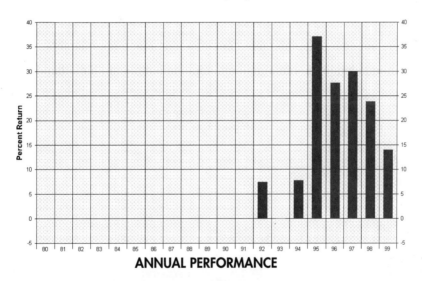

ANNUAL PERFORMANCE

TOP 10 HOLDINGS

Microsoft	Merck & Co.
American Power Conv.	McDonald's
Intel	Hewlett-Packard
Interpublic Group	General Electric
State Street	Molex

RAINIER CORE EQUITY

OBJECTIVE:	Large-Cap Growth	
MANAGER:	James R. Margard	**11**

FUND OVERVIEW:

Although the Rainier Core Equity portfolio is composed primarily of companies in the S&P 500 index, manager James Margard can invest in stocks of all sizes. This highly diversified fund is spread across a broad range of industries. To reduce risk, Margard purposely makes sure not to overweight any single industry. He adheres to a "growth at a reasonable price" philosophy, believing it allows him to generate competitive returns in all market environments.

When evaluating individual securities, Margard emphasizes companies likely to experience superior earnings growth, relative to their peers. He also favors businesses with a competitive advantage operating in a favorable regulatory environment, and he wants them at the right price. Strong management, insider ownership, and financial integrity are other requirements. A stock is sold when it reaches a predetermined target price, or if Margard finds a more attractive idea and needs the money to purchase it.

Even though the minimum investment requirement is a steep $25,000, you can get in for much less through one of the NTF programs (see Chapter 4).

ANNUALIZED RETURNS		PORTFOLIO STATISTICS	
1-Year	15.90%	**Beta**	1.05
3-Year	20.92%	**Turnover**	82.98%
5-Year	24.80%	**12-Month Yield**	0.00%
Overall Rank	2	**12b-1 Fee**	0.25%
Risk Rank	3	**Expense Ratio**	1.11%
MINIMUM INVESTMENT		**CONTACT INFORMATION**	
Regular	$25,000	*Rainier Core Equity Portfolio*	
IRA	$25,000	*Telephone: (800) 248-6314*	
		www.rainierfunds.com	

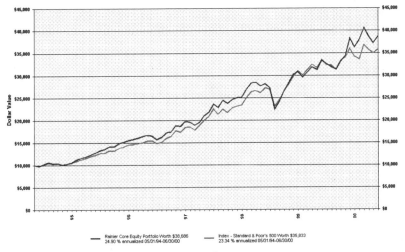

Rainier Core Equity Portfolio Worth $38,686
24.90 % annualized 05/31/94-06/30/00

Index - Standard & Poor's 500 Worth $35,833
23.34 % annualized 05/31/94-06/30/00

GROWTH OF $10,000

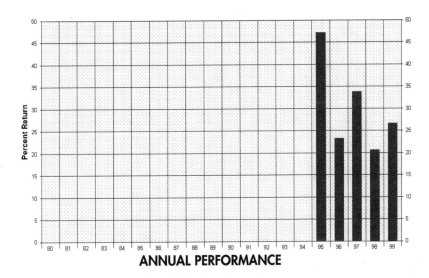

ANNUAL PERFORMANCE

TOP 10 HOLDINGS

Microsoft	Marsh & McLennan
General Electric	Intel
Cisco Systems	Nokia Corp. ADR
Sun Microsystems	Texas Instruments
Nortel Networks	Citigroup

REYNOLDS BLUE CHIP

OBJECTIVE: *Large-Cap Growth*
MANAGER: *Frederick Reynolds*

12

FUND OVERVIEW:

Fritz Reynolds fills his Reynolds Blue Chip Growth Fund with stocks of what he considers to be the "world's best companies." True to the fund's name, he buys mostly blue-chips with: long histories of profitability; leadership positions in their markets; superior and pragmatic growth strategies; proprietary products, processes, or services; experienced and tested management; strong balance sheets; above-average records of dividend consistency and growth; and high returns on equity. (Notice I said he buys *mostly* blue-chips. By prospectus, Reynolds can put up to 35 percent of the portfolio in smaller or foreign names if he thinks that's a wise course of action.)

Reynolds' stock-picking process goes something like this: He starts off by determining the strongest sectors in the market. He then finds individual companies within these sectors with the most favorable earnings prospects. From here, he buys those names he feels are trading at the most attractive valuations. He'll sell a company when it loses its leadership position in its industry or when its price-to-earnings ratio is no longer greater than its future growth prospects.

ANNUALIZED RETURNS		PORTFOLIO STATISTICS	
1-Year	26.40%	Beta	1.12
3-Year	34.34%	Turnover	23.00%
5-Year	33.03%	12-Month Yield	0.00%
Overall Rank	1	12b-1 Fee	0.00%
Risk Rank	4	Expense Ratio	1.30%
MINIMUM INVESTMENT		**CONTACT INFORMATION**	
Regular	$1,000	*Reynolds Blue Chip Growth Fund*	
IRA	$ 100	*Telephone: (800) 773-9665*	
		www.reynoldsfunds.com	

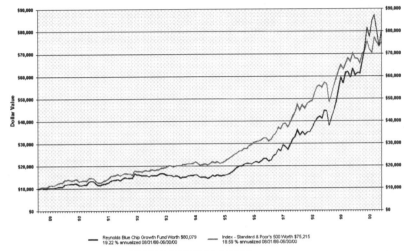

GROWTH OF $10,000

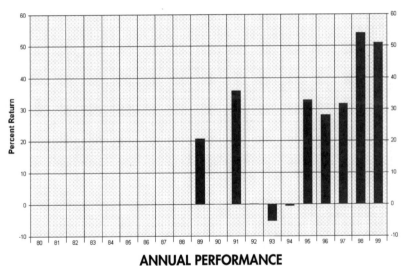

ANNUAL PERFORMANCE

TOP 10 HOLDINGS

Microsoft	Intel
Cisco Systems	Sun Microsystems
Nokia Corp. ADR	Motorola
Yahoo!	America Online
Texas Instruments	Qualcomm

SPECTRA

OBJECTIVE:	*Large-Cap Growth*	
MANAGER:	*David Alger*	*13*

FUND OVERVIEW:

Although I have placed Spectra in the large-cap growth category, it is technically an "all-cap" portfolio. Manager David Alger will buy anything if it meets his criteria. Specifically, he looks for companies experiencing rapid change caused by high unit-volume growth and positive changes in the product life cycle. He and his staff follow 1,400 companies in their database, and like to marry research talent and technology when evaluating potential ideas. Alger refers to his investment style as being an "hourglass method," because he uses both bottom-up and top-down analysis to run this highly concentrated portfolio.

Spectra has been around since 1968, but it was a closed-end fund until February, 1996. This means it was a fixed portfolio traded on the stock exchange. It had a relatively small shareholder base, comprised mostly of members of the Alger family. David Alger has an excellent track record. Unfortunately, the rest of the funds he manages carry steep front-end sales loads. Spectra was converted into a no-load a few years ago, giving investors a chance to tap into Alger's talent without paying a commission. The fund's expense ratio is higher than normal, but it has been justified by stellar performance.

ANNUALIZED RETURNS		PORTFOLIO STATISTICS	
1-Year	31.80%	Beta	1.18
3-Year	35.36%	Turnover	102.54%
5-Year	30.51%	12-Month Yield	0.00%
Overall Rank	2	12b-1 Fee	0.00%
Risk Rank	4	Expense Ratio	1.83%
MINIMUM INVESTMENT		**CONTACT INFORMATION**	
Regular	$1,000	*Spectra Fund*	
IRA	$250	*Telephone: (800) 711-6141*	
		www.spectrafund.com	

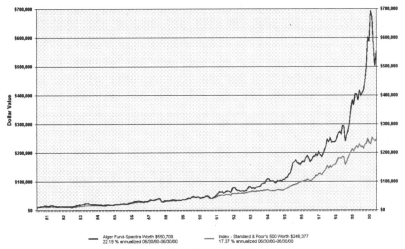

Alger Fund-Spectra Worth $550,709
22.19 % annualized 06/30/80-06/30/00

Index - Standard & Poor's 500 Worth $246,377
17.37 % annualized 06/30/80-06/30/00

GROWTH OF $10,000

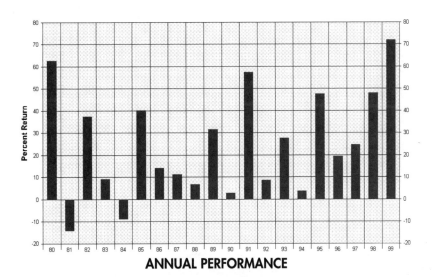

ANNUAL PERFORMANCE

TOP 10 HOLDINGS

Yahoo!	Xilinx
America Online	Cisco Systems
Ebay	Microsoft
Sun Microsystems	Motorola
Exodus Comm.	Home Depot

STEIN ROE YOUNG INVESTOR

OBJECTIVE:	*Large-Cap Growth*	
MANAGER:	*Erik Gustafson and David Brady*	**14**

FUND OVERVIEW:

Even though Stein Roe Young Investor does buy companies of interest to children, the fund's performance has been anything but kid stuff. It has handily outperformed the S&P 500 since inception in 1994, while maintaining a well-diversified portfolio of between 50 and 70 holdings. Although it can invest in both large and small companies, most of the stocks are established blue-chip names. This fund is primarily marketed as a vehicle for growing savings to pay for a young person's college education. However, it is open to all investors.

One reason I like this fund is that Stein Roe writes all shareholder material with its young audience in mind. Big type and graphics are features of every annual report, to make sure children understand how their money is being managed. As a result, the fund gives kids an educational experience while helping them to grow their portfolios. The fund even has its own quarterly newsletter, *Dollar Digest,* and asks shareholders to send in their own investment ideas for future consideration. If you agree to add at least $50 per month to the fund, you can get in for a minimum initial investment of only $100.

ANNUALIZED RETURNS		PORTFOLIO STATISTICS	
1-Year	16.40%	Beta	1.05
3-Year	20.30%	Turnover	43.00%
5-Year	25.48%	12-Month Yield	0.00%
Overall Rank	2	12b-1 Fee	0.00%
Risk Rank	3	Expense Ratio	1.48%
MINIMUM INVESTMENT		**CONTACT INFORMATION**	
Regular	$2,500	*Stein Roe Young Investor Fund*	
IRA	$500	*Telephone: (800) 338-2550*	
		www.steinroe.com	

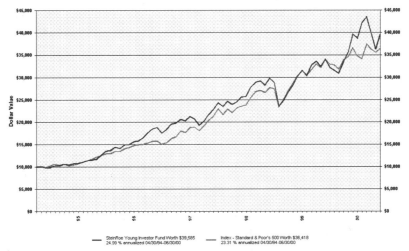

SteinRoe Young Investor Fund Worth $39,585
24.99 % annualized 04/30/94-06/30/00

Index - Standard & Poor's 500 Worth $36,418
23.31 % annualized 04/30/94-06/30/00

GROWTH OF $10,000

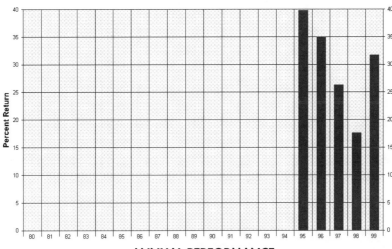

ANNUAL PERFORMANCE

TOP 10 HOLDINGS

Cisco Systems
Microsoft
General Electric
Sun Microsystems
Nortel Networks

Marsh & McLennan
Intel
Nokia Corp. ADR
Texas Instruments
Citigroup

TCW GALILEO SELECT EQUITIES

OBJECTIVE:	*Large-Cap Growth*	
MANAGER:	*Glen Bickerstaff*	**15**

FUND OVERVIEW:

Glen Bickerstaff may be the biggest secret in the mutual fund industry. He has outperformed the S&P 500 in 11 of the 12 years he's been managing money, which is the best record I know of. However, since he's only been running a publicly traded mutual fund for about the past five years, he hasn't received the attention he deserves. After posting great results at the Transamerica Premier Equity Fund, Bickerstaff moved to Trust Company of the West in 1998 and now runs the TCW Galileo Select Equities Fund.

Bickerstaff uses a bottom-up approach and looks for high-quality companies with leadership positions in their respective industries. Among management, he seeks what he calls "patterns of perfection." He wants to make sure they have ownership positions in the companies along with specific plans to capitalize on positive fundamental changes. He also seeks businesses that use cash flow to generate the highest return for shareholders, and he doesn't want to pay too much for the future growth he expects. Bickerstaff keeps a somewhat concentrated portfolio of around 40 names. Because he doesn't do a lot of trading, the fund tends to be pretty tax efficient.

ANNUALIZED RETURNS		PORTFOLIO STATISTICS	
1-Year	43.77%	Beta	N/A
3-Year	34.89%	Turnover	48.00%
5-Year	28.82%	12-Month Yield	0.00%
Overall Rank	N/A	12b-1 Fee	0.25%
Risk Rank	N/A	Expense Ratio	1.46%
MINIMUM INVESTMENT		**CONTACT INFORMATION**	
Regular	$2,000	*TCW Galileo Select Equities Fund*	
IRA	$500	*Telephone: (800) 386-3829*	
		www.tcwgroup.com	

VALUE LINE GROWTH OF $10,000 CHART
NOT AVAILABLE FOR THIS FUND

GROWTH OF $10,000

VALUE LINE ANNUAL PERFORMANCE CHART
NOT AVAILABLE FOR THIS FUND

ANNUAL PERFORMANCE

TOP 10 HOLDINGS

Cisco Systems	EMC Corp.
Network Appliance	Safeway
Microsoft	Maxim Integrated Products
Atmel	Veritas Software
Apple Comupter	General Electric

VANGUARD U.S. GROWTH

OBJECTIVE:	*Large-Cap Growth*	
MANAGER:	*J. Parker Hall III and David Fowler*	**16**

FUND OVERVIEW:

To make it into the Vanguard U.S. Growth portfolio, a company must be attractively priced, financially strong, have an excellent earnings record, enjoy a dominant position in its market, offer above-average prospects for continued growth, and be big in size. To identify such companies, managers J. Parker Hall and David Fowler rigorously research the 200 or so names that meet their initial screening criteria, which include market capitalizations above $1 billion, strong performance records, relatively low sensitivity to changing economic conditions, and a favorable outlook for continued growth. In the end, fewer than 60 companies usually survive this inspection and ultimately find their way into the fund.

The kinds of companies that meet the managers' stringent standards include market leaders from a broad spectrum of industries. You'll normally find such household names as Coca-Cola, AT&T, Cisco Systems, Johnson & Johnson, and Procter & Gamble among the list of top holdings. The fund doesn't tend to do much trading around, and it boasts an annual turnover rate over the past five years of less than 40 percent. It also has about the lowest expense ratio of any actively managed fund available today.

ANNUALIZED RETURNS		PORTFOLIO STATISTICS	
1-Year	20.50%	Beta	1.02
3-Year	24.58%	Turnover	55.00%
5-Year	26.82%	12-Month Yield	0.43%
Overall Rank	2	12b-1 Fee	0.00%
Risk Rank	3	Expense Ratio	0.39%

MINIMUM INVESTMENT		CONTACT INFORMATION	
Regular	$3,000	*Vanguard U.S. Growth*	
IRA	$1,000	*Telephone: (800) 662-7447*	
		www.vanguard.com	

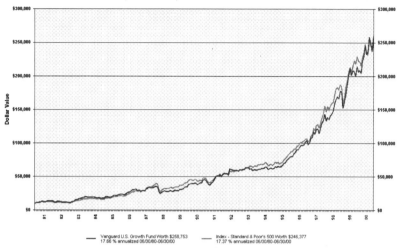

Vanguard U.S. Growth Fund Worth $258,753
17.66 % annualized 06/30/80-06/30/00

Index - Standard & Poor's 500 Worth $246,377
17.37 % annualized 06/30/80-06/30/00

GROWTH OF $10,000

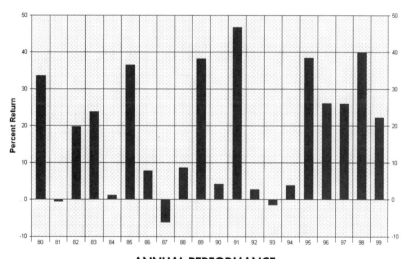

ANNUAL PERFORMANCE

TOP 10 HOLDINGS	
EMC Corp.	Cisco Systems
Microsoft	America Online
General Electric	Sun Microsystems
Texas Instruments	Applied Materials
Intel	Nokia Corp. ADR

WARBURG PINCUS CAPITAL APPRECIATION

OBJECTIVE:	*Large-Cap Growth*	*17*
MANAGER:	*Susan Black*	

FUND OVERVIEW:

Warburg Pincus Capital Appreciation invests across a broadly diversified portfolio of U.S. securities. Portfolio manager Susan Black first tries to find sectors she expects will outperform the overall market for one reason or another. She then searches for the most promising companies within those sectors. Black may also look for positive themes or patterns within businesses (like a change in management, the generation of large free cash flow, or a company share buy-back program), which could make them even more compelling.

This is a pure growth fund, but Black tries to uncover companies she believes are selling at a reasonable price, considering their projected growth. To see whether the valuation makes sense, she analyzes such factors as a company's growth rate, debt-to-equity ratio, and amount of inside ownership. She also tries to identify whether today's growth is sustainable into the future. Some areas of recent interest include financial services, energy, and technology. In particular, she likes financial services because of the sector's significant top-line growth and ongoing consolidation in the industry.

ANNUALIZED RETURNS		PORTFOLIO STATISTICS	
1-Year	41.00%	Beta	0.98
3-Year	31.30%	Turnover	144.00%
5-Year	30.17%	12-Month Yield	0.00%
Overall Rank	1	12b-1 Fee	0.00%
Risk Rank	3	Expense Ratio	1.01%

MINIMUM INVESTMENT		CONTACT INFORMATION
Regular	$2,500	*Warburg Pincus Capital Appreciation*
IRA	$500	*Telephone: (800) 927-2874*
		www.warburg.com

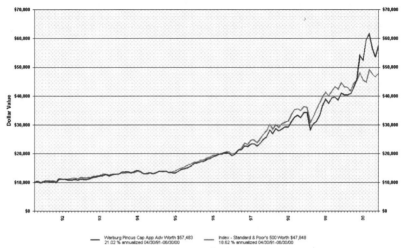

Warburg Pincus Cap App Adv Worth $57,483
21.02 % annualized 04/30/91 -06/30/00

Index - Standard & Poor's 500 Worth $47,848
18.52 % annualized 04/30/91 -06/30/00

GROWTH OF $10,000

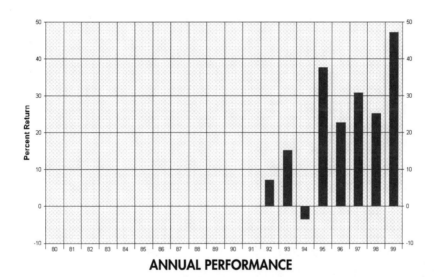

ANNUAL PERFORMANCE

TOP 10 HOLDINGS	
Nextel Communications	Warner-Lambert
General Electric	Cisco Systems
EMC	Intel
Microsoft	CBS Corp.
Sun Microsystems	AT&T Liberty Media A

WHITE OAK GROWTH

OBJECTIVE:	*Large-Cap Growth*	***18***
MANAGER:	*James D. Oelschlager*	

Fund Overview:

White Oak Growth has showered its investors with plenty of money in recent years. This concentrated fund contains around 25 stocks focused in three primary market sectors: financials, technology, and drugs. Manager James Oelschlager has been investing in these areas for the past decade, even before starting this fund. He believes in staying put and running with his winners, which makes the portfolio extremely tax-efficient. With such concentration comes volatility, of course, and this fund can give investors a bumpy ride. Over the long haul, however, it has been a big winner.

White Oak Growth owns established large-cap companies selling at attractive valuations based on expected future earnings. Stocks are monitored based on their five-year growth rates relative to their price-to-earnings multiple. Oelschlager doesn't try to time the market; he generally stays fully invested at all times. He continues to be excited about technology, his largest sector, believing that, going forward, it will be the strongest area for growth in the economy. Furthermore, he remains positive on the pipeline for new drugs and continuing consolidation in the financial services area.

ANNUALIZED RETURNS		PORTFOLIO STATISTICS	
1-Year	61.10%	Beta	1.31
3-Year	41.75%	Turnover	7.19%
5-Year	39.72%	12-Month Yield	0.00%
Overall Rank	1	12b-1 Fee	0.00%
Risk Rank	4	Expense Ratio	1.00%

MINIMUM INVESTMENT		CONTACT INFORMATION
Regular	$2,000	*White Oak Growth*
IRA	$2,000	*Telephone: (888) 462-5386*
		www.oakassociates.com

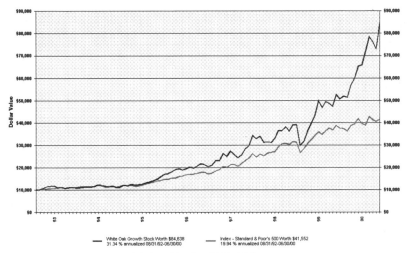

GROWTH OF $10,000

White Oak Growth Stock Worth $84,638
31.34 % annualized 08/31/92–06/30/00

Index – Standard & Poor's 500 Worth $41,552
19.94 % annualized 08/31/92–06/30/00

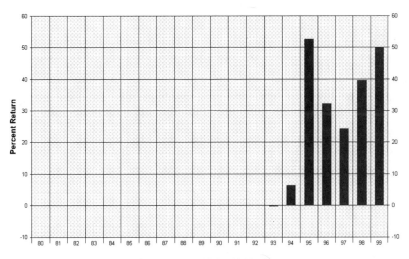

ANNUAL PERFORMANCE

TOP 10 HOLDINGS

Eli Lilly	Intel
Applied Materials	Sun Microsystems
EMC Corp.	Ciena Corp.
Cisco Systems	American International Group
Merck & Co.	Charles Schwab

WILSHIRE TARGET LARGE CO. GROWTH

OBJECTIVE: *Large-Cap Growth*

MANAGER: *Thomas Stevens*

19

FUND OVERVIEW:

You might think of Wilshire Target Large Company Growth as a stylized index fund. The process of putting the portfolio together begins by culling through the 2,500 largest companies from the Wilshire 5000 index (a benchmark consisting of all publicly traded U.S. stocks). From here, manager Thomas Stevens picks out 200 or so of the biggest names with above-average earnings or sales growth. Stevens further favors established companies with solid market recognition, as opposed to up-and-coming turnaround situations. He remains fully invested, opting to switch among holdings as economic conditions change, instead of raising cash.

Stevens reports that five-year earnings growth on the companies in his portfolio remains well above that of the S&P 500, demonstrating the high quality and record of success exemplified by his chosen companies. The fund's sector weighting makeup is also much different from the S&P 500, with almost 30 percent of the portfolio in technology stocks. Its heavy exposure to this area has been beneficial so far, but it could hurt the fund more than its peers if techs take a tumble.

ANNUALIZED RETURNS		PORTFOLIO STATISTICS	
1-Year	21.80%	Beta	1.08
3-Year	27.39%	Turnover	44.00%
5-Year	29.17%	12-Month Yield	0.00%
Overall Rank	1	12b-1 Fee	0.25%
Risk Rank	3	Expense Ratio	0.84%
MINIMUM INVESTMENT		**CONTACT INFORMATION**	
Regular	$2,500	*Wilshire Target Large Co. Growth*	
IRA	$ 750	*Telephone: (888) 200-6796*	
		www.wilfunds.com	

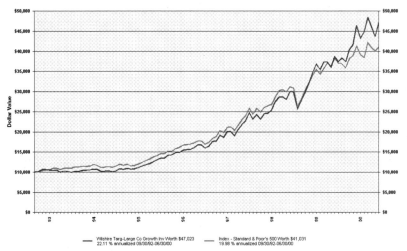

Wilshire Targ-Large Co Growth Inv Worth $47,023
22.11 % annualized 09/30/92-06/30/00

Index - Standard & Poor's 500 Worth $41,031
19.98 % annualized 09/30/92-06/30/00

GROWTH OF $10,000

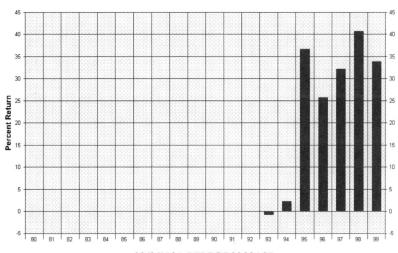

ANNUAL PERFORMANCE

TOP 10 HOLDINGS	
General Electric	Lucent Technologies
Microsoft	Intel
Oracle Corp.	Sun Microsystems
Merck & Co.	Hewlett-Packard
Wal-Mart	Cisco Systems

AMERICAN CENTURY EQUITY GROWTH

OBJECTIVE:	*Large-Cap Value*	***20***
MANAGER:	*William Martin and Jeff Tyler*	

FUND OVERVIEW:

American Century Equity Growth managers William Martin and Jeff Tyler use a quantitative approach to running their fund. They begin by combing through the 2,500 largest companies traded in the United States, which means there are plenty of small caps represented as well. Using a portfolio optimization model, they make sure holdings in the fund match the risk characteristics of the S&P 500, while seeing to it that no more than 25 percent of all assets are invested in the same industry. "This gives the fund balance and stability, which are favorable characteristics during periods of increased market volatility," the managers note.

When it comes to picking individual stocks, the model takes many factors into consideration, including whether a company is underpriced based on earnings growth, business fundamentals, or intrinsic value. Martin and Tyler remain fully invested at all times and tend to focus on the largest names. However, they often include a number of small companies in an effort to enhance returns. They are also working to reduce turnover, which has grown with the increase in assets. This should make the portfolio more tax-efficient.

ANNUALIZED RETURNS		PORTFOLIO STATISTICS	
1-Year	9.40%	Beta	1.04
3-Year	19.96%	Turnover	86.00%
5-Year	23.60%	12-Month Yield	0.54%
Overall Rank	3	12b-1 Fee	0.00%
Risk Rank	3	Expense Ratio	0.68%
MINIMUM INVESTMENT		**CONTACT INFORMATION**	
Regular	$2,500	*American Century Equity*	
IRA	$1,000	*Growth Fund*	
		Telephone: (800) 345-2021	
		www.americancentury.com	

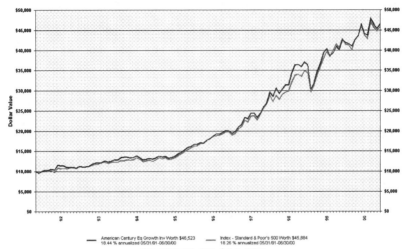

American Century Eq Growth Inv Worth $46,523
18.44 % annualized 05/31/91 -06/30/00

Index - Standard & Poor's 500 Worth $45,884
18.25 % annualized 05/31/91 -06/30/00

GROWTH OF $10,000

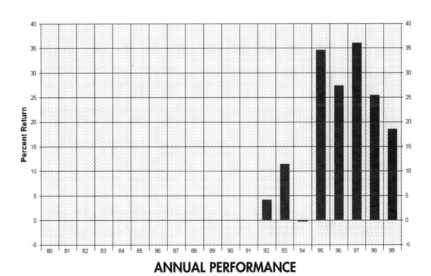

ANNUAL PERFORMANCE

TOP 10 HOLDINGS

Microsoft	Applied Materials
Wal-Mart	Home Depot
Cisco Systems	Hewlett-Packard
Morgan Stanley Dean Witter	Adaptec
Chase Manhattan	General Electric

AMERISTOCK

OBJECTIVE:	*Large-Cap Value*	
MANAGER:	*Nicholas D. Gerber*	**21**

FUND OVERVIEW:

It's no surprise that Nicholas Gerber adheres to a strict combination of active and passive strategies when running his Ameristock mutual fund. After all, before going out on his own, Gerber managed a series of index funds for Bank of America. On the "active" side of the equation, he looks for stocks with low price-to-earnings ratios, high dividend yields, consistent sales growth, and impressive earnings track records. On the "passive" side, he adheres to a low turnover strategy, which keeps commissions and taxable gains down.

Gerber's universe is the largest and most successful companies, which he ranks according to value. He then buys those names that meet his "active" requirements. Gerber started Ameristock in 1995 and operates it out of his California home. In fact, the company is so small, if you call to get information about the fund, Gerber himself might answer the phone.

Nevertheless, Ameristock has everything you could want in a large-cap value fund: relatively low expenses, high tax efficiency, and excellent performance.

ANNUALIZED RETURNS

1-Year	−8.70%
3-Year	14.14%
5-Year	N/A
Overall Rank	2
Risk Rank	3

MINIMUM INVESTMENT

Regular	$1,000
IRA	$1,000

PORTFOLIO STATISTICS

Beta	0.79
Turnover	9.22%
12-Month Yield	1.18%
12b-1 Fee	0.00%
Expense Ratio	0.93%

CONTACT INFORMATION

Ameristock Mutual Fund
Telephone: (800) 394-5064
www.ameristock.com

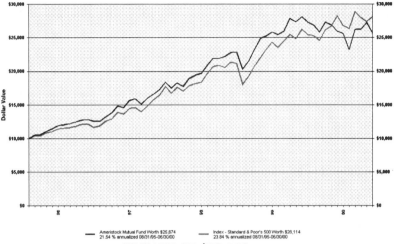

Ameristock Mutual Fund Worth $25,674
21.54 % annualized 08/31/95-06/30/00

Index - Standard & Poor's 500 Worth $28,114
23.84 % annualized 08/31/95-06/30/00

GROWTH OF $10,000

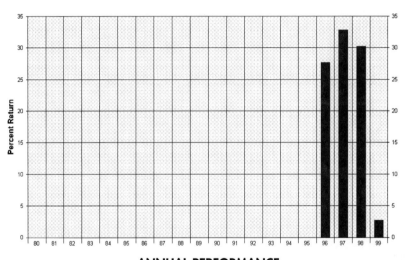

ANNUAL PERFORMANCE

TOP 10 HOLDINGS

PNC Financial Services	Bank of America
Sears Roebuck	Sara Lee
Associates First Cap.	IBM
Washington Mutual	Citigroup
Allstate	Fannie Mae

CLIPPER FUND

OBJECTIVE:	*Large-Cap Value*	
MANAGER:	*James Gipson*	*22*

FUND OVERVIEW:

Clipper Fund skipper James Gipson runs a tight ship. He looks for a few select large-cap stocks that are priced right, and he will hold large amounts of cash when he can't find any. His portfolio may contain as few as 10 to 15 names, as it has recently, especially when he's gloomy about the outlook for the overall market. A cautious approach? You bet. Yet Gipson has managed to perform right in line with the S&P 500, a tough job for even the most aggressive fund.

Gipson is most concerned about preserving capital. He looks for industry leaders selling below intrinsic value. That number is determined either by using a dividend and cash flow discounting model, or by looking at price-to-earnings ratios and comparing the sales transactions of like businesses. Balance sheet strength and the ability to generate earnings are other key factors in the appraisal process. Gipson attempts to keep turnover down, to reduce taxes. But he won't hesitate to trim a holding when he feels the time is right to do so. "Our first choice is to buy stock in a good company cheaply and then hold it forever," he says. "We will sell overvalued stocks, however, rather than expose (the) portfolio to potential loss."

ANNUALIZED RETURNS		PORTFOLIO STATISTICS	
1-Year	−3.40%	Beta	0.52
3-Year	9.74%	Turnover	63.00%
5-Year	16.44%	12-Month Yield	3.08%
Overall Rank	3	12b-1 Fee	0.00%
Risk Rank	2	Expense Ratio	1.10%

MINIMUM INVESTMENT		CONTACT INFORMATION	
Regular	$5,000	*Clipper Fund*	
IRA	$2,000	*Telephone: (800) 776-5033*	
		www.clipperfund.com	

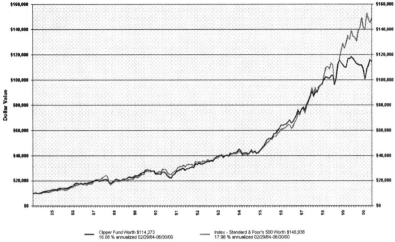

Clipper Fund Worth $114,273
16.08 % annualized 02/29/84-06/30/00

Index - Standard & Poor's 500 Worth $148,938
17.98 % annualized 02/29/84-06/30/00

GROWTH OF $10,000

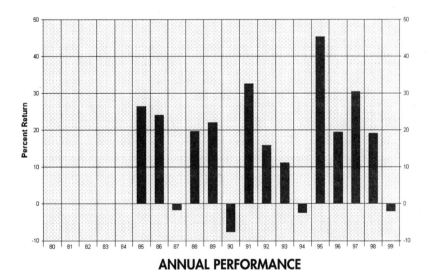

ANNUAL PERFORMANCE

TOP 10 HOLDINGS	
Federal Home Loan	Equity Residential Properties
Fannie Mae	UST Inc.
Philip Morris	Bear Sterns
DeBeers	Manpower
Columbia/HCA	Tenet Healthcare

DODGE & COX STOCK

| OBJECTIVE: | *Large-Cap Value* | **23** |
| MANAGER: | *Team Managed* | |

FUND OVERVIEW:

The Dodge & Cox Stock fund, founded in 1965, takes a price-disciplined approach to investing in large-cap companies. The management team won't buy or sell a stock unless it meets their projected price target. They use a bottom-up approach to company selection, emphasizing fundamental analysis. Still, several themes stand out. The fund has a high weighting in cyclically sensitive areas, such as chemicals, autos, paper/forest products, and transportation. It also maintains a lower exposure than the S&P 500 to the consumer products, health care, and telephone sectors, because valuations in these areas are too high, given the managers' assessment of future earnings potential. "We strive to invest in companies with strong business franchises, good prospects for improving profitability, and current valuations that we believe reflect relatively low investor expectations," notes fund president John A. Gunn.

Stocks in the portfolio generally have below-average price-to-earnings, price-to-book, and market cap-to-sales ratios. Because every investment is made with a three- to five-year time horizon, turnover is consistently low, which increases the overall tax efficiency of this time-tested performer.

ANNUALIZED RETURNS		PORTFOLIO STATISTICS	
1-Year	−3.30%	Beta	0.82
3-Year	10.50%	Turnover	18.00%
5-Year	16.92%	12-Month Yield	1.72%
Overall Rank	3	12b-1 Fee	0.00%
Risk Rank	3	Expense Ratio	0.55%
MINIMUM INVESTMENT		**CONTACT INFORMATION**	
Regular	$2,500	*Dodge & Cox Stock Fund*	
IRA	$1,000	*Telephone: (800) 621-3979*	
		www.dodgeandcox.com	

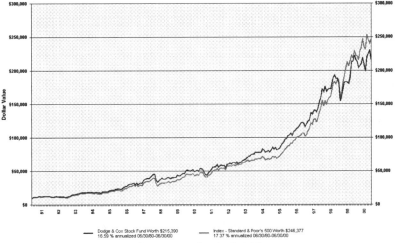

GROWTH OF $10,000

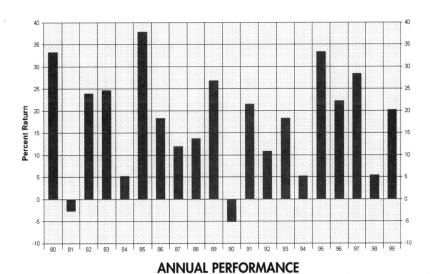

ANNUAL PERFORMANCE

TOP 10 HOLDINGS	
Fox Corp.	Golden West Financial
Matsushita	Hewlett-Packard
News Corp. Pfd.	Citigroup
Rio Tinto PLC ADR	Dow Chemical
Alcoa	Sony Corp. ADR

GABELLI WESTWOOD EQUITY

OBJECTIVE:	*Large-Cap Value*	*24*
MANAGER:	*Susan Byrne*	

FUND OVERVIEW:

Susan Byrne's number-one rule of investing is "Try not to ever lose money." It's a goal she doesn't always achieve, of course. But when she buys each stock for Gabelli Westwood Equity's portfolio, she first attempts to figure out how much it could go down. In her search for individual companies, Byrne employs a top-down approach, beginning with an analysis of overall economic trends to identify sectors or industries poised for growth. Once that work has been done, she starts looking for individual securities that are most likely to benefit.

Byrne's analysis includes searching for a catalyst that can drive a stock higher. When she finds one, she checks out what other analysts are saying about the company. She'll only buy if she feels her peers are underestimating a company's potential. Specifically, Byrne wants to invest in businesses that she is almost certain will come through with positive earnings surprises, surpassing all Wall Street estimates. She sets a target for every stock in the portfolio, and revises it up or down based on the actual reported numbers. This sometimes means she gets out of high-fliers before they run out of steam. But she'd rather play it safe than risk being shocked by a disappointment.

ANNUALIZED RETURNS		PORTFOLIO STATISTICS	
1-Year	7.20%	Beta	0.78
3-Year	14.24%	Turnover	67.00%
5-Year	21.30%	12-Month Yield	0.18%
Overall Rank	2	12b-1 Fee	0.25%
Risk Rank	2	Expense Ratio	1.48%

MINIMUM INVESTMENT		CONTACT INFORMATION
Regular	$1,000	*Gabelli Westwood Equity Fund*
IRA	$1,000	*Telephone: (800) 422-3554*
		www.gabelli.com

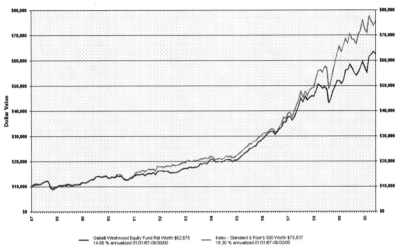

Gabelli Westwood Equity Fund Ret Worth $62,875
14.66 % annualized 01/31/87-06/30/00

Index - Standard & Poor's 500 Worth $75,837
16.30 % annualized 01/31/87-06/30/00

GROWTH OF $10,000

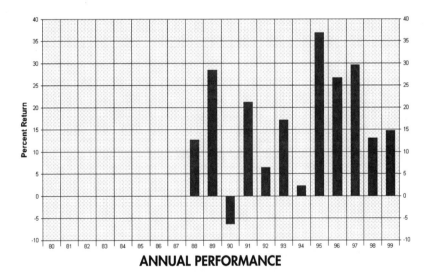

ANNUAL PERFORMANCE

TOP 10 HOLDINGS

Apache Corp.	Pharmacia & Upjohn
Limited	IBM
PNC Financial Svcs.	Time Warner
Delta Air Lines	Chase Manhattan
Reliant Energy	Federated Dept. Stores

LEGG MASON VALUE TRUST

OBJECTIVE:	*Large-Cap Value*	
MANAGER:	*William H. Miller III*	**25**

FUND OVERVIEW:

Let's get the bad news out of the way first. Legg Mason Value Trust has a huge 12b-1 fee of .95 percent, which normally would be reason enough for me to stay away from it. It has also grown quite large in a short period of time. But there is a good reason for that. Manager Bill Miller has steered the fund to excellent returns, thanks to shrewd stock picking, low turnover, and a flexible value bias. For that reason, I'm willing to overlook these negatives, assuming that Miller can continue to deliver despite the obstacles in his way.

Miller is quick to point out that he is an *investor,* not a speculator. He doesn't try to guess the direction of the market or which industries are most likely to outperform. He builds his portfolio one name at a time. "We do intensive research on our holdings and try to buy companies whose prices represent large discounts to our assessment of the intrinsic value of the business," he says. "We use an economic value approach to our analytical process, which involves going well beyond simple accounting-based measures of value." He runs a tightly focused portfolio of about 35 to 40 names, and will hold on to his biggest winners, even when they mature from being "value" stocks and become "growth" stocks.

ANNUALIZED RETURNS		PORTFOLIO STATISTICS	
1-Year	3.80%	Beta	1.22
3-Year	26.76%	Turnover	19.70%
5-Year	31.85%	12-Month Yield	0.02%
Overall Rank	1	12b-1 Fee	0.94%
Risk Rank	4	Expense Ratio	1.67%
MINIMUM INVESTMENT		**CONTACT INFORMATION**	
Regular	$1,000	*Legg Mason Value Trust*	
IRA	$1,000	*Telephone: (800) 822-5544*	
		www.leggmason.com	

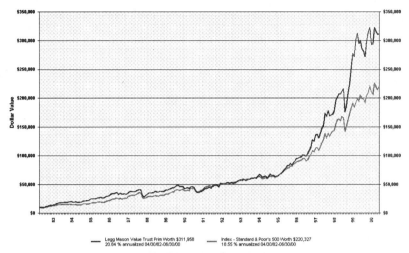

GROWTH OF $10,000

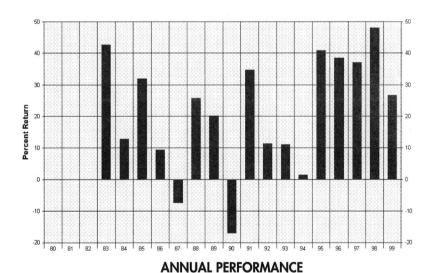

ANNUAL PERFORMANCE

TOP 10 HOLDINGS

Dell Computer	Citigroup
America Online	WPP Group PLC
Gateway	MCI WorldCom
Nextel Communications	Nokia Corp. ADR
Chase Manhattan	United Healthcare

SELECTED AMERICAN SHARES

| OBJECTIVE: | *Large-Cap Value* | *26* |
| MANAGER: | *Christopher Davis and Kenneth Feinberg* | |

FUND OVERVIEW:

If you had to make a short list of the best mutual fund managers of all time, there's no question that Shelby Davis would show up near the top. His New York Venture Fund has been an outstanding performer since its inception in 1969. Perhaps he inherited much of his investment skill from his late father, who was a Wall Street legend in his own right. Unfortunately, New York Venture is a load fund, meaning you pay a commission to get in. In 1993, Shelby took over management of Selected American Shares, which is a nearly identical fund that is available on a no-load basis. Shelby relinquished day-to-day portfolio management duties to his son, Chris, in 1997, although he remains the firm's chief investment officer. Shelby still spends his days providing guidance on investment themes, strategies, and individual stock selection, while Chris and co-manager Kenneth Feinberg pull the trigger.

The Davis investment philosophy calls for finding overlooked, undervalued companies with promising long-term prospects. The Davises believe in doing rigorous research, visiting with management, and actively managing risk. They also favor proven businesses with long histories of earnings growth.

ANNUALIZED RETURNS		PORTFOLIO STATISTICS	
1-Year	10.50%	Beta	1.02
3-Year	19.41%	Turnover	20.00%
5-Year	24.80%	12-Month Yield	0.27%
Overall Rank	2	12b-1 Fee	0.25%
Risk Rank	3	Expense Ratio	0.92%

MINIMUM INVESTMENT		CONTACT INFORMATION	
Regular	$1,000	*Selected American Shares*	
IRA	$ 250	*Telephone: (800) 243-1575*	
		Website: www.selectedfunds.com	

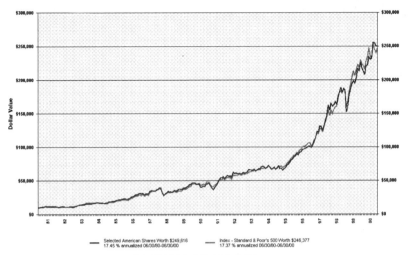

Selected American Shares Worth $249,616
17.45 % annualized 06/30/80-06/30/00

Index - Standard & Poor's 500 Worth $246,377
17.37 % annualized 06/30/80-06/30/00

GROWTH OF $10,000

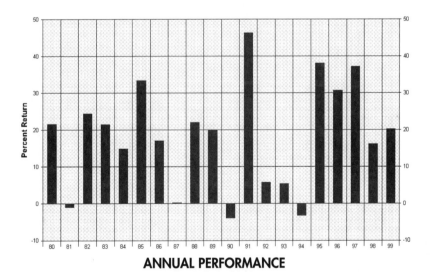

ANNUAL PERFORMANCE

TOP 10 HOLDINGS

Wells Fargo & Co.	American Intl. Group
American Express	Household International
Hewlett-Packard	Citigroup
McDonald's	Texas Instruments
IBM	Morgan Stanley Dean Witter

THE TORRAY FUND

OBJECTIVE:	*Large-Cap Value*	**27**
MANAGER:	*Robert E. Torray*	

FUND OVERVIEW:

Robert Torray is finally getting some much-deserved recognition. His Torray Fund went relatively unnoticed by investors for years, despite its standout performance compared to the S&P 500. Then people began to pay attention, and assets in the fund increased fourfold in one short year. Is all that new money impacting Torray's ability to keep posting strong numbers? No, he insists. And he has no plans to close the fund at this time. "So far, cash flow from shareholders has proven to be a tremendous advantage," he claims. "It has funded promising new investments and additions to existing holdings that otherwise could not have been made without selling stocks we prefer to maintain."

Torray says his investment style is simple. He'll buy stocks in the best companies at a fair price and keep them indefinitely. He'll consider small, medium, or large capitalization companies, although the latter have been getting most of his attention lately. His chosen companies have favorable economic characteristics, like rising sales and earnings, a strong competitive position, capable management, and a solid balance sheet. Torray runs a concentrated portfolio. More than half of all assets are placed in his top 20 holdings.

ANNUALIZED RETURNS		PORTFOLIO STATISTICS	
1-Year	−4.90%	Beta	1.01
3-Year	14.46%	Turnover	14.86%
5-Year	22.10%	12-Month Yield	0.36%
Overall Rank	2	12b-1 Fee	0.00%
Risk Rank	3	Expense Ratio	1.08%
MINIMUM INVESTMENT		**CONTACT INFORMATION**	
Regular	$10,000	*The Torray Fund*	
IRA	$10,000	*Telephone: (800) 443-3036*	
		www.torray.com	

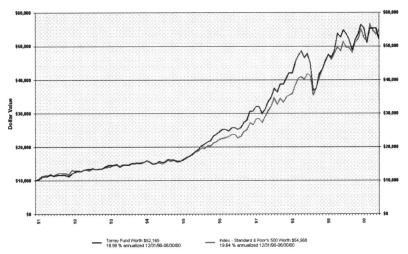

Torray Fund Worth $52,165
18.99 % annualized 12/31/90-06/30/00

Index - Standard & Poor's 500 Worth $54,968
19.64 % annualized 12/31/90-06/30/00

GROWTH OF $10,000

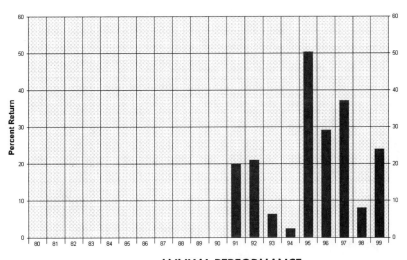

ANNUAL PERFORMANCE

TOP 10 HOLDINGS

SLM Holding Corp.
Electronic Data Systems
Boston Scientific
JP Morgan
Illinois Tool Works

Abbott Labs
Loral Space & Communications
PanamSat Corp.
Amgen
Citigroup

BONNEL GROWTH

OBJECTIVE:	*Mid-Cap Growth*	
MANAGER:	*Art Bonnel*	***28***

FUND OVERVIEW:

In Art Bonnel's mind, a company's financial numbers tell the whole story. That's why he places such an emphasis on locating companies with strong earnings and a solid balance sheet. Working out of his Reno, Nevada home, along with wife Wanda, Bonnel begins most mornings by going through all of the Wall Street earnings reports, in search of potential candidates for his portfolio. If the numbers look good, he'll dig deeper, making sure the company has a leading position in its market niche and a management team with a substantial ownership stake.

While Bonnel has the freedom to buy any stocks he wants, he usually focuses on companies with market capitalizations of under $5 billion. Bonnel has been managing money since 1970, and especially shines when investors are attracted to stocks with rising earnings momentum. He often loads up on technology stocks, which can lead to some frequent turbulence. But, over the long term, Bonnel has done a good job of staying ahead of the market. What's more, running this fund is the only thing Bonnel does, unlike many of his peers who are left juggling a couple of funds and a number of private accounts on the side.

ANNUALIZED RETURNS		PORTFOLIO STATISTICS	
1-Year	68.60%	Beta	0.90
3-Year	37.20%	Turnover	197.00%
5-Year	31.83%	12-Month Yield	0.00%
Overall Rank	2	12b-1 Fee	0.25%
Risk Rank	5	Expense Ratio	1.77%

MINIMUM INVESTMENT		CONTACT INFORMATION
Regular	$5,000	*Bonnel Growth Fund*
IRA	$0	*Telephone: (800) 873-8637*
		www.usfunds.com

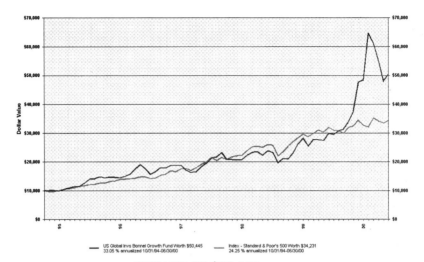

GROWTH OF $10,000

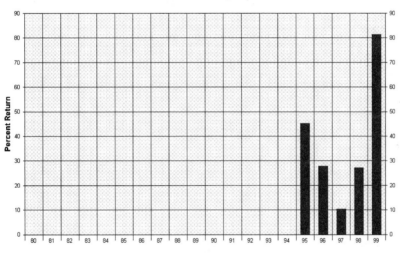

ANNUAL PERFORMANCE

TOP 10 HOLDINGS	
JDS Uniphase	Mercury Air Group
Cisco Systems	Sun Microsystems
QLogic	Idec Pharmaceuticals
Power Integrations	Macrovision
Xilinx	Advent Software

BRAMWELL GROWTH

| **OBJECTIVE:** | *Mid-Cap Growth* | *29* |
| **MANAGER:** | *Elizabeth R. Bramwell* | |

FUND OVERVIEW:

Elizabeth Bramwell uses a blended approach to find stocks for her Bramwell Growth Fund portfolio. She begins from a top-down perspective, looking at such macroeconomic variables as inflation and interest rates. This helps her determine which broad industries or themes are likely to benefit most from current conditions. From here, she does bottom-up analysis, focusing on company-specific variables like competitive industry dynamics, uniqueness of products and services, market leadership, and management expertise. On the financial side, Bramwell searches for stocks with high returns on sales and equity, favorable debt-to-equity ratios, and strong earnings and cash flow growth. She gets information from many sources, and she meets with management by attending the frequent analyst meetings held near her New York office.

Bramwell has been managing money for some three decades. Before launching her own fund in 1994, she built a great record at Gabelli Growth. Her present focus is on companies offering innovative new products and services that are beneficiaries of lower interest rates and effective users of technology. She also likes stocks that exploit the rising standard of living around the globe.

ANNUALIZED RETURNS		PORTFOLIO STATISTICS	
1-Year	22.50%	Beta	1.03
3-Year	26.82%	Turnover	10.00%
5-Year	24.30%	12-Month Yield	0.00%
Overall Rank	1	12b-1 Fee	0.25%
Risk Rank	3	Expense Ratio	1.54%

MINIMUM INVESTMENT		CONTACT INFORMATION	
Regular	$1,000	*Bramwell Growth Fund*	
IRA	$500	*Telephone: (800) 272-6227*	
		www.bramcap.com	

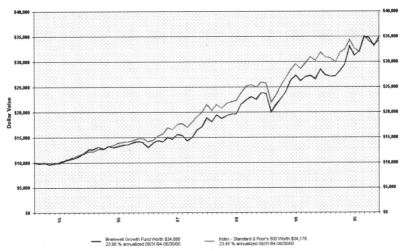

GROWTH OF $10,000

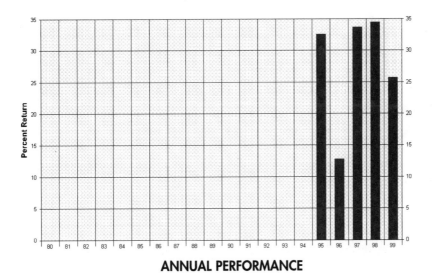

ANNUAL PERFORMANCE

TOP 10 HOLDINGS	
EMC	Tiffany
Computer Sciences	Kohl's Corp.
Walgreen	Applied Materials
General Electric	Nortel Networks
Home Depot	Cisco Systems

FIRSTHAND TECHNOLOGY VALUE

OBJECTIVE:	*Mid-Cap Growth*
MANAGER:	*Kevin Landis*

30

FUND OVERVIEW:

I'm normally not a very big fan of sector investing, but Kevin Landis is such an excellent technology stock picker, I'm willing to make an exception. I stuck this fund in the mid-cap growth list, although Firsthand Technology Value is technically a sector fund. And despite its name, this is, in fact, a growth fund.

Landis came to investment management from the technology field. This was his first fund, and it has had an outstanding track record—the best in the field.

In evaluating potential holdings, Landis looks for companies he thinks are worth more than their current market price. He's pretty good about spotting trends before they happen, which is key in this sector. When grilling management, Landis looks for technical vision, marketing acumen, proprietary technological advantages, and the ability to respond rapidly to changing marketing conditions. Landis is headquartered in the Silicon Valley and once told me he spends part of his weekends driving around the parking lots of the companies he invests in to see if their employees are dedicated enough to be in the office. Now that's what I call dedicated research.

ANNUALIZED RETURNS		PORTFOLIO STATISTICS	
1-Year	120.00%	**Beta**	1.23
3-Year	59.38%	**Turnover**	41.00%
5-Year	59.03%	**12-Month Yield**	0.00%
Overall Risk	2	**12b-1 Fee**	0.00%
Risk Rank	5	**Expense Ratio**	1.90%

MINIMUM INVESTMENT		CONTACT INFORMATION
Regular	$10,000	*Firsthand Technology Value Fund*
IRA	$2,000	*Telephone: (888) 884-2675*
		www.firsthandfunds.com

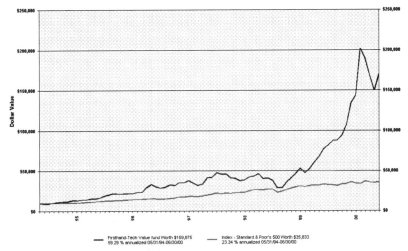

Firsthand-Tech Value fund Worth $169,875
59.29 % annualized 05/31/94-06/30/00

Index - Standard & Poor's 500 Worth $35,833
23.34 % annualized 05/31/94-06/30/00

GROWTH OF $10,000

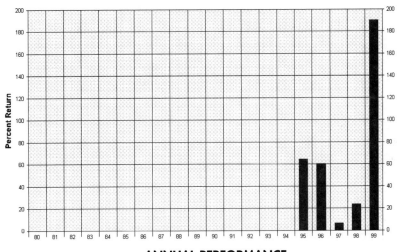

ANNUAL PERFORMANCE

TOP 10 HOLDINGS

TriQuint Semiconductor	Legato Systems
Applied Micro Circuits	Transwitch Corp.
PMC-Sierra	Nokia Corp. ADR
Digital Microwave	Globix Corp.
AT&T	Immune X

MAIRS & POWER GROWTH

OBJECTIVE:	*Mid-Cap Growth*	*31*
MANAGER:	*George A. Mairs*	

FUND OVERVIEW:

George Mairs likes to find investment ideas in his own backyard. That's why his Mairs & Power Growth fund has a large concentration of companies based in Minnesota. In fact, he focuses his research efforts on finding good businesses in the upper Midwest. His rationale is that he can add value to the research process this way. After all, he understands these local firms better than Wall Street and can visit them in person. That doesn't mean he won't consider companies in other parts of the country. He will, but usually only when he can't find an equivalent idea in the same sector locally. This regional focus certainly hasn't hampered performance. Mairs & Power Growth continually seems to outshine the competition.

Mairs looks for high-quality companies with predictable earnings, above-average return on equity, market dominance, and financial strength. He stays fully invested at all times and favors a buy-and-hold strategy. Mairs will sell a holding once he believes it has become fully priced. He'll then use the proceeds to either establish a new position or add to an existing one. He likes mid-caps because they offer comparable returns to small-caps with less risk.

ANNUALIZED RETURNS		PORTFOLIO STATISTICS	
1-Year	4.80%	Beta	0.75
3-Year	10.97%	Turnover	5.55%
5-Year	19.94%	12-Month Yield	0.88%
Overall Rank	3	12b-1 Fee	0.00%
Risk Rank	2	Expense Ratio	0.79%
MINIMUM INVESTMENT		**CONTACT INFORMATION**	
Regular	$2,500	*Mairs & Power Growth Fund*	
IRA	$1,000	*Telephone: (800) 304-7404*	

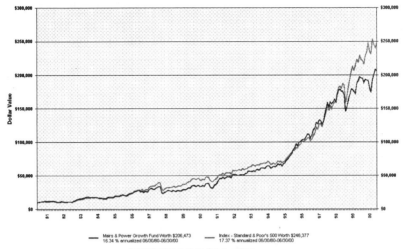

Mairs & Power Growth Fund Worth $206,473
16.34 % annualized 06/30/80-06/30/00

Index - Standard & Poor's 500 Worth $246,377
17.37 % annualized 06/30/80-06/30/00

GROWTH OF $10,000

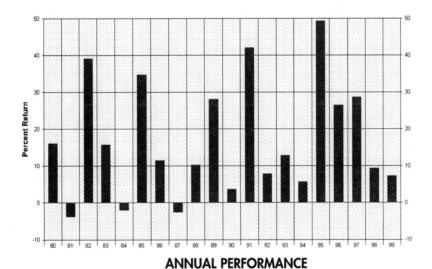

ANNUAL PERFORMANCE

TOP 10 HOLDINGS

Medtronic	Graco Inc.
ADC Telecommunications	Ecolab
Wells Fargo & Co.	Johnson & Johnson
Dayton Hudson	Minnesota Mining & Mfg.
Natl. Computer Systems	Emerson Electric

NEVIS FUND

OBJECTIVE:	*Mid-Cap Growth*	*32*
MANAGER:	*David Wilmerding and Jon Baker*	

FUND OVERVIEW:

Talk about risky. The Nevis Fund loads up on high-octane stocks hoping to produce stunning returns. So far, that's exactly what managers David Wilmerding and Jon Baker have done. They limit the portfolio to less than 30 names and place big bets on a handful of small, relatively unknown companies.

The fund is fairly new, having been launched in June of 1998. But Wilmerding and Baker have been managing money together for foundations, endowments, and wealthy families since 1991.

The two look for companies with management capable of producing rapid sustained earnings growth over the long term. They feel that by concentrating their money in a handful of good ideas, they can keep a closer eye on their holdings.

Since inception, more than half of the fund's money has been put into high-tech companies, a smart move that has powered the fund to chart-topping returns. Although the fund's stunning performance has attracted significant assets, because of the fund's high initial minimum investment, growth has been rather controlled, which is a good sign.

ANNUALIZED RETURNS		PORTFOLIO STATISTICS	
1-Year	69.95%	Beta	N/A
3-Year	N/A	Turnover	N/A
5-Year	N/A	12-Month Yield	0.00%
Overall Risk	N/A	12b-1 Fee	0.00%
Risk Rank	N/A	Expense Ratio	1.50%
MINIMUM INVESTMENT		**CONTACT INFORMATION**	
Regular	$10,000	*Nevis Fund*	
IRA	$2,000	*Telephone: (888) 263-5597*	
		www.nevisfund.com	

VALUE LINE GROWTH OF $10,000 CHART
NOT AVAILABLE FOR THIS FUND

GROWTH OF $10,000

VALUE LINE ANNUAL PERFORMANCE CHART
NOT AVAILABLE FOR THIS FUND

ANNUAL PERFORMANCE

TOP 10 HOLDINGS

Primus Knowledge Solutions	Ariba
American Tower Cl. A	Conductus
Rational Software	Clear Channel Communications
SBA Communications	CSG Systems Intl.
Vitesse Semiconductor	BEA Systems

NICHOLAS

OBJECTIVE:	*Mid-Cap Growth*	
MANAGER:	*Albert O. Nicholas*	*33*

FUND OVERVIEW:

When Albert Nicholas first started managing this fund in 1969, he concentrated mostly on big, blue-chip names. Over the years, however, you could say he has downsized somewhat, favoring more midsize companies. This has been especially true in recent years. As a value investor, Nicholas insists that many of the larger names are highly overpriced.

Patience is a virtue in the Nicholas investment strategy. He is a fundamentally oriented manager who looks for stocks with low price-to-earnings ratios and consistent, above-average earnings growth. He holds his positions, on average, three years or more. He doesn't try to forecast short-term market swings, but will preserve gains by selling what he deems to be overvalued securities. Even though Nicholas is now cautious about the direction of the economy, the fund remains fully invested in companies he considers to be fairly priced with rapid earnings growth. Current earnings momentum is an important factor in his overall investment process. Nicholas generally won't buy Initial Public Offerings or foreign stocks, because they are too risky. This fund has consistently outperformed its peers over time, with lower-than-average volatility.

ANNUALIZED RETURNS		PORTFOLIO STATISTICS	
1-Year	−18.40%	Beta	0.92
3-Year	3.62%	Turnover	39.72%
5-Year	13.16%	12-Month Yield	0.50%
Overall Rank	4	12b-1 Fee	0.00%
Risk Rank	3	Expense Ratio	0.72%
MINIMUM INVESTMENT		**CONTACT INFORMATION**	
Regular	$500	*Nicholas Fund*	
IRA	$500	*Telephone: (800) 227-5987*	
		www.nicholasfunds.com	

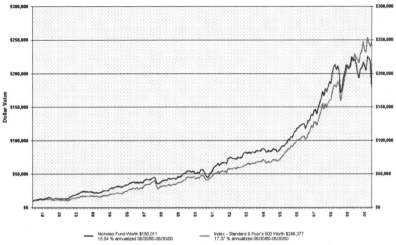

Nicholas Fund Worth $180,011
15.54 % annualized 06/30/80-06/30/00

Index - Standard & Poor's 500 Worth $246,377
17.37 % annualized 06/30/80-06/30/00

GROWTH OF $10,000

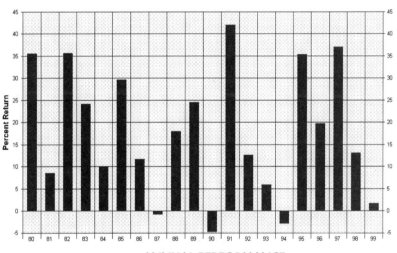

ANNUAL PERFORMANCE

TOP 10 HOLDINGS

Berkshire Hathaway	Mercury General
CVS Corp.	Motorola
Cintas Corp.	General Motors Cl. H
ADC Telecommunication	Intel
Marshall & Ilsley	Sybron Intl.

PIN OAK AGGRESSIVE STOCK

OBJECTIVE:	Mid-Cap Growth	
MANAGER:	James Oelschlager and Douglas MacKay	*34*

FUND OVERVIEW:

Within the mid-cap growth category, you'll find plenty of funds with the kind of rapid trading that can make your head spin. But that's not the case at Pin Oak Aggressive Stock. Managers Jim Oelschlager and Doug MacKay tend to have incredible patience with their holdings, which keeps turnover and annual taxable gains to a minimum. You can think of this as the more aggressive sibling to Oelschlager's White Oak Growth (a Powerhouse Performer in the large-cap area).

Oelschlager and MacKay are big believers in technology, a sector that always has a hefty representation in the portfolio. That, combined with the relatively small number of total holdings, provides for incredible volatility. You can expect that in periods when mid-cap stocks do well, this fund will shine, as it has over the past few years. When large-caps steal the show, as they did throughout the mid-1990s, White Oak will likely do better, although there is some overlap in the holdings. All in all, Pin Oak is an excellent choice for those looking for exposure to this aggressive segment of the market.

ANNUALIZED RETURNS		PORTFOLIO STATISTICS	
1-Year	119.60%	Beta	1.17
3-Year	58.35%	Turnover	26.47%
5-Year	38.25%	12-Month Yield	0.00%
Overall Risk	2	12b-1 Fee	0.00%
Risk Rank	5	Expense Ratio	1.00%

MINIMUM INVESTMENT		CONTACT INFORMATION	
Regular	$2,000	*Pin Oak Aggressive Stock*	
IRA	$2,000	*Telephone: (888) 462-5386*	
		www.oakassociates.com	

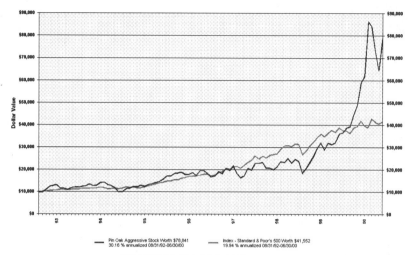

Pin Oak Aggressive Stock Worth $78,841
30.16 % annualized 08/31/92-06/30/00

Index - Standard & Poor's 500 Worth $41,552
19.94 % annualized 08/31/92-06/30/00

GROWTH OF $10,000

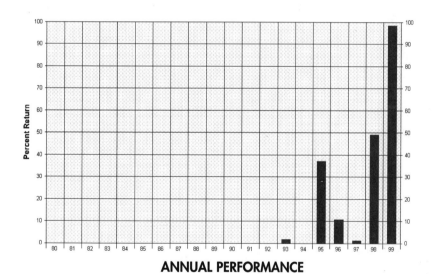

ANNUAL PERFORMANCE

TOP 10 HOLDINGS	
Cisco Systems	Advent Software
Vitesse Semiconductor	Tellabs
JDS Uniphase	Foundry Networks
Brocade Communications	Exodus Communications
MBNA Corp.	Juniper Networks

STRONG GROWTH 20

OBJECTIVE:	*Mid-Cap Growth*	*35*
MANAGER:	*Ronald Ognar*	

FUND OVERVIEW:

Strong Growth 20 manager Ronald Ognar doesn't care what size a company is. He just wants to make sure it's growing and in an industry with solid fundamentals. There is a good and bad side to this investment approach. The good is that Ognar can exploit the best performing part of the market at any given time (assuming he's right). The downside is that Ognar is a style drifter, switching around from small- and large-caps all the time, so you don't always know what kind of fund you own. That's why when you look at the portfolio in total, you can only conclude that this is a true mid-cap offering. And since it is concentrated in only 20 to 30 of Ognar's favorite names, it's extremely aggressive and volatile.

Ognar favors companies with demonstrated earnings growth. He especially likes businesses with good financial and accounting policies, competitive edges, signs that capital is producing high returns, effective marketing and product development departments, prospects for above-average sales and profit growth, and stable managements. Ognar also likes to buy stocks trading at significant discounts to their projected growth rates.

ANNUALIZED RETURNS		PORTFOLIO STATISTICS	
1-Year	88.70%	**Beta**	0.93
3-Year	54.39%	**Turnover**	262.90%
5-Year	N/A	**12-Month Yield**	0.00%
Overall Rank	1	**12b-1 Fee**	0.00%
Risk Rank	4	**Expense Ratio**	1.39%

MINIMUM INVESTMENT		CONTACT INFORMATION
Regular	$2,500	*Strong Growth 20 Fund*
IRA	$250	*Telephone: (800) 368-1030*
		www.strong-funds.com

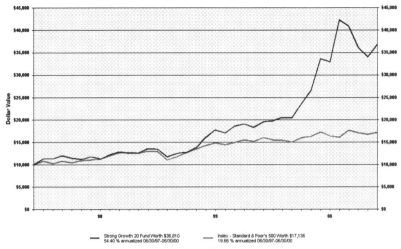

Strong Growth 20 Fund Worth $36,810
54.40 % annualized 06/30/97-06/30/00

Index - Standard & Poor's 500 Worth $17,136
19.66 % annualized 06/30/97-06/30/00

GROWTH OF $10,000

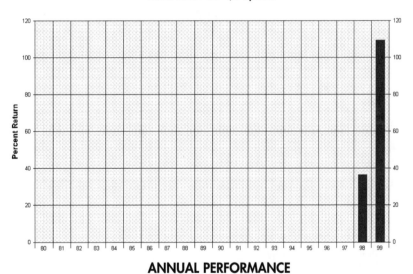

ANNUAL PERFORMANCE

TOP 10 HOLDINGS	
JDS Uniphase	Veritas Software
Cisco Systems	Freemarkets
Verisign	E-Tek Dynamics
Vignette Corp.	Medimmune
Home Depot	Sycamore Networks

T. ROWE PRICE MID-CAP GROWTH

OBJECTIVE:	Mid-Cap Growth	**36**
MANAGER:	Brian W. H. Berghuis	

FUND OVERVIEW:

Brian Berghuis is convinced his mid-cap stock universe is quite attractive going into the new millennium. He feels many of his companies are poised to do extremely well after being somewhat neglected in recent years. Berghuis looks for stocks with market values in the $300 million to $4 billion range and with earnings that are growing at a faster-than-average rate. He sticks mostly with domestic equities, although he'll buy other securities if he feels a purchase is appropriate.

Berghuis invests based on the belief that good research, not opinions on the overall economic environment, are what will lead him to superior long-term results. "We devote our time to carefully researching and evaluating company fundamentals," he says. "While we typically examine a multitude of factors before we invest, and virtually never invest before a face-to-face meeting with a company's management, several of the criteria we focus on include the growth in the company's industry sector, the growth rate we foresee for the company over the next several years, the strength of a company's business model, management we respect, strong financial characteristics, and reasonable valuations."

ANNUALIZED RETURNS		PORTFOLIO STATISTICS	
1-Year	17.60%	Beta	1.01
3-Year	21.17%	Turnover	53.30%
5-Year	22.89%	12-Month Yield	0.00%
Overall Rank	2	12b-1 Fee	0.00%
Risk Rank	3	Expense Ratio	0.86%
MINIMUM INVESTMENT		**CONTACT INFORMATION**	
Regular	$2,500	T. Rowe Price Mid-Cap Growth Fund	
IRA	$1,000	Telephone: (800) 638-5660	
		www.troweprice.com	

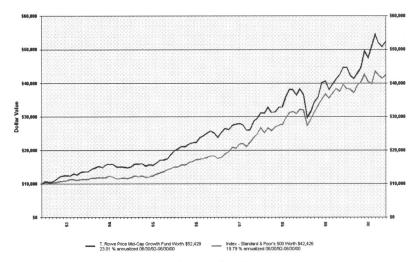

GROWTH OF $10,000

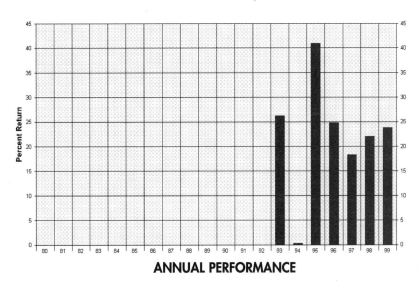

ANNUAL PERFORMANCE

TOP 10 HOLDINGS	
Affiliated Computer Svcs.	BJ Services
Voicestream Wireless	Tera Pharmaceutical
SCI Systems	Ciber Inc.
Circuit City	Analog Devices
Nora Corp.	Western Wireless

TCW GALILEO AGGRESSIVE GROWTH EQUITIES

OBJECTIVE:	*Mid-Cap Growth*	**37**
MANAGER:	*Christopher Ainley and Douglas Foreman*	

FUND OVERVIEW:

The TCW Galileo Aggressive Growth Equities Fund buys mid-sized companies that portfolio managers Christopher Ainley and Douglas Foreman believe are "reshaping the competitive landscape of the industries in which they compete." They believe that investors are generally slow to recognize these trends, and feel if they can spot such companies early enough, they can profit handsomely once the rest of Wall Street catches on.

Ainley and Foreman narrow the mid-cap universe of more than 2,700 issues down to around 200 securities through a computerized screening process. They look for companies with earnings growth of at least 15 percent over the last three years and a similar return on equity. When all is said and done, they get a list of about 80 companies from which to choose.

This is among the most volatile funds in the mid-cap growth category, largely because the two managers often concentrate money in their favorite holdings. In fact, during the most recent period, almost half of the portfolio was invested in the fund's top 10 names. But the fund's overall performance record has been excellent.

ANNUALIZED RETURNS		PORTFOLIO STATISTICS	
1-Year	83.64%	Beta	N/A
3-Year	65.06%	Turnover	N/A
5-Year	N/A	12-Month Yield	N/A
Overall Rank	N/A	12b-1 Fee	0.25%
Risk Rank	N/A	Expense Ratio	1.70%
MINIMUM INVESTMENT		**CONTACT INFORMATION**	
Regular	$2,000	*TCW Galileo Aggressive Growth*	
IRA	$500	*Equities Fund*	
		Telephone: (800) 386-3829	
		www.tcwgroup.com	

VALUE LINE GROWTH OF $10,000 CHART
NOT AVAILABLE FOR THIS FUND

GROWTH OF $10,000

VALUE LINE ANNUAL PERFORMANCE CHART
NOT AVAILABLE FOR THIS FUND

ANNUAL PERFORMANCE

TOP 10 HOLDINGS	
Siebel Systems	Vignette
VeriSign	Maxim Integrated Products
Xilinx	Ariba
Yahoo!	Abgenix
Juniper Net	Human Genome Sciences

TURNER MIDCAP GROWTH

OBJECTIVE:	*Mid-Cap Growth*	*38*
MANAGER:	*Christopher McHugh*	

FUND OVERVIEW:

Chris McHugh selects stocks for the Turner Midcap portfolio based on the belief that earnings drive stock prices. His universe is equities with market capitalizations between $1 billion and $10 billion.

Unlike other funds in this category, McHugh attempts to keep his sector concentrations in line with the Russell Midcap Growth Index, which means you won't find him overweighted in any one area, including technology. That diversification is designed to lower risk, and it certainly hasn't compromised on performance so far.

In addition, by prospectus, the fund normally won't keep more than 2 percent of its assets in any one security.

McHugh buys those stocks he believes will show impressive earnings and generally sells for one of two reasons: Either the earnings don't pan out, or the stock grows outside of his capitalization range. As a result, there is a lot of trading going on in this portfolio, which can create some hefty year-end capital gains distributions. Therefore, this fund will best fit into the tax-deferred portion of your investment portfolio.

ANNUALIZED RETURNS		PORTFOLIO STATISTICS	
1-Year	80.50%	Beta	0.93
3-Year	57.95%	Turnover	290.79%
5-Year	N/A	12-Month Yield	0.00%
Overall Risk	1	12b-1 Fee	0.00%
Risk Rate	4	Exchange Ratio	1.08%

MINIMUM INVESTMENT		CONTACT INFORMATION	
Regular	$2,500	*Turner Midcap Growth*	
IRA	$2,000	*Telephone: (800) 224-6312*	
		www.turner-invest.com	

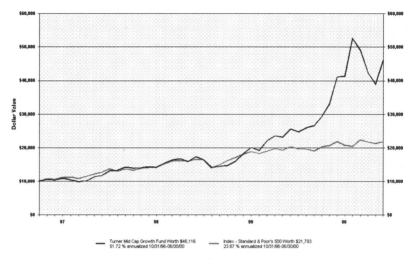

GROWTH OF $10,000

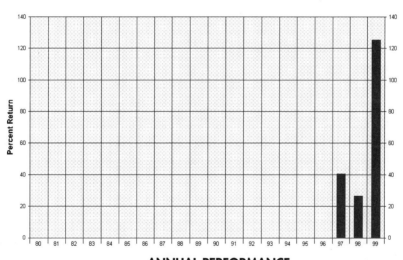

ANNUAL PERFORMANCE

TOP 10 HOLDINGS

Network Solutions	Bausch & Lomb
Best Buy	Circuit City
Double Click	Lexmark Intl.
Paychex	SPX Corp.
Interpublic Group	JDS Uniphase

TURNER TOP 20

OBJECTIVE:	*Mid-Cap Growth*	*39*
MANAGER:	*Team Managed*	

FUND OVERVIEW:

Two of the top small company funds out there are Turner Small Cap and Turner Micro Cap Growth. Unfortunately, both of those funds are closed to new investors. However, you can tap into the best picks of the managers of those funds and others through the Turner Top 20 fund. This non-diversified fund holds a concentrated portfolio of the 15-25 favorite stocks of the managers at Turner Investment Partners, including Chris McHugh (who manages the previous Powerhouse Performer Turner Mid-cap Growth.)

As a result, this portfolio is likely to contain a mix of micro-, small-, mid-, and large-cap stocks. Blended, it's similar to owning a mid-cap portfolio.

The fund isn't shy about concentrating assets in a few holdings, although they do try to spread the portfolio around a number of sectors. It's also ripe for frequent trading, since the Turner approach calls for ousting a holding once earnings begin to disappoint. Therefore, you should be prepared to ride out some wild price swings, and will probably be hit with some stiff year-end taxable gains. So, as with the other Turner funds, this is best held in an IRA or other tax-deferred account.

ANNUALIZED RETURNS		PORTFOLIO STATISTICS	
1-Year	N/A	Beta	N/A
3-Year	N/A	Turnover	N/A
5-Year	N/A	12-Month Yield	N/A
Overall Risk	N/A	12b-1 Fee	0.00%
Risk Rank	N/A	Expense Ratio	1.10%
MINIMUM INVESTMENT		**CONTACT INFORMATION**	
Regular	$2,500	*Turner Top 20 Fund*	
IRA	$2,000	*Telephone: (800) 224-6312*	
		www.turner-invest.com	

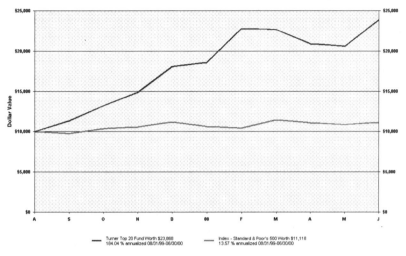

Turner Top 20 Fund Worth $23,868
184.04 % annualized 08/31/99-06/30/00

Index - Standard & Poor's 500 Worth $11,118
13.57 % annualized 08/31/99-06/30/00

GROWTH OF $10,000

VALUE LINE ANNUAL PERFORMANCE CHART
NOT AVAILABLE FOR THIS FUND

ANNUAL PERFORMANCE

TOP 10 HOLDINGS

America Online	LAM Research
JDS Uniphase	Nortel Networks
Cisco Systems	Yahoo!
EMC Corp.	Qualcomm
KLA Tencor	Intel

EXCELSIOR VALUE AND RESTRUCTURING

		40
OBJECTIVE:	*Mid-Cap Value*	
MANAGER:	*David Williams*	

FUND OVERVIEW:

For years, David Williams's Excelsior Value and Restructuring Fund was one of the best kept secrets in the mutual funds world. Then word of his great performance started to trickle into the media. Even though the sudden exposure brought a huge inflow of new assets, Williams has been able to handle the fresh cash without a problem, even in a market where "value" has been out of favor.

This astute U.S. Trust manager looks for stocks that are predicted to benefit from either an expected restructuring or the redeployment of assets and operations. Such companies may include those involved in prospective mergers, consolidations, liquidations, spin-offs, or financial reorganizations. Because these stocks are troubled to begin with, Williams can usually pick them up on the cheap, often for less than 15 times earnings. But such a strategy is fraught with risk. After all, these businesses are often in bad shape to begin with. If the restructuring isn't successful, they might not survive. Williams increases his chances for success by first meeting with management. Then he makes sure the portfolio is diversified among close to 90 names. With that strategy, he surmises, there's a good chance something will always be working.

ANNUALIZED RETURNS		PORTFOLIO STATISTICS	
1-Year	15.30%	Beta	1.08
3-Year	20.37%	Turnover	20.00%
5-Year	24.89%	12-Month Yield	1.92%
Overall Rank	2	12b-1 Fee	0.00%
Risk Rank	3	Expense Ratio	0.90%
MINIMUM INVESTMENT		**CONTACT INFORMATION**	
Regular	$500	*Excelsior Value and Restructuring*	
IRA	$250	*Fund*	
		Telephone: (800) 446-1012	
		www.excelsiorfunds.com	

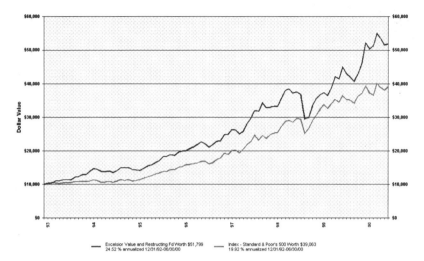

Excelsior Value and Restructuring Fd Worth $51,799
24.52 % annualized 12/31/92-06/30/00

Index - Standard & Poor's 500 Worth $39,063
19.92 % annualized 12/31/92-06/30/00

GROWTH OF $10,000

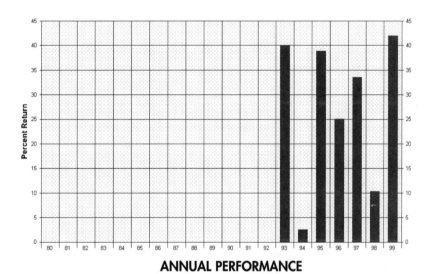

ANNUAL PERFORMANCE

TOP 10 HOLDINGS

General Motors C1. H
IBM
AT&T Liberty Media
Qualcomm
Nokia

Kansas City Southern
Vishay Intertechnology
Texas Instruments
Global Crossing
News Corp. Ltd. ADR

FIRST EAGLE FUND OF AMERICA

OBJECTIVE:	Mid-Cap Value	41
MANAGER:	Team Managed	

FUND OVERVIEW:

The focus of the First Eagle Fund of America is to find quality companies undergoing significant change. Lead portfolio manager Harold Levy contends that positive change can have a tremendous impact on a business, although the market is slow to realize that fact. This creates inefficiencies in the market, which he hopes to capitalize on. Among the changes Levy looks for: new management, acquisitions, share repurchases, divestitures, technological breakthroughs, or changes in strategy. Then, he figures out whether the stock is worth owning from a valuation perspective. "We look at a company as if we were buying the whole business, [which is] the way a rational businessman would price an acquisition," Levy says. He targets a return of 50 percent over a 12- to 18-month time frame for every idea under consideration. If he thinks a stock can achieve that ambitious goal, it will likely find its way into the portfolio.

You can never be certain that change will be good for a company. That's why Levy is constantly reevaluating his decisions. He hopes to limit his errors by doing extensive research and visiting his holdings on a regular basis to get a firsthand sense of how things are progressing.

ANNUALIZED RETURNS		PORTFOLIO STATISTICS	
1-Year	−8.90%	Beta	0.89
3-Year	13.48%	Turnover	89.00%
5-Year	20.26%	12-Month Yield	0.00%
Overall Rank	3	12b-1 Fee	0.00%
Risk Rank	3	Expense Ratio	1.39%
MINIMUM INVESTMENT		**CONTACT INFORMATION**	
Regular	$2,500	First Eagle Fund of America	
IRA	$500	Telephone: (800) 451-3623	
		www.firsteaglefunds.com	

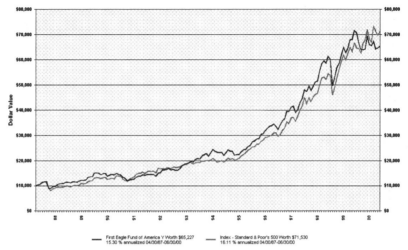

GROWTH OF $10,000

First Eagle Fund of America Y Worth $65,227
15.30 % annualized 04/30/87-06/30/00

Index - Standard & Poor's 500 Worth $71,530
16.11 % annualized 04/30/87-06/30/00

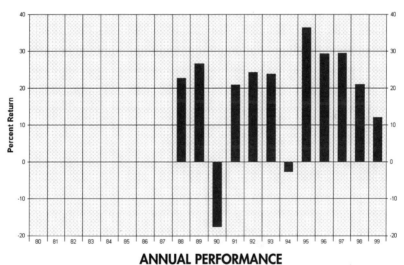

ANNUAL PERFORMANCE

TOP 10 HOLDINGS

St. Jude Medical	General Dynamics
Bausch & Lomb	L-3 Communications
Comdisco	News Corp. Ltd. ADR
Genzyme Corp.	Amgen
NCR Corp.	Dun & Bradstreet

GABELLI ASSET

| **OBJECTIVE:** | *Mid-Cap Value* | *42* |
| **MANAGER:** | *Mario Gabelli* | |

FUND OVERVIEW:

Mario Gabelli doesn't mind that some people view his investment style as being boring. He focuses on a company's free cash flow, defined as earnings before interest, taxes, depreciation, and amortization, less the capital expenditures needed to grow the business. "Rising free cash flow often foreshadows net earnings improvement," he says. "Unlike Wall Street's ubiquitous earnings momentum players, we do not try to forecast earnings with accounting precision and then trade stocks based on quarterly expectations and realities." Instead, he positions himself in front of long-term earnings uptrends.

Gabelli also closely analyzes assets and liabilities, paying attention to inventories, receivables, and potential legal issues. His goal is to come up with a private market value estimate of what a company is worth. He then wants to buy the company's stock for less than that number. Often, Gabelli finds a catalyst that leads him to believe earnings will rise, thus increasing the private market value. At other times, he's attracted by a management change or spin-off. Once he has put his money on the line, Gabelli tends to be patient, though vocal, in seeing that his companies perform up to expectations.

ANNUALIZED RETURNS		PORTFOLIO STATISTICS	
1-Year	8.40%	Beta	0.81
3-Year	19.32%	Turnover	32.00%
5-Year	20.44%	12-Month Yield	0.00%
Overall Rank	3	12b-1 Fee	0.25%
Risk Rank	2	Expense Ratio	1.37%
MINIMUM INVESTMENT		**CONTACT INFORMATION**	
Regular	$1,000	*Gabelli Asset Fund*	
IRA	$1,000	*Telephone: (800) 422-3554*	
		www.gabelli.com	

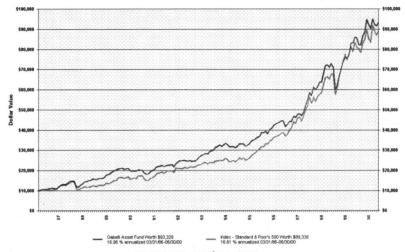

Gabelli Asset Fund Worth $93,329
16.96 % annualized 03/31/86–06/30/00

Index - Standard & Poor's 500 Worth $89,338
16.61 % annualized 03/31/86–06/30/00

GROWTH OF $10,000

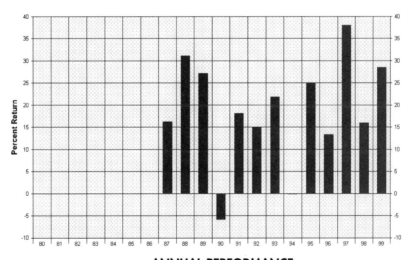

ANNUAL PERFORMANCE

TOP 10 HOLDINGS

Liberty Digital	Telephone & Data Systems
Time Warner	MediaOne Group
Cablevision	USA Networks
Viacom Cl. A	Chris Craft Inds.
American Express	United Television

LEGG MASON OPPORTUNITY TRUST

OBJECTIVE:	*Mid-Cap Value*	*43*
MANAGER:	*William Miller*	

FUND OVERVIEW:

Among the list of Large-Cap Value "Powerhouse Performers," you may remember reading about the Legg Mason Value Trust run by Bill Miller. At the end of 1999, he was given a new fund to manage that gives him much more freedom to buy whatever stocks he wants, small or large. In fact, the fund's prospectus makes it clear that Miller's not limited by investment style, industry sector, location, size, or market capitalization.

As an added twist, he can also sell securities short, which is an aggressive maneuver. In essence, it's a bet that a stock's price is going to fall. Plus, since this fund is considerably smaller than Value Trust, Miller's able to be more flexible.

Miller looks for companies trading at a discount to their intrinsic value. Before buying a security, he and his team assess a potential holding's products, strategy, competitive positioning, and industry dynamics. A stock is sold for a variety of reasons, including when it no longer seems to offer long-term growth, when a more compelling investment opportunity comes around, to realize gains, or to limit losses.

ANNUALIZED RETURNS		PORTFOLIO SALES	
1-Year	N/A	Beta	N/A
3-Year	N/A	Turnover	N/A
5-Year	N/A	12-Month Yield	N/A
Overall Rank	N/A	12b-1 Fee	N/A
Risk Rank	N/A	Expense Ratio	N/A

MINIMUM INVESTMENT		CONTACT INFORMATION
Regular	$1,000	*Legg Mason Opportunity Trust*
IRA	$1,000	*Telephone: (800) 577-8589*
		www.leggmasonfunds.com

VALUE LINE GROWTH OF $10,000 CHART
NOT AVAILABLE FOR THIS FUND

GROWTH OF $10,000

VALUE LINE ANNUAL PERFORMANCE CHART
NOT AVAILABLE FOR THIS FUND

ANNUAL PERFORMANCE

TOP 10 HOLDINGS

Republic Services	Tricon Global Restaurants
Gateway	Abercrombie & Fitch
U.S. Bancorp	Unum Provident Corporation
U.S. Foodservice	Toys R Us
Ames Dept. Stores	Washington Mutual

MUHLENKAMP FUND

OBJECTIVE:	*Mid-Cap Value*	*44*
MANAGER:	*Ronald Muhlenkamp*	

FUND OVERVIEW:

Ron Muhlenkamp will fill his portfolio with whatever he thinks will make the most money. That usually means a heavy weighting in stocks, although he'll emphasize bonds when interest rates exceed the return he expects to get from equities. Muhlenkamp doesn't believe in applying historical standards to today's market, because economic conditions are always changing. Instead, he constantly evaluates the current business cycle to see which industries appear to be most attractive.

Muhlenkamp is a value-oriented investor. He views a company's return on equity and price-to-book value ratio as important numbers for determining whether a stock is attractively priced. Instead of buying growth at a reasonable price, he wants *profitability* at a reasonable price.

Muhlenkamp strives to generate a maximum total return for shareholders consistent with taking a reasonable amount of risk. He will only invest in securities that he expects to outpace the rate of inflation by at least 5 to 6 percent for stocks, and at least 3 percent for bonds.

ANNUALIZED RETURNS		PORTFOLIO STATISTICS	
1-Year	8.30%	**Beta**	0.85
3-Year	13.98%	**Turnover**	15.56%
5-Year	20.69%	**12-Month Yield**	0.00%
Overall Rank	3	**12b-1 Fee**	0.00%
Risk Rank	3	**Expense Ratio**	1.35%
MINIMUM INVESTMENT		CONTACT INFORMATION	
Regular	$1,500	*Muhlenkamp Fund*	
IRA	$1,500	*Telephone: (800) 860-3863*	
		www.muhlenkamp.com	

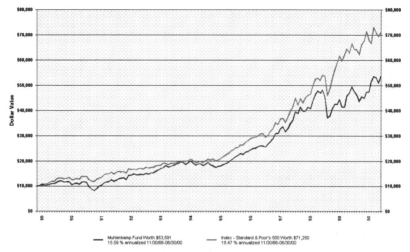

Muhlenkamp Fund Worth $53,591
15.59 % annualized 11/30/88-06/30/00

Index - Standard & Poor's 500 Worth $71,250
18.47 % annualized 11/30/88-06/30/00

GROWTH OF $10,000

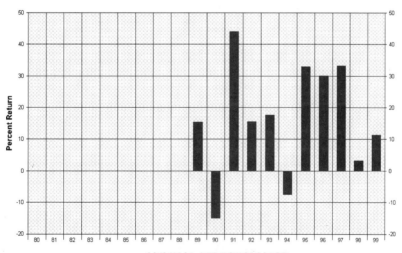

ANNUAL PERFORMANCE

TOP 10 HOLDINGS	
Conseco	Ford Motor Corp.
Merrill Lynch	Applied Materials
Calpine Corp.	Intel
Morgan Stanley Dean Witter	Citigroup
Computer Associates	Southwest Securities Group

NEUBERGER & BERMAN PARTNERS

OBJECTIVE:	*Mid-Cap Value*	
MANAGER:	*Michael Kassen and Robert Gendelman*	

FUND OVERVIEW:

The number-one rule managers of the Neuberger & Berman Partners follow is: "Never forget the fundamentals when pursuing growth." "Whenever we analyze a stock, we ask ourselves, 'If we had all the money in the world, would we be interested in buying the company for the price represented by the stock?'" explains portfolio comanager Michael Kassen. "To decide, we look at the fundamentals: earnings, cash flow, plus the company's track record through all parts of the market cycle." You won't find many Fortune 100 stocks in this fund. Kassen and fellow manager Robert Gendelman feel it's too hard to gain an edge over other investors with these big companies. Instead, they focus primarily on mid-caps, which are small enough to give them access to management. They also attend industry conferences and look for ideas. Before making an investment, they examine a company's balance sheet, contact suppliers, and talk with competitors about the business.

Kassen and Gendelman hope to buy stocks at a discount to their underlying value. They are especially fond of "fallen angels"—growth stocks that have tumbled to new lows but remain fundamentally strong.

ANNUALIZED RETURNS		PORTFOLIO STATISTICS	
1-Year	−5.30%	Beta	0.89
3-Year	8.18%	Turnover	100.00%
5-Year	16.01%	12-Month Yield	1.07%
Overall Rank	4	12b-1 Fee	0.00%
Risk Rank	3	Expense Ratio	0.84%

MINIMUM INVESTMENT		CONTACT INFORMATION
Regular	$1,000	*Neuberger & Berman Partners Fund*
IRA	$250	*Telephone: (800) 877-9700*
		www.nbfunds.com

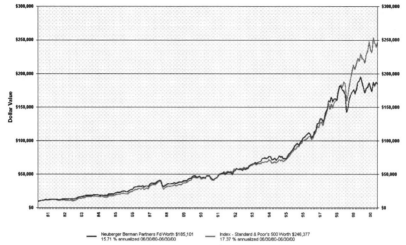

GROWTH OF $10,000

Neuberger Berman Partners Fd Worth $185,101
15.71 % annualized 06/30/80-06/30/00

Index - Standard & Poor's 500 Worth $246,377
17.37 % annualized 06/30/80-06/30/00

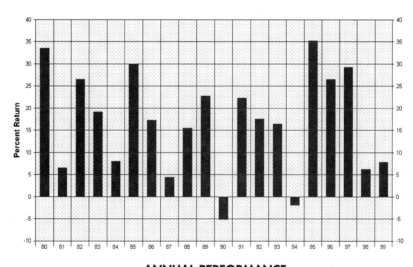

ANNUAL PERFORMANCE

TOP 10 HOLDINGS

Ericsson	Cigna
News Corp. Ltd ADR	Honeywell
GTE Corp.	Parametric Technology
IBM	Computer Associates
Williams Cos.	Bank of New York

OAKMARK SELECT

OBJECTIVE:	*Mid-Cap Value*	*46*
MANAGER:	*William Nygren and Henry Berghoef*	

FUND OVERVIEW:

Concentrating your money in mid-cap value-oriented securities over the past few years would seem to be a recipe for disaster. After all, the market hasn't been very interested in value. But Bill Nygren has done a great job of keeping his shareholders in the black at a time when many value investors are seeing red. At Oakmark Select, he and co-manager Henry Berghoef run a tight ship of around 20 stocks, and place big commitments in their top holdings. They look to buy stocks at a significant discount (60-75 percent) to what they consider to be the company's underlying economic value. They also invest in companies with owner-oriented management who think independently.

Nygren and Berghoef concentrate so much because they believe that allows their best ideas to have a meaningful impact on performance. And, because they go into each position hoping to own it for at least two to three years, turnover is pretty low, although that doesn't always translate into tax efficiency. Still, they set price targets for every stock, and generally sell once that target is met. Nygren also took over management of the firm's flagship and larger Oakmark Fund in early 2000.

ANNUALIZEED RETURNS		PORTFOLIO STATISTICS	
1-Year	–0.60%	Beta	1.11
3-Year	19.71%	Turnover	54.00%
5-Year	N/A	12-Month Yield	0.86%
Overall Rank	2	12b-1 Fee	0.00%
Risk Rank	4	Expense Ratio	1.17%

MINIMUM INVESTMENT		CONTACT INFORMATION
Regular	$1,000	*The Oakmark Select Fund*
IRA	$1,000	*Telephone: (800) 625-6275*
		www.oakmark.com

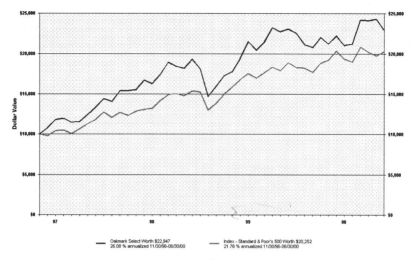

GROWTH OF $10,000

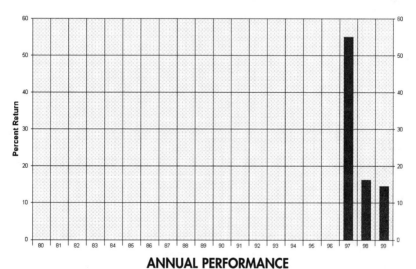

ANNUAL PERFORMANCE

TOP 10 HOLDINGS

Washington Mutual	Liz Clairborne
USG Corp.	U.S. Industries
Reynolds & Reynolds	Thermo Electron
Toys R Us	Partner Re
Dun & Bradstreet	Times Mirror

T. ROWE PRICE VALUE

OBJECTIVE:	*Mid-Cap Value*	*47*
MANAGER:	*Brian Rogers*	

FUND OVERVIEW:

T. Rowe Price Value is one of two funds on my Powerhouse Performers list for 1999 that are managed by Brian Rogers. (The other is T. Rowe Price Equity Income, entry 62 in this chapter.) Although Value is only a few years old, it has managed to beat the return of the S&P 500 every year since inception, a feat only a handful of funds have achieved. Rogers also has a terrific record at Equity Income. (Value, a much smaller fund, allows him to focus on stock picking, without worrying about the dividend component required at Equity Income.).

"We emphasize investments in companies we determine to be undervalued in terms of price/earnings, price/cash flow, and price/asset ratios; replacement value calculations; or a range of other analytical frameworks," Rogers explains. "Many of our holdings are contrarian in nature, since we purchase shares of companies that have been out-of-favor and priced accordingly in the marketplace. We believe companies meeting our criteria prove an attractive combination of limited downside risk and reasonable upside potential." It's not surprising that many of Rogers's ideas are restructuring plays. He's also enamored of financial stocks.

ANNUALIZED RETURNS

1-Year	−9.50%
3-Year	8.47%
5-Year	16.83
Overall Rank	3
Risk Rank	3

MINIMUM INVESTMENT

Regular	$2,500
IRA	$1,000

PORTFOLIO STATISTICS

Beta	0.84
Turnover	67.80%
12-Month Yield	0.58%
12b-1 Fee	0.00%
Expense Ratio	0.92%

CONTACT INFORMATION

T. Rowe Price Value Fund
Telephone: (800) 638-5660
www.troweprice.com

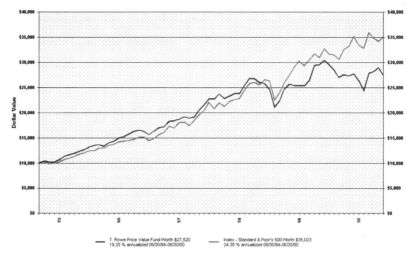

GROWTH OF $10,000

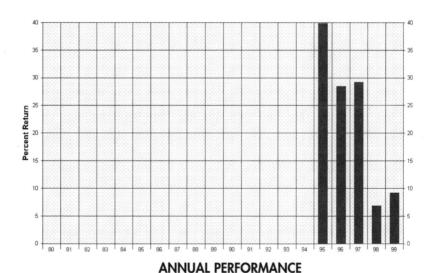

ANNUAL PERFORMANCE

TOP 10 HOLDINGS	
Phelps Dodge	Hillenbrand Industries
Sprint	US West
Stanley Works	Boeing
Amerada Hess	Lockheed Martin
Great Lakes Chemical	American Home Products

TWEEDY, BROWNE AMERICAN VALUE

OBJECTIVE:	*Mid-Cap Value*	*48*
MANAGER:	*Team Managed*	

FUND OVERVIEW:

The managers of Tweedy, Browne American Value aren't shy about telling you they run their portfolio using the principles espoused in *Security Analysis,* the classic written by the late Columbia University Business School Professor Benjamin Graham. Graham talked about evaluating companies based on their "intrinsic value," which is the amount a rational businessperson would pay for the entire business. Graham claimed that investments made at a 40 to 50 percent discount to intrinsic value provided investors with a margin of safety. Once the market price rises toward intrinsic value, he recommended selling the stock and reinvesting the proceeds in other, more attractive ideas.

Therefore, Tweedy, Browne American Value holds stocks with one or more of the following characteristics: low stock price in relation to book value, low price-to-earnings ratio, low price-to-cash flow ratio, above-average dividend yield, and recent stock purchases by insiders. Managers Christopher Browne, John Spears, and William Browne own some 200 small, medium, and large stocks, including a few foreign companies. This conservative fund has consistently managed to keep up with the S&P 500 while incurring less risk.

ANNUALIZED RETURNS		PORTFOLIO STATISTICS	
1-Year	−9.40%	Beta	0.79
3-Year	8.33%	Turnover	19.00%
5-Year	15.98%	12-Month Yield	1.22%
Overall Rank	3	12b-1 Fee	0.00%
Risk Rank	2	Expense Ratio	1.37%
MINIMUM INVESTMENT		**CONTACT INFORMATION**	
Regular	$2,500	*Tweedy, Browne American*	
IRA	$500	*Value Fund*	
		Telephone: (800) 432-4789	
		www.tweedy.com	

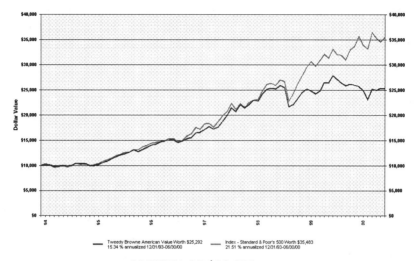

GROWTH OF $10,000

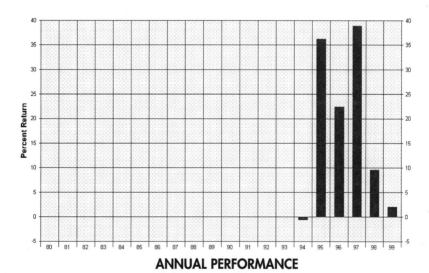

ANNUAL PERFORMANCE

TOP 10 HOLDINGS	
Pharmacia & Upjohn	Rayonier
MBIA	Transatlantic Holdings
Federal Home Loan	Comcast Corp.
McDonald's	Panamerican Beverages
American Express	GATX Corp.

WEITZ PARTNERS VALUE

OBJECTIVE:	*Mid-Cap Value*	*49*
MANAGER:	*Wallace Weitz*	

FUND OVERVIEW:

Weitz Partners Value is a non-diversified fund that seeks companies trading for half of their intrinsic value, or what they would be worth whole if bought out entirely by an interested suitor. This is the same philosophy espoused by both Warren Buffett and Benjamin Graham. Manager Wallace Weitz notes that he favors businesses he can understand, which keeps him from owning many technology companies. He also wants businesses with a niche or franchise that insulate them from competition. Next, a potential company must generate more cash flow than it needs to conduct operations. To make the final cut, a business must have what Weitz calls "honest, intelligent management who treat shareholders as partners in the business, rather than necessary evils." Weitz is also quick to point out that he wants good companies, not just cheap stocks. Although he prefers to stay fully invested, he will hold cash reserves when he can't find enough promising ideas.

You'll notice this fund has a high minimum investment requirement of $25,000, even for IRAs. However, you can get in for much less by using a discount broker.

ANNUALIZED RETURNS		PORTFOLIO STATISTICS	
1-Year	3.10%	**Beta**	0.66
3-Year	23.85%	**Turnover**	5.00%
5-Year	24.76%	**12-Month Yield**	1.37%
Overall Rank	2	**12b-1 Fee**	0.00%
Risk Rank	2	**Expense Ratio**	1.18%

MINIMUM INVESTMENT		CONTACT INFORMATION
Regular	$25,000 (less through some discount brokers)	*Weitz Partners Value Fund*
IRA	$25,000 (less through some discount brokers)	*Telephone: (800) 232-4161*
		www.weitzfunds.com

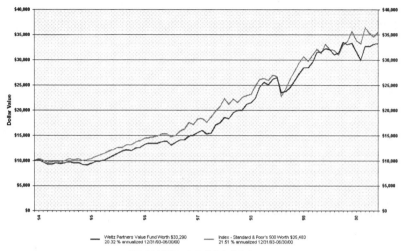

Weltz Partners Value Fund Worth $33,290
20.32 % annualized 12/31/93-06/30/00

Index - Standard & Poor's 500 Worth $35,483
21.51 % annualized 12/31/93-06/30/00

GROWTH OF $10,000

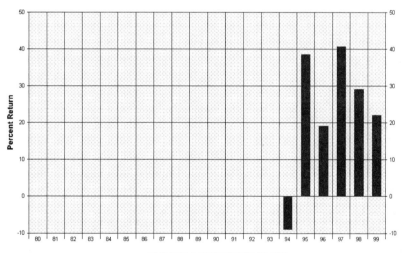

ANNUAL PERFORMANCE

TOP 10 HOLDINGS

Telephone & Data Systems	AT&T Liberty Media
Adelphia Comms. Corp.	Washington Mutual
Berkshire Hathaway	Citizens Utilities
Host Marriot	Countrywide
Greenpoint Financial	Golden St. Bancorp

BARON SMALL CAP

OBJECTIVE:	*Small-Cap Growth*	*50*
MANAGER:	*Cliff Greenberg*	

FUND OVERVIEW:

Even though Cliff Greenberg hasn't been managing a mutual fund for long, he has been making money in small-cap stocks for years. Before joining Baron in 1997, Greenberg spent 12 years running a prominent New York hedge fund. He tries to find companies with superior prospects that can be purchased at attractive prices. Greenberg won't buy a stock unless he thinks it can go up at least 50 percent over a two-year period, and he won't hesitate to overweight his favorite ideas in the portfolio.

Greenberg has an eclectic style. He says most of his investments fall into one of the following categories: growth stocks, fallen angels, or special situations. Growth companies either have new products or are involved in blossoming industries. They are also growing by at least 20 percent a year. Fallen angels are stocks that have tumbled dramatically in price. This often happens because Wall Street is concerned about current earnings prospects. Greenberg digs deeper to see whether the long-term fundamentals have materially changed. If not, he's interested. Finally, special situations encompass spin-offs, recapitalizations, equity stubs, and the like. One thing you won't find is many technology companies, since they rarely meet his price criteria.

ANNUALIZED RETURNS		PORTFOLIO STATISTICS	
1-Year	33.90%	Beta	N/A
3-Year	N/A	Turnover	39.00%
5-Year	N/A	12-Month Yield	0.00
Overall Rank	N/A	12b-1 Fee	0.25%
Risk Rank	N/A	Expense Ratio	1.35%

MINIMUM INVESTMENT		CONTACT INFORMATION
Regular	$2,000	*Baron Small Cap Fund*
IRA	$2,000	*Telephone: (800) 992-2766*
		www.baronfunds.com

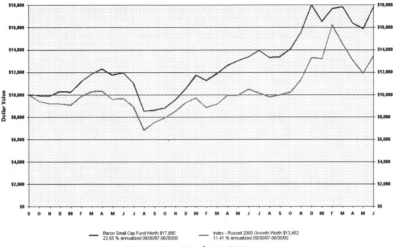

GROWTH OF $10,000

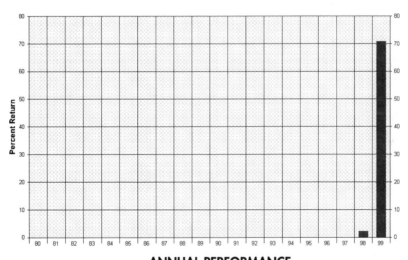

ANNUAL PERFORMANCE

TOP 10 HOLDINGS

United Globalcom	Westwood One
Rural Cellular	Hendrick & Struggles
Radio One	Commonwealth Tel. Ent.
SBA Communications	Corecomm
Kenneth Cole Prods.	Career Education

BJURMAN MICRO-CAP GROWTH

OBJECTIVE:	*Small-Cap Growth*	**51**
MANAGER:	*Team Managed*	

FUND OVERVIEW:

The Bjurman Micro-Cap Growth Fund looks for high-growth companies with market capitalizations between $30 million and $300 million at the time of initial investment. The management team, lead by O. Thomas Barry, seeks out undervalued stocks with superior earnings growth characteristics. They typically screen through a universe of 1,900 companies, using five different models. The models look at such attributes as earnings growth, earnings strength, and earnings revisions. They also take into account price-to-earnings, price-to-growth, and price-to-cash flow ratios. Then the managers perform a top-down analysis of the economy to identify the 10 to 15 most promising industries to be invested in over the next 12 to 18 months. With the two lists in hand, Barry and his associates compile a list of up to 200 of the most attractive companies and begin doing additional fundamental and technical research.

To make sure the portfolio is well diversified, no more than 5 percent of assets are placed in any one stock, nor more than 15 percent in a single industry. This fund is fairly new, although its adviser, George D. Bjurman & Associates, has been managing money for more than 29 years.

ANNUALIZED RETURNS		PORTFOLIO STATISTICS	
1-Year	106.00%	Beta	0.77
3-Year	45.27%	Turnover	234.00%
5-Year	N/A	12-Month Yield	0.00%
Overall Rank	1	12b-1 Fee	0.25%
Risk Rank	5	Expense Ratio	1.80%
MINIMUM INVESTMENT		CONTACT INFORMATION	
Regular	$5,000	*Bjurman Micro-Cap Growth Fund*	
IRA	$2,000	*Telephone: (800) 227-7264*	
		www.bjurmanfunds.com	

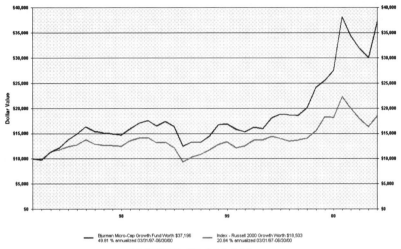

GROWTH OF $10,000

Bjurman Micro-Cap Growth Fund Worth $37,196
49.81 % annualized 03/31/97-06/30/00

Index - Russell 2000 Growth Worth $18,503
20.84 % annualized 03/31/97-06/30/00

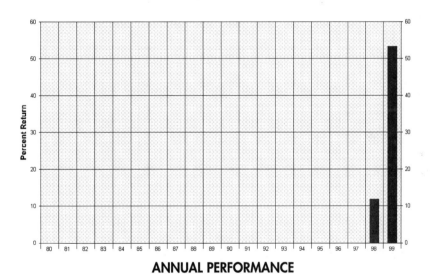

ANNUAL PERFORMANCE

TOP 10 HOLDINGS	
Keithley Instruments	Hall, Kinion & Associates
Tollgrade Communications	Symmetricon
Elantec Semicon	ACT Mfg.
Parlex	Diodes
Cyberoptics	Pericom Semicon

BRAZOS/JMIC MICRO-CAP GROWTH

OBJECTIVE:	*Small-Cap Growth*	
MANAGER:	*Team Managed*	*52*

FUND OVERVIEW:

The mission statement of the Brazos/JMIC Micro-Cap Growth Fund calls for investing in smaller, rapidly growing companies with highly predictable revenue and profit streams, while subjecting the portfolio to moderate risk. The fund's management team focuses on the smallest 10 percent of all stocks, as measured by the Wilshire 5000 index. Many such companies have market capitalizations of less than $200 million.

Although this is a relatively new fund, the firm that manages it, John McStay Investment Counsel (thus the JMIC in the name) has a solid long-term record of managing institutional small-cap accounts. The senior members of the management team each have an average of 20 years experience in the investment field.

JMIC uses a bottom-up research process and selects companies based on their potential for strong revenue, earnings, and cash flow. Other fundamental screens include returns on capital and equity, plus price-to-earnings ratios. The folks who run this fund also look for seasoned management, and try to visit almost every company before making an investment.

ANNUALIZED RETURNS		PORTFOLIO STATISTICS	
1-Year	58.60%	Beta	N/A
3-Year	N/A	Turnover	73.00%
5-Year	N/A	12-Month Yield	0.00%
Overall Rank	N/A	12b-1 Fee	0.00%
Risk Rank	N/A	Expense Ratio	1.52%
MINIMUM INVESTMENT		**CONTACT INFORMATION**	
Regular	$10,000	*Brazos/JMIC Micro-Cap Growth Fund*	
IRA	$2,000	*Telephone: (800) 426-9157*	
		www.brazosfund.com	

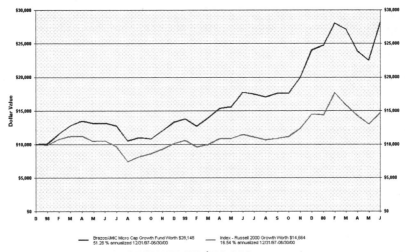

Brazos/JMIC Micro Cap Growth Fund Worth $28,148
51.28 % annualized 12/31/97-06/30/00

Index - Russell 2000 Growth Worth $14,664
16.54 % annualized 12/31/97-06/30/00

GROWTH OF $10,000

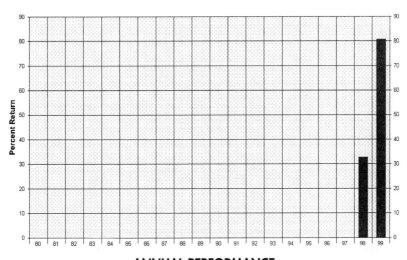

ANNUAL PERFORMANCE

TOP 10 HOLDINGS	
Bright Horizons Family Sol.	Tollgrade Comms.
ILEX Oncology	Accredo Health
Net Scout Sys.	Invitrogen
Mobile Mini	Triad Guaranty
Sierracities.com	Professional Retailing

FMI FOCUS FUND

OBJECTIVE:	*Small-Cap Growth*	*53*
MANAGER:	*Ted Kellner and Richard Lane*	

FUND OVERVIEW:

FMI Focus is one of the most concentrated small-cap funds you'll run across. Managers Ted Kellner and Richard Lane, who have a combined 37 years of investment experience, look for companies they consider to be undiscovered or undervalued by Wall Street. They follow a process designed to find good businesses at value prices. To uncover ideas, they go through computer databases, brokerage reports, newspapers, trade journals, and other outside sources. From here, they study each candidate's business model, determine whether a strong business franchise exists, and fill in the gaps by talking with management, competitors, customers, and industry experts.

Valuation is a critical factor in their process, although I wouldn't consider this to be a pure "value" fund. Stocks are sold when they are considered to be overpriced, because of dramatic appreciation, or if they simply determine they were wrong about a story in the first place. Kellner and Lane generally keep about 40 stocks in the portfolio, which is about half of what you'll find in most small-cap portfolios. But this concentration has provided, even though their general value style of investing has been out of favor.

ANNUALIZED RETURNS		PORTFOLIO STATISTICS	
1-Year	79.089%	Beta	N/A
3-Year	53.96%	Turnover	N/A
5-Year	N/A	12-Month Yield	0.00%
Overall Rank	N/A	12b-1 Fee	0.00%
Risk Rank	N/A	Expense Ratio	1.81%
MINIMUM INVESTMENT		**CONTACT INFORMATION**	
Regular	$1,000	*FMI Focus Fund*	
IRA	$1,000	*Telephone: (800) 811-5311*	
		www.fiduciarymgt.com	

VALUE LINE GROWTH OF $10,000 CHART
NOT AVAILABLE FOR THIS FUND

GROWTH OF $10,000

VALUE LINE ANNUAL PERFORMANCE CHART
NOT AVAILABLE FOR THIS FUND

ANNUAL PERFORMANCE

TOP 10 HOLDINGS

Tollgrade Comms.	Adelphia Business Solutions
Primedia	Vishay Intertechnology
Quest Diagnostics	Adelphia Comms. Cl. A
MGIC Investments	Voicestream Wireless
HNC Software	MKS Instruments

HENLOPEN

| OBJECTIVE: | Small-Cap Growth | *54* |
| MANAGER: | Team Managed | |

FUND OVERVIEW:

Henlopen's three managers—Michael Hershey, Paul Larson, and Lorenzo Villalon—look for dominant small companies with rapid earnings growth. Their eclectic investment philosophy calls for purchasing stocks with strong momentum that they believe can carry the share price significantly higher over a one- or two-year period. But this isn't a pure momentum play, since they will also buy cyclical and out-of-favor companies if the price is right. The fund's average holding reported annual gains of 25 percent over the past three years, which is well ahead of companies in the S&P 500.

The experienced trio remain true to their convictions. They will overweight favorite names and quickly pull out of companies they no longer like. This "quick draw" approach means the fund is more volatile than many of its peers, but past performance has more than compensated for its inherently bumpy ride. Henlopen has landed among the top 15 percent of all small-cap funds since inception in 1992 and has easily surpassed its direct benchmark, the Russell 2000. Henlopen also has a small asset base, which gives it an extra advantage as it navigates through this risk-laden area of the market.

ANNUALIZED RETURNS		PORTFOLIO STATISTICS	
1-Year	53.70%	Beta	0.94
3-Year	33.45%	Turnover	82.80%
5-Year	28.12%	12-Month Yield	0.00%
Overall Rank	3	12b-1 Fee	0.00%
Risk Rank	4	Expense Ratio	1.39%
MINIMUM INVESTMENT		**CONTACT INFORMATION**	
Regular	$2,000	*Henlopen Fund*	
IRA	$2,000	*Telephone: (800) 922-0224*	

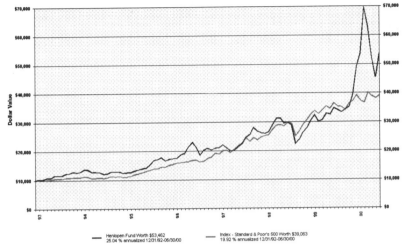

GROWTH OF $10,000

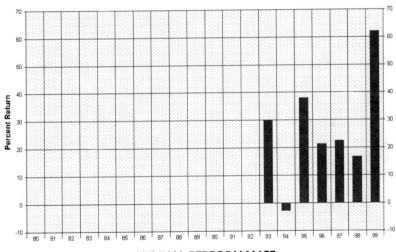

ANNUAL PERFORMANCE

TOP 10 HOLDINGS

Igen Intl.	FVC Com.
Gene Logic	Polycom
Level 8 Systems	Excalibur Technologies
Natural Microsystems	Information Res. Engr.
Tollgrade Communications	Aeroflex

MANAGERS SPECIAL EQUITY

OBJECTIVE:	*Small-Cap Growth*	**55**
MANAGER:	*Team Managed*	

FUND OVERVIEW:

Managers Special Equity gives you access to four leading small-cap stock pickers in one portfolio. It farms out 26 percent of the portfolio to Timothy Ebright of Liberty Investment Management, 36 percent to Andrew Knuth of Westport Asset Management, 30 percent to Gary Pilgrim of Pilgrim Baxter & Associates (who also runs the popular PBHG Growth Fund), and 8 percent to Bob Kern of Kern Capital Management. Each person has a unique style and approach to small-cap investing. Ebright searches for companies that have predictable earnings and are selling at less than intrinsic value. Knuth will only buy stocks trading at or below the market's price-to-earnings multiple. Pilgrim focuses on companies with high earnings momentum. And Kern, who also runs the closed Fremont U.S. Micro-Cap Fund, directs his efforts toward finding micro-cap stocks that are succeeding through new product innovation. Therefore, you get a blend of growth, earnings momentum, and value in one package.

Because of all the managers involved, Managers Special Equity's portfolio is quite diversified. This is a great fund for investors seeking to keep only one small-cap name in their portfolio.

ANNUALIZED RETURNS		PORTFOLIO STATISTICS	
1-Year	55.40%	**Beta**	0.79
3-Year	25.37%	**Turnover**	49.00%
5-Year	26.23%	**12-Month Yield**	0.00%
Overall Rank	2	**12b-1 Fee**	0.00%
Risk Rank	4	**Expense Ratio**	1.33%
MINIMUM INVESTMENT		**CONTACT INFORMATION**	
Regular	$2,000	*Managers Special Equity Fund*	
IRA	$500	*Telephone: (800) 835-3879*	
		www.managersfunds.com	

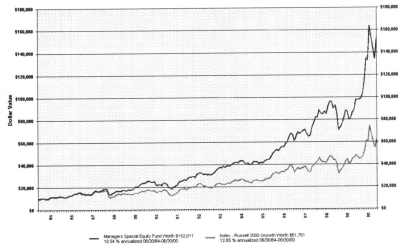

GROWTH OF $10,000

Managers Special Equity Fund Worth $152,011
18.54 % annualized 06/30/84-06/30/00

Index - Russell 2000 Growth Worth $61,761
12.05 % annualized 06/30/84-06/30/00

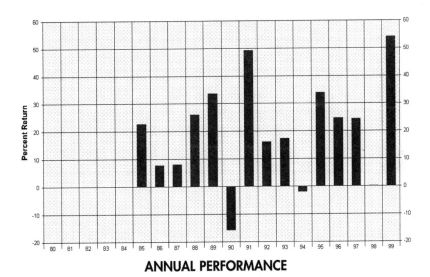

ANNUAL PERFORMANCE

TOP 10 HOLDINGS

Emmis Communications	**Verisign**
Teletech Holdings	**Applied Micro Circuits**
Puma Technology	**Conexant**
Anadigits	**Infospace**
Alpha Industries	**CYTYC**

NICHOLAS LIMITED EDITION

OBJECTIVE:	*Small-Cap Growth*	**56**
MANAGER:	*David O. Nicholas*	

FUND OVERVIEW:

David Nicholas describes his approach to investing as seeking growth at a reasonable price. He buys small- and mid-cap stocks in companies that appear to be attractively priced relative to their growth prospects. He's much more concerned about individual company selection than about the overall market. He also believes that reducing the downside is essential to achieving superior long-term results. Accordingly, he won't invest more than 5 percent of total assets in companies with track records shorter than three years. Nicholas hunts for stocks with price-to-earnings ratios that are low in relation to earnings growth. Alternatively, he likes stocks that are cheap compared to book value. Above-average secular earnings growth and strong current earnings momentum are other important factors he looks for.

The Nicholas Limited Edition portfolio is made up of around 60 stocks in such diversified industries as health care, financial services, media, and industrial products. Nicholas is convinced that large multinational company growth could be restrained at some point, which would further benefit the smaller companies he invests in.

ANNUALIZED RETURNS		PORTFOLIO STATISTICS	
1-Year	3.20%	Beta	0.76
3-Year	6.45%	Turnover	36.01%
5-Year	14.30%	12-Month Yield	0.21%
Overall Rank	4	12b-1 Fee	0.00%
Risk Rank	3	Expense Ratio	0.86%
MINIMUM INVESTMENT		**CONTACT INFORMATION**	
Regular	$2,000	*Nicholas Limited Edition*	
IRA	$2,000	*Telephone: (800) 227-5987*	
		www.nicholasfunds.com	

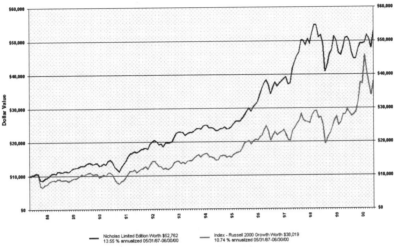

GROWTH OF $10,000

Nicholas Limited Edition Worth $52,762
13.55 % annualized 05/31/87-06/30/00

Index - Russell 2000 Growth Worth $38,019
10.74 % annualized 05/31/87-06/30/00

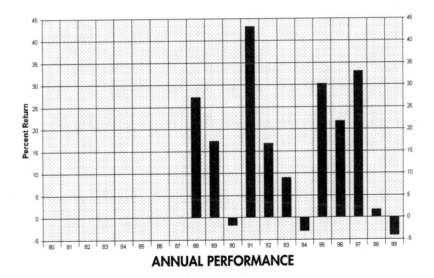

ANNUAL PERFORMANCE

TOP 10 HOLDINGS

International Speedway
Knight Transportation
Renal Care Group
Thermo Bioanalysis
DBT Online

Heartland Express
Brown & Brown
CH Robinson Worldwide
Asia Satellite Tele.
Conmed

RS DIVERSIFIED GROWTH

OBJECTIVE:	*Small-Cap Growth*	**57**
MANAGER:	*John Wallace and John Seabern*	

FUND OVERVIEW:

True to his flexible approach to stock picking, RS Diversified Growth manager John Wallace has the freedom to choose from the broad universe of small- and mid-cap stocks. But, more often than not, he latches on to the tinier names, which is why I have placed this fund in the small-cap category.

Wallace and co-manager John Seabern look for a catalyst in each company they buy that they believe will drive earnings and valuations higher over a one- to three-year time horizon. That catalyst could be new management, enhanced products, or expanding markets. The managers will consider selling when a stock reaches their price objective, when it falls 15 percent from their purchase price, or when something negative happens with management, product definition, or the overall economic environment. They'll also unload one holding to replace it with another.

The overwhelming majority of the fund's assets are in technology-related companies, including the fast-growing biotech area. This fund has been a real category killer. Before joining RS Investment Management, Wallace managed the Oppenheimer Main Street Income & Growth fund to great results.

ANNUALIZED RETURNS		PORTFOLIO STATISTICS	
1-Year	73.80%	Beta	1.02
3-Year	52.32%	Turnover	279.00%
5-Year	N/A	12-Month Yield	0.00%
Overall Rank	1	12b-1 Fee	0.25%
Risk Rank	5	Expense Ratio	1.89%
MINIMUM INVESTMENT		**CONTACT INFORMATION**	
Regular	$5,000	*RS Diversified Growth*	
IRA	$1,000	*Telephone: (800) 766-3863*	
		www.rsfunds.com	

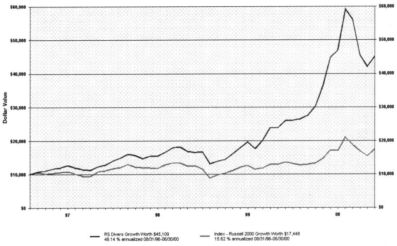

GROWTH OF $10,000

RS Divers Growth Worth $45,109
48.14 % annualized 08/31/96-06/30/00

Index - Russell 2000 Growth Worth $17,448
15.62 % annualized 08/31/96-06/30/00

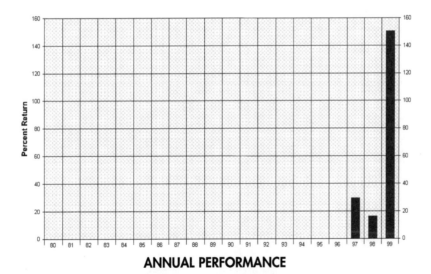

ANNUAL PERFORMANCE

TOP 10 HOLDINGS

Primus Telecomm	Ziff-Davis
Startec Global	Stamps.com
Computer Associates	United Shipping & Technology
Verity	Lodgenet Entertainment
Value Vision Intl.	United Globalcom

T. ROWE PRICE SMALL-CAP STOCK

OBJECTIVE:	*Small-Cap Growth*	*58*
MANAGER:	*Greg A. McCrickard*	

FUND OVERVIEW:

I classify T. Rowe Price Small-Cap Stock as a growth fund, but manager Greg McCrickard actually invests in both growth- and value-oriented securities. He says this flexible approach gives him access to more opportunities, and the value component helps to temper overall volatility. The fund is also highly diversified; the average holding makes up less than 1.5 percent of the portfolio. This is both good and bad. It reduces risk, but it can prevent the fund from reaping the full rewards of its biggest winners. McCrickard is prone to take his gains sooner than most (although he's not a frequent trader), and he generally avoids concentrating too heavily in any one sector or industry.

McCrickard uses a variety of fundamental checkpoints to evaluate potential holdings. Among other things, he wants companies with sound financial structures, good management, attractive niches, pricing flexibility, and strong insider ownership. Because of his value component, McCrickard keeps a close eye on how much he's willing to pay for a stock, checking to see whether price-to-cash flow and price-to-earnings ratios are attractive relative to estimated earnings growth.

ANNUALIZED RETURNS		PORTFOLIO STATISTICS	
1-Year	24.32%	Beta	0.80
3-Year	12.81%	Turnover	42.00%
5-Year	17.58%	12-Month Yield	0.30%
Overall Rank	4	12b-1 Fee	0.00%
Risk Rank	3	Expense Ratio	1.01%
MINIMUM INVESTMENT		**CONTACT INFORMATION**	
Regular	$2,500	*T. Rowe Price Small-Cap Stock Fund*	
IRA	$1,000	*Telephone: (800) 638-5660*	
		www.troweprice.com	

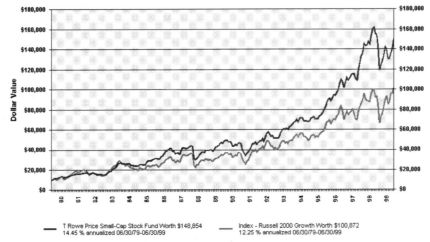

T Rowe Price Small-Cap Stock Fund Worth $148,854   Index - Russell 2000 Growth Worth $100,872
14.45 % annualized 06/30/79-06/30/99   12.25 % annualized 06/30/79-06/30/99

GROWTH OF $10,000

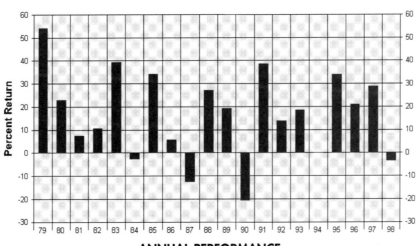

ANNUAL PERFORMANCE

TOP 10 HOLDINGS

US Foodservice	New England Business Svc.
AO Smith	Young Broadcasting
Aliant Communications	Casey's General Stores
Partner RE	Ronac Intl.
Analogic Corp.	Outback Steakhouse

USAA AGGRESSIVE GROWTH

OBJECTIVE:	*Small-Cap Growth*	*59*
MANAGER:	*Eric Efron and John Cabell Jr.*	

FUND OVERVIEW:

Eric Efron and John Cabell spend a lot of time asking themselves where the world is going and how they can take advantage of that. They want to fill the USAA Aggressive Growth Fund with companies that will prosper from these future trends. Efron and Cabell also seek businesses with rapidly growing earnings that can continue to build value over time.

There are several things that set this fund apart from others in the category. For one, it has a fairly low expense ratio. For another, turnover is below average for a small-cap fund because the two managers tend to keep their core holdings for several years. The downside to this, if you're a small-cap purist, is that you'll often find names in the portfolio that fall into the large-cap range, such as Cisco Systems. Another negative: The fund is getting pretty big to be nimble in the small-cap universe.

There's no question this is a volatile fund that either tends to knock the lights out or significantly underperform the S&P 500 (even though its more accurate benchmark is the Russell 2000). However, over time the results have been impressive, especially over the past few years.

ANNUALIZED RETURNS		PORTFOLIO STATISTICS	
1-Year	65.10%	Beta	1.16
3-Year	37.47%	Turnover	43.52
5-Year	31.62%	12-Month Yield	0.00%
Overall Rank	3	Expense Ratio	0.64%
Risk Rank	5		

MINIMUM INVESTMENT		CONTACT INFORMATION	
Regular	$3,000	*USAA Aggressive Growth*	
IRA	$250	*Telephone: (800) 382-8722*	
		www.usaa.com	

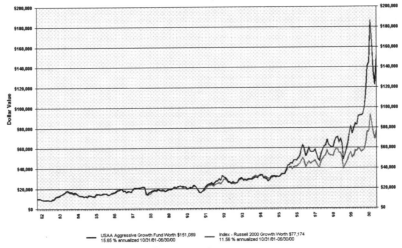

GROWTH OF $10,000

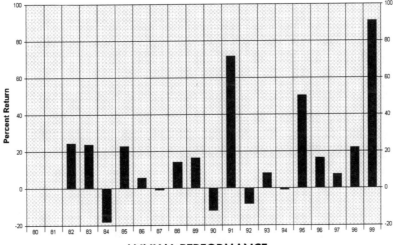

ANNUAL PERFORMANCE

TOP 10 HOLDINGS	
Metromedia Fiber Network	JDS Uniphase
Network Solutions	IDEC Pharmeceuticals
Harmonic	Sandisk Corp.
Applied Micro Circuits	Human Genome Sciences
Medimmune	Genentech

VAN WAGONER POST-VENTURE

OBJECTIVE:	*Small-Cap Growth*	
MANAGER:	*Garrett Van Wagoner*	*60*

FUND OVERVIEW:

If you like action and adventure, you'll probably love the Van Wagoner Post-Venture Fund. Manager Garrett Van Wagoner is no stranger to risk. In fact, he thrives on it. Van Wagoner takes aggressive positions in small, often unseasoned companies, and isn't shy about trading in and out of stocks on a frequent basis. He holds a fairly diversified portfolio, but his style can send investors on occasional roller coaster rides. Still, over the long term, those who have stuck with him through the rough times have made a lot of money.

Van Wagoner runs five funds altogether, with the help of two analysts, although two funds are currently closed to new investors. He prides himself in doing deep fundamental research on his holdings, including talking with company management, competitors, suppliers, and partners. He also demands projected revenue and earnings growth of 20 percent or more, plus a strong business strategy, market leadership, and experienced company management. Van Wagoner sells out when a company fails to execute on its business strategy, there is a weakening economic outlook for the company or industry, or insiders start selling shares. Even with the high turnover, this fund has been tax-efficient.

ANNUALIZED RETURNS		PORTFOLIO STATISTICS	
1-Year	83.00%	Beta	1.20
3-Year	64.43%	Turnover	234.00%
5-Year	N/A	12-Month Yield	0.00%
Overall Rank	3	12b-1 Fee	0.25%
Risk Rank	5	Expence Ratio	1.94%
MINIMUM INVESTMENT		**CONTACT INFORMATION**	
Regular	$1,000	*Van Wagoner Post-Venture Fund*	
IRA	$500	*Telephone: (800) 228-2121*	
		www.vanwagoner.com	

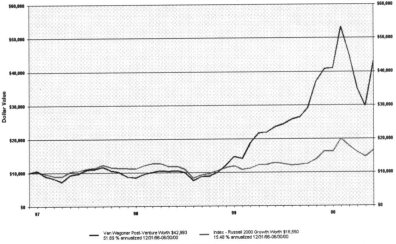

GROWTH OF $10,000

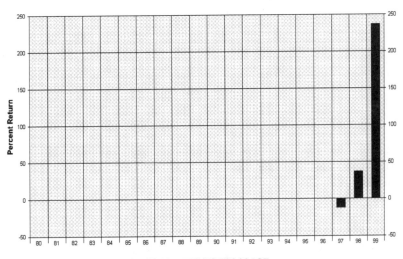

ANNUAL PERFORMANCE

TOP 10 HOLDINGS	
Ariba	Interwoven
OnHealth Network	Netro Corp.
Cobalt Networks	Preview Systems
Bluestone Software	JDS Uniphase
Phone Com	Transwitch

MERIDIAN VALUE

OBJECTIVE:	*Small-Cap Value*	*61*
MANAGER:	*Richard Aster and Kevin O'Boyle*	

FUND OVERVIEW:

When a growth stock messes up and gets sold off by the rest of Wall Street, it peaks the interest of Meridian Value managers Richard Aster and Kevin O'Boyle. O'Boyle discovered that once investors beat up a stock, it usually goes on to enjoy a period of positive results, especially during the subsequent two quarters. It's during that time that Aster and O'Boyle investigate to see whether the company's prospects have, in fact, improved. If so, they'll add the holding to their portfolio, hoping that what is now a value stock will become a growth stock once again. Given Wall Street's tendency to punish stocks that disappoint, the two never have a shortage of ideas to choose from.

Meridian Value's portfolio is concentrated in the handful of holdings these managers have the greatest conviction in. You might say that Aster and O'Boyle are often buying what the skippers of momentum-oriented small-cap funds are trying to sell. What's impressive is that they have been able to perform at the head of their asset class in recent years, without relying heavily on technology. This is a good small-cap choice for more conservative investors.

ANNUALIZED RETURNS		PORTFOLIO STATEMENTS	
1-Year	29.60%	Beta	0.64
3-Year	24.76%	Turnover	124.00%
5-Year	28.42%	12-Month Yield	2.47%
Overall Risk	1	12b-1 Fee	0.00%
Risk Rank	3	Expense Ratio	1.62%
MINIMUM INVESTMENT		**CONTACT INFORMATION**	
Regular	$1,000	*Meridian Value*	
IRA	$1,000	*Telephone: (800) 446-6662*	

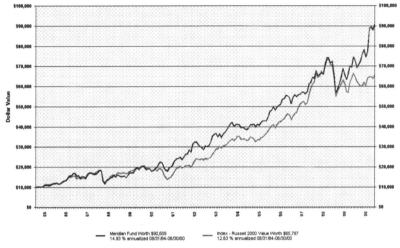

Meridian Fund Worth $90,609
14.93 % annualized 08/31/84-06/30/00

Index - Russell 2000 Value Worth $65,787
12.63 % annualized 08/31/84-06/30/00

GROWTH OF $10,000

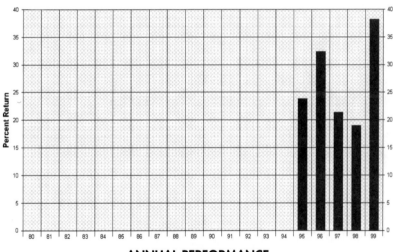

ANNUAL PERFORMANCE

TOP 10 HOLDINGS

Active Voice Corp.	Buffets
Convergys	Haemonetics
Filenet	AVX Corp.
Aventis ADR	Wolverine World Wide
Arrow Electrics	International Rectifier

SCUDDER SMALL COMPANY VALUE

OBJECTIVE:	*Small-Cap Value*	*62*
MANAGER:	*Team Managed*	

FUND OVERVIEW:

Scudder Small Company Value targets tiny companies with big potential. This team-managed fund uses proprietary computer models to find small U.S. companies selling at prices that don't reflect their long-term potential. Stocks are valued based on such measures as price-to-earnings, price-to-book value, and price-to-cash flow ratios. Managers look for favorable trends that could lead to strong earnings growth and therefore stock price momentum.

In line with this style, many of the fund's holdings are often out-of-favor with the rest of Wall Street. "We seek to exploit inefficiencies in the small-cap segment of the U.S. stock market and add value through quantitative equity analysis, portfolio construction, and efficient trading," explain lead managers James Eysenbach and Philip Fortuna. "We do not attempt to add value through market timing, either by moving between stocks and cash or among various segments of the equity markets."

This fund is more quantitative than others in the small-cap value category. It has historically been less volatile than both the Russell 2000 and S&P 500 indexes, which is what you would expect from an offering of this nature.

ANNUALIZED RETURNS		PORTFOLIO STATISTICS	
1-Year	−19.10%	Beta	0.64
3-Year	−3.25%	Turnover	34.00%
5-Year	N/A	12-Month Yield	0.12%
Overall Rank	4	12b-1 Fee	0.00%
Risk Rank	2	Expense Ratio	1.32%

MINIMUM INVESTMENT		CONTACT INFORMATION
Regular	$2,500	*Scudder Small Company Value Fund*
IRA	$500	*Telephone: (800) 343-2890*
		investments.scudder.com

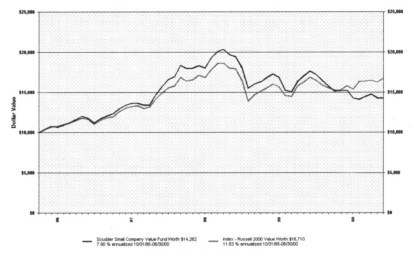

Scudder Small Company Value Fund Worth $14,262
7.90 % annualized 10/31/95-06/30/00

Index - Russell 2000 Value Worth $16,710
11.63 % annualized 10/31/95-06/30/00

GROWTH OF $10,000

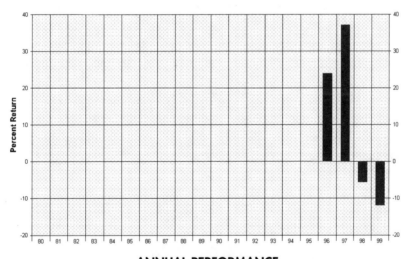

ANNUAL PERFORMANCE

TOP 10 HOLDINGS

CTS Corp.	Ames Dept. Stores
Black Hills	El Paso Electric
Cleco Corp.	Florida Rock Inds.
Scotsman Industries	TNP Enterprises
Laclede Gas	Southwest Secs. Group

STRATTON SMALL-CAP VALUE

OBJECTIVE:	Small-Cap Value	*63*
MANAGER:	Frank Reichel	

FUND OVERVIEW:

Small-cap stocks are not normally considered a good source of dividends, but Frank Reichel begs to differ. His Stratton Small-Cap Value fund seeks to generate both capital appreciation and current income by investing in the common and convertible stock of companies with market capitalizations from $50 million to $500 million. He also tries to keep risk under control by buying only companies that have been around for more than three years and pay an established dividend. Reichel reasons that the dividend requirement helps to reduce price volatility.

The portfolio is invested using both a top-down and a bottom-up approach. Reichel looks for equities with yields greater than the small-cap benchmark Russell 2000 index. Once he has his list narrowed down, he screens for companies with low price-to-earnings and price-to-cash flow multiples. He further favors stocks with demonstrated earnings growth and positive earnings revisions. By charter, Reichel is prohibited from investing in IPOs or tobacco-related stocks. It's also interesting to note that the management fee is based on performance. It goes up if Reichel beats the index, down if he trails it.

ANNUALIZED RETURNS		PORTFOLIO STATISTICS	
1-Year	−5.00%	Beta	0.61
3-Year	2.35%	Turnover	43.00%
5-Year	11.34%	12-Month Yield	1.36%
Overall Rank	5	12b-1 Fee	0.00%
Risk Rank	2	Expense Ratio	1.36%

MINIMUM INVESTMENT		CONTACT INFORMATION
Regular	$2,000	*Stratton Small-Cap Value Fund*
IRA	None	*Telephone: (800) 472-4226*
		www.strattonmgt.com

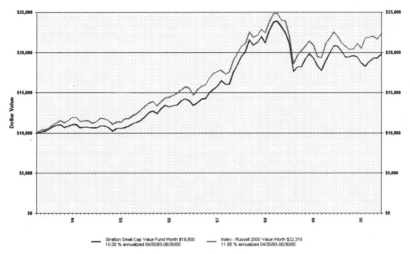

Stratton Small-Cap Value Fund Worth $19,800
10.00 % annualized 04/30/93-06/30/00

Index - Russell 2000 Value Worth $22,316
11.85 % annualized 04/30/93-06/30/00

GROWTH OF $10,000

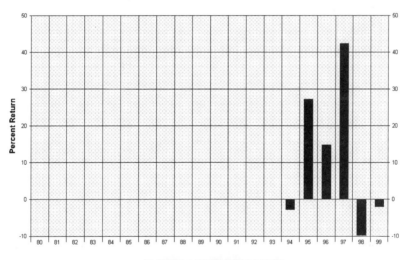

ANNUAL PERFORMANCE

TOP 10 HOLDINGS

Quixote Corp.	Technitrol
Primex Technologies	Bel Fuse
Florida Rock Inds.	Morrison Mgt. Specialists
LSI Industries Ohio	True North Communications
Eaton Vance	National Data Corp.

THIRD AVENUE SMALL-CAP VALUE

OBJECTIVE:	*Small-Cap Value*	**64**
MANAGER:	*Martin J. Whitman/Curtis Jensen*	

FUND OVERVIEW:

Marty Whitman isn't offended when people refer to him as a vulture. After all, that's what he calls himself. Whitman is a dedicated value investor, but not in the traditional sense. He looks for special situations where he can get in cheap, often because investors worry about the businesses' ability to continue as a going concern. His ideal company has an exceptionally strong financial position, as measured by a lack of debt and the presence of high-quality assets. To Whitman and co-manager Curtis Jensen (Whitman's former student), a perfect stock also has a "reasonable" management team, understandable business, and can be had for no more than 50 cents on the $1 for what it would be worth if taken over by another entity. "There are trade-offs involved in following our approach," Whitman admits. "In almost all cases, when we acquire a security, the near-term earnings outlook is terrible." But that, he believes, also reduces his downside; the stock is presumably trading at a low level because this bleak prognosis has already been factored in.

When Whitman can't find enough equities, he'll buy distressed bonds or even hold cash. He's even been known to close his funds to new investors when he can't find enough bargains.

ANNUALIZED RETURNS		PORTFOLIO STATISTICS	
1-Year	11.20%	Beta	0.54
3-Year	5.33%	Turnover	10.00%
5-Year	N/A	12-Month Yield	0.66%
Overall Rank	5	12b-1 Fee	0.00%
Risk Rank	3	Expense Ratio	1.28%
MINIMUM INVESTMENT		**CONTACT INFORMATION**	
Regular	$1,000	*Third Avenue Small-Cap Value Fund*	
IRA	$500	*Telephone: (800) 443-1021*	
		www.mjwhitman.com	

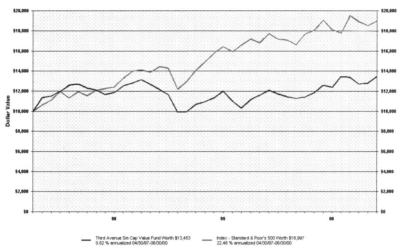

GROWTH OF $10,000

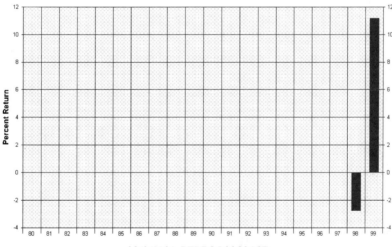

ANNUAL PERFORMANCE

TOP 10 HOLDINGS	
MBIA	Value Vision Intl.
Nissan Fire & Marine	Deltic Timber
TimberWest Timber	Alexander & Baldwin
Skyline	Spectran Corp.
Tejon Ranch	Electroglas

JANUS EQUITY INCOME

OBJECTIVE:	*Equity Income*	**65**
MANAGER:	*Karen L. Reidy*	

FUND OVERVIEW:

Janus Equity Income seeks a combination of current income and long-term growth. Managed by Karen L. Reidy, this is a more aggressive choice than many others in the category. Her job is to uncover the most compelling growth and income stocks, although this is no ordinary equity income fund. She takes it one step further by diversifying across smaller, lesser-known names as well as big, dominant franchises. In other words, she and the other Janus analysts are out there looking for great companies with great business models.

Still, Reidy hopes to keep volatility below that of the S&P 500 by investing in both stocks and bonds. At least 65 percent of the fund's assets are to be kept in income-producing securities (including dividend-paying stocks and convertibles). When selecting companies, she places high importance on earnings-growth stability. She also likes companies that generate above-average free cash flow, along with those that are low-cost leaders in their industries. Furthermore, Reidy seeks out management that is repurchasing stock and avoids economically sensitive businesses, since they generally have unpredictable earnings.

ANNUALIZED RETURNS		PORTFOLIO STATISTICS	
1-Year	16.10%	Beta	0.95
3-Year	29.46	Turnover	125.00%
5-Year	N/A	12-Month Yield	0.52%
Overall Rank	1	12b-1 Fee	0.00%
Risk Rank	3	Expense Ratio	0.95%
MINIMUM INVESTMENT		**CONTACT INFORMATION**	
Regular	$2,500	*Janus Equity Income Fund*	
IRA	$500	*Telephone: (800) 525-3713*	
		www.janus.com	

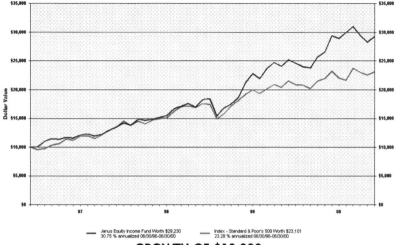

Janus Equity Income Fund Worth $29,230
30.75 % annualized 06/30/96-06/30/00

Index - Standard & Poor's 500 Worth $23,101
23.28 % annualized 06/30/96-06/30/00

GROWTH OF $10,000

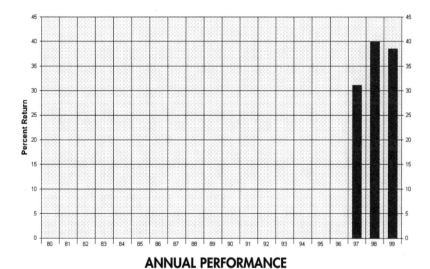

ANNUAL PERFORMANCE

TOP 10 HOLDINGS	
General Electric	Univision
Nokia Corp. ADR	American Express
EMC	Texas Instruments
Enron	Cisco Systems
AT&T Liberty Media	Automatic Data Processing

T. ROWE PRICE EQUITY INCOME

OBJECTIVE:	*Equity Income*	
MANAGER:	*Brian Rogers*	**66**

FUND OVERVIEW:

T. Rowe Price Equity Income takes a conservative approach to generating both consistent income and long-term capital growth. It is managed by Brian Rogers, whose value-oriented strategy has made this fund a real standout. (You may be familiar with Rogers from his regular appearances as a rotating panelist on the PBS program *Wall $treet Week.*) Rogers looks for dividend-paying stocks that appear to be temporarily undervalued for one reason or another. The yield component offers some downside protection against both overall market declines and potential future disappointments from these sometimes troubled companies.

Research is the cornerstone of Rogers's investment approach. He and his analysts screen through hundreds of stocks looking for promising candidates. They then do a bottom-up evaluation of each business to see whether the story really checks out. To make the cut, a company must have an established operating history, a high dividend, a low price-to-earnings ratio relative to the S&P, and a sound balance sheet. The portfolio contains mostly large blue-chip names and is extremely diversified, making it an attractive conservative equity investment.

ANNUALIZED RETURNS		PORTFOLIO STATISTICS	
1-Year	−10.05%	Beta	0.65
3-Year	7.49%	Turnover	22.60%
5-Year	14.74%	12-Month Yield	2.03%
Overall Rank	3	12b-1 Fee	0.00%
Risk Rank	2	Expense Ratio	0.77%
MINIMUM INVESTMENT		**CONTACT INFORMATION**	
Regular	$2,500	*T. Rowe Price Equity Income*	
IRA	$1,000	*Telephone: (800) 638-5660*	
		www.troweprice.com	

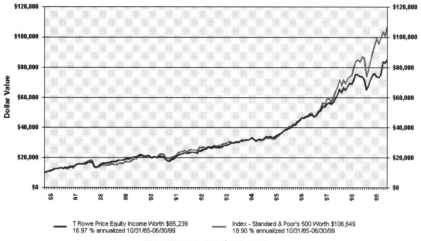

T Rowe Price Equity Income Worth $85,239
16.97 % annualized 10/31/85-06/30/99

Index - Standard & Poor's 500 Worth $106,649
18.90 % annualized 10/31/85-06/30/99

GROWTH OF $10,000

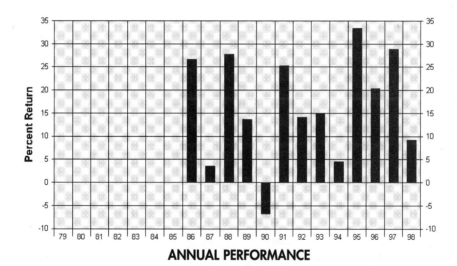

ANNUAL PERFORMANCE

TOP 10 HOLDINGS

SBC Communications	BP Amoco
Alltel	GTE
Mellon Financial	Citigroup
American Home Products	International Paper
ExxonMobil	General Mills

AMERICAN CENTURY INCOME & GROWTH

OBJECTIVE:	*Growth and Income*	
MANAGER:	*John Schniedwind and Kurt Borgwardt*	

FUND OVERVIEW:

Armed with a computer database of 2,500 stocks, John Schniedwind and Kurt Borgwardt search for attractive ideas to put in their American Century Income & Growth Portfolio. Every company is ranked according to earnings momentum and valuation characteristics, to make sure the fund pays a fair price for its holdings. The model also verifies that no more than 25 percent of the portfolio is put in any one industry. The overall goal of this quantitatively driven strategy is to beat the S&P 500 index while generating a yield that's at least 30 percent higher. This is a stiff challenge, but the fund has been able to meet it since inception.

Like most of the other funds in this category, this one doesn't have much of an income component. The portfolio does hold some high-yielding utility and energy stocks, but there are almost no bonds. In the past, the fund experienced a high degree of turnover stemming from strong new asset growth; fresh cash causes the model to reallocate holdings to keep everything in balance. However, Schniedwind and Borgwardt have vowed to make an effort to reduce this frequent trading.

ANNUALIZED RETURNS		PORTFOLIO STATISTICS	
1-Year	3.80%	Beta	1.02
3-Year	18.32%	Turnover	54.00%
5-Year	22.73%	12-Month Yield	1.00%
Overall Rank	3	12b-1 Fee	0.00%
Risk Rank	3	Expense Ratio	0.70%

MINIMUM INVESTMENT		CONTACT INFORMATION	
Regular	$2,500	*American Century Income &*	
IRA	$1,000	*Growth Fund*	
		Telephone: (800) 345-2021	
		www.americancentury.com	

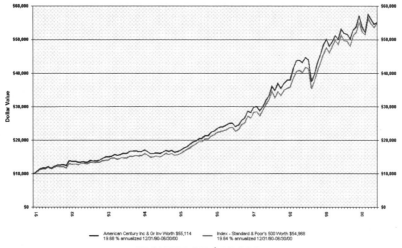

American Century Inc & Gr Inv Worth $55,114
19.68 % annualized 12/31/90-06/30/00

Index - Standard & Poor's 500 Worth $54,968
19.64 % annualized 12/31/90-06/30/00

GROWTH OF $10,000

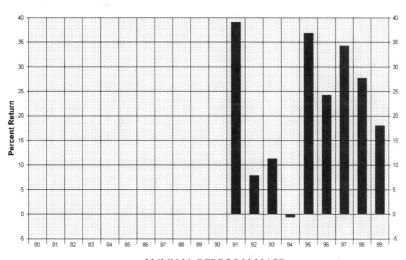

ANNUAL PERFORMANCE

TOP 10 HOLDINGS	
Microsoft	Citigroup
AT&T	Lucent Technologies
Cisco Systems	Wal-Mart
General Electric	SEC Communications
Morgan Stanley Dean Witter	Chase Manhattan

LEXINGTON CORPORATE LEADERS

OBJECTIVE:	*Growth and Income*	*68*
MANAGER:	*Lawrence Kantor*	

FUND OVERVIEW:

Lexington Corporate Leaders was set up as a unit trust in 1935. Its objective was to generate long-term capital growth and income by buying an equal number of shares from a fixed list of 30 American blue-chip companies. Today, that number has been reduced to 25. Because of this unusual policy, if a stock splits, the extra shares are promptly sold and the proceeds are reinvested among other positions. In addition, the fund is prohibited from adding new positions, except in the case of a spin-off. As a result, Lexington Corporate Leaders doesn't own companies in industries that have evolved since its founding, such as computer technology and airlines. Still, most companies in the fund are highly diversified, giving investors some exposure to virtually every segment of the economy, both in the United States and abroad. A stock is removed from the portfolio only if it fails to pay a dividend or is delisted from the exchange.

Fund manager Lawrence Kantor clearly has little flexibility when it comes to adding or deleting names from the fund's list of holdings. That hasn't hurt, though. The fund has consistently been a strong performer since inception, giving the S&P 500 a good run for its money.

ANNUALIZED RETURNS		PORTFOLIO STATISTICS	
1-Year	−8.90%	**Beta**	0.75
3-Year	5.95%	**Turnover**	N/A
5-Year	14.72%	**12-Month Yield**	1.99%
Overall Rank	3	**12b-1 Fee**	0.00%
Risk Rank	2	**Expense Ratio**	0.60%

MINIMUM INVESTMENT		CONTACT INFORMATION
Regular	$1,000	*Lexington Corporate Leaders Trust Fund*
IRA	$250	*Telephone: (800) 526-0056*
		www.lexingtonfunds.com

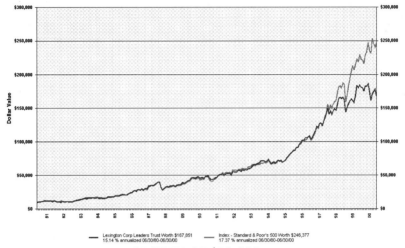

GROWTH OF $10,000

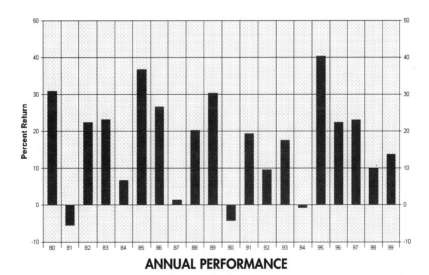

ANNUAL PERFORMANCE

TOP 10 HOLDINGS

General Electric	AT&T
Procter & Gamble	Citigroup
Columbia Energy Group	Eastman Kodak
ExxonMobil	Union Carbide
Chevron	DuPont

MARSICO GROWTH & INCOME

OBJECTIVE:	*Growth and Income*	*69*
MANAGER:	*Tom Marsico*	

FUND OVERVIEW:

One of the best all-around growth and income funds over the past decade has been Janus Growth & Income. For much of that time, the man responsible was Tom Marsico. Marsico managed Janus Growth & Income from May 31, 1991, to August 7, 1997, steering it to a 21.19 percent annualized gain, compared to 18.59 percent for the S&P 500. Now, Marsico has a new fund with the same mandate. Marsico Growth & Income was launched at the beginning of 1998. Because it looks and feels just like the portfolio he ran at Janus, it's reasonable to expect Marsico's winning ways at his own shop will continue, as they have. Plus, his new fund is much smaller, which is always a major advantage.

Marsico Growth & Income tries to identify quality companies with high growth potential before they are fully recognized by Wall Street. Marsico buys mostly blue chips, especially those experiencing a positive element of change. He further looks for globally diverse companies with strong franchises and brand names. The investment objective of this fund is long-term capital growth, with minimal emphasis on income. Marsico can also own bonds and other fixed-income securities, but you should think of this fund as a pure stock offering.

ANNUALIZED RETURNS		PORTFOLIO STATISTICS	
1-Year	22.10%	Beta	N/A
3-Year	N/A	Turnover	137.00%
5-Year	N/A	12-Month Yield	0.00%
Overall Rank	N/A	12b-1 Fee	0.25%
Risk Rank	N/A	Expense Ratio	1.42%
MINIMUM INVESTMENT		**CONTACT INFORMATION**	
Regular	$2,500	*Marsico Growth & Income Fund*	
IRA	$1,000	*Telephone: (888) 860-8686*	
		www.marsicofunds.com	

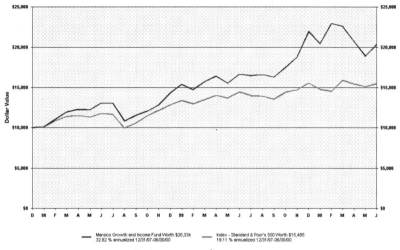

Marsico Growth and Income Fund Worth $20,334
32.82 % annualized 12/31/97-06/30/00

Index - Standard & Poor's 500 Worth $15,485
19.11 % annualized 12/31/97-06/30/00

GROWTH OF $10,000

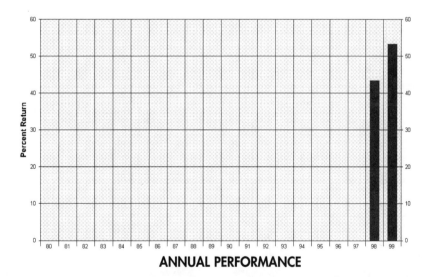

ANNUAL PERFORMANCE

TOP 10 HOLDINGS

EMC	Genentech
Citigroup	Qualcomm
Time Warner	Oracle Corp.
Cisco Systems	Sprint
Sony Corp.	Sun Microsystems

SMITH BREEDEN EQUITY MARKET PLUS

| OBJECTIVE: | *Growth and Income* | *70* |
| MANAGER: | *John Sprow* | |

FUND OVERVIEW:

The Smith Breeden Equity Market Plus Fund's objective is to provide a greater return than the S&P 500 without taking on any additional risk. Manager John Sprow divides the portfolio into two segments: one for the S&P 500 index and the other for fixed-income investments. Sprow doesn't generally buy individual stocks for the S&P 500 segment. Instead, he gets his equity exposure through S&P 500 futures and swaps. This generates index-like returns without requiring any up-front money to enter into these contracts.

Therefore, most of the portfolio's cash gets put to work in the fixed-income segment, namely in U.S. government, mortgage-backed, and corporate debt securities. These investments generate income and have the potential to achieve capital appreciation. The income component allows the fund to outperform the S&P 500 when properly constructed. In other words, you get the market's return (from the S&P 500 derivatives), any dividends, plus the yield and appreciation from the fixed-income instruments.

If this seems like an exotic strategy, it is. But Sprow has consistently achieved his objective with less volatility than the S&P.

ANNUALIZED RETURNS		PORTFOLIO STATISTICS	
1-Year	4.90%	Beta	0.98
3-Year	17.57%	Turnover	2.58%
5-Year	23.05%	12-Month Yield	6.38%
Overall Rank	3	12b-1 Fee	0.00%
Risk Rank	3	Expense Ratio	0.88%
MINIMUM INVESTMENT		**CONTACT INFORMATION**	
Regular	$1,000	*Smith Breeden Equity Market Plus*	
IRA	$250	*Fund*	
		Telephone: (800) 221-3137	
		www.smithbreeden.com	

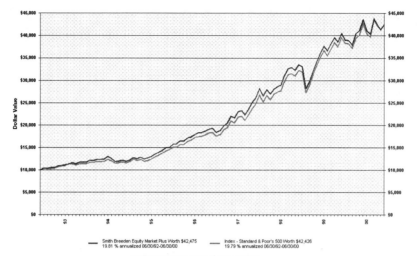

Smith Breeden Equity Market Plus Worth $42,475
19.81 % annualized 06/30/92-06/30/00

Index - Standard & Poor's 500 Worth $42,426
19.79 % annualized 06/30/92-06/30/00

GROWTH OF $10,000

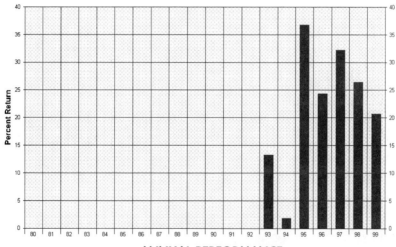

ANNUAL PERFORMANCE

TOP 10 HOLDINGS	
FHLMC 15 yr. 6.5%	FHLMC 15 yr. 6.5%
FHLMC 15 yr. 6.5%	FHLMC 15 yr. 6.5%
FHLMC 15 yr. 6.5%	FHLMC 15 yr. 6.5%
FHLMC 15 yr. 6.5%	FHLMC 15 yr. 6.5%
FHLMC 15 yr. 6.5%	FHLMC 15 yr. 6.5%

SSgA GROWTH & INCOME

OBJECTIVE:	*Growth and Income*	
MANAGER:	*L. Emerson Tuttle*	*71*

FUND OVERVIEW:

Like many other funds in this category, SSgA Growth & Income is purely a stock portfolio. It contains a combination of small- and mid-cap companies, many of which pay only a very small dividend. Nevertheless, the fund's investment objective is to achieve both long-term capital growth and current income. Manager L. Emerson Tuttle's goal is to provide greater long-term returns than the overall U.S. equity market, without incurring more risk. His portfolio strategy combines market economics with fundamental research. He begins by assessing current economic conditions and forecasting his expectations for the coming months. Then he examines each sector in the S&P 500 index to see how it is performing relative to the overall market. Tuttle gives greater weight in the portfolio to those sectors he expects will outperform the index. In that pursuit, he selects those stocks in each sector that appear to be most attractive.

SSgA is part of State Street Global Advisors, an international investment firm with more than $280 billion in assets. The company stresses performance and expects its managers to stay ahead of the pack. Tuttle joined State Street in 1981 and is assisted by four other portfolio managers in running this fund.

ANNUALIZED RETURNS		PORTFOLIO STATISTICS	
1-Year	10.90%	Beta	1.00
3-Year	24.00%	Turnover	49.83%
5-Year	25.07%	12-Month Yield	0.25%
Overall Rank	2	12b-1 Fee	0.14%
Risk Rank	3	Expense Ratio	1.01%

MINIMUM INVESTMENT		CONTACT INFORMATION	
Regular	$1,000	*SSgA Growth and Income Fund*	
IRA	$250	*Telephone: (800) 647-7327*	
		www.ssgafunds.com	

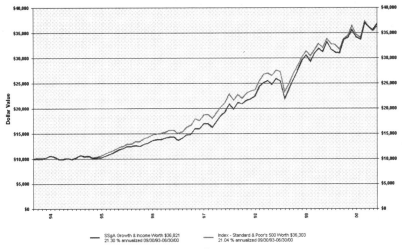

GROWTH OF $10,000

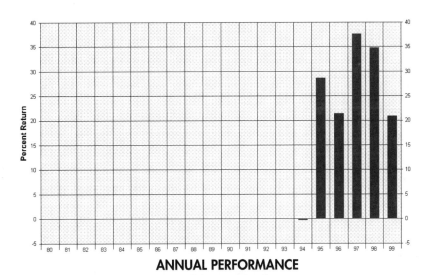

ANNUAL PERFORMANCE

TOP 10 HOLDINGS	
Microsoft	Duke Energy
EMC	Medtronic
Cisco Systems	Wal-Mart
Linear Technologies	Automatic Data Processing
Pharmacia & Upjohn	General Electric

BRIDGEWAY ULTRA-LARGE 35 INDEX

OBJECTIVE:	*Index*	*72*
MANAGER:	*John Montgomery*	

FUND OVERVIEW:

Bridgeway Ultra-Large 35 Index calls itself a hybrid between the Dow and S&P 500. This unique offering, which has the lowest expense ratio of any fund in this book, consists of equal percentages of the 35 largest U.S. companies, excluding tobacco stocks and allowing for industry diversification. Holdings include General Motors, GTE, Intel, AT&T, Merck, Coca-Cola, Fannie Mae, and DuPont. What's great about this fund, besides its bare-bones costs, is that manager John Montgomery runs it with an eye on keeping taxes to an absolute minimum. In fact, his goal is to never have a capital gains distribution. (The fund is fairly new, having been launched in July 1997, so it's too soon to tell how successful he is at reaching this objective over the long term.)

Bridgeway Ultra-Large 35 Index has everything you could want in a fund: Low expenses, tax efficiency, and quality management. By the way, you won't find the past performance of the index Montgomery follows anywhere. He made it up. This fund has done better than the S&P 500 since inception, an accomplishment few funds can boast about. And if the recent large-cap stock dominance continues in the year 2000, this fund should continue to shine.

ANNUALIZED RETURNS		PORTFOLIO STATISTICS	
1-Year	11.70%	Beta	N/A
3-Year	N/A	Turnover	48.50%
5-Year	N/A	12-Month Yield	0.75%
Overall Rank	N/A	12b-1 Fee	0.00%
Risk Rank	N/A	Expense Ratio	0.14%

MINIMUM INVESTMENT		CONTACT INFORMATION
Regular	$2,000	*Bridgeway Ultra Large 35 Index*
IRA	$500	*Telephone: (800) 661-3550*
		www.bridgewayfund.com

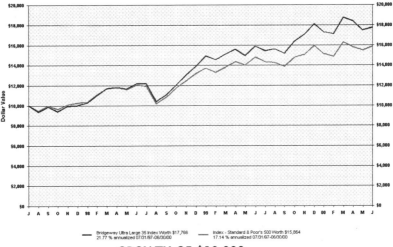

Bridgeway Ultra Large 35 Index Worth $17,766
21.77 % annualized 07/31/97-06/30/00

Index - Standard & Poor's 500 Worth $15,864
17.14 % annualized 07/31/97-06/30/00

GROWTH OF $10,000

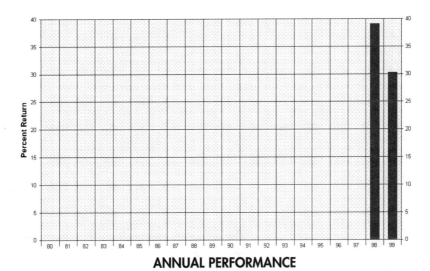

ANNUAL PERFORMANCE

TOP 10 HOLDINGS

Ford Motor	Cisco Systems
Bank of America	Wal-Mart
IBM	Coca-Cola
Intel	Lucent Technologies
General Electric	Chevron

DOMINI SOCIAL EQUITY

OBJECTIVE:	*Index*	**73**
MANAGER:	*Team Managed*	

FUND OVERVIEW:

Domini Social Equity is an index fund with a twist. It invests in a unique index made up of about 400 companies which pass multiple social screens. Specifically, to make it into the Domini Social Index, companies must have positive records for making safe and useful products, good employee relations, positive corporate citizenship, and good track records for protecting the environment. What's more, the index excludes companies deriving more than 2 percent of gross revenues from the sale of military weapons, and an included company must not have any revenue coming from tobacco products, alcoholic beverages, gambling operations, or nuclear power plants.

Clearly, if you are concerned about such social issues, this fund makes perfect sense. But investing with your conscience historically hasn't been very profitable, since most socially aware funds have lousy track records. Domini Social Equity is a rare exception. It has slightly outperformed the S&P 500 since inception. That's an amazing accomplishment for any fund, let alone one which requires its holdings to pass such rigorous and subjective requirements and has a higher expense ratio than most others in this category.

ANNUALIZED RETURNS		PORTFOLIO STATISTICS	
1-Year	7.00%	Beta	1.07
3-Year	21.25%	Turnover	4.00%
5-Year	24.30%	12-Month Yield	0.00%
Overall Rank	3	12b-1 Fee	0.00%
Risk Rank	3	Expense Ratio	0.96%
MINIMUM INVESTMENT		**CONTACT INFORMATION**	
Regular	$1,000	*Domini Social Equity Fund*	
IRA	$250	*Telephone: (800) 582-6757*	
		www.domini.com	

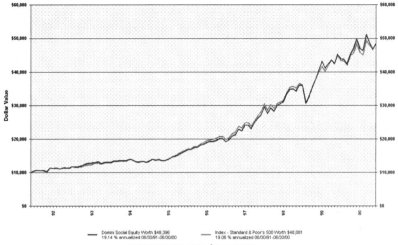

GROWTH OF $10,000

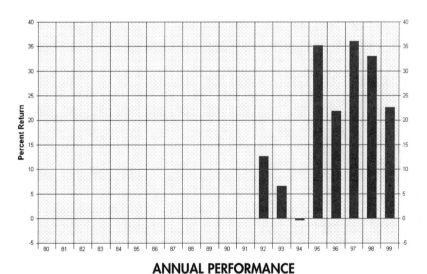

ANNUAL PERFORMANCE

TOP 10 HOLDINGS	
Microsoft	Lucent Technologies
Intel	Wal-Mart
Cisco Systems	American Intl. Group
Merck & Co.	AT&T
Coca-Cola	SBC Communications

RYDEX OTC

OBJECTIVE:	*Index*
MANAGER:	*Michael Byrum*

74

FUND OVERVIEW:

Without question, the index everyone has been talking about over the past few years is the Nasdaq 100. After all, it has posted incredible returns, thanks to its large tech weighting. Until recently, there weren't many ways to gain access to this index. But that has changed. There are now a number of no-load funds tracking the Nasdaq 100, plus the so-called "QQQ" Nasdaq tracking shares traded on the American Stock Exchange. The oldest fund following the Nasdaq 100 is Rydex OTC. It's also the largest.

Manager Mike Byrum puts together a portfolio of stocks that he feels will adequately replicate the performance of the Nasdaq 100. While the fund's expense ratio is higher than most other index funds, investors aren't complaining because of the great performance.

Keep in mind that the Nasdaq 100 is basically an index of large technology stocks, such as Microsoft, Intel, Cisco Systems, Dell Computer, and Oracle. Although there are a few service companies and retailers thrown in—such as Starbucks, Costco, and Amazon.com—a bet on the Nasdaq 100 is a bet on technology stocks. Also note the fund's high minimum investment requirement of $25,000 for both individual accounts and IRAs.

ANNUALIZED RETURNS		PORTFOLIO STATISTICS	
1-Year	61.70%	**Beta**	1.35
3-Year	57.47%	**Turnover**	770.00%
5-Year	47.97%	**12-Month Yield**	0.00%
Overall Rank	1	**12b-1 Fee**	0.00%
Risk Rank	5	**Expense Ratio**	1.14%
MINIMUM INVESTMENT		**CONTACT INFORMATION**	
Regular	$25,000	*Rydex OTC Fund*	
IRA	$25,000	*Telephone: (800) 820-0888*	
		www.rydexfunds.com	

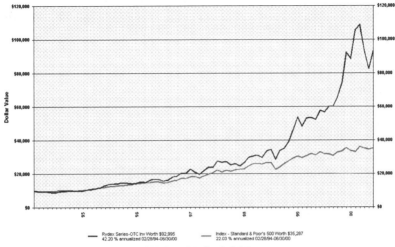

GROWTH OF $10,000

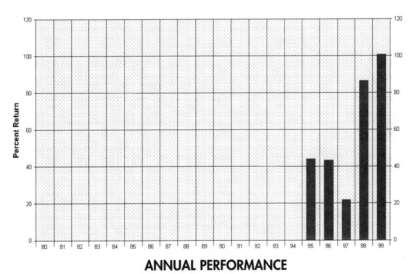

ANNUAL PERFORMANCE

TOP 10 HOLDINGS	
Cisco Systems	JDS Uniphase
Microsoft	Nextel Communications
Intel	Sun Microsystems
Qualcomm	Veritas Software
Oralife	Dell Computer

SCHWAB 1000

OBJECTIVE:	*Index*	
MANAGER:	*Geri Hom*	**75**

FUND OVERVIEW:

Schwab 1000 is a proprietary index set-up by discount broker Charles Schwab & Co. This fund is predictably designed to mimic that index. The index contains the 1,000 largest publicly traded companies in the U.S., in terms of market capitalization. Schwab calls it an index of both large- and mid-cap stocks. Interestingly enough, although there are more than 7,200 publicly traded American stocks, the companies in Schwab 1000 make up some 87 percent of the total value of all U.S. stocks.

Like most index funds, Schwab 1000 is very tax-efficient. In fact, the fund's goal is to never pay out a capital gains distribution, although it does distribute annual dividends which are taxed as ordinary income. To accomplish this goal, the fund may adjust its weightings of certain stocks and even continue to hold companies no longer included in the index to avoid having to realize gains.

Schwab offers this fund in two classes: investor shares and select shares. Select shares have a slightly lower expense ratio, but a much higher initial minimum investment requirement of $50,000.

ANNUALIZED RETURNS		PORTFOLIO STATISTICS	
1-Year	8.30%	Beta	1.00
3-Year	19.55%	Turnover	2.00%
5-Year	23.01%	12-Month Yield	0.64%
Overall Rank	3	12b-1 Fee	0.00%
Risk Rank	3	Expense Ratio	0.46%
MINIMUM INVESTMENT		**CONTACT INFORMATION**	
Regular	$1,000	*Schwab 1000*	
IRA	$500	*Telephone: (800) 435-4000*	
		www.schwab.com	

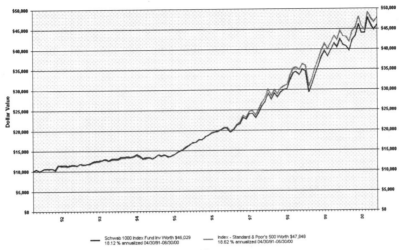

GROWTH OF $10,000

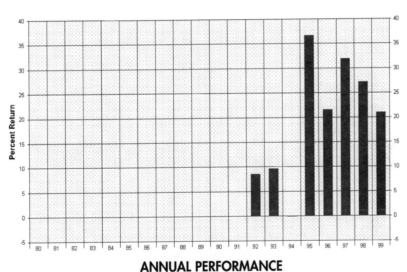

ANNUAL PERFORMANCE

TOP 10 HOLDINGS	
General Electric	SBC Communications
Microsoft	Wal-Mart
ExxonMobil	Lucent Technologies
Coca-Cola	Intel
Merck & Co.	Cisco Systems

VANGUARD INDEX 500

OBJECTIVE:	*Index*	*76*
MANAGER:	*George Sauter*	

FUND OVERVIEW:

Vanguard Index 500 is the granddaddy of all index funds. It is the largest and best performing of the portfolios that try to replicate the price and yield performance of the S&P 500. It does so by following a computer model that guides the fund to invest in all 500 stocks in the index in approximately the exact same proportions. (The S&P 500, as you probably know by now, is dominated by large blue-chip stocks and represents approximately 70 percent of the total capitalization of all U.S. equities.) By nature, the fund will be close to fully invested at all times, holding only a tiny level of cash to meet redemptions. The fund's returns since inception have been virtually identical to the S&P 500, less Vanguard's bare-bones expense ratio.

Assuming no mass redemption requests come in, this fund should be highly tax-efficient because turnover is low. It would make a nice large-cap core holding in almost any portfolio, although I tend to prefer the Vanguard Total Stock Market Portfolio (which we will discuss next) even more, for those who want to own just one index fund. For more on the role indexing should play in your overall portfolio, you might want to reread my comments in Chapter 3.

ANNUALIZED RETURNS		PORTFOLIO STATISTICS	
1-Year	7.30%	Beta	1.00
3-Year	19.67%	Turnover	6.00%
5-Year	23.76%	12-Month Yield	1.01%
Overall Rank	2	12b-1 Fee	0.00%
Risk Rank	3	Expense Ratio	0.17%
MINIMUM INVESTMENT		CONTACT INFORMATION	
Regular	$3,000	*Vanguard Index 500 Portfolio*	
IRA	$1,000	*Telephone: (800) 662-7447*	
		www.vanguard.com	

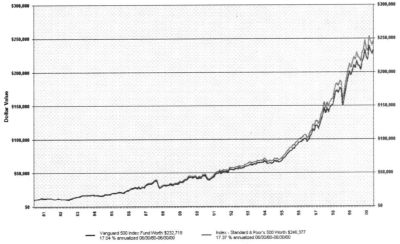

Vanguard 500 Index Fund Worth $232,718
17.04 % annualized 06/30/80-06/30/00

Index - Standard & Poor's 500 Worth $246,377
17.37 % annualized 06/30/80-06/30/00

GROWTH OF $10,000

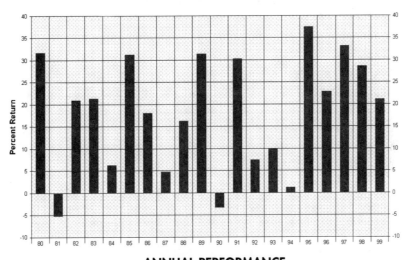

ANNUAL PERFORMANCE

TOP 10 HOLDINGS

Microsoft   Lucent Technologies
General Electric   IBM
Intel   Citigroup
Wal-Mart   America Online
ExxonMobil   Cisco Systems

VANGUARD TOTAL STOCK MARKET

OBJECTIVE:	*Index*	*77*
MANAGER:	*George Sauter*	

FUND OVERVIEW:

Unlike the Vanguard Index 500 fund, which only gives you exposure to blue-chip America, Vanguard Total Stock Market allows you to invest in equities of all sizes—large and small. Although 70 percent of the portfolio looks just like the S&P 500, 20 percent is in mid-cap stocks and the remaining 10 percent is in small caps. This gives you access to the entire U.S. equity market. The fund is designed to parallel the performance of the Wilshire 5000 Index, which consists of all regularly traded U.S. stocks on the three major exchanges. However, it normally will hold only a representative sample of some 2,000 positions because the cost of owning all 5,000 would be quite high.

If you are looking for the simplest approach to gaining exposure to the entire stock market without having to do any work, this fund is a great choice. It is so diversified, it could technically be the only fund you own for your U.S. market exposure. I'm not recommending that approach, but as far as index funds are concerned, this one is my favorite. The actual manager isn't that important; the fund is run by a computer, so this can truly be a buy-and-hold investment.

ANNUALIZED RETURNS		PORTFOLIO STATISTICS	
1-Year	9.90%	Beta	0.97
3-Year	19.08%	Turnover	3.00%
5-Year	22.28%	12-Month Yield	0.99%
Overall Rank	3	12b-1 Fee	0.00%
Risk Rank	3	Expense Ratio	0.20%
MINIMUM INVESTMENT		**CONTACT INFORMATION**	
Regular	$3,000	*Vanguard Total Stock Market*	
IRA	$1,000	*Portfolio*	
		Telephone: (800) 662-7447	
		www.vanguard.com	

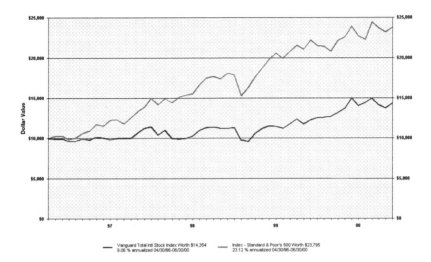

Vanguard Total Intl Stock Index Worth $14,354
9.06 % annualized 04/30/96-06/30/00

Index - Standard & Poor's 500 Worth $23,795
23.12 % annualized 04/30/96-06/30/00

GROWTH OF $10,000

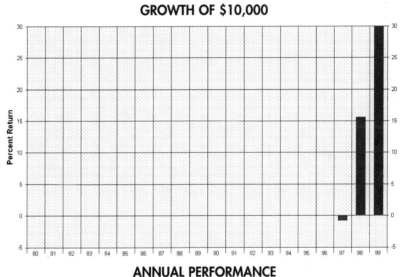

ANNUAL PERFORMANCE

TOP 10 HOLDINGS	
Microsoft	Cisco Systems
General Electric	IBM
Intel	Citigroup
Wal-Mart	American Intl. Group
ExxonMobil	Lucent Technologies

WILSHIRE 5000 INDEX PORTFOLIO

OBJECTIVE:	*Index*	
MANAGER:	*Tom Stevens and Dave Borger*	*78*

FUND OVERVIEW:

The Wilshire 5000 Index Portfolio is similar to the Vanguard Total Stock Market fund in many respects. It tracks the same basket of 7,000-plus stocks and gives you a chance to invest in the entire U.S. equity market. One big difference is that this fund, launched at the beginning of 1999, is run by the same firm that created the index in 1974. That doesn't mean the fund is any better, but these folks certainly know how to run an index fund.

So why buy this fund over Vanguard? The primary reason, as I see it, is to simplify your life if you do business with one of the discount brokers, such as Charles Schwab, Fidelity, or Waterhouse. That's because the Wilshire fund can be purchased through these brokers without any transaction fees. The Vanguard fund, by contrast, is subject to a commission charge at these brokers for both your initial purchase and additional investments. The Wilshire fund does have a slightly higher expense ratio. But that likely won't have much of an impact in the long term and is probably worth it for the added convenience, especially if you own several other funds in your brokerage account and want to add this one to the mix.

ANNUALIZED RETURNS		PORTFOLIO STATISTICS	
1-Year	8.80	Beta	N/A
3-Year	N/A	Turnover	N/A
5-Year	N/A	12-Month Yield	N/A
Overall Rank	N/A	12b-1 Fee	0.00%
Risk Rank	N/A	Expense Ratio	0.53%
MINIMUM INVESTMENT		**CONTACT INFORMATION**	
Regular	$1,000	*Wilshire 5000 Index Portfolio*	
IRA	$1,000	*Telephone: (888) 200-6796*	
		www.wilfunds.com	

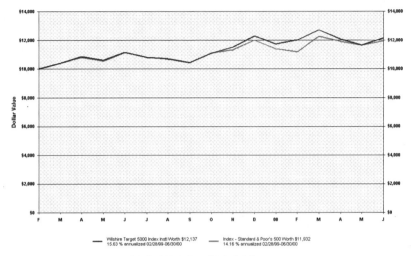

Wilshire Target 5000 Index Instl Worth $12,137
15.63 % annualized 02/28/99-06/30/00

Index - Standard & Poor's 500 Worth $11,932
14.16 % annualized 02/28/99-06/30/00

GROWTH OF $10,000

VALUE LINE ANNUAL PERFORMANCE CHART
NOT AVAILABLE FOR THIS FUND

ANNUAL PERFORMANCE

TOP 10 HOLDINGS	
Microsoft	Citigroup
General Electric	Cisco Systems
Wal-Mart	ExxonMobil
Intel	Lucent Technologies
Merck	IBM

ALLEGHANY MONTAG & CALDWELL BALANCED

OBJECTIVE:	*Balanced*	*79*
MANAGER:	*Ronald E. Canakaris*	

FUND OVERVIEW:

Alleghany Montag & Caldwell Balanced takes a total return approach to investing by spreading the fund across blue-chip companies, corporate and U.S. government bonds, and a slight reserve of cash. Instead of worrying about which asset classes to put the money to work in, manager Ronald Canakaris focuses on finding the best investments for each area of the portfolio. The fund's strategic target allocation calls for stocks to make up 50 to 70 percent of total assets, with the bulk of the rest in senior fixed-income securities. However, if Canakaris believes one asset class is exceedingly more attractive than another, he can navigate outside of these parameters.

Canakaris is positive on the outlook for stocks, assuming the economy and corporate profits continue to grow. He also believes bonds still provide attractive yields and appreciation potential. "With economic growth likely to slow and inflation well-controlled, we think there is the potential for positive bond market returns in the period ahead," he predicts. In addition to gradually lengthening maturities, he will continue to seek high-yielding corporate and agency issues. Meantime, the fund's cash component is at under 5 percent.

ANNUALIZED RETURNS		PORTFOLIO STATISTICS	
1-Year	6.90%	Beta	0.64
3-Year	14.58%	Turnover	55.00%
5-Year	17.58%	12-Month Yield	1.69%
Overall Rank	2	12b-1 Fee	0.25%
Risk Rank	2	Expense Ratio	1.25%
MINIMUM INVESTMENT		**CONTACT INFORMATION**	
Regular	$2,500	*Alleghany Montag & Caldwell*	
IRA	$500	*Balanced Fund*	
		Telephone: (800) 992-8151	
		www.alleghanyfunds.com	

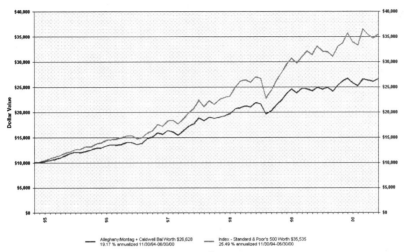

GROWTH OF $10,000

Alleghany/Montag + Caldwell Bal Worth $26,628
19.17 % annualized 11/30/94-06/30/00

Index - Standard & Poor's 500 Worth $35,535
25.49 % annualized 11/30/94-06/30/00

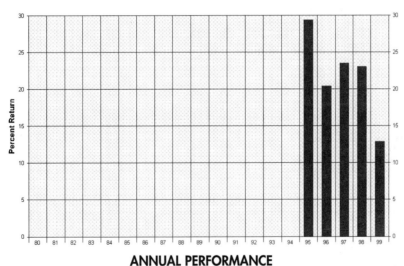

ANNUAL PERFORMANCE

TOP 10 HOLDINGS

Johnson & Johnson	Bristol-Myers Squibb
Pfizer	Coca-Cola
Procter & Gamble	General Electric
McDonald's	MCI WorldCom
Gillette	Home Depot

GABELLI WESTWOOD BALANCED

OBJECTIVE:	*Balanced*	*80*
MANAGER:	*Susan Byrne*	

FUND OVERVIEW:

Gabelli Westwood Balanced manager Susan Byrne takes a top-down approach to investing. She begins by looking at the overall economic environment, paying special attention to inflation. If conditions seem right for equities, she'll place up to 70 percent of the portfolio in stocks, with the remainder in fixed-income instruments and cash. Byrne also buys preferreds, real estate investment trusts (REITs), and high-grade convertible securities.

Westwood Balanced seeks to provide shareholders with both capital appreciation and current income. No less than 25 percent of the portfolio will be invested in bonds and other fixed-income instruments at all times. If Byrne believes the outlook for equities is bleak, she can temporarily put the entire portfolio in U.S. government securities, certificates of deposit, or other cash-equivalent investments to preserve capital.

A few years ago, Byrne entered into an agreement with prominent fund manager Mario Gabelli for the marketing of her Westwood family of funds. When you call for information, you'll be connected to Gabelli's office, even though he has nothing to do with the fund's management.

ANNUALIZED RETURNS		PORTFOLIO STATISTICS	
1-Year	5.30%	Beta	0.50
3-Year	10.96%	Turnover	86.00%
5-Year	15.80%	12-Month Yield	2.06%
Overall Rank	2	12b-1 Fee	0.25%
Risk Rank	1	Expense Ratio	1.55%
MINIMUM INVESTMENT		**CONTACT INFORMATION**	
Regular	$1,000	*Gabelli Westwood Balanced*	
IRA	$1,000	*Telephone: (800) 422-3554*	
		www.gabelli.com	

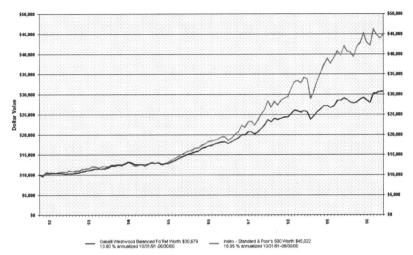

GROWTH OF $10,000

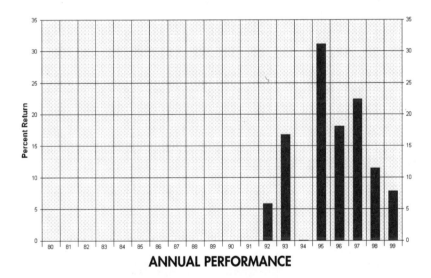

ANNUAL PERFORMANCE

TOP 10 HOLDINGS	
Delta Air Lines	Time Warner
Conoco	Alcoa
United Parcel Service	Limited
IBM	Anheuser-Busch
Deere & Co.	Pharmacia & Upjohn

RAINIER BALANCED PORTFOLIO

OBJECTIVE:	*Balanced*	*81*
MANAGER:	*Team Managed*	

FUND OVERVIEW:

Rainier Balanced is designed to provide long-term capital appreciation and regular income, with less return and risk than the S&P 500. The portfolio is allocated among equities, fixed-income instruments, and short-term cash equivalents. Stocks will normally make up 35 to 65 percent of the portfolio, and bonds will constitute from 30 to 55 percent. The remainder will be in cash. The management team uses a strategic asset allocation approach, putting money where it is expected to do best, given short-term trends in the economy. Shifts from one asset to another are gradual, though, and aggressive market timing is avoided.

The equity portion of the portfolio is invested by Jim Margard, who also runs another Powerhouse Performer, Rainier Core Equity (see entry 10). This fund is appropriate for conservative investors who prefer to have their stock and bond exposure in one place. Note that the fund has a minimum initial investment requirement of $25,000. I realize that's steep for most people. However, if you buy it through a no-load, no-transaction-fee program at one of the discount brokers, which is my preference, you can get in for as little as $2,500.

ANNUALIZED RETURNS		PORTFOLIO STATISTICS	
1-Year	11.10%	Beta	0.68
3-Year	15.03%	Turnover	68.78%
5-Year	17.08%	12-Month Yield	1.51%
Overall Rank	3	12b-1 Fee	0.25%
Risk Rank	2	Expense Ratio	1.19%
MINIMUM INVESTMENT		**CONTACT INFORMATION**	
Regular	$25,000	*Rainier Balanced Portfolio*	
IRA	$25,000	*Telephone: (800) 248-6314*	
		www.rainierfunds.com	

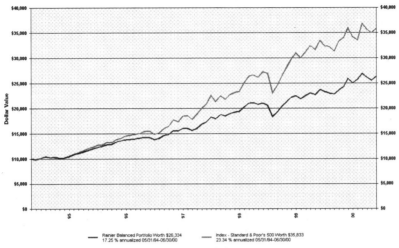

GROWTH OF $10,000

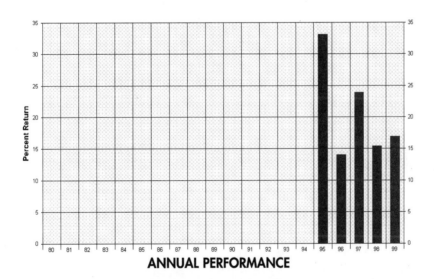

ANNUAL PERFORMANCE

TOP 10 HOLDINGS	
Microsoft	Marsh & McLennan
Cisco Systems	Intel
General Electric	Texas Instruments
Sun Microsystems	Citigroup
Nortel Networks	Nokia Corp. ADR

VALUE LINE ASSET ALLOCATION

OBJECTIVE:	*Balanced*	*82*
MANAGER:	*Team Managed*	

FUND OVERVIEW:

Unlike a traditional balanced fund, which maintains a pretty steady weighting of stocks, bonds, and cash, Value Line Asset Allocation's managers shift exposure to these asset classes, depending on what their computer model tells them. What's amazing is that even though the fund has averaged less than a 50 percent exposure to equities since inception, it has managed to keep up with the S&P 500 all-stock index. And it has done so in spite of owning a highly diversified list of some 200 mostly small- and mid-cap companies across a wide variety of industries. "Our highly disciplined strategy is to invest exclusively in stocks with strong earnings and strong price momentum, quickly selling issues that fail to make the grade," fund chairman Jean Bernhard Buttner notes.

Because Value Line's proprietary stock model is currently somewhat cautious, the fund's equity exposure is slightly below its neutral benchmark of 55 percent. Another 30 percent is in U.S. Treasuries, and the remainder is resting in cash. Value Line Asset Allocation is great for investors looking for both stock and bond diversification in one fund. But if you already have elements of both in your portfolio, this fund might be redundant.

ANNUALIZED RETURNS		PORTFOLIO STATISTICS	
1-Year	15.00%	Beta	0.70
3-Year	19.89%	Turnover	41.00%
5-Year	22.76%	12-Month Yield	1.10%
Overall Rank	2	12b-1 Fee	0.25%
Risk Rank	3	Expense Ratio	1.04%
MINIMUM INVESTMENT		**CONTACT INFORMATION**	
Regular	$1,000	*Value Line Asset Allocation Fund*	
IRA	$100	*Telephone: (800) 223-0818*	
		www.valueline.com	

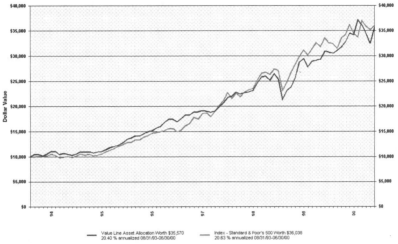

GROWTH OF $10,000

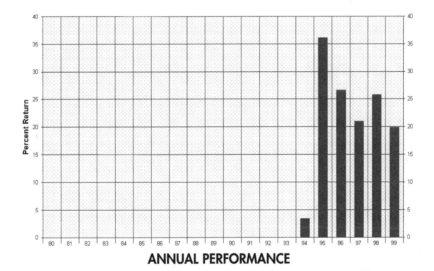

ANNUAL PERFORMANCE

TOP 10 HOLDINGS

General Electric	Peregrine Systems
Wal-Mart	Transwitch
Cisco Systems	PMC-Sierra
JDS Uniphase	Exodus Communications
Mercury Interactive	Polycom

AMERICAN AADVANTAGE INTERNATIONAL EQUITY

OBJECTIVE:	*International*	*83*
MANAGER:	*Team Managed*	

FUND OVERVIEW:

It's not every day that you come across a fund run by an airline. AMR Investments is a multibillion-dollar asset management firm that has long run pension funds for employees of American Airlines. Several years ago, the company decided to offer its investment products to the general public by forming a series of mutual funds. AMR has hired the managers of three other top-notch international funds to run American AAdvantage International. The team includes Sarah Ketterer of Hotchkis & Wiley International, Dominic Caldecott of Morgan Stanley International Equity, and Gary Motyl of Franklin Capital Accumulator. Each manages one-third of the portfolio, and they all follow a value approach to selecting companies around the globe. Collectively, they have put together a highly diversified, mostly large-cap portfolio with some 300 names.

The managers are limited by prospectus to investing only in the more developed markets of Europe and Asia, which means you won't get much exposure to emerging countries. Note that you should invest in the fund's "Plan Ahead" shares, which have a lower expense ratio.

ANNUALIZED RETURNS		PORTFOLIO STATISTICS	
1-Year	15.40%	Beta	0.69
3-Year	10.77%	Turnover	N/A
5-Year	13.73%	12-Month Yield	1.22%
Overall Rank	3	12b-1 Fee	0.00%
Risk Rank	2	Expense Ratio	1.01%
MINIMUM INVESTMENT		**CONTACT INFORMATION**	
Regular	$2,500	*American AAdvantage International*	
IRA	$2,500	*Equity Fund*	
		Telephone: (800) 388-3344	
		www.aafunds.com	

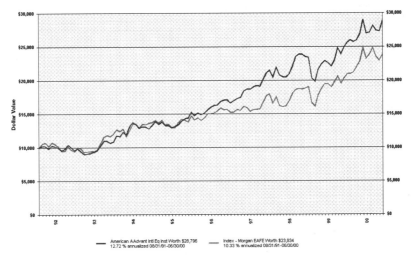

American AAdvant Intl Eq Inst Worth $28,796
12.72 % annualized 08/31/91-06/30/00

Index - Morgan EAFE Worth $23,834
10.33 % annualized 08/31/91-06/30/00

GROWTH OF $10,000

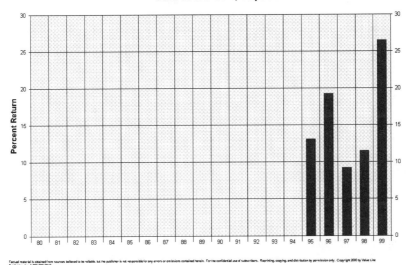

Factual material is obtained from sources believed to be reliable, but the publisher is not responsible for any errors or omissions contained herein. For the confidential use of subscribers. Reprinting, copying, and distribution by permission only. Copyright 2000 by Value Line Publishing, Inc. 1-800-800-0046.

ANNUAL PERFORMANCE

TOP 10 HOLDINGS

Total France Pete
Banque Nationale de Paris
Nintendo
Telefonica de Espana
Veba AG

Philips Electronics
Sony Corp.
National Westminster Bank
NTT Mobile Comm. Network
Electrolux

ARTISAN INTERNATIONAL

OBJECTIVE:	*International*	
MANAGER:	*Mark Yockey*	*84*

FUND OVERVIEW:

Mark Yockey begins the process of investing his Artisan International Fund by looking around the world and figuring out where he would most like to put his money to work. He favors those countries with improving economic conditions, and avoids those that appear to be overvalued. He pays attention to such measures as gross domestic product growth, corporate profitability, current accounting and currency issues, and changes in interest rates. Having made those decisions, he looks for individual companies that are best positioned to profit. He concentrates on stocks with above-average financials and accelerating earnings per share. He also keeps an eye on price, avoiding businesses trading at unsustainable or unusually high valuations.

Yockey is presently most enthusiastic about Europe, where he has invested the biggest bulk of his assets. "To our mind, Europe offers the greatest investment potential in a generation," he insists. "The reasons include privatization, deregulation, increasing competition, merger activity, and a burgeoning commitment to enhancing shareholder value." In Asia, he's most positive on Hong Kong, which he's convinced has favorable long-term prospects.

ANNUALIZED RETURNS		PORTFOLIO STATISTICS	
1-Year	65.60%	Beta	0.82
3-Year	34.14%	Turnover	81.76%
5-Year	N/A	12-Month Yield	0.07%
Overall Rank	1	12b-1 Fee	0.00%
Risk Rank	4	Expense Ratio	1.27%
MINIMUM INVESTMENT		**CONTACT INFORMATION**	
Regular	$1,000	*Artisan International Fund*	
IRA	$1,000	*Telephone: (800) 344-1770*	
		www.artisanfunds.com	

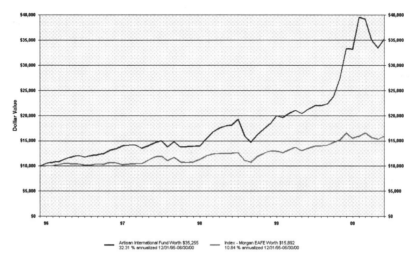

GROWTH OF $10,000

Artisan International Fund Worth $35,255
32.31 % annualized 12/31/95-06/30/00

Index - Morgan EAFE Worth $15,892
10.84 % annualized 12/31/95-06/30/00

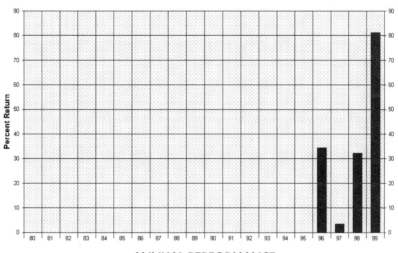

ANNUAL PERFORMANCE

TOP 10 HOLDINGS

COLT Telecom Group
AT&T Canada
Trans Cosmos
BCE
Nortel Networks

United Global
Telecom Italia Mobil
Bipop SPA
Global Telesystems
Mannesmann

DEUTSCHE INTERNATIONAL EQUITY

OBJECTIVE:	*International*	***85***
MANAGER:	*Team Managed*	

FUND OVERVIEW:

There are three managers at the helm of Deutsche International Equity: Michael Levy, Robert Reiner, and Julie Wang. They search the world for attractive investment ideas, and are currently most keen on Europe. "In our opinion, continental European markets continue to offer the best prospects, especially in France and in the periphery," the managers say. "European unification should reward companies that have taken the crucial steps required to be successful in the increasingly competitive marketplace."

As a result, a large majority of the portfolio has been placed in Europe, with only small allotments to Asia. The managers view Japan as a trading market that will remain extremely volatile until serious measures are taken to restructure the economy. They also feel Southeast Asia is a risky place for investors, and thus maintain only a token weighting there.

This fund, which has one of the best records in the international growth category, invests in both large and small securities around the world. The primary emphasis, however, is on established companies in developed countries.

ANNUALIZED RETURNS		PORTFOLIO STATISTICS	
1-Year	23.40%	Beta	0.73
3-Year	13.24%	Turnover	60.00%
5-Year	17.58%	12-Month Yield	0.24%
Overall Rank	3	12b-1 Fee	0.00%
Risk Rank	3	Expense Ratio	1.50%
MINIMUM INVESTMENT		**CONTACT INFORMATION**	
Regular	$2,500	*Deutsche International Equity Fund*	
IRA	$500	*Telephone: (800) 730-1313*	
		www.deam-us.com	

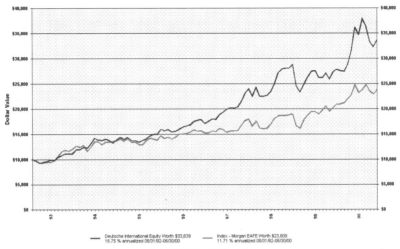

GROWTH OF $10,000

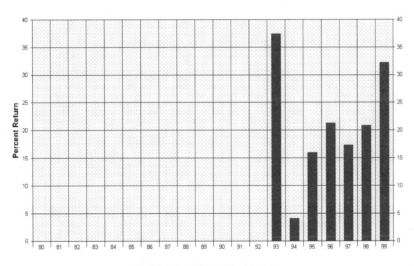

ANNUAL PERFORMANCE

TOP 10 HOLDINGS	
Total Fina Elf	Nokia Corp. ADR
Murata Mfg.	Mannesmann
NTT Mobile Communications	Vodafine Airtouch PLC
COLT Telecom	Ing Groep
Nortel Networks	Fujitsu

MANAGERS INTERNATIONAL EQUITY

OBJECTIVE:	*International*	**86**
MANAGER:	*Team Managed*	

FUND OVERVIEW:

Managers International Equity gives one half of the portfolio to each of two different managers: William Holzer of Scudder Kemper Investments and John Reinsberg of Lazard Asset Management. The concept is similar to the one described for American AAdvantage International Equity. In other words, you get two approaches to selecting overseas investments in one fund. Holzer is a top-down thematic investor who views the world as a single global economy. He first develops themes that target the fastest growing or most profitable segments. He then works with Scudder's analysts to identify companies that could benefit from the effects of these themes. Reinsberg uses a bottom-up value approach. He focuses on individual stocks that are believed to be financially strong and inexpensively priced.

The end result is a broad portfolio of names from around the world. Because part of the diversification benefit of international investing is the result of currency fluctuations, the portfolio managers don't hedge their exposure back to U.S. dollars. Both Holzer and Reinsberg are fairly conservative, take a long-term view on investing, and are normally diversified across at least three countries.

ANNUALIZED RETURNS		PORTFOLIO STATISTICS	
1-Year	13.80%	Beta	0.72
3-Year	10.77%	Turnover	43.00%
5-Year	13.28%	12-Month Yield	0.59%
Overall Rank	4	12b-1 Fee	0.00%
Risk Rank	2	Expense Ratio	1.39%

MINIMUM INVESTMENT		CONTACT INFORMATION	
Regular	$2,000	*Managers International Equity*	
IRA	$500	*Telephone: (800) 835-3879*	
		www.managersfunds.com	

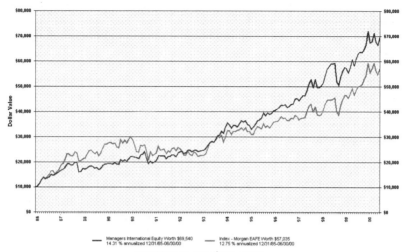

Managers International Equity Worth $69,540
14.31 % annualized 12/31/85-06/30/00

Index - Morgan EAFE Worth $57,035
12.75 % annualized 12/31/85-06/30/00

GROWTH OF $10,000

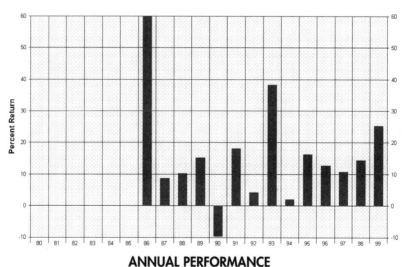

ANNUAL PERFORMANCE

TOP 10 HOLDINGS

Sony Corp.	TDK Corp.
NTT Mobile Comm.	Orix Corp.
Nippon Telegraph & Telephone	Alcatel Alsthom
Broken Hill Properties	Sharp
Siemens	Telefonica SA

OAKMARK INTERNATIONAL

| OBJECTIVE: | *International* | **87** |
| MANAGER: | *David Herro and Michael Welsh* | |

FUND OVERVIEW:

Oakmark International's David Herro and Michael Welsh are very dedicated to their value-oriented investment style. They have strict guidelines for determining whether a stock is worth buying or selling. They choose companies from around the world, that trade at a discount to current or potential free cash flow, where management will use that money to enhance shareholder value. A stock must also sell at no less than a 15 percent discount from what Herro and Welsh consider to be its fair market value. Once a holding approaches fair value, they get rid of it. Herro and Welsh feel currency is a separate issue, and will only hedge when they think the portfolio will suffer if they don't.

When evaluating an individual business, Herro and Welsh consider the relative political and economic stability in the issuer's home country, the applicable accounting practices, and the company's ownership structure. The fund invests in both mature markets (Japan, Canada, and the United Kingdom), as well as less developed areas (Mexico and Thailand), and select parts of the emerging markets. There are no limits on the fund's geographic distribution, though Herro and Walsh are normally spread over at least five countries outside the United States.

ANNUALIZED RETURNS		PORTFOLIO STATISTICS	
1-Year	8.30%	Beta	0.90
3-Year	7.05%	Turnover	54.00%
5-Year	13.56%	12-Month Yield	3.09%
Overall Rank	4	12b-1 Fee	0.00%
Risk Rank	3	Expense Ratio	1.29%
MINIMUM INVESTMENT		CONTACT INFORMATION	
Regular	$1,000	*Oakmark International*	
IRA	$1,000	*Telephone: (800) 625-6275*	
		www.oakmark.com	

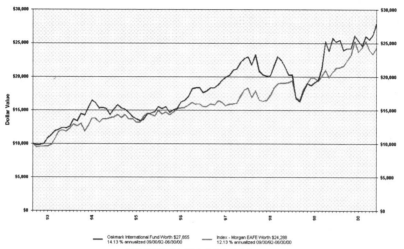

GROWTH OF $10,000

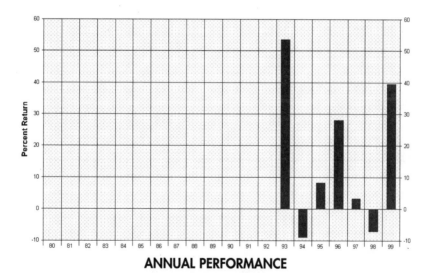

ANNUAL PERFORMANCE

TOP 10 HOLDINGS	
Metso Corp.	SK Telecom
Somerfield PLC	Banco Latinoamericano
Quilmes Indl.	Chargeurs
Citizen Watch Co.	Fila Holdings
Canon	Hunter Douglas NV

AMERICAN CENTURY GLOBAL GROWTH

OBJECTIVE:	*Global*	**88**
MANAGER:	*Team*	

FUND OVERVIEW:

The international investing team at American Century is talented, yet aggressive. This newer offering lets investors tap into their stock picking powers both in the U.S. and abroad.

American Century Global Growth owns companies from around the world with accelerating earnings growth and strong revenue trends. Lead manager Henrik Strabo and his team also run American Century International Growth (a pure overseas fund and fellow Powerhouse Performer) plus the American Century International Discovery Fund, which was closed to new investors in 2000.

Global Growth is off to a promising start. It has not only outperformed the S&P 500, but also the equivalent international index. Since the portfolio is highly diversified, you should expect this fund to be less risky than its two siblings.

Why buy a global fund versus a pure international fund? It's really a matter of preference. For those looking to get some foreign exposure without taking undue risk, a global fund like this one is probably an excellent solution. But, as global funds go, this one will likely be more volatile than normal due to the managers' style of buying high-octane stocks.

ANNUALIZED RETURNS		PORTFOLIO STATISTICS	
1-Year	60.60%	**Beta**	N/A
3-Year	N/A	**Turnover**	N/A
5-Year	N/A	**12-Month Yield**	0.00%
Overall Rank	N/A	**12b-1 Fee**	0.00%
Risk Rank	N/A	**Expense Ratio**	1.30%

MINIMUM INVESTMENT		CONTACT INFORMATION
Regular	$2,500	*American Century Global Growth*
IRA	$1,000	*Telephone: (800) 345-3533*
		www.americancentury.com

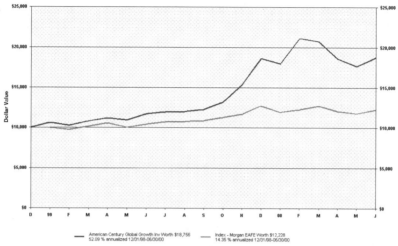

American Century Global Growth Inv Worth $18,756
52.09 % annualized 12/31/98-06/30/00

Index - Morgan EAFE Worth $12,228
14.35 % annualized 12/31/98-06/30/00

GROWTH OF $10,000

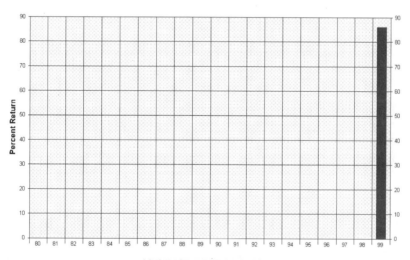

ANNUAL PERFORMANCE

TOP 10 HOLDINGS

Vodafone Airtouch PLC	Nokia Corp. ADR
Cisco Systems	Marschollek, Lautenschlaeger
Microsoft	China Telecom HK
NTT DoCoMo	General Electric
Vivendi	Skandia Foersaekrings

CITIZENS GLOBAL EQUITY

| OBJECTIVE: | *Global* | ***89*** |
| MANAGER: | *Sevgi Ipek* | |

FUND OVERVIEW:

Sevgi Ipek proves that you don't have to sacrifice returns when investing with your heart. Citizens Global Equity manager Sevgi Ipek buys stocks in companies from around the world that pass a series of social screens. For instance, she avoids companies that pollute. She also makes sure that company management treats workers well, and that there is solid representation on the board by women. In addition, tobacco and arms manufacturers are automatically excluded. The result is a portfolio of fast-growing companies with progressive management policies.

For one reason or another, it is mostly the so-called new economy stocks that rate highest on Ipek's various social screens. These are also the companies that have been fueling the growth of the economy.

Citizens Global Equity is one of the only funds to apply this screening strategy to companies from around the world. Yet even with the strict criteria, the fund's performance has been excellent. For investors looking to add international exposure, without completely leaving the U.S., Citizens Global Equity is a fine, relatively conservative choice.

ANNUALIZED RETURNS		PORTFOLIO STATISTICS	
1-Year	53.30%	Beta	0.78
3-Year	31.69%	Turnover	86.00%
5-Year	25.62%	12-Month Yield	0.00%
Overall Rank	1	12b-1 Fee	0.25%
Risk Rank	4	Expense Ratio	1.75%

MINIMUM INVESTMENT		CONTACT INFORMATION	
Regular	$2,500	*Citizens Global Equity*	
IRA	$1,000	*Telephone: (800) 223-7010*	
		www.citizensfunds.com	

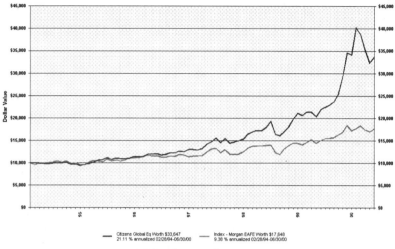

Citizens Global Eq Worth $33,647
21.11 % annualized 02/28/94-06/30/00

Index - Morgan EAFE Worth $17,648
9.38 % annualized 02/28/94-06/30/00

GROWTH OF $10,000

VALUE LINE ANNUAL PERFORMANCE CHART
NOT AVAILABLE FOR THIS FUND

ANNUAL PERFORMANCE

TOP 10 HOLDINGS	
Softbank	Sun Microsystems
Nokia Corp. ADR	Icon Medialab
Information Highway	Time Warner
Cisco Systems	Nortel Networks
COLT Telecom	Ericsson

MONTGOMERY GLOBAL OPPORTUNITIES

OBJECTIVE: *Global*	
MANAGER: *John Boich and Oscar Castro*	*90*

FUND OVERVIEW:

They say the world is full of opportunities. This fund gives managers John Boich and Oscar Castro a chance to go out and find them. Montgomery Global Opportunities is required to invest in at least three different countries, one of which can be the U.S. However, with the exception of the U.S., no country can represent more than 40 percent of total assets.

Boich and Castro seek well-managed companies with sustainable sales and earnings growth. They also purchase shares of companies believed to be relatively cheap compared to their long-term prospects. The managers favor businesses with competitive advantages and those offering innovative products or services. They also look for companies that might profit from such trends as deregulation and privatization, especially overseas.

Boich and Castro often travel to the countries they invest in, to get firsthand insight into the economic, political, and social trends affecting investments around the world. If they find a given country with especially promising fundamentals, they have the freedom to concentrate portfolio assets in that area.

ANNUALIZED RETURNS		PORTFOLIO STATISTICS	
1-Year	21.50%	**Beta**	1.00
3-Year	21.32%	**Turnover**	350.00%
5-Year	22.19%	**12-Month Yield**	0.00%
Overall Rank	2	**12b-1 Fee**	0.00%
Risk Rank	4	**Expense Ratio**	1.95%

MINIMUM INVESTMENT		CONTACT INFORMATION
Regular	$1,000	*Montgomery Global Opportunities*
IRA	$1,000	*Telephone: (800) 572-3863*
		www.montgomeryfunds.com

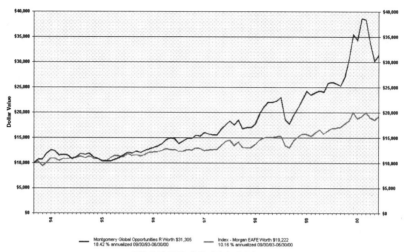

GROWTH OF $10,000

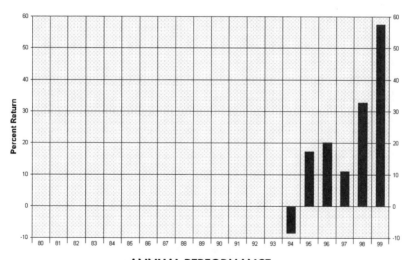

ANNUAL PERFORMANCE

TOP 10 HOLDINGS	
Global Telesystems	Atmel
Sony Corp.	Global Crossing
Sogecable	Nippon Telegraph & Telephone
Mannesmann	Telecom Italia
Sprint	VNV NV

TWEEDY, BROWNE GLOBAL VALUE

OBJECTIVE:	*Global*	
MANAGER:	*Team Managed*	**91**

FUND OVERVIEW:

Tweedy, Browne Global Value's three managers apply the time-tested value approach of the late Benjamin Graham to international investing. Graham, a former Columbia University Business School professor, wrote the 1934 classic *Security Analysis.* He suggested buying companies that could be had for a minimum 40 percent discount from their true intrinsic value. He also advised paying attention to price-to-earnings ratios, book value, and similar benchmarks. This is the same discipline these managers follow at their other Powerhouse Performer fund, American Value (see entry 42). The difference is that this portfolio is made up mostly of foreign securities, although you will find a few U.S. companies inside as well.

You could argue that this is one of the less risky international offerings available, because all overseas investments are hedged back to the U.S. dollar. This eliminates currency risk, which can be either good or bad, depending on the direction of the dollar. When the dollar is declining, you're better off in an unhedged fund because the return from currency fluctuations alone will be impressive. Conservative investors wanting international exposure should feel very comfortable entrusting their money to Tweedy, Browne.

ANNUALIZED RETURNS		PORTFOLIO STATISTICS	
1-Year	7.40%	Beta	0.58
3-Year	15.36%	Turnover	5.00%
5-Year	18.64%	12-Month Yield	1.17%
Overall Rank	1	12b-1 Fee	0.00%
Risk Rank	2	Expense Ratio	1.38%
MINIMUM INVESTMENT		**CONTACT INFORMATION**	
Regular	$2,500	*Tweedy, Browne Global Value Fund*	
IRA	$500	*Telephone: (800) 432-4789*	
		www.tweedy.com	

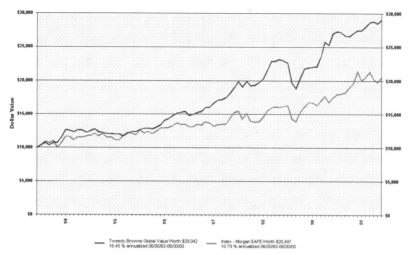

Tweedy Browne Global Value Worth $29,042
16.45 % annualized 06/30/93-06/30/00

Index - Morgan EAFE Worth $20,497
10.79 % annualized 06/30/93-06/30/00

GROWTH OF $10,000

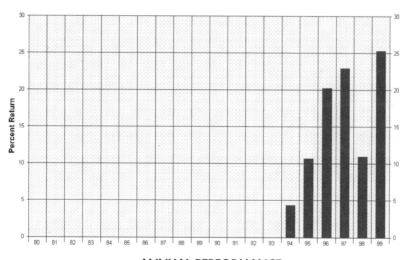

ANNUAL PERFORMANCE

TOP 10 HOLDINGS	
Procordia	Independent Newsp.
Nestle	PanAmerican Beverages
Merck KGAA	Matsushita Elec. Works
Financiere Richemont	Aiful Corp.
Telegraaf Holding	Shionogi & Co.

LOOMIS SAYLES BOND

OBJECTIVE:	*Corporate Bond (Intermediate)*	*92*
MANAGER:	*Daniel J. Fuss*	

FUND OVERVIEW:

Loomis Sayles Bond manager Daniel J. Fuss is one of the best fixed-income investors around. He strives to generate a high total return through a combination of current income and capital appreciation. He invests most of his fund's assets in bonds, although up to 20 percent of the portfolio can be placed in preferred stocks. The fixed-income side can include corporate and U.S. government obligations, plus commercial paper, zero coupon bonds, and mortgage-backed securities. In addition, the prospectus allows Fuss to invest up to 20 percent of the portfolio overseas, and up to 35 percent in junk bonds. Fuss isn't shy about exploiting this flexibility when he thinks conditions warrant it. In early 1998, for example, he was busy looking for battered bargains in Southeast Asia and Latin America.

Loomis Sayles Bond should be viewed as a long-term investment because the securities tend to have extended maturities, and thus a heightened degree of volatility. You'll notice the fund's minimum investment is $25,000. However, that can be reduced to just $2,500 by going through one of the many no-load, no-transaction-fee programs offered by the nation's leading discount brokers.

ANNUALIZED RETURNS		PORTFOLIO STATISTICS	
1-Year	3.40%	Beta	1.13
3-Year	6.13%	Turnover	N/A
5-Year	N/A	12-Month Yield	24.00%
Overall Rank	N/A	12b-1 Fee	0.25%
Risk Rank	N/A	Expense Ratio	1.00%

MINIMUM INVESTMENT		CONTACT INFORMATION
Regular	$25,000	*Loomis Sayles Bond Fund*
IRA	$25,000	*Telephone: (800) 633-3330*
		www.loomissayles.com

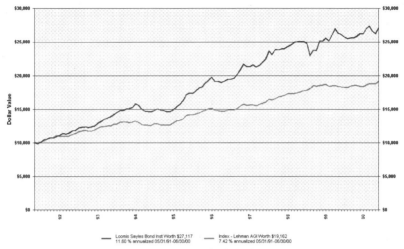

Loomis Sayles Bond Inst Worth $27,117
11.60 % annualized 05/31/91-06/30/00

Index - Lehman AGI Worth $19,162
7.42 % annualized 05/31/91-06/30/00

GROWTH OF $10,000

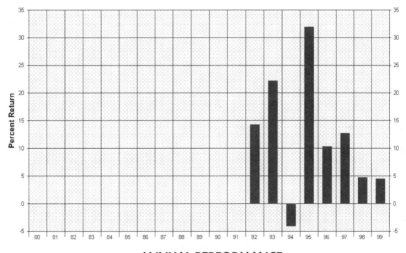

ANNUAL PERFORMANCE

TOP 10 HOLDINGS

Intl Bk Reconstr/Dev 0%	US Treasury Bond 6%
Loews Cv. 3.125%	US Treasury Bond 5.5%
Govt. of Canada 0%	Time Warner 6.95%
Bell Atlantic Finl. 4.25%	Province of Manitoba 7.75%
Philip Morris 7.75%	Bangkok Bk 144A 9.025%

STRONG CORPORATE BOND

OBJECTIVE:	*Corporate Bond (Intermediate)*	***93***
MANAGER:	*Jeffrey Koch and John Bender*	

FUND OVERVIEW:

The Strong Corporate Bond fund is designed for investors seeking a high level of current income with a moderate degree of share price fluctuation. This is not a short-term parking place for your money. Instead, it is designed to be part of the fixed-income mix of a long-term portfolio. Strong Corporate Bond doesn't come with any specific maturity restrictions, but the fund's average maturity will normally be in the 7- to 12-year range. At least 65 percent of the portfolio's total assets will usually be invested in the bonds of corporate issuers. The rest can be in any type of fixed-income security, such as U.S. government and mortgage-backed issues. A majority of the fund is placed in investment-grade debt obligations—those rated BBB or higher by Standard & Poor's. Up to 25 percent can be invested in lower-grade junk bonds and preferred stocks.

Managers Jeffrey Koch and John Bender believe careful research is paramount to their success. They use intense analysis to uncover securities that are ignored, dismissed, or underappreciated by other investors. Koch and Bender feel they can add the most value by attempting to be positioned in the right industries and sectors of the market at the right time.

ANNUALIZED RETURNS		PORTFOLIO STATISTICS	
1-Year	3.90%	Beta	1.15
3-Year	5.69%	Turnover	224.20%
5-Year	7.25%	12-Month Yield	7.19%
Overall Rank	2	12b-1 Fee	0.00%
Risk Rank	4	Expense Ratio	0.90%
MINIMUM INVESTMENT		**CONTACT INFORMATION**	
Regular	$2,500	*Strong Corporate Bond Fund*	
IRA	$250	*Telephone: (800) 368-1683*	
		www.strong-funds.com	

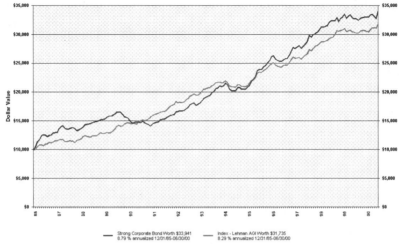

GROWTH OF $10,000

Strong Corporate Bond Worth $33,941
8.79 % annualized 12/31/85-06/30/00

Index - Lehman AGI Worth $31,735
8.29 % annualized 12/31/85-06/30/00

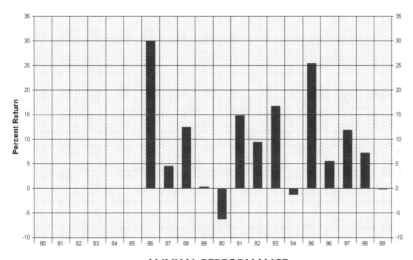

ANNUAL PERFORMANCE

TOP 10 HOLDINGS

GS Escrow 7%	Southdown 10%
Occidental Petro 8.45%	Stop & Shop 9.75%
Riggs Cap 144A 8.625%	LCI Intl. 7.25%
Texas Utilities Elec. 6.501%	El Paso Elec. 9.4%
Cendant 7.75%	Resolution Tr. 6.9%

LEXINGTON GNMA

OBJECTIVE:	Mortgage-Backed Securities (Intermediate)	**94**
MANAGER:	Denis Jamison	

FUND OVERVIEW:

If you're looking for high current yield, credit safety, and liquidity, few investments compare to mortgage-backed Government National Mortgage Association (GNMA) certificates, or Ginnie Maes. The GNMA is a U.S. government agency that pools mortgages together and sells them in the form of certificates. Each certificate represents an undivided part-ownership in one of these pools. Every mortgage in the pool is guaranteed by a certain government agency, meaning they are very safe. In fact, Ginnie Maes and the other securities in the Lexington GNMA portfolio are guaranteed as to the timely payment of principal and interest by Uncle Sam.

Still, the price and yield of shares in the fund will fluctuate with interest rates. GNMAs are also subject to early prepayments from homeowners wishing to refinance their loans at lower rates. High prepayments will have a negative impact on the fund's relative performance. And because prepayments tend to get reinvested at lower yields, the dividend-per-share payouts will be reduced. You shouldn't expect to see much overall volatility, in this fund and you will enjoy a generous yield that currently comes in at around 7 percent.

ANNUALIZED RETURNS		PORTFOLIO STATISTICS	
1-Year	3.50%	Beta	0.68
3-Year	6.17%	Turnover	44.65%
5-Year	6.65%	12-Month Yield	6.27%
Overall Rank	3	12b-1 Fee	0.00%
Risk Rank	2	Expense Ratio	1.62%

MINIMUM INVESTMENT		CONTACT INFORMATION	
Regular	$1,000	*Lexington GNMA Income Fund*	
IRA	$1,000	*Telephone: (800) 526-0056*	
		www.lexingtonfunds.com	

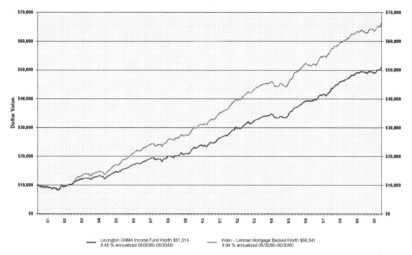

GROWTH OF $10,000

Lexington GNMA Income Fund Worth $51,014
8.48 % annualized 06/30/80-06/30/00

Index - Lehman Mortgage Backed Worth $66,541
9.94 % annualized 06/30/80-06/30/00

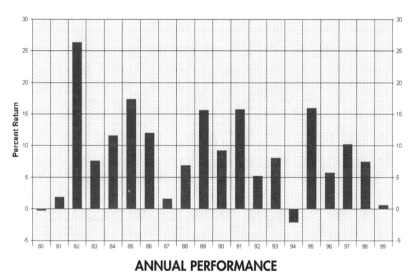

ANNUAL PERFORMANCE

TOP 10 HOLDINGS	
GNMA 7%	GNMA 7%
GNMA 6.5%	US Treasury Note 5.625%
GNMA Project Loan 7.45%	GNMA 8%
GNMA 8%	GNMA Project Loan 8.15%
GNMA 8.125%	GNMA Project Loan 7.9%

VANGUARD GNMA

| OBJECTIVE: | *Mortgage-Backed Securities (Intermediate)* | |
| MANAGER: | *Paul D. Kaplan* | |

FUND OVERVIEW:

Here's another vehicle for capturing monthly income, liquidity, and relative safety through investing in a portfolio of mortgage-backed Government National Mortgage Association (GNMA) certificates, or Ginnie Maes. You'll remember from the previous profile that the GNMA is a U.S. government agency that pools mortgages together and sells them in the form of certificates. These pools are guaranteed by the government.

What's the difference between the Vanguard and Lexington funds? Not much. Both are excellent choices. In fact, even though Lexington's expense ratio is slightly higher, the performance of the two funds has been almost identical. The one advantage to the Lexington fund is its availability through many of the no-load, no-transaction-fee programs. You have to pay a commission to purchase the Vanguard GNMA through a discount broker, although you can buy it directly from the fund at no charge.

The other difference of note is that Vanguard GNMA's manager, Paul Kaplan, considers himself to be a bargain hunter. He buys issues that he feels offer the best relative value. He also runs the portfolio with an eye toward reducing its exposure to interest-rate risk.

ANNUALIZED RETURNS		PORTFOLIO STATISTICS	
1-Year	5.40%	Beta	0.72
3-Year	5.83%	Turnover	4.00%
5-Year	6.51%	12-Month Yield	6.82%
Overall Rank	1	12b-1 Fee	0.00%
Risk Rank	2	Expense Ratio	0.28%
MINIMUM INVESTMENT		**CONTACT INFORMATION**	
Regular	$3,000	*Vanguard GNMA Portfolio*	
IRA	$3,000	*Telephone: (800) 662-7447*	
		www.vanguard.com	

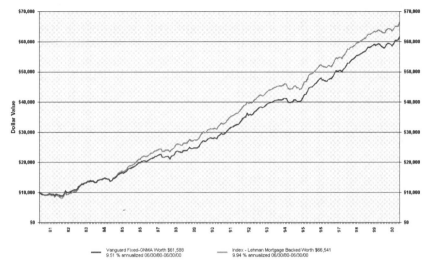

Vanguard Fixed-GNMA Worth $61,588
9.51 % annualized 06/30/80-06/30/00

Index - Lehman Mortgage Backed Worth $66,541
9.94 % annualized 06/30/80-06/30/00

GROWTH OF $10,000

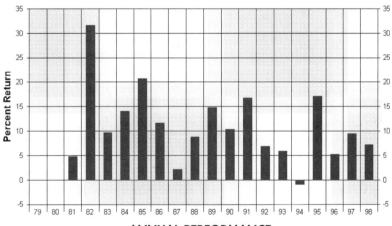

ANNUAL PERFORMANCE

TOP 10 HOLDINGS	
GNMA 6.5%	GNMA 7.5%
GNMA 7%	GNMA 7%
GNMA 6%	GNMA 6.5%
GNMA 7%	GNMA 7.5%
GNMA 7%	GNMA 7%

STRONG GOVERNMENT SECURITIES

OBJECTIVE:	*General Government Bond*	*96*
MANAGER:	*Bradley Tank*	

FUND OVERVIEW:

The Strong Government Securities Fund works to produce a high level of current income with a moderate degree of share price fluctuation. It is appropriate for investors who need a greater level of monthly income than shorter-term funds can provide, but wish to enjoy the low credit risk associated with securities backed by the U.S. government.

Manager Bradley Tank will normally keep at least 90 percent of the fund's assets in U.S. government securities at all times, with the remainder in other investment-grade debt obligations. There are no maturity restrictions on the portfolio, although the average maturity is usually between 5 and 10 years. "Our fixed-income management process includes a top-down analysis of the economy, interest rates, and the supply of and demand for credit," Tank explains. "We then conduct a rigorous security analysis of any issue we're considering."

One advantage to this fund is that, by law, interest income earned from U.S. Treasury securities is exempt from state and local taxes, which is good for investors in high-tax states.

ANNUALIZED RETURNS		PORTFOLIO STATISTICS	
1-Year	4.00%	Beta	0.96
3-Year	5.54%	Turnover	87.50%
5-Year	5.83%	12-Month Yield	5.84%
Overall Rank	2	12b-1 Fee	0.00%
Risk Rank	2	Expense Ratio	0.80%

MINIMUM INVESTMENT		CONTACT INFORMATION
Regular	$2,500	*Strong Corporate Bond Fund*
IRA	$250	*Telephone: (800) 368-1683*
		www.strong-funds.com

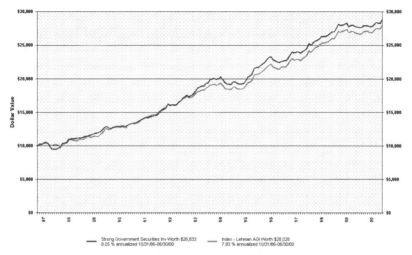

GROWTH OF $10,000

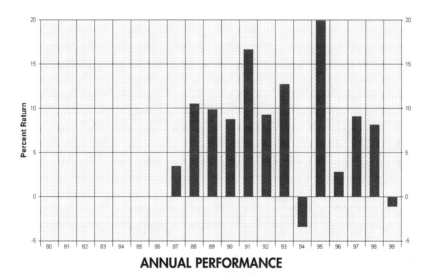

ANNUAL PERFORMANCE

TOP 10 HOLDINGS

US Treasury Note 6%	US Treasury Note 7.875%
US Treasury Bond 8.125%	US Treasury Note 5.5%
US Treasury Bond 5.25%	FNMA Commercial 8.4%
FNMA ARM	US Treasury Bond 7.25%
US Treasury Note 7%	FNMA 6.5%

STRONG HIGH-YIELD MUNICIPAL BOND

| OBJECTIVE: | *Federal Municipal Bond* | *97* |
| MANAGER: | *Mary-Kay H. Bourbulas* | |

FUND OVERVIEW:

Investors seeking income that is federally tax-exempt should consider the Strong High-Yield Municipal Bond Fund. This portfolio invests primarily in long-term, medium- and lower-quality municipal obligations. There are no maturity restrictions; the fund's average portfolio maturity is between 15 and 25 years, which means its share price will fluctuate significantly as interest rates change.

"Our goal is to deliver steady performance by diversifying our investments with respect to position size, sectors, and state concentration," explains portfolio manager Mary-Kay Bourbulas. "Another element of our strategy is keeping a comfortable portion of the portfolio in liquid, rated municipal issues." Bourbulas likes to invest along themes that she believes offer solid growth potential. The most prominent one is the aging of America, which got her interested in hospitals, retirement facilities, and assisted-living centers. "Before we purchase any unrated bond, we conduct thorough research," she adds. "The research process is essential to identifying issues that are attractive on their own merits, regardless of changes in interest rates or in the economy's growth."

ANNUALIZED RETURNS		PORTFOLIO STATISTICS	
1-Year	−5.50%	Beta	0.95
3-Year	2.41%	Turnover	28.90%
5-Year	4.73%	12-Month Yield	6.57%
Overall Rank	3	12b-1 Fee	0.00%
Risk Rank	3	Expense Ratio	0.69%

MINIMUM INVESTMENT		CONTACT INFORMATION
Regular	$2,500	*Strong High-Yield Municipal*
IRA	$250	*Bond Fund*
		Telephone: (800) 368-1683
		www.strong-funds.com

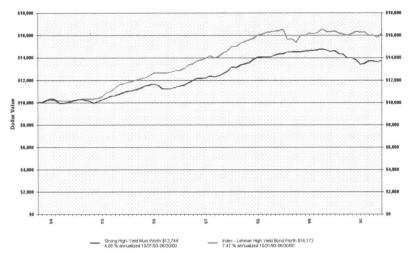

Strong High-Yield Muni Worth $13,744
4.88 % annualized 10/31/93-06/30/00

Index - Lehman High Yield Bond Worth $16,173
7.47 % annualized 10/31/93-06/30/00

GROWTH OF $10,000

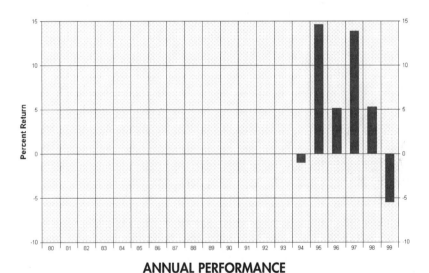

ANNUAL PERFORMANCE

TOP 10 HOLDINGS

NC Fletcher Hsg Averys	NJ ED Kapkowski Rd. 6.5%
IN Health Fac 6.5%	ND Ward Health Care
NJ ED Kapkowski Rd. 6.375%	SC Jobs/Econ Dev.
VA Alexandria Redev/Hsng.	PA Econ. Dev. 6.13%
AL West Jefferson Amusement	OH Cleveland Airport

NORTHEAST INVESTORS TRUST

OBJECTIVE:	*High-Yield Corporate*	*98*
MANAGER:	*Ernest Monrad and Bruce Monrad*	

FUND OVERVIEW:

The father-and-son team of Ernest and Bruce Monrad tries to generate income for shareholders through investing in both corporate bonds and stocks. But, unlike other managers of funds of this nature, the Monrads also try to achieve as much capital appreciation as possible. The proportions of stocks and bonds vary based on market conditions. Since 1970, about 80 percent of all assets have been held in fixed-income securities, preferred stocks, and cash. Only a small portion has been put in common stocks, usually for liquidity purposes and to increase the potential for capital gains. The Monrads also avoid keeping more than 25 percent of the portfolio exposed to any one industry.

A combination of in-house and Wall Street research is used for selecting and evaluating securities for the fund. The Monrads place heavy emphasis on value. When they find an attractive bond, they'll also consider adding shares of the company's stock if the price is right. As an added booster, the Monrads can use leverage, borrowing up to 25 percent of the portfolio's net assets. This enhances the fund's buying power when they are bullish, and gives them adequate cash to meet redemptions without having to liquidate any holdings.

ANNUALIZED RETURNS		PORTFOLIO STATISTICS	
1-Year	−2.60%	Beta	−0.11
3-Year	2.64%	Turnover	16.57%
5-Year	8.00%	12-Month Yield	12.08%
Overall Rank	4	12b-1 Fee	0.00%
Risk Rank	5	Expense Ratio	0.60%
MINIMUM INVESTMENT		**CONTACT INFORMATION**	
Regular	$1,000	*Northeast Investors Trust*	
IRA	$500	*Telephone: (800) 225-6704*	
		www.northeastinvestors.com	

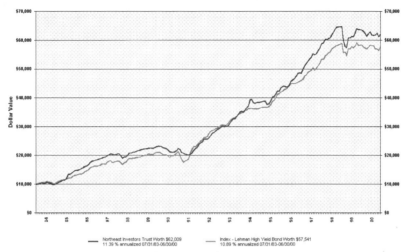

GROWTH OF $10,000

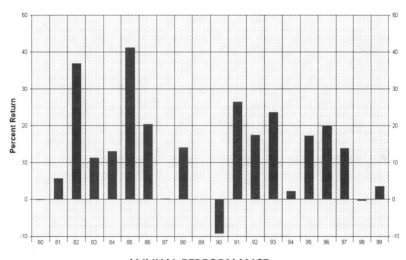

ANNUAL PERFORMANCE

TOP 10 HOLDINGS	
Trump Atlantic City 11.25%	Stone Container 12.58%
Advantica Rest. 11.25%	Specialty Foods 10.25%
Kaiser Alum/Chem 12.75%	Westpoint Stevens
Boyd Gaming 9.5%	Aztar 13.75%
Grand Casinos 10.125%	Huntsman 144A FRN

STRONG HIGH-YIELD BOND

OBJECTIVE:	*High-Yield Corporate*	
MANAGER:	*Jeffrey Koch*	*99*

FUND OVERVIEW:

Strong High-Yield Bond Fund manager Jeffrey Koch follows a straight-forward discipline. "Our approach to investing in the high-yield market begins with a top-down review of macroeconomic factors likely to influence both the real economy and financial asset prices," he says. "Among others, these factors include worldwide economic growth, inflation, interest rates, monetary policy, fiscal policy, and governmental regulation." Once Koch formulates an opinion on these factors, he positions the portfolio according-ingly. "Because the success of an investment in a high-yield bond is ultimately a result of the issuer's creditworthiness, our research analysts rigorously examine the fundamentals of all of the securities in which we invest," he adds.

Strong High-Yield Bond primarily owns medium- and lower-quality corporate debt obligations, or junk bonds, in the pursuit of current income and capital growth. It offers both a higher yield and a greater degree of risk than other bond funds. In addition, keep in mind that high-yield bonds tend to be impacted more by the economy than interest rates, which makes them especially unattractive in times of recession.

ANNUALIZED RETURNS		PORTFOLIO STATISTICS	
1-Year	4.00%	Beta	0.25
3-Year	6.67%	Turnover	78.80%
5-Year	N/A	12-Month Yield	11.02%
Overall Rank	1	12b-1 Fee	0.00%
Risk Rank	5	Expense Ratio	0.80%
MINIMUM INVESTMENT		**CONTACT INFORMATION**	
Regular	$2,500	*Strong High-Yield Bond Fund*	
IRA	$250	*Telephone: (800) 368-1683*	
		www.strong-funds.com	

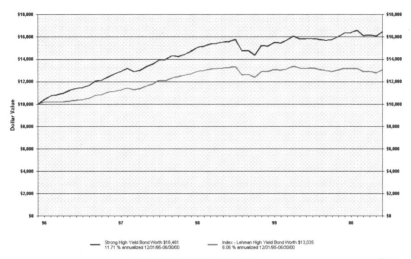

GROWTH OF $10,000

— Strong High Yield Bond Worth $16,461
11.71 % annualized 12/31/95-06/30/00

— Index - Lehman High Yield Bond Worth $13,035
6.06 % annualized 12/31/95-06/30/00

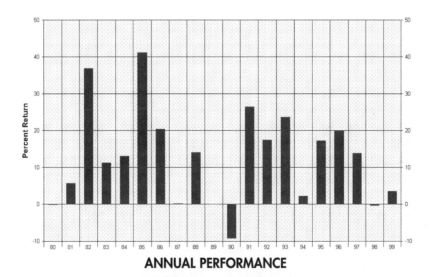

ANNUAL PERFORMANCE

TOP 10 HOLDINGS

Atlas Air 10.75%   Jordan Telecom 0%
Global Crossing 9.625%   Chancellor Media 144A 8%
Fresenius Medical Care 7.875%   TransWestern Pub. 9.625%
Nextlink Comm 144A 10.75%   Rogers Cablesystems 10%
Mohegan Gaming 144A 8.125%   Scotts 144A 8.625%

VALUE LINE AGGRESSIVE INCOME TRUST

OBJECTIVE:	*High-Yield Corporate*	
MANAGER:	*Team Managed*	***100***

FUND OVERVIEW:

Value Line Aggressive Income invests primarily in lower-rated, fixed-income securities issued by smaller and unseasoned companies. These securities are otherwise known as "junk bonds." You take more risk that your money will be returned, and therefore are compensated by a higher yield. The fund's objective is to maximize current income. Capital appreciation, although a secondary consideration, can come from the improved credit rating of a company in the portfolio or from lower interest rates in general. At least 80 percent of the bonds in this fund are rated B++ or lower by the *Value Line Investment Survey*. The rest of the mix may include U.S. government securities, convertible bonds, and warrants. Value Line follows about 3,500 companies, which are rated from A++ to C. Companies with the best financial strength are given an A++, followed by A+, and so on. Those rated C usually have serious financial troubles. The bonds in this fund are right on the border.

You face many risks when investing in junk bonds, including limited liquidity. That's why it's important to own a number of different issues in a fund like this, to quell volatility.

ANNUALIZED RETURNS		PORTFOLIO STATISTICS	
1-Year	−1.80%	Beta	0.17
3-Year	2.12%	Turnover	140.00%
5-Year	8.32%	12-Month Yield	10.75%
Overall Rank	3	12b-1 Fee	0.00%
Risk Rank	5	Expense Ratio	0.81%
MINIMUM INVESTMENT		**CONTACT INFORMATION**	
Regular	$1,000	*Value Line Aggressive Income Trust*	
IRA	$1,000	*Telephone: (800) 223-0818*	
		www.valueline.com	

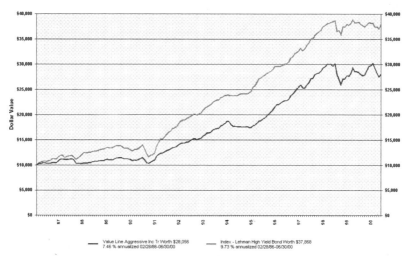

GROWTH OF $10,000

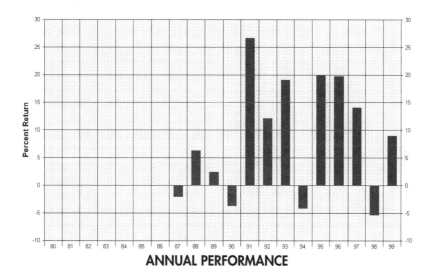

ANNUAL PERFORMANCE

TOP 10 HOLDINGS	
Telegroup Step 0%	Econophone 13.5%
Hyperion Telecom 0%	Rogers Cablesystems 10%
DTI Holdings 144A 0%	Optel 13%
Commemorative Brands 11%	Viatel Step 0%
Ram Energy 11.5%	Adelphia Comm. 9.875%

6

PUTTING YOUR
PORTFOLIO TOGETHER

Now that you know what mutual funds are, how they work, what to look for when choosing them, and which ones appear to be most promising for the year ahead, it's time to put together your own personal investment plan. In a moment, I'll give you an asset allocation test, to help you determine which types of funds might be most appropriate for you, given your stage in life and your comfort level. Then I will reveal my specific portfolio recommendations (complete with the precise percentage allocations to selected funds from the Powerhouse Performers list) that correspond to your score on the test.

WHAT IS ASSET ALLOCATION?

=== You may have heard the term *asset allocation* before. But what exactly does it mean? In a nutshell, asset allocation is the process of figuring out how much of your investment capital should be placed in each of the three main asset classes: stocks, bonds, and cash. (I'm leaving out precious metals, artwork, limited partnerships, commodities, options, futures, and various other possibilities. For most people, these asset classes aren't practical.)

"Investment capital," for purposes of our continuing discussion in this chapter, includes only money you have set aside for the long term. It is an amount above and beyond the money you need to live on. It *does not* include a home that you own, cash in a savings account that you plan to spend soon (say, on a car or vacation), insurance policies, or any emergency funds you may have set aside to get you through rough financial

250

periods. It *does* include your 401(k)s, 403(b)s, and IRAs, although you will probably have to assemble separate fund portfolios for these accounts, because most company retirement plans give you a select list to choose from. (Nevertheless, the principles and allocation guidelines we are about to discuss apply to them as well.)

RISK VERSUS REWARD

===== You've no doubt heard the cliché "No pain, no gain." It certainly applies to investing. Every investment comes with some degree of risk. With stocks, you risk that the overall market will fall or that your underlying companies will suffer financially—or even go out of business. The same is true for corporate bonds. Even bank savings accounts carry the risk that your financial institution will fail, and your balance may be above the amount covered by federal depository insurance. The only no-risk investments out there are Treasury bills, notes, and bonds, which will fluctuate in value as interest rates change (assuming you don't hold on through maturity).

THE $150,000 LUNCH?

You may have more money to invest than you think. Simply cutting back on some of life's indulgences can pump up your portfolio by almost $400,000 over time. Here are just a few examples:

Cut Back On	Savings per Month	Savings per Year	30-Year Growth
Eating lunch out	$ 65	$ 780	$148,702
Coffee	22	260	49,567
Impulse Purchases	43	520	99,135
Clothes	40	480	91,173
Total savings	$170	$2,040	$388,577

These hypothetical figures assume a 10 percent annual rate of return compounded at the same rate as contributions over a 30-year period in a tax-deferred account. All numbers are in today's dollars. The tabulation is for illustrative purposes only. Actual investment returns will vary.

As you might have guessed, the level of return you can expect to receive from an investment corresponds directly with the degree of risk you take. Small-company and foreign stocks, the most volatile of all, have historically showered investors with the highest returns. Equities in general have done much better than fixed-income investments. Corporate bonds pay higher rates than risk-free Treasuries. And insured bank savings accounts normally pay the least.

But there is another risk that most people don't think about: "opportunity risk." If you aren't willing to endure the volatility associated with stocks, at least for a portion of your portfolio, you risk suffering low returns that might not even keep up with the rate of inflation. Consider these statistics. Stocks have provided a rate of return far superior to that of any other asset class over time. From 1979 to 1998, according to data provided by Smith Barney, the S&P 500 rose at an annualized rate of 17.22 percent, including reinvested dividends. That compares to 7.17 percent for 90-day Treasury bills and 11.07 percent for long-term government bonds. The returns during the most recent 10-year bull market have been even higher for stocks: 18.07 percent annually for the S&P, while 90-day bills provided a paltry 5.35 percent, and long-term government bonds returned 11.12 percent. If this trend continues in the future, and I have every reason to believe it will, you will build more wealth from stocks than from any other asset class. (Interestingly, although small and foreign stocks have done better than the S&P 500 over extended periods of time, both have lagged the index considerably over the past decade.)

It is generally assumed that the younger you are, the more your portfolio should be allocated to stocks. This makes sense for two reasons. First, equities generally don't provide much income, a disadvantage that becomes increasingly important in retirement. Second, stocks can be extremely volatile over the short term, so the longer your time horizon, the less you will be impacted by such fluctuations. Nevertheless, some of the most

RISK/REWARD SPECTRUM

Lower   RISK / RETURN   Higher

Cash/Cash Equivalents   Bonds   Stocks

astute elderly investors I know keep anywhere from 80 to 100 percent of their portfolios in equities at all times, even as they near the age of eligibility to receive a televised happy birthday greeting from Willard Scott.

Dollar Cost Averaging

Investors of all ages can profit from volatility by using a technique known as "dollar cost averaging." Simply put, this means investing a fixed amount in your favorite funds on a regular basis, regardless of what's going on with the market. In that way, you buy more shares when the market is down, and fewer shares when it is up. This is precisely what you do when you contribute to your 401(k), SEP-IRA, or 403(b) plan at work. Your company (or you, if you're self-employed) takes regular contributions out of your paycheck and sends them in to your selected funds each month or quarter. Dollar cost averaging doesn't necessarily increase your overall returns, especially during strong bull markets. But it certainly lessens your volatility, and it's often the only way people can afford to invest. (See below.)

Dollar Cost Averaging at Work

Regular Investment	Per-Share Price	Shares Acquired
$ 200	$10	20
200	8	25
200	5	40
200	8	25
200	10	20
Total $1,000	$41	130

Average Cost Per Share = $7.69 ($1,000 ÷ 130 shares)

Average Price Per Share = $8.20 ($41 ÷ 5)

By regularly investing the same dollar amount in your account, you take advantage of market fluctuations by buying more fund shares when prices are low, fewer as prices rise. This strategy, however, does not guarantee profit or protection against loss in declining markets. This is only a hypothetical illustration. It does not project the future performance of any particular investment.

By the way, don't think you can't get a monthly income check from your non-dividend-paying stock funds. You can. Simply sign up for what's called "systematic withdrawal." This program allows you to have a certain amount redeemed automatically from your funds each month. You might think of it as dollar cost averaging in reverse.

INVESTOR PROFILE

≡ Now back to that test I told you about. Discount broker Charles Schwab & Co. has created an investor profile quiz to help people determine which asset allocation plan is most appropriate for them. The quiz takes into consideration such things as age, personality, and tolerance for risk. In the end, you get an overall score, which can be matched up with the model portfolios that follow. (The portfolios are mine, not Schwab's.) Keep in mind that the test assumes we're talking about *investment capital,* or money being set aside for at least five years.

Take a few moments to circle the most appropriate answer for each question in the test. Better yet, make a copy of the test first, so that your spouse (or significant other) can take it too.

Calculate your total and match it up with the appropriate model portfolio. Is this an accurate reflection of your actual investment risk tolerance? Read all five portfolio descriptions before you decide.

1. AGGRESSIVE ALL-STOCK PORTFOLIO: 86 TO 100 POINTS

≡ This portfolio is most appropriate for those under age 40, who have a 20- to 30-year time horizon before needing the money. It assumes you are looking for high growth and are willing to endure substantial year-to-year volatility in that pursuit. The suggested subasset class breakdown for this portfolio is as follows:

40% Large-Cap Funds
20% Mid-Cap Funds
20% Small-Cap Funds
20% International Funds

INVESTOR PROFILE TEST

Points

1. My current age is:
   a) under 31.. 8
   b) 31 to 40. 6
   c) 41 to 50. 4
   d) 51 to 60. 2
   e) over 60. 0

2. Over the next few years, I expect my income to:
   a) decline.. 0
   b) stay about the same. 1
   c) increase. 2
   d) fluctuate.. 0

3. My investment experience is best described as follows:
   a) I've never invested in stocks, either directly or through stock
      mutual funds. 2
   b) I've invested a small amount of money in stocks or stock funds. . . . 6
   c) I've occasionally invested a fair amount in stocks or stock funds. . . 10
   d) I've invested in commodities, options, international stocks, or
      limited partnerships. 14
   e) I have money in a company retirement plan (i.e., a 401(k) or
      SEP-IRA), but am not sure whether I'm invested in stock funds
      or other types of investments. 0

4. I plan to start withdrawing money from my investments in:
   a) less than 5 years. 0
   b) 5 to 10 years. 10
   c) 11 to 15 years. 20
   d) more than 15 years.. 30

5. When I begin withdrawing the money I've accumulated, I plan to
   spend it in:
   a) less than a year. 0
   b) less than 5 years. 2
   c) less than 10 years.. 8
   d) at least 10 years. 10

(Continued)

6. How might you respond to fluctuations in your investment?

   a) I'm very concerned any time my investments lose value and will sell quickly if they start to lose money. 0

   b) Day-to-day market moves make me uncomfortable. If an investment loses 5 percent or more over a full quarter, I am likely to sell it and look for a better alternative. 4

   c) I realize there are lots of random day-to-day movements in the market. I usually wait until I have watched the performance of an investment for at least a year before making changes. 10

   d) Even if poor market conditions result in losses of up to 20 percent in a given year, I try to follow a consistent, long-term investment plan. 14

7. Consider the range of high and low returns that might result from a $10,000 investment in four different areas over a 10-year period. Keep in mind that investments offering higher returns often involve greater risks. Which range of possible outcomes would be most acceptable to you?

Value of $10,000 after 10 years:

Investment A

Best case $45,412

Worst case   6,979. . . . . 10 pts.

Investment B

Best case $82,425

Worst case   4,186. . . . . 15 pts.

Investment C

Best case $27,000

Worst case   9,622 . . . . 5 pts.

Investment D

Best case $12,689

Worst case   10,118 . . . . 2 pts.

8. When I buy car insurance, I:

   a) choose the lowest deductible amount to ensure maximum coverage even though my policy costs more. 0

   b) choose a moderate deductible level in order to reduce the premium. . 2

   c) choose a high deductible in order to pay a low premium, even though many losses may not be covered. 5

   d) choose to carry no insurance. 7

Your Total Points . . . . ____

Reprinted with the permission of Charles Schwab & Co.

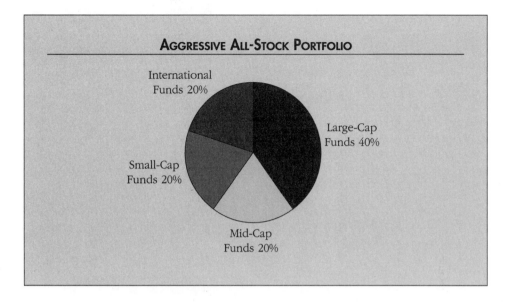

Specific Recommended Funds and Weightings for a $20,000 Portfolio:

$4,000 White Oak Growth (20%)

$4,000 TCW Galileo Select Equities (20%)

$4,000 Turner Midcap Growth (20%)

$2,000 Bjurman Microcap Growth (10%)

$2,000 RS Diversified Growth (10%)

$4,000 Artisan International (20%)

2. MODERATE ALL-STOCK PORTFOLIO: 71 TO 85 POINTS

≡ This portfolio is most appropriate for those ages 40 to 50 who have a 10- to 20-year time horizon, or for younger investors seeking a lower-risk approach to equity investing. It is fully invested, primarily in the stocks of more seasoned and value-oriented companies, yet it assumes you are willing to endure substantial year-to-year volatility in the pursuit of high growth. The suggested sub-asset class breakdown for this portfolio is as follows:

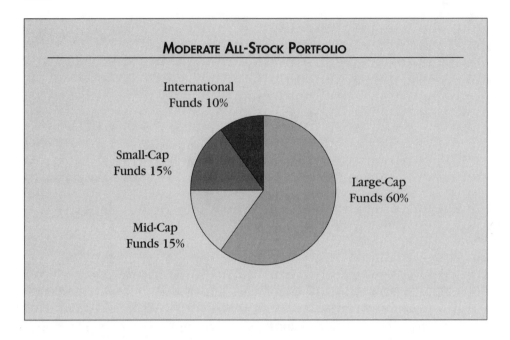

60% Large-Cap Funds

15% Mid-Cap Funds

15% Small-Cap Funds

10% International Funds

Specific Recommended Funds and Weightings for a $20,000 Portfolio:

$6,000 Reynolds Blue Chip (30%)

$6,000 TCW Galileo Select Equity (30%)

$3,000 Excelsior Value and Restructuring (15%)

$3,000 FMI Focus (15%)

$2,000 Artisan International (10%)

3. MODERATE STOCK AND BOND PORTFOLIO: 56 TO 70 POINTS

═══ This portfolio is designed for those ages 50 to 70 who are looking to maintain a majority weighting in stocks, but with a solid fixed-income component to temper volatility. It assumes you are willing to enjoy slightly lower returns in exchange for less risk. The suggested subasset class fund breakdown for this portfolio is:

40% Large-Cap Funds

10% Mid-Cap Funds

10% International Funds

20% Corporate Bond Funds

20% Mortgage-Backed Securities Funds

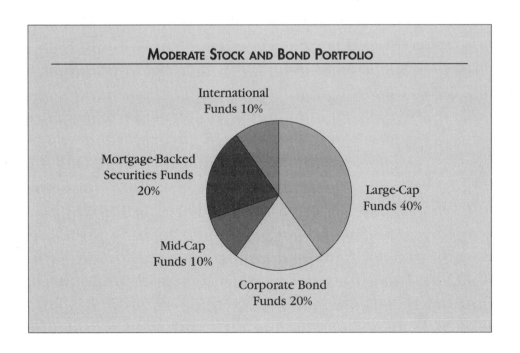

MODERATE STOCK AND BOND PORTFOLIO

International Funds 10%

Mortgage-Backed Securities Funds 20%

Large-Cap Funds 40%

Mid-Cap Funds 10%

Corporate Bond Funds 20%

Specific Recommended Funds and Weightings for a $20,000 Portfolio:

$4,000 Reynolds Blue Chip (20%)

$4,000 TCW Galileo Select Equity (20%)

$2,000 Excelsior Value and Restructuring (10%)

$2,000 Artisan International (10%)

$4,000 Strong Corporate Bond (20%)

$4,000 Vanguard GNMA (20%)

4. BALANCED STOCK AND BOND PORTFOLIO: 41 TO 55 POINTS

═══ This portfolio is most appropriate for those over age 50 seeking a balanced portfolio with 50 percent stocks and 50 percent bonds. While it will provide a moderate degree of income, its primary goal is to grow capital

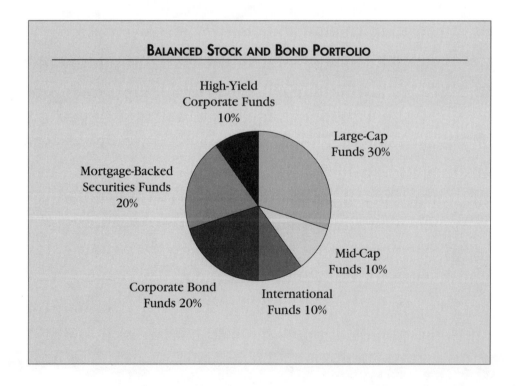

BALANCED STOCK AND BOND PORTFOLIO

High-Yield Corporate Funds 10%

Large-Cap Funds 30%

Mortgage-Backed Securities Funds 20%

Mid-Cap Funds 10%

Corporate Bond Funds 20%

International Funds 10%

without subjecting investors to a high degree of risk. The suggested subasset class breakdown for this portfolio is as follows:

30% Large-Cap Funds

10% Mid-Cap Funds

10% International Funds

20% Corporate Bond Funds

20% Mortgage-Backed Securities Funds

10% High-Yield Corporate Funds

Specific Recommended Funds and Weightings for a $20,000 Portfolio:

$3,000 Gabelli Growth (15%)

$3,000 TCW Galileo Select Equity (15%)

$2,000 Excelsior Value and Restructuring (10%)

$2,000 Artisan International (10%)

$4,000 Strong Corporate Bond (20%)

$4,000 Vanguard GNMA (20%)

$2,000 Northeast Investors Trust (10%)

5. CONSERVATIVE INCOME PRODUCER: 0 TO 40 POINTS

This portfolio maintains a small exposure to dividend-paying stocks for growth, but concentrates on bond investments to provide a steady stream of monthly income. It is most appropriate for people in retirement who are looking to live off their investments while enduring only a minimal amount of volatility. The suggested subasset class breakdown for this portfolio is:

30% Large-Cap Funds

30% Corporate Bond Funds

20% Mortgage-Backed Securities Funds

20% High-Yield Corporate Funds

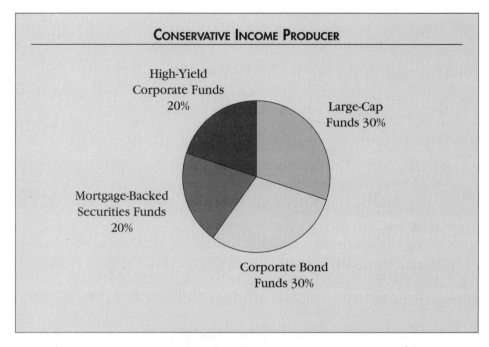

CONSERVATIVE INCOME PRODUCER

High-Yield
Corporate Funds
20%

Large-Cap
Funds 30%

Mortgage-Backed
Securities Funds
20%

Corporate Bond
Funds 30%

Specific Recommended Funds and Weightings for a $20,000 Portfolio:

$3,000 TCW Galileo Select Equities (15%)

$3,000 American Century Equity Growth (15%)

$6,000 Strong Corporate Bond (30%)

$4,000 Vanguard GNMA (20%)

$4,000 Northeast Investors Trust (20%)

HOW THE PORTFOLIOS WERE PUT TOGETHER

═══ The five model portfolios assume you have at least $20,000 to invest. If you have less, that's perfectly fine. Make the necessary adjustments, keeping in mind that each fund has a minimum initial investment requirement. This means you may not be able to buy as many funds as suggested, at least in the beginning. For example, let's say your score leads you to the

Aggressive All-Stock Portfolio. This 100 percent globally diversified equity plan calls for putting 40 percent in large caps, 20 percent in mid caps, 20 percent in small caps, and 20 percent in international funds. If you have only $10,000 to invest, you won't be able to meet the minimums for both White Oak Growth and TCW Galileo Select Equities, so consider putting the entire 40 percent in just one of those funds instead. If you have only $5,000, you might start with one large-cap fund and one mid-cap fund, with the goal of adding a small-cap fund and an international offering when you can afford them. The secret is to get started as early as possible.

You don't have to buy the exact funds I recommend. These just happen to be among my favorite Powerhouse Performers in each category that have the lowest minimum investment requirements. Almost all of them are available through the various no-load, no-transaction-fee supermarkets, which is my preferred way of buying them. Feel free to mix, match, and substitute as you feel is appropriate. If you would rather buy Gabelli Growth or Marsico Focus instead of Reynolds Blue Chip, for instance, go ahead. All are large-cap growth funds from my Powerhouse Performers list. If you have a bigger portfolio and can meet the minimum requirements of funds like Bonnel Growth or Weitz Partners Value, these are excellent choices as well. Likewise, if you're in a high tax bracket, you might consider replacing a corporate or high-yield bond fund with a tax-free municipal fund instead. (By the way, I will be updating these portfolios, recommended funds, and the entire "Powerhouse Performers" roster in each annual edition of this book. So be sure to look for the *Mutual Funds Investor's Guide 2002,* which will be available in bookstores by next January.)

Most of the portfolios are heavily weighted in "growth" funds, but you can add in some "value" funds if you like. After all, growth and value aren't always in vogue at the same time. Therefore, part of your diversification plan might call for holding funds that adhere to both disciplines. I also believe that a maximum 20 percent international weighting is appropriate for aggressive investors. Some advisers recommend putting even more money overseas. But given that most U.S. companies are global anyway, and considering the political and economic turmoil in many foreign countries right now, I'm perfectly comfortable capping this weighting at 20 percent. Again, this is something you can modify to your own personal preferences.

IRA FACTS

Every investor who qualifies should consider putting the maximum $2,000 a year into an IRA account. Even if you can't deduct the contribution, this money will compound tax-free until you withdraw it. Keep in mind that IRA stands for Individual *Retirement* Account, which means this money should not be touched until you need it in your golden years. If you try to tap into an IRA before you turn 59½, the government slaps you with a 10 percent penalty in addition to any income taxes due, unless you have a qualified reason.

There are now two types of IRAs: Traditional and Roth. What follows is a brief rundown of the benefits and requirements for both:

Eligibility

Traditional IRA: Individuals under age 70½ (and their spouses) who have earned income, regardless of the amount.

Roth IRA: Individuals of any age (and their spouses) with earned income and with adjusted gross income below $110,000 (for single filers) or $160,000 (for those filing a joint return).

Deductibility of Contribution

Traditional IRA: Contribution is fully deductible if the investor is not covered by an employer-sponsored retirement plan. If the investor is covered by an employer-sponsored retirement plan, a partial deduction may be permitted for those falling within these income guidelines: $30,000 to $40,000 for single filers; $50,000 to $60,000 for those filing jointly. Above these amounts, you can still contribute to a traditional IRA, but will not receive a tax deduction.

Roth IRA: No deduction permitted.

Annual Contribution Limits

Traditional IRA: Individuals (and their spouses) may contribute up to $2,000 per year (or 100 percent of compensation, whichever is less).

Roth IRA: Individuals (and their spouses) may contribute up to $2,000 (or 100 percent of compensation, whichever is less) with the following limits: The ability to contribute phases out at income levels between $95,000 and $110,000 for individuals and between $150,000 and $160,000 for those filing joint returns.

Tax Treatment of Distributions

Traditional IRA: Total deductible contributions and interest taxed as ordinary income in the year of withdrawal. Nondeductible contributions are not taxed, although the interest earned from them is. Distributions made before age 59½ may be subject to a 10 percent penalty. Early penalty-free withdrawals can be made prior to age 59½ upon death, disability, the purchase of a first-time home (up to $10,000 lifetime maximum), to fund higher education expenses, to pay for medical expenses in excess of 7.5 percent of adjusted gross income, or for health insurance premiums if unemployed more than 12 weeks.

Roth IRA: Distributions made after age 59½ are tax-free if the Roth IRA has been held for more than five years. Distributions made before age 59½ may be subject to a 10 percent penalty. Early penalty-free withdrawals can be made prior to age 59½ upon death, disability, the purchase of a first home (up to $10,000 lifetime maximum), to fund higher education expenses, to pay for medical expenses in excess of 7.5 percent of adjusted gross income, or for health insurance premiums if unemployed more than 12 weeks. You can also withdraw your contributed principal from a Roth IRA without tax or penalty at any time.

Minimum Distribution Requirements

Traditional IRA: Distributions must start by age 70½.

Roth IRA: No requirements.

TIMING THE MARKET

▦ After you have set your asset allocation plan, it makes sense to review it as you grow older and/or as your needs change. But once you have decided on the right program for *you,* stick with it and avoid trying to time the market. If you have made a decision to be 100 percent invested in a globally diversified equity portfolio, don't get creative by switching back and forth from stocks to bonds, based on whether you're bullish or bearish at the moment. The reason? No one has proven that you can successfully time the market over the long haul. It simply can't be done.

The only thing we know for sure is that the market has an upward bias. I can't tell you where it will be tomorrow, next week, or even next year, but I have faith that it will be higher 10 years from now than it is today. It would be great to be able to avoid every bear market. The problem is, the nasty bears creep up without warning. And study after study has shown that investors who simply stay put and ride out the inevitable market swings always come out far ahead of traders who try to guess what will happen next by switching back and forth, which is an exercise in futility.

I continually reinforce the idea that investment capital is money you are willing to put away for long periods of time. In this way, you can afford to ride out the sometimes grueling short-term volatility that I guarantee you will be forced to endure. One of the questions on the test you just took asked how you would feel if your $10,000 investment fell to a mere $4,186 over a 10-year period. If that kind of possibility scares you to death, lighten up on or entirely avoid stocks. But as the question also implies, that $10,000 could grow significantly. Again, the more risk you take, the greater your potential reward, but the more fluctuations you will be forced to endure.

7

THE 25 BEST
INTERNET SITES FOR
MUTUAL FUND INVESTORS

If you have a computer with access to the Internet, you can now tap into more information about mutual funds than you ever dreamed possible, by visiting the plethora of financial sites that pop up daily on the World Wide Web. These locations allow you to do research, download performance charts, track your portfolio online, and even chat in real time with other investors. The bad news is that most of these sites aren't worth your time. A majority of the so-called investment sites out there are mere advertisements for certain products or services. They contain little, if any, objective investment information. Others with more substance charge a subscription fee, which can get pretty steep.

In this chapter, I uncover 25 of the best sites I have run across for mutual fund investors. The sites can be accessed absolutely free. A few have premium content you have to pay for, but you'll do fine just sticking with the stuff that's available at no cost.

I offer a few caveats before you proceed. Anyone can set up and contribute to an Internet site, so always be suspicious of advice you receive online; much of it is self-serving. Occasionally, you'll find companies touting their own stock under the auspices of a seemingly legitimate financial column. Another thing: think twice before giving your e-mail address to anyone, unless you're open to being deluged with junk announcements. In some cases, you must reveal this information to gain access to a site. Otherwise, keep all personal data to yourself.

Finally, beyond what you can access through the Internet, a number of helpful computer software programs are available to help monitor and improve the results of your portfolio. Quicken and Microsoft Money, for example, will keep track of your cost basis for every fund. These programs are complete personal finance solutions, and they allow for such other features as check writing and budgeting. For fund analysis, you should consider the Value Line No-Load Analyzer for Windows program, which is available on CD-ROM. This service contains a database of more than 3,000 no-load and low-load funds, and features sophisticated sorting, screening, filtering, portfolio analysis, and graphics capabilities. A special trial offer to receive this service can be found at the back of this book. I admit to being somewhat biased; Value Line provided much of the data used in this Guide. However, this powerful and comprehensive tool is easy to use and is accessible without logging on to the Internet.

Now that the formalities are out of the way, here (in no particular order) are my picks for the year's 25 best Websites for mutual fund investors. Be sure to look for an updated list of new sites in each annual edition of this book.

1. **CBS MarketWatch** www.marketwatch.com

   If you enjoy reading late-breaking business news and information, you'll love CBS MarketWatch. In addition to quotes and stock charting tools, the site has a dedicated mutual funds channel. This area contains insightful articles and fund manager profiles, plus profiles on new funds and fund industry commentary. One of my favorite sections is called "Betting on the Jockey." It contains one-on-one interviews with leading fund managers. There are also some great fund monitoring and screening tools, plus links to various fund family sites. Best of all, everything is accessible at no charge.

2. **Morningstar.com** www.morningstar.com

   Fund-rating service Morningstar has put together a rather impressive site full of fund manager interviews, late-breaking financial news, chat rooms, market analysis, and snapshot fund profiles containing the company's trademark star ratings. For a fee, the site allows you to monitor your fund portfolio online, and an X-ray feature shows how broadly diversified your overall holdings are, across various asset classes and investment styles. Of greatest value are the archive of reports and insightful articles on the personalities and trends within the fund industry.

3. **Quicken.com**   www.quicken.com

   While not strictly a site for fund investors, Quicken.com contains an array of useful areas covering everything from tracking your investments to running your small business more effectively. The mutual fund page contains not only fund profiles and manager interviews, but also broad-based articles on subjects like the wisdom of small-cap investing. Quicken's Mutual Fund Finder lets you search for funds using your own specific criteria, like low minimum investment requirements. It also has direct links to other helpful sites for investors, and analyses of various fund investment strategies.

4. **Dr. Ed Yardeni's Economics Network**   www.yardeni.com

   Ed Yardeni is the respected chief economist of Deutsche Morgan Grenfell in New York. He says he hopes his site will be the number-one source of economic and financial information for investors. Yardeni has filled it with more economic data and analysis than you could ever hope for, including the portfolio strategy reports presented to Deutsche Morgan Grenfell's clients. Yardeni also includes his past speeches, commentaries, and latest forecasts for interest rates and economic growth around the world. Although his predictions don't always pan out, the plethora of insightful economic data here is well worth the trip.

5. **Invest-O-Rama**   www.investorama.com

   Invest-O-Rama, run by a freelance financial journalist, is more of a directory to other interesting Internet sites than anything else. The home page gives you access to market commentaries from various contributors (mostly newsletter writers), stock and fund quotes, and charting capabilities. But the real attraction is Invest-O-Rama's ability to connect you with company and fund research material from other online sources. It contains direct links to virtually every major fund family's Internet site, along with articles on topics such as "The Advantage of No-Load Mutual Funds" and "How Many Funds Should I Own?"

6. **Investor Words**   www.investorwords.com

   I think the glossary in the back of this book is pretty comprehensive, but it's nothing compared to what you'll find at the Investor Words Internet site. Billed as "the biggest, best investing glossary on the Web," it contains definitions for some 4,000 investment-related words, from *alpha* to *zero-coupon bond*. Within most definitions, you will find links to other related words, to further your understanding of every concept. Given the financial industry's knack for throwing around confusing gobbledygook, this site is bound to be a frequent stop for every serious investor.

7. **MAXfunds.com** www.maxfunds.com

While the stated goal of MAXfunds.com is to bring investors information about tiny and new mutual funds, the site contains valuable performance report cards for all no-load equity mutual funds. The site's founders focus on undiscovered funds since they believe (as do I) that portfolios with smaller asset bases have a better chance of outperforming. In addition to performance information, you'll find fund manager interviews, lessons on such topics as shorting stocks and style drift, plus many helpful articles. One of my favorites is "Think Twice Before Abandoning Your Funds for Individual Stocks."

8. **Yahoo Finance** www.finance.yahoo.com

It's not that pretty to look at, but Yahoo Finance is a great source of comprehensive, up-to-the-minute investment information. On the stock side, it reports on the day's major corporate developments. It also has a page devoted exclusively to news relating to mutual funds, such as new fund launches, cash flow trends, and manager changes. Additionally, it includes links to fund-related stories by reporters from TheStreet.com and other publications. What's more, Yahoo Finance has a fund message board and can provide a quick printout of top performers across various time periods.

9. **Wall Street Research Net** www.wsrn.com

Wall Street Research Net contains thousands of links to help you conduct fundamental research on both actively traded companies and mutual funds. It can also assist you in locating important economic data that could impact the market. In addition to mutual fund news, collected from various sources on the Web, the site provides a daily list of the fund world's biggest gainers and losers. Furthermore, you will find a glossary of commonly used mutual fund terms here, profiles of Morningstar's managers of the year, and insightful commentary on other important business topics of interest to investors.

10. **Daily Rocket**   www.dailyrocket.com

When you call up the Daily Rocket site on your computer, you'll be greeted with a recap of the day on Wall Street, followed by several somewhat dated features primarily of interest to stock investors. What's of more value to fund lovers can be found by clicking on the "articles" icon at the top of the home page and selecting "mutual funds." There you will find a small archive of stories of special appeal to beginning investors. Subjects include "Navigating Through a Mutual Fund Prospectus," "Deciphering the Mutual Fund Rating System," and "Open-End Funds vs. Closed-End Funds."

11. **FinanCenter.com**   www.financenter.com

How much will you need to save to enjoy the retirement of your dreams? What is the total return you have actually earned from your least favorite mutual fund? Do you make enough to buy that brand new home you've been eyeing on the other side of town? For the answers to these questions and more, log in to FinanCenter.com. You'll find dozens of calculators here that work through various "what if" scenarios with you. You supply the raw data and the calculators give numerical responses to everything from estimated living expenses 30 years in the future to the amount you must save to become a millionaire.

12. **ICI Mutual Fund Connection**   www.ici.org

The Investment Company Institute is the trade association for the fund industry. Its Website is packed with statistical fund information, along with the association's most recent press releases and research reports. You can also listen to ICI's weekly 60-second "Informed Investor" radio reports, which cover topics of interest to fund shareholders. This site will give you a better understanding of the various issues affecting the fund industry. In addition, the "About Mutual Fund Shareholders" section contains some fascinating information on the demographic characteristics of the average fund investor.

13. **U.S. Securities and Exchange Commission**   www.sec.gov

By tapping in to the SEC Website, you'll be able to access the huge database of legal documents that mutual funds are required to file with the government. You can pull down prospectuses and other detailed papers filed by every fund company. This is an effective and quick way to do research on funds you own or are considering. It can also lead you to brand new funds that have registered with the SEC but are not yet available to the public. Incidentally, you can use this same database to search for 10-Ks, 10-Qs, and other material that must be filed with the SEC by public companies as well.

14. **Vanguard Online**   www.vanguard.com

Almost every major fund company now has its own Internet site, but this one from the Vanguard Group stands out. It is more than just a commercial message for the company's various funds. Instead, it contains a wealth of educational material. Vanguard Online has an area called "The University," which features a series of ten courses answering such questions as "What is a mutual fund?" "How do you build a portfolio?" and "What are the best ways to rebalance your portfolio?" You'll also find help tools for retirement planning and a library of in-depth fund material.

15. **Find a Fund**   www.findafund.com

Find a Fund is one of the newest Internet sites built especially for mutual fund investors. It contains a spotlight article, which examines recent trends and changes in a new market sector each week. The site also includes a library of mutual fund basics and performance profiles for almost every fund. Find a Fund allows you to compare the holdings and sector weightings of two different funds, to see if owning both really offers diversification. In addition, you will find average performance numbers for various fund categories here, which is useful for evaluating how your funds compare to their peers.

16. **Mutual Fund Investor's Center**   www.mfea.com

This site, sponsored by the Mutual Fund Education Alliance, contains in-depth profiles of select fund managers, thoughts from leaders in the field, and a news center with recent developments in the industry. The education center teaches users about the basics of fund investing, goes over the various types of funds available, discusses the tax ramifications of fund ownership, and has a special feature on investing for women. Finally, the site's planning center lets you go through various scenarios to make informed decisions about everything from investing for college to retirement.

17. **Fund Alarm**   www.fundalarm.com

    Almost every fund site gives you some kind of advice on buying funds. Fund Alarm is the only one specializing in telling you when to *sell*. It is updated at the beginning of each month and follows more than 1,900 funds. A fund is likely to earn a "three alarm" sell signal if it undergoes a bad change in management or its performance lags behind its benchmark over a consistent time period. Fund Alarm is run by Roy Weitz, who is not even in the investment business. His offbeat thoughts about key personalities and changes in the industry are enlightening, even if you don't always agree with him.

18. **Bloomberg**   www.bloomberg.com

    Michael Bloomberg's investment information empire is into just about every medium imaginable now (radio, TV, print, computer terminals), so it was only a matter of time before he put up his own Internet address as well. The site is flush with news straight from the Bloomberg wires, including a section packed with mutual fund-related stories. If you're looking for the latest developments on fund companies and the industry in general, this is about the most comprehensive source around. The site also updates the equity indexes throughout the day and lets you tap into Bloomberg Radio and TV live.

19. **Fund $pot**   www.fundspot.com

    Fund $pot is a site that connects you to other areas on the Internet that are of interest to fund investors. You'll find links to mutual fund news, portfolio manager interviews, and fund family Websites. "Interactive Spot" will take you to worksheets and financial calculators useful for college, retirement, and general financial planning. If you feel like chatting about your newest fund discovery, the site can direct you to an investor forum where you can talk to your heart's content. To round things out, Fund $pot leads you to sites with portfolio tracking capabilities, research, and current quotes.

20. **Mutual Funds Interactive**   www.fundsinteractive.com

    Mutual Funds Interactive is awash with useful information and articles written by its founder, Marla Brill, and by a team of contributing fund experts. This isn't the best looking site around, but there are discussion groups where you can chat about everything from retirement planning to which Websites you like the most. You'll also find Value Line screening tools, the results of various fund-related surveys, manager profiles, and links to fund family home pages. The "Mutual Fund Features" section is especially interesting. It contains dozens of articles culled from numerous columnists and publications.

21. **Mutual Fund Café**   www.mfcafe.com

This cleverly named site invites you to pull up a modem, grab some hot java, and catch up on the freshest fund industry information. Written primarily for fund professionals, the Mutual Fund Café is loaded with behind-the-scenes news that will be of interest to any serious investor. Categorized into such cleverly named sections as "Top Bananas," "Market Share Pie," "Burgers 'n' Acquisitions," "Legal Stew," and "Bean Counters," the site won't teach you the basics of fund investing (there are plenty of previously mentioned online locations that do that). But it will show you how the fund business *really* works.

22. **BuckInvestor.com** www.buckinvestor.com

Even though this site is written with young people in mind, it is appropriate for investors of all ages. Dubbed as "The Most Comprehensive Guide for Investors Under 35," BuckInvestor.com contains many easy-to-digest articles on all aspects of investing. The featured channels let you learn about such topics as becoming a millionaire, being part of an investment club, and, of course, mutual fund investing. Unfortunately, the site is rarely updated. And, while you won't find any earth-shattering information, it's a good way for beginning investors to add even more education to their growing arsenal.

23. **iMoneyNet.com**   www.imoneynet.com

You'll notice that there are no money market funds among my list of "100 Powerhouse Performers." That's because money market yields change so often, it's hard to keep track of who is offering the best deals. One way to stay ahead of the curve is by visiting the iMoneyNet.com site. iMoneyNet is in the business of tracking money funds and yields. You can't access all of its services without paying a fee, but the freebies are all you need. A click of the mouse gives you a rundown of the highest yielding funds. Another section goes over the finer points of selecting and evaluating these cash-equivalent investments.

24. **Index Funds Online**   www.indexfundsonline.com

   If you opt to keep part of your portfolio in index funds, or just want to learn more about how these investments work, you'll find the content of Index Funds Online to be of interest. The site, run by a diehard indexer, has excerpts from books on indexing and reprints of related articles from various publications. The "Index Information" center contains short descriptions for each of the major global indexes (i.e., number of stocks included and market capitalizations), along with a listing of funds available to track these indexes. The site also updates how well the various indexes have performed on a weekly basis, and contains articles about non-index funds as well.

25. **Mutual Funds Online**   www.mfmag.com

   Mutual Funds Online is the Internet site for *Mutual Funds* magazine. You can read most articles found in the magazine here at no cost, including profiles on the "fund of the month" and "undiscovered funds." In-depth interviews with popular managers make for interesting reading and show how some of today's top stock pickers do their stuff. Mutual Funds Online contains an archive of stories from past issues, plus regular chats with both fund managers and writers from the magazine. The site also regularly screens for funds with specific characteristics, such as tax-efficiency, and reviews books of interest to investors.

8

VALUE LINE PERFORMANCE DATA FOR SOME 9,000 FUNDS

What follows are comprehensive performance results and rankings for some 9,000 stock and bond mutual funds from the *Value Line Mutual Fund Survey*. I believe this is the most exhaustive collection of fund data you will find in any book on the market today. The directory starts out with a listing of stock funds, and then gives a roster of bond offerings. The following information (where available) is provided for each entry:

Fund Name.   Funds are listed in alphabetical order, with stock funds up front, and bond funds in the back. Almost every fund you own or are considering can probably be found somewhere on these pages.

Objective.   This is a brief description of the fund's investment objective (i.e., growth, foreign, corporate bond, and so on).

Annualized Return for 1, 3, and 5 Years.   Here you will find every fund's average annual return over the past one-, three- and five-year periods, where applicable, as compiled by Value Line. (All performance data is as of June 30, 2000, unless otherwise noted.)

Overall Rank.   This number, compiled exclusively by Value Line, shows how a given fund stacks up next to its peers. Ratings are on a scale of 1 through 5. Funds with a 1 ranking have performed best, and those rated 5 have done the poorest.

Risk Rank. Another proprietary Value Line statistic, the risk rank number tells you how much volatility a fund has subjected its investors to. It is also based on a scale of 1 through 5, with 1 being least risky, and 5 being riskiest.

Maximum Sales Load. If a fund has a front-end sales load, it will be noted here. (Remember: If you're making fund selections on your own, you should favor no-load funds.) Also, many load funds have several share classes which come with back-ended redemption fees, instead of up-front sales commissions. In other words, you pay on the way "out" rather than on the way "in." Therefore, although some load funds in this directory may have several other share classes with "0" listed as the maximum sales load, be aware that you can almost always count on being hit with steep exit fees on these funds.

Expense Ratio. Every fund has an expense ratio. This number represents the percentage that gets deducted from the fund's net asset value each year, to cover all charges related to managing your money.

Toll-Free Telephone. This is the toll-free telephone number you can call to request a prospectus and more information on the listed fund.

Many thanks to the good folks at Value Line who helped to put this performance directory together. They truly did a first-rate job.

| Stock Fund Name | Objective | Annualized Return for | | | Rank | | Max Load | Expense Ratio | Toll-Free Telephone |
		1 Year	3 Years	5 Years	Overall	Risk			
			STOCK FUNDS						
1st Source Monogram Dvrs Equity	Growth/Inc	5.3	13.19		4	3	1.1	1.42	800 554-3862
1st Source Monogram Income Equity	Income	-5.5	8.32		3	2	1	1.2	800 554-3862
1st Source Monogram Special Eq	Small Co	34.8	11.5		4	4	1	1.23	800 554-3862
59 Wall St International Equity Fd	Foreign	29.6	16.41		2	3	0.65	1.5	800 625-5759
59 Wall St Tax Efficient Equity	Growth	10.4					0.65	1.29	800 625-5759
59 Wall Street European Equity	European	20.7	16.85	17.36	2	3	0.65	1.28	800 625-5759
59 Wall Street Pacific Basin Eq	Pacific	42.5	19.88	17.63	3	4	0.65	1.38	800 625-5759
59 Wall Street U.S. Equity Fund	Growth/Inc	2	8.75	15.73	4	3	0.65	1.39	800 625-5759
AAL Balanced Fund A	Balanced	6.1					0.56	1.14	800 553-6319
AAL Balanced Fund B	Balanced	5.1					0.56	1.97	800 553-6319
AAL Balanced Fund I	Balanced	6.7					0.56	0.88	800 553-6319
AAL Capital Growth Fund A	Growth	8.9	21.52	23.71	2	3	0.54	0.93	800 553-6319
AAL Capital Growth Fund B	Growth	7.7	20.3		3	3	0.54	1.98	800 553-6319
AAL Capital Growth Fund I	Growth	9					0.54	0.59	800 553-6319
AAL Equity Income A	Growth/Inc	-4.1	9.62	11.66	3	2	0.46	1.05	800 553-6319
AAL Equity Income Fund B	Growth/Inc	-5.1	8.52		3	2	0.46	2.08	800 553-6319
AAL Equity Income Fund I	Growth/Inc	-3.6					0.46	0.59	800 553-6319
AAL International A	Foreign	26.3	10.1		3	2	0.7	1.73	800 553-6319
AAL International Fund B	Foreign	24.9	8.86		3	2	0.7	2.85	800 553-6319
AAL International Fund I	Foreign	27					0.7	1.09	800 553-6319
AAL Mid Cap Stock A	Small Co	21.9	13.98	16.48	4	3	0.67	1.37	800 553-6319
AAL Mid Cap Stock Fund B	Small Co	20.5	12.66		4	3	0.67	2.56	800 553-6319
AAL Mid Cap Stock Fund I	Small Co	22.2					0.67	0.84	800 553-6319
AAL Small Cap Stock A	Small Co	34.3	11.54		4	4	0.71	1.82	800 553-6319
AAL Small Cap Stock Fund B	Small Co	32.9	10.43		4	4	0.71	2.89	800 553-6319
AAL Small Cap Stock Fund I	Small Co	35.4					0.71	1.08	800 553-6319
AARP Balanced Stock & Bond	Balanced	-2.5	6.65	11.2	3	1	0.46	0.88	800 253-2277
AARP Capital Growth Fund	Growth	25.3	23.49	25.54	1	3	0.59	0.9	800 253-2277
AARP Diversified Growth Fund	Growth	6.9	9.89		3	1	0	0	800 253-2277
AARP Diversified Inc w/Growth Fd	Income	4.7	5.94		3	1	0	0	800 253-2277
AARP Global Growth Fund	Global	13.5	11.63		3	2	0.82	1.64	800 253-2277
AARP Growth & Income Fund	Growth/Inc	-3.6	8.3	15.94	3	2	0.46	0.75	800 253-2277
AARP International Stk Gr & Inc Fd	Foreign	24	12.09		3	3	0.83	1.75	800 253-2277
AARP Small Company Stock Fund	Small Co	-9.5	0.65		5	3	0.6	1.69	800 253-2277
AARP US Stock Index Fund	Growth	7.2	19.6		2	3	0	0.5	800 253-2277
ABN AMRO Asian Tigers Inv	Pacific	-1.3	-9.18	-2.19	5	5	1	2.06	800 443-4725
ABN AMRO Asian Tigers Tr	Pacific	-1	-8.74	-1.62	5	5	1	1.62	800 443-4725
ABN AMRO Balanced Inv	Balanced	1.4	8.36	12.37	3	2	0.69	1.5	800 443-4725
ABN AMRO Balanced Tr	Balanced	2	8.74	12.72	3	2	0.69	1	800 443-4725
ABN AMRO Growth Inv	Growth	14	16.41	19.39	3	3	0.8	1.52	800 443-4725
ABN AMRO Growth Tr	Growth	14.6	19.25	21.26	2	3	0.8	1.03	800 443-4725
ABN AMRO Intl Equity Inv	Foreign	23.4	13.1	14.03	3	3	1	1.8	800 443-4725
ABN AMRO Intl Equity Tr	Foreign	24	13.58	14.52	3	3	1	1.31	800 443-4725
ABN AMRO Intl Fixed Inv	Intl Bond	-2.3	-0.79	-0.13	4	5	0.8	1.97	800 443-4725
ABN AMRO Intl Fixed Tr	Intl Bond	-1.8	-0.41	0.21	5	5	0.8	1.47	800 443-4725
ABN AMRO Latin America Equity Tr	Foreign	29.5	-0.07		4	5	1	1.87	800 443-4725
ABN AMRO Real Estate Tr	Real Est	4.6					0.5	1.52	800 443-4725
ABN AMRO Small Cap Growth Inv	Small Co	28.6	6.9	12.97	3	4	0.8	1.69	800 443-4725
ABN AMRO Small Cap Tr	Small Co	29.4	8.35	14	3	4	0.8	1.19	800 443-4725
ABN AMRO Value Inv	Growth	-10	6.14	14.02	4	3	0.8	1.53	800 443-4725
ABN AMRO Value Tr	Growth	-9.6	6.58	14.44	4	3	0.8	1.03	800 443-4725
AFBA Five Star Balanced Fund	Balanced	7.2	8.44		3	1	1.08	1.08	800 243-9865
AFBA Five Star Equity Fund	Growth	13.7	12.59		3	2	1.04	1.08	800 243-9865
AFBA Five Star USA Global Fund	Global	36.5	19.1		1	2	1.04	1.08	800 243-9865
AHA Balanced Portfolio	Balanced	4.8	11.69	15.74	3	2	0.75	0.23	800 445-1341
AHA Diversified Equity	Growth	6.1	16.51	21.96	3	3	0	0.1	800 445-1341

278

Stock Fund Name	Objective	Annualized Return for			Rank		Max Load	Expense Ratio	Toll-Free Telephone
		1 Year	3 Years	5 Years	Overall	Risk			
AIM Advisor Flex Fund A	AssetAlloc	-11	5.73		3	2	0.75	1.12	800 347-4246
AIM Advisor Flex Fund B	AssetAlloc	-11.6					0.75	1.87	800 347-4246
AIM Advisor Flex Fund C	AssetAlloc	-11.6	4.97	10.26	3	2	0.75	1.86	800 347-4246
AIM Advisor Intl Value A	Foreign	16.1	9.48		4	3	1.31	1.59	800 347-4246
AIM Advisor Intl Value B	Foreign	15.3					1.31	2.33	800 347-4246
AIM Advisor Intl Value C	Foreign	15.2	8.66	14.14	4	3	1.31	2.27	800 347-4246
AIM Advisor Large Cap Value A	Growth/Inc						0.75	1.19	800 347-4246
AIM Advisor Large Cap Value B	Growth/Inc						0.75	1.94	800 347-4246
AIM Advisor Real Estate A	Real Est	7.5	0.03		4	2	0.9	1.48	800 347-4246
AIM Advisor Real Estate B	Real Est	6.8					0.9	2.24	800 347-4246
AIM Advisor Real Estate C	Real Est	6.8	-0.67	8.36	4	2	0.75	2.24	800 347-4246
AIM Aggressive Growth A	Agg Growth	64.6	25.73	22	3	4	0.64	1.09	800 347-4246
AIM Aggressive Growth B	Agg Growth	63.1					0.64	1.96	800 347-4246
AIM Aggressive Growth C	Agg Growth	63.1					0.64	1.96	800 347-4246
AIM Asian Growth A	Pacific	22.6					0.94	1.91	800 347-4246
AIM Asian Growth B	Pacific	21.4					0.94	2.72	800 347-4246
AIM Asian Growth C	Pacific	21.6					0.94	2.72	800 347-4246
AIM Balanced Fund A	Balanced	15.5	15.1	18.32	2	2	0.51	0.93	800 347-4246
AIM Balanced Fund B	Balanced	14.6	14.19	17.37	3	2	0.51	1.78	800 347-4246
AIM Balanced Fund C	Balanced	14.6					0.51	1.78	800 347-4246
AIM Basic Value A	Growth	8.6	17.54		3	3	0.72	1.72	800 347-4246
AIM Basic Value B	Growth	7.9	16.79		3	3	0.72	2.37	800 347-4246
AIM Basic Value C	Growth	7.9					0.72	2.37	800 347-4246
AIM Blue Chip Fund A	Growth	18.7	23.56	25.33	1	3	0.69	1.18	800 347-4246
AIM Blue Chip Fund B	Growth	17.9	22.69		1	3	0.69	1.9	800 347-4246
AIM Blue Chip Fund C	Growth	17.9					0.69	1.9	800 347-4246
AIM Capital Development A	Growth	42.7	19.89		3	4	0.66	1.37	800 347-4246
AIM Capital Development B	Growth	41.7	19		3	4	0.66	2.1	800 347-4246
AIM Capital Development C	Growth	41.7					0.66	2.1	800 347-4246
AIM Charter Fund A	Growth/Inc	18.2	22.51	23.42	2	3	0.63	1.06	800 347-4246
AIM Charter Fund B	Growth/Inc	17.2	21.6	22.5	2	3	0.63	1.8	800 347-4246
AIM Charter Fund C	Growth/Inc	17.3					0.63	1.8	800 347-4246
AIM Constellation Fund A	Agg Growth	44.5	24.97	21.86	3	4	0.63	1.1	800 347-4246
AIM Constellation Fund B	Agg Growth	43.3					0.63	1.98	800 347-4246
AIM Constellation Fund C	Agg Growth	43.3					0.63	1.94	800 347-4246
AIM Dent Demographics Trends A	Growth						0.84	1.6	800 347-4246
AIM Dent Demographics Trends B	Growth						0.84		800 347-4246
AIM Dent Demographics Trends C	Growth						0.84		800 347-4246
AIM Developing Markets A	Foreign	3.6	-9.29	1.67	5	4	0.97	2.37	800 347-4246
AIM Developing Markets B	Foreign	3					0.97	2.5	800 347-4246
AIM Developing Markets C	Foreign	3					0.97	2.5	800 347-4246
AIM Euroland Growth A	European	45.1	18.33	18.08	3	4	0.96	1.83	800 347-4246
AIM Euroland Growth B	European	44.2	17.53	17.3	3	4	0.96	2.5	800 347-4246
AIM Euroland Growth C	European	44.1					0.96	2.5	800 347-4246
AIM Global Aggr Growth Fund A	Global	58.4	19.2	20.64	3	4	0.86	1.8	800 347-4246
AIM Global Aggr Growth Fund B	Global	57.5	18.53	19.96	3	4	0.9	2.33	800 347-4246
AIM Global Aggr Growth Fund C	Global	57.5					0.9	2.33	800 347-4246
AIM Global Cons Prods & Svcs A	Growth	20.9	24.63	27.05	1	3	0.97	1.93	800 347-4246
AIM Global Cons Prods & Svcs B	Growth	20.3	24	26.4	1	3	0.97	2.41	800 347-4246
AIM Global Cons Prods & Svcs C	Growth	20.3					0.97	2.43	800 347-4246
AIM Global Financial Services A	Financial	9.1	16.26	20.28	3	4	0.97	1.97	800 347-4246
AIM Global Financial Services B	Financial	8.5	15.66	19.7	3	4	0.97	2.62	800 347-4246
AIM Global Financial Services C	Financial	8.5					0.97	2.47	800 347-4246
AIM Global Growth Fund A	Global	35.9	21.82	22.17	2	3	0.84	1.66	800 347-4246
AIM Global Growth Fund B	Global	35.2	21.15	21.51	2	3	0.84	2.25	800 347-4246
AIM Global Growth Fund C	Global	35.2					0.84	2.25	800 347-4246
AIM Global Health Care A	Health	15.5	15.57	20.32	3	3	0.96	1.82	800 347-4246
AIM Global Health Care B	Health	15	14.98	19.72	3	3	0.97	2.33	800 347-4246

279

Stock Fund Name	Objective	Annualized Return for			Rank		Max Load	Expense Ratio	Toll-Free Telephone
		1 Year	3 Years	5 Years	Overall	Risk			
AIM Global Health Care C	Health	15					0.96	2.33	800 347-4246
AIM Global Infrastructure A	Other	37	13.75	14.56	3	4	0.97	2.22	800 347-4246
AIM Global Infrastructure B	Other	36.4	13.18	13.95	3	4	0.97	2.5	800 347-4246
AIM Global Infrastructure C	Other	36.2					0.97	2.5	800 347-4246
AIM Global Resources A	Energy/Res	-3	-6.55	2.93	5	4	0.97	2	800 347-4246
AIM Global Resources B	Energy/Res	-3.5	-6.99	2.43	5	4	0.97	2.5	800 347-4246
AIM Global Resources C	Energy/Res	-3.5					0.97	2.5	800 347-4246
AIM Global Telecom and Tech A	Technology	61.2	34.14	24.77	2	5	0.93	1.86	800 347-4246
AIM Global Telecom and Tech B	Technology	60.3	33.48	24.13	3	5	0.93	2.35	800 347-4246
AIM Global Telecom and Tech C	Technology	60.3					0.93	2.35	800 347-4246
AIM Global Trends A	Growth	27.2					0	0.5	800 347-4246
AIM Global Trends Adv	Growth	25.7					0	0	800 347-4246
AIM Global Trends B	Growth	26.6					0	1	800 347-4246
AIM Global Trends C	Growth	26.7					0	1	800 347-4246
AIM Global Utilities Fund A	Utilities	31.8	22.76	21.29	1	3	0.56	1.1	800 347-4246
AIM Global Utilities Fund B	Utilities	30.8	21.85	20.39	1	3	0.56	1.87	800 347-4246
AIM Global Utilities Fund C	Utilities	30.8					0.56	1.87	800 347-4246
AIM International Equity A	Foreign	34	14.44	16.51	3	3	0.89	1.47	800 347-4246
AIM International Equity B	Foreign	32.9	13.55	15.6	3	3	0.92	2.27	800 347-4246
AIM International Equity C	Foreign	33					0.89	2.27	800 347-4246
AIM Japan Growth A	Pacific	14.1	9.65	9.26	4	4	0.97	1.87	800 347-4246
AIM Japan Growth B	Pacific	13.3	8.96	8.57	4	4	0.97	2.62	800 347-4246
AIM Japan Growth C	Pacific	13.4					0.97	2.64	800 347-4246
AIM Latin American Growth A	Foreign	18.4	-8.23	2.08	4	5	0.97	2.58	800 347-4246
AIM Latin American Growth B	Foreign	17.7	-8.69	1.59	4	5	0.97	2.5	800 347-4246
AIM Latin American Growth C	Foreign	17.7					0.97	2.5	800 347-4246
AIM Mid Cap Equity A	Growth	34.9	19.32	13.88	3	4	0.72	1.45	800 347-4246
AIM Mid Cap Equity B	Growth	34.1	18.54	13.12	3	4	0.71	2.16	800 347-4246
AIM Mid Cap Equity C	Growth	33.9					0.72	2.16	800 347-4246
AIM Mid Cap Growth A	Growth						0.8		800 347-4246
AIM Mid Cap Growth B	Growth						0.8		800 347-4246
AIM Mid Cap Growth Fund C	Growth						0.8		800 347-4246
AIM Mid Cap Opportunities A	Growth	82					1	2.25	800 347-4246
AIM Select Growth Fund A	Growth	44.4	30.51	26.4	1	4	0.66	1.09	800 347-4246
AIM Select Growth Fund B	Growth	43.3	29.44	25.35	2	4	0.66	1.09	800 347-4246
AIM Select Growth Fund C	Growth	43.2					0.66	1.9	800 347-4246
AIM Small Cap Growth A	Small Co	83.9	50.88		1	5	0.75	1.54	800 347-4246
AIM Small Cap Growth B	Small Co	82.6	49.82		1	5	0.75	2.29	800 347-4246
AIM Small Cap Growth C	Small Co	82.6					0.75	2.27	800 347-4246
AIM Small Cap Opportunities A	Small Co	104.1					1	1.79	800 347-4246
AIM Small Cap Opportunities B	Small Co	102.6					1	2.47	800 347-4246
AIM Small Cap Opportunities C	Small Co	102.6					1	2.47	800 347-4246
AIM Strategic Income A	Intl Bond	-1.7	-1.36	5.94	4	5	0.72	1.35	800 347-4246
AIM Strategic Income B	Intl Bond	-2.3	-1.98	5.24	4	5	0.72	2	800 347-4246
AIM Strategic Income C	Intl Bond	-2.3					0.72	2	800 347-4246
AIM Summit Fund I	Growth	35.1	32.04	28.01	2	4	0.64	0.67	800 347-4246
AIM Value Fund A	Growth	13	22.41	21.76	2	3	0.64	1	800 347-4246
AIM Value Fund B	Growth	12.1	21.44	20.78	2	3	0.6	1.81	800 347-4246
AIM Value Fund C	Growth	12.1					0.6	1.8	800 347-4246
AIM Weingarten Fund A	Growth	27.2	27.6	25.38	1	3	0.63	1.03	800 347-4246
AIM Weingarten Fund B	Growth	26.1	26.6	24.38	1	3	0.63	1.82	800 347-4246
AIM Weingarten Fund C	Growth	26.1					0.63	1.82	800 347-4246
AMCAP Fund	Growth	16	24.66	22.56	1	2	0.38	0.68	800 421-9900
AMIDEX35 Fund A	Small Co						0.5		
AMIDEX35 No Load	Small Co						0.5		888 876-3566
API Trust Multiple Index Trust	Growth/Inc	17.9					0.69	1.22	800 544-6060
API Trust-Capital Income	Income	-3.6	9.19	13.9	4	2	0.59	1.34	800 544-6060
API Trust-Growth	Global	23.9	17.41	16.45	3	3	1	2.41	800 544-6060

Stock Fund Name	Objective	Annualized Return for			Rank		Max Load	Expense Ratio	Toll-Free Telephone
		1 Year	3 Years	5 Years	Overall	Risk			
API-Yorktown Classic Value Trust	Growth	-6.2	5.08	9.91	5	4	0.9	2.43	800 544-6060
ASAF Alliance Growth A	Growth	34.9					1.75	1.8	800 752-6342
ASAF Alliance Growth B	Growth	34.3					1.75	2.29	800 752-6342
ASAF Alliance Growth C	Growth	34.3					1.75	2.29	800 752-6342
ASAF Alliance Growth X	Growth	34.3					1.75	2.29	800 752-6342
ASAF American Century Strat Bal A	Balanced	6.5					0.9	1.6	800 752-6342
ASAF American Century Strat Bal B	Balanced	5.9					0.9	2.1	800 752-6342
ASAF American Century Strat Bal C	Balanced	5.9					0.9	2.1	800 752-6342
ASAF American Century Strat Bal X	Balanced	5.9					0.9	2.1	800 752-6342
ASAF Founders Intl Small Cap A	Foreign	55.4					1.1	2.1	800 752-6342
ASAF Founders Intl Small Cap B	Foreign	54.7					1.1	2.6	800 752-6342
ASAF Founders Intl Small Cap C	Foreign	54.3					1.1	2.6	800 752-6342
ASAF Founders Intl Small Cap X	Foreign	54.7					1.1	2.6	800 752-6342
ASAF INVESCO Equity Income A	Income	3.4					0.75	1.55	800 752-6342
ASAF INVESCO Equity Income B	Income	3					0.75	2.04	800 752-6342
ASAF INVESCO Equity Income C	Income	2.9					0.75	2.04	800 752-6342
ASAF INVESCO Equity Income X	Income	2.9					0.75	2.04	800 752-6342
ASAF Janus Capital Growth A	Growth/Inc	19.3					1	1.69	800 752-6342
ASAF Janus Capital Growth B	Growth/Inc	18.7					1	2.2	800 752-6342
ASAF Janus Capital Growth C	Growth/Inc	18.6					1	2.2	800 752-6342
ASAF Janus Capital Growth X	Growth/Inc	18.7					1	2.2	800 752-6342
ASAF Janus Overseas Growth A	Foreign	58.2					1	2.1	800 752-6342
ASAF Janus Overseas Growth B	Foreign	57.5					1	2.6	800 752-6342
ASAF Janus Overseas Growth C	Foreign	57.6					1	2.6	800 752-6342
ASAF Janus Overseas Growth X	Foreign	57.5					1	2.6	800 752-6342
ASAF Janus Small Cap Growth A	Small Co	53.9					0.9	1.69	800 752-6342
ASAF Janus Small Cap Growth B	Small Co	53.2					0.9	2.2	800 752-6342
ASAF Janus Small Cap Growth C	Small Co	53.2					0.9	2.2	800 752-6342
ASAF Janus Small Cap Growth X	Small Co	53.1					0.9	2.2	800 752-6342
ASAF Marsico Capital Growth A	Growth	21.8					1	1.75	800 752-6342
ASAF Marsico Capital Growth B	Growth	21.2					1	2.25	800 752-6342
ASAF Marsico Capital Growth C	Growth	21.2					1	2.25	800 752-6342
ASAF Marsico Capital Growth X	Growth	21.2					1	2.25	800 752-6342
ASAF Neuberger&Berman Mid Cap Gr A	Growth	63.6					0.9	1.75	800 752-6342
ASAF Neuberger&Berman Mid Cap Gr B	Growth	62.9					0.9	2.25	800 752-6342
ASAF Neuberger&Berman Mid Cap Gr C	Growth	63					0.9	2.25	800 752-6342
ASAF Neuberger&Berman Mid Cap Gr X	Growth	62.9					0.9	2.25	800 752-6342
ASAF Neuberger&Berman Mid Cp Val A	Growth	1.9					0.9	1.75	800 752-6342
ASAF Neuberger&Berman Mid Cp Val B	Growth	1.4					0.9	2.25	800 752-6342
ASAF Neuberger&Berman Mid Cp Val C	Growth	1.5					0.9	2.25	800 752-6342
ASAF Neuberger&Berman Mid Cp Val X	Growth	1.4					0.9	2.25	800 752-6342
ASAF T. Rowe Price Sm Co Value A	Small Co	6.2					1	1.75	800 752-6342
ASAF T. Rowe Price Sm Co Value B	Small Co	5.7					1	2.25	800 752-6342
ASAF T. Rowe Price Sm Co Value C	Small Co	5.6					1	2.25	800 752-6342
ASAF T. Rowe Price Sm Co Value X	Small Co	5.7					1	2.25	800 752-6342
AXP Blue Chip A	Growth	6.2	15.77	21.22	3	3	0.42	0.82	800 328-8300
AXP Discovery A	Small Co	-3.5	4.34	10.36	5	4	0.59	1.05	800 328-8300
AXP Diversified Equity Income A	Income	-9	7.36	13.05	4	2	0.48	0.89	800 328-8300
AXP Equity Select A	Growth	22.1	21.83	23.91	2	4	0.58	0.93	800 328-8300
AXP Equity Value B	Growth/Inc	-9.2	5.72	12.99	4	2	0.48	1.66	800 328-8300
AXP Global Bond A	Intl Bond	-0.3	1.67	3.66	5	5	0.75	1.19	800 328-8300
AXP Global Growth A	Global	18.8	17.2	15.13	3	3	0.75	1.25	800 328-8300
AXP Growth Fund A	Growth	27.3	24.55	26.57	1	4	0.53	1.78	800 328-8300
AXP International Fund A	Foreign	18.2	11.42	12.54	4	3	0.66	1.34	800 328-8300
AXP Managed Allocation A	Flexible	5.2	8.04	10.94	4	2	0.48	0.81	800 328-8300
AXP Mutual A	Balanced	-4.4	6.83	10.91	3	1	0.47	0.82	800 328-8300
AXP New Dimensions Fund A	Growth	20.6	23.96	25.07	1	3	0.53	0.93	800 328-8300
AXP Precious Metals Fund A	Prec Metal	-12.7	-18.67	-10.07	5	5	0.81	1.7	800 328-8300

Stock Fund Name	Objective	Annualized Return for			Rank		Max Load	Expense Ratio	Toll-Free Telephone
		1 Year	3 Years	5 Years	Overall	Risk			
AXP Progressive Fund A	Small Co	-3.7	4.72	10.62	4	3	0.61	0.98	800 328-8300
AXP Research Opportunities Fund A	Growth	5.7	16.34		3	3	0.65	1.12	800 328-8300
AXP Research Opportunities Fund B	Growth	4.9	15.45		3	3	0.65	1.86	800 328-8300
AXP Research Opportunities Y	Growth	5.8	16.48		3	3	0.65	1.04	800 328-8300
AXP Small Company Index Fund A	Small Co	13.2	8.85		4	3	0	0.98	800 328-8300
AXP Small Company Index Fund B	Small Co	12.5	8.05		4	3	0	1.76	800 328-8300
AXP Small Company Index Y	Small Co	13.5	8.94		4	3	0	0.86	800 328-8300
AXP Stock Fund A	Growth/Inc	7.2	13.98	17.41	3	2	0.46	0.85	800 328-8300
AXP Strategist Total Return Fund	Growth/Inc	4.6	7.64		4	2	0.48	1.28	800 328-8300
AXP Strategy Aggressive Fund Y	Agg Growth	27.7	16.5	15.05	4	5	0.58	0.91	800 328-8300
AXP Strategy-Aggressive Growth A	Agg Growth	27.2	16.26	14.83	4	5	0.58	1.05	800 328-8300
AXP Strategy-Aggressive Growth B	Agg Growth	56.8	32.79	26.83	3	5	0.58	1.81	800 328-8300
AXP Utilities Fund A	Utilities	1.5	16.12	17.32	3	2	0.58	1.04	800 328-8300
Accessor Fd-Growth Portf Adv	Growth	16.2	26.66	26.95	2	3	0.66	0.96	800 759-3504
Accessor Fd-International Equity	Foreign	17.8	13.8	16.24	3	3	1.14	1.37	800 759-3504
Accessor Fd-Small-Mid Cap Port	Growth	14.4	20.15	23.15	3	4	0.92	1.25	800 759-3504
Accessor Fd-Value & Inc Portf	Income	-11.7	8.72	16.04	4	3	0.75	0.96	800 759-3504
Achievement Balanced Fund Retail B	Balanced	8.1					0.51	1.89	800 472-0577
Achievement Balanced Inst	Balanced	9.1	12.47	14.07	3	2	0.51	0.9	800 472-0577
Achievement Balanced Ret	Balanced	8.9	12.28	13.82	3	2	0.51	1.14	800 472-0577
Achievement Equity Fund Retail B	Growth	12.9					0.51	1.89	800 472-0577
Achievement Equity Inst	Growth	14.1	17.09	19.92	3	3	0.51	0.9	800 472-0577
Achievement Equity Ret	Growth	13.8	16.73	18.24	3	3	0.51	1.14	800 472-0577
Acorn Foreign Forty Fund	Foreign	51.4					0.94	1.54	800 922-6769
Acorn Fund	Small Co	17.8	16.32	18.27	3	3	0.75	0.84	800 922-6769
Acorn International Fund	Foreign	47.6	22.58	20.62	2	4	0.81	1.11	800 922-6769
Acorn Twenty Fund	Growth	9.8					0.9	1.37	800 922-6769
Acorn USA	Small Co	-4.6	8.11		3	3	0.94	1.17	800 922-6769
Activa Growth Fund	Growth						0.68		800 346-2670
Activa International Fund	Foreign						0.84		800 346-2670
Activa Value Fund A	Growth	-18.3	2.76	11.81	3	3	0.55	0.5	800 346-2670
Advantus Cornerstone Fund A	Growth	-12.1	-0.45	11.34	5	2	0.69	1.25	800 665-6005
Advantus Cornerstone Fund B	Growth	-12.8	-1.26	10.49	5	2	0.69	1.96	800 665-6005
Advantus Cornerstone Fund C	Growth	-12.7	-1.25	10.45	5	2	0.69	1.96	800 665-6005
Advantus Enterprise Fund A	Small Co	40.3	15.12	13.5	4	5	0.8	1.33	800 665-6005
Advantus Enterprise Fund B	Small Co	39.1	14.13	13.36	4	5	0.8	2.18	800 665-6005
Advantus Enterprise Fund C	Small Co	39.1	14.14	13.35	4	5	0.8	2.18	800 665-6005
Advantus Horizon Fund A	Growth	19.8	23.47	23.32	2	3	0.8	1.37	800 665-6005
Advantus Horizon Fund B	Growth	18.9	22.74	22.55	2	3	0.8	2.02	800 665-6005
Advantus Horizon Fund C	Growth	18.7	22.92	22.62	2	3	0.8	2.02	800 665-6005
Advantus Index 500 Fund A	Growth/Inc	6	18.39		2	3	0.34	0.75	800 665-6005
Advantus Index 500 Fund B	Growth/Inc	5.1	17.41		2	3	0.34	1.6	800 665-6005
Advantus Index 500 Fund C	Growth/Inc	5.1	17.37		2	3	0.34	1.6	800 665-6005
Advantus International Balanced A	Balanced	11	5.96	9.42	4	2	0.85	1.7	800 665-6005
Advantus International Balanced C	Balanced	9.8	5.01	8.53	4	2	0.85	2.52	800 665-6005
Advantus Real Estate Securities A	Real Est	4.5					0.75	1.5	800 665-6005
Advantus Spectrum Fund A	AssetAlloc	14.7	16.31	16.05	3	2	0.59	1.1	800 665-6005
Advantus Spectrum Fund B	AssetAlloc	13.8	15.52	15.31	3	2	0.59	1.81	800 665-6005
Advantus Spectrum Fund C	AssetAlloc	13.8	15.58	15.3	3	2	0.59	1.81	800 665-6005
Advantus Venture Fund A	Growth	0.1	3.37		5	3	0.8	1.39	800 665-6005
Advantus Venture Fund B	Growth	-0.7	2.4		5	3	0.8	2.25	800 665-6005
Advantus Venture Fund C	Growth	-0.7	2.5		5	3	0.8	2.25	800 665-6005
Aetna Ascent A	AssetAlloc	6.7	8.54		3	2	0.8	1.44	800 238-6263
Aetna Ascent B	AssetAlloc	6					0.8	2.2	800 238-6263
Aetna Ascent C	AssetAlloc	5.9					0.8	2.18	800 238-6263
Aetna Ascent I	AssetAlloc	7.5	9.08	14.79	3	2	0.8	1.19	800 238-6263
Aetna Balanced A	Balanced	8.8	13.65	15.25	3	1	0.8	1.37	800 238-6263
Aetna Balanced B	Balanced	8.4					0.8	2.14	800 238-6263

Stock Fund Name	Objective	Annualized Return for			Rank		Max Load	Expense Ratio	Toll-Free Telephone
		1 Year	3 Years	5 Years	Overall	Risk			
Aetna Balanced C	Balanced	8.4					0.8	2.1	800 238-6263
Aetna Balanced I	Balanced	9.7	14.2	15.91	2	1	0.8	1.11	800 238-6263
Aetna Crossroads B	AssetAlloc	4.3					0.8	2.2	800 238-6263
Aetna Crossroads C	AssetAlloc	4.2					0.8	2.2	800 238-6263
Aetna Crossroads Fund A	AssetAlloc	5.2	6.95		3	1	0.8	1.44	800 238-6263
Aetna Crossroads I	AssetAlloc	5.6	7.32	12.1	3	1	0.8	1.19	800 238-6263
Aetna Growth & Income A	Growth/Inc	5.4	13.72	19.89	3	3	0.66	1.12	800 238-6263
Aetna Growth & Income B	Growth/Inc	3.6					0.66	1.87	800 238-6263
Aetna Growth & Income C	Growth/Inc	3.6					0.66	1.87	800 238-6263
Aetna Growth & Income I	Growth/Inc	5.7	14.11	20.56	3	3	0.66	0.85	800 238-6263
Aetna Growth Fund A	Growth	28.3	28.77	27	1	3	0.69	1.19	800 238-6263
Aetna Growth Fund B	Growth	26.2					0.69	1.91	800 238-6263
Aetna Growth Fund C	Growth	26.1					0.69	1.93	800 238-6263
Aetna Growth Fund I	Growth	28.7	29.21	27.63	1	3	0.69	0.93	800 238-6263
Aetna Index Plus Large Cap B	Growth	9.2					0.45	1.66	800 238-6263
Aetna Index Plus Large Cap C	Growth	9.5					0.45	1.43	800 238-6263
Aetna Index Plus Mid Cap A	Growth	7.8					0.25	1	800 238-6263
Aetna Index Plus Mid Cap B	Growth	7.2					0.25	1.73	800 238-6263
Aetna Index Plus Mid Cap C	Growth	7.2					0.25	1.47	800 238-6263
Aetna Index Plus Mid Cap I	Growth	8.1					0.25	0.75	800 238-6263
Aetna Index Plus Small Cap A	Small Co	7.6					0.25	1	800 238-6263
Aetna Index Plus Small Cap B	Small Co	6.9					0.25	1.73	800 238-6263
Aetna Index Plus Small Cap C	Small Co	7.1					0.25	1.5	800 238-6263
Aetna Index Plus Small Cap I	Small Co	8					0.25	0.75	800 238-6263
Aetna International A	Foreign	38.5	21.11	22.24	2	3	0.63	1.61	800 238-6263
Aetna International B	Foreign	36.5					0.63	2.35	800 238-6263
Aetna International C	Foreign	36.2					0.63	2.35	800 238-6263
Aetna International I	Foreign	38.7	21.33	22.72	2	3	0.63	1.35	800 238-6263
Aetna Legacy A	AssetAlloc	6	6.92		3	1	0.8	1.44	800 238-6263
Aetna Legacy B	AssetAlloc	5.2					0.8	2.2	800 238-6263
Aetna Legacy C	AssetAlloc	5.2					0.8	2.2	800 238-6263
Aetna Legacy I	AssetAlloc	6.3	7.24	10.47	3	1	0.8	1.19	800 238-6263
Aetna Mid Cap A	Growth	19.5					0.65	1.39	800 238-6263
Aetna Mid Cap B	Growth	18.7					0.65	2.14	800 238-6263
Aetna Mid Cap C	Growth	18.7					0.65	2.14	800 238-6263
Aetna Mid Cap I	Growth	19.7					0.65	1.14	800 238-6263
Aetna Real Estate Sec A	Real Est	-2.4					0.8	1.55	800 238-6263
Aetna Real Estate Sec B	Real Est	-2.8					0.8	2.29	800 238-6263
Aetna Real Estate Sec C	Real Est	-3.2					0.8	2.29	800 238-6263
Aetna Real Estate Sec I	Real Est	-3.1					0.8	1.3	800 238-6263
Aetna Small Company A	Small Co	42.7	21.95	22.95	3	4	0.67	1.22	800 238-6263
Aetna Small Company B	Small Co	40.9					0.67	2.22	800 238-6263
Aetna Small Company C	Small Co	40.9					0.67	2.22	800 238-6263
Aetna Small Company I	Small Co	43	22.38	23.55	3	4	0.67	1.22	800 238-6263
Aetna Value Opportunity A	Growth	12					0.59	1.35	800 238-6263
Aetna Value Opportunity B	Growth	11.1					0.59	2.1	800 238-6263
Aetna Value Opportunity C	Growth	11.2					0.59	2.1	800 238-6263
Aetna Value Opportunity I	Growth	12.2					0.59	1.1	800 238-6263
Al Frank Fund (The)	Growth	42.4					1	2.25	888 263-6443
Alger Fund-Balanced Port A	Balanced	16.4	23.57		2	2	0.75	1.51	800 992-3863
Alger Fund-Balanced Port B	Balanced	15.5	22.67	19.24	2	2	0.75	2.18	800 992-3863
Alger Fund-Balanced Port C	Balanced	15.5					0.75	2.27	800 992-3863
Alger Fund-Capital App Port A	Growth	35.8	34.6		1	4	0.84	1.31	800 992-3863
Alger Fund-Capital App Port B	Growth	35	33.67	30.66	2	4	0.84	2.12	800 992-3863
Alger Fund-Capital App Port C	Growth	34.9					0.84	2.08	800 992-3863
Alger Fund-Capital App Retirement	Agg Growth	36.1	47.52	34.98	1	4	0.84		800 992-3863
Alger Fund-Growth Port A	Growth	18.9	29.04		1	3	0.75	1.19	800 992-3863
Alger Fund-Growth Port B	Growth	18	28.08	24.52	2	3	0.75	1.95	800 992-3863

Stock Fund Name	Objective	Annualized Return for			Rank		Max Load	Expense Ratio	Toll-Free Telephone
		1 Year	3 Years	5 Years	Overall	Risk			
Alger Fund-Growth Port C	Growth	18					0.75	1.95	800 992-3863
Alger Fund-Growth Retirement Port	Growth	20	31.43	26.82	1	3	0.75	1.07	800 992-3863
Alger Fund-MidCap Gr Port A	Growth	38.8	31.03		1	4	0.8	1.3	800 992-3863
Alger Fund-MidCap Gr Port B	Growth	37.6	30.02	24.6	2	4	0.8	2.06	800 992-3863
Alger Fund-MidCap Gr Port C	Growth	37.6					0.8	2.08	800 992-3863
Alger Fund-MidCap Gr Retirement	Growth	43.5	37.67	30.74	1	4	0.8	1.22	800 992-3863
Alger Fund-Small Cap Port A	Small Co	15.9	16		3	4	0.84	1.35	800 992-3863
Alger Fund-Small Cap Port B	Small Co	15	15.23	12.72	4	4	0.84	2.14	800 992-3863
Alger Fund-Small Cap Port C	Small Co	15.1					0.84	2.1	800 992-3863
Alger Fund-Small Cap Retirement	Small Co	27.5	28.18	23.88	3	4	0.84	1.02	800 992-3863
Alger Fund-Spectra	Agg Growth	31.8	35.37	30.51	2	4	1.5	1.83	800 711-6141
Alleghany/Blairlogie Emrg Mkt I	Foreign	11.9	-3.31	1.53	5	4	0.52	1.42	800 992-3863
Alleghany/Blairlogie Emrg Mkt N	Foreign	11.6	-3.6	1.24	5	4	0.52	1.67	800 992-3863
Alleghany/Blairlogie Intl Dev I	Foreign	12.6	8.98	11.03	5	3	0.84	1.15	800 992-3863
Alleghany/Blairlogie Intl Dev N	Foreign	11.7	8.45	10.59	5	3	0.84	1.4	800 992-3863
Alleghany/Chicago Trust Bal Fd	Balanced	7.7	15.82		2	1	0.69	1.06	800 992-8151
Alleghany/Chicago Trust Gr & Inc	Growth/Inc	10.5	21.97	25.54	2	3	0.69	1.06	800 992-8151
Alleghany/Chicago Trust Sm Cap Val	Small Co	0.2					1	1.39	800 992-8151
Alleghany/Chicago Trust Talon Fd	Growth	21.9	10.74	17.05	3	3	0.8	1.3	800 992-8151
Alleghany/Montag + Caldwell Bal	Balanced	6.9	14.57	17.58	2	1	0.75	1.25	800 992-8151
Alleghany/Montag + Caldwell Gr Fd	Growth	7.8	19.48	25.04	3	3	0.72	1.05	800 992-8151
Alleghany/Veredus Aggressive Gr Fd	Agg Growth	82.9					1	1.41	800 992-8151
Alliance All-Asia Investment A	Pacific	47.9	6.49	4.82	4	4	1	3.02	800 221-5672
Alliance All-Asia Investment Adv	Pacific	47.9	6.75		3	4	1	2.74	800 221-5672
Alliance All-Asia Investment B	Pacific	46.5	5.64	4.04	4	4	1	3.47	800 221-5672
Alliance All-Asia Investment C	Pacific	46.7	5.72	4.07	4	4	1	3.72	800 221-5672
Alliance Balanced Shares A	Balanced	2.6	13.24	14.08	3	2	0.58	1.12	800 221-5672
Alliance Balanced Shares Adv	Balanced	2.9	13.53		3	2	0.58	0.96	800 221-5672
Alliance Balanced Shares B	Balanced	1.9	12.39	13.02	3	2	0.58	1.98	800 221-5672
Alliance Balanced Shares C	Balanced	2	12.43	13.06	3	2	0.58	1.95	800 221-5672
Alliance Conservative Invest A	Balanced	5.1	8.76	9.25	3	1	0.75	1.39	800 221-5672
Alliance Conservative Invest B	Balanced	4.3	8	8.49	3	1	0.75	2.1	800 221-5672
Alliance Conservative Invest C	Balanced	4.3	8	8.48	3	1	0.75	2.1	800 221-5672
Alliance Fund A	Growth	-0.3	10.71	15.35	4	4	0.68	1.06	800 221-5672
Alliance Fund Adv	Growth	-0.3	10.96		5	4	0.68	0.86	800 221-5672
Alliance Fund B	Growth	-1.2	9.8	14.38	5	4	0.68	1.89	800 221-5672
Alliance Fund C	Growth	-1.3	9.67	14.29	5	4	0.68	1.87	800 221-5672
Alliance Global Environment Fd A	Global	3.2	8.68	15.83	4	4	1.1	4.12	800 221-5672
Alliance Global Environment Fd Adv	Global	3.5					1.1	3.72	800 221-5672
Alliance Global Environment Fd B	Global	2.5					1.1	4.78	800 221-5672
Alliance Global Environment Fd C	Global	2.4					1.1	4.61	800 221-5672
Alliance Global Small Cap A	Global	40.6	16.43	19.41	3	3	1	2.12	800 221-5672
Alliance Global Small Cap Adv	Global	41	16.75		3	3	1	2.12	800 221-5672
Alliance Global Small Cap B	Global	39.4	15.55	18.53	3	3	1	3.14	800 221-5672
Alliance Global Small Cap C	Global	39.5	15.52	18.54	3	3	1	3.14	800 221-5672
Alliance Greater China 97 Fund A	Pacific	14.6					1	2.52	800 221-5672
Alliance Greater China 97 Fund Adv	Pacific	14.7					1	2.22	800 221-5672
Alliance Greater China 97 Fund B	Pacific	13.5					1	3.22	800 221-5672
Alliance Greater China 97 Fund C	Pacific	13.5					1	3.22	800 221-5672
Alliance Growth Fund A	Growth	8.6	20.7	21.95	3	3	0.68	1.17	800 221-5672
Alliance Growth Fund Adv	Growth	9	21.07		3	3	0.68	0.88	800 221-5672
Alliance Growth Fund B	Growth	7.8	19.85	21.1	3	3	0.68	1.89	800 221-5672
Alliance Growth Fund C	Growth	7.8	19.86	21.1	3	3	0.68	1.88	800 221-5672
Alliance Growth Investors Fd A	Growth/Inc	9.9	14.6	15.25	3	2	0.75	1.56	800 221-5672
Alliance Growth Investors Fd B	Growth/Inc	9.2	13.8	14.44	3	2	0.75	2.29	800 221-5672
Alliance Growth Investors Fd C	Growth/Inc	9.2	13.76	14.43	3	2	0.75	2.27	800 221-5672
Alliance Health Care Fund A	Health						0.94		800 221-5672
Alliance Health Care Fund Adv	Health						0.94		800 221-5672

Stock Fund Name	Objective	Annualized Return for			Rank		Max Load	Expense Ratio	Toll-Free Telephone
		1 Year	3 Years	5 Years	Overall	Risk			
Alliance Health Care Fund B	Health						0.94		800 221-5672
Alliance Health Care Fund C	Health						0.94		800 221-5672
Alliance International A	Foreign	29.2	9.83	10.9	4	3	0.94	1.9	800 221-5672
Alliance International Adv	Foreign	29.6	10.15		3	3	0.94	1.69	800 221-5672
Alliance International B	Foreign	28.3	9.04	10.04	4	3	0.94	2.74	800 221-5672
Alliance International C	Foreign	28.3	9	10.02	4	3	0.94	2.64	800 221-5672
Alliance Intl Premier Growth A	Foreign	28.8					1	2.52	800 221-5672
Alliance Intl Premier Growth Adv	Foreign	29.4					1	2.22	800 221-5672
Alliance Intl Premier Growth B	Foreign	28.2					1	3.22	800 221-5672
Alliance Intl Premier Growth C	Foreign	28.1					1	3.22	800 221-5672
Alliance Multi-Market Strategy A	Intl Bond	2	4.39	7.93	2	1	0.59	1.34	800 221-5672
Alliance Multi-Market Strategy B	Intl Bond	1.3	2.33	6.3	3	2	0.59	2.04	800 221-5672
Alliance Multi-Market Strategy C	Intl Bond	1.2	3.54	7.12	3	2	0.59	2.04	800 221-5672
Alliance Muni Income II-FL A	Muni State	0.6	4.16	6.01	3	3	0.62	0.72	800 221-5672
Alliance Muni Income II-FL B	Muni State	-0.1	3.43	5.25	3	3	0.62	1.42	800 221-5672
Alliance Muni Income II-FL C	Muni State	-0.1	3.41	5.27	3	3	0.62	1.42	800 221-5672
Alliance New Europe A	European	21	16.76	17.73	2	3	0.94	1.72	800 221-5672
Alliance New Europe Adv	European	21.3	17.06		2	3	0.94	1.51	800 221-5672
Alliance New Europe B	European	20.1	15.92	16.89	2	3	0.94	2.5	800 221-5672
Alliance New Europe C	European	20.1	15.93	16.9	2	3	0.94	2.5	800 221-5672
Alliance North American Govt A	Intl Bond	12.4	9.34	15.49	2	5	0.72	2.06	800 221-5672
Alliance North American Govt B	Intl Bond	11.6	8.6	14.59	2	5	0.72	2.75	800 221-5672
Alliance North American Govt C	Intl Bond	11.6	8.6	14.59	2	5	0.72	2.75	800 221-5672
Alliance Premier Growth A	Growth	18.2	30.16	29.98	2	4	0.94	1.47	800 221-5672
Alliance Premier Growth Adv	Growth	18.5	30.62		2	4	0.94	1.14	800 221-5672
Alliance Premier Growth B	Growth	17.4	29.31	29.1	2	4	0.94	2.18	800 221-5672
Alliance Premier Growth C	Growth	17.4	29.3	29.1	2	4	0.94	2.16	800 221-5672
Alliance Premier Growth Instl I	Growth	18.3					0.9	1.28	800 221-5672
Alliance Premier Growth Instl II	Growth	17.9					0.9	1.3	800 221-5672
Alliance Quasar Fund A	Small Co	11.1	6.36	17.35	4	4	1.01	1.66	800 221-5672
Alliance Quasar Fund Adv	Small Co	11.3	6.62		5	4	1.01	1.39	800 221-5672
Alliance Quasar Fund B	Small Co	10.2	5.53	16.45	5	4	1.01	2.43	800 221-5672
Alliance Quasar Fund C	Small Co	10.2	5.54	16.44	5	4	1.01	2.43	800 221-5672
Alliance Quasar Instl Fund I	Growth	33.4					1	2.08	800 221-5672
Alliance Quasar Instl Fund II	Growth	33.1					0.9	1.35	800 221-5672
Alliance Real Estate Inv Instl I	Real Est	0.2					0.9	3.54	800 221-5672
Alliance Real Estate Inv Instl II	Real Est	0.3					0.9	1.39	800 221-5672
Alliance Real Estate Invt A	Real Est	2.2	-0.26		4	2	0.9	1.58	800 221-5672
Alliance Real Estate Invt Adv	Real Est	2.6	-0.03		4	2	0.9	1.3	800 221-5672
Alliance Real Estate Invt B	Real Est	1.5	-0.96		5	2	0.9	2.31	800 221-5672
Alliance Real Estate Invt C	Real Est	1.5	-0.96		5	2	0.9	2.31	800 221-5672
Alliance Select Inv Premier Ptf A	Growth	19.1					1.1	2.24	800 221-5672
Alliance Select Inv Premier Ptf B	Growth	18.3					1.1	2.95	800 221-5672
Alliance Select Inv Premier Ptf C	Growth	18.3					1.1	2.93	800 221-5672
Alliance Technology Fund A	Technology	65.9	46.5	33.11	1	4	1.1	1.57	800 221-5672
Alliance Technology Fund Adv	Technology	66.5	46.95		1	4	1.1	1.27	800 221-5672
Alliance Technology Fund B	Technology	64.7	45.46	32.18	1	4	1.1	2.29	800 221-5672
Alliance Technology Fund C	Technology	64.7	45.44	32.17	1	4	1.1	2.27	800 221-5672
Alliance Utility Income Fund A	Utilities	7.8	23.07	18.16	2	2	0.75	1.51	800 221-5672
Alliance Utility Income Fund Adv	Utilities	8.1	23.4		2	2	0.75	1.2	800 221-5672
Alliance Utility Income Fund B	Utilities	7	22.22	17.35	2	2	0.75	2.2	800 221-5672
Alliance Utility Income Fund C	Utilities	7	22.18	17.35	2	2	0.75	2.2	800 221-5672
Alliance WorldWide Privatiztn A	Foreign	24.3	14.22	17.32	3	3	1	1.85	800 221-5672
Alliance WorldWide Privatiztn Adv	Foreign	24.7	14.54		3	3	1	1.62	800 221-5672
Alliance WorldWide Privatiztn B	Foreign	23.5	13.29	16.44	3	3	1	2.62	800 221-5672
Alliance WorldWide Privatiztn C	Foreign	23.4	13.26	16.43	3	3	1	2.62	800 221-5672
Alpine Intl Real Estate A	Real Est	-11.7	1.68	2.05	5	3	1	2.27	888 785-5578
Alpine Intl Real Estate B	Real Est	-12.4	0.96	1.32	5	3	1	3.02	888 785-5578

285

Stock Fund Name	Objective	Annualized Return for			Rank		Max Load	Expense Ratio	Toll-Free Telephone
		1 Year	3 Years	5 Years	Overall	Risk			
Alpine Intl Real Estate Y	Real Est	-11.5	1.9	2.25	5	3	1	2.08	888 785-5578
Alpine Realty Inc & Growth A	Real Est	13.2					1	1.75	888 785-5578
Alpine Realty Inc & Growth B	Real Est	12.9					1	2.47	888 785-5578
Alpine Realty Inc & Growth Y	Real Est	13.4					1	1.47	888 785-5578
Alpine U.S. Real Estate Eq A	Real Est	-13	-2.76	9.54	4	3	1	2.41	888 785-5578
Alpine U.S. Real Estate Eq B	Real Est	-13.6	-3.47	8.77	4	3	1	3.16	888 785-5578
Alpine U.S. Real Estate Eq Y	Real Est	-12.6	-2.48	9.87	4	3	1	2.68	888 785-5578
AmSouth-Balanced Fd A	Balanced	-4.2	7.34	10.21	3	1	0.8	1.35	800 451-8382
AmSouth-Balanced Trust	Balanced	-4	7.54	10.32	3	1	0.8	1.09	800 451-8382
AmSouth-Cap Gr A	Growth	17.1	23.64		2	3	0.8	1.31	800 852-0045
AmSouth-Cap Gr B	Growth	16.4					0.8	1.9	800 852-0045
AmSouth-Cap Gr Tr	Growth	6.5					0.8	0.95	800 451-8382
AmSouth-Equity Income Trust	Growth/Inc	21.7	17.44		2	2	0.8	1.15	800 451-8382
AmSouth-FL T/F Bond Fd A	Muni State	3.3	3.74	4.19	3	3	0.65	0.58	800 451-8382
AmSouth-FL T/F Bond Fd Trust	Muni State	3.4	3.87	4.27	3	3	0.65	0.48	800 451-8382
AmSouth-Intl Eq A	Foreign	14.5					1.25	1.54	800 451-8382
AmSouth-Intl Eq Tr	Foreign	14.6					1.25	1.54	800 451-8382
AmSouth-Large Cap A	Growth/Inc	15.5	24.25	25.64	2	2	0.8	1.04	800 451-8382
AmSouth-Large Cap B	Growth/Inc	14.5					0.8	1.96	800 451-8382
AmSouth-Large Cap Tr	Growth/Inc	15.5					0.8	1.04	800 451-8382
AmSouth-Value Fd A	Growth	-12.4	7.91	13.71	4	3	0.8	1.35	800 451-8382
AmSouth-Value Fd Trust Shares	Growth	-12.4	8.16	13.86	4	3	0.8	1.08	800 451-8382
Amana Mutual Fund Tr-Income	Income	-7.4	7.05	12.54	3	2	0.94	0.69	800 728-8762
Amer Independence Intl Stock Instl	Foreign	15.4	9.9		4	2	1.25	1.37	888 266-8787
Amer Independence Stock Fund Svc	Growth	-13.7	2.59		4	3	1	1.3	888 266-8787
American AAdvant Bal Inst	Balanced	-9	4.21	9.6	3	1	0.28	0.58	800 967-9009
American AAdvant Bal Mileage	Balanced	-9.5	3.8	9.16	3	1	0.28	0.98	800 967-9009
American AAdvant Bal PlanAhead	Balanced	-9.3	3.86	9.27	3	1	0.28	0.91	800 967-9009
American AAdvant Intl Eq Inst	Foreign	15.8	11.05	14.86	3	2	0.4	0.64	800 967-9009
American AAdvant Intl Eq Mileage	Foreign	15.1	10.39	14.07	3	2	0.4	1.47	800 967-9009
American AAdvant Intl Eq PlanAhd	Foreign	15.4	10.78	13.72	3	2	0.4	1.01	800 967-9009
American AAdvant Lg Cp Val Inst	Growth/Inc	-16.7	2.73	11.42	4	3	0.28	0.58	800 967-9009
American AAdvant Lg Cp Val Mileage	Growth/Inc	-17.2	2.3	10.95	4	3	0.28	0.98	800 967-9009
American AAdvant Lg Cp Val PlanAhd	Growth/Inc	-17	2.4	11.07	4	3	0.28	0.9	800 967-9009
American AAdvantage S&P 500 Instl	Growth	6.7	18.99		3	3	0.08	0.17	800 967-9009
American AAdvantage S&P 500 Mlge	Growth	6.4					0.08	0.54	800 967-9009
American AAdvantage S&P 500 Pl Ah	Growth	6.5					0.08	0.53	800 967-9009
American Balanced Fund	Balanced	-2.1	8.33	12.64	3	1	0.28	0.64	800 421-9900
American Century Balanced Adv	Balanced	6.8	11.18		3	1	1	1.25	800 345-2021
American Century Balanced Inv	Balanced	7	11.46	12.89	3	1	1	1	800 345-2021
American Century Emerge Mkt Inv	Foreign	32.8					2	2	800 345-2021
American Century Eq Growth Adv	Growth	9.1					0.68	0.93	800 345-2021
American Century Eq Growth Inst	Growth	9.6					0.68	0.47	800 345-2021
American Century Eq Growth Inv	Growth	9.3	19.95	23.6	3	3	0.68	0.68	800 345-2021
American Century Eq Income Adv	Growth/Inc	-7.5	7.69		3	2	0.8	1.25	800 345-2021
American Century Eq Income Inst	Growth/Inc	-7.3					0.8	0.8	800 345-2021
American Century Eq Income Inv	Growth/Inc	-7.4	8.28	14.54	3	2	0.8	1	800 345-2021
American Century FL Interm Muni	Muni State	4.1	4.72	5.22	1	2	0.51	0.51	800 345-2021
American Century Giftrust	Small Co	99.1	25.09	16.53	3	5	1	1	800 345-2021
American Century Glb Ntrl Res	Energy/Res	7.9	4.05	8.54	5	3	0.68	0.68	800 345-2021
American Century Global Gold Adv	Prec Metal	-11.1					0.68	0.93	800 345-2021
American Century Global Gold Fd	Prec Metal	-10.9	-18.78	-16.4	5	5	0.68	0.68	800 345-2021
American Century Global Growth Adv	Global	60.3					1.3	1.55	800 345-2021
American Century Global Growth Inv	Global	60.6					1.3		800 345-2021
American Century Growth Adv	Growth	29.3	28.93		1	3	1	1.25	800 345-2021
American Century Growth Inst	Growth	29.8	29.49		1	3	1	0.8	800 345-2021
American Century Growth Inv	Growth	29.6	29.24	24.23	1	3	1	1	800 345-2021
American Century Heritage Adv	Growth	51.9					1	1.25	800 345-2021

286

Stock Fund Name	Objective	Annualized Return for			Rank		Max Load	Expense Ratio	Toll-Free Telephone
		1 Year	3 Years	5 Years	Overall	Risk			
American Century Heritage Inst	Growth	52.7	21.43		3	4	1	0.8	800 345-2021
American Century Heritage Inv	Growth	52.4	21.41	20.36	3	4	1	1	800 345-2021
American Century Inc & Gr Adv	Growth/Inc	3.4					0.68	0.93	800 345-2021
American Century Inc & Gr Inst	Growth/Inc	3.9					0.68	0.47	800 345-2021
American Century Inc & Gr Inv	Growth/Inc	3.8	18.33	22.73	3	3	0.68	0.7	800 345-2021
American Century Intl Bond Adv	Intl Bond	-8.8					0.83	1.11	800 345-2021
American Century Intl Bond Inv	Intl Bond	-2.6	1.05	2.6	5	5	0.83	0.85	800 345-2021
American Century Intl Disc Adv	Foreign	59.5					1.3	1.84	800 345-2021
American Century Intl Disc Inst	Foreign	59.9					1.3	1.59	800 345-2021
American Century Intl Disc Inv	Foreign	59.5	31.03	30.15	2	4	1.3	1.55	800 345-2021
American Century Intl Gr Adv	Foreign	45.5	22.7		1	4	1.02	1.53	800 345-2021
American Century Intl Gr Inst	Foreign	46.5					1.02	1.28	800 345-2021
American Century Intl Gr Inv	Foreign	46.1	22.97	22.77	2	4	1.02	1.08	800 345-2021
American Century New Opp	Small Co	151.5	53.69		2	5	1.5	1.5	800 345-2021
American Century Real Estate Adv	Real Est	1.7					1.19	1.44	800 345-2021
American Century Real Estate Inst	Real Est	2.1	1.23		4	2	1.19	1	800 345-2021
American Century Real Estate Inv	Real Est	1.8	0.82		4	2	1.19	1.19	800 345-2021
American Century SC Quant Inv	Growth	18.7					0.88	0.88	800 345-2021
American Century SC Value Instl	Growth	2.9					1.25	1.05	800 345-2021
American Century SC Value Inv	Growth	2.6					1.25	1.25	800 345-2021
American Century Select Adv	Growth	12					1	1.25	800 345-2021
American Century Select Inst	Growth	12.2	22.85		2	3	1	0.8	800 345-2021
American Century Select Inv	Growth	12.1	22.63	23.05	2	3	1	1	800 345-2021
American Century Str Alloc:Agg Adv	AssetAlloc	27.3	18.29		1	2	1.19	1.44	800 345-2021
American Century Str Alloc:Agg Inv	AssetAlloc	27.5	18.55		1	2	1.19	1.19	800 345-2021
American Century Str Alloc:Con Adv	AssetAlloc	7.9	9.37		3	1	1	1.25	800 345-2021
American Century Str Alloc:Con Inv	AssetAlloc	8.2	9.63		3	1	1	1	800 345-2021
American Century Str Alloc:Mod Adv	AssetAlloc	17	14.13		3	1	1.1	1.35	800 345-2021
American Century Str Alloc:Mod Inv	AssetAlloc	17.3	14.41		3	1	1.1	1.1	800 345-2021
American Century Ultra Adv	Agg Growth	20.9	24.4		2	4	1	1.25	800 345-2021
American Century Ultra Inst	Agg Growth	21	24.82		2	4	1	0.8	800 345-2021
American Century Ultra Inv	Agg Growth	21	24.63	23.99	2	4	1	1	800 345-2021
American Century Utilities Adv	Utilities	2.9					0.68	0.93	800 345-2021
American Century Value Adv	Growth	-15.8	3.43		5	3	1	1.25	800 345-2021
American Century Value Inst	Growth	-15.5					1	0.8	800 345-2021
American Century Value Inv	Growth	-15.7	3.69	11.87	4	3	1	1	800 345-2021
American Century Vista Adv	Agg Growth	99.3	25.95		3	5	1	1.25	800 345-2021
American Century Vista Inst	Agg Growth	99.1	26.33		3	5	1	0.8	800 345-2021
American Century Vista Inv	Agg Growth	99.2	26.15	18.6	3	5	1	1	800 345-2021
American Growth Fund A	Growth	2.9	3.29		5	3	0.81	2.06	800 525-2406
American Growth Fund B	Growth	2.2	2.54		5	3	0.81	2.81	800 525-2406
American Growth Fund C	Growth	2.1	2.5		5	3	0.81	2.97	800 525-2406
American Growth Fund D	Growth	3.4	3.58	7.87	5	3	0.81	1.94	800 525-2406
American Heritage Fund	Agg Growth	42.3	-28.2	-10.65	4	5	1	8.88	800 828-5050
American Performance Equity Fund	Growth	5.2	12.94	19.49	3	3	0.5	1.27	800 762-7085
Amerindo Technology A	Technology	16.2					1.5	2.64	888 TECHFUND
Amerindo Technology D	Technology	16.6	70.83		2	5	1.5	2.43	888 TECHFUND
Ameristock Mutual Fund	Growth/Inc	-8.7	14.14		2	3	1	0.93	800 394-5064
Analysts Internet Fund	Technology	21.9					0.75		
Anchor International Bond Trust	Intl Bond	0.7	-0.84	-3.2	4	5	0.75	1.23	
Aon Asset Allocation Fund	Flexible	11	12.79	16.08	3	2	0.25	0.35	800 266-3637
Aon REIT Index Fund	Real Est	3.3	0.4		4	2	0.59	0.26	800 266-3637
Apex Mid-Cap Growth Fund	Agg Growth	-23.7	4.4	-3.87	5	5	1	1.18	800 446-2987
Aquila Cascadia Equity A	Growth	18.9	14.55		3	3	1.5	1.91	800 228-4227
Aquila Cascadia Equity C	Growth	18	13.65		3	3	1.5	2.64	800 228-4227
Aquila Cascadia Equity Y	Growth	19.2	14.79		3	3	1.5	1.65	800 228-4227
Aquila Rocky Mountain Equity A	Growth	11	11.81	13.37	3	3	1.5	1.29	800 228-4227
Aquila Rocky Mountain Equity C	Growth	10.3	10.97		4	3	1.5	2.04	800 228-4227

287

Stock Fund Name	Objective	Annualized Return for			Rank		Max Load	Expense Ratio	Toll-Free Telephone
		1 Year	3 Years	5 Years	Overall	Risk			
Aquila Rocky Mountain Equity Y	Growth	11.4	11.97		3	3	1.5	1.04	800 228-4227
Aquila Tax-Free Fd For Utah A	Muni State	0.5	3.3	4.94	4	4	0.5	0.45	800 228-4227
Aquila Tax-Free Fd For Utah C	Muni State	-0.2	2.31		4	4	0.5	1.44	800 228-4227
Aquila Tax-Free Fd For Utah Y	Muni State	0.8	3.35		4	4	0.5	0.42	800 228-4227
Aquinas Balanced Fund	Balanced	1.3	8.28	11.49	3	1	1	1.5	800 423-6369
Aquinas Equity Growth Fund	Growth	24.1	22.36	23.41	1	3	1	1.4	800 423-6369
Aquinas Equity Income Fund	Income	-13.5	3.81	11.62	3	3	1	1.36	800 423-6369
Arbor Golden Oak Growth A	Agg Growth	33.8	34.39	27.4	1	3	0.73	1.32	800 545-6331
Arbor Golden Oak Growth I	Agg Growth	34.3	36.12	28.51	1	3	0.73	1.06	800 545-6331
Arbor Golden Oak Value A	Growth	-2.4	4.92		5	3	0.73	1.35	800 545-6331
Arbor Golden Oak Value I	Growth	-2	5.25		5	3	0.73	1.1	800 545-6331
Ariel Appreciation Fund	Growth	-9.9	11.83	17.55	3	3	0.75	1.29	800 292-7435
Ariel Fund	Small Co	1.2	10.59	16.03	3	3	0.65	1.23	800 292-7435
Ark Fds-Balanced Inst	Balanced	19.9	20.6	18.58	2	2	0.65	0.84	888 427-5386
Ark Fds-Balanced Retail A	Balanced	19.7	20.38	18.32	2	2	0.65	1.01	888 427-5386
Ark Fds-Balanced Retail B	Balanced	18.8					0.65	1.75	888 427-5386
Ark Fds-Blue Chip Equity Inst	Growth	16.7	22.2		1	2	0.59	0.91	888 427-5386
Ark Fds-Blue Chip Equity Retail A	Growth	16.5	22		1	2	0.59	1.08	888 427-5386
Ark Fds-Blue Chip Equity Retail B	Growth	15.7					0.59	1.84	888 427-5386
Ark Fds-Capital Growth Inst	Growth	41.8	35.65	29.7	1	3	0.65	1	888 427-5386
Ark Fds-Capital Growth Retail A	Growth	41.7	35.46	29.5	1	3	0.65	1.09	888 427-5386
Ark Fds-Capital Growth Retail B	Growth	40.6					0.65	1.87	888 427-5386
Ark Fds-Equity Income Inst	Income	4.6	10.55		3	2	0.59	0.95	888 427-5386
Ark Fds-Equity Income Retail A	Income	4.5	10.35		3	2	0.59	1.08	888 427-5386
Ark Fds-Equity Index Inst	Growth	7.5					0.2	0.23	888 427-5386
Ark Fds-Equity Index Retail A	Growth	7.2					0.13	0.5	888 427-5386
Ark Fds-Intl Eq Selection A	Foreign	32.1					0.55	0.88	888 427-5386
Ark Fds-Intl Eq Selection Inst	Foreign	32.7					0.55	0.88	888 427-5386
Ark Fds-Mid Cap Equity Inst	Growth	32.3	26.18		1	4	0.69	1.1	888 427-5386
Ark Fds-Small Cap Equity Inst	Small Co	107.8	47.25		2	5	0.59	1.15	888 427-5386
Ark Fds-Small Cap Equity Retail A	Small Co	107.6	47.09		2	5	0.59	1.32	888 427-5386
Ark Fds-Value Equity A	Growth/Inc	7					0.86	0.28	888 427-5386
Ark Fds-Value Equity B	Growth/Inc	6.2					0.86	0.47	888 427-5386
Ark Fds-Value Equity Inst	Growth/Inc	7.1					0.86	1.18	888 427-5386
Armada Balanced Allocation A	Balanced	0.3					0.75	1.31	800 622-3863
Armada Balanced Allocation B	Balanced	-0.4					0.75	2.02	800 622-3863
Armada Balanced Allocation C	Balanced						0.75		800 622-3863
Armada Balanced Allocation Instl	Balanced	0.4					0.75	1.06	800 622-3863
Armada Core Equity A	Growth	5.2					0.75	1.22	800 622-3863
Armada Core Equity B	Growth	4.7					0.75	1.93	800 622-3863
Armada Core Equity C	Growth						0.75		800 622-3863
Armada Core Equity Inst	Growth	5.6					0.75	0.97	800 622-3863
Armada Equity Growth A	Growth	14.5	21.62	24.08	2	3	0.75	1.16	800 622-3863
Armada Equity Growth B	Growth	14					0.75	1.87	800 622-3863
Armada Equity Growth C	Growth						0.75		800 622-3863
Armada Equity Growth Inst	Growth	14.8	21.98	24.32	2	3	0.75	0.9	800 622-3863
Armada Equity Income A	Income	-16.2	4.15	11.81	4	3	0.75	1.17	800 622-3863
Armada Equity Income B	Income	-16.5					0.75	1.88	800 622-3863
Armada Equity Income C	Income						0.75		800 622-3863
Armada Equity Income Inst	Income	-15.9	4.63	12.12	4	3	0.75	0.96	800 622-3863
Armada Equity Index A	Growth/Inc	6.6					0.34	0.35	800 622-3863
Armada Equity Index B	Growth/Inc						0.34		800 622-3863
Armada Equity Index C	Growth/Inc						0.34		800 622-3863
Armada Equity Index Inst	Growth/Inc	6.8					0.34	0.2	800 622-3863
Armada International Equity A	Foreign	34.7					1.14	1.67	800 622-3863
Armada International Equity B	Foreign	25.1					1.14	2.43	800 622-3863
Armada International Equity C	Foreign						1.14		800 622-3863
Armada International Equity Instl	Foreign	35					1.14	1.42	800 622-3863

Stock Fund Name	Objective	Annualized Return for			Rank		Max Load	Expense Ratio	Toll-Free Telephone
		1 Year	3 Years	5 Years	Overall	Risk			
Armada Small Cap Growth A	Growth	52.1					1	1.51	800 622-3863
Armada Small Cap Growth B	Growth	42.9					1		800 622-3863
Armada Small Cap Growth C	Growth						1		800 622-3863
Armada Small Cap Growth Inst	Growth	52.5					1	1.27	800 622-3863
Armada Small Cap Value B	Growth/Inc	9.4					1	2.08	800 622-3863
Armada Small Cap Value C	Growth/Inc						1		800 622-3863
Armada Small Cap Value Inst	Growth/Inc	10.4	7.62	14.19	3	3	1	1.12	800 622-3863
Armada Tax Managed Equity A	Growth/Inc	14.7					0.75	1.09	800 622-3863
Armada Tax Managed Equity B	Growth/Inc	13.8					0.75	1.79	800 622-3863
Armada Tax Managed Equity C	Growth/Inc						0.75		800 622-3863
Armada Tax Managed Equity I	Growth/Inc	14.8					0.75	0.82	800 622-3863
Armstrong Associates	Growth	20.4	16.61	15.81	3	3	0.8	1.19	
Artisan International Fund	Foreign	65.6	34.13		1	4	0.98	1.27	800 344-1770
Artisan Mid Cap Fund	Growth	72.9	50.8		1	4	1	2	800 344-1770
Artisan Small Cap Fund	Small Co	32.5	8.03	14.66	3	3	1	1.37	800 344-1770
Artisan Small Cap Value	Small Co	4.2					1	1.65	800 344-1770
Atlas Balanced Fund A	Balanced	-10.9	3.94	9.31	3	1	0.69	1.22	800 933-2852
Atlas Balanced Fund B	Balanced	-11.2	3.47	8.78	3	1	0.69	1.63	800 933-2852
Atlas Emerging Growth Fund A	Foreign	45.2	13.8		4	5	0.8	1.53	800 933-2852
Atlas Emerging Growth Fund B	Foreign	44.2	13.06		4	5	0.8	2.1	800 933-2852
Atlas Global Growth Fund A	Global	52.3	27.78		1	3	0.8	1.55	800 933-2852
Atlas Global Growth Fund B	Global	51.7	27.14		1	3	0.8	2.04	800 933-2852
Atlas Growth & Income Fund A	Growth/Inc	21.9	25.29	26.27	1	2	0.64	1.05	800 933-2852
Atlas Growth & Income Fund B	Growth/Inc	21.3	24.62	24.3	1	2	0.64	1.4	800 933-2852
Atlas Strategic Growth Fund A	Growth	46	24.9	24	2	3	0.69	1.17	800 933-2852
Atlas Strategic Growth Fund B	Growth	45.2	24.38	21.97	2	3	0.69	1.65	800 933-2852
Avondale Hester Total Return Fund	Growth/Inc	11.7	16.51	16.03	2	2	0.69	1.52	800 998-3190
BB&K Diversa	AssetAlloc	-0.2	6.95	9.75	4	1	0.94	1.94	800 882-8383
BB&K International Equity	Foreign	14.7	10.11	11.92	4	3	0.94	1.57	800 882-8383
BB&T Balanced Inv	Balanced	-5.4	7.12	10.54	3	1	0.5	1.15	800 228-1872
BB&T Balanced Tr	Balanced	-5.1	7.4	10.82	3	1	0.5	0.91	800 228-1872
BB&T Capital Manager Conserv Inv	Growth	5.8					0.05	0.41	800 228-1872
BB&T Capital Manager Conserv Tr	Growth	6.5					0.05	0.65	800 228-1872
BB&T Capital Manager Growth Tr	Growth	9.8					0.05	0.48	800 228-1872
BB&T Capital Manager Mod Gr Tr	Growth	8.9					0.05	0.46	800 228-1872
BB&T Cptl Mngr Growth Inv A	Growth	-2.5					0.05	0.7	800 228-1872
BB&T Cptl Mngr Moderate Growth A	Growth	5.3					0.05	0.71	800 228-1872
BB&T Growth & Inc Stock Tr	Growth/Inc	-10.7	7.2	14.74	3	2	0.73	0.84	800 228-1872
BB&T International Equity B	Foreign	18.6	9.14		2	3	1	2.54	800 228-1872
BB&T International Equity Tr	Foreign	19.4	10.14		2	3	1	1.55	800 228-1872
BB&T Large Company Growth A	Growth	31.3					0.5	1.25	800 228-1872
BB&T Large Company Growth B	Growth	30.6					0.5	1.98	800 228-1872
BB&T Large Company Growth Tr	Growth	32.5					0.5	1.01	800 228-1872
BB&T SC Interm Tax Free A	Muni State	2.8					0.5	0.95	800 228-1872
BB&T SC Interm Tax Free Tr	Muni State	2.9					0.5	0.81	800 228-1872
BB&T Small Company Growth B	Small Co	64.3	25.97		3	5	1	2.56	800 228-1872
BB&T Small Company Growth Inv	Small Co	65.4	26.25	24.68	3	5	1	1.82	800 228-1872
BB&T Small Company Growth Tr	Small Co	66	27.23	25.47	3	5	1	1.57	800 228-1872
BIA Growth Equity Fund	Growth						0.75		800 540-6807
BIA Small-Cap Growth Fund	Small Co						1		800 540-6807
BJB Global Income A	Intl Bond	0.9	3.54	3.9	5	3	0.65	1.32	800 435-4659
BJB International Equity A	Foreign	59.5	30.55	26.18	2	4	1	1.36	800 435-4659
BNY Hamilton Equity Income Inst	Income	11.7	14.57		3	2	0.8	0.91	800-426-9363
BNY Hamilton Equity Income Inv	Income	11.5	14.28	17.91	2	2	0.8	1.14	800-426-9363
BNY Hamilton Intl Equity Inst	Foreign	22.2	12.72		3	3	1.05	1.27	800-426-9363
BNY Hamilton Intl Equity Inv	Foreign	22	12.46		3	3	1.05	1.62	800-426-9363
BNY Hamilton Large Cap Gr Inst	Growth	33	27.53		1	3	0.8	0.84	800-426-9363
BNY Hamilton Large Cap Gr Inv	Growth	32.8	27.22		1	3	0.8	1.13	800-426-9363

289

Stock Fund Name	Objective	Annualized Return for			Rank		Max Load	Expense Ratio	Toll-Free Telephone
		1 Year	3 Years	5 Years	Overall	Risk			
BNY Hamilton Small Cap Gr Inst	Small Co	80.4	34.11		1	5	0.94	1.02	800-426-9363
BNY Hamilton Small Cap Gr Inv	Small Co	80.3	33.3		3	5	0.94	1.37	800-426-9363
BT Institutional-EAFE Eq. Index	European	17.4	10.16		3	2	0.25	0.4	800 368-4031
BT Institutional-Equity 500 Index	Growth	7.1	19.56	23.66	2	3	0.65	0.1	800 368-4031
BT Institutional-Small Cap Index	Small Co	13.7	10.04		4	4	0.34	0.25	800 368-4031
BT Investment-Lifecycle Lng Range	AssetAlloc	8.1	14.72	16.51	2	1	0.34	1	800 730-1313
BT Investment-Lifecycle Mid Range	AssetAlloc	7.1	11.83	12.98	3	1	0.39	1	800 730-1313
BT Investment-Lifecycle Sh Range	AssetAlloc	5.4	8.53	9.31	3	1	0.42	1	800 730-1313
BT Investment-Small Cap Fund	Small Co	41.2	23.87	20.11	3	4	0.65	1.25	800 730-1313
BT Pyramid-Equity Appreciation	Growth	48.2	32.34	24.74	2	4	0.06	1	800 730-1313
BT Pyramid-Instl Asset Management	AssetAlloc	8.6	15.16	16.99	2	1	0.39	0.59	800 730-1313
BT Pyramid-Inv Equity 500 Index	Growth	6.6	19.28	23.44	2	3	0.07	0.25	800 368-4031
Babson Enterprise Fund-I	Small Co	2.8	2.16	9.97	4	3	1.1	1.13	800 422-2766
Babson Enterprise Fund-II	Growth	5.6	7.68	15.11	4	3	1.19	1.26	800 422-2766
Babson Growth Fund	Growth	20.7	21.87	23.43	2	3	0.78	0.79	800 422-2766
Babson Stewart Ivory Intl	Foreign	22.6	10.65	12.09	3	2	0.94	1.26	800 422-2766
Babson Value Fund	Growth/Inc	-15.9	3.56	11.7	5	3	0.94	0.95	800 422-2766
Barclays Gbl Inv Asset All Fd	AssetAlloc	7.5	17.04	16.6	2	2	0.34	0.75	888 204-3956
Barclays Gbl Inv LifePath 2000 Fd	AssetAlloc	5.7	7.57	8.13	2	1	0.55	0.94	888 204-3956
Barclays Gbl Inv LifePath 2010 Fd	AssetAlloc	6.9	10.95	12.54	3	1	0.55	0.94	888 204-3956
Barclays Gbl Inv LifePath 2020 Fd	AssetAlloc	8	13.9	15.8	3	1	0.55	0.94	888 204-3956
Barclays Gbl Inv LifePath 2030 Fd	AssetAlloc	10.5	16.36	18.44	2	2	0.55	0.94	888 204-3956
Barclays Gbl Inv LifePath 2040 Fd	AssetAlloc	10.4	17.85	20.71	3	3	0.55	0.94	888 204-3956
Barclays Gbl Inv S&P500 Stock Fd	Growth	6.9	19.29	23.44	2	3	0.05	0.2	888 204-3956
Baron Asset Fund	Small Co	-4.3	11.62	17.69	4	4	1	1.31	800 992-2766
Baron Growth Fund	Growth	8.2	16.1	21.53	3	4	1	1.36	800 992-2766
Baron Small Cap Fund	Small Co	33.9					1	1.35	800 992-2766
Barr Rosenberg Dbl Alpha Mkt Inst	Growth	-9.9					0.1	1.97	800 447-3332
Barr Rosenberg Dbl Alpha Mkt Inv	Growth	-10					0.1	2.14	800 447-3332
Barr Rosenberg Intl Sm Cap Instl	Foreign	20.3	5.61		3	2	1	1.62	800 447-3332
Barr Rosenberg Japan Instl	Pacific	24.5	-0.13	-1.41	5	4	1		800 447-3332
Barr Rosenberg Market Neutral Inst	Growth	-12.5					1.89	3.06	800 447-3332
Barr Rosenberg Market Neutral Inv	Growth	-12.8					1.89	3.47	800 447-3332
Barr Rosenberg Sel Sec Mkt Neu Inst	Growth	3.2					1	3.89	800 447-3332
Barr Rosenberg Sel Sec Mkt Neu Inv	Growth	4.2					1	3.72	800 447-3332
Barr Rosenberg Ser Tr Intl Sm Cap S	Foreign	19.9	5.2		3	2	1	2.66	800 447-3332
Barr Rosenberg Ser Tr Japan Select	Pacific	24.5	-0.3		5	4	1	1.8	800 447-3332
Barr Rosenberg US Small Cap Adv	Small Co	10.7	7.79		5	3	0.75	1.35	800 447-3332
Barr Rosenberg US Small Cap Instl	Small Co	10.9	8.03	16.26	4	3	0.75	1.2	800 447-3332
Barr Rosenberg US Small Cap Sel	Small Co	10.8	7.66		5	3	0.75	1.77	800 447-3332
Bartlett Basic Value A	Growth	-4.3	5.54	11.72	4	3	0.75	1.14	800 800-3609
Bartlett Value International A	Foreign	13.9	4.03	9.73	5	3	1.25	1.8	800 800-3609
Bear Stearns Balanced A	Balanced	-3.1					0.65	1.19	800 766-4111
Bear Stearns Balanced B	Balanced	-3.6					0.59	1.69	800 766-4111
Bear Stearns Balanced C	Balanced	-3.6					0.65	1.69	800 766-4111
Bear Stearns Balanced Y	Balanced	-2.7					0.8	0.69	800 766-4111
Bear Stearns Emerg Mkts Debt A	Intl Bond	19.1	5.31	16.39	3	5	1.14	1.75	800 766-4111
Bear Stearns Emerg Mkts Debt C	Intl Bond	18.4	4.67		3	5	1.14	2.39	800 766-4111
Bear Stearns Focus List Ptfl A	Growth	6.6					0.65	1.39	800 766-4111
Bear Stearns Focus List Ptfl B	Growth	6.2					0.65	1.89	800 766-4111
Bear Stearns Focus List Ptfl C	Growth	6.1					0.65	1.89	800 766-4111
Bear Stearns Insiders Select A	Growth	-7	8.48	15.15	4	3	1	1.64	800 766-4111
Bear Stearns Insiders Select B	Growth	-7.4					1	2.14	800 766-4111
Bear Stearns Insiders Select C	Growth	-7.4	7.92	14.55	3	3	1	2.14	800 766-4111
Bear Stearns Insiders Select Y	Growth	-6.7	8.94	15.56	3	3	1	1.14	800 766-4111
Bear Stearns International Eq A	Foreign	53.6					1	1.75	800 766-4111
Bear Stearns International Eq B	Foreign	52.7					1	2.25	800 766-4111
Bear Stearns International Eq C	Foreign	52.7					1	2.25	800 766-4111

Stock Fund Name	Objective	Annualized Return for			Rank		Max Load	Expense Ratio	Toll-Free Telephone
		1 Year	3 Years	5 Years	Overall	Risk			
Bear Stearns Large Cap Value A	Growth/Inc	-10.3	7.28	14.63	3	3	0.75	1.5	800 766-4111
Bear Stearns Large Cap Value C	Growth/Inc	-10.8	6.74	14.06	3	3	0.75	2	800 766-4111
Bear Stearns Large Cap Value Y	Growth/Inc	-9.8	7.82		4	3	0.75	1	800 766-4111
Bear Stearns S&P STARS A	Growth/Inc	39.2	33.49	29.86	1	3	0.75	1.5	800 766-4111
Bear Stearns S&P STARS B	Growth/Inc	38.5					0.75	2	800 766-4111
Bear Stearns S&P STARS C	Growth/Inc	38.5	32.7	29.14	1	3	0.75	2	800 766-4111
Bear Stearns S&P STARS Y	Growth/Inc	39.9	34.11		1	3	0.75	1	800 766-4111
Bear Stearns Small Cap Value A	Small Co	7.8	11.5	16.27	3	3	0.75	1.5	800 766-4111
Bear Stearns Small Cap Value B	Small Co	9.7					0.75	2	800 766-4111
Bear Stearns Small Cap Value C	Small Co	10.9	12.13	16.39	3	3	0.75	2	800 766-4111
Bear Stearns Small Cap Value Y	Small Co	8.2	12.06	16.8	3	3	0.75	1	800 766-4111
Berger Balanced Fund	Balanced	26.3					0.25	1.34	800 333-1001
Berger Growth & Income Fund	Growth/Inc	44.5	32.46	27.05	1	4	0.75		800 333-1001
Berger Growth Fund	Growth	46.7	26.54	22.04	3	4	0.75	1.36	800 333-1001
Berger Information Tech Fund Instl	Technology	118.6	69.34		1	5	0.94	1.5	
Berger MidCap Growth Fund	Growth	93.1					0.75	2	800 333-1001
Berger MidCap Value Fund	Growth	8.5					0.75	1.62	800 333-1001
Berger New Generation Fund	Growth	76.4	56.48		1	5	0.9	1.71	800 333-1001
Berger Select Fund	Growth	50.2					0.75	1.3	800 333-1001
Berger Small Cap Value Inst	Small Co	3.1	12.63		4	3	0.9	1.1	800 333-1001
Berger Small Cap Value Ret	Small Co	2.9	12.46		4	3	0.9	1.48	800 333-1001
Berger Small Company Growth Fund	Small Co	105.6	40.96	33.35	3	5	0.9	1.6	800 333-1001
Berger/BIAM International Fd	Foreign	20.1	12.22		2	3	0.81	1.76	800 333-1001
Berkshire Focus Fund	Growth	144.5					0.5	1	877 526-0707
Bernstein International Value II	Foreign	9.8					0.94		
Bernstein Intl Value II	Foreign	11.2	10.34	14.34	4	2	0.93	1.25	
Berwyn Fund	Small Co	-16.1	-8.16	0.65	5	3	1	1.38	800 992-6757
Berwyn Income Fund	Flexible	-2	1.41	6.23	3	1	0.5	0.77	800 992-6757
Bishop Street Equity Inst	Growth	10.6	21.05		3	3	0.73	1	800 262-9565
Bishop Street Equity Retail A	Growth	10.2					0.73	1.25	800 262-9565
Bjurman Micro-Cap Growth Fund	Small Co	106	45.27		1	5	1	1.8	800 227-7264
BlackRock Balanced Fund Inv C	Balanced	3	9.4		3	1	0.55	2	800 388-8734
BlackRock Intl Equity Inv C	Foreign	14.4	9.28		3	3	0.75	2.25	800 388-8734
BlackRock Micro-Cap Equity Inv C	Small Co	150.9					1.1	2.66	800 388-8734
BlackRock Midcap Growth Eqty Svc	Growth	89.4	47.65		1	4	0.8	1.4	800 388-8734
BlackRock Midcap Value Equity Svc	Growth/Inc	-6.5	3.2		4	3	0.8	1.39	800 388-8734
BlackRock Select Equity Invest C	Growth/Inc	8	17.26		2	3	0.52	2.02	800 388-8734
BlackRock-Balanced Inst	Balanced	4.6	13.58	16.61	2	1	0.55	0.85	800 388-8734
BlackRock-Balanced Inv A	Balanced	4.2	13.06	16.1	3	1	0.55	1.25	800 388-8734
BlackRock-Balanced Inv B	Balanced	3.3	12.18	15.22	3	1	0.55	2.06	800 388-8734
BlackRock-Balanced Svc	Balanced	4.3	13.24	16.25	2	1	0.55	1.15	800 388-8734
BlackRock-Index Eq Inst	Growth/Inc	7	19.35	22.12	2	3	0.55	0.19	800 388-8734
BlackRock-Index Eq Inv A	Growth/Inc	6.3	18.77	21.57	3	3	0.55	0.65	800 388-8734
BlackRock-Index Eq Inv B	Growth/Inc	5.5	17.85		3	3	0.55	1.38	800 388-8734
BlackRock-Index Eq Inv C	Growth/Inc	5.5	17.84		3	3	0.55	1.37	800 388-8734
BlackRock-Index Eq Svc	Growth/Inc	6.5	18.97	22.85	2	3	0.55	0.48	800 388-8734
BlackRock-Intl Bond Inst	Intl Bond	4.7	7.42		2	2	0.55	1.03	800 388-8734
BlackRock-Intl Bond Inv A	Intl Bond	4.3	6.93		2	2	0.55	1.5	800 388-8734
BlackRock-Intl Bond Inv B	Intl Bond	3.5	6.14		3	2	0.55	2.24	800 388-8734
BlackRock-Intl Bond Inv C	Intl Bond	3.5	6.15		2	2	0.55	2.24	800 388-8734
BlackRock-Intl Bond Svc	Intl Bond	4.3	7.03	8.47	2	2	0.55	1.33	800 388-8734
BlackRock-Intl Emg Mkt Inst	Foreign	8.1	-11.24	-2.64	5	4	1.25	1.73	800 388-8734
BlackRock-Intl Emg Mkt Inv A	Foreign	7.8	-11.61	-3.08	5	4	1.25	2.22	800 388-8734
BlackRock-Intl Emg Mkt Inv B	Foreign	6.7	-12.31		5	4	1.25	2.95	800 388-8734
BlackRock-Intl Emg Mkt Inv C	Foreign	6.7	-12.31		4	4	1.25	2.97	800 388-8734
BlackRock-Intl Emg Mkt Svc	Foreign	7.8	-11.5	-2.94	5	4	1.25	2.02	800 388-8734
BlackRock-Intl Eq Inst	Foreign	13.4	9.84	11.09	4	3	0.75	1.04	800 388-8734
BlackRock-Intl Eq Inv A	Foreign	12.9	9.27	10.57	4	3	0.75	1.34	800 388-8734

Stock Fund Name	Objective	Annualized Return for			Rank		Max Load	Expense Ratio	Toll-Free Telephone
		1 Year	3 Years	5 Years	Overall	Risk			
BlackRock-Intl Eq Inv B	Foreign	12	8.5	9.77	5	3	0.75	2.25	800 388-8734
BlackRock-Intl Eq Svc	Foreign	13	9.49	10.74	4	3	0.75	1.34	800 388-8734
BlackRock-Intl Sm Cap Eq A	Foreign	123.1					1	1.8	800 388-8734
BlackRock-Intl Sm Cap Eq B	Foreign	121.7					1	2.54	800 388-8734
BlackRock-Intl Sm Cap Eq C	Foreign	121.7					1	2.56	800 388-8734
BlackRock-Intl Sm Cap Eq Inst	Foreign	124.1					1	1.33	800 388-8734
BlackRock-Intl Sm Cap Eq Serv	Foreign	123.2					1	1.62	800 388-8734
BlackRock-Lrg Cap Gr Inst	Growth	27.4	29.03	28.15	1	3	0.55	0.8	800 388-8734
BlackRock-Lrg Cap Gr Inv B	Growth	25.8	27.44		1	3	0.55	2.02	800 388-8734
BlackRock-Lrg Cap Gr Inv C	Growth	25.7	27.42		1	3	0.55	2	800 388-8734
BlackRock-Lrg Cap Gr Svc	Growth	26.8	28.58	27.75	1	3	0.55	1.12	800 388-8734
BlackRock-Lrg Cap Val Inst	Growth	-13.6	6.19	14.62	4	3	0.53	0.79	800 388-8734
BlackRock-Lrg Cap Val Inv A	Growth	-13.9	6.29	14.49	4	3	0.53	1.19	800 388-8734
BlackRock-Lrg Cap Val Inv B	Growth	-14.5	4.91		3	3	0.53	2	800 388-8734
BlackRock-Lrg Cap Val Inv C	Growth	-14.5	4.94		3	3	0.53	2	800 388-8734
BlackRock-Lrg Cap Val Svc	Growth	-13.8	5.89	14.23	4	3	0.53	1.09	800 388-8734
BlackRock-Micro Cap Equity A	Small Co	152.8					1.1	1.89	800 388-8734
BlackRock-Micro Cap Equity B	Small Co	151					1.1	2.66	800 388-8734
BlackRock-Micro Cap Equity Inst	Small Co	153.9					0.34	1.44	800 388-8734
BlackRock-Micro Cap Equity Svc	Small Co	152.3					0.65	1.75	800 388-8734
BlackRock-Mid Cp Gr Inst	Growth	90.1	48.12		1	4	0.8	1.11	800 388-8734
BlackRock-Mid Cp Gr Inv A	Growth	89.1	47.32		1	4	0.8	1.58	800 388-8734
BlackRock-Mid Cp Gr Inv B	Growth	87.7	46.26		1	4	0.8	2.31	800 388-8734
BlackRock-Mid Cp Gr Inv C	Growth	87.2	46.13		1	4	0.8	2.31	800 388-8734
BlackRock-Mid Cp Val Inst	Growth/Inc	-6.2	3.42		4	3	0.8	1.11	800 388-8734
BlackRock-Mid Cp Val Inv A	Growth/Inc	-6.7	3.05		4	3	0.8	1.59	800 388-8734
BlackRock-Mid Cp Val Inv B	Growth/Inc	-7.4	2.34		4	3	0.8	2.33	800 388-8734
BlackRock-Mid Cp Val Inv C	Growth/Inc	-7.4	2.34		4	3	0.8	2.33	800 388-8734
BlackRock-Select Eq Inst	Growth/Inc	4.5	16.88	21.95	3	3	0.55	0.81	800 388-8734
BlackRock-Sm Cap Gr Inv A	Small Co	74.2	30.5	28.23	3	5	0.55	1.23	800 388-8734
BlackRock-Sm Cap Gr Inv B	Small Co	73.1	29.42		3	5	0.54	2	800 388-8734
BlackRock-Sm Cap Gr Inv C	Small Co	73.1	29.41		3	5	0.54	2.04	800 388-8734
BlackRock-Sm Cap Val Inst	Small Co	-1	2.33	11.19	4	3	0.55	0.85	800 388-8734
BlackRock-Sm Cap Val Inv A	Small Co	-1.3	1.87	10.73	4	3	0.55	1.29	800 388-8734
BlackRock-Sm Cap Val Inv B	Small Co	-2.1	1.11	9.76	5	3	0.55	2.08	800 388-8734
BlackRock-Sm Cap Val Inv C	Small Co	-2.1	1.11		4	3	0.55	2.08	800 388-8734
BlackRock-Sm Cap Val Svc	Small Co	-1.3	2.02	10.86	4	3	0.55	1.15	800 388-8734
Blue Ridge Total Return	Growth	4.5					1.64	1.52	800 525-3863
Boston 1784 Funds-Asset Alloc A	AssetAlloc	31.5	19	18.38	3	2	0.73	1	800 252-1784
Boston 1784 Funds-FL Tax-Ex Inc	Muni State	2.5	4.62		1	3	0.59	0.8	800 252-1784
Boston 1784 Funds-Growth Inst	Growth	60.4	22.75		3	4	0.73	0.93	800 252-1784
Boston 1784 Funds-Intl Equity A	Foreign	140.6	36.04	28.15	4	5	1	1.19	800 252-1784
Boston Balanced Fund	Balanced	-0.3	11.6		3	1	0.75	1.09	800 252-1784
Boyle Marathon	Growth	56.5					1.5	3.35	888 882-6953
Bramwell Focus Fund	Growth						1		800 272-6227
Bramwell Growth Fund	Growth	22.5	26.82	24.29	1	3	1	1.54	800 272-6227
Brandes Instl Intl Equity Fund	Foreign	34	23.78		1	3	1	1.19	800 237-7119
Brandywine Blue Fund INC	Growth	40.6	18.89	19.64	3	4	1	1.08	800 656-3017
Brandywine Fund INC	Growth	50.4	20.4	20.68	3	4	1		800 656-3017
Brazos Real Estate Secs	Real Est	1.9	1.05		4	2	0.9	1.2	800 336-9970
Brazos Small Cap Growth	Small Co	29.7	24.78		2	4	0.9	1.1	800 336-9970
Brazos/JMIC Growth Portfolio	Agg Growth	59.7					0.9	1.35	800 336-9970
Brazos/JMIC Micro Cap Growth Fund	Agg Growth	58.6					1.19	1.52	800 336-9970
Bremer Growth Stock Fund	Growth	15.1	20.58		2	3	0.69	0.88	800 595-5552
Bridges Investment Fund	Growth/Inc	15.3	20.63	21.56	1	3	0.5	0.76	
Bridgeway Aggressive Growth Fund	Agg Growth	113.1	49.71	41.96	1	5	1.6	1.76	800 661-3550
Bridgeway Micro-Cap Limited	Small Co	28.7					0.9	1.54	800 661-3550
Bridgeway Social Responsibility	Growth	37.6	32.95	28.31	1	3	1.6	1.5	800 661-3550

Stock Fund Name	Objective	Annualized Return for			Rank		Max Load	Expense Ratio	Toll-Free Telephone
		1 Year	3 Years	5 Years	Overall	Risk			
Bridgeway Ultra Large 35 Index	Growth	11.7					0.08	0.14	800 661-3550
Bridgeway Ultra Small Company	Small Co	44.8	13.38	22.92	3	4	1.48	1.97	800 661-3550
Bridgeway Ultra Small Index	Small Co	33.9					0.5	0.75	800 661-3550
Brinson Fund-Global Bond I	Intl Bond	-0.3	1.81	4.85	5	4	0.9	0.9	800 448-2430
Brinson Fund-Global Equity I	Global	2.7	7.22	13.43	4	2	0.8	1	800 448-2430
Brinson Fund-Global Fund I	Global	-0.5	4.12	9.31	3	1	0.8	0.95	800 448-2430
Brinson Fund-Non U.S. Equity I	Foreign	11.8	6.66	12.52	4	2	0.8	0.98	800 448-2430
Brinson Fund-U.S. Balanced I	Balanced	-5	3.71	7.9	3	1	0.69	0.8	800 448-2430
Brinson Global (EX-US) Equity N	Foreign	11.5	6.37		4	2	0.8	1.23	800 448-2430
Brinson Global Bond	Intl Bond	-0.8	1.32	4.35	5	5	0.9	1.38	800 448-2430
Brinson Global Bond Fund N	Intl Bond	-0.6	1.52		5	4	0.9	1.14	800 448-2430
Brinson Global Equity	Global	2	6.41	12.59	4	2	0.8	1.76	800 448-2430
Brinson Global Equity Fund N	Global	2.5	6.91		4	2	0.8	1.25	800 448-2430
Brinson Global Fund	Global	-1	3.44	8.63	4	1	0.8	1.61	800 448-2430
Brinson Global Fund N	Global	-0.8	3.79		3	1	0.8	1.2	800 448-2430
Brinson Non-U.S. Equity	Foreign	13.4	6.59	12.14	5	2	0.8	1.83	800 448-2430
Brinson U.S. Balanced Fund	Balanced	-5.5	3.23	7.41	3	1	0.69	1.3	800 448-2430
Brinson U.S. Equity	Growth/Inc	-17.4	4.57	14.33	3	3	0.69	1.32	800 448-2430
Brinson US Balanced Fund N	Balanced	-6.1	3.15		3	1	0.69	1.05	800 448-2430
Brinson US Equity Fund N	Growth/Inc	-17.2	4.79		4	3	0.69	1.05	800 448-2430
Brinson US Large Cap Equity Fund I	Growth/Inc	-19.2					0.69	0.8	800 448-2430
Brinson US Large Cap Equity Fund N	Growth/Inc	-24.3					0.69	1.05	800 448-2430
Brinson US Large Cap Growth Fund I	Growth	17.5					0.69	0.8	800 448-2430
Brinson US Large Cap Growth Fund N	Growth	17.1					0.69	1.05	800 448-2430
Brinson US Small Cap Growth Fund I	Small Co	76.7					1	1.14	800 448-2430
Brinson US Small Cap Growth Fund N	Small Co	76.3					1	1.39	800 448-2430
Brown Capital Mgmt Intl Fund Instl	Foreign	13.8					1	2	800 525-3863
Brown Capital Mgmt-Balanced	Flexible	4.1	13.22	14.94	3	2	0.65	1.67	800 525-3863
Brown Capital Mgmt-Equity	Growth	7.4	16.58	18.48	3	3	0.65	1.19	800 525-3863
Brown Capital Mgmt-Small Company	Small Co	45.8	26.85	24.03	3	4	1	1.5	800 525-3863
Bruce Fund	Flexible	1.4	4.44	7.87	4	2	1	1.63	800 872-7823
Brundage Story&Rose Equity Fund	Growth	12	14.34	18.41	3	3	0.65	1.14	800 320-2212
Buffalo Balanced Fund	Balanced	6.1	6.01	9.91	3	1	1	1.07	800 492-8332
Buffalo Equity Fund	Growth	15.2	15.67	19.92	2	3	1	1.05	800 492-8332
Buffalo Small Cap Fund	Small Co	45.2					1	0.02	800 492-8332
Buffalo USA Global Fund	Global	39.8	21.5	24.76	1	3	1	1.07	800 492-8332
Bull & Bear Special Equities	Agg Growth	13.8	4.23	5.77	5	4	0.9	3.12	800 400-6432
Bull & Bear US And Overseas Fund	Global	7.3	2.16	4.32	5	4	1	3.37	800 400-6432
Burnham Dow 30 Fund	Growth	-7.4					0.59	1.19	800 874-3863
Burnham Financial Services A	Financial	0.9					0.75	1.6	800 874-3863
Burnham Financial Services B	Financial	0.1					0.75	2.29	800 874-3863
Burnham Fund A	Growth/Inc	31.1	24.57	23.69	1	3	0.59	1.3	800 874-3863
Burnham Fund B	Growth/Inc	30	25.71	24.11	1	3	0.59	2.1	800 874-3863
Buttonwood Capital Appreciation	Growth	-12	-0.43	10.43	5	2	0.75	2	800 526-6397
CG Cap Mkt Fds-Balanced	Balanced	6.2	8.35	13.1	3	1	0.54	1	800 544-7835
CG Cap Mkt Fds-Emerging Mkts	Foreign	12.4	-6.22	1.32	5	4	0.98	1.56	800 544-7835
CG Cap Mkt Fds-Intl Equity Invts	Foreign	27.4	14.01	14.09	3	3	0.9	0.85	800 544-7835
CG Cap Mkt Fds-Intl Fixed Invt	Intl Bond	-0.2	2.4	3.83	5	5	0.5	0.92	800 544-7835
CG Cap Mkt Fds-Large Cap Grwth	Growth	24.9	27.1	26.39	1	3	0.59	0.66	800 544-7835
CG Cap Mkt Fds-Large Cap Val Eq	Growth/Inc	-8.9	8.77	15.62	4	3	0.76	0.75	800 544-7835
CG Cap Mkt Fds-Small Cap Growth	Small Co	38.4	19.26	19.77	3	4	0.79	0.93	800 544-7835
CG Cap Mkt Fds-Small Cap Val Eq	Small Co	-8.1	1.3	10.74	4	2	0.75	0.95	800 544-7835
CGM Capital Development	Growth	6.9	6.58	17.1	4	4	1	1.08	800 345-4048
CGM Focus Fund	Growth	6.5					1	1.21	800 345-4048
CGM Mutual Fund	Balanced	0.6	6.38	11.88	5	3	0.83	1.02	800 345-4048
CGM Realty Fund	Real Est	6	3.08	14.22	3	2	0.84	1.06	800 345-4048
CNI Charter Large Cap Growth Eq I	Growth						0.65		888 889-0799
CNI Charter Large Cap Value Eq I	Growth						0.61		888 889-0799

Stock Fund Name	Objective	Annualized Return for			Rank		Max Load	Expense Ratio	Toll-Free Telephone
		1 Year	3 Years	5 Years	Overall	Risk			
CRA Realty Shares Instl	Real Est	6.1	2.73		4	2	0.83	1	877 362-4099
CRM Large Cap Value Fund	Growth	-4.4					0.75	1.5	800 943-6786
CRM Mid Cap Value Fund Instl	Growth	19					0.75	1.14	800 943-6786
CRM Small Cap Value Fund Instl	Small Co	9.1					0.75	1.07	800 943-6786
CRM Small Cap Value Inv	Small Co	8.8	2.28		4	3	0.75	1.38	800 943-6786
Calamos Global Growth & Income A	Global	32.6	19.71		1	3	0.75	2	800 823-7386
Calamos Global Growth & Income C	Global	31.8	19.65		2	3	0.75	2.5	800 823-7386
Calamos Global Growth and Income I	Global	32.2					0.75	1.5	800 823-7386
Calamos Growth Fund A	Growth	112.1	52.32	41.05	1	5	0.75	2	800 823-7386
Calamos Growth Fund C	Growth	111	51.61		1	5	0.75	2.5	800 823-7386
Calamos Growth Fund I	Growth	112.5					0.75	1.5	800 823-7386
Caldwell & Orkin Mkt Opportunity	AssetAlloc	3.7	14.3	19.46	2	1	0.9	1.37	800 237-7073
California Invest Tr-S&P 500 Idx	Growth/Inc	7.3	19.68	23.67	2	3	0.2	0.36	800 225-8778
California Invest Tr-S&P MdCap Idx	Growth	18.2	20.58	21.17	2	3	0.4	0.4	800 225-8778
Calvert New Africa Fund	Foreign	-36.7	-23.79	-13.56	5	3	1.75	3.27	800 368-2745
Calvert Social Inv Balanced B	Balanced	4.6					0.69	2.37	800 368-2745
Calvert Social Inv Equity Port B	Growth	14.9					0.69	2.2	800 368-2745
Calvert Social Inv Managed Index B	Growth	8.5					0.69	2.5	800 368-2745
Calvert Social Inv Managed Index I	Growth	10.4					0.69	0.81	800 368-2745
Calvert Social-Balanced Portf A	Balanced	5.4	11.8	12.84	3	1	0.69	1.16	800 368-2745
Calvert Social-Balanced Portf C	Balanced	4.5	10.69	11.65	3	1	0.69	2.16	800 368-2745
Calvert Social-Equity A	Growth	15.9	16.12	18.49	3	3	0.69	1.29	800 368-2745
Calvert Social-Managed Index A	Growth	9.8					0.69	1.31	800 368-2745
Calvert Social-Managed Index C	Growth	8.6					0.69	2.56	800 368-2745
Calvert World Values Intl Eqty A	Foreign	15.2	10.92	12.94	3	3	0.69	1.83	800 368-2745
Canandaigua Equity Fund	Growth	26.6	21.29	22.26	2	4	1	1.35	
Capital Advisors Growth Fund	Growth						0.75		800 576-8229
Capital Income Builder	Income	-3.8	6.98	12.52	3	1	0.32	0.64	800 421-9900
Capital Management Mid-Cap Inst	Growth	16.3	12.31	16.25	3	3	1	1.5	800 525-3863
Capital Management Mid-Cap Inv	Growth	15.6	11.46	15.61	3	3	1	2.25	800 525-3863
Capital Management Sm Cap Fund Inst	Small Co	15.2					1	1.5	800 525-3863
Capital Management Sm Cap Fund Inv	Small Co	14.2					1	2.25	800 525-3863
Capital Value Fund	AssetAlloc	26.7	22.36	18.55	2	3	0.59	2.14	800 525-3863
Capital World Bond Fund	Intl Bond	-0.2	1.69	3.58	5	4	0.64	0.54	800 421-9900
Capital World Gr & Inc Fund	Global	19.3	16.33	19.31	2	2	0.41	0.8	800 421-9900
Cappiello-Rushmore Emerging Gr	Small Co	30.4	7.56	6.84	4	5	0.5	1.51	800 343-3355
Cappiello-Rushmore Growth Fund	Growth	-8.9	10.7	12.76	5	4	0.5	1.5	800 343-3355
Cappiello-Rushmore Utility Income	Utilities	-7.1	9.37	10.28	3	2	0.34	1.02	800 343-3355
Capstone Growth Fund	Growth	7.4	17.21	20.34	3	3	0.68	1.17	800 262-6631
Capstone Japan Fund	Pacific	22.3	2.47	2.31	5	3	0.75	4.61	800 262-6631
Capstone New Zealand Fund	Foreign	-12.9	-12.65	-1.85	5	3	0.75	4.29	800 262-6631
Carl Domino Equity Income Fund	Growth/Inc	-11.3	4.8		4	3	1.5	1.53	800 506-9922
Carolinas Fund Inst	Growth	-27	-8.18	0.28	4	3	1	2	800 543-8721
Carolinas Fund Inv	Growth	-27.7	-8.86	-0.48	5	3	1	2.31	800 543-8721
Century Shares Trust	Financial	-15.4	3.58	14.03	4	4	0.69	0.81	800 321-1928
Century Small Cap Select Fund	Small Co						0.94		800 321-1928
Chartwell Large Cap Value Fund	Growth						0.5		
Chartwell Small Cap Value Fund	Small Co						0.8		
Chase Balanced Inv	Balanced	11.6					0.75	1.23	888 524-2730
Chase Balanced Premier	Balanced	11.9	16.83	17.03	2	1	0.75	1	888 524-2730
Chase Core Equity Fund Prem	Growth	10.3	22.06	24.5	3	3	0.75	1	888 524-2730
Chase Core Equity Inv	Growth	10.1					0.75	1.23	888 524-2730
Chase Equity Growth Fund Prem	Growth	20.1	28.05	27.8	1	3	0.75	1	888 524-2730
Chase Equity Growth Inv	Growth	19.8					0.75	1.23	888 524-2730
Chase Equity Income Inv	Growth/Inc	3.6					0.75	1.22	888 524-2730
Chase Equity Income Prem	Growth/Inc	3.8	16.4	20.72	3	2	0.75	1	888 524-2730
Chase Growth Fund	Growth	19.7					1	2.72	888 861-7556
Chase Small Capitalization Prem	Small Co	21	11.49	18.78	3	3	0.75	1	888 524-2730

294

| Stock Fund Name | Objective | Annualized Return for | | | Rank | | Max Load | Expense Ratio | Toll-Free Telephone |
		1 Year	3 Years	5 Years	Overall	Risk			
Chase Small-Cap Inv	Small Co	20.6					0.75	1.26	888 524-2730
Chase Vista Balanced A	Balanced	3.1	11.5	14.18	3	1	0.5	1.25	800 348-4782
Chase Vista Balanced B	Balanced	2.4	10.71	13.39	3	1	0.5	1.9	800 348-4782
Chase Vista Balanced C	Balanced	2.3					0.5	1.9	800 348-4782
Chase Vista Capital Growth A	Growth	15.1	12.55	15.98	3	3	0.4	1.3	800 348-4782
Chase Vista Capital Growth B	Growth	14.5	11.98	15.4	3	3	0.4	1.78	800 348-4782
Chase Vista Capital Growth C	Growth	14.6					0.4	1.78	800 348-4782
Chase Vista Capital Growth I	Growth	15.5	12.98		3	3	0.4	0.91	800 348-4782
Chase Vista Core Equity A	Growth/Inc						0.75		800 348-4782
Chase Vista Core Equity B	Growth/Inc						0.75		800 348-4782
Chase Vista Core Equity C	Growth/Inc						0.75		800 348-4782
Chase Vista Equity Growth A	Growth						0.75		800 348-4782
Chase Vista Equity Growth B	Growth						0.75		800 348-4782
Chase Vista Equity Growth C	Growth						0.75		800 348-4782
Chase Vista Equity Income A	Income	1.3	11.15	18.75	3	2	0.4	1.44	800 348-4782
Chase Vista Equity Income B	Income	0.8	10.64		3	2	0.4	1.93	800 348-4782
Chase Vista Equity Income C	Income	0.8					0.4	1.93	800 348-4782
Chase Vista European Shares A	European	34.1	22.43		2	3	1	1.73	800 348-4782
Chase Vista European Shares B	European	33.2	21.78		2	3	1	2.5	800 348-4782
Chase Vista European Shares C	European	33.2					1	2.35	800 348-4782
Chase Vista Focus A	Agg Growth	6.5					0.4	1.25	800 348-4782
Chase Vista Focus B	Agg Growth	5.9					0.4	1.85	800 348-4782
Chase Vista Focus C	Agg Growth	5.8					0.4	1.85	800 348-4782
Chase Vista Focus I	Agg Growth	6.6					0.4	1	800 348-4782
Chase Vista Growth & Income A	Growth/Inc	-1.6	10.76	15.57	3	3	0.4	1.3	800 348-4782
Chase Vista Growth & Income B	Growth/Inc	-2.2	10.17	14.98	3	3	0.4	1.75	800 348-4782
Chase Vista Growth & Income C	Growth/Inc	-2.2					0.4	1.75	800 348-4782
Chase Vista Growth & Income I	Growth/Inc	-1.3	11.12		2	3	0.4	0.84	800 348-4782
Chase Vista International Equity A	Foreign	26.4	9.03	9.46	4	3	1	1.98	800 348-4782
Chase Vista International Equity B	Foreign	25.9	8.49	8.93	4	3	1	2.49	800 348-4782
Chase Vista Japan Fund A	Pacific	18	-1.91		5	3	1	1.72	800 348-4782
Chase Vista Japan Fund B	Pacific	18.3	-2.5		5	3	1	2.47	800 348-4782
Chase Vista Large Cap Equity A	Growth	1.4	15.25		2	2	0.4	0.79	800 348-4782
Chase Vista Large Cap Equity B	Growth	0.9	14.7		2	2	0.4	1.29	800 348-4782
Chase Vista Large Cap Equity C	Growth	0.9					0.4	1.62	800 348-4782
Chase Vista Large Cap Equity I	Growth	1.9	15.8	20.36	3	2	0.4	0.8	800 348-4782
Chase Vista Select Balanced	Balanced	4.7	12.76		3	1	0.5	0.05	800 348-4782
Chase Vista Select Equity Income	Income	-0.4	9.64		3	2	0.4	0.02	800 348-4782
Chase Vista Select Growth & Income	Growth/Inc	-1					0.4	0.58	800 348-4782
Chase Vista Select Intl Equity	Foreign	28	12.57		2	3	1	0.05	800 348-4782
Chase Vista Select Large Cap Equity	Growth	6.4	18.21		2	3	0.4	0.05	800 348-4782
Chase Vista Select Large Cap Growth	Growth	19.1	30.04		1	3	0.4	0.02	800 348-4782
Chase Vista Select New Growth Opp	Growth	22.7	18.63		2	3	0.65	0.07	800 348-4782
Chase Vista Select Small Cap Value	Small Co	2.7	5.49		4	3	0.65	0.04	800 348-4782
Chase Vista Small Cap Equity A	Small Co	28.3	13.39	19.57	3	3	0.65	1.39	800 348-4782
Chase Vista Small Cap Equity B	Small Co	27.4	12.58	18.72	3	3	0.65	2.08	800 348-4782
Chase Vista Small Cap Equity I	Small Co	29	13.91		3	3	0.65	0.88	800 348-4782
Chase Vista Small Cap Opports A	Small Co	54.3	28.52		3	4	0.65	1.48	800 348-4782
Chase Vista Small Cap Opports B	Small Co	53.2	27.63		3	4	0.65	2.22	800 348-4782
Chase Vista Small Cap Opports C	Small Co	53.1					0.65	2.22	800 348-4782
Chase Vista Small Cap Opports I	Small Co	54.7					0.65	1.09	800 348-4782
Chesapeake Aggressive Growth Fund	Agg Growth	44.1	14.96	14.27	3	4	1.25	1.38	800 525-3863
Chesapeake Core Growth Fund	Growth	48					1	1.38	800 525-3863
Chesapeake Growth Fund A	Growth	66.7	27.21	22.75	3	4	1	1.53	800 525-3863
Chesapeake Growth Fund Instl	Growth	67.2	27.67	23.13	3	4	1	1.14	800 525-3863
Chesapeake Growth Fund Super Instl	Growth	67.5	27.85		3	4	1	0.98	800 525-3863
Choice Focus Fund	Growth						1		800 392-7107
CitiFunds Balanced Fund A	Balanced	-5.5	6.14	9.28	3	1	0.69	1.02	800 721-1899

Stock Fund Name	Objective	Annualized Return for			Rank		Max Load	Expense Ratio	Toll-Free Telephone
		1 Year	3 Years	5 Years	Overall	Risk			
CitiFunds Balanced Portfolio B	Balanced	-15.2					0.69	1.77	800 721-1899
CitiFunds Growth & Income Port A	Growth/Inc	-12.3					1	1.3	800 721-1899
CitiFunds Growth & Income Port B	Growth/Inc	-12.8					0.8	2.04	800 721-1899
CitiFunds International Equity A	Foreign	22	11.89	10.81	3	3	1	1.75	800 721-1899
CitiFunds International Growth B	Foreign	12.5					1	2.5	800 721-1899
CitiFunds Intl Growth & Income A	Foreign	13.3					0.25	1.64	800 721-1899
CitiFunds Intl Growth & Income B	Foreign	12.5					0.29	2.39	800 721-1899
CitiFunds Large Cap Growth A	Growth	12.3	21.09	22.11	2	3	0.29	1.05	800 721-1899
CitiFunds Large Cap Growth Port B	Growth	11.5					0.29	1.8	800 721-1899
CitiFunds Small Cap Value Port A	Small Co	-9.3					0.25	1.35	800 721-1899
CitiFunds Small Cap Value Port B	Small Co	-10					0.25	2.1	800 721-1899
CitiSelect Folio 200 A	AssetAlloc	1.8	3.88		3	1	0.75	1.5	800 721-1899
CitiSelect Folio 300 A	AssetAlloc	4.5	5.21		3	1	0.75	1.5	800 721-1899
CitiSelect Folio 400 A	AssetAlloc	7.2	5.53		4	1	0.75	1.44	800 721-1899
CitiSelect Folio 500 A	AssetAlloc	9.8	6		4	2	0.75	1.44	800 721-1899
Citizens Emerg Gr	Agg Growth	82.1	48.83	22.9	1	4	1	1.82	800 223-7010
Citizens Emerging Growth Fund Instl	Agg Growth						1.1		800 223-7010
Citizens Global Eq	Global	53.3	31.68	25.61	1	4	1	1.75	800 223-7010
Citizens Global Equity Fund Instl	Global						1.1		800 223-7010
Citizens Index Fd	Growth	12.8	26.54	27.71	2	3	0.5	1.58	800 223-7010
Citizens Index Inst	Growth	13.7			2	3	0.58	0.82	800 223-7010
Clipper Fund	Growth	-3.4	9.74	16.44	3	2	1	1.1	800 776-5033
Clover Equity Value Fund	Growth/Inc	-0.5	6.03	10.23	4	2	0.73	1.08	800 224-6312
Clover Max Cap Value Fd	Growth/Inc	2.5					0.73	0.94	800 224-6312
Clover Small Cap Value Fund	Small Co	20.1	12.49		3	3	0.84	1.39	800 224-6312
Cohen & Steers Equity Income A	Income	2					0.75	1.61	800 437-9912
Cohen & Steers Equity Income B	Income	1.8					0.75	2.6	800 437-9912
Cohen & Steers Equity Income C	Income	1.8					0.75	2.27	800 437-9912
Cohen & Steers Equity Income Instl	Income	2.2					0.75	1.21	800 437-9912
Cohen & Steers Realty Shrs	Real Est	3.8	1.57	11.03	3	2	0.83	1.07	800 437-9912
Cohen & Steers Special Equity	Real Est	0.7	-1.43		5	4	0.9	1.94	800 437-9912
Colonial Value Fund A	Growth/Inc	-13.8	7.32		4	3	0.8	1	800 345-6611
Colonial Value Fund B	Growth/Inc	-14.4	6.65		4	3	0.8	1.75	800 345-6611
Colonial Value Fund C	Growth/Inc	-14.4	6.65		4	3	0.8	1.75	800 345-6611
Columbia Balanced Fund	Balanced	11.8	15.22	16	2	1	0.5	0.66	800 547-1707
Columbia Common Stock Fund	Growth/Inc	18.3	22.3	24.25	1	3	0.59	0.65	800 547-1707
Columbia Growth Fund	Growth	21.5	25.89	25.72	1	3	0.55	0.65	800 547-1707
Columbia International Stock	Foreign	28.9	14.09	17.71	3	3	1	1.47	800 547-1707
Columbia Real Estate Equity	Real Est	5.4	3.98	13.66	3	2	0.75	0.98	800 547-1707
Columbia Small Cap Fund	Small Co	81	32.34		2	4	1	1.31	800 547-1707
Columbia Special Fund	Growth	62.3	26.64	23.01	3	4	0.91	1.09	800 547-1707
Commerce Balanced Fd	Balanced	6	10.3	13.02	3	1	1	1.12	800 995-6365
Commerce Growth Fd	Growth	7.6	18.51	21.28	3	3	0.75	1.07	800 995-6365
Commerce Intl Equity Fd	Foreign	22.2	10.46	12.55	3	3	1.5	1.53	800 995-6365
Commerce Mid Cap Fd	Agg Growth	33.4	22.57	20.2	3	4	0.75	1.12	800 995-6365
Comstock Partners Capital Value A	AssetAlloc	-19.3	-24.82	-18.97	5	3	0.75	1.46	800 645-6561
Comstock Partners Capital Value B	AssetAlloc	-19.9	-25.36	-19.59	5	3	0.75	2.2	800 645-6561
Comstock Partners Capital Value C	AssetAlloc	-19.9	-25.29		5	3	0.75	2.18	800 645-6561
Comstock Partners Capital Value R	AssetAlloc	-18.8	-24.45		5	3	0.75	1.23	800 645-6561
Comstock Partners Strategy A	Intl Bond	-11.7	-13.97	-8.98	5	5	0.59	1.75	800 645-6561
Comstock Partners Strategy C	Intl Bond	-11.8	-14.54		5	5	0.59	2.47	800 645-6561
Comstock Partners Strategy O	Intl Bond	-11.4	-13.72	-8.73	5	5	0.59	1.48	800 645-6561
Concert Invmt Series Mid Cap A	Growth	34.6					0.75		800 221-3627
Concert Invmt Series Mid Cap B	Growth	41.6					0.75		800 221-3627
Concert Invmt Series Small Cap 1	Small Co	17.8	17.22		3	4	0.65	1.22	800 221-3627
Concorde Income Fund	Income	1.7	1.94		3	1	0.69	2	800 294-1699
Concorde Value Fund	Growth	3.9	8.44	14.28	3	2	0.9	1.55	800 294-1699
Conseco Fd Grp-20 Fund A	Growth	63.1					0.69	1.75	800 986-3384

Stock Fund Name	Objective	Annualized Return for			Rank		Max Load	Expense Ratio	Toll-Free Telephone
		1 Year	3 Years	5 Years	Overall	Risk			
Conseco Fd Grp-20 Fund B	Growth	62					0.69	2.25	800 986-3384
Conseco Fd Grp-20 Fund C	Growth	61.9					0.69	2.25	800 986-3384
Conseco Fd Grp-20 Fund Y	Growth	63.1					0.69	1.25	800 986-3384
Conseco Fd Grp-Balanced Fund A	AssetAlloc	36.5	21.83		1	3	0.69	1.5	800 986-3384
Conseco Fd Grp-Balanced Fund Y	AssetAlloc	37.3	22.43		1	3	0.69	1	800 986-3384
Conseco Fd Grp-Equity Fd A	Growth	70.4	35.16		2	4	0.69	1.5	800 986-3384
Conseco Fd Grp-Equity Fd Y	Growth	71.1	35.82		2	4	0.69	1	800 986-3384
Copley Fund	Growth/Inc	-8.1	7.72	9.91	3	2	0.64	1.01	800 424-8570
CornerCap Balanced Fund	Balanced	-12.7	3.23		4	1	1	1.3	888 813-8637
CornerCap Sm. Cap Value Fd	Growth	-14.8	-0.02	9.06	5	3	1	1.19	888 813-8637
Countrywide Aggressive Growth A	Agg Growth	97.5	38.87		2	5	1	1.94	800 638-8194
Countrywide Equity Fund A	Growth	11.5	18.1	20.35	2	3	0.75	1.29	800 638-8194
Countrywide Equity Fund C	Growth	0.1	13.19	16.95	2	2	0.75	2.41	800 638-8194
Countrywide Growth/Value A	Growth	72.7	41.54		1	4	1	1.65	800 638-8194
Countrywide Utility Income A	Utilities	-1.7	12.75	13.39	3	2	0.75	2.5	800 638-8194
Countrywide Utility Income C	Utilities	-2.6	11.63	12.38	3	2	0.75	2.5	800 638-8194
Crabbe Huson Small Cap Instl	Small Co	20	-2.91		4	4	0.17	1	800 345-6611
Croft-Leominster Value	Growth	2.8	7.91	15.55	3	3	0.93	1.5	800 551-0990
Cutler Core Fund	Income	8.6	15.08	20.86	2	2	0.75	1.07	800 228-8537
Cutler Value Fund	Income	-9.3	10.21	16.66	2	3	0.75	1.19	800 228-8537
DFA Continental Small Company	European	10.5	7.59	7.97	3	2	0.5	0.71	
DFA Emerging Markets	Foreign	7.4	-0.32	3.83	5	4	0.1	0.94	
DFA Global Fixed Income Fund	Intl Bond	4.2	6.21	8.15	1	1	0.25	0.39	
DFA International Small Cap Value	Foreign	3	-1.04		5	3	0.65	0.85	
DFA International Value I	Foreign	10.1	6.08	8.77	5	3	0.2	0.52	
DFA Japanese Small Co	Pacific	6.5	-9.87	-8.85	4	5	0.5	0.73	
DFA Large Cap International	Foreign	17.2	10.72	12.15	4	2	0.25	0.53	
DFA Large Cap Value I	Growth	-16	6.28	13.56	3	3	0.25	0.33	
DFA Pacific Rim Small Company	Pacific	-5.4	-12.38	-3.74	5	5	0.5	0.82	
DFA Real Estate Securities Port	Real Est	4.7	2.18	10.18	3	2	0.29	0.46	
DFA Small Cap Value I	Small Co	6.2	7.64	14.27	4	3	0.2	0.26	
DFA US 6-10 Small Company Portf	Small Co	21.7	12.31	15.59	4	4	0.02	0.44	
DFA US 9-10 Small Company Portf	Small Co	29.8	14.4	14.55	4	4	0.1	0.6	
DFA US Large Company	Growth/Inc	6.9	19.45	23.53	1	3	0.23	0.16	
DFA United Kingdom Small Co	European	10.5	7.28	10.25	5	2	0.1	0.73	
DLJ Winthrop Growth A	Growth	20.3	23.55	24.25	1	3	0.75	1.22	800 225-8011
DLJ Winthrop Growth B	Growth	19.4	21.78		2	3	0.75	1.93	800 225-8011
DLJ Winthrop Sm Company Value A	Small Co	7.3	5.32	10.47	4	3	0.79	1.22	800 225-8011
DLJ Winthrop Sm Company Value B	Small Co	8.8	5.26		4	3	0.79	2.02	800 225-8011
Davis Financial A	Financial	-2.5	12.91	22.8	3	4	0.64	1.04	800 279-0279
Davis Financial B	Financial	-3.3	11.93	21.71	3	4	0.64	1.9	800 279-0279
Davis Financial Fund C	Financial	-3.3					0.64	1.9	800 279-0279
Davis Financial Y	Financial	-2.3	12.48		4	4	0.64	0.88	800 279-0279
Davis Growth & Income Fund A	Growth/Inc	-1.8					0.75	1.15	800 279-0279
Davis Growth & Income Fund B	Growth/Inc	-2.7					0.75	2.16	800 279-0279
Davis Growth & Income Fund C	Growth/Inc	-2.5					0.75	2.16	800 279-0279
Davis Growth & Income Fund Y	Growth/Inc	-1.6					0.75	1.13	800 279-0279
Davis Growth Opportunity A	Growth	28.9	16.35	18.52	3	4	0.75	1.31	800 279-0279
Davis Growth Opportunity B	Growth	27.8	15.47	17.65	3	4	0.75	2.16	800 279-0279
Davis Growth Opportunity Fund C	Growth	27.7					0.75	2.35	800 279-0279
Davis Growth Opportunity Fund Y	Growth	29.4					0.75	1.1	800 279-0279
Davis Intl Total Return A	Foreign	4.8	0.33	3.6	5	3	1	1.45	800 279-0279
Davis Intl Total Return B	Foreign	3.8	-0.66	2.74	5	3	1	2.58	800 279-0279
Davis Intl Total Return Fund C	Foreign	4.3					1	2.72	800 279-0279
Davis New York Venture Fund A	Growth	9.2	17.6	22.61	2	3	0.53	0.86	800 279-0279
Davis New York Venture Fund B	Growth	8.3	16.6	21.49	2	3	0.53	1.73	800 279-0279
Davis New York Venture Fund C	Growth	8.3	16.67	21.55	2	3	0.53	1.71	800 279-0279
Davis New York Venture Fund Y	Growth	9.5	16.53		3	3	0.53	0.61	800 279-0279

Stock Fund Name	Objective	Annualized Return for			Rank		Max Load	Expense Ratio	Toll-Free Telephone
		1 Year	3 Years	5 Years	Overall	Risk			
Davis Real Estate A	Real Est	1.1	0.62	11.63	4	2	0.7	1.2	800 279-0279
Davis Real Estate B	Real Est	0.3	-0.19	10.66	4	2	0.7	2.02	800 279-0279
Davis Real Estate Fund C	Real Est	-0.8					0.7	2	800 279-0279
Davis Real Estate Y	Real Est	1.5	0.34		4	2	0.7	0.82	800 279-0279
Dean Balanced Fund A	Balanced	-7.3	1.42		3	1	0.75	1.85	800 543-8721
Dean Balanced Fund C	Balanced	-8.7					0.75	2.6	800 543-8721
Dean International Value A	Foreign	46.4					0.75	2.89	800 543-8721
Dean International Value C	Foreign	45.7					0.75	2.83	800 543-8721
Dean Large Cap Value A	Growth	-9.1	2.17		4	3	0.75	1.85	800 543-8721
Dean Large Cap Value C	Growth	-11.7					0.75	2.6	800 543-8721
Dean Small Cap Value A	Small Co	-19.1	-1.52		5	3	0.75	1.85	800 543-8721
Dean Small Cap Value C	Small Co	-19.7					0.75	2.6	800 543-8721
Delafield Fund	Growth	-7.8	-0.11	9.64	5	3	0.8	1.23	800 221-3079
Delaware Balanced A	Balanced	-9.1	5.91	11.12	3	2	0.63	1.12	800 523-4640
Delaware Balanced B	Balanced	-9.8	5.09	10.25	3	2	0.63	1.73	800 523-4640
Delaware Balanced C	Balanced	-9.8	5.1		3	2	0.63	1.73	800 523-4640
Delaware Balanced I	Balanced	-8.9	6.14	11.32	3	2	0.63	0.73	800 523-4640
Delaware Blue Chip A	Growth/Inc	5.1	14.13		3	3	0.65	1.53	800 523-4640
Delaware Blue Chip B	Growth/Inc	4.3	13.35		3	3	0.65	2.22	800 523-4640
Delaware Blue Chip C	Growth/Inc	4.3	13.31		3	3	0.65	2.22	800 523-4640
Delaware Blue Chip Inst	Growth/Inc	5.3	14.45		3	3	0.65	1.22	800 523-4640
Delaware Decatur Equity Income A	Income	-13.5	3.31	11.96	4	2	0.6	1.03	800 523-4640
Delaware Decatur Equity Income B	Income	-14.1	2.52	11.07	3	2	0.6	1.78	800 523-4640
Delaware Decatur Equity Income C	Income	-14.2	2.53		4	2	0.6	1.78	800 523-4640
Delaware Decatur Equity Income I	Income	-13.3	3.54	12.18	4	2	0.6	0.78	800 523-4640
Delaware Emerging Markets A	Foreign	10	-10.4		5	4	1.25	1.94	800 523-4640
Delaware Emerging Markets B	Foreign	9.2	-11.03		5	4	1.25	2.7	800 523-4640
Delaware Emerging Markets C	Foreign	9.1	-11.04		5	4	1.25	2.7	800 523-4640
Delaware Emerging Markets I	Foreign	10.2	-10.15		5	4	1.25	1.69	800 523-4640
Delaware Foundation Balanced A	Balanced	4.8					0.1	0.8	800 523-4640
Delaware Foundation Balanced B	Balanced	4					0.1	1.55	800 523-4640
Delaware Foundation Balanced C	Balanced	4.1					0.1	1.55	800 523-4640
Delaware Foundation Balanced I	Balanced	5.1					0.1	0.55	800 523-4640
Delaware Foundation Growth A	Growth	6.5					0.1	0.8	800 523-4640
Delaware Foundation Growth B	Growth	5.6					0.1	1.55	800 523-4640
Delaware Foundation Growth C	Growth	5.7					0.1	1.55	800 523-4640
Delaware Foundation Growth I	Growth	6.7					0.1	0.55	800 523-4640
Delaware Foundation Income A	Income	3.7					0.1	0.8	800 523-4640
Delaware Foundation Income B	Income	3.1					0.1	1.55	800 523-4640
Delaware Foundation Income C	Income	3					0.1	1.55	800 523-4640
Delaware Foundation Income I	Income	4					0.1	0.55	800 523-4640
Delaware Global Equity A	AssetAlloc	-4.4	3.76	9.22	5	2	0.84	1.85	800 523-4640
Delaware Global Equity B	AssetAlloc	-5	3.05	8.48	5	2	0.84	2.54	800 523-4640
Delaware Global Equity C	AssetAlloc	-5.1	3.03		5	2	0.84	2.54	800 523-4640
Delaware Global Equity I	AssetAlloc	-4.1	4.09	9.56	4	2	0.84	1.55	800 523-4640
Delaware Growth & Income A	Growth/Inc	-14.3	3.48	12.6	3	3	0.6	1.19	800 523-4640
Delaware Growth & Income B	Growth/Inc	-14.8	2.76	11.8	4	3	0.6	1.87	800 523-4640
Delaware Growth & Income C	Growth/Inc	-14.8	2.77		4	3	0.6	1.87	800 523-4640
Delaware Growth & Income I	Growth/Inc	-14	3.79	12.93	4	3	0.6	0.88	800 523-4640
Delaware Growth Opportunities A	Growth	56.6	30.77	24.96	3	4	0.75	1.2	800 523-4640
Delaware Growth Opportunities B	Growth	55.6	29.85	24.1	3	4	0.75	2.06	800 523-4640
Delaware Growth Opportunities C	Growth	55.5	29.85		3	4	0.75	2.06	800 523-4640
Delaware Growth Opportunities I	Growth	57.1	31.17	25.34	2	4	0.75	1.07	800 523-4640
Delaware Growth Stock A	Growth	-8.8	7.72	13.97	3	3	0.65	1.67	800 523-4640
Delaware Growth Stock B	Growth	-9.5	6.21		4	2	0.65	2.43	800 523-4640
Delaware Growth Stock C	Growth	-9.4	6.15		4	2	0.65	2.43	800 523-4640
Delaware Growth Stock I	Growth	-8.5					0.65	1.42	800 523-4640
Delaware Intl Eq A	Foreign	5.6	4.59	10.64	5	2	0.84	1.86	800 523-4640

298

Stock Fund Name	Objective	Annualized Return for			Rank		Max Load	Expense Ratio	Toll-Free Telephone
		1 Year	3 Years	5 Years	Overall	Risk			
Delaware Intl Eq B	Foreign	4.9	3.76	9.83	5	2	0.84	2.49	800 523-4640
Delaware Intl Eq C	Foreign	4.9	3.76		5	2	0.84	2.49	800 523-4640
Delaware Intl Eq I	Foreign	5.8	4.92	10.98	5	2	0.84	1.48	800 523-4640
Delaware New Pacific A	Pacific	12.3	-10.16	-2.69	5	4	0.84	2	800 523-4640
Delaware New Pacific B	Pacific	11.4	-10.7	-3.32	5	4	0.84	2.7	800 523-4640
Delaware New Pacific C	Pacific	11.5	-10.78	-3.37	5	4	0.84	2.7	800 523-4640
Delaware Overseas Equity A	Global	9.8	0.92	5.87	5	3	1	1.85	800 523-4640
Delaware Overseas Equity B	Global	8.8	-0.12	5.54	5	3	1	2.54	800 523-4640
Delaware Overseas Equity C	Global	8.8	0.15	5.67	5	3	1	2.54	800 523-4640
Delaware Overseas Equity I	Global	9.8	1.09	5.76	5	3	1	1.55	800 523-4640
Delaware Pooled Tr-Intl Equity	Foreign	8.8	6.23	11.71	5	3	0.75	0.9	800 523-4640
Delaware Pooled Tr-Labor Intl Eq	Foreign	9.1	8.25		3	2	0.56	0.69	800 523-4640
Delaware Pooled Tr-Mid Cap Gr	Agg Growth	57.1	32.38	25.85	2	4	0.33	1.12	800 523-4640
Delaware REIT A	Real Est	7.5	5.55		3	2	0.75	1.19	800 523-4640
Delaware REIT B	Real Est	6.6					0.75	1.94	800 523-4640
Delaware REIT C	Real Est	6.6					0.75	1.94	800 523-4640
Delaware Select Growth A	Agg Growth	44.2	48.07	37.78	1	4	0.75	1.2	800 523-4640
Delaware Select Growth B	Agg Growth	43.2	46.94		2	4	0.75	2.79	800 523-4640
Delaware Select Growth C	Agg Growth	43.1	46.24	36.26	1	4	0.75	2.79	800 523-4640
Delaware Select Growth I	Agg Growth	44.5					0.75	1.81	800 523-4640
Delaware Small Cap Value A	Small Co	-9.6	0.31	10.25	5	3	0.75	1.6	800 523-4640
Delaware Small Cap Value B	Small Co	-10.3	-0.37	9.49	5	3	0.75	2.16	800 523-4640
Delaware Small Cap Value C	Small Co	-10.3	-0.37		5	3	0.75	2.16	800 523-4640
Delaware Small Cap Value I	Small Co	-9.3	0.61	10.58	5	3	0.75	1.15	800 523-4640
Delaware Social Awareness A	Growth	8.1	15.28		4	3	0.75	1.47	800 523-4640
Delaware Social Awareness B	Growth	7.3	14.41		4	3	0.75	2.22	800 523-4640
Delaware Social Awareness C	Growth	7.3	14.41		4	3	0.75	2.22	800 523-4640
Delaware Social Awareness I	Growth	8.3	15.55		3	3	0.75	1.22	800 523-4640
Delaware TF Florida A	Muni State	-0.2	3.81	5.45	3	3	0.55	0.57	800 523-4640
Delaware TF Florida B	Muni State	-0.9	3.02		4	3	0.55	1.33	800 523-4640
Delaware TF Florida C	Muni State	-0.9	2.97	4.66	4	3	0.55	1.33	800 523-4640
Delaware TF Florida Ins A	Muni State	1.5	4.3	5.45	2	3	0.5	0.81	800 523-4640
Delaware TF Florida Ins B	Muni State	0.8	3.56	4.77	3	3	0.5	1.57	800 523-4640
Delaware Tax Efficient Eq A	Growth	-9.3	8.54		4	2	0.75	1.44	800 523-4640
Delaware Tax Efficient Eq B	Growth	-10.1	7.77		4	2	0.75	2.2	800 523-4640
Delaware Tax Efficient Eq C	Growth	-9.9	7.83		4	2	0.75	2.2	800 523-4640
Delaware Tax Efficient Eq I	Growth	-8.7					0.75		800 523-4640
Delaware Trend Fund A	Agg Growth	63.9	36.39	28.45	2	4	0.75	1.05	800 523-4640
Delaware Trend Fund B	Agg Growth	62.7	35.36	27.5	2	4	0.75	1.44	800 523-4640
Delaware Trend Fund C	Agg Growth	62.7	35.36		2	4	0.75	2.16	800 523-4640
Delaware Trend Fund I	Agg Growth	64.4	36.73	28.77	2	4	0.75	1.16	800 523-4640
Delaware US Growth A	Growth	35.3	28.5	25.89	1	4	0.65	1.48	800 523-4640
Delaware US Growth B	Growth	34.3	27.57	25	2	4	0.65	2.18	800 523-4640
Delaware US Growth C	Growth	34.3	27.71	25.1	2	4	0.65	2.18	800 523-4640
Delaware US Growth I	Growth	35.7	28.88	26.28	2	4	0.65	1.18	800 523-4640
Deutsche International Equity	Foreign	23.4	13.24	17.59	3	3	0.65	1.5	800 730-1313
Deutsche Intl Equity I Instl	Foreign	24.1	14		3	3	0.57	0.94	800 368-4031
Deutsche Intl Equity II Instl	Foreign	23.7	14.16		3	3	0.57	1.25	800 368-4031
Deutsche Micro Cap Svc	Small Co	58.6					1.5	1.73	800 550-6426
Deutsche Mid Cap Inv	Growth	46.8	32.57	24.42	2	4	0.65	1.25	800 730-1313
Deutsche Quantitative Equity Inv	Growth	9.1					0.9	0.9	800 730-1313
Deutsche Smaller Company Svc	Small Co	42.8					1	1.5	800 550-6426
Dodge & Cox Balanced Fund	Balanced	-0.7	8.95	12.84	2	1	0.5	0.53	800 621-3979
Dodge & Cox Stock Fund	Growth/Inc	-3.3	10.5	16.93	3	3	0.5	0.55	800 621-3979
Domini Social Equity	Growth	7	21.25	24.3	3	3	0.94	0.96	800 762-6814
Dreyfus Appreciation Fund	Growth	6.6	16.51	22.64	2	3	0.55	0.88	800 645-6561
Dreyfus Balanced Fund	Balanced	5.2	8.92	11.73	3	1	0.59	1.02	800 645-6561
Dreyfus Basic S&P 500 Stock Idx	Growth/Inc	7	19.35	23.47	2	3	0.2	0.1	800 645-6561

Stock Fund Name	Objective	Annualized Return for			Rank		Max Load	Expense Ratio	Toll-Free Telephone
		1 Year	3 Years	5 Years	Overall	Risk			
Dreyfus Disciplined Stock Fund	Growth/Inc	7.5	18.8	23.25	3	3	0.9	0.5	800 645-6561
Dreyfus Emerging Markets Fund	Foreign	10.8	3.01		4	4	0.85	1.87	800 645-6561
Dreyfus Equity Income	Growth/Inc	-5.7	6.31		3	2	0.75	0.61	800 645-6561
Dreyfus FL Intermediate Muni	Muni State	2.6	3.43	4.2	3	2	0.59	0.81	800 645-6561
Dreyfus Founders Balanced Fund F	Balanced	-3	5.6	12.14	3	1	0.56	0.96	800 525-2440
Dreyfus Founders Discovery Fund F	Small Co	85.5	44.03	32.33	2	5	1	1.44	800 525-2440
Dreyfus Founders Growth Fund F	Growth	20.3	21.36	24.04	2	3	0.67	1.08	800 525-2440
Dreyfus Founders International Eq	Foreign	43	21.55		2	3	1	1.8	800 525-2440
Dreyfus Founders Mid Cap Growth F	Agg Growth	38.1	16.66	16.09	3	4	0.79	1.39	800 525-2440
Dreyfus Founders Passport Fund F	Foreign	54.1	21.29	20.72	3	4	1	1.62	800 525-2440
Dreyfus Founders Worldwide Gr F	Global	35.2	16.13	16.34	3	3	0.94	1.53	800 525-2440
Dreyfus Fund	Growth/Inc	9.6	12.88	13.97	4	3	0.63	0.71	800 645-6561
Dreyfus Global Growth Fund	Global	31.1	10.41	12.41	4	4	0.75	1.39	800 645-6561
Dreyfus Gr & Value-Aggressive Gr	Agg Growth	35.5	-6.59		4	4	0.75	1.19	800 645-6561
Dreyfus Gr & Value-Aggressive Val	Small Co	8.8	8.57		3	3	0.75	1.29	800 645-6561
Dreyfus Gr & Value-Emerg Leaders	Growth	26.6	23.85		2	3	0.9	1.37	800 645-6561
Dreyfus Gr & Value-Intl Value	Foreign	13	9.19		4	2	1	0.69	800 645-6561
Dreyfus Gr & Value-Large Co Val	Growth	-5.2	6.3	16.31	4	3	0.75	1.25	800 645-6561
Dreyfus Gr & Value-Midcap Val	Growth	15.9	14.75		3	4	0.75	1.28	800 645-6561
Dreyfus Gr & Value-Sm Co Val	Small Co	9.3	9.6	19.62	3	4	0.75	1.22	800 645-6561
Dreyfus Growth & Income	Growth/Inc	3.9	10.8	13.58	4	2	0.75	1.03	800 645-6561
Dreyfus Growth Opportunity	Growth	8.2	11.31	15.85	4	3	0.75	1.03	800 645-6561
Dreyfus International Growth	Foreign	39.6	8.98	10.39	4	4	0.75	2	800 645-6561
Dreyfus Intl Stock Index	Foreign	16.4	9.3		3	3	0.25	0.29	800 645-6561
Dreyfus MidCap Index Fund	Growth	16.3	19.59	20.53	2	3	0.25	0.25	800 645-6561
Dreyfus New Leaders Fund	Growth	30.4	16.69	18.41	3	3	0.75	1.12	800 645-6561
Dreyfus Premier Aggr Growth A	Agg Growth	34.8	-4.83	-2.81	4	4	0.75	0.71	888 338-8084
Dreyfus Premier Aggr Growth B	Agg Growth	33.6	-5.64		4	4	0.75	1.14	888 338-8084
Dreyfus Premier Aggr Growth C	Agg Growth	33.7	-5.49		4	4	0.75	1.17	888 338-8084
Dreyfus Premier Aggr Growth R	Agg Growth	34.6	-5		4	4	0.75	0.58	888 338-8084
Dreyfus Premier Balanced Fd A	Balanced	2.3	12.23	16.44	3	1	1	0.61	888 338-8084
Dreyfus Premier Balanced Fd B	Balanced	1.5	11.39	15.56	3	1	1	0.98	888 338-8084
Dreyfus Premier Balanced Fd C	Balanced	1.5	11.41	15.48	3	1	1	0.98	888 338-8084
Dreyfus Premier Balanced Fd R	Balanced	2.5	12.52	16.74	3	1	1	1	888 338-8084
Dreyfus Premier Core Value A	Growth	-1.6	9.64	16.55	2	3	0.9	1.14	888 338-8084
Dreyfus Premier Core Value B	Growth	-2.3					0.9	0.94	888 338-8084
Dreyfus Premier Core Value C	Growth	-2.3					0.9	0.95	888 338-8084
Dreyfus Premier Core Value Inst	Growth	-1.5	9.75	16.72	3	3	0.9	0.52	888 338-8084
Dreyfus Premier Core Value R	Growth	-1.4	9.82	16.86	3	3	0.9	0.45	888 338-8084
Dreyfus Premier Emerging Markets A	Foreign	20.1					1.25	1.12	888 338-8084
Dreyfus Premier Emerging Markets B	Foreign	19.1					1.25	1.5	888 338-8084
Dreyfus Premier Emerging Markets C	Foreign	19.2					1.25	1.48	888 338-8084
Dreyfus Premier Emerging Markets R	Foreign	29.1					1.25	0.98	888 338-8084
Dreyfus Premier European Eq A	European	41.6					0.9	0.88	888 338-8084
Dreyfus Premier European Eq B	European	40.6					0.9	1.16	888 338-8084
Dreyfus Premier European Eq C	European	40.6					0.9	1.16	888 338-8084
Dreyfus Premier European Eq R	European	41.9					0.9	0.78	888 338-8084
Dreyfus Premier FL Muni A	Muni State	0.1	2.65	3.72	4	3	0.55	0.92	888 338-8084
Dreyfus Premier FL Muni B	Muni State	-0.4	2.18	3.23	5	3	0.55	1.41	888 338-8084
Dreyfus Premier FL Muni C	Muni State	-0.7	1.86		5	3	0.55	1.75	888 338-8084
Dreyfus Premier Global Alloc A	Global	7.8					1	0.92	888 338-8084
Dreyfus Premier Global Alloc B	Global	6.9					1	1.29	888 338-8084
Dreyfus Premier Global Alloc C	Global	6.9					1	1.29	888 338-8084
Dreyfus Premier Global Alloc R	Global	8					1	0.8	888 338-8084
Dreyfus Premier Greater China A	Pacific	51					1.25	1.11	888 338-8084
Dreyfus Premier Greater China B	Pacific	49.7					1.25	1.48	888 338-8084
Dreyfus Premier Greater China C	Pacific	49.8					1.25	1.48	888 338-8084
Dreyfus Premier Greater China R	Pacific	51.3					1.25	0.98	888 338-8084

Stock Fund Name	Objective	Annualized Return for			Rank		Max Load	Expense Ratio	Toll-Free Telephone
		1 Year	3 Years	5 Years	Overall	Risk			
Dreyfus Premier Growth & Inc A	Growth/Inc	3.8	10.65		4	2	0.75	0.67	888 338-8084
Dreyfus Premier Growth & Inc B	Growth/Inc	3	9.85		4	2	0.75	1.04	888 338-8084
Dreyfus Premier Growth & Inc C	Growth/Inc	3.1	9.86		4	2	0.75	1.02	888 338-8084
Dreyfus Premier Growth & Inc R	Growth/Inc	3.8	10.73		3	2	0.75	0.61	888 338-8084
Dreyfus Premier HY Debt + Eq A	Flexible	-18.5					0.75	1	888 338-8084
Dreyfus Premier HY Debt + Eq B	Flexible	-19.6					0.75	1.75	888 338-8084
Dreyfus Premier HY Debt + Eq C	Flexible	-19.6					0.75	1.75	888 338-8084
Dreyfus Premier HY Debt + Eq T	Flexible	-19.2					0.75	1.25	888 338-8084
Dreyfus Premier Intl Growth A	Foreign	40.1	12.35	13.7	4	4	0.75	1.39	888 338-8084
Dreyfus Premier Intl Growth B	Foreign	39.1	11.5	12.83	4	4	0.75	1.07	888 338-8084
Dreyfus Premier Intl Growth C	Foreign	39	11.46		4	4	0.75	1.08	888 338-8084
Dreyfus Premier Intl Growth R	Foreign	40.4	12.35		4	4	0.75	0.63	888 338-8084
Dreyfus Premier Intl Value A	Foreign	15.1					1	0.98	888 338-8084
Dreyfus Premier Intl Value B	Foreign	14.1					1	1.37	888 338-8084
Dreyfus Premier Intl Value C	Foreign	14.2					1	1.36	888 338-8084
Dreyfus Premier Intl Value R	Foreign	15.4					1	0.88	888 338-8084
Dreyfus Premier Large Co Stock A	Growth/Inc	7.4	18.8	23.01	3	3	0.9	0.56	888 338-8084
Dreyfus Premier Large Co Stock B	Growth/Inc	6.5					0.9	0.93	888 338-8084
Dreyfus Premier Large Co Stock C	Growth/Inc	6.5					0.9	0.93	888 338-8084
Dreyfus Premier Large Co Stock R	Growth/Inc	7.6	19.1	23.31	3	3	0.9	0.9	888 338-8084
Dreyfus Premier Market Neutral A	Growth	-7.2					1.5	0.7	888 338-8084
Dreyfus Premier Market Neutral B	Growth	-7.9					1.5	1.09	888 338-8084
Dreyfus Premier Market Neutral C	Growth	-7.9					1.5	1.09	888 338-8084
Dreyfus Premier Market Neutral R	Growth	-7					1.5	0.58	888 338-8084
Dreyfus Premier Midcap Stock A	Growth	14.2	14.61	20.98	3	3	1.1	0.67	888 338-8084
Dreyfus Premier Midcap Stock B	Growth	13.3					1.1	1.04	888 338-8084
Dreyfus Premier Midcap Stock C	Growth	13.3					1.1	1.04	888 338-8084
Dreyfus Premier Midcap Stock R	Growth	14.5	14.91	21.31	3	3	1.1	1.1	888 338-8084
Dreyfus Premier Real Estate Mtg A	Real Est	8					0.59	2.75	800 645-6561
Dreyfus Premier Small Cap Val A	Small Co	-3.4					1.25	0.73	888 338-8084
Dreyfus Premier Small Cap Val B	Small Co	-4.3					1.25	1.12	888 338-8084
Dreyfus Premier Small Cap Val C	Small Co	-4.2					1.25	1.12	888 338-8084
Dreyfus Premier Small Cap Val R	Small Co	-3.3					1.25	0.61	888 338-8084
Dreyfus Premier Small Co Stk A	Small Co	12.5	6.35	12.81	4	3	1.25	0.73	888 338-8084
Dreyfus Premier Small Co Stk B	Small Co	11.6	5.5	11.92	4	3	1.25	1.12	888 338-8084
Dreyfus Premier Small Co Stk C	Small Co	11.6	5.52	11.94	4	3	1.25	1.12	888 338-8084
Dreyfus Premier Small Co Stk R	Small Co	12.8	6.58	13.06	4	3	1.25	0.61	888 338-8084
Dreyfus Premier Tax Mgd Grwth A	Growth	6.7					1.1	1.35	888 338-8084
Dreyfus Premier Tax Mgd Grwth B	Growth	5.9					1.1	0.67	888 338-8084
Dreyfus Premier Tax Mgd Grwth C	Growth	5.9					1.1	1.04	888 338-8084
Dreyfus Premier Tax Mgd Grwth T	Growth	6.5					1.1	1.04	888 338-8084
Dreyfus Premier Tech Growth A	Technology	94.8					0.75	1.19	888 338-8084
Dreyfus Premier Tech Growth B	Technology	93.1					0.75	0.81	888 338-8084
Dreyfus Premier Tech Growth C	Technology	93.1					0.75	0.81	888 338-8084
Dreyfus Premier Tech Growth R	Technology	94.1					0.75	0.44	888 338-8084
Dreyfus Premier Third Century Fd Z	Growth	18.5	23.81	26	2	3	0.75	0.92	800 645-6561
Dreyfus Premier Value A	Small Co	-4.3	5.8	12.18	5	3	0.75	0.57	888 338-8084
Dreyfus Premier Value B	Small Co	-5.1	4.98	11.34	5	3	0.75	0.95	888 338-8084
Dreyfus Premier Value C	Small Co	-5.2	4.87		5	3	0.75	0.93	888 338-8084
Dreyfus Premier Value R	Small Co	-4.4	5.49		5	3	0.75	0.71	888 338-8084
Dreyfus Premier Wrldwde Growth A	Global	13.8	17.35	21.08	2	2	0.75	1.15	888 338-8084
Dreyfus Premier Wrldwde Growth B	Global	12.9	16.48	20.18	2	2	0.75	0.94	888 338-8084
Dreyfus Premier Wrldwde Growth C	Global	13	16.49	20.15	2	2	0.75	0.93	888 338-8084
Dreyfus Premier Wrldwde Growth R	Global	14.1	17.67		2	2	0.75	0.45	888 338-8084
Dreyfus S&P 500 Index Fund	Growth/Inc	6.6	19.02	23.11	2	3	0.25	0.5	800 645-6561
Dreyfus Small Cap Stock Index Fd	Small Co	14.3	9.84		4	3	0.25	0.25	800 645-6561
Driehaus Asia Pacific Growth Fund	Pacific	80.9					1.5	2.77	800 560-6111
Driehaus Emerging Markets Growth	Foreign	52.5					1.5	2.7	800 560-6111

Stock Fund Name	Objective	Annualized Return for			Rank		Max Load	Expense Ratio	Toll-Free Telephone
		1 Year	3 Years	5 Years	Overall	Risk			
Driehaus European Opportunity Fund	European	192.3					1.5	2.1	800 560-6111
Driehaus International Discovery Fd	Foreign	141.9					1.5	2.47	800 560-6111
Driehaus International Growth Fund	Foreign	58.1	25.97		3	4	1.5	1.84	800 560-6111
Duncan-Hurst Aggressive Growth I	Agg Growth						1		800 558-9105
Duncan-Hurst International Growth I	Foreign						1.25		800 558-9105
Duncan-Hurst International Growth R	Foreign						1.25		800 558-9105
Duncan-Hurst Large Cap Growth-20	Growth	62.8					1		800 558-9105
Duncan-Hurst Technology Fund R	Technology						1		800 558-9105
E-Trade S&P 500 Index Fund	Growth	6.5					0.07		800 786-2575
Eagle Growth Shares	Growth	-5.7	-0.13	6.21	5	2	0.75	3.35	800 749-9933
Eastcliff Contrarian Value Fund	Agg Growth	-6.5					1	1.3	800 595-5519
Eastcliff Emerging Growth Fund	Agg Growth						1		800 595-5519
Eastcliff Growth Fund	Growth	22.5	21.08		2	4	1	1.3	800 595-5519
Eastcliff Regional Sm Cap Value	Small Co	-11.8	-1.08		5	3	1	1.3	800 595-5519
Eastcliff Total Return	Growth/Inc	20.8	25.16	25.81	1	3	1	1.3	800 811-5311
Eaton Vance Asian Small Companies A	Pacific	78.5					1.25		800 225-6265
Eaton Vance Asian Small Companies B	Pacific						1.25		800 225-6265
Eaton Vance Balanced A	Balanced	-1.9	7.59	12.23	3	1	0.6	0.96	800 225-6265
Eaton Vance Balanced B	Balanced	-2.7	6.77	11.27	3	1	0.6	1.75	800 225-6265
Eaton Vance Capital Exchange Fund	Growth/Inc	13.6	19.85	23.43	2	2	0.5	0.47	800 225-6265
Eaton Vance Emerging Mkts A	Foreign	29.3	-3.13	6.84	4	5	1.25	2.95	800 225-6265
Eaton Vance Emerging Mkts B	Foreign	28.5	-3.58	6.26	4	5	1.25	3.39	800 225-6265
Eaton Vance FL Ins Muni A	Muni State	1.3	3.84	5.03	4	4	0.45	0.66	800 225-6265
Eaton Vance FL Ins Muni B	Muni State	0.6	3.04	4.3	5	4	0.45	1.43	800 225-6265
Eaton Vance FL Ltd Mat Muni B	Muni State	0.7	2.24	2.85	4	2	0.46	1.62	800 225-6265
Eaton Vance FL Ltd Mat Muni C	Muni State	0.7	2.21	2.79	4	2	0.46	1.65	800 225-6265
Eaton Vance FL Muni A	Muni State	-0.3	3.47	4.83	4	4	0.45	0.72	800 225-6265
Eaton Vance FL Muni B	Muni State	-1	2.71	4.01	5	4	0.45	1.56	800 225-6265
Eaton Vance Greater China A	Pacific	23.4	-7.93	1.92	4	5	1.25	2.33	800 225-6265
Eaton Vance Greater China B	Pacific	22.8	-8.45	1.38	4	5	1.25	2.6	800 225-6265
Eaton Vance Greater China C	Pacific	22.8	-8.47	1.18	4	5	1.25	2.6	800 225-6265
Eaton Vance Greater India A	Foreign	25.6	7.47	2.77	4	4	1.25	3.52	800 225-6265
Eaton Vance Greater India B	Foreign	24.7	7.24	2.14	4	4	1.25	3.68	800 225-6265
Eaton Vance Growth & Income A	Growth/Inc	-4.7	11.77	17.47	3	3	0.62	1.08	800 225-6265
Eaton Vance Growth & Income B	Growth/Inc	-5.5	10.81	16.27	3	3	0.62	1.83	800 225-6265
Eaton Vance Growth Fund A	Growth	-10.6	6.79	14.04	3	3	1	1.06	800 225-6265
Eaton Vance Growth Fund B	Growth	-11.4	6	12.92	4	3	1	1.87	800 225-6265
Eaton Vance Growth Fund C	Growth	-11.4	5.72	11.8	3	3	1	1.89	800 225-6265
Eaton Vance Info Age A	Technology	47.3	32.85		1	3	0.75	2.45	800 225-6265
Eaton Vance Info Age B	Technology	46.9	32.5		1	3	0.75	2.79	800 225-6265
Eaton Vance Info Age C	Technology	46.7	32.42		1	3	0.75	2.87	800 225-6265
Eaton Vance SC Muni A	Muni State	0.4	2.92	4.55	4	4	0.28	0.8	800 225-6265
Eaton Vance SC Muni B	Muni State	-0.6	2.12	3.92	5	3	0.28	1.54	800 225-6265
Eaton Vance Special Eq A	Growth	49.5	26.2	24.21	2	4	0.63	1.16	800 225-6265
Eaton Vance Special Eq B	Growth	43.9	23.82	21.46	3	4	0.63	2.02	800 225-6265
Eaton Vance Tax-Managed Growth A	Growth	13.3	19.71		2	2	0.45	0.68	800 225-6265
Eaton Vance Tax-Managed Growth B	Growth	12.5	18.82		2	2	0.45	1.42	800 225-6265
Eaton Vance Tax-Managed Growth C	Growth	12.4	18.59		2	2	0.45	1.58	800 225-6265
Eaton Vance Tax-Managed Intl Gr A	Global	31.6					1	1.91	800 225-6265
Eaton Vance Tax-Managed Intl Gr B	Global	30.6					1	2.66	800 225-6265
Eaton Vance Tax-Managed Intl Gr C	Global	30.6					1	2.91	800 225-6265
Eaton Vance Tax-Mgd Emerg Gr A	Growth	49.2					0.62	0.95	800 225-6265
Eaton Vance Tax-Mgd Emerg Gr B	Growth	48					0.62	1.73	800 225-6265
Eaton Vance Tax-Mgd Emerg Gr C	Growth	47.9					0.62	1.9	800 225-6265
Eaton Vance Utilities A	Utilities	23.1	23.84	20.14	2	2	0.65	1.08	800 225-6265
Eaton Vance Utilities B	Utilities	22.3	22.86	19.18	2	2	0.65	1.82	800 225-6265
Eaton Vance WW Health Sciences A	Health	113.9	35.29	34.08	2	4	1.13	1.68	800 225-6265
Eaton Vance WW Health Sciences B	Health	112.4	34.38		2	4	1.13	2.16	800 225-6265

Stock Fund Name	Objective	Annualized Return for			Rank		Max Load	Expense Ratio	Toll-Free Telephone
		1 Year	3 Years	5 Years	Overall	Risk			
Eaton Vance WW Health Sciences C	Health	112.4					1.13	2.29	800 225-6265
Eclipse Balanced Fund	Balanced	-6.1	5.74	9.93	3	1	0.84	0.93	800 872-2710
Eclipse MidCap Value Fund	Growth/Inc	-10.5	6.56	13.81	4	3	0.9	1.05	800 872-2710
Eclipse Small Cap Value Fund	Small Co	-7.3	5.71	14.16	3	3	1	1.17	800 872-2710
Edgar Lomax Value Fund	Growth/Inc	-19.6					1	1.75	800 385-7003
Ehrenkrantz Growth Fund	Growth	28.9	14.86	11.81	3	2	1	2.39	800 424-8570
Elfun Diversified Fund	Flexible	10.1	13.84	15.67	3	1	0.07	0.25	800 242-0134
Elfun International Fund	Global	27.9	17.7	17.22	2	3	0.05	0.3	800 242-0134
Elfun Trusts	Growth	8.7	19.38	23.32	2	2	0.02	0.11	800 242-0134
Endowments Growth & Income	Growth/Inc	-5.4	9.69	14.91	3	2	0.5	0.75	800 421-9900
Enterprise Global Financial Serv A	Global	-14.7					0.84	1.75	800 432-4320
Enterprise Global Financial Serv B	Global	-15.1					0.84	2.29	800 432-4320
Enterprise Global Financial Serv C	Global	-15.2					0.84	2.29	800 432-4320
Enterprise-Balanced A	Balanced						0.75		800 432-4320
Enterprise-Balanced B	Balanced						0.75		800 432-4320
Enterprise-Balanced C	Balanced						0.75		800 432-4320
Enterprise-Capital Appreciation A	Growth	18.7	22.86	20.31	3	4	0.75	1.52	800 432-4320
Enterprise-Capital Appreciation B	Growth	18	22.2	19.66	3	4	0.75	2.04	800 432-4320
Enterprise-Capital Appreciation C	Growth	18.2	16.44		2	4	0.75	2.04	800 432-4320
Enterprise-Equity A	Growth	24.7					0.75	1.6	800 432-4320
Enterprise-Equity B	Growth	23.8	17.56		3	3	0.75	2.14	800 432-4320
Enterprise-Equity C	Growth	23.9	16.72		3	3	0.75	2.14	800 432-4320
Enterprise-Equity Income A	Income	-8.5	7.04	14.85	3	2	0.75	1.5	800 432-4320
Enterprise-Equity Income B	Income	-9	6.4	14.19	3	2	0.75	2.04	800 432-4320
Enterprise-Equity Income C	Income	-8.9	3.35		4	2	0.75	2.04	800 432-4320
Enterprise-Growth Portfolio A	Growth	7.6	18.83	24.65	2	3	0.75	1.39	800 432-4320
Enterprise-Growth Portfolio B	Growth	7	18.25	24	3	3	0.75	1.94	800 432-4320
Enterprise-Growth Portfolio C	Growth	7	17.41		2	3	0.75	1.94	800 432-4320
Enterprise-Growth and Income A	Growth/Inc	17.7					0.75	1.5	800 432-4320
Enterprise-Growth and Income B	Growth/Inc	17.1					0.75	2.04	800 432-4320
Enterprise-Growth and Income C	Growth/Inc	17.2					0.75	2.04	800 432-4320
Enterprise-International Growth A	Foreign	21.5	9.25	12.58	3	3	0.84	2	800 432-4320
Enterprise-International Growth B	Foreign	20.7	27.59	24.58	3	5	0.84	2.54	800 432-4320
Enterprise-International Growth C	Foreign	20.7	6.08		3	3	0.84	2.54	800 432-4320
Enterprise-Internet Fund A	Technology						1		800 432-4320
Enterprise-Internet Fund B	Technology						1		800 432-4320
Enterprise-Internet Fund C	Technology						1		800 432-4320
Enterprise-Managed Portfolio A	AssetAlloc	-1.8	6.1	12.72	3	2	0.75	1.44	800 432-4320
Enterprise-Managed Portfolio B	AssetAlloc	-2.3	5.47	12.1	3	2	0.75	2	800 432-4320
Enterprise-Managed Portfolio C	AssetAlloc	-2.4	3.75		5	2	0.75	2	800 432-4320
Enterprise-Multi-Cap Growth A	Growth						1		800 432-4320
Enterprise-Multi-Cap Growth B	Growth						1		800 432-4320
Enterprise-Multi-Cap Growth C	Growth						1		800 432-4320
Enterprise-Small Co Growth A	Small Co	31.4					1	1.85	800 432-4320
Enterprise-Small Co Growth B	Small Co	30.9					1	2.39	800 432-4320
Enterprise-Small Co Growth C	Small Co	30.8					1	2.39	800 432-4320
Enterprise-Small Co Value A	Small Co	8.1	13.32	16.14	3	2	0.75	1.62	800 432-4320
Enterprise-Small Co Value B	Small Co	7.6	12.68	15.48	3	2	0.75	2.18	800 432-4320
EquiTrust Blue Chip Fund Trad	Growth	-0.1	11.59	17.6	3	2	0.25	1.44	800 247-4170
EquiTrust Managed Fund Trad	Flexible	-0.5	-2.67	4.74	3	1	0.45	1.94	800 247-4170
EquiTrust Value Growth Trad	Growth/Inc	-11.9	-11.27	0.25	5	3	0.5	1.73	800 247-4170
Euclid Market Neutral A	Growth	-3.3					1.5	3.64	800 243-4361
Euclid Market Neutral B	Growth	-4					1.5	4.34	800 243-4361
Euclid Market Neutral C	Growth	-4.1					1.5	4.34	800 243-4361
Eureka Equity Fund A	Growth	3.3					0.65	1.25	800 300-8893
Eureka Equity Fund Trust	Growth	3.6					0.65	1	800 300-8893
Eureka Global Asset Allocation A	Balanced	7.4					0.8	1.61	800 300-8893
Eureka Global Asset Allocation Tr	Balanced	7.7					0.8	1.37	800 300-8893

303

Stock Fund Name	Objective	Annualized Return for			Rank		Max Load	Expense Ratio	Toll-Free Telephone
		1 Year	3 Years	5 Years	Overall	Risk			
EuroPacific Growth Fund	Foreign	33.2	18.86	19.59	2	3	0.46	0.83	800 421-9900
Evergreen Aggressive Growth A	Agg Growth	53.3	32.77	26.08	2	4	0.81	1.12	800 343-2898
Evergreen Aggressive Growth B	Agg Growth	52.2	31.79		3	4	0.81	1.97	800 343-2898
Evergreen Aggressive Growth C	Agg Growth	52.2	31.8		2	4	0.81	1.97	800 343-2898
Evergreen Aggressive Growth Y	Agg Growth	53.8	33.25		2	4	0.81	0.97	800 343-2898
Evergreen Balanced A	Balanced	8.1					0.42	0.95	800 343-2898
Evergreen Balanced B	Balanced	7.4	10.82	14.26	3	1	0.42	1.65	800 343-2898
Evergreen Balanced C	Balanced	7.3					0.42	1.7	800 343-2898
Evergreen Balanced Y	Balanced	8.5					0.42	0.7	800 343-2898
Evergreen Blue Chip A	Growth/Inc	12.4					0.64	1.19	800 343-2898
Evergreen Blue Chip B	Growth/Inc	11.5	18.03	21.36	2	2	0.64	1.94	800 343-2898
Evergreen Blue Chip C	Growth/Inc	11.5					0.64	1.94	800 343-2898
Evergreen Blue Chip Fund Y	Growth/Inc	12.6					0.64	0.94	800 343-2898
Evergreen Capital Balanced A	Balanced	0.8	5.09	9.22	3	1	0.84	1.37	800 343-2898
Evergreen Capital Balanced B	Balanced						0.75	2.22	800 343-2898
Evergreen Capital Balanced C	Balanced	0	5.04	8.88	3	1	0.84	2.12	800 343-2898
Evergreen Capital Balanced Fund Y	Balanced	0.1					0.75	1.13	800 343-2898
Evergreen Capital Growth A	Growth	0.3	12.84	16.59	3	4	0.8	1.36	800 343-2898
Evergreen Capital Growth C	Growth	-0.2	14.64	19.43	3	3	0.8	2.43	800 343-2898
Evergreen Emerging Markets Fd A	Foreign	12.7	0.87	7.24	5	4	1.5	2.25	800 343-2898
Evergreen Emerging Markets Fd B	Foreign	11.8	-0.09	6.36	5	4	1.5	3.02	800 343-2898
Evergreen Emerging Markets Fd C	Foreign	12.1	0	6.42	5	4	1.5	3.02	800 343-2898
Evergreen Emerging Markets Fd Y	Foreign	13.1	1.21	7.55	5	4	1.5	1.9	800 343-2898
Evergreen Equity Income A	Income	-6.2	8.09	15.59	3	2	0.63	1.19	800 343-2898
Evergreen Equity Income B	Income	-6.9	7.24	14.66	3	2	0.63	1.92	800 343-2898
Evergreen Equity Income C	Income	-6.8	7.27	14.69	3	2	0.63	1.92	800 343-2898
Evergreen Equity Income Y	Income	-6	8.37		4	3	0.63	0.86	800 343-2898
Evergreen Equity Index C	Growth	6.2					0.11	1.31	800 343-2898
Evergreen FL High Income Muni A	Muni State	-2.5	3.33	5.31	2	2	0.59	0.86	800 343-2898
Evergreen FL High Income Muni B	Muni State	-3.1	2.6		3	2	0.59	1.62	800 343-2898
Evergreen FL High Income Muni C	Muni State	-3.1					0.59	1.61	800 343-2898
Evergreen FL High Income Muni Y	Muni State	-2.3	3.6		2	2	0.59	0.61	800 343-2898
Evergreen FL Muni Bond A	Muni State	0.7	3.67	4.97	3	3	0.5	0.33	800 343-2898
Evergreen FL Muni Bond B	Muni State	-0.2	2.78	4.05	4	3	0.5	1.25	800 343-2898
Evergreen FL Muni Bond C	Muni State	-0.2					0.5	1.25	800 343-2898
Evergreen FL Muni Bond Y	Muni State	0.8	3.8	5.08	3	3	0.5	0.25	800 343-2898
Evergreen Foundation Fund A	Balanced	6.3	12.31	14.3	3	1	0.77	1.26	800 343-2898
Evergreen Foundation Fund B	Balanced	5.5	11.45	13.43	3	1	0.77	2	800 343-2898
Evergreen Foundation Fund C	Balanced	5.5	11.45	13.33	3	1	0.77	2	800 343-2898
Evergreen Foundation Fund Y	Balanced	6.6	12.56	14.47	3	1	0.77	0.96	800 343-2898
Evergreen Fund A	Growth	4.4	10.75	15.56	4	2	0.89	1.41	800 343-2898
Evergreen Fund B	Growth	3.6	9.97	14.76	4	2	0.89	2.16	800 343-2898
Evergreen Fund C	Growth	3.6	9.99	14.76	4	2	0.89	2.16	800 343-2898
Evergreen Fund Y	Growth	4.6	11.09	15.92	4	2	0.89	1.13	800 343-2898
Evergreen Global Leaders A	Global	9.3	12.13		3	2	0.88	1.79	800 343-2898
Evergreen Global Leaders B	Global	8.5	11.38		3	2	0.88	2.54	800 343-2898
Evergreen Global Leaders C	Global	8.5	11.35		3	2	0.88	2.54	800 343-2898
Evergreen Global Leaders Y	Global	9.6	12.48		3	2	0.88	1.57	800 343-2898
Evergreen Global Opp A	Global	59.8	22.44	16.49	3	4	0.97	1.77	800 343-2898
Evergreen Global Opp B	Global	58.6	21.53	15.61	3	4	0.97	2.52	800 343-2898
Evergreen Global Opp C	Global	58.6	21.55	15.6	3	4	0.97	2.52	800 343-2898
Evergreen Growth & Income Fund A	Growth/Inc	4.3	9.49		4	2	0.89	1.42	800 343-2898
Evergreen Growth & Income Fund B	Growth/Inc	3.5	8.69	15.06	4	2	0.89	2.18	800 343-2898
Evergreen Growth & Income Fund C	Growth/Inc	3.5	8.7	15.02	4	2	0.89	2.18	800 343-2898
Evergreen Growth & Income Fund Y	Growth/Inc	4.5	9.84	16.19	4	2	0.89	1.2	800 343-2898
Evergreen Growth A	Growth	59.7	19.56	21.62	3	4	0.69	2.04	800 343-2898
Evergreen Growth C	Growth	58.5	18.6	20.89	3	4	0.69	2.04	800 343-2898
Evergreen Income and Growth A	Income	-1.8	7.97	11.41	3	2	1	0.93	800 343-2898

Stock Fund Name	Objective	Annualized Return for			Rank		Max Load	Expense Ratio	Toll-Free Telephone
		1 Year	3 Years	5 Years	Overall	Risk			
Evergreen Income and Growth B	Income	-2.6	7.11	10.56	4	2	1	2.2	800 343-2898
Evergreen Income and Growth C	Income	-2.7	7.09	10.6	4	2	1	2.2	800 343-2898
Evergreen Income and Growth Y	Income	-1.6	8.17	11.65	4	2	1	1.2	800 343-2898
Evergreen International Growth A	Foreign	22.7					0.64	1.25	800 343-2898
Evergreen International Growth B	Foreign	21.9	10.47	13.98	3	2	0.64	2	800 343-2898
Evergreen International Growth C	Foreign	21.8					0.64	2	800 343-2898
Evergreen International Growth Y	Foreign	23					0.64	1	800 343-2898
Evergreen Latin America Fund A	Foreign	28.9	-3.04	8.98	4	5	0.75	2.25	800 343-2898
Evergreen Latin America Fund B	Foreign	28.1	-3.72	8.18	4	5	0.75	3	800 343-2898
Evergreen Latin America Fund C	Foreign	28	-3.8	8.15	4	5	0.75	3.02	800 343-2898
Evergreen Latin America Fund Y	Foreign	29.3					0.75	2.02	800 343-2898
Evergreen Masters Fund A	Growth	23.3					0.94	1.58	800 343-2898
Evergreen Masters Fund B	Growth	22.4					0.94	2.37	800 343-2898
Evergreen Masters Fund C	Growth	22.5					0.94	2.35	800 343-2898
Evergreen Masters Fund Y	Growth	23.6					0.94	0.77	800 343-2898
Evergreen Omega A	Agg Growth	45.1	34.62	28.19	1	4	0.73	1.13	800 343-2898
Evergreen Omega B	Agg Growth	43.9	33.61	27.16	1	4	0.73	2.04	800 343-2898
Evergreen Omega C	Agg Growth	44	33.61	27.16	1	4	0.73	2.04	800 343-2898
Evergreen Omega Y	Agg Growth	45.4	34.92		1	4	0.73	1.04	800 343-2898
Evergreen Perpetual Global A	Global	13.1	14.28	17.47	3	3	1.03	2.16	800 343-2898
Evergreen Perpetual Global C	Global	12.3	13.49	16.6	3	3	1.03	2.5	800 343-2898
Evergreen Precious Metals A	Prec Metal	-3.8					0.75	1.98	800 343-2898
Evergreen Precious Metals B	Prec Metal	-4.6	-16.92	-12.65	5	5	0.75	2.74	800 343-2898
Evergreen Precious Metals C	Prec Metal	-4.6					0.75	2.85	800 343-2898
Evergreen SC Muni Bond A	Muni State	2.1	3.93	5.45	2	3	0.5	0.69	800 343-2898
Evergreen SC Muni Bond B	Muni State	1.3	2.93	4.59	3	3	0.5	1.44	800 343-2898
Evergreen SC Muni Bond Y	Muni State	2.4	4.17	5.7	2	3	0.5	0.45	800 343-2898
Evergreen Select Balanced I	Balanced	19.5					0.5	0.68	800 343-2898
Evergreen Select Balanced IS	Balanced	18.2					0.5	0.93	800 343-2898
Evergreen Select Core Equity I	Growth	7.6					0.59	0.67	800 343-2898
Evergreen Select Core Equity IS	Growth	7.4					0.59	0.92	800 343-2898
Evergreen Select Diversfd Val I	Growth	6.7					0.5	0.61	800 343-2898
Evergreen Select Diversfd Val IS	Growth	6.4					0.5	0.88	800 343-2898
Evergreen Select Interntl Bond I	Intl Bond	-2.8	1.98	4.01	5	4	0.59	0.67	800 343-2898
Evergreen Select Interntl Bond IS	Intl Bond	-1.7	2.23	4.04	5	4	0.5	0.92	800 343-2898
Evergreen Select Lrg Cap Blend I	Growth	4.7					0.59	0.68	800 343-2898
Evergreen Select Lrg Cap Blend IS	Growth	4.4					0.59	0.93	800 343-2898
Evergreen Select Secular Growth I	Growth	7.6	5.19	3.08			0.69	0.7	800 343-2898
Evergreen Select Secular Growth IS	Growth	49.6					0.69	0.95	800 343-2898
Evergreen Select Sm Comp Value I	Small Co	-1.9					0.65	0.96	800 343-2898
Evergreen Select Small Cap Growth I	Small Co	66.7	24.89		3	5	0.8	1.02	800 343-2898
Evergreen Select Social Princ I	Growth	19.6					0.69	0.83	800 343-2898
Evergreen Select Social Princ IS	Growth	19.1					0.69	1.09	800 343-2898
Evergreen Select Strat Value I	Growth	-7.3					0.69	0.7	800 343-2898
Evergreen Select Strat Value IS	Growth	-7.8					0.69	0.95	800 343-2898
Evergreen Select Strategic Gr I	Growth	52.2					0.59	0.71	800 343-2898
Evergreen Select Strategic Growth S	Growth	51.9					0.59	0.96	800 343-2898
Evergreen Small Cap Value A	Small Co	0.4	3.31	12.5	3	2	0.97	1.66	800 343-2898
Evergreen Small Cap Value B	Small Co	-0.3	2.5	11.66	3	2	0.97	2.41	800 343-2898
Evergreen Small Cap Value C	Small Co	-0.4	2.48	11.63	3	2	0.97	2.41	800 343-2898
Evergreen Small Cap Value Y	Small Co	0.7	3.55	12.81	3	2	0.97	1.38	800 343-2898
Evergreen Small Co Growth A	Small Co	60.8	17.57		3	4	0.47	1.21	800 343-2898
Evergreen Small Co Growth B	Small Co	59.5	18.25	14.32	3	4	0.47	1.92	800 343-2898
Evergreen Small Co Growth C	Small Co	59.7	16.76		3	4	0.47	1.98	800 343-2898
Evergreen Small Co Growth Y	Small Co	61					0.47	1.01	800 343-2898
Evergreen Stock Selector A	Growth	2.2	14.31	20.35	3	3	0.73	1.06	800 343-2898
Evergreen Stock Selector B	Growth	1.5					0.73	1.81	800 343-2898
Evergreen Stock Selector Y	Growth	2.7	14.6	20.7	3	3	0.73	0.81	800 343-2898

305

Stock Fund Name	Objective	Annualized Return for			Rank		Max Load	Expense Ratio	Toll-Free Telephone
		1 Year	3 Years	5 Years	Overall	Risk			
Evergreen Tax Strat Equity A	Growth	5.2					0.94	2.83	800 343-2898
Evergreen Tax Strat Equity Y	Growth	5.4					0.94	2.58	800 343-2898
Evergreen Tax Strat Foundation A	Balanced	1.9	7.49	10.77	3	1	0.88	1.28	800 343-2898
Evergreen Tax Strat Foundation B	Balanced	1.1	6.7	11.76	3	1	0.88	2.08	800 343-2898
Evergreen Tax Strat Foundation C	Balanced	1.1	6.71	10.97	3	1	0.88	2.08	800 343-2898
Evergreen Tax Strat Foundation Y	Balanced	2.2	7.8	11.65	3	1	0.88	1.08	800 343-2898
Evergreen Utility A	Utilities	22.1	22.47	19.57	1	2	0.5	1.03	800 343-2898
Evergreen Utility B	Utilities	21.4	21.63	18.71	2	2	0.5	1.77	800 343-2898
Evergreen Utility C	Utilities	21.2	21.51	18.7	2	2	0.5	1.77	800 343-2898
Evergreen Utility Y	Utilities	22.2	22.59	18.79	1	2	0.5	0.77	800 343-2898
Evergreen Value A	Growth/Inc	-7.9	8.19	13.76	3	2	0.5	1	800 343-2898
Evergreen Value B	Growth/Inc	-8.6	7.38	12.92	3	2	0.5	1.75	800 343-2898
Evergreen Value C	Growth/Inc	-8.6	7.33	12.9	3	2	0.5	1.75	800 343-2898
Evergreen Value Y	Growth/Inc	-7.7	8.45	14.03	3	2	0.5	0.75	800 343-2898
Excelsior Blended Equity Fd	Growth	14.4	22.82	23.08	2	3	0.75	0.96	800 446-1012
Excelsior Emerging Markets	Foreign	29					0.2	1.64	800 446-1012
Excelsior Energy & Natural Res Fd	Energy/Res	24.4	14.09	19.75	3	4	0.55	0.97	800 446-1012
Excelsior Equity Fund	Growth	16.2	22.28	23.09	2	3	0.5	0.69	800 446-1012
Excelsior Instl Value Equity Fund	Growth	10.3	19.03		2	3	0.36	0.8	800 446-1012
Excelsior International	Foreign	35.3	14.48	14.47	3	3	0.93	1.41	800 446-1012
Excelsior Intl Equity Fund	Foreign	41.5	13.86	13.31	3	3	1	0.9	800 446-1012
Excelsior Large Cap Growth Fund	Growth	25.3					0.75	1	800 446-1012
Excelsior Latin America Fund	Foreign	23.5	-11.56	3.15	4	5	0.9	1.66	800 446-1012
Excelsior Optimum Growth	Agg Growth	21.8	39.47		1	4	0.42	0.8	800 446-1012
Excelsior Pacific/Asia Fund	Pacific	22.6	4.6	5.74	4	4	0.91	1.46	800 446-1012
Excelsior Pan European Fund	European	34.8	16.23	18.14	2	3	0.93	1.42	800 446-1012
Excelsior Real Estate Fund	Real Est	0.2					1	1.19	800 446-1012
Excelsior Small Cap Fd	Small Co	43	14.54	10.21	4	4	0.45	0.93	800 446-1012
Excelsior Value and Restructing Fd	Growth	15.3	20.38	24.89	2	3	0.59	0.9	800 446-1012
Expedition Equity Inst	Growth	17.1	23.78		2	3	0.75	1.05	800 992-2085
Expedition Equity Inv-Svc	Growth	16.8					0.75	1.32	800 992-2085
FA Telecom & Util Gr-CL A	Utilities	15.8	29.66		1	3	0.6	1.32	800 522-7297
FA Telecom & Util Gr-CL B	Utilities	15	28.86		1	3	0.6	2.04	800 522-7297
FA Telecom & Util Gr-CL C	Utilities	15					0.6	2.04	800 522-7297
FA Telecom & Util Gr-CL I	Utilities	16.2	29.96		1	3	0.6	0.98	800 522-7297
FA Telecom & Util Gr-CL T	Utilities	15.7	29.55		1	3	0.6	1.55	800 522-7297
FAM Equity-Income Fund	Income	-9.8	3.01		4	2	1	2.56	800 932-3271
FAM Value Fund	Growth	-5.9	7.69	11.66	4	3	1	1.22	800 932-3271
FBP Contrarian Balanced Fund	Balanced	-12.5	6.53	11.71	3	2	0.75	1.03	800 543-8721
FBP Contrarian Equity Fund	Growth	-19.6	6.2	13.71	4	3	0.75	1.04	800 543-8721
FBR Financial Services A	Financial	-18.3	2.26		5	4	0.9	1.83	888 888-0025
FBR Realty Growth A	Real Est	-6.9	-2.81	8.22	4	2	1	0.81	888 888-0025
FBR Small Cap Financial A	Financial	-5.5	3.23		4	3	0.9	1.64	888 888-0025
FBR Small Cap Value A	Small Co	10.2	15.68		3	3	0.9	1.87	888 888-0025
FFTW Worldwide Fixed Income	Intl Bond	1.7	4.12	4.42	4	4	0.45	0.59	800 762-4848
FFTW Worldwide-Hedged	Intl Bond	4.2	7.55	8.78	1	3	0.25	0.45	800 762-4848
FMC Select Fund	Growth	-0.7	12.06	17.86	3	2	0.8	1.08	877 362-4099
FPA Capital Fund Inc	Small Co	-4.5	7.35	14.56	4	3	0.67	0.86	800 982-4372
FRIC Institutional Equity I Fund E	Growth	2.5					0.55		
FRIC Institutional Equity II Fund E	Growth	23.5					0.69		
FRIC Institutional Equity III Fd E	Growth	-14.6					0.55		
FRIC Institutional Equity Q Fund E	Growth	8.3					0.55		
FRIC Institutional International E	Foreign	20.2					0.69		
FRIC LifePoints Aggress Strategy C	Growth	9.1					0.2	1	
FRIC LifePoints Aggress Strategy E	Growth	9.8					0.2	0.25	
FRIC LifePoints Balance Strategy C	Balanced	7.1					0.2	1	
FRIC LifePoints Balance Strategy E	Balanced	7.9					0.2	0.25	
FRIC LifePoints Conserv Strategy C	Income	4.7					0.2	1	

Stock Fund Name	Objective	Annualized Return for			Rank		Max Load	Expense Ratio	Toll-Free Telephone
		1 Year	3 Years	5 Years	Overall	Risk			
FRIC LifePoints Eqty Agg Strategy C	Agg Growth	9.8					0.2	1	
FRIC LifePoints Eqty Agg Strategy E	Agg Growth	10.5					0.2	0.25	
FRIC LifePoints Moderate Strategy C	Growth/Inc	5.9					0.2	1	
FRIC Russell Diversified Equity C	Growth/Inc	0.8					0.72	1.87	
FRIC Russell Diversified Equity E	Growth/Inc	2	16.2		3	3	0.72	1.12	
FRIC Russell Emerging Markets C	Foreign	9.2					0.11	2.93	
FRIC Russell Emerging Markets E	Foreign	9.9					0.11	2.2	
FRIC Russell Emerging Markets S	Foreign	10.1	-7.42	0.57	5	4	0.11	1.6	
FRIC Russell Equity Income Fund C	Growth/Inc	-15.7					0.75	2.1	
FRIC Russell Equity Income Fund E	Growth/Inc	-14.9	5.18		5	3	0.75	1.37	
FRIC Russell International Secs C	Foreign	19.3					0.9	2.2	
FRIC Russell International Secs E	Foreign	20.5	9.36		3	2	0.9	1.47	
FRIC Russell International Secs S	Foreign	16.6	8.45	10.16	4	2	0.9	1.23	
FRIC Russell Quantitative Equity C	Growth	6.6					0.72	1.83	
FRIC Russell Quantitative Equity E	Growth	7.9	19.1		3	3	0.72	1.12	
FRIC Russell Real Estate Secs E	Real Est	5.2	1.8		4	2	0.8	1.4	
FRIC Russell Real Estate Secs S	Real Est	5.5	2.31	9.69	3	2	0.8	0.93	
FRIC Russell Special Growth Fund C	Agg Growth	21.4					0.9	2.29	
FRIC Russell Special Growth Fund E	Agg Growth	22.9	14.4		3	3	0.9	1.5	
Fairmont Fund	Growth	-19.4	-9.65	0.42	5	3	1.67	1.77	800 262-9936
Fasciano Fund	Small Co	3.7	9.39	14.22	3	2	1	1.19	800 338-1579
Federated Aggressive Growth A	Agg Growth	69.2	39.9		3	5	1	2.5	800 245-5051
Federated Aggressive Growth B	Agg Growth	68	38.92		3	5	1	2.5	800 245-5051
Federated Aggressive Growth C	Agg Growth	67.8	38.85		3	5	1	2.5	800 245-5051
Federated American Leaders A	Growth/Inc	-9.2	10.22	16.76	3	2	0.64	1.15	800 245-5051
Federated American Leaders B	Growth/Inc	-9.9	9.37	15.89	3	2	0.64	1.86	800 245-5051
Federated American Leaders C	Growth/Inc	-9.8	9.38	15.9	3	2	0.64	1.86	800 245-5051
Federated American Leaders F	Growth/Inc	-9.2	10.18	16.75	3	2	0.64	1.11	800 245-5051
Federated Asia Pacific Growth A	Pacific	23.5	1.85		4	4	1.1	1.85	800 245-5051
Federated Asia Pacific Growth B	Pacific	22.4	1.14		4	4	1.1	2.6	800 245-5051
Federated Asia Pacific Growth C	Pacific	22.4	1.23		4	4	1.1	2.6	800 245-5051
Federated Capital Appreciation A	Growth/Inc	26.1	25.72	25.96	1	3	0.75	1.26	800 245-5051
Federated Capital Appreciation B	Growth/Inc	25.2	24.83		1	3	0.75	1.98	800 245-5051
Federated Capital Appreciation C	Growth/Inc	25.2	24.76		1	3	0.75	1.98	800 245-5051
Federated Comm Technology A	Technology						0.75		800 245-5051
Federated Comm Technology B	Technology						0.75		800 245-5051
Federated Comm Technology C	Technology						0.75		800 245-5051
Federated Emerging Markets A	Foreign	8.9	-2.7		4	4	1.25	2.6	800 245-5051
Federated Emerging Markets B	Foreign	8.1	-3.4		4	4	1.25	3.31	800 245-5051
Federated Emerging Markets C	Foreign	8.1	-3.42		4	4	1.25	3.31	800 245-5051
Federated Equity Income Fd A	Income	9.1	13.76	19.51	3	2	0.59	1.1	800 245-5051
Federated Equity Income Fd B	Income	8.2	12.92	14.6	3	2	0.59	1.86	800 245-5051
Federated Equity Income Fd C	Income	8.3	12.93	18.62	3	2	0.59	1.86	800 245-5051
Federated Equity Income Fd F	Income	8.8	13.49	19.2	3	2	0.59	1.36	800 245-5051
Federated European Growth Fund A	European	25.2	17		2	3	1	1.85	800 245-5051
Federated European Growth Fund B	European	24.2	16.1		2	3	1	1.84	800 245-5051
Federated European Growth Fund C	European	24.3	16.05		2	3	1	2.6	800 245-5051
Federated Glb Financial Services A	Financial	-0.8					1		800 245-5051
Federated Glb Financial Services B	Financial	-1.6					1		800 245-5051
Federated Glb Financial Services C	Financial	-1.5					1		800 245-5051
Federated Global Equity Income A	Global	30.3					1	2	800 245-5051
Federated Global Equity Income B	Global	29.6					1	2.5	800 245-5051
Federated Global Equity Income C	Global	29.4					1	2.5	800 245-5051
Federated Growth Strategies A	Growth	35.5	29	28.82	2	4	0.84	1.23	800 245-5051
Federated Growth Strategies B	Growth	34.5	28.07		2	4	0.84	1.98	800 245-5051
Federated Growth Strategies C	Growth	34.7	28.25		2	4	0.84	1.96	800 245-5051
Federated International Equity A	Foreign	52.1	24.96	18.73	3	4	1	1.63	800 245-5051
Federated International Equity B	Foreign	50.9	23.99		3	4	1	2.37	800 245-5051

307

Stock Fund Name	Objective	Annualized Return for			Rank		Max Load	Expense Ratio	Toll-Free Telephone
		1 Year	3 Years	5 Years	Overall	Risk			
Federated International Equity C	Foreign	51.3	24.09	15.21	3	4	1	2.37	800 245-5051
Federated International Growth A	Foreign	28.3	9.12		3	3	0.25	0.07	800 245-5051
Federated International Income A	Intl Bond	-6.4	-1.35	1.7	4	5	0.7	1.42	800 245-5051
Federated International Income B	Intl Bond	-7	-2.04	-1.95	4	5	0.7	2.14	800 245-5051
Federated International Income C	Intl Bond	-7.1	-2.06	0.95	4	5	0.7	2.14	800 245-5051
Federated Intl Small Co Fd A	Foreign	44	34.31		2	4	1.25	2.02	800 245-5051
Federated Intl Small Co Fd B	Foreign	43	33.34		2	4	1.25	2.7	800 245-5051
Federated Intl Small Co Fd C	Foreign	42.9	33.34		2	4	1.25	2.7	800 245-5051
Federated Large Cap Growth A	Growth	27.5					0.75	1.19	800 245-5051
Federated Large Cap Growth B	Growth	26.9					0.75	1.94	800 245-5051
Federated Large Cap Growth C	Growth	26.9					0.75	1.96	800 245-5051
Federated Max Cap Fund C	Growth/Inc	5.7					0.29	1.32	800 245-5051
Federated Max Cap Fund Instl	Growth/Inc	6.7	19.11	23.28	1	3	0.29	0.3	800 245-5051
Federated Max Cap Fund Instl-Svc	Growth/Inc	6.4	18.69	22.9	1	3	0.29	0.6	800 245-5051
Federated Mid Cap Fund	Growth	16.2	19.39	20.08	2	3	0.4	0.59	800 245-5051
Federated Mini Cap C	Small Co	11.1					0.5	1.82	800 245-5051
Federated Mini Cap Instl	Small Co	12.2	8.34	12.21	4	4	0.5	0.9	800 245-5051
Federated Mngd Moderate Gr Sel	AssetAlloc	5.4	9.5	10.96	4	1	0.75	1.77	800 245-5051
Federated Small Cap Strategies A	Small Co	12.3	8.03		4	5	0.75	2.14	800 245-5051
Federated Small Cap Strategies B	Small Co	11.4	7.23		4	5	0.75	2.04	800 245-5051
Federated Small Cap Strategies C	Small Co	11.3	7.18		4	5	0.75	2.04	800 245-5051
Federated Stock Trust	Growth/Inc	-11.2	10.03	17.1	3	2	0.66	0.94	800 245-5051
Federated Stock and Bond Fund A	Balanced	-5.2	7.14	11.78	3	1	0.72	1.25	800 245-5051
Federated Stock and Bond Fund B	Balanced	-6	6.34		3	1	0.72	2	800 245-5051
Federated Stock and Bond Fund C	Balanced	-5.9	6.29		3	1	0.72	2	800 245-5051
Federated Utility Fund A	Utilities	-3	9.51	12.73	3	2	1	1.21	800 245-5051
Federated Utility Fund B	Utilities	-3.7	8.71		3	2	1	1.97	800 245-5051
Federated Utility Fund C	Utilities	-3.7	8.69	11.89	3	2	1	1.97	800 245-5051
Federated Utility Fund F	Utilities	-2.9	9.57		3	2	1	1.19	800 245-5051
Federated World Utility Fund A	Utilities	11.4	17.6	19.37	2	3	1	1.61	800 245-5051
Federated World Utility Fund B	Utilities	10.5	16.73		2	3	1	2.33	800 245-5051
Federated World Utility Fund C	Utilities	10.5	16.73		2	3	1	2.33	800 245-5051
Fidelity Adv Asset Allocation A	AssetAlloc	11.6					0.58	1.75	800 522-7297
Fidelity Adv Asset Allocation B	AssetAlloc	10.9					0.58	2.5	800 522-7297
Fidelity Adv Asset Allocation C	AssetAlloc	10.8					0.58	2.5	800 522-7297
Fidelity Adv Asset Allocation I	AssetAlloc	11.9					0.72	1.5	800 522-7297
Fidelity Adv Asset Allocation T	AssetAlloc	11.4					0.58	1.98	800 522-7297
Fidelity Adv Balanced Fund A	Balanced	-0.7	8.92		3	1	0.44	0.9	800 522-7297
Fidelity Adv Balanced Fund B	Balanced	-1.6	8.08		3	1	0.44	1.68	800 522-7297
Fidelity Adv Balanced Fund C	Balanced	-1.6					0.44	1.65	800 522-7297
Fidelity Adv Balanced Fund I	Balanced	-0.5	9.36		3	1	0.44	0.63	800 522-7297
Fidelity Adv Balanced Fund T	Balanced	-1.1	8.74	11.02	3	1	0.44	1.15	800 522-7297
Fidelity Adv Consumer Indust A	Growth	-5.6	14.16		3	3	0.6	1.54	800 522-7297
Fidelity Adv Consumer Indust B	Growth	-6.4	13.26		3	3	0.6	2.29	800 522-7297
Fidelity Adv Consumer Indust C	Growth	-6.3					0.6	2.29	800 522-7297
Fidelity Adv Consumer Indust T	Growth	-5.9	13.82		3	3	0.6	1.77	800 522-7297
Fidelity Adv Cyclical Indust A	Growth	-8.1	5.71		5	3	0.6	1.54	800 522-7297
Fidelity Adv Cyclical Indust B	Growth	-8.7	4.95		5	3	0.6	2.29	800 522-7297
Fidelity Adv Cyclical Indust C	Growth	-8.7					0.6	2.27	800 522-7297
Fidelity Adv Cyclical Indust I	Growth	-7.7	6.02		5	3	0.6	1.29	800 522-7297
Fidelity Adv Cyclical Indust T	Growth	-8.3	5.5		5	3	0.6	1.81	800 522-7297
Fidelity Adv Diversified Intl A	Foreign	33.3					0.73	2	800 522-7297
Fidelity Adv Diversified Intl B	Foreign	32.3					0.73	2.75	800 522-7297
Fidelity Adv Diversified Intl C	Foreign	32.3					0.73	2.75	800 522-7297
Fidelity Adv Diversified Intl I	Foreign	33.7					0.73	1.75	800 522-7297
Fidelity Adv Diversified Intl T	Foreign	32.9					0.73	2.25	800 522-7297
Fidelity Adv Dividend Growth A	Growth	3.3					0.58	1.25	800 522-7297
Fidelity Adv Dividend Growth B	Growth	2.6					0.58	2.27	800 522-7297

Stock Fund Name	Objective	Annualized Return for			Rank		Max Load	Expense Ratio	Toll-Free Telephone
		1 Year	3 Years	5 Years	Overall	Risk			
Fidelity Adv Dividend Growth C	Growth	2.6					0.58	2.25	800 522-7297
Fidelity Adv Dividend Growth I	Growth	3.6					0.72	1.21	800 522-7297
Fidelity Adv Dividend Growth T	Growth	3.1					0.58	1.73	800 522-7297
Fidelity Adv Dynamic Cap App A	Growth	61.9					0.58	1.75	800 522-7297
Fidelity Adv Dynamic Cap App B	Growth	60.9					0.58	2.5	800 522-7297
Fidelity Adv Dynamic Cap App C	Growth	60.9					0.58	2.5	800 522-7297
Fidelity Adv Dynamic Cap App I	Growth	62.4					0.58	1.5	800 522-7297
Fidelity Adv Dynamic Cap App T	Growth	61.7					0.58	2	800 522-7297
Fidelity Adv Emerging Asia A	Pacific						0.72		800 522-7297
Fidelity Adv Emerging Asia B	Pacific						0.72		800 522-7297
Fidelity Adv Emerging Asia C	Pacific						0.72		800 522-7297
Fidelity Adv Emerging Asia I	Pacific						0.72		800 522-7297
Fidelity Adv Emerging Asia T	Pacific						0.72		800 522-7297
Fidelity Adv Emerging Markets Inc C	Intl Bond	23.4					0.68	2.24	800 522-7297
Fidelity Adv Emerging Mkts Inc A	Intl Bond	24.4	5.93		3	5	0.68	1.39	800 522-7297
Fidelity Adv Emerging Mkts Inc B	Intl Bond	23.5	5.42	16.28	3	5	0.68	2.1	800 522-7297
Fidelity Adv Emerging Mkts Inc I	Intl Bond	24.6	6.03		3	5	0.68	1.15	800 522-7297
Fidelity Adv Emerging Mkts Inc T	Intl Bond	24.3	5.86	16.89	3	5	0.68	1.4	800 522-7297
Fidelity Adv Equity Growth A	Growth	25.5	29.09		1	3	0.6	1.12	800 522-7297
Fidelity Adv Equity Growth B	Growth	24.6	28.15		1	3	0.6	1.88	800 522-7297
Fidelity Adv Equity Growth C	Growth	24.6					0.6	1.87	800 522-7297
Fidelity Adv Equity Growth I	Growth	25.9	29.58	26.89	1	3	0.6	0.78	800 522-7297
Fidelity Adv Equity Growth T	Growth	25.3	28.89	26.19	1	3	0.6	1.31	800 522-7297
Fidelity Adv Equity Income A	Income	-8.8	7.78		4	3	0.5	1.01	800 522-7297
Fidelity Adv Equity Income B	Income	-9.4	7.04	12.96	4	3	0.5	1.73	800 522-7297
Fidelity Adv Equity Income C	Income	-9.7					0.5	1.76	800 522-7297
Fidelity Adv Equity Income I	Income	-8.5	8.16	14.18	4	3	0.5	0.69	800 522-7297
Fidelity Adv Equity Income T	Income	-9	7.59	13.52	4	3	0.5	1.22	800 522-7297
Fidelity Adv Europe Captl Apprec A	European	18.3					0.73	2	800 522-7297
Fidelity Adv Europe Captl Apprec B	European	17.3					0.73	2.75	800 522-7297
Fidelity Adv Europe Captl Apprec C	European	17.4					0.73	2.75	800 522-7297
Fidelity Adv Europe Captl Apprec I	European	18.6					0.73	1.75	800 522-7297
Fidelity Adv Europe Captl Apprec T	European	18.1					0.73	2.25	800 522-7297
Fidelity Adv Financial Serv A	Financial	-7.9	10.94		4	4	0.57	1.22	800 522-7297
Fidelity Adv Financial Serv B	Financial	-8.6	10.06		4	4	0.57	1.97	800 522-7297
Fidelity Adv Financial Serv C	Financial	-8.6					0.57	1.93	800 522-7297
Fidelity Adv Financial Serv I	Financial	-7.6	11.1		3	4	0.57	0.92	800 522-7297
Fidelity Adv Financial Serv T	Financial	-8.1	10.66		3	4	0.57	1.45	800 522-7297
Fidelity Adv Global Equity A	Global	21					0.73	2	800 522-7297
Fidelity Adv Global Equity B	Global	20.1					0.73	2.75	800 522-7297
Fidelity Adv Global Equity C	Global	20.2					0.73	2.75	800 522-7297
Fidelity Adv Global Equity Instl	Global	21.4					0.73	1.75	800 522-7297
Fidelity Adv Global Equity T	Global	20.7					0.73	2.25	800 522-7297
Fidelity Adv Gr Opportunity A	Growth	-6.7	11.38		3	2	0.78	0.93	800 522-7297
Fidelity Adv Gr Opportunity B	Growth	-7.5	10.55		4	2	0.78	1.68	800 522-7297
Fidelity Adv Gr Opportunity C	Growth	-7.4					0.78	1.67	800 522-7297
Fidelity Adv Gr Opportunity I	Growth	-6.4	11.75		2	2	0.78	0.61	800 522-7297
Fidelity Adv Gr Opportunity T	Growth	-6.9	11.18	15.87	2	2	0.78	1.11	800 522-7297
Fidelity Adv Growth & Income A	Growth/Inc	9.6	20.92		3	3	0.5	1.04	800 522-7297
Fidelity Adv Growth & Income B	Growth/Inc	8.8	20.59		3	3	0.5	1.81	800 522-7297
Fidelity Adv Growth & Income C	Growth/Inc	8.8					0.5	1.8	800 522-7297
Fidelity Adv Growth & Income I	Growth/Inc	9.9	21.35		3	3	0.5	0.75	800 522-7297
Fidelity Adv Growth & Income T	Growth/Inc	9.4	20.71		3	3	0.5	1.29	800 522-7297
Fidelity Adv Health Care A	Health	23.1	23.44		2	2	0.6	1.2	800 522-7297
Fidelity Adv Health Care B	Health	22.2	22.47		2	2	0.6	1.95	800 522-7297
Fidelity Adv Health Care C	Health	22.2					0.6	1.91	800 522-7297
Fidelity Adv Health Care I	Health	23.5	23.77		2	2	0.6	0.94	800 522-7297
Fidelity Adv Health Care T	Health	22.9	23.19		2	3	0.6	1.42	800 522-7297

| Stock Fund Name | Objective | Annualized Return for | | | Rank | | Max Load | Expense Ratio | Toll-Free Telephone |
		1 Year	3 Years	5 Years	Overall	Risk			
Fidelity Adv Intl Cap Apprec A	Foreign	47.1					0.59	1.71	800 522-7297
Fidelity Adv Intl Cap Apprec B	Foreign	46					0.59	2.47	800 522-7297
Fidelity Adv Intl Cap Apprec I	Foreign	47.7					0.59	1.46	800 522-7297
Fidelity Adv Intl Cap Apprec T	Foreign	46.9					0.59	1.96	800 522-7297
Fidelity Adv Intl Captl Apprec C	Foreign	46.2					0.59	2.47	800 522-7297
Fidelity Adv Japan A	Pacific	57.2					0.73	2	800 522-7297
Fidelity Adv Japan B	Pacific	55.9					0.73	2.75	800 522-7297
Fidelity Adv Japan C	Pacific	56.1					0.73	2.75	800 522-7297
Fidelity Adv Japan Instl	Pacific	57.7					0.73	1.75	800 522-7297
Fidelity Adv Japan T	Pacific	56.8					0.73	2.25	800 522-7297
Fidelity Adv Large Cap Fund A	Growth	17.7	24.39		2	3	0.59	1.3	800 522-7297
Fidelity Adv Large Cap Fund B	Growth	16.8	23.67		2	3	0.6	2.02	800 522-7297
Fidelity Adv Large Cap Fund C	Growth	16.8					0.59	2.04	800 522-7297
Fidelity Adv Large Cap Fund I	Growth	18.1	24.92		2	3	0.6	0.95	800 522-7297
Fidelity Adv Large Cap Fund T	Growth	17.4	24.33		2	3	0.6	1.43	800 522-7297
Fidelity Adv Latin America A	Foreign	16.3					0.73	2	800 522-7297
Fidelity Adv Latin America B	Foreign	15.5					0.73	2.5	800 522-7297
Fidelity Adv Latin America C	Foreign	15.4					0.73	2.75	800 522-7297
Fidelity Adv Latin America Instl	Foreign	16.6					0.73	1.75	800 522-7297
Fidelity Adv Latin America T	Foreign	16.1					0.73	2.25	800 522-7297
Fidelity Adv Mid Cap Fund A	Growth	49.6	29.83		2	4	0.59	1.18	800 522-7297
Fidelity Adv Mid Cap Fund B	Growth	48.5	28.99		2	4	0.6	1.92	800 522-7297
Fidelity Adv Mid Cap Fund C	Growth	48.5					0.6	1.93	800 522-7297
Fidelity Adv Mid Cap Fund I	Growth	50.3	30.39		2	4	0.6	0.86	800 522-7297
Fidelity Adv Mid Cap Fund T	Growth	49.4	29.68		2	4	0.6	1.38	800 522-7297
Fidelity Adv Natural Resources A	Energy/Res	16.9	8.01		4	4	0.59	1.22	800 522-7297
Fidelity Adv Natural Resources B	Energy/Res	16	7.49		4	4	0.6	1.94	800 522-7297
Fidelity Adv Natural Resources C	Energy/Res	16.1					0.59	1.88	800 522-7297
Fidelity Adv Natural Resources I	Energy/Res	17.4	8.59		4	4	0.6	0.81	800 522-7297
Fidelity Adv Natural Resources T	Energy/Res	16.7	8.05	12.9	4	4	0.57	1.39	800 522-7297
Fidelity Adv Overseas Fund A	Foreign	25.7	13.11		3	3	0.68	1.55	800 522-7297
Fidelity Adv Overseas Fund B	Foreign	24.8	12.3		3	3	0.68	2.29	800 522-7297
Fidelity Adv Overseas Fund C	Foreign	24.8					0.68	2.24	800 522-7297
Fidelity Adv Overseas Fund I	Foreign	26.2	13.51		3	3	0.68	1.17	800 522-7297
Fidelity Adv Overseas Fund T	Foreign	25.6	12.95	14.48	3	3	0.68	1.71	800 522-7297
Fidelity Adv Small Cap A	Growth	32.3					0.73	1.38	800 522-7297
Fidelity Adv Small Cap B	Growth	31.3					0.73	2.16	800 522-7297
Fidelity Adv Small Cap C	Growth	31.4					0.73	2.12	800 522-7297
Fidelity Adv Small Cap Instl	Growth	32.3					0.73	1.08	800 522-7297
Fidelity Adv Small Cap T	Growth	33					0.73	1.62	800 522-7297
Fidelity Adv Technology A	Technology	57.8	46.13		2	5	0.6	1.23	800 522-7297
Fidelity Adv Technology B	Technology	56.6	44.96		2	5	0.6	2	800 522-7297
Fidelity Adv Technology C	Technology	56.6					0.6	1.95	800 522-7297
Fidelity Adv Technology I	Technology	58.3	46.47		2	5	0.6	0.96	800 522-7297
Fidelity Adv Technology T	Technology	57.4	46.49		2	5	0.6	1.45	800 522-7297
Fidelity Adv Technoquant Gr A	Growth	25.4	19.94		2	3	0.59	1.3	800 522-7297
Fidelity Adv Technoquant Gr B	Growth	24.3	19.07		2	3	0.59	2.02	800 522-7297
Fidelity Adv Technoquant Gr C	Growth	24.5					0.59	2.47	800 522-7297
Fidelity Adv Technoquant Gr I	Growth	25.6	20.21		2	3	0.59	1.02	800 522-7297
Fidelity Adv Technoquant Gr T	Growth	25	19.65		2	3	0.59	1.52	800 522-7297
Fidelity Adv Value Strategies A	Growth	3.6	10.66		4	3	0.34	1.06	800 522-7297
Fidelity Adv Value Strategies B	Growth	2.8	10.03	11.84	5	3	0.34	1.66	800 522-7297
Fidelity Adv Value Strategies I	Growth	4	11.12	12.67	3	3	0.34	0.57	800 522-7297
Fidelity Adv Value Strategies T	Growth	3.4	10.62	12.44	5	3	0.34	1.15	800 522-7297
Fidelity Aggressive Growth Fund	Agg Growth	55.5	48.38	34.61	2	4	0.71	0.96	800 544-8888
Fidelity Aggressive Int'l Fd	Foreign	29.3	14.45	16.03	3	3	0.84	1.13	800 544-8888
Fidelity Asset Manager	AssetAlloc	11.6	14.62	15.53	3	1	0.54	0.75	800 544-8888
Fidelity Asset Manager Growth	AssetAlloc	7.7	14.63	17.33	2	2	0.58	0.82	800 544-8888

Stock Fund Name	Objective	Annualized Return for			Rank		Max Load	Expense Ratio	Toll-Free Telephone
		1 Year	3 Years	5 Years	Overall	Risk			
Fidelity Asset Manager Income	Balanced	5.6	8.19	9.21	3	1	0.42	0.67	800 544-8888
Fidelity Asset Manager: Aggressive	Agg Growth							0.57	800 544-8888
Fidelity Balanced Fund	Balanced	-0.1	13.23	13.7	3	1	0.45	0.67	800 544-8888
Fidelity Blue Chip Growth	Growth	18.7	23.59	22.68	2	3	0.46	0.81	800 544-8888
Fidelity Canada Fund	Foreign	51.6	12.24	13.32	3	4	0.45	1.08	800 544-8888
Fidelity Capital Appreciation	Growth	19.9	21.35	20.76	2	4	0.78	0.65	800 544-8888
Fidelity Congress Street	Growth	0.9	12.88	19.19	3	2	0.32	0.61	800 544-8888
Fidelity Contrafund	Growth	10.5	21.5	22.38	3	3	0.45	0.66	800 544-8888
Fidelity Contrafund II	Growth	33.9					0.58	0.85	800 544-8888
Fidelity Destiny I Class O	Growth	-8.2	11.68	16.79	3	2	0.65	0.26	800 544-8888
Fidelity Destiny II Class O	Growth	12.4	21.53	22.51	2	3	0.78	0.54	800 544-8888
Fidelity Disciplined Equity	Growth	15.9	21.29	21.46	2	3	0.42	0.65	800 544-8888
Fidelity Diversified Intl Fund	Foreign	32.2	17.95	20.06	2	3	0.85	1.2	800 544-8888
Fidelity Dividend Growth Fund	Growth	4.8	21.01	24.11	2	3	0.64	0.7	800 544-8888
Fidelity Emerging Markets	Foreign	12.2	-11.52	-5.89	5	5	0.76	1.46	800 544-8888
Fidelity Equity Income-I	Income	-7.7	9.21	16.06	3	3	0.48	0.68	800 544-8888
Fidelity Equity Income-II	Income	-7.7	10.27	15.53	3	2	0.48	0.66	800 544-8888
Fidelity Europe	European	23.2	16.07	19.06	2	3	0.72	0.98	800 544-8888
Fidelity European Cap Apprec	European	20.9	15.73	18.64	3	3	0.65	1.09	800 544-8888
Fidelity Exchange Fund	Growth	3	13.58	19.96	3	2	0	0.63	800 544-8888
Fidelity Export Fund	Global	30.3	25.96	26.67	1	3	0.6	0.85	800 544-8888
Fidelity Fifty Fund	Agg Growth	9.3	19.26	20.18	3	4	0.65	0.79	800 544-8888
Fidelity Four-in-One Index Fund	Growth/Inc						0.1	0.08	800 544-8888
Fidelity France Fund	European	37.8	22.9		2	3	0.75	1.96	800 544-8888
Fidelity Freedom 2000 Fund	AssetAlloc	11.1	12.66		3	1	0.1	0.07	800 544-8888
Fidelity Freedom 2010 Fund	AssetAlloc	14.7	16.35		2	1	0.1	0.07	800 544-8888
Fidelity Freedom 2020 Fund	AssetAlloc	18	19.08		2	2	0.1	0.07	800 544-8888
Fidelity Freedom 2030 Fund	AssetAlloc	19.5	19.99		2	2	0.1	0.07	800 544-8888
Fidelity Fund	Growth/Inc	10.5	21.62	23.93	2	3	0.38	0.53	800 544-8888
Fidelity Germany Fund	European	31.9	16.24		3	4	0.75	1.55	800 544-8888
Fidelity Global Balanced Fund	Balanced	15.2	13.07	13.45	3	2	0.73	1.18	800 544-8888
Fidelity Growth Company	Growth	63.9	38.05	31.2	1	4	0.51	0.73	800 544-8888
Fidelity Hong Kong and China Fund	Pacific	28.8	5.6		4	5	0.75	1.34	800 544-8888
Fidelity International Bond	Intl Bond	3.3	2.19	1.88	4	5	0.69	0.65	800 544-8888
Fidelity Intl Growth & Income	Foreign	35.3	16.18	16.09	3	3	0.73	1.12	800 544-8888
Fidelity Japan Fund	Pacific	57.6	23.19	16.1	3	4	0.93	1.23	800 544-8888
Fidelity Japan Small Companies	Pacific	31.2	31.14		3	5	0.72	1.07	800 544-8888
Fidelity Large Cap Stock Fund	Growth	18.5	25.27	24.93	2	3	0.68	0.9	800 544-8888
Fidelity Latin American Fund	Foreign	15.1	-4.08	10.55	4	5	0.76	1.31	800 544-8888
Fidelity Low-Priced Stock	Small Co	3.1	7.94	14.56	2	2	0.81	1.09	800 544-8888
Fidelity Magellan Fund	Growth	9.8	22.16	20.79	3	3	0.78	0.73	800 544-8888
Fidelity Mid-Cap Stock Fund	Growth	50.5	31.05	27.13	2	4	0.66	0.73	800 544-8888
Fidelity New Millennium	Agg Growth	56.5	44.9	39.46	2	5	0.82	0.93	800 544-8888
Fidelity Nordic Fund	European	49.1	29.62		1	4	0.75	1.15	800 544-8888
Fidelity OTC Portfolio	Agg Growth	55.3	38.59	31.05	2	4	0.83	0.75	800 544-8888
Fidelity Overseas Fund	Foreign	26	13.63	15.16	3	3	0.93	1.27	800 544-8888
Fidelity Pacific Basin	Pacific	42.6	16.12	11.54	3	4	1.05	1.36	800 544-8888
Fidelity Puritan Fund	Balanced	-1.3	8.96	13.27	3	1	0.45	0.64	800 544-8888
Fidelity Real Estate Investment	Real Est	7.9	2.11	11.05	3	2	0.57	0.9	800 544-8888
Fidelity Retirement Growth	Growth	47.9	33.86	26.82	2	4	0.4	0.63	800 544-8888
Fidelity Select-Air Transport	Other	14.4	23.9	18.16	3	4	0.57	1.27	800 544-6666
Fidelity Select-Automotive	Other	-22.8	-3.89	4.4	5	3	0.58	1.69	800 544-6666
Fidelity Select-Banking Port	Financial	-20.5	3.49	16.66	4	4	0.58	1.15	800 544-6666
Fidelity Select-Biotech	Health	115.1	51.5	37.02	2	5	0.58	1.16	800 544-6666
Fidelity Select-Brokerage	Financial	20.2	26.45	29.84	3	4	0.58	1.26	800 544-6666
Fidelity Select-Business Svcs	Financial	-2.5					0.58	1.63	800 544-6666
Fidelity Select-Chemicals	Other	-3.9	-0.86	7.41	4	3	0.58	1.6	800 544-6666
Fidelity Select-Computers	Technology	72.8	58.65	42.04	1	5	0.59	1.09	800 544-6666

311

Stock Fund Name	Objective	Annualized Return for			Rank		Max Load	Expense Ratio	Toll-Free Telephone
		1 Year	3 Years	5 Years	Overall	Risk			
Fidelity Select-Cons Industries	Other	-6	15.05	18.67	3	3	0.58	1.32	800 544-6666
Fidelity Select-Const & Hous	Other	-19.1	1.69	9.24	5	3	0.58	2.22	800 544-6666
Fidelity Select-Cyclical Industs	Other	-6.2	5.15		5	3	0.58	2.49	800 544-6666
Fidelity Select-Def & Aero	Technology	0.5	10.63	16.57	3	3	0.57	1.41	800 544-6666
Fidelity Select-Dev Communica	Technology	84.8	63.63	38.29	2	5	0.59	1.12	800 544-6666
Fidelity Select-Electronics	Technology	112.6	60.97	48.59	1	5	0.58	0.98	800 544-6666
Fidelity Select-Energy	Energy/Res	20.5	13.7	17.37	4	4	0.58	1.25	800 544-6666
Fidelity Select-Energy Svcs	Energy/Res	59.3	15.69	26.93	3	5	0.58	1.2	800 544-6666
Fidelity Select-Environmental	Other	-28.8	-10.99	-1.31	5	4	0.58	2.16	800 544-6666
Fidelity Select-Financial	Financial	-9	11.39	20.62	3	4	0.58	1.14	800 544-6666
Fidelity Select-Food/Agri	Other	-7.1	3.54	11.06	4	2	0.58	1.27	800 544-6666
Fidelity Select-Gold	Prec Metal	-3	-14.5	-8.93	4	5	0.58	1.41	800 544-6666
Fidelity Select-Health Care	Health	22.7	22.19	26.06	2	3	0.58	1.06	800 544-6666
Fidelity Select-Home Finance	Financial	-17.9	-5.45	11.43	4	4	0.57	1.33	800 544-6666
Fidelity Select-Ind Equipment	Other	1.1	10.69	16.04	3	3	0.58	1.4	800 544-6666
Fidelity Select-Ind Materials	Other	-19.3	-5.58	0.08	5	4	0.58	1.84	800 544-6666
Fidelity Select-Insurance	Financial	-5.1	11.83	19.94	3	4	0.58	1.28	800 544-6666
Fidelity Select-Leisure	Other	-2.8	26.12	23.25	3	3	0.58	1.23	800 544-6666
Fidelity Select-Med Delivery	Health	-4.5	-7.63	4.06	5	4	0.58	1.66	800 544-6666
Fidelity Select-Multimedia	Other	11.3	28.92	21.98	2	3	0.58	1.17	800 544-6666
Fidelity Select-Natural Gas	Energy/Res	35.2	17.08	16.82	3	4	0.58	1.57	800 544-6666
Fidelity Select-Natural Resources	Energy/Res	21.5	10.39		4	4	0.58	2.47	800 544-6666
Fidelity Select-Paper/Forest	Other	-10.2	-0.52	3.23	5	4	0.58	2.2	800 544-6666
Fidelity Select-Retailing	Other	-10.6	19.24	20.78	3	3	0.58	1.14	800 544-6666
Fidelity Select-Software/CS	Technology	62.6	44.79	34.62	2	5	0.58	1.15	800 544-6666
Fidelity Select-Technology	Technology	92.9	63.59	44.91	1	5	0.59	1.08	800 544-6666
Fidelity Select-Telecom	Technology	27.1	35.5	27.86	2	4	0.58	1.11	800 544-6666
Fidelity Select-Transportation	Other	-9.3	9.59	13.46	4	3	0.57	1.62	800 544-6666
Fidelity Select-Utilities Growth	Utilities	11.4	29.41	26.63	2	2	0.58	1.07	800 544-6666
Fidelity Small Cap Selector	Small Co	22.7	9.91	12.54	4	3	0.63	0.85	800 544-8888
Fidelity Small Cap Stock Fund	Small Co	42.5					0.72	0.98	800 544-8888
Fidelity Southeast Asia Fund	Pacific	25.9	1.01	2.99	4	5	0.89	1.42	800 544-8888
Fidelity Spartan 500 Idx Fund	Growth/Inc	7.1	19.46	23.51	2	3	0.45	0.19	800 544-6666
Fidelity Spartan Extended Mkt Idx	Growth	18.1					0.25	0.3	800 544-6666
Fidelity Spartan FL Muni Income	Muni State	3	4.33	5.49	1	3	0.55	0.54	800 544-6666
Fidelity Spartan Intl Index	Foreign	17					0.4	0.35	800 544-6666
Fidelity Spartan Total Mkt Index	Growth	9.1					0.23	0.27	800 544-6666
Fidelity Stock Selector	Growth	14	17.73	20.1	3	3	0.42	0.61	800 544-8888
Fidelity Tax Managed Stock Fund	Growth	9.9					0.58	1.11	800 544-8888
Fidelity TechnoQuant Growth Fund	Growth	24.3	20.69		2	3	0.6	0.89	800 544-8888
Fidelity Trend Fund	Growth	20.3	13.64	15.54	3	4	0.36	0.57	800 544-8888
Fidelity US Equity Index	Growth/Inc	7.1	19.44	23.55	2	3	0.23	0.19	800 544-6666
Fidelity United Kingdom Fund	European	2.6	9.34		3	2	0.75	1.98	800 544-8888
Fidelity Utilities Fund	Utilities	11.7	25.96	23.26	2	2	0.58	0.79	800 544-8888
Fidelity Value Fund	Growth	-16.3	2.38	10.79	5	3	0.32	0.56	800 544-8888
Fidelity Worldwide Fund	Global	22.2	11.65	13.77	3	3	0.76	1.12	800 544-8888
Fiduciary Capital Growth	Growth	-1.2	6.96	12.67	4	3	0.93	1.3	800 811-5311
Fifth Third Balanced A	Balanced	15.9	16.05	17.19	2	2	0.8	1.25	888 799-5353
Fifth Third Balanced C	Balanced	15.4	15.44		2	2	0.8	1.76	888 799-5353
Fifth Third Balanced I	Balanced	16.2					0.8	1	888 799-5353
Fifth Third Cardinal Fd A	Growth/Inc	16.2	20.73	23.08	2	3	0.59	-0.17	888 799-5353
Fifth Third Cardinal Fd I	Growth/Inc	17					0.59	0.81	888 799-5353
Fifth Third Equity Income A	Income	-8.4	9.28		4	3	0.8	1.27	888 799-5353
Fifth Third Equity Income C	Income	-8.8	8.7		4	3	0.8	1.83	888 799-5353
Fifth Third Equity Income I	Income	-8.1					0.8	1.07	888 799-5353
Fifth Third Intl Equity C	Foreign	14.2	9.65		4	2	1	2.25	888 799-5353
Fifth Third Intl Equity I	Foreign	15.2					1	1.5	888 799-5353
Fifth Third Mid Cap A	Growth/Inc	20	15.9	17.18	3	3	0.8	1.28	888 799-5353

312

Stock Fund Name	Objective	Annualized Return for			Rank		Max Load	Expense Ratio	Toll-Free Telephone
		1 Year	3 Years	5 Years	Overall	Risk			
Fifth Third Mid Cap C	Growth/Inc	19.5	15.26		3	3	0.8	1.85	888 799-5353
Fifth Third Mid Cap I	Growth/Inc	20.4					0.8	0.96	888 799-5353
Fifth Third Pinnacle I	Growth	4.7					0.8	1.2	888 799-5353
Fifth Third Quality Growth A	Growth	18.5	23.03	25.4	1	3	0.8	1.23	888 799-5353
Fifth Third Quality Growth C	Growth	18.1	22.45		2	3	0.8	1.8	888 799-5353
Fifth Third Quality Growth I	Growth	18.8					0.8	1	888 799-5353
First American Balanced C	Balanced	-2.8					0.69	1.81	800 637-2548
First American Emerging Markets B	Foreign	22					1.25	2.45	800 637-2548
First American Emerging Markets C	Foreign						1.25		800 637-2548
First American Emerging Markets Y	Foreign	23.1					1.25	1.44	800 637-2548
First American Equity Income C	Income	-5.5					0.69	1.76	800 637-2548
First American Equity Index C	Growth/Inc	3					0.69	1.35	800 637-2548
First American Health Sciences C	Health						0.69		800 637-2548
First American International Fund C	Foreign	51.3					1.25	2.35	800 637-2548
First American International Indx C	Foreign						0.69		800 637-2548
First American Large Cap Growth C	Growth	23.7					0.69	1.8	800 637-2548
First American Large Cap Value C	Growth/Inc	-10.8					0.69	1.8	800 637-2548
First American Mid Cap Growth B	Small Co	56.2					0.75	1.87	800 637-2548
First American Mid Cap Growth C	Small Co	59.6					0.75	1.88	800 637-2548
First American Mid Cap Value C	Agg Growth	-13.1					0.69	1.89	800 637-2548
First American Real Estate Secs C	Real Est						0.69		800 637-2548
First American Small Cap Growth C	Small Co	60.6					0.69	1.89	800 637-2548
First American Small Cap Value C	Small Co	12.2					0.69	1.88	800 637-2548
First American Technology C	Technology						0.69		800 637-2548
First American-Balanced Fund A	Balanced	-2.1	6.51	11.48	3	1	0.69	1.05	800 637-2548
First American-Balanced Fund B	Balanced	-2.9	5.72	11.94	3	1	0.69	1.8	800 637-2548
First American-Balanced Fund Y	Balanced	-1.9	6.81	11.79	3	1	0.69	0.8	800 637-2548
First American-Emerg Markets A	Foreign	22.8	-6.01	0.36	5	5	1	1.69	800 637-2548
First American-Equity Inc A	Income	-4.9	9.76	14.87	2	2	0.5	1	800 637-2548
First American-Equity Inc B	Income	-5.5	9.04	14.11	3	2	0.5	1.75	800 637-2548
First American-Equity Inc Y	Income	-4.5	10.14	15.25	2	2	0.53	0.75	800 637-2548
First American-Equity Index A	Growth/Inc	6.1	18.87	23.02	2	3	0.2	0.59	800 637-2548
First American-Equity Index B	Growth/Inc	5.2	17.95	22.1	3	3	0.16	1.35	800 637-2548
First American-Equity Index Y	Growth/Inc	6.3	19.14	23.31	2	3	0.17	0.34	800 637-2548
First American-Health Sciences A	Health	41.7	9.5		4	3	0.69	1.15	800 637-2548
First American-Health Sciences B	Health	40.8	8.73		4	3	0	1.89	800 637-2548
First American-Health Sciences Y	Health	42	9.75		4	3	0.56	0.9	800 637-2548
First American-International A	Foreign	52.6	26.17	22.4	3	4	1.25	1.6	800 637-2548
First American-International B	Foreign	51.3	25.19	21.44	3	4	1.25	2.35	800 637-2548
First American-International Y	Foreign	52.7	26.44	22.62	3	4	1.25	1.35	800 637-2548
First American-Intl Index A	Foreign	15.8	9.42		4	2	0.69	1	800 637-2548
First American-Intl Index B	Foreign	14.8					0.69	1.75	800 637-2548
First American-Intl Index Y	Foreign	16	9.7		4	2	0.69	0.75	800 637-2548
First American-Lrg Cap Gr A	Growth	24.6	23.84	23.73	1	3	0.56	1.05	800 637-2548
First American-Lrg Cap Gr B	Growth	23.7	22.95	22.83	2	3	0.56	1.8	800 637-2548
First American-Lrg Cap Gr Y	Growth	24.9	24.17	24.06	1	3	0.56	0.8	800 637-2548
First American-Lrg Cap Val A	Growth/Inc	-10.1	5.5	14.53	4	3	0.69	1.05	800 637-2548
First American-Lrg Cap Val B	Growth/Inc	-10.8	4.75	13.71	4	3	0.69	1.8	800 637-2548
First American-Lrg Cap Val Y	Growth/Inc	-9.9	5.8	14.85	4	3	0.69	0.8	800 637-2548
First American-Mid Cap Growth A	Small Co	60.7	29.51	25.7	3	4	0.75	1.12	800 637-2548
First American-Mid Cap Growth Y	Small Co	61.1	24.88		3	4	0.75	0.86	800 637-2548
First American-Mid Cap Value A	Agg Growth	-12.4	-6.11	7.54	5	4	0.69	1.14	800 637-2548
First American-Mid Cap Value B	Agg Growth	-13	-6.77	6.77	5	3	0.69	1.89	800 637-2548
First American-Mid Cap Value Y	Agg Growth	-12.1	-5.82	7.86	5	4	0.69	0.9	800 637-2548
First American-Real Estate Secs A	Real Est	4.4	1.7		3	2	0.69	1.05	800 637-2548
First American-Real Estate Secs B	Real Est	3.6	0.92		3	2	0.69	1.8	800 637-2548
First American-Real Estate Secs Y	Real Est	4.6	1.96	10.14	3	2	0.69	0.8	800 637-2548
First American-SmallCap Grwth A	Small Co	61.8	30.35	25.44	3	5	0.69	1.29	800 637-2548

313

Stock Fund Name	Objective	Annualized Return for			Rank		Max Load	Expense Ratio	Toll-Free Telephone
		1 Year	3 Years	5 Years	Overall	Risk			
First American-SmallCap Grwth B	Small Co	60.6	24.45		3	5	0.63	1.88	800 637-2548
First American-SmallCap Grwth Y	Small Co	62.2					0.68	0.89	800 637-2548
First American-SmallCap Value A	Small Co	13	4.2	12.74	4	3	0.69	1.13	800 637-2548
First American-SmallCap Value B	Small Co	12.3					0.69	1.88	800 637-2548
First American-SmallCap Value Y	Small Co	13.3	4.44		4	3	0.69	0.89	800 637-2548
First American-Strat Aggress Grw	Agg Growth	18.1	13.5		3	2	0.01	0.27	800 637-2548
First American-Strat Grow & Inc	Growth/Inc	20.9	13.38		3	1	0.01	0.27	800 637-2548
First American-Strat Growth	Growth	4.3	8.17		3	2	0.01	0.27	800 637-2548
First American-Strategy Income	Income	1.7	6.09		3	1	0.01	0.27	800 637-2548
First American-Technology Fund A	Technology	128.5	65.29	43.57	1	5	0.69	1.14	800 637-2548
First American-Technology Fund B	Technology	126.8	64.17	42.49	2	5	0.69	1.89	800 637-2548
First American-Technology Fund Y	Technology	129.2	65.85	43.92	2	5	0.69	0.9	800 637-2548
First Choice Equity Fund I	Growth/Inc	16.3					0.25	0.68	888 347-7816
First Choice Equity Fund R	Growth/Inc	16					0.25	0.53	888 347-7816
First Eagle Fund of America A	Growth	-9.1					1	1.6	800 451-3623
First Eagle Fund of America C	Growth	-9.6					1	2.1	800 451-3623
First Eagle Fund of America Y	Growth	-8.9	13.48	20.27	3	3	1	1.39	800 451-3623
First Eagle International Fund A	Foreign	25.7					1	3	800 451-3623
First Eagle International Fund C	Foreign	25					1	3.1	800 451-3623
First Eagle International Fund Y	Foreign	26.1	8.65	13.57	3	3	1	2.39	800 451-3623
First Eagle SoGen Global Fund A	Global	12.7	6.37	9.87	3	1	0.75	1.28	800 334-2143
First Eagle SoGen Gold Fund	Prec Metal	0.1	-15.51	-11.58	5	4	0.75	1.84	800 334-2143
First Eagle SoGen Overseas Fund A	Foreign	17.9	9.19	12.13	3	2	0.75	1.34	800 334-2143
First Fds-Growth & Income I	Growth/Inc	8.1	21.64	23.43	2	2	0.65	0.79	800 442-1941
First Fds-Growth & Income II	Growth/Inc	7.8	21.33		2	2	0.65	1.1	800 442-1941
First Fds-Growth & Income III	Growth/Inc	7	20.4	22.12	2	2	0.65	1.87	800 442-1941
First Inv Blue Chip A	Growth	16.4	17.77	21.14	2	3	0.84	1.36	800 423-4026
First Inv Global A	Global	17.1	13.42	15.35	3	3	1	1.71	800 423-4026
First Investors FL Ins Tax Free A	Muni State	3	4.18	5.37	2	3	0.75	0.8	800 423-4026
First Investors Mid Cap Opport A	Growth	27.4	21.73	19.22	2	4	1	1.5	800 423-4026
First Investors Special Situation A	Small Co	29.8	14.28	14.28	3	4	0.98	1.56	800 423-4026
First Investors Total Return A	Flexible	12.8	13.38	14.89	3	1	1	1.39	800 423-4026
First Omaha Balanced Fund	Balanced	-13.5	0.2		4	1	0.75	1.1	800 662-4203
First Omaha Equity Fund	Growth	-22	-2.02	6.87	5	2	0.75	1.03	800 662-4203
First Omaha Small Cap Value Fund	Small Co	-2.3	0.92		5	2	0.29	1.7	800 662-4203
Firstar Balanced Growth Inst	Balanced	14.7	12.28	13.98	3	2	0.69	0.93	800 982-8909
Firstar Balanced Growth Ret A	Balanced	14.4	12	13.57	3	2	0.69	1.13	800 982-8909
Firstar Balanced Growth Retail B	Balanced	13.3					0.69	2.14	800 982-8909
Firstar Balanced Income Inst	Balanced	3.9					0.67	0.89	800 982-8909
Firstar Balanced Income Ret A	Balanced	3.6					0.67	1.13	800 982-8909
Firstar Balanced Income Retail B	Balanced	0.6					0.67	2.02	800 982-8909
Firstar Emerging Growth Inst	Small Co	29.2					0.75	1.02	800 982-8909
Firstar Emerging Growth Ret	Small Co	28.9					0.75	1.27	800 982-8909
Firstar Emerging Growth Retail B	Small Co	28.1					0.75		800 982-8909
Firstar Equity Index Inst	Growth/Inc	6.7	19.2	23.31	2	3	0.75	0.34	800 982-8909
Firstar Equity Index Ret A	Growth/Inc	6.4	18.97	22.85	2	3	0.25	0.59	800 982-8909
Firstar Equity Index Retail B	Growth/Inc	5.3					0.25	1.38	800 982-8909
Firstar Growth & Income Inst	Growth/Inc	4.4	15.06	20.83	2	2	0.75	0.9	800 982-8909
Firstar Growth & Income Ret A	Growth/Inc	4.1	14.77	20.53	2	2	0.75	1.18	800 982-8909
Firstar Growth & Income Retail B	Growth/Inc	3.3					0.75	1.93	800 982-8909
Firstar Growth Inst	Growth	17.6	20.56	21.04	2	3	0.73	0.91	800 982-8909
Firstar Growth Ret	Growth	17.3	20.25	20.75	2	3	0.73	1.15	800 982-8909
Firstar Growth Retail B	Growth	16.4					0.73	2.06	800 982-8909
Firstar International Equity Ret B	Foreign	1.2					1.34	2.81	800 982-8909
Firstar Intl Equity Inst	Foreign	2.1	-3.4	1.08	5	3	1.34	1.48	800 982-8909
Firstar Intl Equity Ret	Foreign	1.9	-3.6	1.73	5	3	1.34	1.79	800 982-8909
Firstar Micro Cap Inst	Small Co	136.2	48.54		2	5	1.5	1.77	800 982-8909
Firstar Micro Cap Ret	Small Co	135.6	48.14		2	5	1.5	2.02	800 982-8909

314

| Stock Fund Name | Objective | Annualized Return for | | | Rank | | Max Load | Expense Ratio | Toll-Free Telephone |
		1 Year	3 Years	5 Years	Overall	Risk			
Firstar MicroCap Retail B	Small Co	133.7					1.5	2.87	800 982-8909
Firstar Special Growth Inst	Agg Growth	29.1	9.37	14.78	3	4	0.72	0.92	800 982-8909
Firstar Special Growth Ret	Agg Growth	28.9	9.13	14.49	3	4	0.72	1.16	800 982-8909
Firstar Special Growth Retail B	Agg Growth	27.9					0.72	2	800 982-8909
Firstar Stellar Capital Appre A	Growth	8.9	9.39	9.26	4	3	0.94	1.3	800 677-3863
Firstar Stellar Growth Equity B	Growth	20.6	22.59	24.1	1	2	0.75	1.36	800 677-3863
Firstar Stellar Relative Value A	Growth/Inc	-5.1	11.14	18.28	3	3	0.75	1.3	800 677-3863
Firstar Stellar Select REIT Plus Y	Real Est	4.2	0.37		4	2	0.75	1.45	800 677-3863
Firsthand Technology Innovators	Technology	124.7					1.5	1.91	888 884-2675
Firsthand Technology Leaders Fund	Technology	104.2					1.5	1.93	888 884-2675
Firsthand-Tech Value fund	Technology	120	59.37	59.04	2	5	1.5	1.9	888 884-2675
Flag European Mid-Cap C	European	46					0.84	2.35	800 730-1313
Flag Investors Communications A	Technology	2.2	39.88	33.65	2	4	0.66	0.95	800 767-3524
Flag Investors Communications B	Technology	1.4	38.84	32.65	2	4	0.66	1.7	800 767-3524
Flag Investors Emerging Growth A	Small Co	51.2	18.88	20.67	3	5	0.84	1.39	800 767-3524
Flag Investors Emerging Growth B	Small Co	50	17.98		3	5	0.84	2.12	800 767-3524
Flag Investors Emerging Growth I	Small Co	51.6	19.12		3	5	0.84	1.12	800 767-3524
Flag Investors Equity Partners A	Growth	-15.8	9.78	16.69	3	3	0.65	1.19	800 767-3524
Flag Investors Equity Partners B	Growth	-16.4	8.96	15.8	3	3	0.65	1.94	800 767-3524
Flag Investors Equity Partners Fd I	Growth	-15.6	10.05		3	3	0.65	0.94	800 767-3524
Flag Investors Euro Mid-Cap Fd A	European	47.3					0.84	1.6	800 730-1313
Flag Investors Euro Mid-Cap Fd B	European	45.9					0.84	2.35	800 730-1313
Flag Investors International	Foreign	-9.2	4.1	8.82	5	2	0.65	1.5	800 767-3524
Flag Investors Japanese Eq Fd A	Pacific	54.1					0.84	1.6	800 730-1313
Flag Investors Japanese Eq Fd B	Pacific	50.6					0.84	2.35	800 730-1313
Flag Investors Real Est Sec A	Real Est	4.1	0.5	9.85	4	2	0.65	1.25	800 767-3524
Flag Investors Real Est Sec B	Real Est	3.3	-0.26	9.02	4	2	0.65	2	800 767-3524
Flag Investors Real Estate Sec Inst	Real Est	6.3	1.42		4	2	0.65	1	800 767-3524
Flag Investors Top 50 Asia Fd A	Pacific	39.6					1	1.6	800 730-1313
Flag Investors Top 50 Asia Fd B	Pacific	38.6					1	2.35	800 730-1313
Flag Investors Top 50 Europe Fd A	European	23.9					1	1.6	800 730-1313
Flag Investors Top 50 Europe Fd B	European	22.8					1	2.35	800 730-1313
Flag Investors Top 50 US A	Growth	13.4					0.84	1.5	800 730-1313
Flag Investors Top 50 US B	Growth	12.4					0.84	2.25	800 730-1313
Flag Investors Top 50 World A	Global	16					1	1.6	800 730-1313
Flag Investors Top 50 World B	Global	15.1					1	2.35	800 730-1313
Flag Investors Value Builder A	Balanced	-6.1	10.83	16.44	3	2	0.75	1.09	800 767-3524
Flag Investors Value Builder B	Balanced	-6.8	10.1	15.63	2	2	0.75	1.87	800 767-3524
Flag Investors Value Builder Inst	Balanced	-5.8	11.12		2	2	0.75	0.86	800 767-3524
Flag Top 50 Europe Fund C	European	22.8					1	2.35	800 730-1313
Flag Top 50 US Fund Cl C	Growth	12.5					0.84	2.25	800 730-1313
Flex Fund-Highlands Gr Fd	Growth	4.7	18.17	18.22	3	3	1	1.54	800 325-3539
Flex Fund-Muirfield	AssetAlloc	-8.5	10.58	12.98	4	2	0.79	1.2	800 325-3539
Flex Fund-Total Ret Utilities	Utilities	11.9	18.76	18.41	2	2	1	1.8	800 325-3539
Fortis Advantage-Asset Alloc A	AssetAlloc	12	15.04	14.79	3	2	0.89	1.41	800 800-2000
Fortis Advantage-Asset Alloc B	AssetAlloc	11.5	14.43	9.65	3	2	0.89	1.96	800 800-2000
Fortis Advantage-Asset Alloc C	AssetAlloc	11.5	14.43	9.67	3	2	0.89	1.96	800 800-2000
Fortis Advantage-Asset Alloc H	AssetAlloc	11.4	14.42	14.16	3	2	0.89	1.96	800 800-2000
Fortis Advantage-Cap Apprec A	Small Co	101.7	46.16	29.33	3	5	0.93	1.5	800 800-2000
Fortis Advantage-Cap Apprec B	Small Co	100.6	45.39	28.66	3	5	0.93	2.06	800 800-2000
Fortis Advantage-Cap Apprec C	Small Co	100.5	45.38	28.67	3	5	0.93	2.06	800 800-2000
Fortis Advantage-Cap Apprec H	Small Co	100.5	45.38	28.65	3	5	0.93	2.06	800 800-2000
Fortis Capital Fund A	Growth	19.3	22.77	20.74	2	3	0.78	1.07	800 800-2000
Fortis Capital Fund B	Growth	18.4	21.85	19.83	2	3	0.78	1.87	800 800-2000
Fortis Capital Fund C	Growth	18.5	21.85	19.85	2	3	0.78	1.87	800 800-2000
Fortis Capital Fund H	Growth	18.4	21.85	19.85	2	3	0.78	1.87	800 800-2000
Fortis Growth & Income A	Growth/Inc	2.6	10.27		3	2	1	1.43	800 800-2000
Fortis Growth & Income B	Growth/Inc	1.8	9.44		2	2	1	2.18	800 800-2000

315

Stock Fund Name	Objective	Annualized Return for			Rank		Max Load	Expense Ratio	Toll-Free Telephone
		1 Year	3 Years	5 Years	Overall	Risk			
Fortis Growth & Income C	Growth/Inc	1.9	9.47		2	2	1	2.18	800 800-2000
Fortis Growth & Income H	Growth/Inc	1.8	9.45		2	2	1	2.18	800 800-2000
Fortis Growth Fund A	Agg Growth	68.2	30.24	24.16	3	4	0.75	1.05	800 800-2000
Fortis Growth Fund B	Agg Growth	66.9	29.27	23.26	3	4	0.75	1.81	800 800-2000
Fortis Growth Fund C	Agg Growth	66.9	29.29	23.27	3	4	0.75	1.81	800 800-2000
Fortis Growth Fund H	Agg Growth	66.9	29.28	23.28	3	4	0.75	1.81	800 800-2000
Fortis International Equity A	Foreign	57.5					1	1.69	800 800-2000
Fortis International Equity B	Foreign	56.4					1	2.45	800 800-2000
Fortis International Equity C	Foreign	56.4					1	2.45	800 800-2000
Fortis International Equity H	Foreign	56.3					1	2.45	800 800-2000
Fortis Value A	Growth/Inc	-1.1	9.08		3	3	1	1.43	800 800-2000
Fortis Value B	Growth/Inc	-1.8	8.25		3	3	1	2.18	800 800-2000
Fortis Value C	Growth/Inc	-1.8	8.28		3	3	1	2.18	800 800-2000
Fortis Value H	Growth/Inc	-1.8	8.27		3	3	1	2.18	800 800-2000
Fortis Worldwide-Global Growth A	Global	37	18.32	18.75	3	4	1	1.39	800 800-2000
Fortis Worldwide-Global Growth B	Global	36	17.48	17.89	3	4	1	2.14	800 800-2000
Fortis Worldwide-Global Growth C	Global	36.3	17.57	17.95	3	4	1	2.14	800 800-2000
Fortis Worldwide-Global Growth H	Global	35.9	17.46	17.87	3	4	1	2.14	800 800-2000
Forum Austin Global Equity	Global	43.9	26.3	23.25	2	4	1.5	2.39	800 943-6786
Forum Equity Index	Growth	6.9					0.14	0.25	800 943-6786
Forum Investors Equity	Growth	11.5					0.65	1.1	800 943-6786
Forum Investors Growth	Growth	-11					0.65	1.1	800 943-6786
Forum Payson Balanced	Balanced	-1.2	4.76	10.05	4	2	0.59	1.14	800 805-8258
Forum Payson Value	Growth	2.7	11.79	16.86	3	3	0.8	1.44	800 805-8258
Forward Garzarelli US Equity Fund	Growth/Inc	8.8					0.63	1.39	800 999-6809
Forward Hansberger Intl Grwth Fund	Foreign	7.7					1.05	2.12	800 999-6809
Forward Hoover Small Cap Equity	Small Co	20					1.05	1.86	800 999-6809
Forward Uniplan RE Investment	Real Est	5.6					0.5	3.68	800 999-6809
Fountainhead Kaleidoscope Fund	Small Co						1.75		800 868-9535
Fountainhead Special Value Fund	Growth	47.3	33.47		2	4	1.25	1.25	800 868-9535
Franklin Aggressive Growth A	Agg Growth						0.5		800 342-5236
Franklin Aggressive Growth Adv	Agg Growth						0.5		800 342-5236
Franklin Aggressive Growth B	Agg Growth						0.5		800 342-5236
Franklin Aggressive Growth C	Agg Growth						0.5		800 342-5236
Franklin Asset Allocation A	AssetAlloc	9.5	12.08	14.64	3	1	0.63	1.1	800 342-5236
Franklin Balance Sheet Investmt A	Small Co	-3.7	3.48	10.49	3	2	0.46	1.27	800 342-5236
Franklin Biotechnology Discovery A	Health	212.3					0.56	1.45	800 342-5236
Franklin Blue Chip A	Growth	24.2	16.04		2	3	0.86	1.25	800 342-5236
Franklin California Growth A	Growth	90.7	39.89	34.2	1	4	0.56	0.95	800 342-5236
Franklin California Growth B	Growth	89.1					0.56	1.75	800 342-5236
Franklin California Growth C	Growth	89.2	38.89		2	4	0.56	1.75	800 342-5236
Franklin Equity A	Growth	52.1	28.12	27.23	1	3	0.5	0.93	800 342-5236
Franklin Equity Adv	Growth	52.5	28.46		1	3	0.5	0.69	800 342-5236
Franklin Equity B	Growth	50.9					0.5	1.56	800 342-5236
Franklin Equity C	Growth	50.9	27.2	26.26	1	3	0.5	1.67	800 342-5236
Franklin Equity Inc A	Income	-5.3	7.28	11.98	3	2	0.5	0.93	800 342-5236
Franklin Equity Inc B	Income	-5.8					0.5	1.66	800 342-5236
Franklin Equity Inc C	Income	-6	6.49		3	2	0.5	1.67	800 342-5236
Franklin FL Ins Tax-Free Inc A	Muni State	1.4	4.39	5.57	3	4	0.63	0.41	800 342-5236
Franklin Florida Tax-Free Inc A	Muni State	1.3	3.94	4.94	3	3	0.46	0.6	800 342-5236
Franklin Florida Tax-Free Inc C	Muni State	0.7	3.38	4.38	4	3	0.46	1.16	800 342-5236
Franklin Global Communications A	Utilities	32.8	21.81	21.67	2	3	0.56	1.05	800 342-5236
Franklin Global Communications B	Utilities	31.8					0.56	1.8	800 342-5236
Franklin Global Communications C	Utilities	31.8	20.89	20.82	2	3	0.56	1.8	800 342-5236
Franklin Global Government Inc A	Intl Bond	2.4	2.97	5.65	5	5	0.59	1.1	800 342-5236
Franklin Global Government Inc C	Intl Bond	1.9	2.47	5.11	5	5	0.59	1.62	800 342-5236
Franklin Global Health Care A	Health	68.9	10.67	19.26	4	4	0.58	1.34	800 342-5236
Franklin Global Health Care B	Health	67.8					0.58	1.84	800 342-5236

316

Stock Fund Name	Objective	Annualized Return for 1 Year	3 Years	5 Years	Rank Overall	Risk	Max Load	Expense Ratio	Toll-Free Telephone
Franklin Global Health Care C	Health	67.6	9.88		4	4	0.58	2.06	800 342-5236
Franklin Gold & Precious Metals A	Prec Metal	-1.5	-9.67	-8.11	5	5	0.55	1.21	800 342-5236
Franklin Gold & Precious Metals B	Prec Metal	-2.6					0.54	1.97	800 342-5236
Franklin Gold & Precious Metals C	Prec Metal	-2.1	-10.24	-8.78	5	5	0.54	2.06	800 342-5236
Franklin Gold & Precious Metls Ad	Prec Metal	-1.2	-8.98		5	5	0.54	1.08	800 342-5236
Franklin Growth A	Growth	10.7	15.32	18.25	2	1	0.47	0.9	800 342-5236
Franklin Growth Adv	Growth	11	15.6		2	1	0.47	0.64	800 342-5236
Franklin Growth B	Growth	9.9					0.47	1.63	800 342-5236
Franklin Growth C	Growth	9.9	14.44	17.36	2	1	0.47	1.63	800 342-5236
Franklin Income A	Flexible	3.2	5.61	8.42	3	1	0.46	0.72	800 342-5236
Franklin Income Adv	Flexible	2.9	5.59		3	1	0.46	0.57	800 342-5236
Franklin Income B	Flexible	2.6					0.46	1.23	800 342-5236
Franklin Income C	Flexible	2.2	4.9	7.86	3	1	0.46	1.21	800 342-5236
Franklin Large Cap Growth A	Growth						0.5		800 342-5236
Franklin Large Cap Growth Adv	Growth						0.5		800 342-5236
Franklin Large Cap Growth B	Growth						0.5		800 342-5236
Franklin Large Cap Growth C	Growth						0.5		800 342-5236
Franklin MicroCap Value A	Small Co	-2.7	2.97		4	2	0.75	1.27	800 342-5236
Franklin MidCap Growth A	Growth	65.1	24.5		3	4	0.65	1.23	800 342-5236
Franklin Natural Resources A	Energy/Res	24.3	5.49	13.39	4	4	0.28	1.12	800 342-5236
Franklin Natural Resources Adv	Energy/Res	24.7	6.63		4	4	0.28	0.65	800 342-5236
Franklin Real Estate Sec A	Real Est	4.6	1.45	10.84	3	2	0.51	1	800 342-5236
Franklin Real Estate Sec Adv	Real Est	4.9	-0.58		4	2	0.51	0.7	800 342-5236
Franklin Real Estate Sec B	Real Est	3.9					0.51	1.57	800 342-5236
Franklin Real Estate Sec C	Real Est	3.9	0.73	10.01	4	2	0.51	1.7	800 342-5236
Franklin Rising Dividends A	Growth/Inc	-13.7	2.29	11.85	4	3	0.75	1.42	800 342-5236
Franklin Rising Dividends B	Growth/Inc	-14.2					0.75	2	800 342-5236
Franklin Rising Dividends C	Growth/Inc	-14.2	1.73	11.24	4	3	0.75	1.97	800 342-5236
Franklin Small Cap Growth I A	Small Co	85.9	32.98	29.32	3	4	0.46	0.91	800 342-5236
Franklin Small Cap Growth I Adv	Small Co	86.5	33.39		1	4	0.46	0.68	800 342-5236
Franklin Small Cap Growth I C	Small Co	84.6	32.04		3	4	0.46	1.68	800 342-5236
Franklin Templeton Conserv Tgt A	Growth/Inc	18.3	9.95		3	1	0.56	0.75	800 342-5236
Franklin Templeton Conserv Tgt C	Growth/Inc	17.4	9.06		3	1	0.56	1.5	800 342-5236
Franklin Templeton Growth Tgt A	Growth	39.7	16.24		2	3	0.59	0.75	800 342-5236
Franklin Templeton Growth Tgt C	Growth	38.7	15.63		3	3	0.59	1.5	800 342-5236
Franklin Templeton Moderate Tgt A	Growth	27.9	11.85		3	2	0.4	0.84	800 342-5236
Franklin Templeton Moderate Tgt C	Growth	27.1	10.88		3	2	0.4	1.6	800 342-5236
Franklin Utilities A	Utilities	-7.1	4.39	6.99	4	2	0.46	0.8	800 342-5236
Franklin Utilities Adv	Utilities	-7.1	4.61		3	2	0.46	0.61	800 342-5236
Franklin Utilities B	Utilities	-8.7					0.46	1.29	800 342-5236
Franklin Utilities C	Utilities	-7.6	3.88	6.45	4	2	0.46	0.61	800 342-5236
Franklin Value A	Growth/Inc	-4.5	-4.3		5	3	0.67	1.48	800 342-5236
Franklin Value Adv	Growth/Inc	-4.1	-3.92		5	3	0.59	1.21	800 342-5236
Franklin Value B	Growth/Inc	-5.1					0.73	2.2	800 342-5236
Franklin Value C	Growth/Inc	-5.2	-4.91		5	3	1.98	2.2	800 342-5236
Fremont Emerging Markets Fund	Foreign	35.1	-2.02		4	4	1	1.5	800 548-4539
Fremont Global Fund	Global	17.8	11.08	13.31	4	2	0.59	0.85	800 548-4539
Fremont Growth Fund	Growth	5.2	14.9	19.93	3	3	0.5	0.81	800 548-4539
Fremont Institutional US Micro-Cap	Small Co	126.5					1.14	1.25	800 548-4539
Fremont International Growth	Foreign	29.8	12.7	12.06	3	3	1	1.5	800 548-4539
Fremont Real Estate Securities	Real Est	-0.4					1	1.5	800 548-4539
Fremont US Micro-Cap Inst	Small Co	107	43.58	42.21	2	5	1.82	1.82	800 548-4539
Fremont US Small Cap Fund	Small Co	70.5					1	1.5	800 548-4539
Friends Ivory Europe Soc Awar Adv	European						0.84		800 481-4404
Friends Ivory Social Awareness Adv	Growth						0.75		800 481-4404
Frontegra Opportunity	Small Co	-6.7					0.65	0.9	888 825-2100
Fundamental Investors	Growth/Inc	12.8	18.65	21.44	2	2	0.28	0.64	800 421-9900
GAM Europe Fund A	European	39.4	15.26	18.3	3	3	1	2.41	800 426-4685

317

Stock Fund Name	Objective	Annualized Return for			Rank		Max Load	Expense Ratio	Toll-Free Telephone
		1 Year	3 Years	5 Years	Overall	Risk			
GAM Europe Fund B	European	38.2					1	4.58	800 426-4685
GAM Europe Fund C	European	37.5					1	6.2	800 426-4685
GAM Global Fund A	Global	-0.7	3.85	10.59	4	3	1	1.88	800 426-4685
GAM Global Fund B	Global	-1.4					1	2.75	800 426-4685
GAM Global Fund C	Global	-1.4					1	2.79	800 426-4685
GAM Global Fund D	Global	-1	3.65		4	3	1	2.02	800 426-4685
GAM International Fund A	Foreign	-0.5	0.31	7.36	4	4	1	1.7	800 426-4685
GAM International Fund B	Foreign	-1.2					1	2.47	800 426-4685
GAM International Fund C	Foreign	-1.2					1	2.45	800 426-4685
GAM International Fund D	Foreign	-0.6	0.18		4	4	1	1.91	800 426-4685
GAM Japan Capital Fund A	Pacific	32.7	11.03	14.51	3	3	1	2.06	800 426-4685
GAM Japan Capital Fund B	Pacific	31.2					1	5.76	800 426-4685
GAM Japan Capital Fund C	Pacific	31.6					1	5.29	800 426-4685
GAM North America Fund A	Global	6	15.83	21.81	2	2	1	1.72	800 426-4685
GAM North America Fund B	Global	5.2					1	3.5	800 426-4685
GAM North America Fund C	Global	5.1					1	3	800 426-4685
GAM Pacific Basin Fund A	Pacific	9.7	-3.69	1.18	5	4	1	2.25	800 426-4685
GAM Pacific Basin Fund B	Pacific	8.9					1	9.16	800 426-4685
GAM Pacific Basin Fund C	Pacific	8.6					1	14.38	800 426-4685
GAM Pacific Basin Fund D	Pacific	9	-4.29		5	4	1	2.97	800 426-4685
GAMerica Capital A	Growth	20.1	30.62	24.95	2	3	1	1.84	800 426-4685
GAMerica Capital B	Growth	19.3					1	3.58	800 426-4685
GAMerica Capital C	Growth	19.2					1	3.08	800 426-4685
GE Global Equity Fund A	Global	24.6	15.75	17.02	3	3	0.75	1.35	800 242-0134
GE Global Equity Fund B	Global	23.7	14.91	16.29	3	3	0.75	2.1	800 242-0134
GE Global Equity Fund Y	Global	24.9	16.05	17.39	3	3	0.75	1.1	800 242-0134
GE Institutional Emerging Mkts	Foreign	36.7					1.05	1.05	800 242-0134
GE Institutional Intl Equity	Foreign	27.1					1	0.63	800 242-0134
GE Institutional Mid Cap	Growth	13.2					0.55	0.55	800 242-0134
GE Institutional S&P 500 Index Inv	Growth	7.8					0.14		800 242-0134
GE Institutional US Equity Inv	Growth	5.3					0.4	0.42	800 242-0134
GE International Equity Fd A	Foreign	25.8	13.03	14.18	3	3	1	1.35	800 242-0134
GE International Equity Fd B	Foreign	24.9	12.2	13.4	3	3	1	2.1	800 242-0134
GE International Equity Fd Y	Foreign	26.2	13.36	14.5	3	3	1	1.1	800 242-0134
GE Mid-Cap Growth A	Growth	12.5	11.31	15.5	3	3	0.59	1.37	800 242-0134
GE Mid-Cap Growth B	Growth	11.7	10.67	14.78	3	3	0.59	1.89	800 242-0134
GE Mid-Cap Growth Y	Growth	12.9					0.59	0.9	800 242-0134
GE Premier Growth Equity A	Growth	12.7	27.84		1	3	0.59	1.1	800 242-0134
GE Premier Growth Equity B	Growth	11.9	26.97		1	3	0.59	1.87	800 242-0134
GE Premier Growth Equity Y	Growth	13	28		1	3	0.59	0.86	800 242-0134
GE S&S Program Mutual Fund	Growth/Inc	5.5	18.52	22.62	2	2	0.04	0.08	800 242-0134
GE Strategic Investment Fd A	Flexible	9.6	13.17	14.5	3	1	0.34	0.86	800 242-0134
GE Strategic Investment Fd B	Flexible	8.8	12.25	13.66	3	1	0.34	1.62	800 242-0134
GE Strategic Investment Fd Y	Flexible	9.9	13.43	14.75	3	1	0.34	0.63	800 242-0134
GE US Equity Fund A	Growth	4.8	17.96	21.23	2	2	0.4	0.81	800 242-0134
GE US Equity Fund B	Growth	4.1	17.06	20.36	3	2	0.4	1.5	800 242-0134
GE US Equity Fund Y	Growth	5.1	18.24	21.48	2	2	0.4	0.5	800 242-0134
GE Value Equity Fund A	Growth/Inc	4.6	16.47	21.82	2	2	0.55	1.29	800 242-0134
GE Value Equity Fund B	Growth/Inc	3.8	15.77	21.12	2	2	0.55	1.82	800 242-0134
GE Value Equity Fund Y	Growth/Inc	4.9					0.55	0.81	800 242-0134
GE Value Equity Instl	Growth/Inc	3.6					0.55		800 242-0134
GMO Tr Core II	Growth	6.7	18.85		3	3	0.33	0.55	
GMO Tr Core III	Growth	6.7	18.91	22.74	3	3	0.33	1.47	
GMO Tr Core IV	Growth	6.7					0.3	0.43	
GMO Tr Curr Hedged Intl Core III	Foreign	9.6					0.54	0.68	
GMO Tr Curr Hedged Intl Core IV	Foreign	9.6					0.54	0.63	
GMO Tr Emerging Markets III	Foreign	5.8	-3.58	3.25	5	5	0.81	1.14	
GMO Tr Emerging Markets IV	Foreign	5.8					0.81	1.11	

Stock Fund Name	Objective	Annualized Return for			Rank		Max Load	Expense Ratio	Toll-Free Telephone
		1 Year	3 Years	5 Years	Overall	Risk			
GMO Tr Foreign II	Foreign	13.7	10.21		3	2	0.59	0.81	
GMO Tr Foreign III	Foreign	13.8	9.14		4	2	0.59	0.75	
GMO Tr Foreign IV	Foreign	13.8					0.59	0.68	
GMO Tr Fundamental Value III	Growth	64.7	31.67	28.44	1	3	0.59	0.75	
GMO Tr Global Balance Alloc III	Global	6.2	8.8		3	1	0	0	
GMO Tr Global Equity Allocation III	Global	7.9	5.49		5	2	0	0	
GMO Tr Global Hedged Equity III	Global	0.7	-0.05	1.11	3	1	0.5	0.22	
GMO Tr Growth III	Growth	34.8	20.89	23.98	2	3	0.33	0.47	
GMO Tr International Core II	Foreign	5.6	6.64		4	2	0.54	0.76	
GMO Tr International Core III	Foreign	5.6	2.44	5.75	5	2	0.54	0.68	
GMO Tr International Core IV	Foreign	5.6					0.54	0.63	
GMO Tr International Eqty Alloc III	Global	5.9	1.06		5	3	0	0	
GMO Tr International Small Co III	Foreign	6.8	2.03	5.61	5	2	0.59	0.75	
GMO Tr Japan III	Pacific	24.9	4.05	3.29	5	3	0.54	0.68	
GMO Tr Pelican Fund	Growth	-7.1	8.69	13.85	3	2	0.9	0.94	
GMO Tr REIT III	Real Est	2.4	-4.88		5	2	0.54	0.68	
GMO Tr Small Cap Growth III	Small Co	33.3	16.55		3	4	0.33	0.47	
GMO Tr Small Cap Value III	Small Co	-1.8	-3.79	6.57	5	3	0.33	0.47	
GMO Tr Tobacco-Free Core	Growth	7.4	14.5	20.14	3	3	0.33	0.47	
GMO Tr US Bond Global Alpha A III	Intl Bond	4.6	2.41		4	5	0.25	0.4	
GMO Tr US Bond Global Alpha B III	Intl Bond	3.5					0.2	0.34	
GMO Tr US Sector III	Growth	8.9	13.97	18.88	3	2	0.33	0	
GMO Tr Value III	Growth	-10.6	-3.7	7.39	5	3	0.46	0.6	
GMO Tr World Equity Allocation III	Global	6.8	7.56		4	2	0	0	
Gabelli ABC Fund	Growth	7.4	10.45	10.1	3	1	1	1.68	800 422-3554
Gabelli Asset Fund	Growth	8.4	19.32	20.44	3	2	1	1.37	800 422-3554
Gabelli Blue Chip Value Fund	Growth						1		800 422-3554
Gabelli Equity Income	Income	0.9	11.9	16.4	3	2	1	1.64	800 422-3554
Gabelli Global Int Couch Potato	Technology	39.6	44.6	33.59	1	4	1	1.53	800 422-3554
Gabelli Global Opportunity Fund	Global	43.3					1	1.1	800 422-3554
Gabelli Global Telecom	Technology	28.7	37.26	29.3	1	3	1	1.47	800 422-3554
Gabelli Gold Fund	Prec Metal	-2.4	-18.38	-14.95	5	5	1	2.37	800 422-3554
Gabelli Growth Fund	Growth	33.8	33.65	31.45	1	3	1	1.37	800 422-3554
Gabelli International Growth	Foreign	36.7	18.18	19.34	2	3	1	2	800 422-3554
Gabelli Small Cap Growth	Small Co	11.2	11.34	15.5	3	2	1	1.39	800 422-3554
Gabelli Utility Fund	Utilities						1		800 422-3554
Gabelli Value Fund	Agg Growth	5.2	24.08	22.7	3	3	1	1.37	800 422-3554
Gabelli Westwood Balanced Fd Ret	Balanced	5.3	10.96	15.79	2	1	0.75	1.55	800 422-3554
Gabelli Westwood Balanced Fd Svc	Balanced	5	10.65	15.52	2	1	0.16	1.43	800 422-3554
Gabelli Westwood Equity Fund Ret	Growth/Inc	7.2	14.24	21.31	2	2	1	1.48	800 422-3554
Gabelli Westwood Equity Fund Svc	Growth/Inc	6.9	13.96	20.97	2	2	1	1.75	800 422-3554
Gabelli Westwood Mighty Mites Fund	Small Co	21.4					1	1.01	800 422-3554
Gabelli Westwood Realty Fund	Real Est	5.8					1	1.68	800 422-3554
Gabelli Westwood Sm Cap Equity Ret	Small Co	37.9	26.92		3	4	0.3	1.63	800 422-3554
Galaxy Asset Allocation B	Balanced	8.5	12.03		3	1	0.75	1.94	800 628-0414
Galaxy Asset Allocation Inst	Balanced	9.5	12.97	15.41	2	1	0.75	1.09	800 628-0414
Galaxy Asset Allocation Ret A	Balanced	9.2	12.78	15.21	2	1	0.75	1.32	800 628-0414
Galaxy Equity Growth B	Growth	17.4	22.85		1	3	0.75	1.97	800 628-0414
Galaxy Equity Growth Inst	Growth	18.8	24.19	24.8	1	3	0.75	0.93	800 628-0414
Galaxy Equity Growth Ret A	Growth	18.3	23.7	24.28	1	3	0.75	1.31	800 628-0414
Galaxy Equity Income Inst	Growth/Inc	0.2	10.66	15.95	3	2	0.75	0.91	800 628-0414
Galaxy Equity Income Ret A	Growth/Inc	-0.3	10.18	15.45	3	2	0.75	1.33	800 628-0414
Galaxy Equity Value B	Growth/Inc	-8.2	10.97		3	3	0.75	2.04	800 628-0414
Galaxy Equity Value Inst	Growth/Inc	-7.2	12.13	16.89	3	3	0.75	1	800 628-0414
Galaxy Equity Value Ret A	Growth/Inc	-7.6	11.73	16.44	3	3	0.75	1.37	800 628-0414
Galaxy Growth & Income Inst	Growth/Inc	-4.1	11.84	16.86	2	2	0.75	1.05	800 628-0414
Galaxy Growth & Income Ret B	Growth/Inc	-5	10.79		3	2	0.75	2.02	800 628-0414
Galaxy II-Large Company Idx Inv	Growth/Inc	6.8	19.2	23.35	2	3	0.1	0.46	800 628-0414

Stock Fund Name	Objective	Annualized Return for			Rank		Max Load	Expense Ratio	Toll-Free Telephone
		1 Year	3 Years	5 Years	Overall	Risk			
Galaxy II-Small Company Idx Inv	Small Co	14.7	9.74	14.68	4	3	0.1	0.4	800 628-0414
Galaxy II-Utility Idx Inv	Utilities	2.8	13.09	13.98	3	2	0.1	0.4	800 628-0414
Galaxy International Eq Inst	Foreign	23.1	15.72	17.11	3	3	0.9	0.93	800 628-0414
Galaxy International Eq Ret A	Foreign	22.5	15.07	16.42	3	3	0.9	1.42	800 628-0414
Galaxy Small Cap Value Inst	Small Co	8.6	8.47	16.12	3	2	0.75	0.94	800 628-0414
Galaxy Small Cap Value Ret A	Small Co	8.2	8.05	15.7	3	2	0.75	1.31	800 628-0414
Galaxy Small Company Eq B	Small Co	59.1	13.81		3	4	0.75	2.16	800 628-0414
Galaxy Small Company Eq Inst	Small Co	60.9	15.01	17.78	3	4	0.75	1.12	800 628-0414
Galaxy Small Company Eq Ret	Small Co	60	14.49	17.21	3	4	0.75	1.53	800 628-0414
Gateway Cincinnati Fund	Growth	-9.3	5.75	12.59	4	2	0.5	1.28	800 354-6339
Gateway Fund	Growth/Inc	11.4	12.81	11.85	3	1	0.66	0.97	800 354-6339
Gateway Small Cap Index Fund	Small Co	21.7	13.22	15.18	3	4	0.9	1.5	800 354-6339
General Securities	Flexible	48.9	20.33	20.52	2	3	1	1.48	800 577-9217
George Putnam Fund of Boston C	Balanced						0.47		800 225-1581
Gintel Fund	Growth	29.9	13.45	18.7	3	5	1	1.89	800 243-5808
Glenmede Emerging Mkts	Foreign	-6.1	-9.04	-2.8	5	4	1.25	1.75	800 442-8299
Glenmede International Equity Fd	Foreign	11.1	10.99	13.93	3	2		0.13	800 442-8299
Glenmede International I	Foreign	8.7	9.83	12.76	3	2	0.75	0.85	800 442-8299
Glenmede Large Cap Value Fd	Growth	-12.8	7.69	13.77	4	3	1	0.13	800 442-8299
Glenmede Small Cap Equity Adv	Small Co	8.9	2.36	11.85	4	3	0.55	0.89	800 442-8299
Golden Rainbow Fund	Flexible	5	7.43	9.26	3	1	0.73	1.04	800 621-7227
Goldman S. Aggr Gr Strategy A	Growth	10.4					0.34	1.02	800 292-4726
Goldman S. Aggr Gr Strategy B	Growth	9.6					0.34	1.77	800 292-4726
Goldman S. Aggr Gr Strategy C	Growth	9.7					0.34	1.77	800 292-4726
Goldman S. Asia Growth A	Pacific	5.9	-10.59	-4.79	5	5	0.85	1.92	800 292-4726
Goldman S. Asia Growth B	Pacific	5.3	-10.97		5	5	0.85	2.35	800 292-4726
Goldman S. Asia Growth C	Pacific	5.3					0.85	2.35	800 292-4726
Goldman S. Balanced B	Balanced	3	6.23		3	1	0.65	1.85	800 292-4726
Goldman S. Balanced C	Balanced	3.1					0.65	1.85	800 292-4726
Goldman S. Balanced Inst	Balanced	4.4					0.65	0.69	800 292-4726
Goldman S. Balanced Svc	Balanced	3.8					0.65	1.19	800 292-4726
Goldman S. CORE Intl Eq A	Foreign	14					0.75	1.65	800 292-4726
Goldman S. CORE Intl Eq B	Foreign	13.4					0.75	2.16	800 292-4726
Goldman S. CORE Intl Eq C	Foreign	13.5					0.75	2.16	800 292-4726
Goldman S. CORE Intl Eq Inst	Foreign	14.8					0.75	1.01	800 292-4726
Goldman S. CORE Intl Eq Svc	Foreign	14.2					0.75	1.51	800 292-4726
Goldman S. CORE Lrg Cap Gr C	Growth	24.7					0.75	1.79	800 292-4726
Goldman S. CORE Sm Cap Eq A	Small Co	14.4					0.84	1.33	800 292-4726
Goldman S. CORE Sm Cap Eq B	Small Co	13.5					0.84	2.08	800 292-4726
Goldman S. CORE Sm Cap Eq C	Small Co	13.6					0.84	2.08	800 292-4726
Goldman S. CORE Sm Cap Eq Inst	Small Co	14.9					0.84	0.93	800 292-4726
Goldman S. CORE Sm Cap Eq Svc	Small Co	14.3					0.84	1.42	800 292-4726
Goldman S. CORE US Equity A	Growth/Inc	8	17.79	21.61	3	3	0.75	1.13	800 292-4726
Goldman S. CORE US Equity B	Growth/Inc	7.1	16.79		2	3	0.75	1.88	800 292-4726
Goldman S. CORE US Equity C	Growth/Inc	7.1					0.75	1.88	800 292-4726
Goldman S. Capital Growth A	Growth	14.7	24.57	24.65	2	3	1	1.43	800 292-4726
Goldman S. Capital Growth B	Growth	13.9	23.6		2	3	1	2.18	800 292-4726
Goldman S. Capital Growth C	Growth	13.9					1	2.18	800 292-4726
Goldman S. Capital Growth Inst	Growth	15.2					1	1.04	800 292-4726
Goldman S. Capital Growth Svc	Growth	14					1	1.54	800 292-4726
Goldman S. Emerg Mkts Eq A	Foreign	14.7					0.89	2.04	800 292-4726
Goldman S. Emerg Mkts Eq B	Foreign	14.3					0.89	2.54	800 292-4726
Goldman S. Emerg Mkts Eq C	Foreign	14					0.89	2.54	800 292-4726
Goldman S. European Equity A	Foreign	29.5					0.89	1.79	800 292-4726
Goldman S. European Equity B	Foreign	28.8					0.89	2.29	800 292-4726
Goldman S. European Equity C	Foreign	28.5					0.89	2.29	800 292-4726
Goldman S. Global Income A	Intl Bond	3.1	5.28	7.27	2	3	0.9	1.34	800 292-4726
Goldman S. Global Income B	Intl Bond	2.6	4.7		2	3	0.9	1.84	800 292-4726

Stock Fund Name	Objective	Annualized Return for			Rank		Max Load	Expense Ratio	Toll-Free Telephone
		1 Year	3 Years	5 Years	Overall	Risk			
Goldman S. Global Income C	Intl Bond	2.6					0.9	1.84	800 292-4726
Goldman S. Gr & Inc Strategy A	Growth/Inc	8.2					0.34	0.86	800 292-4726
Goldman S. Gr & Inc Strategy B	Growth/Inc	7.4					0.34	1.62	800 292-4726
Goldman S. Gr & Inc Strategy C	Growth/Inc	7.5					0.34	1.62	800 292-4726
Goldman S. Growth & Income A	Growth/Inc	-5.8	2.35	12.14	4	2	0.69	1.18	800 292-4726
Goldman S. Growth & Income B	Growth/Inc	-6.5	1.62		5	2	0.69	1.93	800 292-4726
Goldman S. Growth & Income C	Growth/Inc	-6.5					0.69	1.93	800 292-4726
Goldman S. Growth Strategy A	Growth	9.3					1	0.89	800 292-4726
Goldman S. Growth Strategy B	Growth	8.5					1	1.63	800 292-4726
Goldman S. Growth Strategy C	Growth	8.5					1	1.63	800 292-4726
Goldman S. Internet Tollkeeper A	Technology						1		800 292-4726
Goldman S. Internet Tollkeeper B	Technology						1		800 292-4726
Goldman S. Internet Tollkeeper C	Technology						1		800 292-4726
Goldman S. Intl Equity A	Foreign	25.3	11.95	16.01	3	2	0.89	1.79	800 292-4726
Goldman S. Intl Equity B	Foreign	24.7	11.34		3	2	0.89	2.29	800 292-4726
Goldman S. Intl Equity C	Foreign	24.8					0.89	2.29	800 292-4726
Goldman S. Intl Sm-Cap Equity A	Foreign	36.2					0.75	2.04	800 292-4726
Goldman S. Intl Sm-Cap Equity B	Foreign	34.8					0.75	2.54	800 292-4726
Goldman S. Intl Sm-Cap Equity C	Foreign	35.5					0.75	2.54	800 292-4726
Goldman S. Japanese Equity A	Pacific	34.6					0.8	1.69	800 292-4726
Goldman S. Japanese Equity B	Pacific	34.1					0.8	2.2	800 292-4726
Goldman S. Japanese Equity C	Pacific	33.9					0.8	2.2	800 292-4726
Goldman S. Mid-Cap Equity A	Growth	-11.5					0.75	1.29	800 292-4726
Goldman S. Mid-Cap Equity B	Growth	-12.1					0.75	2.04	800 292-4726
Goldman S. Mid-Cap Equity C	Growth	-12.2					0.75	2.04	800 292-4726
Goldman S. Small Cap Value A	Small Co	-2.5	0.36	8.88	4	4	1	1.5	800 292-4726
Goldman S. Small Cap Value B	Small Co	-3.4	-0.41		4	4	1	2.25	800 292-4726
Goldman S. Small Cap Value C	Small Co	-3.3					1	2.25	800 292-4726
Goldman S. Small Cap Value Inst	Small Co	-2.2					1	1.1	800 292-4726
Goldman S. Small Cap Value Svc	Small Co	-2.7					1	1.6	800 292-4726
Goldman Sachs Real Estate Secs A	Real Est	4.7					1	1.43	800 292-4726
Goldman Sachs Real Estate Secs B	Real Est	4.9					1	2.18	800 292-4726
Goldman Sachs Real Estate Secs C	Real Est	5					1	2.18	800 292-4726
Government Street Equity Fund	Growth	8.4	16.99	20.73	2	2	0.59	0.82	800 543-8721
Governor Aggressive Growth Ret	Agg Growth	16.3	12.27		3	4	0.59	1.04	800 766-3960
Governor Established Gr Ret	Growth	9.3	17.27		3	3	0.5	0.91	800 766-3960
Governor International Equity Fund	Foreign	12.9					0.4	0.97	800 766-3960
Governor Lifestyle Conservative Gr	Growth	4.9					0.14	1.79	800 766-3960
Governor Lifestyle Growth	Growth	4.2					0.14	1.81	800 766-3960
Governor Lifestyle Moderate Gr	Growth	6.8					0.14	1.76	800 766-3960
Govett Emerging Markets A	Foreign	10.8	-8.57	-0.71	5	4	1	1.85	800 821-0803
Govett Global Income Fund A	Intl Bond	-1.8	1.13	0.9	5	4	0.75	2.35	800 821-0803
Govett International Equity A	Foreign	-1.8	4.64	8.46	4	3	1	2.35	800 821-0803
Govett International Equity Fund I	Foreign	-1.7					1	2	800 821-0803
Govett Intl Smaller Companies A	Foreign	10.7					1	1.82	800 821-0803
Govett Intl Smaller Companies Instl	Foreign	10.9					1	1.5	800 821-0803
Govett Smaller Companies A	Small Co	36.4	13.65	8.15	4	4	1	2.35	800 821-0803
Grand Prix Fund A	Growth	116.7					1	1.71	800 432-4741
Granum Value Fund	Growth	9.7	8.5		3	3	2		
Green Century Balanced	Balanced	115.9	30.59	25.56	3	4	0.75	2.5	800 934-7336
Green Century Equity	Growth	6.5	20.74		2	3	0.2	1.5	800 934-7336
Greenspring Fund	Growth/Inc	3.4	0	7.75	4	2	0.75	1.07	800 366-3863
Growth Fund of America (The)	Growth	42	35.95	27.99	1	3	0.34	0.75	800 421-9900
Growth Fund of Washington	Growth	-15.6	6.95	14.15	4	3	0.73	1.17	800 972-9274
Guardian Asset Allocation A	AssetAlloc	13.6	15.36	17.79	2	1	0.65	0.47	800 221-3253
Guardian Baillie Giff Emerg Mkts A	Foreign	35.6	0.55		4	4	1	2.5	800 221-3253
Guardian Baillie Giff Emerg Mkts B	Foreign	53.3	3.02		3	5	1	5.37	800 221-3253
Guardian Baillie Gifford Intl A	Foreign	20	13.08	15.74	3	3	0.8	1.43	800 221-3253

321

Stock Fund Name	Objective	Annualized Return for			Rank		Max Load	Expense Ratio	Toll-Free Telephone
		1 Year	3 Years	5 Years	Overall	Risk			
Guardian Park Avenue Fund A	Growth	23.9	22.74	25.27	2	3	0.5	0.77	800 221-3253
Guardian Park Avenue Small Cap A	Small Co	54.8	19.05		3	4	0.75	1.35	800 221-3253
Guardian Park Avenue Small Cap B	Small Co	53.4	18		3	4	0.75	2.25	800 221-3253
Guinness Flight Asia Blue Chip	Pacific	12.8	-6.89		4	5	1	1.97	800 915-6565
Guinness Flight Asia Small Cap	Pacific	-8	-22.01		5	5	1	1.97	800 915-6565
Guinness Flight China & Hong Kong	Pacific	25.2	-1.28	10.34	4	5	1	1.86	800 915-6565
Guinness Flight Internet.Com Fd	Growth						0.9		800 915-6565
Guinness Flight Mainland China Fd	Pacific	-4.8					1	1.97	800 915-6565
Guinness Flight Wired Index Fund	Growth	43.3					0.9	1.35	800 915-6565
HLM Emerging Markets Portfolio	Foreign	40.4					1.25	1.75	
HLM Multi-Asset Global Portfolio	Global	13.8					1	1.25	
HSBC Growth & Income Fund	Growth/Inc	10.6	18.49	21.33	2	3	0.55	0.9	800 662-3343
Harbor Fund-Capital Apprec	Growth	29.2	32.24	28.72	1	4	0.59	0.66	800 422-1050
Harbor Fund-Growth	Growth	95.1	39.69	30.28	2	4	0.75	0.9	800 422-1050
Harbor Fund-International	Foreign	14.6	9.73	15.57	3	3	0.8	0.92	800 422-1050
Harbor Fund-International Grwth	Foreign	14.4	10.42	15.46	3	3	0.65	0.91	800 422-1050
Harbor Fund-International II	Foreign	30	11.31		4	3	0.75	0.92	800 422-1050
Harbor Fund-Value	Growth/Inc	-11.2	7.59	14.89	4	3	0.59	0.76	800 422-1050
Harding Loevner Global Equity	Global	30.6	13.25		3	3	1	1.25	
Harding Loevner Intl Equity	Foreign	28.4	12.53		2	3	0.75	1	
Harris Insight Balanced Fund A	Balanced	3.4					0.56	1.22	800 982-8782
Harris Insight Balanced Inst	Balanced	3.8	8.22		3	1	0.59	0.88	800 982-8782
Harris Insight Balanced N	Balanced	3.5	7.92		3	1	0.59	1.12	800 982-8782
Harris Insight Emerging Mkt Inst	Foreign	3.9					1.25	1.75	800 982-8782
Harris Insight Emerging Mkt N	Foreign	3.3					1.25	2	800 982-8782
Harris Insight Emerging Mkts A	Foreign	3.3					0.91		800 982-8782
Harris Insight Equity Fund A	Growth/Inc	1.2					0.69	1.25	800 982-8782
Harris Insight Equity Income A	Income	-4.4					0.69	1.28	800 982-8782
Harris Insight Equity Income Inst	Income	-4.1	12.83		2	3	0.69	0.93	800 982-8782
Harris Insight Equity Income N	Income	-4.4	12.53		3	3	0.25	1.17	800 982-8782
Harris Insight Equity Inst	Growth/Inc	0.7	11.24		3	3	0.69	0.9	800 982-8782
Harris Insight Equity N	Growth/Inc	0.4	10.93	17.53	3	3	0.69	1.14	800 982-8782
Harris Insight Growth Fund A	Growth	7.9					0.89	1.44	800 982-8782
Harris Insight Growth Inst	Growth	8.1	17.76		2	3	0.9	1.1	800 982-8782
Harris Insight Growth N	Growth	7.8	17.47		2	3	0.9	1.35	800 982-8782
Harris Insight Index Inst	Growth/Inc	6.7	19.16		2	3	0.25	0.45	800 982-8782
Harris Insight Index N	Growth/Inc	6.5	18.9		1	3	0.25	0.69	800 982-8782
Harris Insight International Inst	Foreign	3.9	-0.21		4	3	1.05	1.34	800 982-8782
Harris Insight International N	Foreign	3.6	-0.55		5	3	1.05	1.59	800 982-8782
Harris Insight Intl Equity A	Foreign	3.6					1.03	1.68	800 982-8782
Harris Insight Small Cap Opp A	Small Co	33.3					0.98	1.55	800 982-8782
Harris Insight Small Cap Oppt Inst	Small Co	33.7	19.48		3	4	1	1.19	800 982-8782
Harris Insight Small Cap Oppt N	Small Co	33.4	19.15		3	4	1	1.44	800 982-8782
Harris Insight Small Cap Val A	Small Co	6.1					0.72		800 982-8782
Harris Insight Small Cap Val Inst	Small Co	7.1	5.33		4	3	1	0.98	800 982-8782
Harris Insight Small Cap Val N	Small Co	7	5.13		4	3	0.8	1.23	800 982-8782
Hartford Advisers (The) A	Growth	6.3	14.35		3	1	0.75	1.32	888 843-7824
Hartford Advisers (The) B	Growth	5.6	13.58		3	1	0.75	2.02	888 843-7824
Hartford Advisers (The) C	Growth	5.5					0.75	2.04	888 843-7824
Hartford Advisors Fund Y	Growth	5.8	14.52		3	1	0.75	0.83	888 843-7824
Hartford Capital Apprec (The) A	Agg Growth	40.9	28.4		1	4	0.8	1.37	888 843-7824
Hartford Capital Apprec (The) B	Agg Growth	39.9	27.5		1	4	0.8	2.08	888 843-7824
Hartford Capital Apprec (The) C	Agg Growth	39.8					0.8	2.1	888 843-7824
Hartford Capital Appreciation Y	Agg Growth	34.6	26.83		2	4	0.8	0.91	888 843-7824
Hartford Dividend & Growth (The) A	Growth/Inc	-3.9	9.15		3	2	0.75	1.36	888 843-7824
Hartford Dividend & Growth (The) B	Growth/Inc	-4.4	8.45		3	2	0.75	2.06	888 843-7824
Hartford Dividend & Growth (The) C	Growth/Inc	-4.6					0.75	2.08	888 843-7824
Hartford Dividend & Growth Y	Growth/Inc	-4.2	9.39		3	3	0.75	0.9	888 843-7824

Stock Fund Name	Objective	Annualized Return for			Rank		Max Load	Expense Ratio	Toll-Free Telephone
		1 Year	3 Years	5 Years	Overall	Risk			
Hartford Global Leaders A	Global	35.2					0.84	1.78	888 843-7824
Hartford Global Leaders B	Global	34.4					0.84	2.49	888 843-7824
Hartford Global Leaders C	Global	34.3					0.84	2.49	888 843-7824
Hartford Global Leaders Fund Y	Global	35.2					0.84	1.3	888 843-7824
Hartford Growth & Income (The) A	Growth/Inc	8.8					0.8	1.46	888 843-7824
Hartford Growth & Income (The) B	Growth/Inc	8					0.8	2.16	888 843-7824
Hartford Growth & Income (The) C	Growth/Inc	8					0.8	2.18	888 843-7824
Hartford Growth and Income Y	Growth/Inc	8.5					0.8	0.96	888 843-7824
Hartford Intl Opportunity (The) A	Foreign	20	11.17		3	3	0.84	1.68	888 843-7824
Hartford Intl Opportunity (The) B	Foreign	19	10.38		3	3	0.84	2.39	888 843-7824
Hartford Intl Opportunity (The) C	Foreign	19					0.84	2.39	888 843-7824
Hartford Intl Opportunity Y	Foreign	20.1	11.54		3	3	0.84	1.21	888 843-7824
Hartford Mid Cap Fd (The) A	Small Co	45.8					0.84	1.48	888 843-7824
Hartford Mid Cap Fd (The) B	Small Co	44.7					0.84	2.18	888 843-7824
Hartford Mid Cap Fd (The) C	Small Co	44.8					0.84	2.22	888 843-7824
Hartford MidCap Fund Y	Small Co	41.5					0.84	1.02	888 843-7824
Hartford Small Company (The) A	Small Co	41.5	27.17		2	4	0.84	1.48	888 843-7824
Hartford Small Company (The) B	Small Co	40.4	26.27		3	4	0.84	2.18	888 843-7824
Hartford Small Company (The) C	Small Co	40.4					0.84	2.2	888 843-7824
Hartford Small Company Y	Small Co	42.1	27.74		2	4	0.84	1.01	888 843-7824
Hartford Stock (The) A	Growth	8.2	20.92		2	3	0.8	1.38	888 843-7824
Hartford Stock (The) B	Growth	7.5	20.09		2	3	0.8	2.08	888 843-7824
Hartford Stock (The) C	Growth	7.5					0.8	2.1	888 843-7824
Hartford Stock Fund Y	Growth	7.8	21.15		2	3	0.8	0.9	888 843-7824
Haven Fund	Growth	17.8	14.4	18.34	2	3	0.59	1.2	800 844-4836
Heartland Select Value Fd	Growth/Inc	-1.2	4.87		5	3	0.75	0.53	800 432-7856
Heartland Value Fund	Small Co	4.4	3.7	10.86	5	3	0.75	1.34	800 432-7856
Heartland Value Plus Fund	Income	-4.9	3.03	11.29	5	2	0.69	1.23	800 432-7856
Henlopen Fund	Growth	53.7	33.44	28.13	3	5	1	1.39	800 922-0224
Henssler Equity Fund	Growth	13					0.5	1.19	800 936-3863
Heritage Aggressive Growth A	Agg Growth	45.8					1	1.64	800 421-4184
Heritage Aggressive Growth B	Agg Growth	44.7					1	2.39	800 421-4184
Heritage Aggressive Growth C	Agg Growth	44.7					1	2.39	800 421-4184
Heritage Capital Appreciation A	Agg Growth	17.7	29.55	27.21	1	3	0.75	1.25	800 421-4184
Heritage Capital Appreciation B	Agg Growth	17					0.75	1.94	800 421-4184
Heritage Capital Appreciation C	Agg Growth	17	28.76	26.59	1	3	0.75	1.94	800 421-4184
Heritage Income Growth Trust A	Growth/Inc	-4.4	6.23	13.53	3	2	0.73	1.27	800 421-4184
Heritage Income Growth Trust B	Growth/Inc	-5.1					0.73	2.04	800 421-4184
Heritage Income Growth Trust C	Growth/Inc	-5.1	5.41	12.69	3	2	0.73	2.04	800 421-4184
Heritage Ser Tr-Eagle Intl Eq A	Foreign	21.1	11.99		3	3	1	1.96	800 421-4184
Heritage Ser Tr-Eagle Intl Eq B	Foreign	20.2					1	2.72	800 421-4184
Heritage Ser Tr-Eagle Intl Eq C	Foreign	20.2	11.15		3	3	1	2.72	800 421-4184
Heritage Ser Tr-Eagle Intl Eq Eagl	Foreign	20.3	11.28	13.09	3	3	1	2.6	800 421-4184
Heritage Ser Tr-Growth Eq A	Growth	60	42.31		1	4	0.75	1.23	800 421-4184
Heritage Ser Tr-Growth Eq B	Growth	58.8					0.75	2.02	800 421-4184
Heritage Ser Tr-Growth Eq C	Growth	58.8	41.26		1	4	0.75	2.02	800 421-4184
Heritage Ser Tr-Mid Cap Growth A	Growth	40.3					0.75	1.6	800 421-4184
Heritage Ser Tr-Mid Cap Growth B	Growth	39.2					0.75	2.35	800 421-4184
Heritage Ser Tr-Mid Cap Growth C	Growth	39.2					0.75	2.35	800 421-4184
Heritage Ser Tr-Small Cap Stk A	Small Co	12.7	5.41	16.18	4	4	0.8	1.26	800 421-4184
Heritage Ser Tr-Small Cap Stk B	Small Co	11.8					0.8	2.02	800 421-4184
Heritage Ser Tr-Small Cap Stk C	Small Co	11.8	4.63	15.37	4	4	0.8	2.02	800 421-4184
Heritage Ser Tr-Value Eq A	Growth/Inc	-8.2	1.54	9.93	5	3	0.75	1.44	800 421-4184
Heritage Ser Tr-Value Eq B	Growth/Inc	-8.9					0.75	2.2	800 421-4184
Heritage Ser Tr-Value Eq C	Growth/Inc	-9	0.77	9.09	5	3	0.75	2.2	800 421-4184
Heritage West Dividend Capture Inc	Income	-5.3					1	1.97	800 596-1213
Hibernia Capital Appreciation A	Growth/Inc	9.4	18.64	22.9	2	3	0.75	1.2	800 999-0124
Hibernia Capital Appreciation B	Growth/Inc	8.6	17.74		2	3	0.75	1.95	800 999-0124

Stock Fund Name	Objective	Annualized Return for			Rank		Max Load	Expense Ratio	Toll-Free Telephone
		1 Year	3 Years	5 Years	Overall	Risk			
Highmark Balanced A	Balanced	1.3	8.47	12.31	3	1	0.59	1.16	800 433-6884
Highmark Balanced Fid	Balanced	1.7	8.77	12.59	3	1	0.59	0.88	800 433-6884
Highmark Balanced Fund C	Balanced						0.59		800 433-6884
Highmark Growth Fund A	Growth	9.8	20.67	22.96	2	3	0.59	1.13	800 433-6884
Highmark Growth Fund C	Growth						0.59		800 433-6884
Highmark Growth Fund Fid	Growth	10.1	20.96	23.13	2	3	0.59	0.9	800 433-6884
Highmark Income Equity A	Income	-14.1	5.9	13.4	4	2	0.94	1.12	800 433-6884
Highmark Income Equity C	Income						0.94		800 433-6884
Highmark Income Equity Fid	Income	-13.9	6.16	13.58	4	2	0.94	0.88	800 433-6884
Highmark International Equity A	Foreign						0.94		800 433-6884
Highmark International Equity B	Foreign						0.94		800 433-6884
Highmark International Equity C	Foreign						0.94		800 433-6884
Highmark Intl Equity Fid	Foreign	18.1	6.66	6.68	4	3	0.94	1.36	800 433-6884
Highmark Small Cap Value A	Small Co	16.6					1	1.77	800 433-6884
Highmark Small Cap Value B	Small Co	16.3					1	2.39	800 433-6884
Highmark Small Cap Value C	Small Co						1		800 433-6884
Highmark Small Cap Value Fid	Small Co	17.1					1	1.54	800 433-6884
Highmark Value Momentum A	Growth/Inc	1.9	11.17	17.92	3	2	1	1.06	800 433-6884
Highmark Value Momentum Fid	Growth/Inc	2.1	11.43	18.18	3	2	1	0.81	800 433-6884
Highmark Value Momentum Fund C	Growth/Inc						1		800 433-6884
Hilliard-Lyons Growth Fund	Growth	-3.7	11.04	17.34	2	2	0.8	1.29	800 444-1854
Hodges Fund	Growth	-9.6	11.88	17.45	4	4	0.84	1.75	800 388-8512
Homestate Banking & Finance	Small Co	-15.9	-0.25		5	4	1	2.6	800 232-0224
Homestate PA Growth Fund	Growth	66.4	23.64	23.71	3	4	0.75	1.56	800 232-0224
Homestead Funds-Value Fund	Growth/Inc	-20.3	2.53	11.04	4	3	0.58	0.72	800 258-3030
Homestead Small Company Stock Fund	Small Co	-15.4					0.01	2.24	800 258-3030
Hotchkis & Wiley Balanced Income	Balanced	-9.3	2.24	7.32	4	1	0.75	0.94	800 236-4479
Hotchkis & Wiley Equity Income	Growth/Inc	-19.8	1.79	9.81	4	3	0.75	0.99	800 236-4479
Hotchkis & Wiley Global Equity	Global	-1.4	3.88		4	2	0.75	1.09	800 236-4479
Hotchkis & Wiley International	Foreign	15.6	9.09	13.36	3	2	0.75	1.01	800 236-4479
Hotchkis & Wiley Mid Cap Fund	Growth	10.4	10.97		4	3	0.75	1.05	800 236-4479
Hotchkis & Wiley Small Cap	Small Co	-18.6	-5.12	4.84	5	3	0.75	1.28	800 236-4479
Howard Equity Fund	Growth	32.3					1	1.94	
Huntington Growth Inv	Growth	8	16.45	19.92	2	2	0.59	1.06	800 253-0412
Huntington Growth Tr	Growth	7.8	16.61	20.15	2	2	0.59	0.81	800 253-0412
Huntington Income Equity Inv	Income	-14.2	4.9		3	2	0.59	1.07	800 253-0412
Huntington Income Equity Tr	Income	-13.7	5.3	12.09	3	2	0.59	0.81	800 253-0412
IAA Trust Asset Allocation	AssetAlloc	8.1	11.85	14	3	1	0.75	1.34	800 245-2100
IAA Trust Growth Fund	Growth	10.3	15.56	19.23	2	3	0.75	1.04	800 245-2100
IAI Balanced	Balanced	-2.9	7.5	12.76	3	1	1.25	1.25	800 945-3863
IAI Capital Appreciation	Growth	47.6	19.13		3	4	1.39	1.39	800 945-3863
IAI Emerging Growth	Small Co	49.2	23.91	20.13	3	4	1.25	1.25	800 945-3863
IAI Growth & Income Fund	Growth/Inc	1.3	10.66	15.92	3	3	1.25	1.25	800 945-3863
IAI Growth Fund	Growth	20.7	21.85	19.89	2	3	1.25	1.25	800 945-3863
IAI International Fund	Foreign	-4.7	-2.82	3.24	5	2	1.69	1.83	800 945-3863
IAI Midcap Growth	Growth	28.7	24.41	20.48	2	4	1.25	1.25	800 945-3863
IAI Regional Fund	Growth	6.3	4.33	11.5	4	3	1.22	1.22	800 945-3863
IAI Value Fund	Growth	-3.3	8.82	12.28	4	5	1.25	1.3	800 945-3863
ICAP Discretionary Equity	Growth/Inc	-4.6	9.15	16.85	3	2	0.8	0.94	888 221-4227
ICAP Equity	Growth/Inc	-4.1	9.83	17.94	3	3	0.8	0.86	888 221-4227
ICAP Euro Select Equity	Global	7.9					0.8	1	888 221-4227
ICAP Select Equity Portfolio	Growth	6					0.8	0.8	888 221-4227
ICM/Isabelle Small Cap Value Instl	Small Co	39.8					1	1.69	800 472-6114
ICM/Isabelle Small Cap Value Inv	Small Co	39.3					1	4.79	800 472-6114
ICON Fds-Asia Region	Pacific	10.8	-1.34		4	4	1	1.58	888 389-ICON
ICON Fds-Basic Materials	Other	-12	-10		5	4	1	1.43	888 389-ICON
ICON Fds-Consumer Cyclicals	Technology	-11.5					1	1.35	888 389-ICON
ICON Fds-Energy	Energy/Res	45.4					1	1.46	888 389-ICON

Stock Fund Name	Objective	Annualized Return for			Rank		Max Load	Expense Ratio	Toll-Free Telephone
		1 Year	3 Years	5 Years	Overall	Risk			
ICON Fds-Financial Services	Financial	-8.6					1	1.44	888 389-ICON
ICON Fds-Healthcare	Health	22.9	15.43		3	3	1	1.37	888 389-ICON
ICON Fds-Leisure	Other	-12.2	9.1		3	3	1	1.36	888 389-ICON
ICON Fds-North Europe Region	European	19.1	12.75		2	2	1	1.56	888 389-ICON
ICON Fds-South Europe Region	European	9.6	10.55		4	3	1	1.77	888 389-ICON
ICON Fds-Technology	Technology	68.4	45.63		2	5	1	1.36	888 389-ICON
ICON Fds-Telecomm & Utilities	Utilities	-3.6					1	1.51	888 389-ICON
ICON Fds-Transportation	Other	-19.2	-0.68		5	3	1	1.39	888 389-ICON
IDEX Alger Aggressive Growth A	Agg Growth	30.1	35.04	26.62	1	4	0.8	1.71	888 233-4339
IDEX Alger Aggressive Growth B	Agg Growth	29.5	34.54		1	4	1	2.37	888 233-4339
IDEX Alger Aggressive Growth C	Agg Growth						0.8		888 233-4339
IDEX Alger Aggressive Growth M	Agg Growth	29.6	34.61	26.25	2	4	1	2.27	888 233-4339
IDEX C.A.S.E. Growth A	Growth	-3.6	5.96		5	4	1	1.75	888 233-4339
IDEX C.A.S.E. Growth B	Growth	-4.1	5.34		5	4	1	2.39	888 233-4339
IDEX C.A.S.E. Growth C	Growth						0.8		888 233-4339
IDEX C.A.S.E. Growth M	Growth	-4	5.45		5	4	1	2.29	888 233-4339
IDEX Dean Asset Alloc A	AssetAlloc	-6.4	2.81		4	1	0.8	1.75	888 233-4339
IDEX Dean Asset Alloc B	AssetAlloc	-6.9	2.18		4	1	1	2.39	888 233-4339
IDEX Dean Asset Alloc C	AssetAlloc						0.8		888 233-4339
IDEX Dean Asset Alloc M	AssetAlloc	-6.8	2.26		4	1	1	2.29	888 233-4339
IDEX GE International Equity A	Foreign	28.8	11.48		3	3	1	2	888 233-4339
IDEX GE International Equity B	Foreign	28.1	10.83		3	3	1	2.64	888 233-4339
IDEX GE International Equity C	Foreign						0.8		888 233-4339
IDEX GE International Equity M	Foreign	28.3	10.92		3	3	1	2.54	888 233-4339
IDEX Goldman Sachs Growth A	Growth	13.7					0.8	1.55	888 233-4339
IDEX Goldman Sachs Growth B	Growth	12.9					0.8	2.2	888 233-4339
IDEX Goldman Sachs Growth C	Growth						0.8		888 233-4339
IDEX Goldman Sachs Growth M	Growth	13.1					0.8	2.1	888 233-4339
IDEX JCC Balanced A	Balanced	11.7	20.9	21.08	3	2	1	1.87	888 233-4339
IDEX JCC Balanced B	Balanced	11.1	20.17		3	2	1	2.45	888 233-4339
IDEX JCC Balanced C	Balanced						1		888 233-4339
IDEX JCC Balanced M	Balanced	11.2	20.28	20.45	3	2	1	2.35	888 233-4339
IDEX JCC Capital Appreciation A	Growth	57.5	43.43	32.67	2	5	1	1.84	888 233-4339
IDEX JCC Capital Appreciation B	Growth	56.9	42.89		2	5	1	2.5	888 233-4339
IDEX JCC Capital Appreciation C	Growth						1		888 233-4339
IDEX JCC Capital Appreciation M	Growth	54.9	42.31	31.85	2	5	1	2.39	888 233-4339
IDEX JCC Global A	Global	48.4	28.11	28.29	1	3	1	1.71	888 233-4339
IDEX JCC Global B	Global	47.8	27.59		1	3	1	2.37	888 233-4339
IDEX JCC Global C	Global						1		888 233-4339
IDEX JCC Global M	Global	47.9	27.7	28.03	1	3	1	2.27	888 233-4339
IDEX JCC Growth A	Growth	29.5	38.9	33.01	1	4	0.9	1.39	888 233-4339
IDEX JCC Growth B	Growth	28.8	38.39		1	4	0.9	2.04	888 233-4339
IDEX JCC Growth C	Growth						0.9		888 233-4339
IDEX JCC Growth M	Growth	29	38.49	32.63	1	4	0.9	1.94	888 233-4339
IDEX LKCM Strategic Total Return A	Balanced	1.8	8.23	13.32	3	1	0.8	1.63	888 233-4339
IDEX LKCM Strategic Total Return B	Balanced	1.2	7.66		3	1	1	2.39	888 233-4339
IDEX LKCM Strategic Total Return C	Balanced						0.8		888 233-4339
IDEX LKCM Strategic Total Return M	Balanced	1.3	7.77	13.44	3	1	1	2.29	888 233-4339
IDEX NWQ Value Equity A	Growth/Inc	-6.6	6.89		5	3	1	1.75	888 233-4339
IDEX NWQ Value Equity B	Growth/Inc	-7.3	2.93		5	3	1	2.39	888 233-4339
IDEX NWQ Value Equity C	Growth/Inc						0.8		888 233-4339
IDEX NWQ Value Equity M	Growth/Inc	-7.1	3.02		5	3	1	2.29	888 233-4339
IDEX Pilgrim Baxter Mid Cap Gr A	Growth	81.9					0.8	1.55	888 233-4339
IDEX Pilgrim Baxter Mid Cap Gr B	Growth	81.2					0.8	2.2	888 233-4339
IDEX Pilgrim Baxter Mid Cap Gr C	Growth						0.8		888 233-4339
IDEX Pilgrim Baxter Mid Cap Gr M	Growth	81.3					0.8	2.1	888 233-4339
IDEX Salomon All Cap A	Growth	26.4					0.8	1.55	888 233-4339
IDEX Salomon All Cap B	Growth	25.8					0.8	2.2	888 233-4339

Stock Fund Name	Objective	Annualized Return for			Rank		Max Load	Expense Ratio	Toll-Free Telephone
		1 Year	3 Years	5 Years	Overall	Risk			
IDEX Salomon All Cap C	Growth						0.8		888 233-4339
IDEX Salomon All Cap M	Growth	25.8					0.8	2.1	888 233-4339
IDEX T.Rowe Price Dividend Gr A	Income	-4.7					0.8	1.55	888 233-4339
IDEX T.Rowe Price Dividend Gr B	Income	-6					0.8	2.2	888 233-4339
IDEX T.Rowe Price Dividend Gr C	Income						0.8		888 233-4339
IDEX T.Rowe Price Dividend Gr M	Income	-5.9					0.8	2.1	888 233-4339
IDEX T.Rowe Price Small Cap A	Small Co	30.6					0.8	1.55	888 233-4339
IDEX T.Rowe Price Small Cap B	Small Co	29.9					0.8	2.2	888 233-4339
IDEX T.Rowe Price Small Cap C	Small Co						0.8		888 233-4339
IDEX T.Rowe Price Small Cap M	Small Co	30.1					0.8	2.1	888 233-4339
ING European Equity A	European	16.3					1.14	2.93	877 463-6464
ING European Equity B	European	15.6					1.14	2.27	877 463-6464
ING European Equity C	European	15.2					1.14	2.27	877 463-6464
ING European Equity X	European	15.6					1.14	2.27	877 463-6464
ING Focus Fund A	Growth	13					1	1.32	877 463-6464
ING Focus Fund B	Growth	12.3					1	1.93	877 463-6464
ING Focus Fund C	Growth	12.2					1	1.91	877 463-6464
ING Focus Fund X	Growth	12.2					1	1.91	877 463-6464
ING Global Brand Names A	Global	16.4					1	1.43	877 463-6464
ING Global Brand Names B	Global	15.6					1	2.08	877 463-6464
ING Global Brand Names C	Global	15.7					1	2.06	877 463-6464
ING Global Brand Names X	Global	15.7					1	1.98	877 463-6464
ING Global Info Tech A	Technology	115.7					0.3	1.5	877 463-6464
ING Global Info Tech B	Technology	114.5					0.3	2.16	877 463-6464
ING Global Info Tech C	Technology	114.6					0.3	2.14	877 463-6464
ING Global Info Tech X	Technology	114.4					0.3	2.14	877 463-6464
ING Growth & Income A	Growth/Inc	5.1					0.75	1.26	877 463-6464
ING Growth & Income B	Growth/Inc	4.3					0.75	1.89	877 463-6464
ING Growth & Income C	Growth/Inc	4.3					0.75	1.89	877 463-6464
ING Growth & Income X	Growth/Inc	4.3					0.75	1.88	877 463-6464
ING International Eq A	Foreign	16.3					1.25	1.59	877 463-6464
ING International Eq B	Foreign	15.6					1.25	2.24	877 463-6464
ING International Eq C	Foreign	15.5					1.25	2.24	877 463-6464
ING International Eq X	Foreign	15.7					1.25	2.24	877 463-6464
ING Internet Fund A	Technology						0.3		877 463-6464
ING Internet Fund B	Technology						0.3		877 463-6464
ING Internet Fund C	Technology						0.3		877 463-6464
ING Internet Fund X	Technology						0.3		877 463-6464
ING Large Cap Growth A	Growth	17.1					0.75	1.29	877 463-6464
ING Large Cap Growth B	Growth	16.5					0.75	1.93	877 463-6464
ING Large Cap Growth C	Growth	16.4					0.75	1.93	877 463-6464
ING Large Cap Growth X	Growth	16.4					0.75	1.93	877 463-6464
ING Mid Cap Growth Fund A	Growth	27.8					1	1.35	877 463-6464
ING Mid Cap Growth Fund B	Growth	26.9					1	2	877 463-6464
ING Mid Cap Growth Fund C	Growth	27					1	2	877 463-6464
ING Mid Cap Growth Fund X	Growth	27					1	2	877 463-6464
ING Small Cap Growth A	Small Co	49.2					1	1.35	877 463-6464
ING Small Cap Growth B	Small Co	48.3					1	2	877 463-6464
ING Small Cap Growth C	Small Co	48					1	2	877 463-6464
ING Small Cap Growth X	Small Co	48.2					1	2	877 463-6464
ING Tax Efficient Eq A	Growth	3.2					0.8	1.22	877 463-6464
ING Tax Efficient Eq B	Growth	2.6					0.8	1.86	877 463-6464
ING Tax Efficient Eq C	Growth	2.6					0.8	1.76	877 463-6464
ING Tax Efficient Eq X	Growth	2.6					0.8	1.85	877 463-6464
INVESCO Balanced Ret	Balanced	6.3	14.61	18.18	3	1	0.59	0.6	800 525-8085
INVESCO Blue Chip C	Growth						0.55		800 525-8085
INVESCO Blue Chip Growth	Growth	36.4	32.1	29.94	1	4	0.55	1.04	800 525-8085
INVESCO Dynamics	Agg Growth	53.3	40.02	31.4	1	4	0.59	1.05	800 525-8085

Stock Fund Name	Objective	Annualized Return for			Rank		Max Load	Expense Ratio	Toll-Free Telephone
		1 Year	3 Years	5 Years	Overall	Risk			
INVESCO Dynamics Fund C	Agg Growth						0.52		800 525-8085
INVESCO Endeavor Fund	Agg Growth	52.7					0.75	1.48	800 525-8085
INVESCO Endeavor Fund C	Agg Growth						0.75		800 525-8085
INVESCO Energy Fund C	Energy/Res						0.75		800 525-8085
INVESCO Energy Ret	Energy/Res	40	15.46	20.78	4	5	0.75	1.67	800 525-8085
INVESCO Equity Income Fund C	Income						0.47		800 525-8085
INVESCO Equity Income Ret	Income	3.7	13.1	16.51	2	2	0.47	0.9	800 525-8085
INVESCO European	European	49.8	25.28	24.64	2	4	0.69	1.45	800 525-8085
INVESCO European Fund C	European						0.69		800 525-8085
INVESCO Financial Services	Financial	-3.8	11.04	21	3	4	0.63	1.26	800 525-8085
INVESCO Financial Services Fund C	Financial						0.63		800 525-8085
INVESCO Gold	Prec Metal	-10.2	-26.01	-15.51	5	5	0.75	2.2	800 525-8085
INVESCO Gold Fund C	Prec Metal						0.75		800 525-8085
INVESCO Growth and Income Fund	Growth/Inc	31.5					0.75	1.52	800 525-8085
INVESCO Growth and Income Fund C	Growth/Inc						0.75		800 525-8085
INVESCO Health Sciences Fund C	Health						0.61		800 525-8085
INVESCO Hlth Sciences	Health	23	20.38	24.26	3	4	0.61	1.21	800 525-8085
INVESCO International Blue Chip	Foreign	18.2					0.75	1.05	800 525-8085
INVESCO International Blue Chip C	Foreign						0.75		800 525-8085
INVESCO Latin Amer Gr	Foreign	16.3	-11.27	3.06	4	5	0.75	2.16	800 525-8085
INVESCO Latin American Growth C	Foreign						0.75		800 525-8085
INVESCO Leisure	Other	19.7	31.83	23.64	2	3	0.73	1.43	800 525-8085
INVESCO Leisure Fund C	Other						0.73		800 525-8085
INVESCO Pacific Basin	Pacific	10.7	-11.12	-4.06	5	4	0.75	2.1	800 525-8085
INVESCO Pacific Basin C	Pacific						0.75		800 525-8085
INVESCO Real Estate Opportunity Fd	Real Est	4.2	-2.34		5	2	0.75	1.34	800 525-8085
INVESCO Realty Fund C	Real Est						0.75		800 525-8085
INVESCO S&P 500 Index Fund Class I	Growth	6.5					0.25	0.34	800 525-8085
INVESCO S&P 500 Index Fund Class II	Growth	6.6					0.25	0.59	800 525-8085
INVESCO Small Company Growth	Small Co	69.1	35.14	28.52	3	5	0.75	1.5	800 525-8085
INVESCO Small Company Growth Fund C	Small Co						0.71		800 525-8085
INVESCO Technology Fund C	Technology						0.59		800 525-8085
INVESCO Technology Fund I	Technology	112.6					1	0.23	800 525-8085
INVESCO Technology II	Technology	111.8	54.44	41.4	1	5	0.75	1.19	800 525-8085
INVESCO Telecommunications	Technology	75.2	61.69	44.76	1	5	0.61	1.23	800 525-8085
INVESCO Telecommunications Fund C	Technology						0.61		800 525-8085
INVESCO Total Return Fund	AssetAlloc	-12.1	5.3	10.78	3	1	0.47	0.46	800 525-8085
INVESCO Total Return Fund C	AssetAlloc						0.56		800 525-8085
INVESCO Util Fd Ret	Utilities	11.2	21.52	19.84	2	2	0.75	1.26	800 525-8085
INVESCO Utilities Fund C	Utilities						0.75		800 525-8085
INVESCO Value Equity	Growth/Inc	-8.5	6.28	13.5	4	2	0.75	1.27	800 525-8085
IPO Plus Aftermarket Fund	Growth	64.2					1.5	2.5	888 476-3863
ISI Strategy A	Growth	5.9					0.5	1	800 882-8585
Income Fund of America (The)	Income	-4.4	6.6	11.54	3	1	0.28	0.58	800 421-9900
Independence One Equity Plus	Growth	12.7	22.83		2	3	0.4	0.56	800 622-4644
Internet 100 Fund	Technology						0.75		877 655-1110
Internet Fund (The)	Technology	7	101.33		1	5	1.25	2	888 386-3999
Investment Company of America	Growth/Inc	6.4	17.31	20.65	2	2	0.23	0.55	800 421-9900
Investors Research Fund	Growth	11.3	9.81	13.35	3	2	0.5	1.85	800 732-1733
Ivy Asia Pacific Fund Advisor	Pacific						1	2.1	800 456-5111
Ivy European Opportunities I	European	146.7					1		800 456-5111
Ivy Fund-Asia Pacific A	Pacific	-5.7	-10.72		5	5	1	2.58	800 456-5111
Ivy Fund-Asia Pacific B	Pacific	-6.5	-11.47		5	5	1	3.37	800 456-5111
Ivy Fund-Asia Pacific C	Pacific	-6.5	-11.35		5	5	1	3.29	800 456-5111
Ivy Fund-China Region A	Pacific	5.7	-6.81	2	5	5	1	2.83	800 456-5111
Ivy Fund-China Region Adv	Pacific	6					1	2.64	800 456-5111
Ivy Fund-China Region B	Pacific	4.9	-7.54	1.16	5	5	1	2.97	800 456-5111
Ivy Fund-China Region C	Pacific	4.8	-7.52		5	5	1	2.99	800 456-5111

327

Stock Fund Name	Objective	Annualized Return for			Rank		Max Load	Expense Ratio	Toll-Free Telephone
		1 Year	3 Years	5 Years	Overall	Risk			
Ivy Fund-Developing Nations A	Foreign	1.8	-8.68	0.27	5	5	1	2.27	800 456-5111
Ivy Fund-Developing Nations Adv	Foreign	2.3					1	1.76	800 456-5111
Ivy Fund-Developing Nations B	Foreign	1.2	-9.37	-0.4	5	5	1	2.93	800 456-5111
Ivy Fund-Developing Nations C	Foreign	1.1	-9.33		5	5	1	2.87	800 456-5111
Ivy Fund-European Opport A	European	151.1					1		800 456-5111
Ivy Fund-European Opport Adv	European	152.9					1		800 456-5111
Ivy Fund-European Opport B	European	150.3					1		800 456-5111
Ivy Fund-European Opport C	European	150.2					1		800 456-5111
Ivy Fund-Gbl Science/Tech A	Technology	88.3	48.7		1	5	1	2	800 456-5111
Ivy Fund-Gbl Science/Tech Adv	Technology	88.5					1	1.87	800 456-5111
Ivy Fund-Gbl Science/Tech B	Technology	86.9	47.56		2	5	1	2.77	800 456-5111
Ivy Fund-Gbl Science/Tech C	Technology	87	47.68		1	5	1	2.7	800 456-5111
Ivy Fund-Global A	Global	6.6	3.48	8.92	5	4	1	2.77	800 456-5111
Ivy Fund-Global Adv	Global	6.8					1	1.95	800 456-5111
Ivy Fund-Global B	Global	5.7	2.64	8.15	4	4	1	3	800 456-5111
Ivy Fund-Global C	Global	5.5	2.38		5	4	1	3.22	800 456-5111
Ivy Fund-Global Nat Resource A	Energy/Res	15	-0.89		5	4	1	1.94	800 456-5111
Ivy Fund-Global Nat Resource B	Energy/Res	14.6	-1.55		5	4	1	2.58	800 456-5111
Ivy Fund-Global Nat Resource C	Energy/Res	14.8	-2.1		5	4	1	2.77	800 456-5111
Ivy Fund-Growth A	Growth	28	17.34	18.22	3	3	0.84	1.37	800 456-5111
Ivy Fund-Growth Adv	Growth	27.9					0.84	1.4	800 456-5111
Ivy Fund-Growth B	Growth	26.8	16.27	16.86	3	3	0.84	2.33	800 456-5111
Ivy Fund-Growth C	Growth	26.6	16.06		3	3	0.84	2.43	800 456-5111
Ivy Fund-Growth with Income A	Growth	-3.1	7.16	12.45	4	3	0.75	1.61	800 456-5111
Ivy Fund-Growth with Income Adv	Growth	-3.1					0.84	1.44	800 456-5111
Ivy Fund-Growth with Income B	Growth	-2	7.06	12.52	4	3	0.75	2.35	800 456-5111
Ivy Fund-Growth with Income C	Growth	-1	7.38	13.61	4	3	0.75	2.47	800 456-5111
Ivy Fund-International A	Foreign	-1.3	2.7	9.83	4	3	1	1.65	800 456-5111
Ivy Fund-International B	Foreign	-2.3	1.83	8.91	5	3	1	2.41	800 456-5111
Ivy Fund-International C	Foreign	-2.3	1.83		5	3	1	2.39	800 456-5111
Ivy Fund-International II A	Foreign	10	4.58		4	3	1	1.71	800 456-5111
Ivy Fund-International II Adv	Foreign	10.4					1	1.39	800 456-5111
Ivy Fund-International II B	Foreign	9.1	3.75		4	3	1	2.52	800 456-5111
Ivy Fund-International II C	Foreign	9.1	3.74		4	3	1	2.47	800 456-5111
Ivy Fund-International Sm Co A	Foreign	45.7	12.41		3	3	1	2.45	800 456-5111
Ivy Fund-International Sm Co B	Foreign	44.6	11.54		3	3	1	3.22	800 456-5111
Ivy Fund-International Sm Co C	Foreign	44.5	11.58		3	3	1	3.16	800 456-5111
Ivy Fund-Pan-Europe Fund A	European	107.2	34.56		5	5	1	2.43	800 456-5111
Ivy Fund-Pan-Europe Fund B	European	106.7	35.57		3	5	1	3.14	800 456-5111
Ivy Fund-Pan-Europe Fund C	European	105.3	35.18		3	5	1	3.2	800 456-5111
Ivy Fund-South America A	Foreign	23.5	-8.17	5.2	4	5	1	2.2	800 456-5111
Ivy Fund-South America B	Foreign	22.7	-8.84	4.32	4	5	1	3	800 456-5111
Ivy Fund-South America C	Foreign	22.4	-8.92		5	5	1	3.02	800 456-5111
Ivy Fund-US Emerging Growth A	Small Co	63.7	28.63	24.18	3	5	0.84	1.68	800 456-5111
Ivy Fund-US Emerging Growth Adv	Small Co	64					0.84	1.45	800 456-5111
Ivy Fund-US Emerging Growth B	Small Co	62.4	27.66	21.49	3	5	0.84	2.45	800 456-5111
Ivy Fund-US Emerging Growth C	Small Co	62.5	27.71		3	5	0.84	2.39	800 456-5111
Ivy International Fund II Cl I	Foreign	8.9	3.96		4	3	1	1.17	800 456-5111
Ivy Intl Small Companies Fund Adv	Foreign						1		800 456-5111
Ivy Pan Europe Fund Advisor	European	9.5					1	2.29	800 456-5111
Ivy South America Fund Advisor	Foreign						1		800 456-5111
Ivy US Blue Chip Fund A	Growth/Inc	6.8					0.75	1.45	800 456-5111
Ivy US Blue Chip Fund Advisor	Growth/Inc	7.1					0.75	1.08	800 456-5111
Ivy US Blue Chip Fund B	Growth/Inc	6					0.75	2.14	800 456-5111
Ivy US Blue Chip Fund C	Growth/Inc	6.2					0.75	2.08	800 456-5111
Ivy US Blue Chip Fund I	Growth/Inc	6.2					0.75		800 456-5111
J. Hancock Balanced A	Balanced	-3	7.78	11.23	3	1	0.75	1.21	800 225-5291
J. Hancock Balanced B	Balanced	-3.3	7.19	9.77	3	1	0.75	1.94	800 225-5291

Stock Fund Name	Objective	Annualized Return for			Rank		Max Load	Expense Ratio	Toll-Free Telephone
		1 Year	3 Years	5 Years	Overall	Risk			
J. Hancock Core Equity A	Growth	1.8	17.14	21.15	3	3	0.75	1.37	800 225-5291
J. Hancock Core Equity B	Growth	1.1	16.3		2	3	0.75	2	800 225-5291
J. Hancock Core Equity C	Growth	1.1					0.75	2	800 225-5291
J. Hancock European Equity A	Foreign	17.4					0.81	1.89	800 225-5291
J. Hancock European Equity B	Foreign	16.7					0.81	2.6	800 225-5291
J. Hancock Global Fund A	Global	6.3	7.31	10.9	4	3	0.94	1.71	800 225-5291
J. Hancock Global Fund B	Global	5.5	6.61	10.16	4	3	0.94	2.25	800 225-5291
J. Hancock Health Sciences A	Health	38.8	18.68	21.75	3	3	0.8	1.6	800 225-5291
J. Hancock Health Sciences B	Health	37.9	17.87	20.9	3	3	0.8	2.25	800 225-5291
J. Hancock International A	Foreign	12.4	3.66	7	4	3	1	1.69	800 225-5291
J. Hancock International B	Foreign	11.7	2.97	6.26	5	3	1	2.39	800 225-5291
J. Hancock International C	Foreign	11.8					0	2.41	800 225-5291
J. Hancock Large Cap Growth A	Growth	5	15.93	17.24	4	3	0.75	1.35	800 225-5291
J. Hancock Large Cap Growth B	Growth	4.2	15.17	16.43	3	3	0.75	1.98	800 225-5291
J. Hancock Large Cap Value A	Growth/Inc	25.6	22.79	25.87	1	3	0.63	1.15	800 225-5291
J. Hancock Large Cap Value B	Growth/Inc	24.7	21.89	25.16	1	3	0.63	1.84	800 225-5291
J. Hancock Large Cap Value C	Growth/Inc	24.7					0.63	1.9	800 225-5291
J. Hancock Mid Cap Growth A	Growth	48.3	25.08	22.56	3	4	0.8	1.64	800 225-5291
J. Hancock Mid Cap Growth B	Growth	47.3	24.26	21.69	3	4	0.8	2.25	800 225-5291
J. Hancock Mid Cap Growth C	Growth	47.2					0.8	2.35	800 225-5291
J. Hancock Pacific Basin A	Pacific	25.3	0.8	4.23	4	4	0.8	2.37	800 225-5291
J. Hancock Pacific Basin B	Pacific	24.4	0.08	3.5	4	4	0.8	3.2	800 225-5291
J. Hancock Regional Bank A	Financial	-26.4	-0.74	12.51	4	4	0.8	1.27	800 225-5291
J. Hancock Regional Bank B	Financial	-26.9	-1.41	11.75	5	4	0.75	1.91	800 225-5291
J. Hancock Small Cap Growth A	Small Co	51	27.88	23.75	3	5	0.75	1.98	800 225-5291
J. Hancock Small Cap Growth B	Small Co	49.8	26.96	22.83	3	5	0.75	2.02	800 225-5291
J. Hancock Small Cap Growth C	Small Co	49.7					0.75	2.08	800 225-5291
J. Hancock Small Cap Value A	Growth	73.2	33.09	27.08	2	4	0.69	1.25	800 225-5291
J. Hancock Small Cap Value B	Growth	72	32.16	26.19	2	4	0.69	1.92	800 225-5291
J. Hancock Sovereign Investors A	Growth/Inc	-4.4	9.03	14.78	2	2	0.54	1.04	800 225-5291
J. Hancock Sovereign Investors B	Growth/Inc	-5.1	8.23	13.91	3	2	0.59	1.68	800 225-5291
J. Hancock Sovereign Investors C	Growth/Inc	-1.2					0.55	1.73	800 225-5291
J. Hancock Technology A	Technology	75.9	55.73	35.45	2	5	0.79	1.35	800 225-5291
J. Hancock Technology B	Technology	74.6	54.64	38.08	2	5	0.84	1.98	800 225-5291
J.P. Morgan Disciplined Equity	Growth	2.5					0.34	0.85	800 766-7722
J.P. Morgan Diversified Fund	Balanced	6.6	12.54	14.89	3	1	0.55	1.01	800 766-7722
J.P. Morgan Emerging Mkts Debt	Intl Bond	25	3.48		4	5	0.69	2.5	800 766-7722
J.P. Morgan Emerging Mkts Equity	Foreign	10.3	-8.1	-0.77	5	4	1	1.9	800 766-7722
J.P. Morgan Europe Equity Fund	European	11.7	13.27		3	3	0.59	2.35	800 766-7722
J.P. Morgan Global 50 Fund	Foreign	22.2					1.25	2.04	800 766-7722
J.P. Morgan Instl-Disciplined Eq	Growth	3	18.98		2	3	0.34	0.59	800 766-7722
J.P. Morgan Instl-Diversified Fd	Balanced	6.7	12.84	15.19	3	1	0.55	0.65	800 766-7722
J.P. Morgan Instl-Emerg Mkts Eq	Foreign	11.5	-7.67	-0.36	5	4	1	1.23	800 766-7722
J.P. Morgan Instl-Europe Equity	European	11.9	13.95		3	3	0.59	2.29	800 766-7722
J.P. Morgan Instl-Intl Equity	Foreign	16.9	8.95	11.21	5	3	0.59	0.96	800 766-7722
J.P. Morgan Instl-Intl Opport Fd	Foreign	20	8.85		4	3	0.59	1.02	800 766-7722
J.P. Morgan Instl-Tax Aware Dis Eq	Growth	2.3	19.11		2	3	0.34	0.67	800 766-7722
J.P. Morgan Instl-US Equity	Growth	-0.3	15.97	19.97	3	3	0.4	0.63	800 766-7722
J.P. Morgan Instl-US Small Comp	Small Co	36.8	15.68	17.89	3	4	0.59	0.84	800 766-7722
J.P. Morgan International Equity	Foreign	16.5	8.73	10.98	5	3	0.59	1.23	800 766-7722
J.P. Morgan Intl Opportunities	Foreign	20.9	9.11		4	3	0.59	1.29	800 766-7722
J.P. Morgan Tax Aware US Equity	Growth	4.9	19.36		3	3	0.45	0.93	800 766-7722
J.P. Morgan US Equity Fund	Growth	-1	15.54	19.61	3	3	0.4	0.78	800 766-7722
J.P. Morgan US Sm Comp Oppts	Small Co	47	25.7		3	5	0.59	1.07	800 766-7722
J.P. Morgan US Small Company	Small Co	36.4	15.43	17.82	3	4	0.59	1	800 766-7722
JP Morgan Instl SmartIndex Fund	Growth/Inc	4.7					0.25	5.44	800 766-7722
Jacob Internet Fund	Technology						1.25		888 522-6239
James Advantage Market Neutral A	Growth	7					1.65	1.93	800 995-2637

Stock Fund Name	Objective	Annualized Return for			Rank		Max Load	Expense Ratio	Toll-Free Telephone
		1 Year	3 Years	5 Years	Overall	Risk			
James Advantage Small Cap Fund A	Growth	-10.6					1.2	1.48	800 995-2637
Jamestown Intl Equity Fund	Foreign	22	15.71		3	3	1	1.51	800 787-7414
Janus Fund	Growth	26.9	31.73	27.97	1	3	0.65	0.84	800 525-3713
Janus Global Life Sciences Fund	Global	73.8					0.65	1.18	800 525-3713
Janus Global Technology Fund	Global	109.6					0.75	1.02	800 525-3713
Jensen Portfolio	Growth/Inc	24.6	18.78	21.13	2	2	0.5	0.95	800 221-4384
John Hancock Balanced Fund C	Balanced	-3.1					0.75		800 225-5291
John Hancock Core Growth A	Growth						0.8		800 225-5291
John Hancock Core Growth B	Growth						0.8		800 225-5291
John Hancock Core Growth C	Growth						0.8		800 225-5291
John Hancock Core Value B	Growth						0.8		800 225-5291
John Hancock Core Value C	Growth						0.8		800 225-5291
John Hancock European Equity C	Foreign	16.7					0.9	2.6	800 225-5291
John Hancock Financial Industries C	Financial	-2.3					0.76	2.06	800 225-5291
John Hancock Global C	Global	1.6					0.94	2.41	800 225-5291
John Hancock Health Science C	Health	37.9					0.8		800 225-5291
John Hancock Large Cap Growth C	Growth	4.2					0.75	2.04	800 225-5291
John Hancock Pacific Basin C	Pacific	21.9					0.8	3.2	800 225-5291
John Hancock Regional Bank C	Financial	-26.9					0.75	1.96	800 225-5291
John Hancock Small Cap Value Fund C	Growth	72					0.1	1.96	800 225-5291
John Hancock Sovereign Investors Y	Growth/Inc	-4.1	5.77	12.79	4	2	0.59	0.68	800 225-5291
John Hancock Technology C	Technology	74.6					0.79	2.02	800 225-5291
JohnsonFamily International Equity	Foreign	17.5					0.9	1.85	
JohnsonFamily Large Cap Equity Fund	Growth	-11.2					0.75	1.36	
JohnsonFamily Small Cap Equity Fund	Small Co	-3.6					0.75	1.44	
Jundt 25 Fund I	Growth	14.4					1.3	2	800 370-0612
Jundt Growth Fund A	Growth	5.4	20.73		3	3	1	1.95	800 370-0612
Jundt Growth Fund B	Growth	8.8	21.48		3	3	1	2.7	800 370-0612
Jundt Growth Fund C	Growth	8.9	21.6		3	3	1	2.7	800 370-0612
Jundt Growth Fund I	Growth	5.4	21.06		2	3	1	1.71	800 370-0612
Jundt Opportunity Fund A	Agg Growth	36.2	44.46		1	3	1.3	2.14	800 370-0612
Jundt Opportunity Fund B	Agg Growth	35.2	43.38		1	3	1.3	2.89	800 370-0612
Jundt Opportunity Fund C	Agg Growth	35.2	43.32		1	3	1.3	2.89	800 370-0612
Jundt Opportunity Fund I	Agg Growth	36.6	44.82		1	3	1.3	1.88	800 370-0612
Jundt Twenty Five Fund A	Growth	14.1					1.3	2.25	800 370-0612
Jundt Twenty Five Fund B	Growth	13.2					1.3	3	800 370-0612
Jundt Twenty Five Fund C	Growth	13.1					1.3	3	800 370-0612
Jundt US Emerging Growth A	Small Co	58.1	38.03		2	4	1	1.8	800 370-0612
Jundt US Emerging Growth B	Small Co	57.1	37.06		2	4	1	2.54	800 370-0612
Jundt US Emerging Growth C	Small Co	57	37.05		2	4	1	2.54	800 370-0612
Jundt US Emerging Growth Fund I	Small Co	58.6	38.41		2	4	1	1.55	800 370-0612
Jurika & Voyles Balanced J	Balanced	7.3	7.17	11.26	3	1	0.69	0.94	800 584-6878
Jurika & Voyles Sm Cap J	Small Co	46.5	15.85	21.39	3	4	1	1.5	800 584-6878
Jurika & Voyles Value + Growth J	Growth	9.1	8.9	13.88	3	3	0.84	1.25	800 584-6878
KOPP Emerging Growth Fund A	Growth	180.4					1	1.5	888 533-5677
Kalmar Growth & Value Small Cap	Small Co	27.1	12.57		4	3	1	1.25	800 282-2319
Kaufmann Fund	Agg Growth	43.3	15.39	18.02	3	4	1.5	1.93	800 261-0555
Kayne Anderson Rising Dividend	Growth/Inc	5.4	14.47	19.88	3	3	0.75	1.06	800 231-7414
Keeley Small Cap Value Fund	Small Co	-5.3	9.25	16.1	3	3	1	1.97	800 533-5344
Kemper Aggressive Growth A	Agg Growth	47.4					0.4	1.41	800 621-1048
Kemper Aggressive Growth B	Agg Growth	45.8					0.4	2.12	800 621-1048
Kemper Asian Growth Fund A	Pacific	6.9	-8.4		4	5	0.84	1.84	800 621-1048
Kemper Asian Growth Fund B	Pacific	6.5	-9.22		4	5	0.84	2.47	800 621-1048
Kemper Asian Growth Fund C	Pacific	6	-9.59		4	5	0.84	4.12	800 621-1048
Kemper Blue Chip Fund A	Growth/Inc	9.9	16.13	21.03	3	2	0.56	1.18	800 621-1048
Kemper Blue Chip Fund B	Growth/Inc	8.9	15.13	20.01	3	2	0.56	1.87	800 621-1048
Kemper Blue Chip Fund C	Growth/Inc	9.1	15.22	20.08	3	2	0.56	2	800 621-1048
Kemper Classic Growth A	Growth	24.7	22.57		2	3	0.69	1.27	800 621-1048

Stock Fund Name	Objective	Annualized Return for			Rank		Max Load	Expense Ratio	Toll-Free Telephone
		1 Year	3 Years	5 Years	Overall	Risk			
Kemper Classic Growth B	Growth	23.6					0.69	2.12	800 621-1048
Kemper Classic Growth C	Growth	23.1					0.69	2.08	800 621-1048
Kemper Contrarian A	Growth/Inc	-24.1	3.5	12.27	4	3	0.73	1.39	800 621-1048
Kemper Contrarian B	Growth/Inc	-24.7	2.61		3	3	0.73	2.25	800 621-1048
Kemper Contrarian C	Growth/Inc	-24.6	2.58		4	3	0.73	2.41	800 621-1048
Kemper Dreman Financial Services A	Financial	-15.6					0.59	1.32	800 621-1048
Kemper Dreman Financial Services B	Financial	-15.6					0.59	2.22	800 621-1048
Kemper Dreman Financial Services C	Financial	-16.3					0.59	2.24	800 621-1048
Kemper Dreman High Return A	Growth/Inc	-16.7	3.7	15.37	3	3	0.68	1.19	800 621-1048
Kemper Dreman High Return B	Growth/Inc	-17.4	2.83		4	3	0.68	2.06	800 621-1048
Kemper Dreman High Return C	Growth/Inc	-17.3	2.87		4	3	0.68	2.06	800 621-1048
Kemper Emerging Mkts Gr Fund A	Foreign	13.6					1.25	2.18	800 621-1048
Kemper Emerging Mkts Gr Fund C	Foreign	12.7					1.25	3.02	800 621-1048
Kemper Global Blue Chip Fund A	Global	14.2					0.56	1.8	800 621-1048
Kemper Global Blue Chip Fund B	Global	13.2					0.56	2.68	800 621-1048
Kemper Global Blue Chip Fund C	Global	12.9					0.56	2.64	800 621-1048
Kemper Global Income A	Intl Bond	-0.2	1.52	2.65	4	4	0.75	1.71	800 621-1048
Kemper Global Income B	Intl Bond	-1	0.79	1.91	5	4	0.75	2.35	800 621-1048
Kemper Global Income C	Intl Bond	-1.1	0.83	1.99	5	4	0.75	2.2	800 621-1048
Kemper Growth Fund A	Growth	29.6	20.76	20.17	2	4	0.54		800 621-1048
Kemper Growth Fund B	Growth	28.4	19.54	18.95	3	4	0.54	1.01	800 621-1048
Kemper Growth Fund C	Growth	28.5	19.81	19.15	3	4	0.54	1.95	800 621-1048
Kemper Horizon 10+ Portfolio A	Growth/Inc	0.3	7.25		4	1	0.56	1.45	800 621-1048
Kemper Horizon 10+ Portfolio B	Growth/Inc	-0.6	6.33		4	1	0.56	2.33	800 621-1048
Kemper Horizon 10+ Portfolio C	Growth/Inc	-0.7	6.14		4	1	0.56	2.5	800 621-1048
Kemper Horizon 20+ Portfolio A	Growth	-2.2	6.18		4	2	0.56	1.89	800 621-1048
Kemper Horizon 20+ Portfolio B	Growth	-2.9	5.35		4	2	0.56	2.6	800 621-1048
Kemper Horizon 20+ Portfolio C	Growth	-3.1	5.18		4	2	0.56	2.87	800 621-1048
Kemper Horizon 5 Portfolio A	Income	0.9	6.12		3	1	0.56	1.54	800 621-1048
Kemper Horizon 5 Portfolio B	Income	0.1	5.43		4	1	0.56	2.2	800 621-1048
Kemper Horizon 5 Portfolio C	Income	0.1	5.34		4	1	0.56	2.39	800 621-1048
Kemper International Fund A	Foreign	25.8	9.72	13.52	4	3	0.73	1.78	800 621-1048
Kemper International Fund B	Foreign	24.9	8.8	11.94	4	3	0.73	2.87	800 621-1048
Kemper International Fund C	Foreign	25	8.85	12.05	4	3	0.73	2.87	800 621-1048
Kemper Latin America Fund A	Foreign	13.8					1.25	3.06	800 621-1048
Kemper New Europe A	European	40.7	16.81		3	3	0.75	1.6	800 621-1048
Kemper New Europe B	European	39.7	15.66		3	3	0.75	2.79	800 621-1048
Kemper New Europe C	European	37.6	15.36		3	3	0.75	2.87	800 621-1048
Kemper Retirement Fund-II	Flexible	8.9	11.11	11.95	3	1	0.5	0.97	800 621-1048
Kemper Retirement Fund-III	Flexible	8.6	11.46	12.5	3	1	0.5	1.04	800 621-1048
Kemper Retirement Fund-IV	Flexible	7.3	10.9	11.76	3	1	0.5	1.03	800 621-1048
Kemper Retirement Fund-V	Flexible	7.9	11.77	12.66	3	1	0.5	1.03	800 621-1048
Kemper Retirement Fund-VII	Flexible	6.6	9.93		3	1	0	1.17	800 621-1048
Kemper Small Cap Equity Fund A	Small Co	41.3	14.04	16.75	4	5	0.35	1.01	800 621-1048
Kemper Small Cap Equity Fund B	Small Co	40	12.75	15.46	3	5	0.47	2.49	800 621-1048
Kemper Small Cap Equity Fund C	Small Co	40.2	13.17	15.73	3	5	0.52	2.12	800 621-1048
Kemper Small Cap Value A	Small Co	-10.9	-4.39	7.09	5	3	0.73	1.52	800 621-1048
Kemper Small Cap Value B	Small Co	-11.6	-5.21		5	3	0.73	1.48	800 621-1048
Kemper Small Cap Value C	Small Co	-11.4	-5.11		5	3	0.73	2.33	800 621-1048
Kemper Small Cap Value I	Small Co	-10.3	-3.15		5	3	0.73	0.93	800 621-1048
Kemper State Tax Free Inc-FL A	Muni State	2.2	3.52	4.89	3	3	0.55	0.81	800 621-1048
Kemper State Tax Free Inc-FL B	Muni State	1.6	2.73	4.1	3	3	0.55	1.62	800 621-1048
Kemper State Tax Free Inc-FL C	Muni State	1.5	2.74	4.05	4	3	0.55	1.62	800 621-1048
Kemper Target 2010	Flexible	9.5	12.51	13.95	3	1	0.5	1.02	800 621-1048
Kemper Technology Fund A	Technology	86.1	52.26	37.15	2	5	0.55	0.93	800 621-1048
Kemper Technology Fund B	Technology	84.1	50.71	35.76	2	5	0.54	1.82	800 621-1048
Kemper Technology Fund C	Technology	84.4	50.96	26.8	2	5	0.52	1.78	800 621-1048
Kemper Total Return Fund A	Balanced	6.6	12.28	15.05	3	1	0.53	1.02	800 621-1048

Stock Fund Name	Objective	Annualized Return for			Rank		Max Load	Expense Ratio	Toll-Free Telephone
		1 Year	3 Years	5 Years	Overall	Risk			
Kemper Total Return Fund B	Balanced	5.5	11.19	13.97	3	1	0.54	2.08	800 621-1048
Kemper Total Return Fund C	Balanced	5.7	11.3	14.07	3	1	0.54	1.77	800 621-1048
Kemper Value Plus Growth A	Growth	7.1	14.04		3	3	0.69	1.41	800 621-1048
Kemper Value Plus Growth B	Growth	6.4	11.24		4	3	0.69	0.2	800 621-1048
Kemper Value Plus Growth C	Growth	6.3	13.16		3	3	0.69	2.16	800 621-1048
Kemper Worldwide 2004	Growth	13.8	9.52	9.94	3	1	0.75	1.3	800 621-1048
Kemper-Dreman High Return Fund I	Growth/Inc	-17.9	3.43		4	3	0.68	0.79	800 621-1048
Kent Fds-Growth & Income Inst	Growth/Inc	4.6	17.29	20.31	3	2	0.69	0.92	800 633-5368
Kent Fds-Growth & Income Inv	Growth/Inc	4.3	17.01	20.02	3	2	0.69	1.16	800 633-5368
Kent Fds-Index Equity Inst	Growth	6.8	19.2	23.16	2	3	0.29	0.4	800 633-5368
Kent Fds-Index Equity Inv	Growth	6.5	18.89	22.7	2	3	0.29	0.66	800 633-5368
Kent Fds-International Gr Inst	Foreign	15.5	9.69	12.54	4	2	0.75	1.02	800 633-5368
Kent Fds-International Gr Inv	Foreign	15.3	9.41	12.24	5	2	0.75	1.27	800 633-5368
Kent Fds-Small Co Growth Inst	Small Co	24.3	12.34	16.73	3	4	0.69	0.93	800 633-5368
Kent Fds-Small Co Growth Inv	Small Co	24	12.08	16.44	3	4	0.69	1.18	800 633-5368
Kent Large Company Growth Instl	Growth						0.69		800 633-5368
Kent Large Company Growth Invest	Growth						0.69		800 633-5368
Kobren Growth	Growth	9.5	12.78		2	3	0.75	0.97	800 895-9936
Kobren Moderate Growth	Growth/Inc	4.5	8.93		4	2	0.75	0.93	800 895-9936
Kobrick Capital Fund B	Growth						1		
Kobrick Capital Fund C	Growth						1		
Kobrick Capital Fund Y	Growth						1		
Kobrick Emerging Growth Fund B	Small Co						1		
Kobrick Emerging Growth Fund C	Small Co						1		
Kobrick Emerging Growth Fund Y	Small Co						1		
Kobrick Growth Fund B	Growth						1		
Kobrick Growth Fund C	Growth						1		
Kobrick Growth Fund Y	Growth						1		
LKCM Balanced Fund	Balanced	3.9					0.65	2.04	800 688-5526
LKCM Equity Fund	Growth	11.2	15.14		2	2	0.69	0.8	800 688-5526
LKCM International Fund	Foreign	38.8					0	1.46	800 688-5526
LKCM Small Cap Equity	Small Co	13.1	8.48	15.42	3	3	0.75	0.93	800 688-5526
LaCrosse Large Cap Stock Fund	Growth	-2.8					0.75	1.11	888 661-7600
Lazard Emerging Markets Inst	Foreign	11.7	-7.3	4.3	5	4	1	1.22	800 823-6300
Lazard Emerging Markets Open	Foreign	11.2	-7.48		5	5	1	1.76	800 823-6300
Lazard Equity Inst	Growth	-9.2	8.3	15.14	2	3	0.75	0.83	800 823-6300
Lazard Equity Open	Growth	-9.4	8.04		4	3	0.75	0.82	800 823-6300
Lazard Global Equity Inst	Global	3	10.29		3	2	0.75	1.05	800 823-6300
Lazard Global Equity Open	Global	2.7	9.99		4	2	0.75	1.9	800 823-6300
Lazard Intl Equity Inst	Foreign	12.4	11.05	14.16	3	2	0.75	0.88	800 823-6300
Lazard Intl Equity Open	Foreign	12	10.65		2	2	0.75	1.15	800 823-6300
Lazard Intl Small Cap Inst	Foreign	19.6	8.58	10.15	4	2	0.75	1.01	800 823-6300
Lazard Intl Small Cap Open	Foreign	19.1	8.2		3	2	0.75	2.1	800 823-6300
Lazard Mid Cap Portfolio - Instl	Growth	-0.6					0.75	1.08	800 823-6300
Lazard Mid Cap Portfolio - Open	Growth	-1					0.75	1.09	800 823-6300
Lazard Small Cap Inst	Small Co	-4.5	0.51	8.85	4	3	0.75	0.81	800 823-6300
Lazard Small Cap Open	Small Co	-4.8	0.23		4	3	0.75	1.09	800 823-6300
Legg Mason American Lead Co Prim	Growth	-10.3	8.65	16.23	4	3	0.7	1.92	800 822-5544
Legg Mason Balanced Fund Prim	Balanced	1.1	5.87		3	1	0.75	1.85	800 822-5544
Legg Mason Emerging Markets Prim	Foreign	28.8	1.78		4	5	1	2.5	800 822-5544
Legg Mason Financial Services A	Financial	-11.9					1	1.5	800 800-3609
Legg Mason Financial Services Prim	Financial	-11.5					1	2.25	800 800-3609
Legg Mason Focus Trust	Growth	-1.4	20.56	20.84	3	3	0.69	1.89	800 822-5544
Legg Mason Global Income Trust	Intl Bond	1.1	0.54	2.79	4	5	1	1.87	800 822-5544
Legg Mason International Eq Prim	Foreign	8.8	1.87	7.79	5	3	0.75	2.14	800 822-5544
Legg Mason Intl Equity Navigator	Foreign	11.9	0.41	0.24	5	2	0.75	1.04	800 822-5544
Legg Mason Special Invest Navigator	Small Co	8	19.64	21.97	3	4	0.72	0.78	800 822-5544
Legg Mason Special Invest Prim	Small Co	11	19.94	21.63	3	4	0.72	1.82	800 822-5544

Stock Fund Name	Objective	Annualized Return for			Rank		Max Load	Expense Ratio	Toll-Free Telephone
		1 Year	3 Years	5 Years	Overall	Risk			
Legg Mason Total Return Prim	Growth/Inc	-15.1	2.7	13.03	4	3	0.75	1.88	800 822-5544
Legg Mason US Sm Cap Value Tr Nav	Small Co	-19.7					0.84		800 822-5544
Legg Mason US Sm-Cap Value Trust	Small Co	-20.5					0.84	2	800 822-5544
Legg Mason Value Trust Navigator	Growth	4.9	27.99	32.63	2	4	0.67	0.71	800 822-5544
Legg Mason Value Trust Prim	Growth	3.8	26.75	31.86	1	4	0.67	1.67	800 822-5544
Lepercq-Istel Fund	Growth/Inc	13.4	14.59	15.06	3	4	0.75	1.39	800 655-7766
Lexington Corp Leaders Trust	Growth/Inc	-8.9	5.95	14.72	3	2	0.4	0.6	800 526-0056
Lexington Global Corporate Leaders	Global	20.7	14.5	16.34	3	2	1	1.95	800 526-0056
Lexington Goldfund	Prec Metal	-8.7	-15.64	-11.64	5	5	0.9	1.93	800 526-0056
Lexington Growth & Inc Fund	Growth/Inc	10.9	16.53	21.3	2	3	0.75	1.05	800 526-0056
Lexington International Fund	Foreign	33.6	16.94	17.1	2	3	1	1.97	800 526-0056
Lexington Silver Fund	Prec Metal	-15.5	-14.48	-8.96	5	4	1	2.1	800 526-0056
Lexington Small Cap Asia Grth Fd	Pacific	3.2	-17.33		5	5	1.25	2.5	800 526-0056
Lexington Troika Dialog Russia	Foreign	32.6	-24.68		4	5	1.25	3.16	800 526-0056
Lexington WorldWide Emerg Mkts	Foreign	34.1	-2.71	1.78	4	5	1	2	800 526-0056
Liberty Stein Roe Adv Tax-Mngd Vl A	Growth	-14.5					1		800 338-2550
Liberty Stein Roe Adv Tax-Mngd Vl B	Growth	-15					1		800 338-2550
Liberty Stein Roe Adv Tax-Mngd Vl C	Growth	-15					1		800 338-2550
Liberty Stein Roe Adv Tax-Mngd Vl Z	Growth	-14.5					1		800 338-2550
Liberty Stein Roe Midcap Growth	Growth	42.5					0.55	1.36	800 338-2550
Liberty-Colonial FL Tax Exempt A	Muni State	1.6	3.89	5.13	3	4	0.07	0.93	800 345-6611
Liberty-Colonial FL Tax Exempt B	Muni State	0.8	3.12	4.36	5	4	0.07	1.68	800 345-6611
Liberty-Colonial FL Tax Exempt C	Muni State	1.1					0.51	1.38	800 345-6611
Liberty-Colonial Fund (The) A	Balanced	6.3	11.17	15.07	3	1	0.54	1.11	800 345-6611
Liberty-Colonial Fund (The) B	Balanced	5.4	10.32	14.18	3	1	0.55	1.87	800 345-6611
Liberty-Colonial Fund (The) C	Balanced	5.4					0.55	1.87	800 345-6611
Liberty-Colonial Glbl Utilities A	Utilities	17.6	17.23	17.15	2	3	0.65	1.28	800 345-6611
Liberty-Colonial Glbl Utilities B	Utilities	16.6	16.31	16.23	2	3	0.65	2.02	800 345-6611
Liberty-Colonial Glbl Utilities C	Utilities	16.7	16.35	16.25	2	3	0.65	2.02	800 345-6611
Liberty-Colonial Global Equity A	Global	3.8	8.4	12.83	4	3	0.94	0.1	800 345-6611
Liberty-Colonial Global Equity B	Global	2.9	7.56	11.92	5	3	0.94	2.39	800 345-6611
Liberty-Colonial Global Equity C	Global	2.9					0.94	2.39	800 345-6611
Liberty-Colonial Intl Horizons A	Foreign	8.2	6.49	10.86	4	3	0.75	1.61	800 345-6611
Liberty-Colonial Intl Horizons B	Foreign	7.6	5.79	10.09	5	3	0.75	2.35	800 345-6611
Liberty-Colonial Intl Horizons C	Foreign	7.6					0.75	2.27	800 345-6611
Liberty-Colonial Select Val Fd A	Growth	7.9	15.41	18.68	3	3	0.69	1.32	800 345-6611
Liberty-Colonial Select Val Fd B	Growth	7.2	14.53	17.79	3	3	0.59	2.08	800 345-6611
Liberty-Colonial Select Val Fd C	Growth	7.2					0.69	2.08	800 345-6611
Liberty-Colonial Sm Cap Val Fd A	Small Co	7.2	4.2	11.11	5	3	0.8	1.48	800 345-6611
Liberty-Colonial Sm Cap Val Fd B	Small Co	6.4	3.43	10.3	5	3	0.59	2.24	800 345-6611
Liberty-Colonial Sm Cap Val Fd C	Small Co	6.4	3.46		5	3	0.8	2.24	800 345-6611
Liberty-Colonial Strategic Bal A	Balanced	4.1	9.27	12.56	3	1	0.69	1.55	800 345-6611
Liberty-Colonial Strategic Bal B	Balanced	3.4	8.66	12.01	3	1	0.69	2.14	800 345-6611
Liberty-Colonial Strategic Bal C	Balanced	3.3	8.67	11.99	3	1	0.69	2.14	800 345-6611
Liberty-Colonial US Gr & Inc A	Growth/Inc	1.4	14.14	18.49	3	3	0.8	1.4	800 345-6611
Liberty-Colonial US Gr & Inc B	Growth/Inc	0.6	13.27	17.59	2	3	0.8	2.16	800 345-6611
Liberty-Colonial US Gr & Inc C	Growth/Inc	0.7	13.28	17.59	2	3	0.8	2.16	800 345-6611
Liberty-Colonial Utilities Fund A	Utilities	6.1	18.33	17.42	2	2	0.65	1.17	800 345-6611
Liberty-Colonial Utilities Fund B	Utilities	5.3	17.46	16.57	2	2	0.65	1.92	800 345-6611
Liberty-Colonial Utilities Fund C	Utilities	5.3					0.65	1.92	800 345-6611
Liberty-Crabbe Huson Equity A	Growth	-0.4	5.7	10.57	4	3	0.98	1.41	800 345-6611
Liberty-Crabbe Huson Mgd Inc&Eq A	AssetAlloc	1.6	7.04	9.06	4	2	1	1.41	800 345-6611
Liberty-Crabbe Huson RealEst Inv A	Real Est	-0.5	1.05	8.65	4	3	0.71	1.5	800 345-6611
Liberty-Crabbe Huson Sm Cap Fd	Small Co	19.3	-3.34		4	4	0.17	1.5	800 345-6611
Liberty-Crabbe Huson Special Fd	Growth	2	-13.02	-3.83	5	4	0.81	1.5	800 345-6611
Liberty-Newport Greater China A	Pacific	38.1					1.39	2.14	800 345-6611
Liberty-Newport Greater China B	Pacific	37.2	0.79		3	5	1.39	2.89	800 345-6611
Liberty-Newport Greater China C	Pacific	37	1.27		3	5	1.39	2.89	800 345-6611

333

Stock Fund Name	Objective	Annualized Return for			Rank		Max Load	Expense Ratio	Toll-Free Telephone
		1 Year	3 Years	5 Years	Overall	Risk			
Liberty-Newport Japan Opp A	Pacific	28.5	21.46		3	4	1.19	2	800 345-6611
Liberty-Newport Japan Opp B	Pacific	27.4	20.51		3	4	1.19	2	800 345-6611
Liberty-Newport Japan Opp C	Pacific	27.3	20.52		3	4	1.19	2.75	800 345-6611
Liberty-Newport Tiger A	Pacific	29.1	-1.65	2.74	4	5	1.02	1.76	800 345-6611
Liberty-Newport Tiger B	Pacific	28.1	-2.41	1.95	4	5	1.02	2.5	800 345-6611
Liberty-Newport Tiger C	Pacific	28.2	-2.39	1.95	4	5	1.02	2.5	800 345-6611
Liberty-Newport Tiger Cub Fd A	Pacific	9.3	-1.87		4	5	1.39	2.25	800 345-6611
Liberty-Newport Tiger Cub Fd B	Pacific	8.3	-2.69		5	5	1.39	3	800 345-6611
Liberty-Newport Tiger Cub Fd C	Pacific	8.3	-2.62		5	5	1.39	3	800 345-6611
Liberty-Newport Tiger T	Pacific	29.5	-1.43	2.97	4	5	1.25	1.52	800 345-6611
Liberty-SteinRoe Adv Tax Mgd Gr A	Growth	10	18.51		2	3	0.72	1.58	800 338-2550
Liberty-SteinRoe Adv Tax Mgd Gr B	Growth	9.2	17.59		2	3	0.72	2.33	800 338-2550
Liberty-SteinRoe Adv Tax Mgd Gr C	Growth	9.2	17.59		2	3	0.72	2.33	800 338-2550
Liberty-SteinRoe Adv Tax Mgd Gr E	Growth	10.1	18.42		2	3	0.72	1.67	800 338-2550
Liberty-SteinRoe Adv Tax Mgd Gr F	Growth	9.6	17.58		2	3	0.72	2.33	800 338-2550
Lighthouse Contrarian Fund	Growth	10.3	-4.75		5	3	1.25	2.18	800 282-2340
Lindner Asset Allocation Inv	AssetAlloc	-5.9	0.65	5.19	5	1	0.51	0.96	800 995-7777
Lindner Large Cap Fund Inv	Growth/Inc	8.6	-2.02	5.23	5	3	0.41	0.84	800 995-7777
Lindner Market Neutral Fund	Flexible	19.4	3.85	2.43	3	1	1.19	4.29	800 995-7777
Lindner Utility Fund Inv	Utilities	32.5	18.46	20.8	2	3	0.69	0.97	800 995-7777
Lindner/Ryback Small-Cap Fd Inv	Small Co	16.3	10.28	16.07	3	3	0.69	1.01	800 995-7777
Lipper Prime Europe Eq Retirement	European	15.4	15.59		3	2	1.1	1.78	800 547-7379
Lipper Prime Europe Equity Prem	European	15.6	15.85		3	2	1.1	1.53	800 547-7379
Lipper Prime Europe Equity Ret	European	15.5	15.55		3	2	1.1	1.78	800 547-7379
Lipper Prime US Equity Retail	Growth	9	10.93		3	2	0.84	1.7	800 547-7379
Lipper U.S. Equity Prem	Growth	9.1	11.16		3	2	0.84	1.45	800 547-7379
Lipper U.S. Equity Ret	Growth	9.3	11.02		3	2	0.84	1.73	800 547-7379
LongLeaf Partners International	Foreign	14					1.5	0.92	800 445-9469
Longleaf Partners Fund	Growth	-13.6	10.2	15.1	3	3	0.77	0.92	800 445-9469
Longleaf Partners Realty Fund	Real Est	-11.3	-3.05		5	2	1.17	1.16	800 445-9469
Longleaf Partners Small-Cap Fund	Small Co	-4.5	9.39	17.37	3	2	0.83	0.96	800 445-9469
Loomis Sayles Aggressive Gr Inst	Growth	124.6	64.9		1	5	0.75	1	800 626-9390
Loomis Sayles Aggressive Gr Ret	Growth	124	64.39		1	5	0.75	1.25	800 626-9390
Loomis Sayles Core Value Inst	Growth/Inc	-13.8	4.63	12.9	4	3	0.5	0.78	800 626-9390
Loomis Sayles Core Value Ret	Growth/Inc	-14	4.34		4	2	0.5	1.1	800 626-9390
Loomis Sayles Global Bond Inst	Intl Bond	-1.9	3.74	9.16	4	5	0.59	0.9	800 626-9390
Loomis Sayles Growth Fund Inst	Growth	31.6	24.55	22.66	2	4	0.5	0.84	800 626-9390
Loomis Sayles Growth Fund Ret	Growth	31.3	24.24		2	4	0.5	1.1	800 626-9390
Loomis Sayles Intl Equity Inst	Foreign	63.2	18.32	16.19	3	4	0.75	1	800 626-9390
Loomis Sayles Intl Equity Ret	Foreign	62.7	17.95		2	4	0.75	1.25	800 626-9390
Loomis Sayles Mid Cap Val Inst	Growth/Inc	-1.6	5.94		5	3	0.75	1	800 626-9390
Loomis Sayles Mid Cap Val Ret	Growth/Inc	-1.7	5.74		4	3	0.75	1.25	800 626-9390
Loomis Sayles Small Cap Gr Inst	Small Co	67.4	39.71		2	5	0.75	1	800 626-9390
Loomis Sayles Small Cap Gr Ret	Small Co	66.9	37.11		1	5	0.75	1.25	800 626-9390
Loomis Sayles Small Cap Val Inst	Small Co	5.9	6.12	15.72	4	3	0.75	0.9	800 626-9390
Loomis Sayles Small Cap Val Ret	Small Co	5.6	5.8		4	3	0.75	1.15	800 626-9390
Loomis Sayles Worldwide Inst	AssetAlloc	52.5	19.34		3	3	0.75	1	800 626-9390
Loomis Sayles Worldwide Ret	AssetAlloc	52.3	19.05		2	3	0.75	1.25	800 626-9390
Lord Abbett Affiliated Fund A	Growth/Inc	1.1	12.12	17.52	2	2	0.3	0.73	888 522-2388
Lord Abbett Affiliated Fund B	Growth/Inc	0.4	11.32		2	2	0.3	1.39	888 522-2388
Lord Abbett Affiliated Fund C	Growth/Inc	0.4	11.35		2	2	0.3	1.39	888 522-2388
Lord Abbett Affiliated Fund P	Growth/Inc	1					0.3	0.85	888 522-2388
Lord Abbett Affiliated Fund Y	Growth/Inc	1.4					0.3	0.85	888 522-2388
Lord Abbett Developing Growth A	Small Co	9	15.22	19.82	3	4	0.56	0.46	888 522-2388
Lord Abbett Developing Growth B	Small Co	8.4	14.45		2	4	0.58	1.67	888 522-2388
Lord Abbett Developing Growth C	Small Co	8.3	14.44		2	4	0.58	1.65	888 522-2388
Lord Abbett Developing Growth P	Small Co	9.5					0.56	1.12	888 522-2388
Lord Abbett Developing Growth Y	Small Co	9.4					0.53	0.34	888 522-2388

Stock Fund Name	Objective	Annualized Return for			Rank		Max Load	Expense Ratio	Toll-Free Telephone
		1 Year	3 Years	5 Years	Overall	Risk			
Lord Abbett Global-Equity A	Global	29.7	10.59	11.95	3	3	0.5	1.78	888 522-2388
Lord Abbett Global-Equity B	Global	28.9	9.83		3	3	0.75	1.47	888 522-2388
Lord Abbett Global-Equity C	Global	28.9	9.84		3	3	0.75	1.47	888 522-2388
Lord Abbett Global-Income A	Intl Bond	-3.2	0.76	2.8	5	4	0.5	1.17	888 522-2388
Lord Abbett Global-Income B	Intl Bond	-3.7	0.12		4	4	0.5	1.89	888 522-2388
Lord Abbett Global-Income C	Intl Bond	-3.9	0.11		4	4	0.5	1.86	888 522-2388
Lord Abbett Global-Income P	Intl Bond	-3.6					0.5	1.28	888 522-2388
Lord Abbett Growth Opportunities B	Growth	44.4					0.9	0.41	888 522-2388
Lord Abbett Growth Opportunities C	Growth	44.4					0.9	0.13	888 522-2388
Lord Abbett Invt Tr-Balanced A	Balanced	1.8	8.6	10.61	3	1	0.75	0.11	888 522-2388
Lord Abbett Invt Tr-Balanced B	Balanced	1.3					0.75	1.76	888 522-2388
Lord Abbett Invt Tr-Balanced C	Balanced	1.1	7.65		3	1	0.75	1.76	888 522-2388
Lord Abbett Lg Cap Growth A	Growth						0.75		888 522-2388
Lord Abbett Lg Cap Growth B	Growth						0.75		888 522-2388
Lord Abbett Lg Cap Growth C	Growth						0.75		888 522-2388
Lord Abbett Mid-Cap Value A	Growth	12	11.97	16.56	2	3	0.71	1.21	888 522-2388
Lord Abbett Mid-Cap Value B	Growth	11.3	11.19		4	3	0.71	1.91	888 522-2388
Lord Abbett Mid-Cap Value C	Growth	11.3	11.22		4	3	0.71	1.91	888 522-2388
Lord Abbett Mid-Cap Value P	Growth	12.1					0.71	1.34	888 522-2388
Lord Abbett Mid-Cap Value Y	Growth	12.2					0.69	0.35	888 522-2388
Lord Abbett Research-Large Cap A	Growth/Inc	-1.4	11.95	17.66	3	2	0.75	1.42	888 522-2388
Lord Abbett Research-Large Cap B	Growth/Inc	-2	11.17		3	2	0.75	1.01	888 522-2388
Lord Abbett Research-Large Cap C	Growth/Inc	-2	11.17		3	2	0.75	1.01	888 522-2388
Lord Abbett Research-Large Cap P	Growth/Inc	-1.2					0.75	0.14	888 522-2388
Lord Abbett Research-Large Cap Y	Growth/Inc	-1.4					0.75	0.08	888 522-2388
Lord Abbett Research-Small Cap A	Small Co	10	7.55		4	3	0.75	1.52	888 522-2388
Lord Abbett Research-Small Cap B	Small Co	9.3	6.79		4	3	0.75	2.14	888 522-2388
Lord Abbett Research-Small Cap C	Small Co	9.3	6.8		4	3	0.75	2.14	888 522-2388
Lord Abbett Research-Small Cap Y	Small Co	10.4					0.75	1.15	888 522-2388
Lord Abbett Sec Tr-Alpha Series A	Growth	12.5					0.5	0.14	888 522-2388
Lord Abbett Sec Tr-Alpha Series B	Growth	11.8					0.5	0.48	888 522-2388
Lord Abbett Sec Tr-Alpha Series C	Growth	11.8					0.5	0.48	888 522-2388
Lord Abbett Sec Tr-Gr & Inc A	Growth/Inc	0.5	13.47		3	2	0.75	1.21	888 522-2388
Lord Abbett Sec Tr-Gr & Inc C	Growth/Inc	0	12.66	17.43	3	2	0.75	1.97	888 522-2388
Lord Abbett Sec Tr-Intl A	Foreign	16.8	16.42		3	4	0.75	1.51	888 522-2388
Lord Abbett Sec Tr-Intl B	Foreign	16	15.59		3	4	0.75	2.1	888 522-2388
Lord Abbett Sec Tr-Intl C	Foreign	16	15.56		3	4	0.75	2.12	888 522-2388
Lord Abbett Sec Tr-Intl P	Foreign	16.8					0.75	0.32	888 522-2388
Lord Abbett Sec Tr-Intl Y	Foreign	17.2					0.75	1.12	888 522-2388
Lord Abbett Tax Free Inc-FL A	Muni State	-0.4	2.99	4.05	4	3	0.5	0.93	888 522-2388
Lord Abbett Tax Free Inc-FL C	Muni State	-0.8	2.34		4	3	0.5	1.58	888 522-2388
Lutheran Brotherhood Fund A	Growth/Inc	7	17.31	20.24	3	3	0.34	0.84	800 328-4552
Lutheran Brotherhood Fund B	Growth/Inc	6.2					0.34	1.59	800 328-4552
Lutheran Brotherhood Fund Y	Growth/Inc	7.1					0.34	0.58	800 328-4552
Lutheran Brotherhood Growth Fund A	Growth						0.42		800 328-4552
Lutheran Brotherhood Growth Fund B	Growth						0.42		800 328-4552
Lutheran Brotherhood Growth Fund Y	Growth						0.42		800 328-4552
Lutheran Brotherhood MidCap Gr A	Growth	47	26.57		1	4	0.69	1.94	800 328-4552
Lutheran Brotherhood MidCap Gr B	Growth	45.9					0.2	2.7	800 328-4552
Lutheran Brotherhood MidCap Gr Y	Growth	47.9					0.45	1.69	800 328-4552
Lutheran Brotherhood Opport Gr A	Agg Growth	29.8	9.96	10.7	4	4	0.42		800 328-4552
Lutheran Brotherhood Opport Gr B	Agg Growth	28.8	4.84				0.42	2.27	800 328-4552
Lutheran Brotherhood Opport Gr Y	Agg Growth	30.2					0.42	1.27	800 328-4552
Lutheran Brotherhood Value Fund A	Growth						0.4		800 328-4552
Lutheran Brotherhood Value Fund B	Growth						0.4		800 328-4552
Lutheran Brotherhood Value Fund Y	Growth						0.4		800 328-4552
Lutheran Brotherhood World Gr A	Foreign	21.7	10.23		3	3	0.75	1.87	800 328-4552
Lutheran Brotherhood World Gr B	Foreign	20.7					0.75	2.62	800 328-4552

335

Stock Fund Name	Objective	Annualized Return for			Rank		Max Load	Expense Ratio	Toll-Free Telephone
		1 Year	3 Years	5 Years	Overall	Risk			
Lutheran Brotherhood World Gr Y	Foreign	22.3					0.75	1.62	800 328-4552
M.S.B. Fund	Growth	-3	14.45	18.4	3	3	0.75	1.26	800 661-3938
MAS Balanced Instl	Balanced	7.9	13.3	15.82	2	1	0.45	0.57	800 354-8185
MAS Equity Instl	Growth	9.3	18.41	21.48	2	3	0.5	0.6	800 354-8185
MAS Funds Small Cap Growth I	Small Co	100.6					1	1.22	800 354-8185
MAS Global Fixed Income Instl	Intl Bond	0.3	2.62	3.48	5	4	0.37	0.53	800 354-8185
MAS Intl Fixed Income Instl	Intl Bond	0.3	1.87	2.09	5	5	0.37	0.52	800 354-8185
MAS Mid Cap Growth Instl	Growth	47.2	43.71	35.71	1	4	0.5	0.6	800 354-8185
MAS Mid Cap Value Instl	Growth	12.5	20.56	25.96	2	3	0.56	0.84	800 354-8185
MAS Multi-Asset-Class Instl	AssetAlloc	6.5	11.03	14.29	3	1	0.65	0.78	800 354-8185
MAS Small Cap Value Instl	Small Co	14.2	13.1	20.28	3	3	0.75	0.85	800 354-8185
MAS Value Instl	Growth/Inc	-17.1	-1.14	10.01	5	3	0.5	0.63	800 354-8185
MDL Large Cap Growth	Growth	3.2					0.73	1.26	877 362-4099
MFS Capital Opportunities A	Agg Growth	35	31.84	29.28	1	3	0.7	1.17	800 343-2829
MFS Capital Opportunities B	Agg Growth	34	30.87	26.01	1	3	0.7	1.96	800 343-2829
MFS Capital Opportunities C	Agg Growth	34	30.88		1	3	0.7	1.96	800 343-2829
MFS Emerging Growth Fund A	Agg Growth	38.7	27.55	26.56	2	4	0.68	1.13	800 343-2829
MFS Emerging Growth Fund B	Agg Growth	37.7	26.59	25.59	2	4	0.68	1.87	800 343-2829
MFS Emerging Growth Fund C	Agg Growth	37.7	26.59		2	4	0.68	1.88	800 343-2829
MFS FL Municipal Bond Fund A	Muni State	2.3	4.08	4.87	3	1	0.55	0.68	800 343-2829
MFS Global Asset Alloc A	AssetAlloc	17.3	9.17	12.36	4	2	0.59	1.43	800 343-2829
MFS Global Asset Alloc B	AssetAlloc	16.7	8.53	11.69	4	2	0.59	1.93	800 343-2829
MFS Global Asset Alloc C	AssetAlloc	16.7	8.53	11.71	4	2	0.59	1.93	800 343-2829
MFS Global Equity A	Global	18	13.35	16.92	3	2	1	1.59	800 343-2829
MFS Global Equity B	Global	17.1	12.5	16.01	3	2	1	2.33	800 343-2829
MFS Global Equity C	Global	17.1	12.39	15.98	3	2	1	2.35	800 343-2829
MFS Global Equity I	Global	17.6	13.4		3	2	1	1.34	800 343-2829
MFS Global Govts Fund A	Intl Bond	0.3	1.11	1.84	4	4	0.75	1.37	800 343-2829
MFS Global Govts Fund B	Intl Bond	-0.5	0.35	1.06	5	4	0.75	2.12	800 343-2829
MFS Global Govts Fund C	Intl Bond	-0.4	0.38	1.1	4	4	0.75	2.12	800 343-2829
MFS Global Growth Fund A	Global	44.9	22.2	21.1	3	4	0.9	1.5	800 343-2829
MFS Global Growth Fund B	Global	43.9	21.33	20.2	3	4	0.9	2.25	800 343-2829
MFS Global Growth Fund C	Global	43.9	21.32	20.23	3	4	0.9	2.22	800 343-2829
MFS Global Total Return A	Balanced	10.8	10.71	12.96	3	1	0.81	1.47	800 343-2829
MFS Global Total Return B	Balanced	10	9.95	12.18	3	1	0.81	2.12	800 343-2829
MFS Global Total Return C	Balanced	10	9.96	12.2	3	1	0.81	2.12	800 343-2829
MFS Growth Opportunities Fund A	Growth	30.2	24.6	24.97	2	4	0.41	0.8	800 343-2829
MFS Growth Opportunities Fund B	Growth	29.2	23.55	23.9	2	4	0.41	1.62	800 343-2829
MFS Intl Gr & Inc A	Foreign	22.3	13.01		3	2	0.97	2.04	800 343-2829
MFS Intl Gr & Inc B	Foreign	21.7	12.46		3	2	0.97	2.6	800 343-2829
MFS Intl Gr & Inc C	Foreign	21.5	12.39		3	2	0.97	2.58	800 343-2829
MFS Intl Gr A	Foreign	29.7	6.89		4	3	0.97	2.14	800 343-2829
MFS Intl Gr B	Foreign	29	6.28		4	3	0.97	2.5	800 343-2829
MFS Intl Gr C	Foreign	29	6.35		4	3	0.97	2.5	800 343-2829
MFS Large Cap Growth A	Growth	27.6	27.82	26.88	1	3	0.75	1.21	800 343-2829
MFS Large Cap Growth B	Growth	26.6	26.85	25.91	1	3	0.75	1.96	800 343-2829
MFS Managed Sectors Fund A	Agg Growth	48.1	28.09	24.82	3	4	0.75	1.36	800 343-2829
MFS Managed Sectors Fund B	Agg Growth	47.1	27.25	23.98	3	4	0.75	1.32	800 343-2829
MFS Mass Investors Growth Stock A	Growth	28.1	33.14	32.07	1	3	0.33	0.88	800 343-2829
MFS Mass Investors Growth Stock B	Growth	27.3	32.24	31.08	1	3	0.33	1.53	800 343-2829
MFS Mass Investors Trust A	Growth/Inc	1.9	13.59	20.8	3	2	0.33	0.88	800 343-2829
MFS MidCap Growth Fund A	Small Co	80.4	42.05	31.42	1	4	0.75	1.37	800 343-2829
MFS MidCap Growth Fund B	Small Co	79	40.95	30.38	1	4	0.75	2.12	800 343-2829
MFS MidCap Growth Fund C	Small Co	7	2.26	1.35			0.75		800 343-2829
MFS Research Fund A	Growth	20.5	19.85	23.39	2	3	0.42	0.95	800 343-2829
MFS Research Fund B	Growth	19.8	19.08	22.55	2	3	0.42	1.63	800 343-2829
MFS Research Fund C	Growth	19.8	19.07	22.1	2	3	0.42	1.63	800 343-2829
MFS SC Municipal Bond Fund A	Muni State	1.2	3.44	4.6	3	3	0.45	1.02	800 343-2829

336

Stock Fund Name	Objective	Annualized Return for			Rank		Max Load	Expense Ratio	Toll-Free Telephone
		1 Year	3 Years	5 Years	Overall	Risk			
MFS Strategic Growth A	Growth	35.9	37.99		1	3	0.75	1.33	800 343-2829
MFS Strategic Growth B	Growth	35.1	36.52		1	3	0.75	2.02	800 343-2829
MFS Strategic Growth C	Growth	35.1	36.99		1	3	0.75	2.02	800 343-2829
MFS Strategic Growth Fund I	Growth	36.4	37.75		1	3	0.75	1.07	800 343-2829
MFS Total Return Fund A	Balanced	1.9	9.14	12.94	3	1	0.34	0.89	800 343-2829
MFS Total Return Fund B	Balanced	1.2	8.49	12.2	3	1	0.34	1.55	800 343-2829
MFS Total Return Fund C	Balanced	1.2	8.46	12.19	3	1	0.34	1.55	800 343-2829
MFS Utilities Fund A	Utilities	24.6	23.71	24.75	1	2	0.55	1.05	800 343-2829
MFS Utilities Fund B	Utilities	23.7	22.82	21.1	1	2	0.55	1.86	800 343-2829
MFS Utilities Fund C	Utilities	23.7	22.79	23.8	1	2	0.55	0.85	800 343-2829
MFS/ Emerging Mkt Equity Fd A	Foreign	10.1	-5.45		5	4	1.25	2.45	800 343-2829
MFS/ Emerging Mkt Equity Fd B	Foreign	9.6	-5.92		5	4	1.25	2.95	800 343-2829
MFS/ Emerging Mkt Equity Fd C	Foreign	9.6	-5.86		5	4	1.25	2.93	800 343-2829
MMA Praxis Growth B	Growth	-3.2	9.04	14.66	3	2	0.73	1.75	800 977-2947
MMA Praxis International B	Foreign	23.7	14.78		2	3	0.5	2	800 977-2947
MSD & T Diversified Real Estate Fd	Real Est	5.7					0.39	1.46	
MSD & T Equity Growth Fund	Growth	12.1					0.4	0.69	
MSD & T Equity Income Fund	Growth/Inc	-37.1					0.47	0.69	
MSDW Aggressive Equity A	Agg Growth	42.7					0.75		800 869-6397
MSDW Aggressive Equity B	Agg Growth	41.6					0.75		800 869-6397
MSDW Aggressive Equity C	Agg Growth	41.6					0.75		800 869-6397
MSDW Aggressive Equity D	Agg Growth	43					0.75		800 869-6397
MSDW American Opportunities A	Growth	25.3					0.51	0.77	800 869-6397
MSDW American Opportunities B	Growth	24.7	28.69	25.77	2	3	0.48	1.33	800 869-6397
MSDW American Opportunities C	Growth	24.3					0.51	0.77	800 869-6397
MSDW American Opportunities D	Growth	25.6					0.51	0.58	800 869-6397
MSDW Balanced Growth A	Balanced	-11.1					0.59	1.01	800 869-6397
MSDW Balanced Growth B	Balanced	-11.9					0.59	1.8	800 869-6397
MSDW Balanced Growth C	Balanced	-11.9	5.21	10.82	2	1	0.59	1.79	800 869-6397
MSDW Balanced Growth D	Balanced	-11					0.59	0.8	800 869-6397
MSDW Balanced Income A	Balanced	-4.2					0.59	1.18	800 869-6397
MSDW Balanced Income B	Balanced	-4.9					0.59	1.93	800 869-6397
MSDW Balanced Income C	Balanced	-5	4.53	7.85	3	1	0.59	1.93	800 869-6397
MSDW Balanced Income D	Balanced	-4					0.59	0.93	800 869-6397
MSDW Capital Growth A	Growth	25.2					2	1	800 869-6397
MSDW Capital Growth B	Growth	24.3	19.32	19.9	2	4	2	1.86	800 869-6397
MSDW Capital Growth C	Growth	24.2					2	1.34	800 869-6397
MSDW Capital Growth D	Growth	25.5					2	0.84	800 869-6397
MSDW Compet Edge Best Ideas A	Growth	17.1					0.65	1.1	800 869-6397
MSDW Compet Edge Best Ideas B	Growth	16.2					0.65	1.86	800 869-6397
MSDW Compet Edge Best Ideas C	Growth	16.3					0.65	1.68	800 869-6397
MSDW Compet Edge Best Ideas D	Growth	17.3					0.65	0.85	800 869-6397
MSDW Developing Growth A	Small Co	54.7					0.48	0.85	800 869-6397
MSDW Developing Growth B	Small Co	53.5	29.87	24.31	2	5	0.48	1.69	800 869-6397
MSDW Developing Growth C	Small Co	53.5					0.48	1.43	800 869-6397
MSDW Developing Growth D	Small Co	55					0.48	0.71	800 869-6397
MSDW Dividend Growth A	Growth/Inc	-15.8					0.39	0.64	800 869-6397
MSDW Dividend Growth B	Growth/Inc	-16	5.03	12.92	4	2	0.34	1.09	800 869-6397
MSDW Dividend Growth C	Growth/Inc	-16.4					0.39	1.42	800 869-6397
MSDW Dividend Growth D	Growth/Inc	-15.6					0.39	0.42	800 869-6397
MSDW Equity A	Growth	8.8					0.84	1.37	800 869-6397
MSDW Equity B	Growth	8					0.84	2.12	800 869-6397
MSDW Equity C	Growth	8.1					0.84	1.9	800 869-6397
MSDW Equity D	Growth	9.2					0.84	1.12	800 869-6397
MSDW European Growth A	European	25.9					0.96	1.36	800 869-6397
MSDW European Growth B	European	24.9	17.33	19.92	1	3	0.91	2.12	800 869-6397
MSDW European Growth C	European	24.9					0.96	2.14	800 869-6397
MSDW European Growth D	European	26.1					0.96	1.13	800 869-6397

Stock Fund Name	Objective	Annualized Return for			Rank		Max Load	Expense Ratio	Toll-Free Telephone
		1 Year	3 Years	5 Years	Overall	Risk			
MSDW Financial Serv Tr A	Financial	-10.3					0.75	1.19	800 869-6397
MSDW Financial Serv Tr B	Financial	-11.1	13.52		3	3	0.75	1.96	800 869-6397
MSDW Financial Serv Tr C	Financial	-11.1					0.75	1.9	800 869-6397
MSDW Financial Serv Tr D	Financial	-10.2					0.75	0.96	800 869-6397
MSDW Fund of Funds Dom A	Growth	10					0	0.22	800 869-6397
MSDW Fund of Funds Dom B	Growth	9.1					0	1	800 869-6397
MSDW Fund of Funds Dom C	Growth	9.2					0	0.25	800 869-6397
MSDW Fund of Funds Dom D	Growth	10.1					0	0	800 869-6397
MSDW Fund of Funds Intl A	Foreign	20.8					0	0.23	800 869-6397
MSDW Fund of Funds Intl B	Foreign	20					0	1	800 869-6397
MSDW Fund of Funds Intl C	Foreign	20					0	0.2	800 869-6397
MSDW Fund of Funds Intl D	Foreign	21.2					0	0	800 869-6397
MSDW Global Dividend Gr A	Global	-2.4					0.71	1.12	800 869-6397
MSDW Global Dividend Gr B	Global	-3.1	5.09	10.92	3	2	0.75	0.9	800 869-6397
MSDW Global Dividend Gr C	Global	-3.2					0.71	1.85	800 869-6397
MSDW Global Dividend Gr D	Global	-2.1					0.71	0.9	800 869-6397
MSDW Global Utilities A	Utilities	15.5					0.65	1.1	800 869-6397
MSDW Global Utilities B	Utilities	14.8	22.4	19.86	1	2	0.65	1.71	800 869-6397
MSDW Global Utilities C	Utilities	14.7					0.65	1.85	800 869-6397
MSDW Global Utilities D	Utilities	15.9					0.65	0.84	800 869-6397
MSDW Growth Fund A	Growth	29.2					0.84	1.18	800 869-6397
MSDW Growth Fund B	Growth	28.8	24.75	22.37	1	3	0.79	1.47	800 869-6397
MSDW Growth Fund C	Growth	28.2					0.84	1.93	800 869-6397
MSDW Growth Fund D	Growth	29.6					0.84	0.93	800 869-6397
MSDW Health Science Tr A	Health	61.5					1	1.46	800 869-6397
MSDW Health Science Tr B	Health	60.1	25.97	22.71	3	4	1	2.27	800 869-6397
MSDW Health Science Tr C	Health	60.2					1	2.27	800 869-6397
MSDW Health Science Tr D	Health	61.8					1	1.27	800 869-6397
MSDW Income Builder A	Growth/Inc	-7					0.75	1.15	800 869-6397
MSDW Income Builder B	Growth/Inc	-7.7	4.29		4	1	0.75	1.89	800 869-6397
MSDW Income Builder C	Growth/Inc	-7.7					0.75	1.92	800 869-6397
MSDW Income Builder D	Growth/Inc	-6.8					0.75	0.93	800 869-6397
MSDW Information Fund A	Technology	96.1					0.75	1.23	800 869-6397
MSDW Information Fund B	Technology	95.3	67.83		1	5	0.75	1.73	800 869-6397
MSDW Information Fund C	Technology	94.7					0.75	2	800 869-6397
MSDW Information Fund D	Technology	96.7					0.75	1.01	800 869-6397
MSDW Inst Asian RE A	Real Est	-14.6					0.01	1.01	800 548-7786
MSDW Inst Asian RE B	Real Est	-14.9					0.01	1.26	800 548-7786
MSDW Inst European RE A	Real Est	-0.8					0.4	1.3	800 548-7786
MSDW Inst European RE B	Real Est	-1.1					0.4	1.59	800 548-7786
MSDW Inst Technology A	Technology	114.1	72.23		1	5	0.47	1.15	800 548-7786
MSDW Inst Technology B	Technology	114	71.92		1	5	0.47	1.4	800 548-7786
MSDW Inst Value Equity B	Growth/Inc	-5.4	12.22		3	3	0.39	1.02	800 548-7786
MSDW Inst-Act Ctry All A	Foreign	14.4	11.02	14.78	4	2	0.44	0.8	800 548-7786
MSDW Inst-Act Ctry All B	Foreign	14.1	10.8		4	2	0.44	1.07	800 548-7786
MSDW Inst-Asian Eq A	Pacific	13.3	-9.87	-5	5	5	0.11	1.07	800 548-7786
MSDW Inst-Asian Eq B	Pacific	13.3	-10.09		4	5	0.11	1.32	800 548-7786
MSDW Inst-Emerg Mkts A	Foreign	37	4.08	9.92	4	5	1.25	1.57	800 548-7786
MSDW Inst-Emerg Mkts B	Foreign	36.7	3.78		4	5	1.25	1.92	800 548-7786
MSDW Inst-Emg Mkt Debt A	Intl Bond	24.1	-3.56	12.76	3	5	1	1.46	800 548-7786
MSDW Inst-Emg Mkt Debt B	Intl Bond	23.4	-3.75		3	5	1	1.71	800 548-7786
MSDW Inst-Equity Gr A	Growth	28.5	26.81	29.04	1	3	0.59	0.8	800 548-7786
MSDW Inst-Equity Gr B	Growth	28.3	26.59		1	3	0.59	1.05	800 548-7786
MSDW Inst-Euro Equity A	European	14	7.71	12.06	3	2	0.4	1.1	800 548-7786
MSDW Inst-Euro Equity B	European	14.9	7.84		3	2	0.4	1.35	800 548-7786
MSDW Inst-Focus Equity A	Agg Growth	25.7	28.2	32.18	1	3	0.59	1.02	800 548-7786
MSDW Inst-Focus Equity B	Agg Growth	25.4	27.89		1	3	0.59	1.27	800 548-7786
MSDW Inst-Global Eq A	Global	4	9.42	14.89	2	2	0.73	1.01	800 548-7786

Stock Fund Name	Objective	Annualized Return for			Rank		Max Load	Expense Ratio	Toll-Free Telephone
		1 Year	3 Years	5 Years	Overall	Risk			
MSDW Inst-Global Eq B	Global	3.7	9.06		3	2	0.73	1.25	800 548-7786
MSDW Inst-Global Fixed A	Intl Bond	-0.3	2.57	3.79	5	4	0.13	0.5	800 548-7786
MSDW Inst-Global Fixed B	Intl Bond	-0.4	2.38		5	4	0.13	0.65	800 548-7786
MSDW Inst-Intl Eq A	Foreign	18.3	13.74	16.75	3	2	0.79	1	800 548-7786
MSDW Inst-Intl Eq B	Foreign	19	13.82		2	2	0.79	1.25	800 548-7786
MSDW Inst-Intl Magnum A	Foreign	15.1	6.35		4	2	0.68	1	800 548-7786
MSDW Inst-Intl Magnum B	Foreign	14.8	6.07		4	2	0.68	1.25	800 548-7786
MSDW Inst-Intl Sm Cap A	Foreign	27.5	11.95	12.25	3	2	0.9	1.14	800 548-7786
MSDW Inst-Japanese Eq A	Pacific	33.6	10.66	13.75	4	3	0.6	1.01	800 548-7786
MSDW Inst-Japanese Eq B	Pacific	35.7	10.92		4	3	0.6	1.26	800 548-7786
MSDW Inst-Latin Amer A	Foreign	22.3	1.58	18.46	3	5	1.1	1.75	800 548-7786
MSDW Inst-Latin Amer B	Foreign	27.5	2.94		3	5	1.1	2	800 548-7786
MSDW Inst-Small Co Growth A	Small Co	78.8	47.96	31.87	2	5	1	1.25	800 548-7786
MSDW Inst-Small Co Growth B	Small Co	80	47.79		2	4	1	1.5	800 548-7786
MSDW Inst-US Real Est B	Real Est	3.4	2.35		3	2	0.76	1.25	800 548-7786
MSDW Inst-Value Eq A	Growth/Inc	-5.2	12.45	16.68	3	3	0.39	0.76	800 548-7786
MSDW Intl Small Cap A	Foreign	21.2					1.25	2.35	800 869-6397
MSDW Intl Small Cap B	Foreign	20.2	8.76	7.36	4	3	1.14	3.12	800 869-6397
MSDW Intl Small Cap C	Foreign	20					1.25	2.89	800 869-6397
MSDW Intl Small Cap D	Foreign	21.2					1.25	2.12	800 869-6397
MSDW Japan Fund A	Pacific	30.9					1	1.71	800 869-6397
MSDW Japan Fund B	Pacific	29.9	8.44		4	3	1	2.58	800 869-6397
MSDW Japan Fund C	Pacific	29.9					1	2.58	800 869-6397
MSDW Japan Fund D	Pacific	31.1					1	1.59	800 869-6397
MSDW Latin American Growth A	Foreign	16.5					1.25	1.87	800 869-6397
MSDW Latin American Growth B	Foreign	15.5	-6.32	7.23	4	5	1.25	3.06	800 869-6397
MSDW Latin American Growth C	Foreign	15.5					1.25	2.41	800 869-6397
MSDW Latin American Growth D	Foreign	16.6					1.25	1.65	800 869-6397
MSDW Market Leader Tr A	Growth	33.8					0.75	1.23	800 869-6397
MSDW Market Leader Tr B	Growth	32.7	25.71		1	3	0.75	2.02	800 869-6397
MSDW Market Leader Tr C	Growth	32.7					0.75	1.35	800 869-6397
MSDW Market Leader Tr D	Growth	34.1					0.75	1.02	800 869-6397
MSDW Mid Cap Dividend Gr A	Growth/Inc	-22.2					0.75	1.3	800 869-6397
MSDW Mid Cap Dividend Gr B	Growth/Inc	-22.8					0.75	2.04	800 869-6397
MSDW Mid Cap Dividend Gr C	Growth/Inc	-23.3					0.75	1.57	800 869-6397
MSDW Mid Cap Dividend Gr D	Growth/Inc	-22.1					0.75	1.05	800 869-6397
MSDW Mid-Cap Equity Trust A	Growth	55					1	1.43	800 869-6397
MSDW Mid-Cap Equity Trust B	Growth	54.3	58.58		2	5	1	1.82	800 869-6397
MSDW Mid-Cap Equity Trust C	Growth	53.9					1	2.2	800 869-6397
MSDW Mid-Cap Equity Trust D	Growth	55.1					1	1.2	800 869-6397
MSDW Multi State-FL	Muni State	2.5	4.14	5.15	1	3	0.34	0.61	800 869-6397
MSDW Natural Resource A	Energy/Res	6.9					0.61	1.13	800 869-6397
MSDW Natural Resource B	Energy/Res	6	2.12	10.34	5	4	0.61	1.9	800 869-6397
MSDW Natural Resource C	Energy/Res	6					0.61	1.89	800 869-6397
MSDW Natural Resource D	Energy/Res	7.2					0.61	0.9	800 869-6397
MSDW Pacific Growth A	Pacific	22.6					0.97	1.84	800 869-6397
MSDW Pacific Growth B	Pacific	21.7	-4.7	-1.49	5	4	0.97	2.62	800 869-6397
MSDW Pacific Growth C	Pacific	21.7					0.97	2.62	800 869-6397
MSDW Pacific Growth D	Pacific	22.9					0.97	1.62	800 869-6397
MSDW S&P 500 Index Fd A	Growth/Inc	6.5					0.23	0.72	800 869-6397
MSDW S&P 500 Index Fd B	Growth/Inc	5.7					0.23	1.5	800 869-6397
MSDW S&P 500 Index Fd C	Growth/Inc	5.7					0.23	1.5	800 869-6397
MSDW S&P 500 Index Fd D	Growth/Inc	6.7					0.23	0.5	800 869-6397
MSDW S&P 500 Select Fund A	Growth/Inc	7.1					0.59	1.28	800 869-6397
MSDW S&P 500 Select Fund B	Growth/Inc	6.2					0.59	2.02	800 869-6397
MSDW S&P 500 Select Fund C	Growth/Inc	6.3					0.59	2.02	800 869-6397
MSDW S&P 500 Select Fund D	Growth/Inc	7.3					0.59	1.03	800 869-6397
MSDW Small Cap Growth A	Small Co	82.9					1	1.5	800 869-6397

| Stock Fund Name | Objective | Annualized Return for | | | Rank | | Max Load | Expense Ratio | Toll-Free Telephone |
		1 Year	3 Years	5 Years	Overall	Risk			
MSDW Small Cap Growth B	Small Co	82.1	43.92	34.36	3	5	1	1.47	800 869-6397
MSDW Small Cap Growth C	Small Co	81.5					1	2.25	800 869-6397
MSDW Small Cap Growth D	Small Co	83.4					1	1.26	800 869-6397
MSDW Special Value Fd A	Small Co	4.6					0.75	1.21	800 869-6397
MSDW Special Value Fd B	Small Co	3.8	5.22		4	2	0.75	1.98	800 869-6397
MSDW Special Value Fd C	Small Co	3.8					0.75	1.87	800 869-6397
MSDW Special Value Fd D	Small Co	4.9					0.75	0.98	800 869-6397
MSDW Strategist Fund A	Flexible	12.1					0.54	0.86	800 869-6397
MSDW Strategist Fund B	Flexible	11.4	14.07	15.56	3	2	0.54	1.54	800 869-6397
MSDW Strategist Fund C	Flexible	11.2					0.54	1.64	800 869-6397
MSDW Strategist Fund D	Flexible	12.3					0.54	0.65	800 869-6397
MSDW Total Return Trust A	Growth/Inc	19.7					0.75	1.3	800 869-6397
MSDW Total Return Trust B	Growth/Inc	19	23.05	22.97	1	3	1	1.89	800 869-6397
MSDW Total Return Trust C	Growth/Inc	18.7					0.75	1.71	800 869-6397
MSDW Total Return Trust D	Growth/Inc	19.9					0.75	1.06	800 869-6397
MSDW Utilities Fund A	Utilities	6.8					0.53	0.82	800 869-6397
MSDW Utilities Fund B	Utilities	6	17.17	15.33	3	1	0.62	1.64	800 869-6397
MSDW Utilities Fund C	Utilities	6.1					0.53	1.66	800 869-6397
MSDW Utilities Fund D	Utilities	6.8					0.53	0.67	800 869-6397
MSDW Value Fund A	Growth	-15.4					1	1.62	800 869-6397
MSDW Value Fund B	Growth	-16.1					1	2.37	800 869-6397
MSDW Value Fund C	Growth	-16.2					1	2.37	800 869-6397
MSDW Value Fund D	Growth	-15.2					1	1.37	800 869-6397
MSDW Value-Added Equity A	Growth/Inc	-3.1					0.46	0.8	800 869-6397
MSDW Value-Added Equity B	Growth/Inc	-3.7	10	14.63	3	3	0.46	1.41	800 869-6397
MSDW Value-Added Equity C	Growth/Inc	-3.8					0.46	1.57	800 869-6397
MSDW Value-Added Equity D	Growth/Inc	-2.9					0.46	0.58	800 869-6397
MSDW World Wide Inc A	Intl Bond	-2.5					0.75	1.43	800 869-6397
MSDW World Wide Inc B	Intl Bond	-3.1	0.74	3.99	5	4	0.75	2.06	800 869-6397
MSDW World Wide Inc C	Intl Bond	-3.1					0.75	2.06	800 869-6397
MSDW World Wide Inc D	Intl Bond	-2.3					0.75	1.2	800 869-6397
Magna Growth & Income	Growth/Inc	12.1	18.37	21.76	2	2	0.5	0.86	800 219-4182
MainStay Asset Manager Inst	AssetAlloc	10.3	15.22	18.43	2	1	0.65	0.78	800 624-6782
MainStay Blue Chip Growth A	Growth	33.1					1	1.95	800 624-6782
MainStay Blue Chip Growth B	Growth	32.1					1	2.7	800 624-6782
MainStay Blue Chip Growth C	Growth	32.1					1	2.7	800 624-6782
MainStay Capital Appreciation A	Agg Growth	17.7	24.67	24.3	2	3	0.71	1.01	800 624-6782
MainStay Capital Appreciation B	Agg Growth	16.8	23.75	23.51	2	3	0.71	1.93	800 624-6782
MainStay Capital Appreciation C	Agg Growth	16.8					0.71	1.76	800 624-6782
MainStay EAFE Index Inst Fd	Foreign	14.9	9.07	10.44	4	2	0.94	0.93	800 624-6782
MainStay Equity Income A	Growth	3.7					0.69	1.64	800 624-6782
MainStay Equity Income B	Growth	2.8					0.69	1.55	800 624-6782
MainStay Equity Income C	Growth	2.8					0.69	2.39	800 624-6782
MainStay Equity Index A	Growth/Inc	6.3	19.54	23.28	2	3	0.5	0.95	800 624-6782
MainStay Growth Equity Inst Fd	Growth	18.4	25.37	25.49	2	3	0.84	0.93	800 624-6782
MainStay Growth Opportunities A	Growth	18.7					0.69	1.64	800 624-6782
MainStay Growth Opportunities B	Growth	17.9					0.69	2.39	800 624-6782
MainStay Growth Opportunities C	Growth	17.9					0.69	2.39	800 624-6782
MainStay Indexed Eq Inst Fd	Growth/Inc	7.1	19.46	23.49	2	3	0.1	0.29	800 624-6782
MainStay Intl Equity A	Foreign	12.3	8.9	11.96	4	2	1	1.93	800 624-6782
MainStay Intl Equity C	Foreign	11.2					1	2.68	800 624-6782
MainStay Intl Equity Inst Fd	Foreign	13.2	10.08	13.32	4	2	0.81	0.98	800 624-6782
MainStay Intl Equity Inst Serv	Foreign	13	9.7	12.93	4	2	0.81	0.98	800 624-6782
MainStay MAP-Equity Fund I	Growth	10	16.26	21.94	2	3	0.75	1.25	800 624-6782
MainStay Map Equity Fund A	Growth	9.7					0.75	1.1	800 624-6782
MainStay Map Equity Fund B	Growth	8.9					0.75	1.85	800 624-6782
MainStay Map Equity Fund C	Growth	8.9					0.75	1.85	800 624-6782
MainStay Research Value A	Growth	12.3					0.84	1.8	800 624-6782

Stock Fund Name	Objective	Annualized Return for			Rank		Max Load	Expense Ratio	Toll-Free Telephone
		1 Year	3 Years	5 Years	Overall	Risk			
MainStay Research Value B	Growth	11.6					0.84	2.54	800 624-6782
MainStay Research Value C	Growth	11.6					0.84	2.54	800 624-6782
MainStay Small Cap Growth A	Small Co	64.3					1	2.29	800 624-6782
MainStay Small Cap Growth B	Small Co	62.9					1	3.04	800 624-6782
MainStay Small Cap Growth C	Small Co	62.9					1	3.04	800 624-6782
MainStay Small Cap Value A	Small Co	15.7					1	1.89	800 624-6782
MainStay Small Cap Value B	Small Co	14.8					1	2.64	800 624-6782
MainStay Small Cap Value C	Small Co	14.8					1	2.64	800 624-6782
MainStay Strategic Value A	AssetAlloc	-3.5					0.75	1.78	800 624-6782
MainStay Strategic Value B	AssetAlloc	-4.2					0.75	1.19	800 624-6782
MainStay Strategic Value C	AssetAlloc	-4.2					0.75	1.19	800 624-6782
MainStay Total Return A	Flexible	13.8	17.77	17.56	2	2	0.63	1.15	800 624-6782
MainStay Total Return B	Flexible	13	16.99	16.86	3	2	0.32	0.56	800 624-6782
MainStay Total Return C	Flexible	13					0.61	0.59	800 624-6782
MainStay Value Equity Inst Fd	Growth/Inc	-10.6	1.51	9.73	5	3	0.25	0.96	800 624-6782
MainStay Value Fund A	Growth/Inc	-11.5	1.35	9.42	5	3	0.65	0.78	800 624-6782
MainStay Value Fund B	Growth/Inc	-12.2	0.62	8.71	5	3	0.56	1.84	800 624-6782
MainStay Value Fund C	Growth/Inc	-12.2					0.56	0.02	800 624-6782
Mairs & Power Balanced Fund	Balanced	3.1	11.53	15.94	2	1	0.59	0.88	800 304-7404
Mairs & Power Growth Fund	Growth	4.8	10.97	19.94	3	2	0.59	0.79	800 304-7404
Managers Capital Appreciation	Growth	60	50.76	35.61	2	5	0.8	1.26	800 835-3879
Managers Emerging Markets Equity	Foreign	27.3					1.14	1.88	800 835-3879
Managers Income Equity	Income	-6.4	8.66	14.82	3	2	0.75	1.34	800 835-3879
Managers International Equity	Foreign	13.8	10.78	13.28	4	2	0.9	1.39	800 835-3879
Managers Special Equity Fund	Small Co	55.4	25.37	26.23	2	4	0.9	1.33	800 835-3879
Markman Aggressive Alloc Portf	Flexible	27.6	24.94	20.26	3	4	0.94	0.94	800 707-2771
Markman Conservative Alloc Portf	Flexible	11.7	12.22	12.06	3	2	0.94	0.94	800 707-2771
Markman Moderate Alloc Portf	Flexible	10.7	15.31	14.64	3	3	0.94	0.94	800 707-2771
Marshall Equity Income A	Growth/Inc	-11.1					0.75	1.16	800 236-8560
Marshall Equity Income Y	Growth/Inc	-11.1	6.91	14.29	3	2	0.75	1.16	800 236-8560
Marshall International Stock Fd A	Foreign	32.1					1	1.47	800 236-8560
Marshall International Stock Fd I	Foreign						1		800 236-8560
Marshall International Stock Fd Y	Foreign	32.1	11.99	14.67	3	4	1	1.47	800 236-8560
Marshall Large-Cap Growth & Inc A	Growth/Inc	7.4					0.75	1.19	800 236-8560
Marshall Large-Cap Growth & Inc Y	Growth/Inc	7.4	17.31	19.94	3	2	0.75	1.19	800 236-8560
Marshall Mid-Cap Growth A	Growth	54.1					0.75	1.22	800 236-8560
Marshall Mid-Cap Growth Y	Growth	54.1	33.17	28.22	2	4	0.75	1.22	800 236-8560
Marshall Mid-Cap Value A	Growth	-8.4					0.75	1.27	800 236-8560
Marshall Mid-Cap Value Y	Growth	-8.4	5.63	10.19	5	3	0.75	1.27	800 236-8560
Marshall Small-Cap Growth A	Small Co	46.3					0.75	1.59	800 236-8560
Marshall Small-Cap Growth Y	Small Co	46.3	17.21		3	4	0.75	1.59	800 236-8560
Marsico Focus Fund	Growth	23.9					0.84	1.31	888 860-8686
Marsico Growth and Income Fund	Growth/Inc	22.1					0.84	1.42	888 860-8686
Mason Street Fds-Aggr Gr Stk A	Agg Growth	52.5	30		2	4	0.75	1.62	888 627-6678
Mason Street Fds-Aggr Gr Stk B	Agg Growth	51.4	29.13		1	4	0.75	1.94	888 627-6678
Mason Street Fds-Asset Alloc A	AssetAlloc	23.5	17.03		2	1	0.69	1.35	888 627-6678
Mason Street Fds-Asset Alloc B	AssetAlloc	22.6	16.26		2	1	0.69	2	888 627-6678
Mason Street Fds-Gr & Inc Stk A	Growth/Inc	-4.6	12.2		3	3	0.65	1.19	888 627-6678
Mason Street Fds-Gr & Inc Stk B	Growth/Inc	-5.2	11.51		3	3	0.65	1.85	888 627-6678
Mason Street Fds-Gr Stk A	Growth	19.2	24.25		2	2	0.75	1.3	888 627-6678
Mason Street Fds-Gr Stk B	Growth	18.5	23.46		2	2	0.75	1.94	888 627-6678
Mason Street Fds-Index 500 Stk A	Growth	6.6	18.85		3	3	0.29	0.84	888 627-6678
Mason Street Fds-Index 500 Stk B	Growth	5.9	18.08		2	3	0.29	1.5	888 627-6678
Mason Street Fds-Intl Equity A	Foreign	8.9	3.55		4	3	0.84	1.64	888 627-6678
Mason Street Fds-Intl Equity B	Foreign	8.1	2.86		4	3	0.84	2.29	888 627-6678
MassMutual Core Equity Fund S	Growth/Inc	-13.1	6.45	13.89	4	3	0.55	0.55	
MassMutual Inst-Balanced S	Balanced	-5.7	6.2	10.14	3	1	0.45	0.55	
MassMutual Inst-Intl Equity S	Foreign	56.9	20.44	19.78	3	4	0.84	1.04	

341

Stock Fund Name	Objective	Annualized Return for			Rank		Max Load	Expense Ratio	Toll-Free Telephone
		1 Year	3 Years	5 Years	Overall	Risk			
MassMutual Inst-Sm Cap Value Eq s	Small Co	3.5	5.13	13	4	3	0.55	0.65	
Masters Select Equity Fund	Growth	-7.8	12.93		2	3	1.1	1.3	800 960-0188
Masters' Select International Fund	Foreign	51.6					1.1	1.89	800 960-0188
Mathers Fund	Flexible	6	1.76	1.07	3	1	0.75	1.13	800 962-3863
Matrix Growth Fund	Growth	6.6	16.8	19.37	3	3	0.9	1.75	800 576 8229
Matrix/LMH Value Fund	Growth/Inc	14.2	15.44	17.36	3	3	1	1.82	800 366-6223
Matterhorn Growth Fund	Growth	17.6	16.57	14.56	3	2	1	3.56	800 637-3901
Matthews Asian Growth & Income	Pacific	22	4.88	7.41	4	3	1	1.89	800 789-2742
Matthews Dragon Century Fund I	Pacific	-0.9					1	2	800 789-2742
Matthews Japan Fund I	Pacific	19.5					1	2	800 789-2742
Matthews Korea Fund I	Pacific	-14.3	-0.17	-6.36	5	5	1	2.02	800 789-2742
Matthews Pacific Tiger Fund I	Pacific	18	0.51	6.27	4	5	1	1.89	800 789-2742
Maxus Aggressive Value Individual	Agg Growth	-4.7					1	2.37	877 593-8637
Maxus Aggressive Value Instl	Agg Growth	-4.4					1	1.87	877 593-8637
Maxus Equity Fund	Growth/Inc	5.6	7.88	13.18	3	3	1	1.86	877 593-8637
Maxus Income Fund	Flexible	1	4	6.32	3	1	1	1.97	877 593-8637
Maxus Laureate Fund	Growth/Inc	34.6	25.83	22.8	1	2	1	2.24	877 593-8637
Maxus Ohio Heartland Individual	Growth/Inc	-7.8					1	3.64	877 593-8637
Maxus Ohio Heartland Instl	Growth/Inc	-8.5					1	2.74	877 593-8637
McM Balanced Fund	Balanced	2.5	12.44	15.62	3	1	0.45	0.64	800 788-9485
McM Equity Investment Fund	Growth	1.6	17.12	22.32	3	2	0.5	0.67	800 788-9485
Members Balanced Fd A	Balanced	6.7					0.65	1.1	800 877-6089
Members Balanced Fd B	Balanced	5.9					0.65	1.1	800 877-6089
Members Capital Appreciation Fd A	Growth	13.9					0.75	1.19	800 877-6089
Members Capital Appreciation Fd B	Growth	13.1					0.75	1.94	800 877-6089
Members Growth & Income Fd A	Growth/Inc	-0.5					0.55	1	800 877-6089
Members Growth & Income Fd B	Growth/Inc	-1.2					0.55	1.75	800 877-6089
Members International Fd A	Foreign	-1.2					1.05	1.6	800 877-6089
Members International Fd B	Foreign	-1.9					1.05	2.35	800 877-6089
Memorial Growth Equity Instl	Growth	16.7					0.45	0.98	888 263-5593
Memorial Value Equity Instl	Growth	-18.7					0.45	0.98	888 263-5593
Mercantile Small Cap Eq Index Instl	Small Co	12.9					0.4	0.81	800 452-2724
Mercantile Small Cap Eq Index Inv A	Small Co	13.1					0.4	0.93	800 452-2724
Mercantile Small Cap Eq Index Trust	Small Co	13.1					0.4	0.56	800 452-2724
Mercantile-Balanced B	Balanced	0	7.98	10.96	3	1	0.75	1.97	800 452-2724
Mercantile-Balanced Inst	Balanced	0.5	8.65	11.68	3	1	0.75	1.26	800 452-2724
Mercantile-Balanced Inv	Balanced	0.6	8.69	11.69	3	1	0.75	1.27	800 452-2724
Mercantile-Balanced Tr	Balanced	0.8	8.97	12.02	3	1	0.75	0.96	800 452-2724
Mercantile-Equity Income B	Growth/Inc	-14.2	4.35		5	3	0.75	1.96	800 452-2724
Mercantile-Equity Income Inst	Growth/Inc	-13.6	5.16		5	3	0.75	1.27	800 452-2724
Mercantile-Equity Income Inv	Growth/Inc	-13.7	5.03		5	3	0.75	1.27	800 452-2724
Mercantile-Equity Income Tr	Growth/Inc	-13.5	5.34		5	3	0.75	0.96	800 452-2724
Mercantile-Equity Index Inst	Growth/Inc	6.6	18.89		2	3	0.29	0.83	800 452-2724
Mercantile-Equity Index Inv	Growth/Inc	6.5	18.82		3	2	0.29	0.83	800 452-2724
Mercantile-Equity Index Tr	Growth/Inc	6.9	19.19		3	3	0.29	0.54	800 452-2724
Mercantile-Growth & Inc Eq B	Growth/Inc	-0.2	10.65	16.13	3	3	0.55	1.73	800 452-2724
Mercantile-Growth & Inc Eq Inst	Growth/Inc	0.5	11.4	16.91	3	3	0.55	1.04	800 452-2724
Mercantile-Growth & Inc Eq Inv	Growth/Inc	0.5	11.4	16.88	3	3	0.55	1.04	800 452-2724
Mercantile-Growth & Inc Eq Tr	Growth/Inc	0.8	11.73	17.25	2	3	0.55	0.73	800 452-2724
Mercantile-Growth Eq B	Growth	19.8					0.75	1.97	800 452-2724
Mercantile-Growth Eq Inst	Growth	22.4					0.75	1.25	800 452-2724
Mercantile-Growth Eq Inv	Growth	22.5					0.75	1.27	800 452-2724
Mercantile-Growth Eq Tr	Growth	22.8					0.75	0.96	800 452-2724
Mercantile-Interl Equity B	Foreign	35.6	16.88	15.46	3	3	1	2.25	800 452-2724
Mercantile-Interl Equity Inst	Foreign	36.6	17.56	16.16	3	3	1	1.58	800 452-2724
Mercantile-Interl Equity Inv	Foreign	36.6	17.57	16.19	3	3	1	1.58	800 452-2724
Mercantile-Interl Equity Tr	Foreign	37	17.91	16.87	3	3	1	1.28	800 452-2724
Mercantile-Small Cap Equity B	Small Co	33.2	10.25	10.86	4	4	0.75	1.94	800 452-2724

Stock Fund Name	Objective	Annualized Return for			Rank		Max Load	Expense Ratio	Toll-Free Telephone
		1 Year	3 Years	5 Years	Overall	Risk			
Mercantile-Small Cap Equity Inst	Small Co	34.1	11	11.62	3	4	0.75	1.23	800 452-2724
Mercantile-Small Cap Equity Inv	Small Co	34.1	10.99	11.58	4	4	0.75	1.25	800 452-2724
Mercantile-Small Cap Equity Tr	Small Co	34.5	11.34	12.01	3	4	0.75	0.94	800 452-2724
Mercury Global Balance A	Balanced	11.2					0.59	1.41	888 763-2260
Mercury Global Balance B	Balanced	10.3					0.59	2.18	888 763-2260
Mercury Global Balance C	Balanced	10.3					0.59	2.18	888 763-2260
Mercury Global Balance I	Balanced	11.2					0.59	1.16	888 763-2260
Mercury International A	Foreign	19.1					0.75	1.82	888 763-2260
Mercury International B	Foreign	18.1					0.75	2.54	888 763-2260
Mercury International C	Foreign	18.1					0.75	2.56	888 763-2260
Mercury International I	Foreign	19.4					0.75	1.56	888 763-2260
Mercury Pan Euro Growth A	European	14.8					0.75	1.65	888 763-2260
Mercury Pan Euro Growth B	European	14					0.75	2.43	888 763-2260
Mercury Pan Euro Growth C	European	14					0.75	2.43	888 763-2260
Mercury Pan Euro Growth I	European	15.1					0.75	1.4	888 763-2260
Mercury US Large Cap A	Growth	10.3					0.5	1.18	888 763-2260
Mercury US Large Cap B	Growth	9.4					0.5	1.95	888 763-2260
Mercury US Large Cap C	Growth	9.4					0.5	1.95	888 763-2260
Mercury US Large Cap I	Growth	10.6					0.5	0.93	888 763-2260
Merger Fund	Growth	17.2	12.91	12.45	3	1	1	1.32	800 343-8959
Meridian Fund	Small Co	21.5	13.51	15.12	3	3	0.78	1.09	800 446-6662
Meridian Value Fund	Growth	29.6	24.76	28.42	1	3	1	1.62	800 446-6662
Merrill Lynch Basic Value A	Growth/Inc	-6	9.88	15.63	2	2	0.4	0.55	800 637-3863
Merrill Lynch Basic Value B	Growth/Inc	-6.9	8.85	14.51	3	2	0.4	1.57	800 637-3863
Merrill Lynch Capital A	Flexible	-3.2	6.59	11.56	3	2	0.4	0.56	800 637-3863
Merrill Lynch Capital B	Flexible	-4.2	5.52	10.44	3	1	0.4	1.59	800 637-3863
Merrill Lynch Dev Cap Market A	Foreign	16	-5.24	2.81	4	4	1	1.87	800 637-3863
Merrill Lynch Disciplined Equity A	Growth/Inc	3.5					0.65		800 637-3863
Merrill Lynch Disciplined Equity B	Growth/Inc	2.5					0.65		800 637-3863
Merrill Lynch Disciplined Equity C	Growth/Inc	2.5					0.65		800 637-3863
Merrill Lynch Disciplined Equity D	Growth/Inc	3.2					0.65		800 637-3863
Merrill Lynch Dragon Fund B	Pacific	9.7	-9.82	-3.32	5	5	1	2.54	800 637-3863
Merrill Lynch Dragon Fund D	Pacific	10.5	-9.08	-2.54	5	5	1	1.77	800 637-3863
Merrill Lynch Eurofund A	European	7.2	16.33	18.15	2	3	0.75	0.98	800 637-3863
Merrill Lynch Eurofund B	European	6.1	14.64	16.63	3	2	0.75	2	800 637-3863
Merrill Lynch Eurofund C	European	6.1	15.16	16.92	3	2	0.75	2.02	800 637-3863
Merrill Lynch Eurofund D	European	7	16.17	17.93	3	3	0.75	1.22	800 637-3863
Merrill Lynch FL Muni A	Muni State	0.4	3.39	4.74	3	3	0.55	0.68	800 637-3863
Merrill Lynch FL Muni B	Muni State	-0.1	2.86	4.21	4	3	0.55	1.19	800 637-3863
Merrill Lynch Fundamental Gr B	Growth	25.5	27.39	27.54	1	3	0.61	1.77	800 637-3863
Merrill Lynch Glbl Allocation B	AssetAlloc	9.3	9.63	12.76	3	2	0.75	1.93	800 637-3863
Merrill Lynch Glbl Allocation D	AssetAlloc	10	10.44	13.61	3	2	0.75	1.26	800 637-3863
Merrill Lynch Global Bond A	Intl Bond	-1.7	2.16	2.85	5	4	0.59	1.02	800 637-3863
Merrill Lynch Global Bond B	Intl Bond	-2.6	1.37	2.05	5	4	0.59	1.8	800 637-3863
Merrill Lynch Global Bond C	Intl Bond	-2.5	1.32	1.99	5	4	0.59	1.85	800 637-3863
Merrill Lynch Global Bond D	Intl Bond	-2	1.9	2.59	5	4	0.59	1.27	800 637-3863
Merrill Lynch Global Resource A	Energy/Res	19.4	2.45	5.82	5	4	0.59	1.28	800 637-3863
Merrill Lynch Global Resource B	Energy/Res	18.2	1.36	4.81	5	4	0.59	2.35	800 637-3863
Merrill Lynch Global Utility A	Utilities	9.3	15.32	16.63	2	2	0.59	1.58	800 637-3863
Merrill Lynch Global Utility B	Utilities	8.4	14.41	15.74	2	2	0.59	1.59	800 637-3863
Merrill Lynch Global Value A	Global	15.9	16.03		2	2	0.75	0.9	800 637-3863
Merrill Lynch Global Value B	Global	14.7	14.86		3	2	0.75	1.92	800 637-3863
Merrill Lynch Global Value C	Global	14.7	14.86		3	2	0.75	1.91	800 637-3863
Merrill Lynch Global Value D	Global	15.6	15.7		2	2	0.75	1.14	800 637-3863
Merrill Lynch Growth A	Growth	35.2	3.47	11.69	3	3	0.65	1.01	800 637-3863
Merrill Lynch Growth B	Growth	33.8	2.4	10.55	3	3	0.65	1.98	800 637-3863
Merrill Lynch Growth C	Growth	33.8	2.39	10.53	3	3	0.65	2.04	800 637-3863
Merrill Lynch Growth D	Growth	34.9	3.2	12.83	3	3	0.65	1.25	800 637-3863

Stock Fund Name	Objective	Annualized Return for			Rank		Max Load	Expense Ratio	Toll-Free Telephone
		1 Year	3 Years	5 Years	Overall	Risk			
Merrill Lynch Health Care A	Health	45.9	27.7	28.5	1	3	1	1.27	800 637-3863
Merrill Lynch Health Care B	Health	44.3	26.38	27.21	2	3	1	2.29	800 637-3863
Merrill Lynch International Index D	Foreign	17.8	13.08		3	3	0.11	1.11	800 637-3863
Merrill Lynch Latin America A	Foreign	31.6	-1.31	10.23	4	5	1	2	800 637-3863
Merrill Lynch Latin America B	Foreign	30.3	-2.33	9.1	4	5	1	2.87	800 637-3863
Merrill Lynch Latin America C	Foreign	30.3	-2.32	9.08	4	5	1	3.08	800 637-3863
Merrill Lynch Latin America D	Foreign	31.3	-1.55	10.02	4	5	1	2.27	800 637-3863
Merrill Lynch Mercury Glb Hldngs A	Global	33.4	17.35	17.01	3	3	1	1.37	800 637-3863
Merrill Lynch Mercury Glb Hldngs B	Global	32	16.16	16.06	3	3	1	2.43	800 637-3863
Merrill Lynch Pacific A	Pacific	32.2	12.22	14.41	3	4	0.59	0.84	800 637-3863
Merrill Lynch Pacific B	Pacific	30.9	11.08	13.25	4	4	0.59	1.91	800 637-3863
Merrill Lynch Phoenix A	Growth/Inc	14.6	20.21	17.84	3	3	0.98	1.27	800 637-3863
Merrill Lynch Phoenix B	Growth/Inc	13.4	18.99	16.64	3	3	0.98	2.25	800 637-3863
Merrill Lynch S&P 500 Index D	Growth/Inc	6.6	18.95		3	3	0.05	0.64	800 637-3863
Merrill Lynch Special Value A	Small Co	24.6	14.04	18.97	3	3	0.75	1.08	800 637-3863
Merrill Lynch Special Value B	Small Co	23.3	12.88	17.75	3	3	0.75	2.1	800 637-3863
Merrill Lynch Strategic Div A	Income	-7.6	8.93	15.29	2	2	0.59	0.86	800 637-3863
Merrill Lynch Strategic Div B	Income	-8.6	7.83	14.11	3	2	0.59	1.88	800 637-3863
Merrill Lynch World Income A	Intl Bond	10	-3.19	1.9	3	5	0.59	0.94	800 637-3863
Merrill Lynch World Income B	Intl Bond	9	-3.99	1.12	4	5	0.59	1.72	800 637-3863
Merriman Asset Allocation	AssetAlloc	9.4	6.79	8.38	3	2	1.25	1.88	800 423-4893
Merriman Cap Appreciation	Growth	12.3	10.39	11.7	4	3	1.25	1.85	800 423-4893
Merriman Growth & Income Fund	Growth/Inc	5.5	9.71	13.27	3	2	1.25	1.79	800 423-4893
Merriman Leveraged Growth Fund	Growth	15.3	14.05	15.11	3	4	1.25	3.08	800 423-4893
MetaMarkets.com Open Fund	Growth						1		877 638-2658
Meyers Pride Value Fund	Growth	7.4	15.86		3	3	1	1.94	800 410-3337
Midas Fund	Prec Metal	-29.9	-35.86	-25.63	5	5	1	2.81	800 400-6432
Midas Investors LTD	Prec Metal	-25.9	-31.12	-24.46	5	4	1	4.17	800 400-6432
Midas Magic Fund	Growth	7.3	5.38	13.43	4	4	1	1.93	800 400-6432
Millennium Growth & Income Fund	Growth/Inc	60.4					0.94	1.44	800 535-9169
Millennium Growth Fund	Growth	55.3					0.94	1.44	800 535-9169
Monetta Fund	Small Co	71.8	21.45	17.32	3	5	1	1.44	800 666-3882
Monetta Trust-Balanced	Balanced	21.4	17.91		2	3	0.4	0.93	800 666-3882
Monetta Trust-Large-Cap Equity	Growth	32.2	24.63		2	4	0.75	1.65	800 666-3882
Monetta Trust-Mid Cap Equity	Growth	57.6	25.74	23.89	2	4	0.75	1.25	800 666-3882
Monetta Trust-Small Cap Equity	Small Co	46.6	25.54		3	5	0.75	2.5	800 666-3882
Montag & Caldwell Balanced I	Balanced	7.1					0.75	0.95	800 992-8151
Monterey Murphy Biotech	Health	102.1	23.57	13.13	3	4	1	1.98	800 628-9403
Monterey Murphy Technology	Technology	37.2	10.09	9.78	4	5	1	2.08	800 628-9403
Monterey OCM Gold Fund	Prec Metal	-5.9	-14.74	-5.71	5	5	1	2.43	800 628-9403
Monterey PIA Equity Fund	Growth	30.6	13.31	18.59	3	4	1	1.8	800 628-9403
Montgomery Balanced Fund R	AssetAlloc	1.6	9.25	13.11	3	1	0	0.6	800 572-3863
Montgomery Emerging Asia R	Pacific	-12.6	-14.22		4	5	1.25	2.18	800 572-3863
Montgomery Emerging Mkts R	Foreign	17.6	-9.45	-0.94	4	4	1.15	2.04	800 572-3863
Montgomery Global Communication R	Technology	47.9	41.48	30.49	2	4	1.21	1.51	800 572-3863
Montgomery Global Long-Short R	Global	67.3					1.5	4.17	800 572-3863
Montgomery Global Opportunities R	Global	21.5	21.33	22.19	2	4	1.25	1.95	800 572-3863
Montgomery Growth Fund R	Growth	-1.3	8.86	14.16	4	3	0.94	1.44	800 572-3863
Montgomery Instl Emerging Mkts R	Foreign	21	-6.29	1.72	4	4	1.05	2.29	800 572-3863
Montgomery Intl Growth Fund P	Foreign	105.5					1.1	1.9	800 572-3863
Montgomery Intl Growth Fund R	Foreign	10.2	11.64		3	3	1.1	1.71	800 572-3863
Montgomery Select 50 Fund R	Growth/Inc	15.9	15.07		3	3	1.25	1.72	800 572-3863
Montgomery Small Capital R	Small Co	34.1	16.57	18.64	3	5	1	1.31	800 572-3863
Montgomery US Emerging Growth R	Small Co	40.9	18.07	19.85	3	3	1.34	1.65	800 572-3863
Monument Internet A	Technology	46.9					1	2.75	888 520-8637
Monument Internet Fund B	Technology						1		888 520-8637
Monument Medical Sciences Fund A	Health	104.8					1	1.75	888 520-8637
Monument Medical Sciences Fund B	Health						1		888 520-8637

Stock Fund Name	Objective	Annualized Return for			Rank		Max Load	Expense Ratio	Toll-Free Telephone
		1 Year	3 Years	5 Years	Overall	Risk			
Monument Telecommunications Fund A	Technology	119.1					1	1.73	888 520-8637
Monument Telecommunications Fund B	Technology						1		888 520-8637
Morgan Grenfell EmergMkt Equity	Foreign	14.4	-5.94	0.46	5	4	1	1.25	800 730-1313
Morgan Grenfell European Equity	European	188.2	53.86		2	5	0.69	0.9	800 730-1313
Morgan Grenfell Global Fixed	Intl Bond	2.2	2.52	3.02	5	5	0.5	1.03	800 550-6426
Morgan Grenfell Intl Equity	Foreign	62.2	30.77	25.62	2	4	0.69	0.9	800 550-6426
Morgan Grenfell Intl Small Cap	Foreign	35.6	16.25	12.37	3	3	1	1.25	800 550-6426
Morgan Grenfell Microcap Fd	Small Co	59.2	28.88		3	4	1.5	1.48	800 550-6426
Morgan Grenfell Smaller Co Fd	Small Co	43.1	18.68	19.64	3	4	1	1.25	800 550-6426
Morgan Keegan Southern Cap	Growth	-0.8	9.33	16.19	4	3	1	1.8	800 564-2113
Mosaic Balanced Fund	Balanced	-2.3	10.59	15.24	3	1	0.75	1.19	888 670-3600
Mosaic Foresight Fund	Foreign	1.2	0.48	6.04	4	2	0.75	1.21	888 670-3600
Mosaic Investors Fund	Growth	-5	13.48	16.77	3	3	0.75	1.12	888 670-3600
Mosaic Mid-Cap Growth Fd	Small Co	11.5	9.75	10.5	4	3	0.75	1.21	888 670-3600
Muhlenkamp Fund	Growth/Inc	8.3	13.97	20.69	3	3	1	1.35	800 860-3863
Munder All Season Aggressive Y	Growth	22.6	14.57		3	3	0.34	0.35	800 438-5789
Munder All Season Moderate A	Growth/Inc	12.8	9.35		3	2	0.34	0.66	800 438-5789
Munder All Season Moderate Y	Growth/Inc	13.1	9.55		3	2	0.34	0.35	800 438-5789
Munder Balanced A	Balanced	27.2	17.73	16.76	2	2	0.65	1.21	800 438-5789
Munder Balanced B	Balanced	26.2	16.88	15.89	3	2	0.65	1.96	800 438-5789
Munder Balanced C	Balanced	26.4	16.89		2	2	0.65	1.96	800 438-5789
Munder Balanced K	Balanced	27	17.68	16.74	2	2	0.65	1.21	800 438-5789
Munder Balanced Y	Balanced	27.5	18.09	17.07	2	2	0.65	0.96	800 438-5789
Munder Equity Income A	Growth/Inc	-16.5	3.25	11.25	4	2	0.75	1.2	800 438-5789
Munder Equity Income B	Growth/Inc	-17.1	-2.99	6.83	5	2	0.75	1.96	800 438-5789
Munder Equity Income C	Growth/Inc	-17	2.44		4	2	0.75	1.96	800 438-5789
Munder Equity Income K	Growth/Inc	-16.5	3.22	11.25	4	2	0.75	1.2	800 438-5789
Munder Equity Income Y	Growth/Inc	-16.3	3.49	11.53	4	2	0.75	0.95	800 438-5789
Munder Equity Selection Y	Growth	19.7					0.75	1.64	800 438-5789
Munder Framlington Emerg Mkts A	Foreign	9.3	0.61		4	5	1.25	1.85	800 438-5789
Munder Framlington Emerg Mkts B	Foreign	9.2	-0.78		4	5	1.25	2.6	800 438-5789
Munder Framlington Emerg Mkts C	Foreign	8.4	-0.44		4	5	1.25	2.6	800 438-5789
Munder Framlington Emerg Mkts K	Foreign	8.8	0.19		4	5	1.25	1.85	800 438-5789
Munder Framlington Emerg Mkts Y	Foreign	9.1	0.47		4	5	1.25	1.6	800 438-5789
Munder Framlington Global Fin Svc Y	Financial	7.9					0.75	1.17	800 438-5789
Munder Framlington Healthcare A	Health	171	38.07		3	5	1	1.61	800 438-5789
Munder Framlington Healthcare B	Health	169.1	37.04		3	5	1	2.35	800 438-5789
Munder Framlington Healthcare C	Health	168.9	37		3	5	1	2.35	800 438-5789
Munder Framlington Healthcare K	Health	170.9	37.5		3	5	1	1.61	800 438-5789
Munder Framlington Healthcare Y	Health	171.7	38.36		3	5	1	1.36	800 438-5789
Munder Framlington Intl Growth A	Foreign	28.9	13.47		3	3	1	1.6	800 438-5789
Munder Framlington Intl Growth B	Foreign	27.9	12.52		3	3	1	2.35	800 438-5789
Munder Framlington Intl Growth C	Foreign	28	12.58		3	3	1	2.35	800 438-5789
Munder Framlington Intl Growth K	Foreign	29	13.38		3	3	1	1.61	800 438-5789
Munder Framlington Intl Growth Y	Foreign	29.3	13.69		3	3	1	1.36	800 438-5789
Munder Growth Opportunities Fund Y	Growth	45.8					0.75	1.17	800 438-5789
Munder Index 500 A	Growth/Inc	6.7	19.13	23.24	2	3	0.1	0.44	800 438-5789
Munder Index 500 B	Growth/Inc	6.4	18.72		3	3	0.1	0.77	800 438-5789
Munder Index 500 K	Growth/Inc	6.6	18.99	23.08	2	3	0.1	0.55	800 438-5789
Munder Index 500 Y	Growth/Inc	6.9	19.29	23.39	2	3	0.1	0.29	800 438-5789
Munder Instl Mid-Cap Index Eq Fund	Growth/Inc	16.4					0.14	0.17	800 438-5789
Munder Instl S&P 500 Index Eq Fund	Growth/Inc	7					0.07	0.08	800 438-5789
Munder International Equity A	Foreign	23.9	12.69	13.87	3	3	0.75	1.29	800 438-5789
Munder International Equity B	Foreign	22.5	11.76	12.92	3	3	0.75	2.04	800 438-5789
Munder International Equity C	Foreign	22.7	11.77		3	3	0.75	2.04	800 438-5789
Munder International Equity K	Foreign	23.5	12.6	13.83	3	3	0.75	1.29	800 438-5789
Munder International Equity Y	Foreign	23.8	12.9	14.14	3	3	0.75	1.06	800 438-5789
Munder Micro-Cap Equity A	Small Co	58.6	33.66		2	5	1	1.36	800 438-5789

345

Stock Fund Name	Objective	Annualized Return for			Rank		Max Load	Expense Ratio	Toll-Free Telephone
		1 Year	3 Years	5 Years	Overall	Risk			
Munder Micro-Cap Equity B	Small Co	57.1	32.46		2	5	1	2.27	800 438-5789
Munder Micro-Cap Equity C	Small Co	57	32.46		2	5	1	2.27	800 438-5789
Munder Micro-Cap Equity K	Small Co	58.4	33.47		2	5	1	1.53	800 438-5789
Munder Micro-Cap Equity Y	Small Co	58.6	33.77		3	5	1	1.28	800 438-5789
Munder Multi-Season Growth A	Growth	0.2	11.76	17.8	3	3	1	1.21	800 438-5789
Munder Multi-Season Growth B	Growth	-0.5	11	17	4	3	1	1.25	800 438-5789
Munder Multi-Season Growth C	Growth	-0.5	11	16.98	4	3	1	1.96	800 438-5789
Munder Multi-Season Growth K	Growth	0.3	11.81	17.85	3	3	1	1.21	800 438-5789
Munder Multi-Season Growth Y	Growth	0.5	12.02	18.11	3	3	1	0.96	800 438-5789
Munder Net Net Fund A	Technology	58.9	85.9		1	5	1	1.61	800 438-5789
Munder Net Net Fund B	Technology	57.7					1	2.33	800 438-5789
Munder Net Net Fund C	Technology	57.7					1	2.33	800 438-5789
Munder NetNet Fund Y	Technology	59.3					1	1.3	800 438-5789
Munder Real Estate Equity A	Real Est	0.6	0.74	9.61	4	2	0.73	1.27	800 438-5789
Munder Real Estate Equity B	Real Est	0	0.02	8.8	4	2	0.73	2.02	800 438-5789
Munder Real Estate Equity C	Real Est	0	0.07		4	2	0.73	2.02	800 438-5789
Munder Real Estate Equity Invst K	Real Est	0.5	0.73		4	2	0.73	1.27	800 438-5789
Munder Real Estate Equity Y	Real Est	1	1.06	9.89	4	2	0.73	1.02	800 438-5789
Munder Small Cap Value A	Small Co	-6.7	3.24		4	3	0.75	1.22	800 438-5789
Munder Small Cap Value B	Small Co	-7.4	2.46		5	3	0.75	1.97	800 438-5789
Munder Small Cap Value C	Small Co	-7.5	2.39		5	3	0.75	1.97	800 438-5789
Munder Small Cap Value K	Small Co	-6.7	3.21		5	3	0.75	0.97	800 438-5789
Munder Small Cap Value Y	Small Co	-6.5	3.48		5	3	0.75	0.97	800 438-5789
Munder Small Company Growth A	Small Co	22.3	6.84	16.54	4	4	0.75	1.21	800 438-5789
Munder Small Company Growth B	Small Co	19.5	5.49	15.17	4	4	0.75	1.96	800 438-5789
Munder Small Company Growth C	Small Co	19.5	5.19		4	4	0.75	1.96	800 438-5789
Munder Small Company Growth K	Small Co	20.4	6.28	16.18	4	4	0.75	1.21	800 438-5789
Munder Small Company Growth Y	Small Co	20.7	6.55	16.46	4	4	0.75	1	800 438-5789
Mutual Beacon A	Growth/Inc	1.8	10.11		3	2	0.59	1.11	800 342-5236
Mutual Beacon B	Growth/Inc	1.2					0.59	1.78	800 342-5236
Mutual Beacon C	Growth/Inc	1.2	9.41		3	2	0.59	1.76	800 342-5236
Mutual Beacon Z	Growth/Inc	2.3	10.52	15.34	3	2	0.59	0.79	800 342-5236
Mutual Discovery A	Global	17.4	12.4		2	2	0.8	1.37	800 342-5236
Mutual Discovery B	Global	16.5					0.8	2.04	800 342-5236
Mutual Discovery C	Global	16.6	11.7		2	2	0.8	2.02	800 342-5236
Mutual Discovery Z	Global	17.8	12.81	17.85	2	2	0.8	1.05	800 342-5236
Mutual European A	European	39.8	21.55		1	3	0.8	1.39	800 342-5236
Mutual European B	European	38.9					0.8	2.06	800 342-5236
Mutual European C	European	39.1	20.99		1	3	0.8	2.04	800 342-5236
Mutual European Z	European	40.4	22.19		1	3	0.8	1.06	800 342-5236
Mutual Financial Svcs A	Financial	-6.4					0.8	1.33	800 342-5236
Mutual Financial Svcs B	Financial	-7.1					0.17	1.98	800 342-5236
Mutual Financial Svcs C	Financial	-7					0.8	1.95	800 342-5236
Mutual Financial Svcs Z	Financial	-6.1					0.8	0.97	800 342-5236
Mutual Qualified A	Growth/Inc	0.5	8.76		3	2	0.59	1.1	800 342-5236
Mutual Qualified B	Growth/Inc	-0.1					0.59	1.78	800 342-5236
Mutual Qualified C	Growth/Inc	-0.1	8.01		4	2	0.59	1.76	800 342-5236
Mutual Qualified Z	Growth/Inc	0.9	9.11	14.79	3	2	0.59	0.8	800 342-5236
Mutual Shares A	Growth/Inc	-1.2	8.57		4	2	0.59	1.09	800 342-5236
Mutual Shares B	Growth/Inc	-1.9					0.59	1.75	800 342-5236
Mutual Shares C	Growth/Inc	-1.8	7.87		4	2	0.59	1.72	800 342-5236
Mutual Shares Z	Growth/Inc	-0.8	8.94	14.9	3	2	0.59	0.77	800 342-5236
Nasdaq 100 Index Fund A	Growth						0.5		877 627-3272
Nasdaq 100 Index Fund C	Growth						0.5		877 627-3272
National Asset Management Core Eq	Growth	5.1					0.5		
Nations Aggressive Growth Inv A	Growth	-6.6	13.25	17.74	2	3	0.65	1.21	800 321-7854
Nations Aggressive Growth Inv B	Growth	-7.3	12.35	16.9	4	3	0.65	1.97	800 321-7854
Nations Aggressive Growth Inv C	Growth	-7.2	12.43	17.08	4	3	0.65	1.96	800 321-7854

Stock Fund Name	Objective	Annualized Return for			Rank		Max Load	Expense Ratio	Toll-Free Telephone
		1 Year	3 Years	5 Years	Overall	Risk			
Nations Aggressive Growth Pr A	Growth	-6.3	13.49	18.01	4	3	0.65	0.96	800 321-7854
Nations Asset Alloc Inv A	AssetAlloc	3.8	12.66	15.26	2	1	0.65	1.22	800 321-7854
Nations Asset Alloc Srf	AssetAlloc						0.65	0.97	800 321-7854
Nations Asset Allocation Inv B	AssetAlloc	6					0.65	1.97	800 321-7854
Nations Asset Allocation Inv C	AssetAlloc	5.9	11.47		3	2	0.65	1.97	800 321-7854
Nations Asset Allocation Pr A	AssetAlloc	2.6					0.65	0.97	800 321-7854
Nations Balanced Assets Inv A	Balanced	-5.6	4.71	10.06	3	1	0.65	1.34	800 321-7854
Nations Balanced Assets Inv B	Balanced	-6.3	4.03	9.41	3	1	0.65	2	800 321-7854
Nations Balanced Assets Inv C	Balanced	-6.3	4.02	9.42	3	1	0.65	2	800 321-7854
Nations Balanced Assets Pr A	Balanced	-5.4	5.03	10.36	3	1	0.65	1.25	800 321-7854
Nations Blue Chip Inv A	Growth	9.2	19.36	23.63	3	3	0.65	1.19	800 321-7854
Nations Blue Chip Inv B	Growth	-1.6					0.65	1.95	800 321-7854
Nations Blue Chip Inv C	Growth	8.4	18.68		3	3	0.65	1.95	800 321-7854
Nations Blue Chip Pr A	Growth	9.6					0.65		
Nations Blue Chip Seafirst	Growth						0.65	0.93	800 321-7854
Nations Capital Growth Inv A	Growth	16	23.36	22.87	2	3	0.65	1.2	800 321-7854
Nations Capital Growth Inv B	Growth	15.1	22.41	21.96	2	3	0.65	1.95	800 321-7854
Nations Capital Growth Inv C	Growth	15.1	22.52	22.19	2	3	0.65	1.95	800 321-7854
Nations Capital Growth Pr A	Growth	16.4	23.68	23.2	2	3	0.65	0.95	800 321-7854
Nations Emerging Markets Inv A	Foreign	34.2	3.9	7.19	4	5	1.1	2.14	800 321-7854
Nations Emerging Markets Inv B	Foreign	33.2	3.13	6.4	4	5	1.1	2.77	800 321-7854
Nations Emerging Markets Inv C	Foreign	33.2	3.16	6.55	4	5	1.1	2.77	800 321-7854
Nations Emerging Markets Pr A	Foreign	34.7	4.2	7.47	4	5	1.1	1.78	800 321-7854
Nations Equity Income Inv A	Income	-8.3	3.88	11.1	3	2	0.65	1.12	800 321-7854
Nations Equity Income Inv B	Income	-9	3.17	10.44	5	2	0.65	1.8	800 321-7854
Nations Equity Income Inv C	Income	-9	3.25	10.53	3	2	0.65	1.63	800 321-7854
Nations Equity Income Pr A	Income	-8.1	4.12	11.39	4	2	0.65	0.8	800 321-7854
Nations FL Interm Muni Inv A	Muni State	2.6	3.75	4.5	3	2	0.4	0.69	800 321-7854
Nations FL Interm Muni Inv B	Muni State	2	3.16	4.03	3	2	0.4	1.3	800 321-7854
Nations FL Interm Muni Inv C	Muni State	2.1	3.19	4.04	3	2	0.4	1.36	800 321-7854
Nations FL Interm Muni Pr A	Muni State	2.9	4.01	4.74	2	2	0.4	0.5	800 321-7854
Nations FL Muni Bond Inv A	Muni State	3.1	4.21	5.25	2	3	0.4	0.8	800 321-7854
Nations FL Muni Bond Inv B	Muni State	2.4	3.39	4.52	3	3	0.4	1.44	800 321-7854
Nations FL Muni Bond Inv C	Muni State	2.3	3.38	4.6	3	3	0.4	1.53	800 321-7854
Nations FL Muni Bond Pr A	Muni State	3.4	4.28	5.38	1	3	0.4	0.59	800 321-7854
Nations International Eq Inv A	Foreign	28.1	12.49	13.41	3	3	0.8	1.37	800 321-7854
Nations International Eq Inv B	Foreign	27	11.49	12.52	3	3	0.8	2.12	800 321-7854
Nations International Eq Inv C	Foreign	26.9	11.52	12.64	3	3	0.8	2.12	800 321-7854
Nations International Eq Pr A	Foreign	28.6	12.73	13.67	3	3	0.8	1.12	800 321-7854
Nations International Growth Pr B	Foreign	47.5	19.13		3	5	0.8	1.37	800 321-7854
Nations International Val Inv A	Foreign	28.3	20.87		2	4	0.9	1.55	800 321-7854
Nations International Val Inv B	Foreign	21.8					0.9	2.29	800 321-7854
Nations International Val Inv C	Foreign	24.7					0.9	2.29	800 321-7854
Nations International Val Pr A	Foreign	28.7	20.94		2	4	0.9	1.3	800 321-7854
Nations Intl Growth Inv A	Foreign	10	-3.42		5	3	0.8	1.37	800 321-7854
Nations Intl Growth Inv B	Foreign	8.9	6.36		4	3	0.8	2.45	800 321-7854
Nations Intl Growth Inv C	Foreign	8.7	6.16		3	3	0.8	2.12	800 321-7854
Nations Large Cap Index Fund Pr A	Growth	7	19.23	23.5	2	3	0.2	0.34	800 321-7854
Nations LifeGoal Bal Growth Inv A	Balanced	13.8	11.61		3	1	0.25	0.5	800 321-7854
Nations LifeGoal Bal Growth Inv B	Balanced	12.9					0.25	1.25	800 321-7854
Nations LifeGoal Bal Growth Inv C	Balanced	12.9	11.07		3	1	0.25	1.25	800 321-7854
Nations LifeGoal Bal Growth Pr A	Balanced	13.9	11.8		3	1	0.25	0.25	800 321-7854
Nations LifeGoal Bal Growth Pr B	Balanced	13.4	11.31		3	1	0.25	0.75	800 321-7854
Nations LifeGoal Growth Inv A	Growth	20	15.41		3	3	0.25	0.5	800 321-7854
Nations LifeGoal Growth Inv B	Growth	17.7					0.25	1.25	800 321-7854
Nations LifeGoal Growth Inv C	Growth	19.2	14.54		3	3	0.25	1.25	800 321-7854
Nations LifeGoal Growth Pr A	Growth	20.3	15.64		3	3	0.25	0.25	800 321-7854
Nations LifeGoal Growth Pr B	Growth	19.6	15.17		3	3	0.25	0.75	800 321-7854

Stock Fund Name	Objective	1 Year	3 Years	5 Years	Overall	Risk	Max Load	Expense Ratio	Toll-Free Telephone
Nations LifeGoal Inc & Gr Inv A	Growth/Inc	4.3	6.97		3	1	0.25	0.5	800 321-7854
Nations LifeGoal Inc & Gr Inv B	Growth/Inc	3.6					0.25	1.25	800 321-7854
Nations LifeGoal Inc & Gr Inv C	Growth/Inc	3.5	6.15		3	1	0.25	1.25	800 321-7854
Nations LifeGoal Inc & Gr Pr A	Growth/Inc	4.3	7.07		3	1	0.25	0.25	800 321-7854
Nations LifeGoal Inc & Gr Pr B	Growth/Inc	0.4	5.23		3	1	0.25	1.25	800 321-7854
Nations Managed Index Inv A	Growth	4.8	17.48		3	3	0.4	0.75	800 321-7854
Nations Managed Index Pr A	Growth	5.3	17.83		3	3	0.4	0.5	800 321-7854
Nations Managed Sm Cap Index Inv A	Small Co	8.1	7.34		4	3	0.4	0.75	800 321-7854
Nations Managed Sm Cap Index Pr A	Small Co	8.3	7.58		4	3	0.4	0.5	800 321-7854
Nations Managed Sm Cap Index Pr B	Small Co	9	7.41		5	3	0.4	1	800 321-7854
Nations Marsico Focused Eq Inv A	Growth	21.8					0.75	1.31	800 321-7854
Nations Marsico Focused Eq Inv B	Growth	20.8					0.75	2.06	800 321-7854
Nations Marsico Focused Eq Inv C	Growth	20.8					0.75	2.06	800 321-7854
Nations Marsico Focused Eq Pr A	Growth	22					0.75	1.06	800 321-7854
Nations Marsico Gr & Inc Inv A	Growth/Inc	24.9					0.75	1.25	800 321-7854
Nations Marsico Gr & Inc Inv B	Growth/Inc	23.9					0.75	2.25	800 321-7854
Nations Marsico Gr & Inc Inv C	Growth/Inc	23.9					0.75	2.25	800 321-7854
Nations Marsico Gr & Inc Pr A	Growth/Inc	25.2					0.75	1.25	800 321-7854
Nations MidCap Growth Fund Inv A	Agg Growth	48.7	24.85	23.08	3	4	0.75	1.28	800 321-7854
Nations MidCap Growth Fund Inv B	Agg Growth	47.7	23.95	22.17	3	4	0.75	1.97	800 321-7854
Nations MidCap Growth Fund Inv C	Agg Growth	47.8	24	22.37	3	4	0.75	1.97	800 321-7854
Nations MidCap Growth Fund Pr A	Agg Growth	49.2	25.18	23.36	3	4	0.75	0.97	800 321-7854
Nations SC Intermed Muni Inv A	Muni State	2.6	3.71	4.52	3	2	0.4	0.69	800 321-7854
Nations SC Intermed Muni Inv B	Muni State	1.8	3.03	3.98	3	2	0.4	1.3	800 321-7854
Nations SC Intermed Muni Inv C	Muni State	1.9	3.03	3.98	3	2	0.4	1.32	800 321-7854
Nations SC Intermed Muni Pr A	Muni State	2.8	3.9	4.71	1	2	0.4	0.5	800 321-7854
Nations SC Muni Bond Inv A	Muni State	2.2	3.77	5.09	2	3	0.5	0.8	800 321-7854
Nations SC Muni Bond Inv B	Muni State	1.5	3.07	4.45	4	3	0.5	1.43	800 321-7854
Nations SC Muni Bond Inv C	Muni State	1.5	3.07	4.51	4	3	0.5	1.43	800 321-7854
Nations SC Muni Bond Pr A	Muni State	2.5	3.99	5.3	1	3	0.5	0.59	800 321-7854
Nations Small Company Fund Inv A	Small Co	68.2	23.56		3	4	0.9	1.19	800 321-7854
Nations Small Company Fund Inv B	Small Co	67	22.73		3	4	0.9	1.94	800 321-7854
Nations Small Company Fund Inv C	Small Co	67	22.88		2	4	0.9	2.1	800 321-7854
Nations Small Company Fund Pr A	Small Co	68.6	23.88		3	4	0.9	0.94	800 321-7854
Nations Value Fund Inv A	Growth/Inc	-11.3	6.8	13.89	2	2	0.65	0.95	800 321-7854
Nations Value Fund Inv B	Growth/Inc	-12.3	5.84	13.04	4	2	0.65	1.93	800 321-7854
Nations Value Fund Inv C	Growth/Inc	-12.2	6.05	13.66	4	2	0.65	1.69	800 321-7854
Nations Value Fund Pr A	Growth/Inc	-11.1	7.04	14.14	2	2	0.65	0.93	800 321-7854
Nationwide Fund A	Growth/Inc	-4.4					0.56	0.93	800 848-0920
Nationwide Fund B	Growth/Inc	-5.1					0.56	1.68	800 848-0920
Nationwide Fund D	Growth/Inc	-4.1	15.02	22.1	3	3	0.56	0.72	800 848-0920
Nationwide Growth A	Growth	0.5					0.56	1.02	800 848-0920
Nationwide Growth B	Growth	-0.3					0.56	1.77	800 848-0920
Nationwide Growth D	Growth	1.1	13.58	17.05	3	3	0.56	0.8	800 848-0920
Nationwide Mid-Cap Growth A	Growth	45.6					0.59	1.25	800 848-0920
Nationwide Mid-Cap Growth B	Growth	45.4					0.59	2	800 848-0920
Nationwide Mid-Cap Growth D	Growth	46.5	25.76	21.97	3	4	0.59	1.25	800 848-0920
Navellier Aggressive Growth	Agg Growth	27.6	24.35		3	4	0.83	1.48	800 887-8671
Navellier Aggressive Micro Cap	Small Co	68.1	26.74		3	4	0.83	1.48	800 887-8671
Navellier Aggressive Small Cap Eq	Small Co	16.2	12.65	14.4	4	4	0.83	1.48	800 887-8671
Navellier International Equity	Foreign	9.3					1	1.75	800 887-8671
Navellier Large-Cap Growth	Growth	61.6					0.83	1.48	800 887-8671
Navellier Large-Cap Value	Growth	-13.9					0.75	1.39	800 887-8671
Navellier Mid Cap Growth	Growth	56.5	43.66		1	5	0.83	1.48	800 887-8671
Navellier Small-Cap Value	Small Co	6.7					0.83	1.48	800 887-8671
Neuberger Berman AMT Balanced	Balanced	44.2	21.06	17.61	3	3	0.29	1.05	800 877-9700
Neuberger Berman AMT Growth Port	Growth	66.8	29.77	24.81	3	4	0.29	0.9	800 877-9700
Neuberger Berman AMT Guardian Port	Growth	6.4					0.84	1	800 877-9700

Stock Fund Name	Objective	Annualized Return for			Rank		Max Load	Expense Ratio	Toll-Free Telephone
		1 Year	3 Years	5 Years	Overall	Risk			
Neuberger Berman AMT Midcap Growth	Growth	63.6					0.29	1.01	800 877-9700
Neuberger Berman Focus Assets	Growth	17.2	19.04		3	4	0.75	1.5	800 877-9700
Neuberger Berman Focus Fd	Growth	17.7	17.91	19.87	3	4	0.75	0.85	800 877-9700
Neuberger Berman Focus Tr	Growth	17.5	17.84	19.81	3	4	0.75	0.84	800 877-9700
Neuberger Berman Genesis Assets	Small Co	15.3	8.39		4	3	0.84	1.5	800 877-9700
Neuberger Berman Genesis Fd	Small Co	15.6	8.67	17.01	3	3	0.96	1.16	800 877-9700
Neuberger Berman Genesis Tr	Small Co	15.6	8.63	16.98	3	3	1.07	1.22	800 877-9700
Neuberger Berman Guardian Assets	Growth/Inc	-4.8	4.84		5	4	0.83	1.5	800 877-9700
Neuberger Berman Guardian Fd	Growth/Inc	-4.2	5.57	11.13	5	4	0.69	0.81	800 877-9700
Neuberger Berman Guardian Tr	Growth/Inc	-4.2	5.5	11.05	5	4	0.69	0.88	800 877-9700
Neuberger Berman International	Foreign	33.6	13.14	16.48	3	4	1.11	1.61	800 877-9700
Neuberger Berman International Tr	Foreign	33.3					1.11	1.69	800 877-9700
Neuberger Berman Manhattan Assets	Agg Growth	64.8	29.08		2	4	0.79	1.5	800 877-9700
Neuberger Berman Manhattan Fd	Agg Growth	66.4	30.02	24.99	3	4	0.79	0.94	800 877-9700
Neuberger Berman Manhattan Tr	Agg Growth	66.5	29.57	24.72	3	4	0.79	1.14	800 877-9700
Neuberger Berman Millenium Fund	Growth	94.2					1.11	1.75	800 877-9700
Neuberger Berman Millenium Tr	Growth	85.2					1.25	1.75	800 877-9700
Neuberger Berman Partners Assets	Growth	-5.7	7.59		4	3	0.7	1.31	800 877-9700
Neuberger Berman Partners Fd	Growth	-5.3	8.19	16.01	4	3	0.7	0.84	800 877-9700
Neuberger Berman Partners Tr	Growth	-5.4	8.2	16.03	4	3	0.7	0.92	800 877-9700
Neuberger Berman Soc Resp Trust	Growth	-8.5	10.41		3	3	0.94	1.29	800 877-9700
Neuberger Berman Socially Resp	Growth	-8.3	8.87	15.43	4	3	0.8	1.16	800 877-9700
New Alternatives Fund	Other	28.7	10.3	11.44	4	3	0.78	1.12	800 423-8383
New Century Balanced	Balanced	12.2	13.12	14.33	3	1	1	1.45	888 639-0102
New Century Capital	Growth	21.2	20.98	21.13	1	3	0.97	1.45	888 639-0102
New Covenant Balance Growth Fund	Growth/Inc	4.5					0.2		800 858-6127
New Covenant Balance Income Fund	Growth/Inc	3.4					0.2		800 858-6127
New Covenant Growth Fund	Growth	7.2					0.98		800 858-6127
New Covenant Income Fund	Income	0.6					0.75		800 858-6127
New Economy Fund (The)	Growth	24.7	28.5	24.6	1	3	0.41	0.8	800 421-9900
New Perspective Fund	Global	29.9	23.61	22	1	2	0.4	0.77	800 421-9900
New York Equity Fund	Growth	37.9	26.87		1	3	0	1.96	888 899-8344
Newport Asia Pacific Fund A	Pacific	36.2					1.25		800 345-6611
Newport Asia Pacific Fund B	Pacific	35.4					1.25		800 345-6611
Newport Asia Pacific Fund C	Pacific	35.2					1.25		800 345-6611
Nicholas Equity Income Fund	Growth/Inc	-11.9	0.5	6.9	5	2	0.5	0.9	800 227-5987
Nicholas Fund	Growth	-18.4	3.62	13.16	4	3	0.75	0.72	800 227-5987
Nicholas II Fund	Small Co	3.3	9.87	15.96	4	3	0.52	0.6	800 227-5987
Nicholas Limited Edition	Small Co	3.2	6.45	14.29	4	3	0.75	0.86	800 227-5987
Nicholas-Applegate Emer Cos I	Foreign	21.5	4.21	12.85	4	4	1.25	1.96	800 551-8043
Nicholas-Applegate Glb Blue Chip I	Global	76.1					0.8	3.14	800 551-8043
Nicholas-Applegate Glb Gr & Inc I	Global	35.7	30.44		2	4	1	4.37	800 551-8043
Nicholas-Applegate Glbl Tech I	Technology	169					1	4.12	800 551-8043
Nicholas-Applegate Gr Equity A	Growth	80.1	40.71	30.79	3	5	0.94	1.39	800 551-8043
Nicholas-Applegate Gr Equity B	Growth	78.6	39.59	29.71	3	5	0.94	2.18	800 551-8043
Nicholas-Applegate Gr Equity C	Growth	78.6	39.59	29.71	3	5	0.94	2.18	800 551-8043
Nicholas-Applegate Int Sm Cap Gr I	Foreign	95.2	46.61	36.29	1	4	1	1.35	800 551-8043
Nicholas-Applegate Intl Core Gr I	Foreign	37.7	22.55		2	4	1	1.39	800 551-8043
Nicholas-Applegate Large Cap Gr I	Growth	60.4	58.29		1	4	1	1.62	800 551-8043
Nicholas-Applegate Latin Amer I	Foreign	42.2					1.25	1.63	800 551-8043
Nicholas-Applegate Mid Cap Gr I	Growth	81.8	41.87	31.97	2	5	0.75	1.04	800 551-8043
Nicholas-Applegate Mini-Cap Gr I	Small Co	104.4	39.63		3	5	1.25	1.59	800 551-8043
Nicholas-Applegate Pacific Rim I	Pacific	44.8					1	1.57	800 551-8043
Nicholas-Applegate Small Cap Gr I	Small Co	62	31.08	26.4	3	5	1	1.25	800 551-8043
Nicholas-Applegate Value I	Growth/Inc	-8.6	12.12		4	3	1	0.98	800 551-8043
Nicholas-Applegate Worldwide Gr I	Global	46.2	36.52	30.37	1	4	1	1.34	800 551-8043
Noah Fund	Growth	18.1	27.94		2	4	1	2.14	
Nomura Pacific Basin Fund	Pacific	21.2	1.17	4.74	4	4	0.75	2.18	800 833-0018

349

Stock Fund Name	Objective	Annualized Return for			Rank		Max Load	Expense Ratio	Toll-Free Telephone
		1 Year	3 Years	5 Years	Overall	Risk			
North American Balanced A	Balanced	0.1	6.37	10.05	3	1	0.77	1.38	800 872-8037
North American Balanced B	Balanced	-0.4	5.71	9.35	3	1	0.77	2.04	800 872-8037
North American Balanced C	Balanced	-0.4	5.72	9.36	3	1	0.77	2.04	800 872-8037
North American Equity Inc A	Income	-15.1	2.55	9.33	4	2	0.8	1.41	800 872-8037
North American Equity Inc B	Income	-15.6	1.89	8.62	3	2	0.8	2.06	800 872-8037
North American Equity Inc C	Income	-15.6	1.91	8.64	4	2	0.75	2.06	800 872-8037
North American Global Equity A	Global	-16	0.42	6.8	5	3	0.9	1.75	800 872-8037
North American Global Equity B	Global	-16.4	0.01	6.28	5	3	0.9	2.39	800 872-8037
North American Global Equity C	Global	-16.5	0	6.27	4	3	0.9	2.39	800 872-8037
North American Gr & Income A	Growth/Inc	4.8	17.58	21.54	2	3	0.72	1.34	800 872-8037
North American Gr & Income B	Growth/Inc	4.1	16.78	20.74	3	3	0.72	1.98	800 872-8037
North American Gr & Income C	Growth/Inc	4.1	16.8	20.74	3	3	0.72	1.98	800 872-8037
North American Growth Equity A	Growth	18.4	20.6		2	3	0.9	1.64	800 872-8037
North American Growth Equity B	Growth	17.5	19.78		2	3	0.9	2.29	800 872-8037
North American Growth Equity C	Growth	17.6	19.78		2	3	0.9	2.29	800 872-8037
North American Int Sm Cap A	Foreign	63.1	22.31		3	5	1.05	1.89	800 872-8037
North American Int Sm Cap B	Foreign	61.7	21.4		3	5	1.05	2.54	800 872-8037
North American Int Sm Cap C	Foreign	62.2	21.58		3	5	1.05	2.54	800 872-8037
North American Intl Equity A	Foreign	12.7	6.36	9.32	5	3	0.9	1.75	800 872-8037
North American Intl Equity B	Foreign	11.9	5.62	8.62	5	3	0.9	2.39	800 872-8037
North American Intl Equity C	Foreign	12	5.61	10.36	4	3	0.9	2.39	800 872-8037
North American Sm/Midcap A	Growth	25.7	25.21		3	4	0.93	1.66	800 872-8037
North American Sm/Midcap B	Growth	24.8	24.26		3	4	0.93	2.31	800 872-8037
North American Sm/Midcap C	Growth	24.8	24.26		3	4	0.93	2.33	800 872-8037
North American Small Cap Growth A	Growth	72.4					0.94	1.69	800 872-8037
North American Small Cap Growth B	Growth	70.1					0.94	2.35	800 872-8037
North American Small Cap Growth C	Growth	70					0.94	2.35	800 872-8037
North American Tax Sensitive Eq A	Growth	-2.3					0.84	1.6	800 872-8037
North American Tax Sensitive Eq B	Growth	-3.4					0.84	2.25	800 872-8037
North American Tax Sensitive Eq C	Growth	-3.6					0.84	2.25	800 872-8037
Northeast Investors Growth	Growth	17.6	25.42	27.48	2	3	0.67	0.84	800 225-6704
Northern FL Interm Tax Exempt Bond	Muni State	3	4.02		2	2	0.69	0.84	800 595-9111
Northern Growth Equity Fund	Growth	16.4	23.84	24.24	1	3	0.84	1	800 595-9111
Northern Income Equity Fund	Income	9.3	12.18	14.94	3	1	0.84	1.34	800 595-9111
Northern Instl Balanced A	Balanced	11.3	15.64	16.05	2	1	0.8	0.6	800 595-9111
Northern Instl Balanced C	Balanced	11	15.18		2	1	0.5	0.84	800 595-9111
Northern Instl Balanced D	Balanced	10.9	14.99		2	1	0.5	1	800 595-9111
Northern Instl Diversified Gr A	Growth	17.7	24.33	24.96	1	3	0.8	0.66	800 595-9111
Northern Instl Diversified Gr D	Growth	15.8	23.31	24.16	1	3	0.55	1.05	800 595-9111
Northern Instl Equity Index A	Growth/Inc	6.7	19.07	23.3	2	3	0.29	0.2	800 595-9111
Northern Instl Equity Index C	Growth/Inc	6.5	18.87		2	3	0.1	0.45	800 595-9111
Northern Instl Equity Index D	Growth/Inc	6.4	18.74	22.98	3	3	0.1	0.59	800 595-9111
Northern Instl Focused Growth A	Growth	25.9	29.54	27.03	1	3	1.1	0.91	800 595-9111
Northern Instl Focused Growth C	Growth	25.7	29.24		1	3	0.8	1.14	800 595-9111
Northern Instl Focused Growth D	Growth	25.5	29.07	26.62	1	3	0.8	1.3	800 595-9111
Northern Instl Int'l Bond A	Intl Bond	-0.6	0.95	2.1	5	5	0.9	0.95	800 595-9111
Northern Instl Int'l Equity Idx A	Foreign	16.3	8.84		3	2	0.5	0.52	800 595-9111
Northern Instl Int'l Growth A	Foreign	21.3	16.7	14.38	3	2	1	1.06	800 595-9111
Northern Instl Intl Bond Fund D	Intl Bond	-2.9	-0.7		4	5	0.69	1.35	800 595-9111
Northern Instl Intl Growth Fund D	Foreign	22.8	16.36	13.99	2	2	0.8	1.44	800 595-9111
Northern Instl Sm Company Index C	Small Co	-0.2					0.2	0.59	800 595-9111
Northern Instl Small Co. Idx A	Small Co	13.6	9.88	13.68	4	4	0.4	0.35	800 595-9111
Northern Instl Small Co. Idx D	Small Co	12.9	11.06	14.31	4	4	0.2	0.75	800 595-9111
Northern Intl Growth Equity	Foreign	20.1	16.06	14.06	3	2	1	1.25	800 595-9111
Northern Intl Select Equity	Foreign	21.7	15.63	12.69	3	2	1	1.25	800 595-9111
Northern Mid Cap Growth Fund	Growth	73					0.84	1.34	800 595-9111
Northern Select Equity Fund	Agg Growth	37.5	31.9	30.1	1	4	1.19	1	800 595-9111
Northern Small Cap Growth Fund	Small Co						1.19		800 595-9111

350

Stock Fund Name	Objective	Annualized Return for			Rank		Max Load	Expense Ratio	Toll-Free Telephone
		1 Year	3 Years	5 Years	Overall	Risk			
Northern Small Cap Index Fund	Small Co						0.65		800 595-9111
Northern Stock Index Fund	Growth	7.6	19.36		3	3	0.4	0.55	800 595-9111
Northern Technology Fund	Technology	87.5	68.48		1	5	1	1.22	800 595-9111
Numeric Investors Small Cap Value	Small Co	-4.3					0.75		800 686-3742
Nuveen Dividend & Growth Fund A	Growth/Inc	-2.8	7.78	9.58	3	1	0.75	1.34	800 621-7227
Nuveen Dividend & Growth Fund C	Growth/Inc	-3.4	7.07	8.89	3	1	0.75	1.98	800 621-7227
Nuveen European Value A	Foreign	17.2					0.94	1.55	800 621-7227
Nuveen European Value B	Foreign	16.3					0.94	2.29	800 621-7227
Nuveen European Value C	Foreign	16.3					0.94	2.29	800 621-7227
Nuveen European Value R	Foreign	17.4					0.94	1.3	800 621-7227
Nuveen Rittenhouse Growth Fund A	Growth	14.9					0.83	1.27	800 621-7227
Nuveen Rittenhouse Growth Fund B	Growth	14					0.83	2	800 621-7227
Nuveen Rittenhouse Growth Fund C	Growth	14					0.83	2	800 621-7227
Nuveen Rittenhouse Growth Fund R	Growth	15.1					0.83	1.03	800 621-7227
Nuveen-Flagship FL Muni Bond A	Muni State	1.1	3.7	4.76	2	3	0.54	0.83	800 621-7227
Nuveen-Flagship FL Muni Bond C	Muni State	0.5	3.11	4.71	3	3	0.54	1.38	800 621-7227
Nuveen-Flagship FL Muni Bond R	Muni State	1.1	3.83	4.98	1	3	0.54	0.64	800 621-7227
Nvest Balanced Fund A	Balanced	-13	1.56	7.85	4	1	0.72	1.34	800 225-5478
Nvest Balanced Fund B	Balanced	-13.7	0.78	7.04	4	1	0.72	2.08	800 225-5478
Nvest Balanced Fund C	Balanced	-13.7	0.67	6.15	4	1	0.72	2.08	800 225-5478
Nvest Balanced Fund Y	Balanced	-12.7	1.96	8.3	4	1	0.72	0.93	800 225-5478
Nvest Bullseye Fund A	Agg Growth	24.9					0.94	1.75	800 225-5478
Nvest Bullseye Fund B	Agg Growth	23.9					0.94	2.5	800 225-5478
Nvest Bullseye Fund C	Agg Growth	23.9					0.94	2.5	800 225-5478
Nvest Capital Growth A	Growth	22.2	21.19	20.17	2	3	0.73	1.38	800 225-5478
Nvest Capital Growth B	Growth	21.3	20.2	19.21	2	3	0.73	2.16	800 225-5478
Nvest Capital Growth C	Growth	21.5	20.27	19.25	2	3	0.73	2.16	800 225-5478
Nvest Equity Income Fund A	Income	-9.4	2.44		5	3	0.69	1.5	800 225-5478
Nvest Growth & Income A	Growth/Inc	-5.5	13.2	18.26	3	2	0.68	1.22	800 225-5478
Nvest Growth & Income B	Growth/Inc	-6.2	12.34		3	2	0.69	1.97	800 225-5478
Nvest Growth & Income C	Growth/Inc	-6.2	12.27	17.29	3	2	0.69	1.97	800 225-5478
Nvest Growth Fund A	Growth	3.2	14.56	18.53	3	3	0.67	1.12	800 225-5478
Nvest Intl Equity A	Foreign	60	16.19	11.88	4	4	0.9	2	800 225-5478
Nvest Intl Equity B	Foreign	58.7	15.34	11.07	4	4	0.84	2.75	800 225-5478
Nvest Intl Equity C	Foreign	58.8	15.37	11.11	4	4	0.84	2.75	800 225-5478
Nvest Intl Equity Y	Foreign	60.6	16.86	12.66	4	4	0.84	1.39	800 225-5478
Nvest Kobrick Capital Fund A	Growth	24.2					1	1.75	
Nvest Kobrick Emerging Growth A	Small Co	39.3					1	1.75	
Nvest Kobrick Growth Fund A	Growth						1	1.39	
Nvest Star Advisers A	Growth	19.9	21.68	22.51	1	3	1.04	1.62	800 225-5478
Nvest Star Advisers B	Growth	19.1	20.77	21.61	2	3	1.04	2.39	800 225-5478
Nvest Star Advisers C	Growth	19	20.77	21.62	2	3	1.04	2.39	800 225-5478
Nvest Star Advisers Y	Growth	20.3	22	22.91	2	3	1.04	1.39	800 225-5478
Nvest Star Small Cap A	Small Co	50.2	26.76		1	4	1.05	2.12	800 225-5478
Nvest Star Small Cap B	Small Co	49.1	25.8		3	4	1.05	2.87	800 225-5478
Nvest Star Small Cap C	Small Co	49	25.78		3	4	1.05	2.87	800 225-5478
Nvest Star Value Fund A	Growth/Inc	-16.4	0.36	9.88	5	3	0.71	1.33	800 225-5478
Nvest Star Value Fund B	Growth/Inc	-17	-0.36	9.1	5	3	0.72	2.08	800 225-5478
Nvest Star Value Fund C	Growth/Inc	-17.1	-0.38	9.1	5	3	1.5	2.08	800 225-5478
Nvest Star Value Fund Y	Growth/Inc	-16.1	0.65	10.2	5	3	0.72	1.08	800 225-5478
Nvest Star Worldwide A	Global	11.4	8.95		4	3	1.05	2.58	800 225-5478
Nvest Star Worldwide B	Global	10.6	8.16		4	3	1.05	2.83	800 225-5478
Nvest Star Worldwide C	Global	10.6	8.18		4	3	1.05	2.83	800 225-5478
O'Shaughnessy Cornerstone Growth	Growth	41.9	20.71		3	4	0.73	1.97	877 673-8637
O'Shaughnessy Cornerstone Value	Growth/Inc	-14.4	4.33		4	3	0.73	1.15	877 673-8637
O.R.I. Funds-Small Cap Equity A	Small Co	40.2	14.32	18.67	3	4	0.75	2	800 407-7298
O.R.I. Funds-Small Cap Equity C	Small Co	39.2	10.97		3	4	0.75	2.7	800 407-7298
OVB Capital Appreciation A	Growth	30	30.49	26.3	2	4	0.94	1.02	800 545-6331

Stock Fund Name	Objective	Annualized Return for			Rank		Max Load	Expense Ratio	Toll-Free Telephone
		1 Year	3 Years	5 Years	Overall	Risk			
OVB Capital Appreciation B	Growth	29.7	30.09	25.96	2	4	0.94	1.27	800 545-6331
Oak Ridge Large Cap Equity A	Growth	95.5					0.59	2	800 407-7298
Oak Ridge Large Cap Equity C	Growth	91.2					0.59		800 407-7298
Oak Value Fund	Growth	-7.9	9.78	18.97	3	3	0.9	1.1	800 680-4199
Oakmark Equity & Income Fd	Balanced	2.3	12.03		2	1	0.75	1.17	800 625-6275
Oakmark Fund (The)	Growth	-24.7	-1.35	9.15	5	3	0.93	1.21	800 625-6275
Oakmark International Fund	Foreign	8.3	7.06	13.56	4	3	1	1.29	800 625-6275
Oakmark Intl Small Cap Fund	Foreign	1.4	5.61		5	4	1.2	1.79	800 625-6275
Oakmark Select	Growth	-0.6	19.7		2	4	0.97	1.17	800 625-6275
Oakmark Small Cap	Small Co	-12.5	-3.38		5	3	1.25	1.47	800 625-6275
Oberweis Emerging Growth Portfolio	Small Co	56.6	16.74	16.7	3	5	0.81	1.59	800 245-7311
Oberweis Micro Cap Portfolio	Small Co	28	12.05		4	5	1	2	800 245-7311
Oberweis Mid Cap Growth Portfolio	Small Co	107.8	47.73		2	5	0.8	2	800 245-7311
Old Dominion Investors Trust	Growth/Inc	-14.4	3.23	10.56	4	3	0.5	1.08	800 441-6580
Olstein Financial Alert C	Growth	13.9	25.55		1	3	1	2.37	800 799-2113
One Group-Balanced A	AssetAlloc	5.5	13.01	14.65	3	1	0.55	1.1	800 480-4111
One Group-Balanced B	AssetAlloc	4.7	12.2	11.82	3	1	0.55	1.85	800 480-4111
One Group-Balanced I	AssetAlloc	5.7	13.33	14.95	2	1	0.55	0.84	800 480-4111
One Group-Diversified Equity A	Growth/Inc	5	18.57	21.54	2	3	0.75	1.18	800 480-4111
One Group-Diversified Equity B	Growth/Inc	-14.5	17.7	20.63	3	4	0.75	1.95	800 480-4111
One Group-Diversified Equity C	Growth/Inc	4.3					0.75	1.95	800 480-4111
One Group-Diversified Equity I	Growth/Inc	5.2	18.88		2	3	0.75	0.94	800 480-4111
One Group-Diversified Intl A	Foreign	20.7	12.78	12.38	3	3	0.8	1.29	800 480-4111
One Group-Diversified Intl B	Foreign	19.9	12.06		3	3	0.8	2.04	800 480-4111
One Group-Diversified Intl C	Foreign	19.8					0.8	2	800 480-4111
One Group-Diversified Intl I	Foreign	21.1	13.07	12.94	3	3	0.8	1.06	800 480-4111
One Group-Diversified Mid Cap A	Growth	13.7	12.82	16.74	3	3	0.73	1.11	800 480-4111
One Group-Diversified Mid Cap B	Growth	13	12.2		3	3	0.73	1.87	800 480-4111
One Group-Diversified Mid Cap C	Growth	12.8					0.73	1.87	800 480-4111
One Group-Diversified Mid Cap I	Growth	14	13.1	17.01	3	3	0.73	0.9	800 480-4111
One Group-Equity Income A	Income	-8.6	7.62	15.1	3	2	0.66	1.17	800 480-4111
One Group-Equity Income B	Income	-9.2	6.82	14.28	3	2	0.66	1.92	800 480-4111
One Group-Equity Income C	Income	-9.1					0.66	1.93	800 480-4111
One Group-Equity Income I	Income	-8.3	7.91	15.41	3	2	0.66	0.85	800 480-4111
One Group-Equity Index A	Growth/Inc	6.6	18.99	23.08	2	3	0.14	0.59	800 480-4111
One Group-Equity Index B	Growth/Inc	5.8	18.14	21.34	3	3	0.14	1.35	800 480-4111
One Group-Equity Index C	Growth/Inc	5.8					0.14	1.35	800 480-4111
One Group-Equity Index I	Growth/Inc	6.9	19.31	23.4	2	3	0.14	0.59	800 480-4111
One Group-Intl Equity Index A	Foreign	17.6	12.65	12.68	4	3	0.55	1.1	800 480-4111
One Group-Intl Equity Index B	Foreign	17	11.81	11.74	3	3	0.55	1.83	800 480-4111
One Group-Intl Equity Index C	Foreign	16.9					0.55	1.86	800 480-4111
One Group-Intl Equity Index I	Foreign	18.1	12.81	12.84	4	3	0.55	0.84	800 480-4111
One Group-Investor Balanced A	Balanced	6.4	11.16		3	1	0.05	0.45	800 480-4111
One Group-Investor Balanced B	Balanced	5.7	10.43		3	1	0.05	1.19	800 480-4111
One Group-Investor Balanced C	Balanced	5.7					0.05	1.19	800 480-4111
One Group-Investor Balanced I	Balanced	6.8	11.57		3	1	0.05	0.2	800 480-4111
One Group-Investor Conserv Gr A	Growth/Inc	4.3	7.75		3	1	0.05	0.45	800 480-4111
One Group-Investor Conserv Gr B	Growth/Inc	3.5	6.98		3	1	0.05	1.19	800 480-4111
One Group-Investor Conserv Gr C	Growth/Inc	3.5					0.05	1.19	800 480-4111
One Group-Investor Conserv Gr I	Growth/Inc	4.5	8.02		3	1	0.05	0.2	800 480-4111
One Group-Investor Gr & Inc A	Growth/Inc	8	13.8		3	1	0.05	0.45	800 480-4111
One Group-Investor Gr & Inc B	Growth/Inc	7.1	12.95		3	1	0.05	1.19	800 480-4111
One Group-Investor Gr & Inc C	Growth/Inc	7.2					0.05	1.19	800 480-4111
One Group-Investor Gr & Inc I	Growth/Inc	8.3	14.15		3	1	0.05	0.2	800 480-4111
One Group-Investor Growth A	Growth	10.1	16.49		2	2	0.05	0.45	800 480-4111
One Group-Investor Growth B	Growth	9.2	15.65		3	2	0.05	1.19	800 480-4111
One Group-Investor Growth C	Growth	9.2					0.05	1.19	800 480-4111
One Group-Investor Growth I	Growth	10.2	16.83		2	2	0.05	0.2	800 480-4111

Stock Fund Name	Objective	Annualized Return for			Rank		Max Load	Expense Ratio	Toll-Free Telephone
		1 Year	3 Years	5 Years	Overall	Risk			
One Group-Large Cap Growth A	Growth	15	25.98	25.37	2	3	0.68	1.17	800 480-4111
One Group-Large Cap Growth B	Growth	14.2	25.07	24.58	2	3	0.68	1.95	800 480-4111
One Group-Large Cap Growth C	Growth	14.2					0.68	1.94	800 480-4111
One Group-Large Cap Growth I	Growth	15.3	26.32	25.78	2	3	0.68	0.95	800 480-4111
One Group-Large Cap Value A	Growth	-5.9	9.8	13.62	3	3	0.73	1.19	800 480-4111
One Group-Large Cap Value B	Growth	-6.5	9.01	12.82	3	3	0.73	1.94	800 480-4111
One Group-Large Cap Value C	Growth	-6.6					0.73	1.94	800 480-4111
One Group-Large Cap Value I	Growth	-5.6	10.37	14.01	3	3	0.73	0.95	800 480-4111
One Group-Market Expansion Index A	Small Co	13.9					0.14	0.84	800 480-4111
One Group-Market Expansion Index B	Small Co	13.1					0.14	1.6	800 480-4111
One Group-Market Expansion Index C	Small Co	13.1					0.14	1.58	800 480-4111
One Group-Market Expansion Index I	Small Co	14.3					0.14	0.56	800 480-4111
One Group-Mid Cap Growth A	Small Co	36.3	31.64	28.28	2	4	0.73	1.23	800 480-4111
One Group-Mid Cap Growth B	Small Co	35.2	30.61	27.44	2	4	0.73	1.98	800 480-4111
One Group-Mid Cap Growth C	Small Co	35.5					0.73	1.98	800 480-4111
One Group-Mid Cap Growth I	Small Co	36.6	32	28.61	2	4	0.73	2	800 480-4111
One Group-Mid Cap Value A	Growth	0.1	9.91	13.84	3	3	0.73	1.2	800 480-4111
One Group-Mid Cap Value B	Growth	-0.6	9.07	12.95	3	3	0.73	1.94	800 480-4111
One Group-Mid Cap Value C	Growth	-0.4					0.73	1.94	800 480-4111
One Group-Mid Cap Value I	Growth	0.4	10.19	14.07	3	3	0.73	0.96	800 480-4111
One Group-Small Cap Growth A	Growth	31.3	17.32	17.24	3	4	0.73	1.31	800 480-4111
One Group-Small Cap Growth B	Growth	30.6	16.29	16.28	3	4	0.73	2.06	800 480-4111
One Group-Small Cap Growth C	Growth	31.2					0.73	2.06	800 480-4111
One Group-Small Cap Growth I	Growth	32	17.51	17.45	3	4	0.73	1.06	800 480-4111
One Group-Small Cap Value A	Small Co	-3.1	0.04	10.96	4	3	0.73	1.16	800 480-4111
One Group-Small Cap Value B	Small Co	-3.8	-0.65	10.28	4	3	0.73	1.93	800 480-4111
One Group-Small Cap Value C	Small Co	-3.6					0.73	1.93	800 480-4111
One Group-Small Cap Value I	Small Co	-2.8	0.31	11.41	4	3	0.73	0.93	800 480-4111
Oppenheimer Capital Appr Fd A	Agg Growth	34.2	28.91	28.12	1	3	0.69	1.06	800 525-7048
Oppenheimer Capital Appr Fd B	Agg Growth	33.2	27.89		1	3	0.75	1.85	800 525-7048
Oppenheimer Capital Appr Fd C	Agg Growth	33.1	27.88	27.13	1	3	0.73	1.85	800 525-7048
Oppenheimer Capital Appr Fd Y	Agg Growth	34.8					0.68	0.69	800 525-7048
Oppenheimer Capital Income Fd A	Income	-7	6.82	13.04	3	2	0.52	0.86	800 525-7048
Oppenheimer Capital Income Fd B	Income	-7.7	5.97	12.12	3	2	0.52	1.76	800 525-7048
Oppenheimer Capital Income Fd C	Income	-7.7	5.96		3	2	0.52	1.66	800 525-7048
Oppenheimer Developing Mkts A	Foreign	53.2	11.77		3	4	1	2.35	800 525-7048
Oppenheimer Developing Mkts B	Foreign	52.2	10.95		3	4	1	3.2	800 525-7048
Oppenheimer Developing Mkts C	Foreign	52.1	10.93		3	4	1	3.2	800 525-7048
Oppenheimer Disciplined Alloc Fd A	AssetAlloc	-2.7	5.69	9.13	3	1	0.61	1.04	800 525-7048
Oppenheimer Disciplined Alloc Fd B	AssetAlloc	-3.4	4.88		4	1	0.61	1.83	800 525-7048
Oppenheimer Disciplined Alloc Fd C	AssetAlloc	-3.4	4.89		3	1	0.61	1.83	800 525-7048
Oppenheimer Disciplined Value A	Growth	-8.5	3.6	11.59	4	3	0.62	1.04	800 525-7048
Oppenheimer Disciplined Value B	Growth	-9.2	2.83		4	3	0.62	1.8	800 525-7048
Oppenheimer Disciplined Value C	Growth	-9.1	2.84		5	3	0.62	1.8	800 525-7048
Oppenheimer Disciplined Value Y	Growth	-8.2	3.93		5	3	0.62	0.66	800 525-7048
Oppenheimer Discovery Fund A	Small Co	55.4	16.7	17.8	4	5	0.67	1.37	800 525-7048
Oppenheimer Discovery Fund B	Small Co	54.2	15.82	16.91	4	5	0.67	2.12	800 525-7048
Oppenheimer Discovery Fund C	Small Co	54.2	15.85		4	5	0.67	2.12	800 525-7048
Oppenheimer Discovery Fund Y	Small Co	55.9	17.06	18.12	3	5	0.67	1.28	800 525-7048
Oppenheimer Enterprise Fund A	Growth	44.3	42.02		3	5	0.75	1.55	800 525-7048
Oppenheimer Enterprise Fund B	Growth	43.2	40.97		3	5	0.73	2.29	800 525-7048
Oppenheimer Enterprise Fund C	Growth	43.3	41.02		3	5	0.73	2.29	800 525-7048
Oppenheimer Enterprise Fund Y	Growth	45					0.75		800 525-7048
Oppenheimer Europe Fund A	European	10.5					0.8		800 525-7048
Oppenheimer Europe Fund B	European	9.7					0.8		800 525-7048
Oppenheimer Europe Fund C	European	9.8					0.8		800 525-7048
Oppenheimer Europe Fund Y	European	10.8					0.8		800 525-7048
Oppenheimer FL Municipal Fund A	Muni State	-0.3	3.22	4.75	3	3	0.59	0.94	800 525-7048

Stock Fund Name	Objective	Annualized Return for			Rank		Max Load	Expense Ratio	Toll-Free Telephone
		1 Year	3 Years	5 Years	Overall	Risk			
Oppenheimer FL Municipal Fund B	Muni State	-1.1	2.43	3.98	5	3	0.59	1.69	800 525-7048
Oppenheimer FL Municipal Fund C	Muni State	-1.1	2.41		5	3	0.59	1.69	800 525-7048
Oppenheimer Global Fund A	Global	52.6	27	24.59	1	3	0.68	1.15	800 525-7048
Oppenheimer Global Fund B	Global	51.4	26.01	23.61	1	3	0.68	1.97	800 525-7048
Oppenheimer Global Fund C	Global	51.4	26.01		1	3	0.68	1.97	800 525-7048
Oppenheimer Global Gr & Inc Fd A	Global	60.7	37.65	30.57	1	4	0.78	1.33	800 525-7048
Oppenheimer Global Gr & Inc Fd B	Global	59.6	36.62		1	4	0.78	2.14	800 525-7048
Oppenheimer Global Gr & Inc Fd C	Global	59.6	36.61	29.6	1	4	0.78	2.14	800 525-7048
Oppenheimer Gold/Spec Min Fd A	Prec Metal	-8.8	-10.67	-7.56	5	5	0.68	1.43	800 525-7048
Oppenheimer Gold/Spec Min Fd B	Prec Metal	-9.5	-11.35		5	5	0.68	2.41	800 525-7048
Oppenheimer Gold/Spec Min Fd C	Prec Metal	-9.4	-11.33		5	5	0.68	2.39	800 525-7048
Oppenheimer Growth Fund A	Growth	51.6	25.59	25.03	1	3	0.68	1.04	800 525-7048
Oppenheimer Growth Fund B	Growth	50.4	24.58	23.97	2	3	0.75	1.86	800 525-7048
Oppenheimer Growth Fund C	Growth	50.4	24.6		2	3	0.75	1.86	800 525-7048
Oppenheimer Growth Fund Y	Growth	52	25.92	25.23	1	3	0.75	0.81	800 525-7048
Oppenheimer International Gr Fd A	Foreign	59.3	22.53		2	4	0.8	1.55	800 525-7048
Oppenheimer International Gr Fd B	Foreign	58.1	21.59		2	4	0.8	2.29	800 525-7048
Oppenheimer International Gr Fd C	Foreign	58.1	21.58		2	4	0.8	2.31	800 525-7048
Oppenheimer Intl Small Comp Fd A	Foreign	21					0.8	2.04	800 525-7048
Oppenheimer Intl Small Comp Fd B	Foreign	20.1					0.8	3.14	800 525-7048
Oppenheimer Intl Small Comp Fd C	Foreign	20.1					0.8	3.14	800 525-7048
Oppenheimer Large Cap Growth A	Growth	23.8					0.75	1.64	800 525-7048
Oppenheimer Large Cap Growth B	Growth	22.8					0.75	2.75	800 525-7048
Oppenheimer Large Cap Growth C	Growth	22.7					0.75	2.72	800 525-7048
Oppenheimer Large Cap Growth Y	Growth	24.3					0.75	1.5	800 525-7048
Oppenheimer Main St Gr & Inc Fd A	Growth/Inc	7.5	17.8	19.62	3	3	0.45	0.91	800 525-7048
Oppenheimer Main St Gr & Inc Fd B	Growth/Inc	6.7	16.9	18.71	2	3	0.45	1.62	800 525-7048
Oppenheimer Main St Gr & Inc Fd C	Growth/Inc	6.7	16.91	18.72	3	3	0.45	1.62	800 525-7048
Oppenheimer Main St Gr & Inc Fd Y	Growth/Inc	7.7	18.02		3	3	0.45	0.82	800 525-7048
Oppenheimer Main Street Small Cap A	Small Co						0.75		800 525-7048
Oppenheimer Main Street Small Cap B	Small Co						0.75		800 525-7048
Oppenheimer Main Street Small Cap C	Small Co						0.75		800 525-7048
Oppenheimer Main Street Small Cap Y	Small Co						0.75		800 525-7048
Oppenheimer Midcap Fund A	Growth	87.6					0.73	1.55	800 525-7048
Oppenheimer Midcap Fund B	Growth	86					0.73	2.31	800 525-7048
Oppenheimer Midcap Fund C	Growth	86.2					0.73	2.31	800 525-7048
Oppenheimer Midcap Fund Y	Growth	88.4					0.73	1.06	800 525-7048
Oppenheimer Multiple Strat Fund A	AssetAlloc	8.2	10.55	13.46	3	1	0.7	1.09	800 525-7048
Oppenheimer Multiple Strat Fund B	AssetAlloc	7.3	9.67		3	1	0.7	1.96	800 525-7048
Oppenheimer Multiple Strat Fund C	AssetAlloc	7.2	9.64	12.31	3	1	0.7	1.96	800 525-7048
Oppenheimer Quest Balanced Val A	Growth/Inc	-2.7	19.18	19.01	3	2	0.84	1.51	800 525-7048
Oppenheimer Quest Balanced Val B	Growth/Inc	-3.3	18.48	18.39	3	2	0.84	2.08	800 525-7048
Oppenheimer Quest Balanced Val C	Growth/Inc	-3.3	18.48	18.35	3	2	0.84	2.08	800 525-7048
Oppenheimer Quest Capital Val A	Growth	5.5	13.19		3	3	1	1.7	800 525-7048
Oppenheimer Quest Capital Val B	Growth	4.9	12.53		3	3	1	2.12	800 525-7048
Oppenheimer Quest Capital Val C	Growth	5	12.52		3	3	1	2.12	800 525-7048
Oppenheimer Quest Gbl Val Inc A	Global	9.9	11.29	14.68	3	2	0.73	1.75	800 525-7048
Oppenheimer Quest Gbl Val Inc B	Global	9.3	10.74	14.11	3	2	0.73	2.25	800 525-7048
Oppenheimer Quest Gbl Val Inc C	Global	9.3	10.74	13.96	3	2	0.73	2.25	800 525-7048
Oppenheimer Quest Opporty Val A	Flexible	-4	6.76	13.13	3	2	0.85	1.57	800 525-7048
Oppenheimer Quest Opporty Val B	Flexible	-4.5	6.2	12.55	3	2	0.85	2.1	800 525-7048
Oppenheimer Quest Opporty Val C	Flexible	-4.5	6.21	12.54	3	2	0.85	2.08	800 525-7048
Oppenheimer Quest Opporty Val Y	Flexible	-3.6	7.25		2	2	0.85	1.38	800 525-7048
Oppenheimer Quest Value Fund A	Growth	-12.2	4.75	13.09	4	3	0.9	1.59	800 525-7048
Oppenheimer Quest Value Fund B	Growth	-12.8	4.17	12.48	4	3	0.9	2.14	800 525-7048
Oppenheimer Quest Value Fund C	Growth	-12.8	4.18	12.48	4	3	0.9	2.12	800 525-7048
Oppenheimer Quest Value Fund Y	Growth	-12.1	4.87		4	3	0.9	1.14	800 525-7048
Oppenheimer Real Asset Fund A	AssetAlloc	55.1	-3.07		4	4	1	1.88	800 525-7048

| Stock Fund Name | Objective | Annualized Return for | | | Rank | | Max Load | Expense Ratio | Toll-Free Telephone |
		1 Year	3 Years	5 Years	Overall	Risk			
Oppenheimer Real Asset Fund B	AssetAlloc	53.9	-3.78		4	4	1	2.64	800 525-7048
Oppenheimer Real Asset Fund C	AssetAlloc	53.9	-3.79		4	4	1	2.64	800 525-7048
Oppenheimer Real Asset Fund Y	AssetAlloc	55.3	-2.88		4	4	1	1.79	800 525-7048
Oppenheimer Trinity Core Fund A	Agg Growth						0.75		800 525-7048
Oppenheimer Trinity Core Fund B	Agg Growth						0.75		800 525-7048
Oppenheimer Trinity Core Fund C	Agg Growth						0.75		800 525-7048
Oppenheimer Trinity Core Fund Y	Agg Growth						0.75		800 525-7048
Oppenheimer Trinity Growth Fund A	Growth						0.75		800 525-7048
Oppenheimer Trinity Growth Fund B	Growth						0.75		800 525-7048
Oppenheimer Trinity Growth Fund C	Growth						0.75		800 525-7048
Oppenheimer Trinity Growth Fund Y	Growth						0.75		800 525-7048
Oppenheimer Trinity Value Fund A	Growth						0.75		800 525-7048
Oppenheimer Trinity Value Fund B	Growth						0.75		800 525-7048
Oppenheimer Trinity Value Fund C	Growth						0.75		800 525-7048
Oppenheimer Trinity Value Fund Y	Growth						0.75		800 525-7048
Oppenheimer Ttl Ret Inc Fd A	Flexible	12.7	19.01	20.97	2	2	0.52	0.86	800 525-7048
Oppenheimer Ttl Ret Inc Fd B	Flexible	11.8	18.05	20.07	2	2	0.56	1.68	800 525-7048
Oppenheimer Ttl Ret Inc Fd C	Flexible	11.8	18.02		2	2	0.52	1.68	800 525-7048
Oppenheimer Ttl Ret Inc Fd Y	Flexible	12.8	19.16	21.12	2	2	0.52	0.66	800 525-7048
Orbitex Focus 30 Fd D	Growth/Inc	-2.8	12	18.44	2	3	0.75	3.1	888 672-4839
Osterweis Fund	Growth	31	26.48	23.06	1	3	1	1.6	800 662-4203
PBHG Core Growth Fund	Growth	92.5	34.71		3	5	0.84	1.44	800 433-0051
PBHG Emerging Growth Fund	Small Co	72.3	20.21	19.35	3	5	0.84	1.27	800 433-0051
PBHG Focus Value	Agg Growth	57.5					0.84	0.5	800 433-0051
PBHG Growth Fd	Small Co	103.9	31.05	24.71	3	5	0.84	1.31	800 433-0051
PBHG Growth II Ins	Growth	90.2	38.36		3	5	0.84	1.19	800 433-0051
PBHG International Fund	Foreign	9.4	5.34	9.43	4	3	1	2.04	800 433-0051
PBHG Large Cap 20	Growth	106.5	63.02		1	5	0.84	1.27	800 433-0051
PBHG Large Cap Growth	Growth	89	42.65	37.06	2	4	0.75	1.27	800 433-0051
PBHG Large Cap Growth Ins	Growth	81.9	40.78		1	4	0.84	1.1	800 433-0051
PBHG Large Cap Value	Growth	8.6	20.66		1	3	0.65	1.01	800 433-0051
PBHG Lg Cap Value Port	Growth	-17.9					0.59	0.98	800 433-0051
PBHG Limited Fund	Small Co	87.3	37.76		3	5	1	1.39	800 433-0051
PBHG Mid-Cap Value	Growth	28.2	31.08		2	3	0.84	1.33	800 433-0051
PBHG New Opportunities Fund	Growth	289.3					1	1.5	800 433-0051
PBHG Select Equity	Growth	220.3	62.85	48.54	3	5	0.84	1.34	800 433-0051
PBHG Small Cap Value Fund	Small Co	49.4	23.72		3	3	1	1.47	800 433-0051
PBHG Small Cap Value Port	Small Co	65.6					0.59	1.19	800 433-0051
PBHG Strategic Small Company	Small Co	76.7	30.3		3	4	1	1.5	800 433-0051
PBHG Technology & Comm Fund	Technology	170	71.16		2	5	0.84	1.27	800 433-0051
PBHG Technology & Communication Ins	Technology	165.3	73.39		2	5	0.84	1.09	800 433-0051
PDP Inst'l Gr Stock Port. X	Growth	24.5	24.82	23.5	1	3	0.59	0.69	800 243-4361
PDP Inst'l Gr Stock Port. Y	Growth	24.2	24.5	23.19	1	3	0.59	0.94	800 243-4361
PDP Real Estate Securities A	Real Est	8.8	2.45	11.27	4	2	0.75	1.3	800 243-4361
PDP Real Estate Securities B	Real Est	7.9	1.69	10.44	4	2	0.75	2.04	800 243-4361
PIMCO 30/70 Portfolio A	AssetAlloc	6.8					0.4	0.65	800 426-0107
PIMCO 30/70 Portfolio B	AssetAlloc	6.1					0.4	1.39	800 426-0107
PIMCO 30/70 Portfolio C	AssetAlloc	6.1					0.4	1.39	800 426-0107
PIMCO 60/40 Portfolio A	AssetAlloc	9.2					0.4	0.65	800 426-0107
PIMCO 60/40 Portfolio B	AssetAlloc	8.4					0.4	1.39	800 426-0107
PIMCO 60/40 Portfolio C	AssetAlloc	8.4					0.4	1.39	800 426-0107
PIMCO 90/10 Portfolio A	AssetAlloc	11.5					0.4	0.65	800 426-0107
PIMCO 90/10 Portfolio B	AssetAlloc	10.6					0.4	1.39	800 426-0107
PIMCO 90/10 Portfolio C	AssetAlloc	10.6					0.4	1.39	800 426-0107
PIMCO Capital Appreciation A	Growth	22.7	21.4		1	3	0.45	1.1	800 426-0107
PIMCO Capital Appreciation Admin	Growth	22.5	21.43		1	3	0.45	0.94	800 426-0107
PIMCO Capital Appreciation B	Growth	21.8	20.51		2	3	0.45	1.85	800 426-0107
PIMCO Capital Appreciation C	Growth	21.9	20.52		2	3	0.45	1.85	800 426-0107

355

Stock Fund Name	Objective	Annualized Return for			Rank		Max Load	Expense Ratio	Toll-Free Telephone
		1 Year	3 Years	5 Years	Overall	Risk			
PIMCO Capital Appreciation D	Growth	22.8					0.45		800 426-0107
PIMCO Capital Appreciation Inst	Growth	22.8	21.76	24.23	1	3	0.69	0.7	800 426-0107
PIMCO Core Equity Fund Admin	Growth	12.5	26.08	23.4	3	3	0.56	1.08	800 426-0107
PIMCO Core Equity Fund Inst	Growth	13.1	26.55	23.8	3	3	0.63	1.01	800 426-0107
PIMCO Emerging Markets Bond A	Intl Bond	22.6					0.84	1.25	800 426-0107
PIMCO Emerging Markets Bond B	Intl Bond	21.7					0.84	2	800 426-0107
PIMCO Emerging Markets Bond C	Intl Bond	21.8					0.84	2	800 426-0107
PIMCO Emerging Markets Bond Inst	Intl Bond	23.1					0.84	0.84	800 426-0107
PIMCO Enhanced Equity Fund Admin	Growth	4.5					0.45	0.95	800 426-0107
PIMCO Enhanced Equity Fund Inst	Growth	4.4	17.69	21.33	2	3	0.69	0.7	800 426-0107
PIMCO Equity Income A	Income	-13.8	5.51		5	3	0.45	1.1	800 426-0107
PIMCO Equity Income Admin	Income	-13.5	5.7	12.59	4	3	0.45	0.95	800 426-0107
PIMCO Equity Income B	Income	-14.2	4.79		4	3	0.45	1.85	800 426-0107
PIMCO Equity Income C	Income	-14.2	4.79		4	3	0.45	1.85	800 426-0107
PIMCO Equity Income D	Income	-13.1					0.45		800 426-0107
PIMCO Equity Income Inst	Income	-13.5	5.86	13.59	3	3	0.45	0.72	800 426-0107
PIMCO Foreign Bond Fund A	Intl Bond	4.8	6.28		1	3	0.5	0.94	800 426-0107
PIMCO Foreign Bond Fund Admin	Intl Bond	5	6.53		1	3	0.5	0.75	800 426-0107
PIMCO Foreign Bond Fund B	Intl Bond	4	5.5		2	3	0.5	1.69	800 426-0107
PIMCO Foreign Bond Fund C	Intl Bond	4	5.53		2	3	0.5	1.69	800 426-0107
PIMCO Foreign Bond Fund D	Intl Bond	4.8					0.5	0.94	800 426-0107
PIMCO Foreign Bond Fund Inst	Intl Bond	5.3	6.79	11.32	1	3	0.5	0.5	800 426-0107
PIMCO Growth Fund A	Growth	32.5	30.39	26.05	2	4	0.5	1.15	800 426-0107
PIMCO Growth Fund Admin	Growth	31.9					0.5	0.96	800 426-0107
PIMCO Growth Fund B	Growth	31.3	29.33	25.06	2	4	0.5	1.89	800 426-0107
PIMCO Growth Fund C	Growth	31.3	29.35	25.07	2	4	0.5	1.89	800 426-0107
PIMCO Growth Fund I	Growth	32.7					0.5	0.73	800 426-0107
PIMCO Innovation Fund A	Technology	115	72.56	48.51	1	5	0.65	1.3	800 426-0107
PIMCO Innovation Fund B	Technology	114.2	71.46	47.5	1	5	0.65	2.04	800 426-0107
PIMCO Innovation Fund C	Technology	114.2	71.48	47.49	1	5	0.65	2.04	800 426-0107
PIMCO Innovation Fund D	Technology	115.9					0.65		800 426-0107
PIMCO Innovation Fund I	Technology	115.3					0.65	0.88	800 426-0107
PIMCO International Fund A	Foreign	11.9	5.57	8.32	5	3	0.55	1.55	800 426-0107
PIMCO International Fund Admin	Foreign	10.8					0.55	1.34	800 426-0107
PIMCO International Fund B	Foreign	10	4.43	7.3	5	3	0.55	2.29	800 426-0107
PIMCO International Fund C	Foreign	9.9	4.41	7.29	5	3	0.55	2.29	800 426-0107
PIMCO International Fund Instl	Foreign	11.1					0.55	1.09	800 426-0107
PIMCO Intl Growth Instl	Foreign	56.3					0.5	1.38	800 426-0107
PIMCO Micro Cap Gr Fund Admin	Small Co	25.3	13.41		4	4	1.25	1.75	800 426-0107
PIMCO Micro Cap Gr Fund Inst	Small Co	25.6	13.69	19.16	3	4	1.25	1.51	800 426-0107
PIMCO Mid Cap Equity Fund Inst	Growth	49.3	33.85	27.67	1	4	0.63	0.89	800 426-0107
PIMCO Mid Cap Growth D	Growth	34.2					0.45		800 426-0107
PIMCO Mid Cap Growth Fund A	Growth	34.3	19.01		3	3	0.45	1.1	800 426-0107
PIMCO Mid Cap Growth Fund Admin	Growth	34.5	19.28	21.79	3	3	0.45	0.94	800 426-0107
PIMCO Mid Cap Growth Fund B	Growth	33.3	18.12		3	3	0.45	1.85	800 426-0107
PIMCO Mid Cap Growth Fund C	Growth	33.3	18.12		3	3	0.45	1.85	800 426-0107
PIMCO Mid Cap Growth Fund Inst	Growth	34.9	19.51	22.06	3	3	0.69	0.69	800 426-0107
PIMCO Opportunity Fund A	Agg Growth	50.8	21.3	16.56	3	5	0.65	1.31	800 426-0107
PIMCO Opportunity Fund Admin	Agg Growth	50.4					0.65	1.12	800 426-0107
PIMCO Opportunity Fund B	Agg Growth	49.8					0.65	2.02	800 426-0107
PIMCO Opportunity Fund C	Agg Growth	49.9	20.46	15.73	3	5	0.65	2.06	800 426-0107
PIMCO Opportunity Fund I	Agg Growth	50.2					0.65	0.88	800 426-0107
PIMCO Renaissance Fund A	Growth/Inc	3.4	14.17	20.55	3	3	0.59	1.26	800 426-0107
PIMCO Renaissance Fund Admin	Growth/Inc	3.4					0.59	1.09	800 426-0107
PIMCO Renaissance Fund B	Growth/Inc	2.6	13.25	19.62	3	3	0.59	2	800 426-0107
PIMCO Renaissance Fund C	Growth/Inc	2.6	13.31	19.66	3	3	0.59	2	800 426-0107
PIMCO Renaissance Fund D	Growth/Inc	3.6					0.59		800 426-0107
PIMCO Renaissance Fund Instl	Growth/Inc	3.3					0.59	0.85	800 426-0107

Stock Fund Name	Objective	Annualized Return for			Rank		Max Load	Expense Ratio	Toll-Free Telephone
		1 Year	3 Years	5 Years	Overall	Risk			
PIMCO Small Cap Gr Fund Admin	Small Co	16	5.24		4	4	1	1.5	800 426-0107
PIMCO Small Cap Gr Fund Inst	Small Co	15.9	5.53	11.11	4	4	1	1.25	800 426-0107
PIMCO Small Cap Value Fund A	Small Co	-9.3	0.19		4	2	0.59	1.25	800 426-0107
PIMCO Small Cap Value Fund Admin	Small Co	-9.1	0.31		4	2	0.59	1.1	800 426-0107
PIMCO Small Cap Value Fund B	Small Co	-9.9	-0.56		4	2	0.59	2	800 426-0107
PIMCO Small Cap Value Fund C	Small Co	-10	-0.56		4	2	0.59	2	800 426-0107
PIMCO Small Cap Value Fund Inst	Small Co	-8.9	0.6	10.39	4	2	0.59	0.84	800 426-0107
PIMCO StocksPLUS Fund A	Growth/Inc	6.4	18.64		2	3	0.4	1.05	800 426-0107
PIMCO StocksPLUS Fund Admin	Growth/Inc	6.6	18.77		3	3	0.4	0.9	800 426-0107
PIMCO StocksPLUS Fund B	Growth/Inc	5.7	17.76		2	3	0.4	1.8	800 426-0107
PIMCO StocksPLUS Fund C	Growth/Inc	6	18.09		2	3	0.4	1.55	800 426-0107
PIMCO StocksPLUS Fund Inst	Growth/Inc	6.9	19.2	23.66	2	3	0.4	0.65	800 426-0107
PIMCO StocksPlus Fund D	Growth/Inc	5.6					0.4	1.05	800 426-0107
PIMCO Strategic Balanced A	Balanced	0.9					0.4		800 426-0107
PIMCO Strategic Balanced Admin	Balanced	1.4					0.4		800 426-0107
PIMCO Strategic Balanced B	Balanced	0.5					0.4		800 426-0107
PIMCO Strategic Balanced C	Balanced	10.9					0.4		800 426-0107
PIMCO Strategic Balanced D	Balanced	1.1					0.4	1.05	800 426-0107
PIMCO Strategic Balanced Inst	Balanced	4.2	13.15		3	1	0.4	0.65	800 426-0107
PIMCO Structured Emerging Mkts I	Foreign	6.4					0.5	0.94	800 426-0107
PIMCO Target Fund A	Growth	90.4	41.07	31.76	2	5	0.55	1.2	800 426-0107
PIMCO Target Fund Admin	Growth	91.1					0.55	1.02	800 426-0107
PIMCO Target Fund B	Growth	89.7	40.23	30.89	2	4	0.55	1.94	800 426-0107
PIMCO Target Fund C	Growth	89.8	40.24	30.88	2	4	0.55	1.94	800 426-0107
PIMCO Target Fund I	Growth	89.9					0.55	0.79	800 426-0107
PIMCO Tax Efficient Emerging Mkts I	Foreign	7.5					0.5	0.94	800 426-0107
PIMCO Tax-Efficient Equity A	Growth	5.6					0.45	1.11	800 426-0107
PIMCO Tax-Efficient Equity Admin	Growth	5.8					0.45	0.92	800 426-0107
PIMCO Tax-Efficient Equity B	Growth	4.8					0.45	1.85	800 426-0107
PIMCO Tax-Efficient Equity C	Growth	4.8					0.45	1.84	800 426-0107
PIMCO Tax-Efficient Equity D	Growth	5.4					0.45		800 426-0107
PIMCO Tax-Efficient Equity I	Growth						0.45		800 426-0107
PIMCO Value Fund A	Growth/Inc	-7.4	7.19		5	3	0.45	1.11	800 426-0107
PIMCO Value Fund Admin	Growth/Inc	-7.4					0.45	0.95	800 426-0107
PIMCO Value Fund B	Growth/Inc	-7.9	6.54		5	3	0.45	1.85	800 426-0107
PIMCO Value Fund C	Growth/Inc	-7.9	6.45		5	3	0.45	1.85	800 426-0107
PIMCO Value Fund D	Growth/Inc	-7.5					0.45		800 426-0107
PIMCO Value Fund Inst	Growth/Inc	-7	7.6	14.8	4	3	0.45	0.7	800 426-0107
Pacific Advisors Balanced C	Balanced	10.3					0.75	2.2	800 282-6693
Pacific Advisors Balanced Fund	Balanced	11.4	10.24	12.18	3	1	0.75	1.65	800 282-6693
Pacific Advisors Growth A	Growth	21.8					0.75	0.3	800 282-6693
Pacific Advisors Growth C	Growth	20.9					0.75	0.32	800 282-6693
Pacific Advisors Income	Growth/Inc	1.6	6.02	5.84	3	1	0.75	0.94	800 282-6693
Pacific Advisors Income & Equity C	Growth/Inc	1.5					0.75	0.98	800 282-6693
Pacific Advisors Small Cap	Small Co	-15.7	-10.8	-1.63	5	3	0.75	3.31	800 282-6693
Pacific Advisors Small Cap C	Small Co	-16.9					0.75	2.14	800 282-6693
Pacific Capital Gr & Inc Stock B	Growth/Inc	21.7	23.36	24.01	1	3	0.8	2.08	800 424-2295
Pacific Capital Gr & Inc Stock I	Growth/Inc	23	24.35	24.71	1	3	0.8	1.1	800 424-2295
Pacific Capital Gr & Inc Stock Ret	Growth/Inc	22.7	24.11	24.46	1	3	0.8	1.35	800 424-2295
Pacific Capital Growth Stock I	Growth	45.1	32.05	28.82	1	3	0.8	1.07	800 424-2295
Pacific Capital New Asia Gr A	Pacific	22.3	3.39	7.7	4	5	0.9	2.14	800 424-2295
Pacific Capital New Asia Gr B	Pacific	23.6	3.46	7.74	4	5	0.9	2.81	800 424-2295
Pacific Capital New Asia Gr I	Pacific	22.5	3.62	7.93	4	5	0.9	1.89	800 424-2295
Pacific Captl International Stock A	Foreign	35.1					1.1	1.93	800 424-2295
Pacific Captl International Stock B	Foreign	33.9					1.1	2.75	800 424-2295
Pacific Captl International Stock Y	Foreign	35.1					1.1	1.64	800 424-2295
Pacific Captl Small Cap A	Small Co	-0.1					1.1	1.84	800 424-2295
Pacific Captl Small Cap B	Small Co	-0.8					1.1	2.58	800 424-2295

Stock Fund Name	Objective	Annualized Return for			Rank		Max Load	Expense Ratio	Toll-Free Telephone
		1 Year	3 Years	5 Years	Overall	Risk			
Pacific Captl Small Cap Y	Small Co	1.9					1.1	1.52	800 424-2295
Pacific Captl Value Equity A	Growth	1					0.8	1.6	800 424-2295
Pacific Captl Value Equity B	Growth	0.2					0.8	2.43	800 424-2295
Pacific Captl Value Equity Y	Growth	1.2					0.8	1.28	800 424-2295
PaineWebber Asia Pacific Growth A	Pacific	11.5	-6.43		4	4	1.19	2.95	800 647-1568
PaineWebber Asia Pacific Growth B	Pacific	10.6	-7.14		4	4	1.19	3.74	800 647-1568
PaineWebber Asia Pacific Growth C	Pacific	10.7	-7.11		4	4	1.19	3.7	800 647-1568
PaineWebber Asia Pacific Growth Y	Pacific	11.8					1.19	2.68	800 647-1568
PaineWebber Balanced Fund A	Balanced	0.6	9.73	12.86	3	1	0.75	1.22	800 647-1568
PaineWebber Balanced Fund B	Balanced	-0.2	8.9	12.02	3	1	0.75	1.97	800 647-1568
PaineWebber Balanced Fund C	Balanced	-0.2	8.95	11.01	3	1	0.75	1.94	800 647-1568
PaineWebber Emerg Mkts Equity A	Foreign	3.9	-6.22	-0.1	5	4	1.19	2.43	800 647-1568
PaineWebber Emerg Mkts Equity B	Foreign	3.1	-6.72	-0.69	5	4	1.19	3.18	800 647-1568
PaineWebber Emerg Mkts Equity C	Foreign	3	-6.99	-1.04	5	4	1.19	3.18	800 647-1568
PaineWebber Financial Services A	Financial	-11.4	3.08	15.38	4	3	0.69	1.17	800 647-1568
PaineWebber Financial Services B	Financial	-12.1	2.31	14.59	4	3	0.69	1.93	800 647-1568
PaineWebber Financial Services C	Financial	-12.1	2.29	14.51	4	3	0.69	1.93	800 647-1568
PaineWebber Global Equity A	Global	12.8	7.62	10.5	5	3	0.84	1.55	800 647-1568
PaineWebber Global Equity B	Global	11.7	6.65		5	3	0.84	2.39	800 647-1568
PaineWebber Global Equity C	Global	12	5.08	9.12	5	3	0.84	2.31	800 647-1568
PaineWebber Global Income A	Intl Bond	1.1	3.41	4.82	5	3	0.73	1.14	800 647-1568
PaineWebber Global Income B	Intl Bond	-0.1	2.42	3.91	5	3	0.73	2.04	800 647-1568
PaineWebber Global Income C	Intl Bond	0.6	2.9	4.33	5	3	0.73	1.64	800 647-1568
PaineWebber Global Income Y	Intl Bond	1	3.56	4.76	4	3	0.73	0.81	800 647-1568
PaineWebber Growth & Income A	Growth/Inc	2.2	11.55	18.18	3	3	0.69	1.08	800 647-1568
PaineWebber Growth & Income B	Growth/Inc	1.4	10.7	17.26	3	3	0.69	1.85	800 647-1568
PaineWebber Growth & Income C	Growth/Inc	1.4	10.68	17.2	3	3	0.69	1.84	800 647-1568
PaineWebber Growth & Income Y	Growth/Inc	2.5	11.85	17.05	3	3	0.69	0.78	800 647-1568
PaineWebber Growth Fund A	Growth	19.5	25.45	22.79	2	3	0.75	1.17	800 647-1568
PaineWebber Growth Fund B	Growth	18.5	24.15	21.72	2	3	0.75	1.98	800 647-1568
PaineWebber Growth Fund C	Growth	18.5	24.15	21.71	2	3	0.75	1.97	800 647-1568
PaineWebber Growth Fund Y	Growth	19.9	25.61	22.97	2	3	0.75	0.89	800 647-1568
PaineWebber Mid Cap Apprec A	Growth	42	22.01	21.32	3	4	1	1.6	800 647-1568
PaineWebber Mid Cap Apprec B	Growth	40.9	21.74	20.8	3	4	1	2.49	800 647-1568
PaineWebber Mid Cap Apprec C	Growth	41	21.05	20.23	3	4	1	2.39	800 647-1568
PaineWebber Mid Cap Apprec Y	Growth	42.5					1	1.37	800 647-1568
PaineWebber PACE Intl Emerg Mkts	Foreign	3	-5.45		5	4	0.9	1.5	800 647-1568
PaineWebber PACE Intl Equity	Foreign	21.2	12.76		3	3	0.69	1.18	800 647-1568
PaineWebber PACE Lrg Company Gr	Growth	14.5	26.01		1	3	0.59	0.93	800 647-1568
PaineWebber PACE Lrg Company Val	Growth/Inc	-17	5.07		4	3	0.59	0.95	800 647-1568
PaineWebber PACE Sm/Med Co Gr	Growth	68.7	39.66		2	4	0.59	0.95	800 647-1568
PaineWebber PACE Sm/Med Co Value	Small Co	-14.2	-0.34		4	3	0.59	1	800 647-1568
PaineWebber S&P 500 Index Fund A	Growth	6.4					0.2	0.59	800 647-1568
PaineWebber S&P 500 Index Fund Y	Growth	6.6					0.2	0.34	800 647-1568
PaineWebber Small Cap A	Small Co	14.4	5.25	9.89	4	4	1	1.59	800 647-1568
PaineWebber Small Cap B	Small Co	13.4	4.36	8.97	4	4	1	2.43	800 647-1568
PaineWebber Small Cap C	Small Co	13.6	4.43	9	4	4	1	2.39	800 647-1568
PaineWebber Strategy Fund A	Small Co						0.75		800 647-1568
PaineWebber Strategy Fund B	Small Co						0.75		800 647-1568
PaineWebber Strategy Fund C	Small Co						0.75		800 647-1568
PaineWebber Strategy Fund Y	Small Co						0.75		800 647-1568
PaineWebber Tactical Alloc A	AssetAlloc	6.4	18.71	22.64	2	2	0.46	0.88	800 647-1568
PaineWebber Tactical Alloc C	AssetAlloc	5.7	17.82	21.78	2	2	0.46	1.6	800 647-1568
PaineWebber Tactical Alloc Y	AssetAlloc	6.8	18.96	22.49	2	2	0.46	0.61	800 647-1568
PaineWebber Tax Managed Eq A	Growth	-5.7					0.75	1.61	800 647-1568
PaineWebber Tax Managed Eq B	Growth	-6.5					0.75	2.35	800 647-1568
PaineWebber Tax Managed Eq C	Growth	-6.5					0.75	2.37	800 647-1568
PaineWebber Tax Managed Eq Y	Growth	-5.5					0.75		800 647-1568

| Stock Fund Name | Objective | Annualized Return for | | | Rank | | Max Load | Expense Ratio | Toll-Free Telephone |
		1 Year	3 Years	5 Years	Overall	Risk			
PaineWebber Utility Income A	Utilities	-4.4	9.81	11.38	3	2	0.69	1.59	800 647-1568
PaineWebber Utility Income B	Utilities	-5.1	8.99	10.55	3	2	0.69	2.35	800 647-1568
PaineWebber Utility Income C	Utilities	-5	9.02	10.54	3	2	0.69	2.35	800 647-1568
Papp America-Abroad Fund	Growth	24.7	18.27	24.69	2	3	1	1.09	800 421-4004
Papp America-Pacific Rim Fund	Pacific	43	24.94		1	3	1.25	1.25	800 421-4004
Papp Focus Fund	Growth	15.9					1	1.25	800 421-4004
Papp L. Roy Stock Fund	Growth	16.1	18.71	23.13	2	3	1	1.13	800 421-4004
Papp Small & Mid-Cap Growth Fund	Growth	45.1					1.25	1.25	800 421-4004
Parnassus Fund	Growth	62	26.09	19.29	3	4	1	1.08	800 999-3505
Parnassus Income Fd-Equity Income	Balanced	22.8	19.93	17.16	2	2	0.75	1.07	800 999-3505
Pax World Fund	Balanced	9.7	18.08	18.7	2	1	0.51	0.89	800 767-1729
Pax World Growth Fund	Growth	17.6	12.18		3	3	0.1	1.57	800 767-1729
Payden & Rygel Euro Gr & Inc R	European	-11.1	2.92		5	2	0.69	0.9	800 572-9336
Payden & Rygel European Aggr Gr R	European	88.3					0.8		800 572-9336
Payden & Rygel Global Balanced R	Balanced	10.7	10.46		3	1	0.5	0.69	800 572-9336
Payden & Rygel Global Fixed Inc R	Intl Bond	4.7	6.98	7.25	1	3	0.33	0.5	800 572-9336
Payden & Rygel Global Short Bond R	Intl Bond	4.4	5.4		1	1	0.29	0.5	800 572-9336
Payden & Rygel Growth & Income R	Growth/Inc	-9.5	8.9		4	2	0.29	0.75	800 572-9336
Payden & Rygel Market Return R	Flexible	3	17.07		3	3	0.28	0.45	800 572-9336
Payden & Rygel US Growth Leaders R	Growth	14.5					0.59		800 572-9336
Penn Capital Sel Financial Svcs	Financial	-13					0.98	1.39	800 224-6312
Pennsylvania Mutual Fd Cons	Small Co	6.5	8.33		4	2	0.78	1.78	800 221-4268
Pennsylvania Mutual Fd Inv	Small Co	7.4	9.14	12.19	3	2	0.8	1.04	800 221-4268
Performance Fds-Lrg Cap Eq Cons	Growth	2.5	16.96	22.19	3	3	0.59	1.14	800 737-3676
Performance Fds-Lrg Cap Eq Inst	Growth	2.8	17.28	22.53	3	3	0.59	0.9	800 737-3676
Performance Fds-Mid Cap Gr A	Growth	5.1	10.39	16.55	3	3	0.75	1.35	800 737-3676
Performance Fds-Mid Cap Gr I	Growth	5.4	10.68	16.86	4	3	0.75	1.09	800 737-3676
Performance Large Cap Equity B	Growth	1.8					0.59	1.87	800 737-3676
Performance Mid Cap Equity B	Growth	4.3					0.75	2.1	800 737-3676
Performance Small Cap Equity A	Small Co	2.4					1	1.64	800 737-3676
Performance Small Cap Equity B	Small Co	1.8					1	2.39	800 737-3676
Performance Small Cap Equity Instl	Small Co	2.8					1	1.39	800 737-3676
Perkins Discovery Fund	Small Co	72					1	2.5	800 998-3190
Perkins Opportunity Fund	Small Co	61	13.11	7.98	4	5	1	2.24	800 998-3190
Permanent Portfolio Aggress Gr	Agg Growth	13.2	21.45	20	3	3	1.12	1.72	800 531-5142
Permanent Portfolio Family Fds	AssetAlloc	5.5	4.18	3.65	3	1	1.12	1.45	800 531-5142
Perritt Micro Cap Opportunities	Small Co	27.8	6.26	12.08	4	4	1	1.52	800 331-8936
Philadelphia Fund	Growth/Inc	-9.7	7.26	12.44	3	2	0.75	1.55	800 749-9933
Phoenix-Aberdeen Global Sm Cap A	Global	41.6	15.95		3	3	0.84	2.1	800 243-4361
Phoenix-Aberdeen Global Sm Cap B	Global	40.5	15.08		3	3	0.84	2.85	800 243-4361
Phoenix-Aberdeen Int'l Port. A	Foreign	16.7	15.09	16.22	3	3	0.75	1.53	800 243-4361
Phoenix-Aberdeen Int'l Port. B	Foreign	15.9	14.25	15.34	3	3	0.75	2.22	800 243-4361
Phoenix-Aberdeen New Asia A	Pacific	6.4	-2.87		5	4	0.84	2.1	800 243-4361
Phoenix-Aberdeen New Asia B	Pacific	5.6	-3.63		5	4	0.84	2.85	800 243-4361
Phoenix-Aberdeen Worldwide Opp A	Global	11.4	16.86	17.04	3	2	0.75	1.57	800 243-4361
Phoenix-Aberdeen Worldwide Opp B	Global	10.6	16.01	16.17	3	2	0.75	2.2	800 243-4361
Phoenix-Duff & Phelps Core Eq A	Growth	-3.3					0.75	1.25	800 243-4361
Phoenix-Duff & Phelps Core Eq B	Growth	-4					0.75	2	800 243-4361
Phoenix-Duff & Phelps Core Eq C	Growth	-4.1					0.75	2	800 243-4361
Phoenix-Engemann Aggressive Gr A	Agg Growth	64	42.64	33.32	2	5	0.69	1.18	800 243-4361
Phoenix-Engemann Aggressive Gr B	Agg Growth	62.7	41.6	32.35	2	5	0.69	1.94	800 243-4361
Phoenix-Engemann Balanced A	Balanced	16	19.46	19.47	2	2	0.73	1.56	800 243-4361
Phoenix-Engemann Balanced B	Balanced	15.2	18.54	18.53	2	2	0.73	2.33	800 243-4361
Phoenix-Engemann Balanced C	Balanced	15.2	18.53	18.53	2	2	0.73	2.33	800 243-4361
Phoenix-Engemann Capital Gr A	Growth	21.3	22.34	21.89	2	3	0.69	1.07	800 243-4361
Phoenix-Engemann Capital Gr B	Growth	20.4	21.44	21	2	3	0.66	1.82	800 243-4361
Phoenix-Engemann Focus Gr A	Growth	32.5	30.39	26.28	1	4	0.65	1.55	800 243-4361
Phoenix-Engemann Focus Gr B	Growth	31.5	29.4	25.28	2	4	0.65	2.29	800 243-4361

359

Stock Fund Name	Objective	Annualized Return for			Rank		Max Load	Expense Ratio	Toll-Free Telephone
		1 Year	3 Years	5 Years	Overall	Risk			
Phoenix-Engemann Focus Gr C	Growth	31.5	29.4	25.28	2	4	0.65	2.29	800 243-4361
Phoenix-Engemann Nifty Fifty A	Growth	21.7	24.05	24.71	2	3	0.81	1.59	800 243-4361
Phoenix-Engemann Nifty Fifty B	Growth	20.8	23.13	23.78	2	3	0.81	2.33	800 243-4361
Phoenix-Engemann Nifty Fifty C	Growth	20.8	23.13	23.79	2	3	0.81	2.33	800 243-4361
Phoenix-Engemann Sm & Mid-Cap A	Agg Growth	81.7	34.48	36.19	3	5	1	1.75	800 243-4361
Phoenix-Engemann Sm Cap A	Small Co	77.7	33.88		3	5	0.75	1.5	800 243-4361
Phoenix-Engemann Sm Cap B	Small Co	76.4	32.89		3	5	0.75	2.2	800 243-4361
Phoenix-Engemann Value 25 A	Growth/Inc	-32.9	-3.49		4	3	0.9	1.75	800 243-4361
Phoenix-Engemann Value 25 B	Growth/Inc	-33.5	-4.26		4	4	0.9	2.5	800 243-4361
Phoenix-Engemann Value 25 C	Growth/Inc	-33.4	-4.23		4	4	0.9	2.5	800 243-4361
Phoenix-Euclid Market Neutral I	Growth	-3					1.5	3.35	800 243-4361
Phoenix-Goodwin Emerging Mkts A	Intl Bond	21.7	-1.2		3	5	0.75	1.57	800 243-4361
Phoenix-Goodwin Emerging Mkts B	Intl Bond	20.8	-1.95		3	5	0.75	2.31	800 243-4361
Phoenix-Goodwin Strategic All. A	Flexible	7.3	13.77	13.43	3	2	0.65	1.19	800 243-4361
Phoenix-Goodwin Strategic All. B	Flexible	6.6	12.93	12.53	3	2	0.65	1.91	800 243-4361
Phoenix-Hollister Sm Cap Value A	Small Co	54.3					0.9		800 243-4361
Phoenix-Hollister Sm Cap Value B	Small Co	53.2					0.9	2.14	800 243-4361
Phoenix-Hollister Sm Cap Value C	Small Co	53.2					0.9	0.91	800 243-4361
Phoenix-Hollister Value Equity A	Growth	6.3					0.75	1.25	800 243-4361
Phoenix-Hollister Value Equity B	Growth	5.5					0.75	2	800 243-4361
Phoenix-Hollister Value Equity C	Growth	5.5					0.75	2	800 243-4361
Phoenix-Oakhurst Balanced A	Balanced	7.3	12.27	13.58	3	2	0.55	0.96	800 243-4361
Phoenix-Oakhurst Balanced B	Balanced	6.5	11.43	12.74	3	2	0.52	1.7	800 243-4361
Phoenix-Oakhurst Gr & Inc A	Growth/Inc	7					0.75		800 243-4361
Phoenix-Oakhurst Gr & Inc B	Growth/Inc	6.3					0.75	2	800 243-4361
Phoenix-Oakhurst Gr & Inc C	Growth/Inc	6.3					0.75	2	800 243-4361
Phoenix-Oakhurst Inc & Gr A	Flexible	4.4	8.6	11.45	3	1	0.69	1.17	800 243-4361
Phoenix-Oakhurst Inc & Gr B	Flexible	3.5	7.79	10.61	3	1	0.69	1.91	800 243-4361
Phoenix-Seneca Gr A	Growth	25.6	25.3		1	3	0.69	1.42	800 243-4361
Phoenix-Seneca Gr B	Growth	24.3					0.69	2.6	800 243-4361
Phoenix-Seneca Gr C	Growth	24.2					0.69	2.6	800 243-4361
Phoenix-Seneca Gr X	Growth	25.9	25.8		1	3	0.69	1.14	800 243-4361
Phoenix-Seneca Real Est. A	Real Est	2.8	-1.98		4	2	0.84	3.04	800 243-4361
Phoenix-Seneca Real Est. B	Real Est	2.1					0.84	3.79	800 243-4361
Phoenix-Seneca Real Est. C	Real Est	2					0.84	3.79	800 243-4361
Phoenix-Seneca Real Est. X	Real Est	4.1	-0.68		4	2	0.84	1.69	800 243-4361
Phoenix-Seneca Strategic Theme A	Growth	46.7	39.76		1	4	0.75	1.37	800 243-4361
Phoenix-Seneca Strategic Theme B	Growth	45.6	38.74		1	4	0.75	2.12	800 243-4361
Phoenix-Seneca Strategic Theme C	Growth	45.6					0.75	2.12	800 243-4361
Phoenix-Zweig Foreign Equity Fund A	Foreign	9.5					1	2.62	800 243-4361
Phoenix-Zweig Foreign Equity Fund B	Foreign	8.7					1	3.33	800 243-4361
Phoenix-Zweig Foreign Equity Fund C	Foreign	8.6					1	3.33	800 243-4361
Phoenix-Zweig Growth & Income I	Growth/Inc	7.8	7.8		3	2	0.75	1.4	800 243-4361
Phoenix-Zweig Ser Tr-Mgd Assets A	AssetAlloc	4.4	9.96	11.22	3	1	1	1.48	800 243-4361
Phoenix-Zweig Ser Tr-Mgd Assets B	AssetAlloc	3.7	9.15		3	1	1	2.18	800 243-4361
Phoenix-Zweig Ser Tr-Mgd Assets C	AssetAlloc	3.7	9.18	10.43	3	1	1	2.2	800 243-4361
Phoenix-Zweig Ser Tr-Strat A	Growth	-1.3	3.62	7.43	5	2	0.75	1.32	800 243-4361
Phoenix-Zweig Ser Tr-Strat B	Growth	-2	2.9		5	2	0.75	2.02	800 243-4361
Phoenix-Zweig Ser Tr-Strat C	Growth	-2	2.88	6.73	5	2	0.75	2.02	800 243-4361
Phoenix-Zweig Series Tr-Apprec A	Small Co	0.5	4.24	9.52	5	2	1	1.61	800 243-4361
Phoenix-Zweig Series Tr-Apprec B	Small Co	-0.1	3.54		5	2	1	2.31	800 243-4361
Phoenix-Zweig Series Tr-Apprec C	Small Co	-0.1	3.52	8.76	5	2	1	2.31	800 243-4361
Phoenix-Zweig Series Tr-Gr & Inc A	Growth/Inc	7.5	7.46		3	2	0.75	1.7	800 243-4361
Phoenix-Zweig Series Tr-Gr & Inc B	Growth/Inc	6.8	6.72		4	2	0.75	2.41	800 243-4361
Phoenix-Zweig Series Tr-Gr & Inc C	Growth/Inc	6.7	6.71		4	2	0.75	2.41	800 243-4361
Pilgrim Asia/Pac Eq A	Pacific	0.1	-12.86		5	5	1.25	2	800 992-0180
Pilgrim Asia/Pac Eq B	Pacific	-0.7	-13.66		5	5	1.25	2.75	800 992-0180
Pilgrim Asia/Pac Eq M	Pacific	-0.4	-13.45		5	5	1.25	2.5	800 992-0180

Stock Fund Name	Objective	Annualized Return for			Rank		Max Load	Expense Ratio	Toll-Free Telephone
		1 Year	3 Years	5 Years	Overall	Risk			
Pilgrim Balanced A	Balanced	-0.1	13.59	14.17	3	1	0.75	1.48	800 992-0180
Pilgrim Balanced B	Balanced	-1	12.86	13.49	3	1	0.75	2.14	800 992-0180
Pilgrim Balanced C	Balanced	-1	12.73	13.38	3	1	0.75	2	800 992-0180
Pilgrim Balanced Q	Balanced	0.2	13.79	14.64	3	1	0.75	1.25	800 992-0180
Pilgrim Bank & Thrift B	Growth	-23					0.76	2.14	800 992-0180
Pilgrim Emer Cos A	Foreign	20.8	3.17	11.94	4	4	1.25	2.06	800 992-0180
Pilgrim Emer Cos C	Foreign	20	2.75	11.38	4	4	1.25	2.12	800 992-0180
Pilgrim Emer Cos Q	Foreign	20.9	3.7	12.45	4	4	1.25	1.89	800 992-0180
Pilgrim Growth + Value A	Growth	67	38.96		2	5	1		800 992-0180
Pilgrim Growth + Value B	Growth	65.9	37.93		2	5	1	2.45	800 992-0180
Pilgrim Growth + Value C	Growth	66	37.91		2	5	1	2.45	800 992-0180
Pilgrim Growth Opportunities A	Growth	50.5	37.62	24	2	4	0.75	1.37	800 992-0180
Pilgrim Growth Opportunities B	Growth	49.4	36.67	30.17	1	4	0.75	2.12	800 992-0180
Pilgrim Growth Opportunities C	Growth	49.5	36.75	30.17	1	4	0.75	2.12	800 992-0180
Pilgrim Growth Opportunities T	Growth	49.4	36.7	30.22	1	4	0.75	2.02	800 992-0180
Pilgrim Int Sm Cap Gr A	Foreign	82.8	42.99	33.97	1	4	1	1.64	800 992-0180
Pilgrim Int Sm Cap Gr B	Foreign	81.6	42.09	33.15	1	4	1	2.49	800 992-0180
Pilgrim Int Sm Cap Gr C	Foreign	81.4	42.07	33.14	1	4	1	2.49	800 992-0180
Pilgrim Int Sm Cap Gr Q	Foreign	83	43.31	34.3	1	4	1	1.64	800 992-0180
Pilgrim Intl Core Gr A	Foreign	33	20.46		2	4	1	1.77	800 992-0180
Pilgrim Intl Core Gr B	Foreign	31.8	19.58		2	4	1	2.35	800 992-0180
Pilgrim Intl Core Gr C	Foreign	31.9	19.63		2	4	1	2.35	800 992-0180
Pilgrim Intl Core Gr Q	Foreign	32.9	20.66		2	4	1	1.54	800 992-0180
Pilgrim Large Cap Gr A	Growth	55.3	57		1	4	0.75	1.42	800 992-0180
Pilgrim Large Cap Gr B	Growth	54.3	56.02		1	4	0.75	2.08	800 992-0180
Pilgrim Large Cap Gr C	Growth	54.3	56.02		1	4	0.75	2.08	800 992-0180
Pilgrim Large Cap Gr Q	Growth	54.8	57.11		1	5	0.75	1.22	800 992-0180
Pilgrim Lrg Cap Leaders A	Growth/Inc	3	13.53		3	3	1	1.75	800 992-0180
Pilgrim Lrg Cap Leaders B	Growth/Inc	2.3	12.7		3	3	1	2.5	800 992-0180
Pilgrim Lrg Cap Leaders M	Growth/Inc	2.5	12.99		2	3	1	2.25	800 992-0180
Pilgrim MagnaCap A	Growth	-0.4	11.66	17.17	3	3	0.71	1.43	800 992-0180
Pilgrim MagnaCap B	Growth	-1.1	10.88		2	3	0.76	2.04	800 992-0180
Pilgrim MagnaCap M	Growth	-0.7	11.2		3	3	0.76	1.8	800 992-0180
Pilgrim Mid Cap Gr A	Growth	77.3	40.21	30.74	3	5	0.75	1.35	800 992-0180
Pilgrim Mid Cap Gr B	Growth	76.3	39.33	29.94	3	5	0.75	2.14	800 992-0180
Pilgrim Mid Cap Gr C	Growth	76.2	39.34	29.98	3	5	0.75	2.22	800 992-0180
Pilgrim Mid Cap Gr Q	Growth	77.9	40.6	31.09	3	5	0.75	1.19	800 992-0180
Pilgrim Small Cap Gr A	Small Co	60.7	30.16	25.56	3	5	1	1.69	800 992-0180
Pilgrim Small Cap Gr B	Small Co	59.5	29.22	24.64	3	5	1	2.56	800 992-0180
Pilgrim Small Cap Gr C	Small Co	59.7	29.32	24.77	3	5	1	2.5	800 992-0180
Pilgrim Small Cap Gr Q	Small Co	61	30.63	26.14	3	5	1	1.44	800 992-0180
Pilgrim Small Cap Value Fund	Small Co						1	2.87	800 526-0056
Pilgrim SmallCap Opportunities A	Small Co	112.7	44.74	32.36	3	5	0.75	1.46	800 992-0180
Pilgrim SmallCap Opportunities B	Small Co	111.3	43.92	30.27	3	5	0.75	2.18	800 992-0180
Pilgrim SmallCap Opportunities C	Small Co	111.2	43.88	30.78	3	5	0.75	2.22	800 992-0180
Pilgrim SmallCap Opportunities T	Small Co	111.6	44.08	31.57	3	5	0.75	2.06	800 992-0180
Pilgrim Worldwide Gr A	Global	42.4	34.94	29.17	1	4	1	1.61	800 992-0180
Pilgrim Worldwide Gr B	Global	41.5	34.14	28.41	1	4	1	2.39	800 992-0180
Pilgrim Worldwide Gr C	Global	41.5	34.09	28.36	1	4	1	2.39	800 992-0180
Pilgrim Worldwide Gr Q	Global	42.6	35.31	29.53	1	4	1	1.55	800 992-0180
Pillar Balanced Fund A	Balanced	4.3	11.55	14.16	3	2	0.75	1.12	800 932-7782
Pillar Balanced Fund B	Balanced	3.6	7.13		3	2	0.75	1.87	800 932-7782
Pillar Balanced Fund I	Balanced	4.6	11.83	14.43	3	2	0.75	0.94	800 932-7782
Pillar Equity Growth A	Growth	32.1	27.41		1	4	0.5	1.12	800 932-7782
Pillar Equity Growth B	Growth	31.2	26.64		1	4	0.5	1.88	800 932-7782
Pillar Equity Growth I	Growth	32.5	28.26		1	4	0.5	0.86	800 932-7782
Pillar Equity Income A	Income	-4.9	7.19	14.78	3	2	0.46	1.12	800 932-7782
Pillar Equity Income B	Income	-5.6	6.19		3	2	0.46	1.87	800 932-7782

Stock Fund Name	Objective	Annualized Return for			Rank		Max Load	Expense Ratio	Toll-Free Telephone
		1 Year	3 Years	5 Years	Overall	Risk			
Pillar Equity Income I	Income	-4.6	7.72	15.4	3	2	0.46	0.93	800 932-7782
Pillar Equity Index A	Growth/Inc	6.1					0.78	1.05	800 932-7782
Pillar Equity Index B	Growth/Inc	5.3					0.78	1.8	800 932-7782
Pillar Equity Index I	Growth/Inc	6.3					0.78	0.8	800 932-7782
Pillar Equity Value A	Growth/Inc	2.5	15.24	19.87	3	2	0.75	1.18	800 932-7782
Pillar Equity Value B	Growth/Inc	1.7	14.27		3	2	0.46	1.87	800 932-7782
Pillar Equity Value I	Growth/Inc	2.8	15.55	20.21	3	2	0.46	0.86	800 932-7782
Pillar International Growth A	Foreign	22.9	7.93	10.59	4	3	1	1.75	800 932-7782
Pillar International Growth B	Foreign	22	6.55		3	3	1	2.5	800 932-7782
Pillar International Growth I	Foreign	23.1	8.01	10.75	4	3	1	1.5	800 932-7782
Pin Oak Aggressive Stock	Small Co	119.6	58.36	38.25	2	5	0.73	1	888 462-5386
Pioneer Balanced Fund A	Balanced	1.9	4.49	7.94	3	1	0.63	1.19	800 225-6292
Pioneer Balanced Fund B	Balanced	1.1	3.53	7.26	3	1	0.65	2.12	800 225-6292
Pioneer Balanced Fund C	Balanced	0.9	3.55		3	1	0.65	2.41	800 225-6292
Pioneer Emerging Markets A	Foreign	33	2.61	10.46	4	5	1.25	2.54	800 225-6292
Pioneer Emerging Markets B	Foreign	31.8	1.79	9.62	4	5	1.25	3.37	800 225-6292
Pioneer Emerging Markets C	Foreign	31.6	1.52		4	5	1.25	4	800 225-6292
Pioneer Emerging Markets Y	Foreign	33.8					1.25	1.73	800 225-6292
Pioneer Equity Income A	Income	-6.5	10.88	15.81	2	2	0.59	1.09	800 225-6292
Pioneer Equity Income B	Income	-7.2	10.01	14.91	3	2	0.59	1.85	800 225-6292
Pioneer Equity Income C	Income	-7.3	9.97		3	2	0.59	1.94	800 225-6292
Pioneer Europe Fund A	European	26.5	16.1	18.66	2	3	1	1.54	800 225-6292
Pioneer Europe Fund B	European	25.5	15.16	17.7	3	3	1	2.37	800 225-6292
Pioneer Europe Fund C	European	25.5	15.24		3	3	1	2.31	800 225-6292
Pioneer Fund A	Growth/Inc	8.7	20.89	23.06	2	2	0.55	1.1	800 225-6292
Pioneer Fund B	Growth/Inc	7.8	19.83		2	2	0.69	2	800 225-6292
Pioneer Fund C	Growth/Inc	7.8	19.86		2	2	0.69	1.97	800 225-6292
Pioneer Fund II A	Growth/Inc	2.1	1.75	10.43	4	3	0.56	0.98	800 225-6292
Pioneer Fund II B	Growth/Inc	0.4	0.44		5	3	0.69	2.06	800 225-6292
Pioneer Fund II C	Growth/Inc	0.7	0.62		5	3	0.69	2.24	800 225-6292
Pioneer Growth Shares A	Growth	-4.1	17.39	23.9	3	3	0.46	0.98	800 225-6292
Pioneer Growth Shares B	Growth	-4.8	16.07	22.53	2	3	0.46	1.79	800 225-6292
Pioneer Growth Shares C	Growth	-4.9	16.13		3	3	0.46	1.69	800 225-6292
Pioneer Growth Shares Y	Growth	-2.7					0.46	0.54	800 225-6292
Pioneer Indo-Asia Fund A	Foreign	13.9	17.09	6.26	4	4	1.25	2.14	800 225-6292
Pioneer Indo-Asia Fund B	Foreign	12.9	16.24	5.45	4	4	1.25	2.68	800 225-6292
Pioneer Indo-Asia Fund C	Foreign	13	15.94		4	4	1.25	2.5	800 225-6292
Pioneer International Growth A	Foreign	19.5	3.25	8.54	5	4	0.94	1.87	800 225-6292
Pioneer International Growth B	Foreign	18.5	2.4	7.72	4	4	0.95	2.74	800 225-6292
Pioneer International Growth C	Foreign	18.2	2.5		4	4	0.95	2.6	800 225-6292
Pioneer Micro-Cap Fund A	Small Co	35.8	16.29		3	4	1	2.08	800 225-6292
Pioneer Micro-Cap Fund B	Small Co	34.6	15.39		3	4	1	2.72	800 225-6292
Pioneer Mid Cap Value A	Growth	-1.6	4.68	9.46	5	3	0.75	1.17	800 225-6292
Pioneer Mid Cap Value B	Growth	-2.4	3.85	8.58	5	3	0.75	2.02	800 225-6292
Pioneer Mid Cap Value C	Growth	-2.5	3.81		5	3	0.75	2.22	800 225-6292
Pioneer Mid-Cap Fund A	Growth	36	18.47	15.01	3	4	0.82	0.89	800 225-6292
Pioneer Mid-Cap Fund B	Growth	34.7	16.87		3	4	0.82	1.91	800 225-6292
Pioneer Mid-Cap Fund C	Growth	34.7	17.04		3	4	0.82	1.92	800 225-6292
Pioneer Real Estate Shares A	Real Est	4	-0.21	9.05	4	2	1	1.68	800 225-6292
Pioneer Real Estate Shares B	Real Est	3.4	-0.92		4	2	1	2.54	800 225-6292
Pioneer Real Estate Shares C	Real Est	3.5	-0.89		4	2	1	2.75	800 225-6292
Pioneer Small Company Fund A	Small Co	23.1	6.88		4	3	0.84	1.67	800 225-6292
Pioneer Small Company Fund B	Small Co	22.2	6.12		4	3	0.84	2.37	800 225-6292
Pioneer Small Company Fund C	Small Co	21	5.73		4	3	0.84	2.41	800 225-6292
Pioneer World Equity Fund A	Global	29.2	11.58		3	3	1	1.76	800 225-6292
Pioneer World Equity Fund B	Global	28.1	10.26		3	3	1	2.41	800 225-6292
Pioneer World Equity Fund C	Global	27.8	10.16		3	3	1	2.37	800 225-6292
Polaris Global Value Fund	Global	1					1	2.06	800 943-6786

Stock Fund Name	Objective	Annualized Return for			Rank		Max Load	Expense Ratio	Toll-Free Telephone
		1 Year	3 Years	5 Years	Overall	Risk			
Polynous Growth Fund	Growth	-12.6	-5.45		5	4	1	1.89	800 924-3863
Potomac OTC Plus Fund	Growth	71.7					0.75	1.56	88 976-8662
Potomac OTC Short Fund	Growth	-49.7					0.9	1.89	88 976-8662
Potomac U.S. Plus Fund	Growth	3					0.75	1.6	88 976-8662
Potomac U.S. Short Fund	Growth	-7.8					0.9	1.83	88 976-8662
Preferred Asset Allocation Fund	AssetAlloc	5.5	14.65	16.59	2	1	0.69	0.88	800 662-2465
Preferred Growth Fund	Growth	30	31.56	27.43	1	4	0.75		800 662-2465
Preferred International Fund	Foreign	14.2	9.47	12.82	4	3	0.94	1.17	800 662-2465
Preferred Small Cap	Small Co	5.2	1.71		4	4	0.75	0.92	800 662-2465
Preferred Value Fund	Growth/Inc	-5.2	8.53	16.1	3	3	0.75	0.83	800 662-2465
Price (T. Rowe) Balanced Fund	Balanced	6	11.61	14.16	3	1	0.46	0.79	800 638-5660
Price (T. Rowe) Cap Opportunity	Growth	13.8	13.33	15.25	3	3	0.67	1.32	800 638-5660
Price (T. Rowe) Div Small Cap Gr	Small Co	34.5	15.18		3	4	0.66	1.25	800 638-5660
Price (T. Rowe) Dividend Growth	Growth/Inc	-5.1	9.13	16.68	3	2	0.52	0.77	800 638-5660
Price (T. Rowe) Emerging Mkts Stk	Foreign	37.4	4.16	7.55	4	5	1.07	1.75	800 638-5660
Price (T. Rowe) Equity Income	Income	-10.3	7.39	14.59	3	2	0.56	0.77	800 638-5660
Price (T. Rowe) Equity Index	Growth/Inc	7	19.33	23.45	2	3	0.4	0.4	800 638-5660
Price (T. Rowe) European Stock	European	20.1	15.99	18.85	2	2	0.81	1.05	800 638-5660
Price (T. Rowe) Ext Eq Mkt Index	Growth/Inc	20.4					0.4	0.4	800 638-5660
Price (T. Rowe) FL Ins Intrm T/F	Muni State	3.4	3.91	4.58	3	2	0.36	0.59	800 638-5660
Price (T. Rowe) Financial Svcs	Financial	0.1	12.56		3	4	0.67	1.13	800 638-5660
Price (T. Rowe) Global Bond	Intl Bond	0.5	1.65	3.28	5	5	0.67	1	800 638-5660
Price (T. Rowe) Global Stock Fd	Global	21.7	16.69		2	3	0.67	1.19	800 638-5660
Price (T. Rowe) Growth & Inc	Growth/Inc	-4.7	8.88	15.74	3	2	0.56	0.77	800 638-5660
Price (T. Rowe) Hlth Sciences	Health	47.1	24.14		3	4	0.67	1.11	800 638-5660
Price (T. Rowe) Internatl Bond	Intl Bond	-1.4	0.57	1.84	5	5	0.67	0.91	800 638-5660
Price (T. Rowe) Intl Discovery	Foreign	105.2	36.21	26.12	2	4	1.07	1.41	800 638-5660
Price (T. Rowe) Intl Growth & Inc	Foreign	12.2					0.67	1.25	800 638-5660
Price (T. Rowe) Intl Stock	Foreign	24	11.26	13.95	3	3	0.67	0.84	800 638-5660
Price (T. Rowe) Japan Fund	Pacific	34	13.02	9.32	4	4	0.81	1.13	800 638-5660
Price (T. Rowe) Latin America	Foreign	28.2	-0.67	11.49	4	5	1.07	1.62	800 638-5660
Price (T. Rowe) Media & Telecomm	Technology	49.2	45.93	32.19	1	4	0.67	0.93	800 638-5660
Price (T. Rowe) Mid-Cap Value	Growth	-0.7	7.16		4	2	0.67	1.08	800 638-5660
Price (T. Rowe) New Asia Fund	Pacific	36.3	1.48	3.28	4	5	0.81	1.2	800 638-5660
Price (T. Rowe) New Era	Energy/Res	6.2	5.14	11.35	4	4	0.56	0.73	800 638-5660
Price (T. Rowe) New Horizons	Small Co	36.3	19.09	20.16	3	4	0.67	0.9	800 638-5660
Price (T. Rowe) Prsnl Strat Bal	Balanced	5.4	10.63	13.56	3	1	0.56	0.95	800 638-5660
Price (T. Rowe) Prsnl Strat Gr	Growth	6.1	12.57	16.29	3	2	0.61	1.1	800 638-5660
Price (T. Rowe) Prsnl Strat Inc	AssetAlloc	4.8	8.86	11.16	3	1	0.46	0.9	800 638-5660
Price (T. Rowe) Real Estate	Real Est	6.9					0.61	1	800 638-5660
Price (T. Rowe) Sci & Tech	Technology	49.5	40.28	30.81	3	5	0.67	0.86	800 638-5660
Price (T. Rowe) Small Cap Stock	Small Co	22.2	12.54	17.54	3	3	0.77	0.95	800 638-5660
Price (T. Rowe) Small Cap Value	Small Co	6.2	3.72	11.46	3	2	0.67	0.92	800 638-5660
Price (T. Rowe) Spectrum Intl	Foreign	27	12		3	3	0	0	800 638-5660
Price (T. Rowe) Tax-Eff Balanced	Balanced	13	15.89		4	4	0.52	1	800 638-5660
Price (T. Rowe) Tax-Eff Growth	Growth						0.61		800 638-5660
Price (T. Rowe) Total Eq Mkt Index	Growth/Inc	10.2					0.4	0.4	800 638-5660
Primary Income Fund	Growth/Inc	-9.7	2.19	8.74	3	1	0.73	1	800 443-6544
Primary Trend Fund	Flexible	-11.1	1.69	8.56	4	2	0.73	1.27	800 443-6544
Principal Balanced Fund A	Balanced	-4	6.26	10.29	3	1	0.58	1.28	800 247-4123
Principal Balanced Fund B	Balanced	-4.7	5.42	9.43	4	1	0.58	1.92	800 247-4123
Principal Balanced Fund C	Balanced	-5.5					0.58		800 247-4123
Principal Blue Chip A	Growth/Inc	-2.9	10.31	16.56	2	2	0.47	1.26	800 247-4123
Principal Blue Chip B	Growth/Inc	-3.6	9.49	15.64	3	2	0.47	1.95	800 247-4123
Principal Blue Chip Fund C	Growth/Inc	-3.7					0.47		800 247-4123
Principal Blue Chip R	Growth/Inc	-3.5	9.73		3	2	0.5	1.75	800 247-4123
Principal Capital Value A	Growth	-19.6	2.32	11.79	4	2	0.38	0.75	800 247-4123
Principal Capital Value B	Growth	-20.3	1.49	10.83	4	2	0.38	1.41	800 247-4123

Stock Fund Name	Objective	Annualized Return for			Rank		Max Load	Expense Ratio	Toll-Free Telephone
		1 Year	3 Years	5 Years	Overall	Risk			
Principal Capital Value Fund C	Growth	-20.4					0.38		800 247-4123
Principal Growth Fund A	Growth	9.3	16.83	18.63	3	3	0.38	1.01	800 247-4123
Principal Growth Fund B	Growth	8.5	16.17	17.91	3	3	0.38	1.33	800 247-4123
Principal Growth Fund C	Growth	8.3					0.38		800 247-4123
Principal Growth Fund R	Growth	8.7	16.15		3	3	0.38	1.42	800 247-4123
Principal International A	Foreign	21.8	10.63	15.26	3	3	0.68	1.21	800 247-4123
Principal International B	Foreign	21.1	9.92	14.45	3	3	0.68	1.87	800 247-4123
Principal International Fund C	Foreign	20.3					0.68		800 247-4123
Principal Intl Emerg Mkts Fd A	Foreign	21.1					1.25	2.72	800 247-4123
Principal Intl Emerg Mkts Fd B	Foreign	20.3					1.25	3.83	800 247-4123
Principal Intl Emerging Market Fd C	Foreign	20.1					1.25		800 247-4123
Principal Intl Small Cap Fund C	Foreign	54					1.19		800 247-4123
Principal Intl SmallCap Fd A	Foreign	55.7					1.19	2.2	800 247-4123
Principal Intl SmallCap Fd B	Foreign	54.8					1.19	3.08	800 247-4123
Principal Mid Cap A	Growth	11.4	8.22	13.94	4	3	0.56	1.21	800 247-4123
Principal Mid Cap B	Growth	10.8	7.75	13.33	4	3	0.56	1.59	800 247-4123
Principal MidCap Fund C	Growth	9.8					0.56		800 247-4123
Principal Presv-Divd Achievers A	Growth/Inc	11.8	16.63	21.28	2	2	0.75	1.3	800 826-4600
Principal Presv-PSE Tech Stk 100 A	Technology	81.4	56.2		1	5	0.5	0.59	800 826-4600
Principal Presv-S&P 100 Plus A	Growth/Inc	13.5	23.32	25.24	2	3	0.57	0.9	800 826-4600
Principal Presv-Select Value A	Small Co	7.1	4.82	13.6	4	3	0.75	1.3	800 826-4600
Principal Real Estate Fd Inc A	Real Est	4.6					0.9	2	800 247-4123
Principal Real Estate Fd Inc B	Real Est	3.7					0.9	2.89	800 247-4123
Principal Real Estate Fund C	Real Est	3.3					0.9		800 247-4123
Principal Small Cap Fund C	Small Co	30.1					0.84		800 247-4123
Principal SmallCap Fd Inc A	Small Co	32.4					0.84	1.91	800 247-4123
Principal SmallCap Fd Inc B	Small Co	31.4					0.84	2.66	800 247-4123
Principal Utilities Fund A	Utilities	-2.2	15.6	15.43	3	2	0.59	1.19	800 247-4123
Principal Utilities Fund B	Utilities	-3	14.77	14.57	3	2	0.59	1.92	800 247-4123
Principal Utilities Fund C	Utilities	-3.4					0.59		800 247-4123
Principal Utilities Fund R	Utilities	-2.8	14.91		3	2	1	1.84	800 247-4123
ProFunds-Bear Fund Inv	Growth	-1.7					0.75	1.37	888 776-3637
ProFunds-Bear Fund Serv	Growth	-15.7					0.75	2.62	888 776-3637
ProFunds-Bull Fund Inv	Growth	3.3					0.75	1.56	888 776-3637
ProFunds-Bull Fund Serv	Growth	2.4					0.75	2.58	888 776-3637
ProFunds-Ultra Bear Fund Inv	Growth	-16.8					0.75	1.37	888 776-3637
ProFunds-Ultra Bear Fund Serv	Growth	-14.1					0.75	2.35	888 776-3637
ProFunds-Ultra Bull Fund Inv	Growth	0.9					0.75	1.33	888 776-3637
ProFunds-Ultra Bull Fund Serv	Growth	-0.2					0.75	2.33	888 776-3637
ProFunds-Ultra OTC Fund Inv	Growth	96.6					0.75	1.3	888 776-3637
ProFunds-Ultra OTC Fund Serv	Growth	94.6					0.75	2.29	888 776-3637
ProFunds-Ultrashort OTC Fund Inv	Growth	-77.8					0.75	1.41	888 776-3637
ProFunds-Ultrashort OTC Fund Serv	Growth	-78.1					0.75	2.43	888 776-3637
Progressive Capital Accumulation	Growth	22.2	16.73	17.31	2	2	0.75	1.75	
Prov Inv Counsel Balanced A	Balanced	18.2	20.06	19.23	2	3	0.59	1.05	800 618-7643
Prov Inv Counsel Growth A	Growth	21.9	25.44		2	4	0.8	1.35	800 618-7643
Prov Inv Counsel Growth B	Growth	21					0.8	2.1	800 618-7643
Prov Inv Counsel Growth I	Growth	21.8	25.45	24.1	2	4	0.8	1.25	800 618-7643
Prov Inv Counsel Mid Cap A	Growth	80.5					0.69	1.38	800 618-7643
Prov Inv Counsel Mid Cap B	Growth	86.8					0.69	2.14	800 618-7643
Prov Inv Counsel Sm Co Gr A	Small Co	90.8	30.73		3	5	0.8	1.55	800 618-7643
Prov Inv Counsel Sm Co Gr B	Small Co	86.7					0.8	2.29	800 618-7643
Prov Inv Counsel Small Cap Gr I	Small Co	89.1	30.67	27.43	3	5	0.8	1	800 618-7643
Prudent Bear	Growth	2	-18.28		5	4	1.25	1.94	888 778-2327
Prudential 20/20 Focus Fd A	Growth	6.4					0.75	0.96	800 225-1852
Prudential 20/20 Focus Fd B	Growth	5.4					0.75	0.96	800 225-1852
Prudential 20/20 Focus Fd C	Growth	5.4					0.75	0.96	800 225-1852
Prudential 20/20 Focus Fd Z	Growth	6.5					0.75	0.96	800 225-1852

Stock Fund Name	Objective	Annualized Return for			Rank		Max Load	Expense Ratio	Toll-Free Telephone
		1 Year	3 Years	5 Years	Overall	Risk			
Prudential Active Balanced A	Balanced	7.7	11.97		3	1	0.65	1.12	800 225-1852
Prudential Active Balanced B	Balanced	7.1	11.14		3	1	0.65	1.12	800 225-1852
Prudential Active Balanced C	Balanced	7.1	11.14		3	1	0.65	1.12	800 225-1852
Prudential Active Balanced Z	Balanced	8.1	12.21	11.27	3	1	0.65	1.12	800 225-1852
Prudential Balanced A	Balanced	6.7	10.01	11.82	3	1	0.65	0.92	800 225-1852
Prudential Balanced B	Balanced	5.8	9.2	10.97	4	1	0.65	1.93	800 225-1852
Prudential Balanced Z	Balanced	6.9	10.32	11.9	3	1	0.65	0.92	800 225-1852
Prudential Developing Mkts Eq A	Foreign	14.8					1.25	3.18	800 225-1852
Prudential Developing Mkts Eq B	Foreign	14					1.25	3.18	800 225-1852
Prudential Developing Mkts Eq C	Foreign	14					1.25	3.18	800 225-1852
Prudential Developing Mkts Eq Z	Foreign	14.9					1.25	3.18	800 225-1852
Prudential Distressed Securities A	Flexible	11.7	5.13		4	3	0.75	1	800 225-1852
Prudential Distressed Securities B	Flexible	11.7	4.65		4	3	0.75	1	800 225-1852
Prudential Distressed Securities C	Flexible	11.7	4.71		4	3	0.75	1	800 225-1852
Prudential Diversified Consv Gr A	Growth	8.2					0.75	1.66	800 225-1852
Prudential Diversified Consv Gr B	Growth	8.2					0.75	1.66	800 225-1852
Prudential Diversified Consv Gr C	Growth	8.2					0.75	1.66	800 225-1852
Prudential Diversified Consv Gr Z	Growth	8.3					0.75	1.66	800 225-1852
Prudential Diversified High Gr A	Growth	17.3					0.75	1.47	800 225-1852
Prudential Diversified High Gr B	Growth	16.2					0.75	1.47	800 225-1852
Prudential Diversified High Gr C	Growth	16.2					0.75	1.46	800 225-1852
Prudential Diversified High Gr Z	Growth	17.5					0.75	1.47	800 225-1852
Prudential Diversified Mod Gr A	Growth	11.8					0.75	1.62	800 225-1852
Prudential Diversified Mod Gr B	Growth	10.8					0.75	1.62	800 225-1852
Prudential Diversified Mod Gr C	Growth	10.8					0.75	1.62	800 225-1852
Prudential Diversified Mod Gr Z	Growth	12.2					0.75	1.62	800 225-1852
Prudential Equity Fund A	Growth	-8.5	7.95	13.52	3	3	0.46	0.6	800 225-1852
Prudential Equity Fund B	Growth	-9.1	7.16	12.67	3	3	0.46	1.71	800 225-1852
Prudential Equity Fund C	Growth	-9.1	7.16	12.65	4	3	0.46	0.6	800 225-1852
Prudential Equity Income A	Income	-10.6	5.96	12.58	5	3	0.5	0.78	800 225-1852
Prudential Equity Income B	Income	-11.3	5.18	11.76	5	3	0.5	1.77	800 225-1852
Prudential Equity Income C	Income	-11.3	5.18	11.76	5	3	0.5	0.78	800 225-1852
Prudential Europe Growth A	European	17.2	16.18	16.75	3	3	0.75	1.17	800 225-1852
Prudential Europe Growth B	European	16.3	15.21	15.82	3	3	0.75	1.43	800 225-1852
Prudential Financial Services Fd A	Financial	-8.6					0.75		800 225-1852
Prudential Financial Services Fd B	Financial	-9.3					0.75		800 225-1852
Prudential Financial Services Fd C	Financial	-9.3					0.75		800 225-1852
Prudential Financial Services Fd Z	Financial	-8.5					0.75		800 225-1852
Prudential Global Genesis A	Global	25.4	9.08	10.25	4	3	1	1.78	800 225-1852
Prudential Global Genesis B	Global	24.7	8.35	9.45	4	3	1	2.77	800 225-1852
Prudential Global Genesis C	Global	24.7	8.35	9.45	4	3	1	1.78	800 225-1852
Prudential Global Utility A	Utilities	-1.3	12.11	14.27	3	2	0.67	1.16	800 225-1852
Prudential Global Utility B	Utilities	-2.1	11.28	13.42	3	2	0.67	0.93	800 225-1852
Prudential Health Sciences Fund A	Health	61.1					0.75		800 225-1852
Prudential Health Sciences Fund B	Health	59.9					0.75		800 225-1852
Prudential Health Sciences Fund C	Health	59.9					0.75		800 225-1852
Prudential Health Sciences Fund Z	Health	59.9					0.75		800 225-1852
Prudential Intl Value Fund A	Foreign	14.1	9.52		4	3	0.75	1.61	800 225-1852
Prudential Intl Value Fund B	Foreign	13.3	8.72		4	3	1	1.36	800 225-1852
Prudential Intl Value Fund C	Foreign	13.3	8.72		4	3	1	1.36	800 225-1852
Prudential Intl Value Fund Z	Foreign	14.5	9.83	12.97	4	3	1	1.36	800 225-1852
Prudential Jennison Growth & Inc A	Growth/Inc	5.8	13.76		3	3	0.59	1.16	800 225-1852
Prudential Jennison Growth & Inc B	Growth/Inc	5	12.89		3	3	0.59	1.16	800 225-1852
Prudential Jennison Growth & Inc C	Growth/Inc	5	12.88		3	3	0.59	1.16	800 225-1852
Prudential Jennison Growth & Inc Z	Growth/Inc	6.1	14.01		3	3	0.59	1.16	800 225-1852
Prudential Jennison Growth Fund A	Growth	27.1	31.36		1	4	0.59	0.84	800 225-1852
Prudential Jennison Growth Fund B	Growth	26.1	30.38		1	4	0.59	0.84	800 225-1852
Prudential Jennison Growth Fund C	Growth	26.1	30.38		1	4	0.59	0.84	800 225-1852

Stock Fund Name	Objective	Annualized Return for			Rank		Max Load	Expense Ratio	Toll-Free Telephone
		1 Year	3 Years	5 Years	Overall	Risk			
Prudential Jennison Growth Fund Z	Growth	27.4	31.7		1	4	0.59	0.84	800 225-1852
Prudential Latin Am Equity A	Foreign	28.4					1.25	8.47	800 225-1852
Prudential Latin Am Equity B	Foreign	27.7					1.25	8.47	800 225-1852
Prudential Latin Am Equity C	Foreign	27.7					1.25	8.47	800 225-1852
Prudential Latin Am Equity Z	Foreign	28.7					1.25	8.47	800 225-1852
Prudential Mid-Cap Value A	Growth	3.4					0.69	1.18	800 225-1852
Prudential Mid-Cap Value B	Growth	3.1					0.69	1.18	800 225-1852
Prudential Mid-Cap Value C	Growth						0.69	1.18	800 225-1852
Prudential Mid-Cap Value Z	Growth	4.4					0.69	1.18	800 225-1852
Prudential Muni-FL A	Muni State	1.9	4.03	5.31	2	3	0.5	0.69	800 225-1852
Prudential Muni-FL B	Muni State	1.6	3.69	4.95	3	3	0.5	0.69	800 225-1852
Prudential Natural Resources A	Energy/Res	22.5	6.24	10.6	4	4	0.75	1.6	800 225-1852
Prudential Natural Resources B	Energy/Res	21.6	5.47	9.65	4	4	0.75	2.25	800 225-1852
Prudential Pacific Growth A	Pacific	9.8	-2.56	1.26	5	3	0.75	1.62	800 225-1852
Prudential Pacific Growth B	Pacific	9.1	-3.25	0.57	5	3	0.75	2.47	800 225-1852
Prudential Pacific Growth C	Pacific	9.1	-3.25	0.57	5	3	0.75	1.62	800 225-1852
Prudential Real Estate Fd A	Real Est	-1.1					0.75	1.31	800 225-1852
Prudential Real Estate Fd B	Real Est	-1.9					0.75	1.31	800 225-1852
Prudential Real Estate Fd C	Real Est	-2.1					0.75	1.31	800 225-1852
Prudential Real Estate Fd Z	Real Est	-1.3					0.75	1.31	800 225-1852
Prudential Sector Utility Fund A	Utilities	11.5	14.5	17.61	2	2	0.4	0.53	800 225-1852
Prudential Sector Utility Fund B	Utilities	10.6	13.59	16.7	2	2	0.4	1.53	800 225-1852
Prudential Sector Utility Fund C	Utilities	10.8	13.64	16.72	2	2	0.4	0.53	800 225-1852
Prudential Sm Cap Quantum A	Small Co	11.4					0.59	1.01	800 225-1852
Prudential Sm Cap Quantum B	Small Co	10.6					0.59	1.01	800 225-1852
Prudential Sm Cap Quantum C	Small Co	10.6					0.59	1.01	800 225-1852
Prudential Sm Cap Quantum Z	Small Co	11.6					0.59	1.01	800 225-1852
Prudential Small Company Fund A	Small Co	5.5	3.8	11.64	4	3	0.69	0.92	800 225-1852
Prudential Small Company Fund B	Small Co	4.7	3.01	10.81	4	3	0.69	2.02	800 225-1852
Prudential Small Company Fund C	Small Co	4.7	3.03	10.83	4	3	0.69	0.92	800 225-1852
Prudential Stock Index Z	Growth	7.1	19.26	23.03	2	5	0.29	0.4	800 225-1852
Prudential Tax Managed Equity A	Growth	8.7					0.65		800 225-1852
Prudential Tax Managed Equity B	Growth	7.9					0.65		800 225-1852
Prudential Tax Managed Equity C	Growth	7.9					1		800 225-1852
Prudential Tax Managed Equity Z	Growth	8.9					0.65		800 225-1852
Prudential Technology Fund A	Technology	81.2					0.75		800 225-1852
Prudential Technology Fund B	Technology	80					0.75		800 225-1852
Prudential Technology Fund C	Technology	80					0.75		800 225-1852
Prudential Technology Fund Z	Technology	81.7					0.75		800 225-1852
Prudential World Global Fund A	Global	33.2	19.19	18.71	3	3	0.75	1.1	800 225-1852
Prudential World Global Fund B	Global	32.2	18.39	17.92	3	3	0.75	1.07	800 225-1852
Prudential World Global Fund C	Global	32	18.29	17.86	3	3	0.75	1.1	800 225-1852
Purisima Total Return Fund	AssetAlloc	14.7	18.55		2	3	1	1.85	800 841-2858
Putnam Asia Pacific Growth A	Pacific	23.8	5.83	6.96	4	4	0.8	1.45	800 225-1581
Putnam Asia Pacific Growth B	Pacific	22.9	5.08	6.17	4	4	0.8	1.15	800 225-1581
Putnam Asia Pacific Growth M	Pacific	23.2	5.32	6.45	4	4	0.8	1.03	800 225-1581
Putnam Asset Alloc-Balanced A	Balanced	13.3	11.55	15.06	3	2	0.58	1.13	800 225-1581
Putnam Asset Alloc-Balanced B	Balanced	12.4	10.73	14.22	3	2	0.58	0.94	800 225-1581
Putnam Asset Alloc-Balanced C	Balanced	12.4	10.7	13.5	3	2	0.58	0.94	800 225-1581
Putnam Asset Alloc-Balanced M	Balanced	12.7	10.97	12.75	4	2	0.58	0.82	800 225-1581
Putnam Asset Alloc-Conserv A	AssetAlloc	6.5	7.52	10.05	3	1	0.67	1.31	800 225-1581
Putnam Asset Alloc-Conserv B	AssetAlloc	5.9	6.65	9.21	4	1	0.67	1.04	800 225-1581
Putnam Asset Alloc-Conserv C	AssetAlloc	5.8	6.79	9.28	4	1	0.67	1.04	800 225-1581
Putnam Asset Alloc-Conserv M	AssetAlloc	6.1	7	8.8	3	1	0.67	0.92	800 225-1581
Putnam Asset Alloc-Growth A	AssetAlloc	11.9	12.88	16.61	3	2	0.6	1.2	800 225-1581
Putnam Asset Alloc-Growth B	AssetAlloc	12	12.36	15.99	3	2	0.6	1	800 225-1581
Putnam Asset Alloc-Growth C	AssetAlloc	12.1	12.36	15.97	3	2	0.6	1	800 225-1581
Putnam Asset Alloc-Growth M	AssetAlloc	12.2	12.69	16.28	3	2	0.6	0.86	800 225-1581

Stock Fund Name	Objective	Annualized Return for			Rank		Max Load	Expense Ratio	Toll-Free Telephone
		1 Year	3 Years	5 Years	Overall	Risk			
Putnam Asset Alloc:Balanced Y	Balanced	13.5	11.75	14.71	3	2	0.58	0.45	800 225-1581
Putnam Asset Alloc:Conservative Y	AssetAlloc	6.9	7.74	9.22	3	1	0.67	0.54	800 225-1581
Putnam Asset Alloc:Growth Y	AssetAlloc	13.1	13.5	17.18	3	2	0.6	0.5	800 225-1581
Putnam Balanced Retirement A	Balanced	-6.1	5.24	10.12	3	1	0.6	1.09	800 225-1581
Putnam Balanced Retirement B	Balanced	-6.9	4.5	9.3	3	1	0.6	0.91	800 225-1581
Putnam Balanced Retirement C	Balanced						0.6		800 225-1581
Putnam Balanced Retirement M	Balanced	-6.6	4.69	9.58	3	1	0.6	0.78	800 225-1581
Putnam Emerging Markets A	Foreign	16.9	-1.51		4	5	1	2.1	800 225-1581
Putnam Emerging Markets B	Foreign	15.9	-2.21		4	5	1	1.41	800 225-1581
Putnam Emerging Markets C	Foreign						1		
Putnam Emerging Markets M	Foreign	16.2	-2.04		4	5	1	1.29	800 225-1581
Putnam Equity Income A	Income	-12.1	6.46	14.11	3	2	0.54	0.93	800 225-1581
Putnam Equity Income B	Income	-12.9	5.66	13.24	3	2	0.54	0.84	800 225-1581
Putnam Equity Income M	Income	-12.6	5.91	13.53	3	2	0.54	0.72	800 225-1581
Putnam Europe Growth A	European	24.1	17.63	19.78	2	3	0.69	0.59	800 225-1581
Putnam Europe Growth B	European	23.2	16.81	18.9	2	3	0.69	1.97	800 225-1581
Putnam Europe Growth M	European	23.6	17.14	19.24	2	3	0.69	1.72	800 225-1581
Putnam FL Tax Exempt Income A	Muni State	1.9	3.69	4.96	2	3	0.5	0.97	800 225-1581
Putnam FL Tax Exempt Income B	Muni State	1	2.92	4.22	4	3	0.5	1.62	800 225-1581
Putnam FL Tax Exempt Income M	Muni State	1.4	3.33	4.62	3	3	0.5	1.28	800 225-1581
Putnam Fund For Growth & Income C	Growth/Inc						0.4		800 225-1581
Putnam Fund for Gr & Inc A	Growth/Inc	-11.2	6.61	14.48	3	3	0.4	0.81	800 225-1581
Putnam Fund for Gr & Inc B	Growth/Inc	-11.8	5.81	13.62	4	3	0.4	0.77	800 225-1581
Putnam Fund for Gr & Inc M	Growth/Inc	-11.7	6.07	11.42	4	3	0.4	1.29	800 225-1581
Putnam George Fund A	Balanced	-6.9	5.91	11.68	3	1	0.47	0.92	800 225-1581
Putnam George Fund B	Balanced	-7.7	5.1	10.84	3	1	0.47	1.67	800 225-1581
Putnam George Fund M	Balanced	-7.4	5.37	11.11	3	1	0.47	1.42	800 225-1581
Putnam Global Equity A	Global	36.9	26.3	25.12	1	3	0.68	1.23	800 225-1581
Putnam Global Equity B	Global	35.9	25.45	24.34	1	3	0.68	0.94	800 225-1581
Putnam Global Equity M	Global	36.3	25.8		1	4	0.68	0.81	800 225-1581
Putnam Global Govt Income A	Intl Bond	0.1	-0.05	3.24	5	5	0.69	0.6	800 225-1581
Putnam Global Govt Income B	Intl Bond	-0.6	-0.8	2.19	5	5	0.69	0.98	800 225-1581
Putnam Global Govt Income Trust C	Intl Bond						0.69		800 225-1581
Putnam Global Growth Fd A	Global	36.3	22.93	22.41	2	4	0.63	1.1	800 225-1581
Putnam Global Growth Fd B	Global	35.2	21.98	21.46	2	4	0.63	0.93	800 225-1581
Putnam Global Growth Fd M	Global	35.6	22.29	21.77	2	4	0.63	0.8	800 225-1581
Putnam Global Growth and Income C	Growth/Inc						0.48		
Putnam Global Natural Resources A	Energy/Res	5.9	5.21	11.57	4	4	0.69	1.15	800 225-1581
Putnam Global Natural Resources B	Energy/Res	5.2	4.1	9.18	5	4	0.69	0.94	800 225-1581
Putnam Global Natural Resources M	Energy/Res	5.4	4.64		4	4	0.69	0.82	800 225-1581
Putnam Growth Opportunities A	Growth	36.3	35.43		1	4	0.58	1	800 225-1581
Putnam Growth Opportunities B	Growth	35.3					0.58	1.76	800 225-1581
Putnam Growth Opportunities M	Growth	35.6					0.58	1.51	800 225-1581
Putnam Health Sciences Trust A	Health	36.1	20.42	25.25	2	3	0.54	0.94	800 225-1581
Putnam Health Sciences Trust B	Health	35.1	19.52	23.6	2	3	0.54	0.83	800 225-1581
Putnam Health Sciences Trust C	Health						0.54		800 225-1581
Putnam International Growth A	Foreign	44	24.74	23.91	2	3	0.64	1.15	800 225-1581
Putnam International Growth B	Foreign	43	23.86	23.02	2	3	0.64	2.02	800 225-1581
Putnam International Growth Fund Y	Foreign	44.4	24.58		2	3	0.64	1.02	800 225-1581
Putnam International Growth M	Foreign	43.3	24.11	23.09	2	3	0.64	1.77	800 225-1581
Putnam International Voyager A	Foreign	74.1	35.56		1	4	1	1.78	800 225-1581
Putnam International Voyager B	Foreign	72.9	34.49		1	4	1	1.28	800 225-1581
Putnam International Voyager C	Foreign						1		
Putnam International Voyager M	Foreign	73.4	34.86		1	4	1	1.14	800 225-1581
Putnam Intl Growth & Inc A	Foreign	16.7	15.29		3	3	0.76	1.3	800 225-1581
Putnam Intl Growth & Inc B	Foreign	15.6	14.43		2	3	0.76	2.04	800 225-1581
Putnam Intl Growth & Inc M	Foreign	15.6	14.56		2	3	0.76	0.83	800 225-1581
Putnam Intl New Opportunities A	Foreign	46.7	21.4	20.59	3	4	0.9	1.54	800 225-1581

Stock Fund Name	Objective	Annualized Return for			Rank		Max Load	Expense Ratio	Toll-Free Telephone
		1 Year	3 Years	5 Years	Overall	Risk			
Putnam Intl New Opportunities B	Foreign	45.7	20.51		3	4	0.9	1.18	800 225-1581
Putnam Intl New Opportunities M	Foreign	46.1	20.83		3	4	0.9	1.06	800 225-1581
Putnam Investors Fund A	Growth	15.6	24.79	26.12	2	3	0.46	0.85	800 225-1581
Putnam Investors Fund B	Growth	14.8	23.87	25.18	2	3	0.46	0.89	800 225-1581
Putnam Investors Fund M	Growth	15.1	24.2	25.49	2	3	0.46	1.38	800 225-1581
Putnam New Opportunities A	Agg Growth	60.5	35.89	30.61	2	4	0.47	0.88	800 225-1581
Putnam New Opportunities B	Agg Growth	59.5	34.98	29.7	2	4	0.47	1.6	800 225-1581
Putnam New Opportunities C	Agg Growth						0.47		
Putnam New Opportunities M	Agg Growth	59.7	35.21	29.96	2	4	0.47	1.42	800 225-1581
Putnam New Value Fund A	Growth	-10.2	4.52	12.99	4	3	0.66	1.12	800 225-1581
Putnam New Value Fund B	Growth	-11	3.61		4	3	0.66	0.91	800 225-1581
Putnam New Value Fund M	Growth	-10.7	3.93		4	3	0.66	0.78	800 225-1581
Putnam OTC & Emerging Growth C	Small Co						0.55		
Putnam OTC & Emerging Growth Y	Small Co	71.3					0.55	0.72	800 225-1581
Putnam OTC Emerging Growth A	Small Co	70.8	33.51	27.78	2	5	0.55	0.97	800 225-1581
Putnam OTC Emerging Growth B	Small Co	69.4	32.52	26.86	2	5	0.55	1.72	800 225-1581
Putnam OTC Emerging Growth M	Small Co	69.9	32.81	27.12	2	5	0.55	1.47	800 225-1581
Putnam Preferred Income A	Income	-2.4	2.29	5.12	4	1	0.65	0.88	800 225-1581
Putnam Research Fund A	Growth	18.8	24.53		1	3	0.63	1.08	800 225-1581
Putnam Research Fund B	Growth	17.9					0.63	1.83	800 225-1581
Putnam Research Fund M	Growth	18.2					0.63	1.58	800 225-1581
Putnam Utilities Gr & Inc A	Utilities	-1.9	11.37	14.41	3	2	0.6	1	800 225-1581
Putnam Utilities Gr & Inc B	Utilities	-2.7	10.52	12.07	3	2	0.6	0.86	800 225-1581
Putnam Utilities Gr & Inc M	Utilities	-2.4	12.79	12.01	3	2	0.6	0.73	800 225-1581
Putnam Utilities Growth & Income C	Utilities						0.6		
Putnam Vista Fund A	Growth	58.6	33.46	30.37	1	4	0.47	0.9	800 225-1581
Putnam Vista Fund B	Growth	57.5	32.49	29.41	2	4	0.47	1.68	800 225-1581
Putnam Vista Fund C	Growth						0.47		
Putnam Vista Fund M	Growth	57.8	32.78	29.79	2	4	0.47	1.43	800 225-1581
Putnam Voyager A	Agg Growth	38	30.27	27.15	2	4	0.46	0.88	800 225-1581
Putnam Voyager B	Agg Growth	36.9	29.29	26.19	2	4	0.46	1.64	800 225-1581
Putnam Voyager Fund II C	Agg Growth						0.58		
Putnam Voyager Fund Y	Agg Growth	38.4	30.61	27.48	1	4	0.46	0.65	800 225-1581
Putnam Voyager II A	Agg Growth	51.9	34.93	28.98	1	4	0.58	1.03	800 225-1581
Putnam Voyager II B	Agg Growth	50.7	33.91		2	4	0.58	0.89	800 225-1581
Putnam Voyager II M	Agg Growth	51.2	34.26		2	4	0.58	0.76	800 225-1581
Putnam Voyager M	Agg Growth	37.4	29.66	26.53	2	4	0.46	1.39	800 225-1581
Quaker Aggressive Growth	Agg Growth	60.5	42.67		1	3	1	1.35	800-220-8888
Quaker Core Equity Fund	Growth	14.2	21.93		1	3	0.75	1.43	800-220-8888
Quaker Large Cap Value	Growth	-16.2	-0.14		5	4	0.5	2.02	800-220-8888
Quaker Mid Cap Value	Growth	-2.3					0.75	1.62	800-220-8888
Quaker Small Cap Value	Small Co	1.3	5.21		5	3	1.64	1.3	800-220-8888
Quant Emerging Markets Instl	Foreign	6.3	-3.54		5	4	0.8	1.73	800 331-1244
Quant Emg-Markets Ord	Foreign	5.8	-4.01	1.85	5	4	0.8	2.24	800 331-1244
Quant Foreign Value Instl	Foreign	3.4					1	1.69	800 331-1244
Quant Foreign Value Ord	Foreign	3.2					1	1.89	800 331-1244
Quant Gr & Inc Inst	Growth/Inc	40.7	29.18	28.23	1	3	0.75	0.14	800 331-1244
Quant Gr & Inc Ord	Growth/Inc	39.9	28.16	27.38	1	3	0.75	1.69	800 331-1244
Quant Intl Eq Inst	Foreign	7.4	2.21	5.33	5	3	1	1.58	800 331-1244
Quant Intl Eq Ord	Foreign	6.9	1.74	4.76	5	3	1	2.08	800 331-1244
Quant Mid Cap Inst	Agg Growth	34.4	24.21	23.03	2	4	1	1.62	800 331-1244
Quant Mid Cap Ord	Agg Growth	33.2	23.79		2	4	1	1.64	800 331-1244
Quant Small Cap Inst	Growth	48.2	16.54	18.74	3	4	1	1.43	800 331-1244
Quant Small Cap Ord	Growth	47.4	15.97	18.05	3	4	1	2	800 331-1244
RBB Fd-NI Growth Fund	Small Co	56	24.33		3	4	0.52	1	800 686-3742
RBB Fd-NI Micro Cap Fund	Small Co	54.4	30.04		2	4	0.51	1	800 686-3742
RBB Fd-NI Mid Cap Fund	Growth	15.4	19.64		3	3	0.36	1	800 686-3742

Stock Fund Name	Objective	Annualized Return for			Rank		Max Load	Expense Ratio	Toll-Free Telephone
		1 Year	3 Years	5 Years	Overall	Risk			
RCB Growth and Income Fund	Growth	0.9					0.59		
RCB Small Cap	Growth	3.3					0.84		
REvest Value Fund	Growth/Inc	-2.4	3.28	9.22	3	2	1	1.3	877 473-8378
RS Contrarian Fd	Global	15.5	-9.73	-1.35	5	4	1.5	2.43	800 766-3863
RS Divers Growth	Growth	73.8	52.33		1	5	1	1.89	800 766-3863
RS Emerging Growth Fd	Small Co	100.6	62.74	44.97	2	5	1	1.51	800 766-3863
RS Glb Natl Res	Energy/Res	3.2	-7.84		4	4	1	2.08	800 766-3863
RS Info Age	Technology	92.2	56.86		1	5	1	1.67	800 766-3863
RS Internet Age Fund	Technology						1.25		800 766-3863
RS Microcap Gr	Small Co	60.2	29.84		3	5	1.25	1.92	800 766-3863
RS MidCap Opport	Growth/Inc	29	25.96		2	4	1	1.58	800 766-3863
RS Partners	Small Co	4.7	-3.61		4	3	1.25	1.92	800 766-3863
RSI Retirement Core Equity	Growth	10.4	19.72	23.21	2	3	0.52	-0.96	800 772-3615
RSI Retirement Emerg Growth Equity	Small Co	68.9	24.43	24.52	3	5	1.12	2.08	800 772-3615
RSI Retirement International Equity	Foreign	21.5	8.85	12.67	4	3	0.9	1.96	800 772-3615
RSI Retirement Value Equity	Growth	5	16.91	22.22	2	3	0.38	-1.02	800 772-3615
RYDEX Arktos Fund Inv	Other	-48.9					0.9	1.37	800 820-0888
RYDEX Banking Fund Inv	Financial	-28.3					0.84	2.22	800 820-0888
RYDEX Basic Materials Fund Inv	Other	-26.9					0.84	1.61	800 820-0888
RYDEX Biotechnology Fund Inv	Health	134.5					0.84	1.55	800 820-0888
RYDEX Consumer Products Fund Inv	Other	-19.2					0.84	1.54	800 820-0888
RYDEX Electronics Fund Inv	Technology	129.6					0.84	1.56	800 820-0888
RYDEX Energy Fund Inv	Energy/Res	10.5					0.84	1.57	800 820-0888
RYDEX Energy Services Fund Inv	Energy/Res	39.1					0.84	1.62	800 820-0888
RYDEX Financial Services Fund Inv	Financial	-12.3					0.84	1.57	800 820-0888
RYDEX Health Care Fund Inv	Health	12.2					0.84	1.42	800 820-0888
RYDEX Leisure Fund Inv	Other	-0.6					0.84	1.59	800 820-0888
RYDEX Technology Fund Inv	Technology	49.6					0.84	1.38	800 820-0888
RYDEX Telecommunications Fund Inv	Utilities	22.5					0.84	1.55	800 820-0888
RYDEX Transportation Fund Inv	Other	-32.4					0.84	1.58	800 820-0888
Rainbow Fund	Growth/Inc	-18	-11.42	0.32	5	3	0.62	3.72	
Rainier Balanced Portfolio	Balanced	11.1	15.04	17.08	3	2	0.69	1.19	800 248-6314
Rainier Small-Mid Cap Eq Portfolio	Small Co	23.9	14.69	20.11	3	3	0.84	1.25	800 248-6314
Red Oak Technology Select Funds	Technology	183.7					0.73	1.35	800 342-5734
Regional Opportunity Fund B	Growth	3.6	24.87		3	4	1.25	2.7	
Regions Aggressive Growth	Growth	60.1					0.75	1.19	800 433-2829
Regions Balanced Fund A	Balanced	5					0.8	1.11	800 433-2829
Regions Balanced Fund B	Balanced	5.1	11.69	13.35	3	1	0.8	1.29	800 433-2829
Regions Growth Fund A	Growth/Inc	18.5		7.08			0.8	0.97	800 433-2829
Regions Growth Fund B	Growth/Inc	18.1	24.73	25.71	2	3	0.8	1.18	800 433-2829
Regions Value Fund A	Growth/Inc	-9.5					0.8	1.04	800 433-2829
Regions Value Fund B	Growth/Inc	-9.7	6.35	13.16	4	2	0.8	1.21	800 433-2829
Republic Equity Inv A	Growth	-5.3	13.9		3	3	0.5	0.8	800 782-8183
Republic Opportunity Fund A	Agg Growth	41.7	21.87		3	4	0.91	1.67	800 782-8183
Republic Overseas Equity	Foreign	36.6	18.31		2	3	0.75	1.79	800 782-8183
Reserve Blue Chip Growth A	Growth	28.4	32.75	25.14	2	4	1.19	1.53	800 637-1700
Reserve Blue Chip Growth Fund I	Growth	33.9					0.9	0.88	800 637-1700
Reserve Informed Investors Gr R	Growth	65.2	43.35	24.35	2	5	1.3	1.61	800 637-1700
Reserve Informed Investors Growth I	Growth	71.8					1	1.06	800 637-1700
Reserve International Equity A	Foreign	50.9	17.23		3	4	1.55	1.87	800 637-1700
Reserve International Equity Fund I	Foreign	50.5					1.25	1.29	800 637-1700
Reserve Large Cap Growth R	Growth	-4.5	13.28		3	3	1.19	1.44	800 637-1700
Reserve Large-Cap Growth I	Growth	-2.6					1.19	0.86	800 637-1700
Reserve Small Cap Growth I	Small Co	104.8					1	1	800 637-1700
Reserve Small Cap R	Small Co	107.2	51.62	33.94	2	5	1.3	1.61	800 637-1700
Reserve Strategic Growth	Growth	18.8					1.19		800 637-1700
Reynolds Blue Chip Growth Fund	Growth	26.4	34.33	33.03	1	4	1	1.3	800 773-9665
Reynolds Fund	Growth						1		800 773-9665

369

Stock Fund Name	Objective	Annualized Return for			Rank		Max Load	Expense Ratio	Toll-Free Telephone
		1 Year	3 Years	5 Years	Overall	Risk			
Reynolds Opportunity Fund	Agg Growth	32.2	38.13	30.78	2	4	1	1.3	800 773-9665
Riggs Large Cap Growth Fund B	Growth						0.75		800 934-3883
Riggs Large Cap Growth R	Growth						0.75		800 934-3883
Riggs Small Company Stock B	Small Co	4.6					0.8	2.33	800 934-3883
Riggs Small Company Stock R	Small Co	5.1	5.62	12.93	4	4	0.8	1.62	800 934-3883
Riggs Stock Fund B	Growth/Inc	-5.1					0.75	2.16	800 934-3883
Riggs Stock Fund R	Growth/Inc	-4.7	9.44	16.39	3	3	0.75	1.38	800 934-3883
Riggs Stock Fund Y	Growth/Inc						0.75		800 934-3883
Rightime Blue Chip Fund	Flexible	-8	8.75	10.12	3	1	0.5	2.08	800 866-9393
Rightime Fund	Flexible	4.3	11.71	9.8	3	2	0.5	2.5	800 866-9393
Rightime Midcap Fund	Flexible	-2.2	14.82	12.46	3	1	0.5	2.16	800 866-9393
Rightime Social Awareness	Growth/Inc	-17.9	5.73	9.27	4	2	0.5	2.2	800 866-9393
Riverfront Balanced A	Balanced	12.1	16.75	14.7	2	1	0.8	1.61	800 424-2295
Riverfront Balanced B	Balanced	11.5	15.89	14.04	3	1	0.8	2.39	800 424-2295
Riverfront Income Equity A	Growth/Inc	2	7.6	14.2	4	2	0.94	1.84	800 424-2295
Riverfront Income Equity B	Growth/Inc	1.2	6.81	13.55	4	2	0.94	2.64	800 424-2295
Riverfront Large Company Fund B	Growth/Inc	18.1	24.7		2	3	0.8	2.25	800 424-2295
Riverfront Large Company Select A	Growth/Inc	19	25.65		2	3	0.8	1.52	800 424-2295
Riverfront Small Company A	Growth	66.9	23.75	20.35	3	5	0.8	1.92	800 424-2295
Riverfront Small Company B	Growth	65.7	22.73		3	5	0.8	2.68	800 424-2295
Rockhaven Fund	Growth/Inc	21.3					1.5	1.5	800 522-3508
Roulston Emerging Growth Fund	Growth	257.3					0.75		800 332-6459
Roulston Growth & Income Fund	Growth/Inc	-19.9	-1.16	8.7	5	3	0.75		800 332-6459
Roulston Growth Fund	Growth	20.7	4.33	10.63	4	3	0.75	1.53	800 332-6459
Roulston International Equity Fund	Foreign						0.75		800 332-6459
Royce Fund-Low Priced Stock	Small Co	29.3	19.01	18.28	3	3	1.5	1.48	800 221-4268
Royce Fund-Micro-Cap Fund	Small Co	24	11.77	13.67	3	3	1.5	1.48	800 221-4268
Royce Fund-Opportunity Fund	Small Co	35.9	21.58		2	3	1	1.48	800 221-4268
Royce Fund-Premier	Small Co	8.8	8.67	12.59	3	2	1	1.23	800 221-4268
Royce Fund-Total Return Fund	Growth/Inc	3	6.47	13.64	3	1	1	1.25	800 221-4268
Royce Fund-Trust & GiftShares Inv	Small Co	30.9	26.98		1	3	1	1.48	800 221-4268
Royce Giftshares Fund Consultant Cl	Small Co	29.7					1	2.49	800 221-4268
Rushmore American Gas Index	Other	9.9	12.28	15.22	3	2	0.4	0.84	800 343-3355
Rydex Series-Nova Fund Inv	Agg Growth	3.7	21.37	27.92	3	4	0.75	1.17	800 820-0888
Rydex Series-OTC Inv	Agg Growth	61.7	57.47	47.97	1	5	0.75	1.14	800 820-0888
Rydex Series-Precious Metals Fd	Prec Metal	-17.1	-17.79	-14.93	5	5	0.75	1.17	800 820-0888
Rydex Series-Ursa Fund Inv	Growth	-1.2	-12.22	-14.18	5	3	0.9	1.37	800 820-0888
SAFECO Advisor Dividend Inc Fund A	Income	-8.6	2.91		5	2	0.68	1.37	800 624-5711
SAFECO Advisor Dividend Inc Fund B	Income	-9.3	2.28		5	2	0.68	2.12	800 624-5711
SAFECO Advisor Growth Oppt Fund A	Growth	7.2	8.99		4	4	0.68	1.18	800 624-5711
SAFECO Advisor Growth Oppt Fund B	Growth	6.3	8.06		4	4	0.68	2.12	800 624-5711
SAFECO Advisor International A	Foreign	19.4	11.19		3	3	1.1	1.98	800 624-5711
SAFECO Advisor International B	Foreign	16.8	10.2		4	3	1.1	2.93	800 624-5711
SAFECO Advisor Small Company Val A	Small Co	20.2	-0.35		4	4	0.84	1.72	800 624-5711
SAFECO Advisor Small Company Val B	Small Co	19.1	-3.93		4	4	0.84	2.5	800 624-5711
SAFECO Advisor US Value Fund A	Growth/Inc	-9.6	4.31		5	2	0.75	1.69	800 624-5711
SAFECO Advisor US Value Fund B	Growth/Inc	-10.1	3.56		5	2	0.75	2.39	800 624-5711
SAFECO Balanced A	Balanced	-5	6.13		3	1	0.69	1.48	800 624-5711
SAFECO Balanced B	Balanced	-5.6	5.37		4	1	0.69	2.24	800 624-5711
SAFECO Balanced Fd	Balanced	-4.6	6.11		3	1	0.69	1.13	800 624-5711
SAFECO Dividend Inc Fd	Income	-8.4	3.2	11.73	3	2	0.68	1.31	800 624-5711
SAFECO Equity A	Growth/Inc	-4.3	11.85		2	3	0.75	0.94	800 624-5711
SAFECO Equity B	Growth/Inc	-4.9	10.83		2	2	0.75	1.95	800 624-5711
SAFECO Equity Fd	Growth/Inc	-3.9	12.18	18.01	3	2	0.75	0.82	800 624-5711
SAFECO Growth Oppt Fd	Growth	7.4	9.08	16.3	3	4	0.68	1.01	800 624-5711
SAFECO International Fd	Foreign	19.7	11.69		3	3	1.1	1.62	800 624-5711
SAFECO Northwest A	Growth	39.6	22.7		2	4	0.75	1.48	800 624-5711
SAFECO Northwest B	Growth	38.9	22.03		3	4	0.75	2.24	800 624-5711

Stock Fund Name	Objective	Annualized Return for			Rank		Max Load	Expense Ratio	Toll-Free Telephone
		1 Year	3 Years	5 Years	Overall	Risk			
SAFECO Northwest Fd	Growth	45.3	23.17	21.8	2	4	0.75	1.1	800 624-5711
SAFECO Small Company Val Fd	Small Co	20.4	0.12		4	4	0.84	1.22	800 624-5711
SAFECO US Value Fd	Growth/Inc	-9.2	6.12		4	3	0.75	1.21	800 624-5711
SCM Strategic Growth Fund	Balanced	-1.1					0.84	1.25	800 773-3863
SEI Asset Alloc-Dvrs Consv A	Growth	6.6	10.13		3	1	0	0.11	800 342-5734
SEI Asset Alloc-Dvrs Consv D	Growth	5.6	9.05		3	1	0	1.12	800 342-5734
SEI Asset Alloc-Dvrs Glb Growth A	Foreign	10	12.79		3	2	0	0.11	800 342-5734
SEI Asset Alloc-Dvrs Glb Growth D	Foreign	8.9	11.64		3	2	0	1.12	800 342-5734
SEI Asset Alloc-Dvrs Glb Mod Gr A	Global	8.4	10.89		3	2	0	0.11	800 342-5734
SEI Asset Alloc-Dvrs Glb Mod Gr D	Global	7.3	9.73		4	4	0	1.12	800 342-5734
SEI Asset Alloc-Dvrs Glb Stock A	Global	11.3	14.33		3	3	0	0.11	800 342-5734
SEI Asset Alloc-Dvrs Glb Stock D	Global	10	13.2		4	3	0	1.12	800 342-5734
SEI Asset Alloc-Dvrs Mod Gr A	Growth	8	12.21		3	1	0	0.11	800 342-5734
SEI Asset Alloc-Dvrs Mod Gr D	Growth	6.9	11.33		3	1	0	1.12	800 342-5734
SEI Asset Alloc-Dvrs US Stock A	Growth	7.8	17.9		3	3	0	0.11	800 342-5734
SEI Asset Alloc-Dvrs US Stock D	Growth	6.8	16.75		2	3	0	0.53	800 342-5734
SEI Index Fds-S&P 500 Idx Fd A	Growth/Inc	6.9	19.17		2	3	0.19	0.4	800 342-5734
SEI Index Fds-S&P 500 Idx Fd E	Growth/Inc	7.1	19.4	23.53	2	3	0.14	0.25	800 342-5734
SEI Instl Managed Tr-Balanced A	Balanced	3.2	12.02	14.56	3	1	0.68	0.75	800 342-5734
SEI Instl Managed Tr-Eqty Inc A	Income	-11	7.61	14.79	3	2	0.75	0.84	800 342-5734
SEI Instl Managed Tr-Lg Cap Val A	Growth/Inc	-13.7	7.61	15.74	4	3	0.34	0.84	800 342-5734
SEI Instl Managed Tr-MidCap Gr A	Agg Growth	3.8	10.68	16	3	3	0.75	1	800 342-5734
SEI Instl Managed Tr-Sm Cap Gr A	Small Co	64.1	29.59	26.16	3	5	0.65	1.1	800 342-5734
SEI Instl Managed Tr-Sm Cap Gr D	Small Co	63.6	29.22	25.77	3	5	0.5	1.42	800 342-5734
SEI Instl Managed Tr-Sm Cap Val A	Small Co	-1.6	2.37	11.33	4	3	0.65	1.1	800 342-5734
SEI Instl Managed Tr-T/M Lg Cap A	Growth	-0.4					0.69	0.84	800 342-5734
SEI Intl Tr-Emerging Mkts Eq	Foreign	12.9	-6.73	0	5	4	0.94	1.94	800 342-5734
SEI Intl Tr-International Eq A	Foreign	20.4	12.26	13.32	3	3	0.51	1.28	800 342-5734
SEI Intl Tr-International Eq D	Foreign	20.2	11.28	12.53	3	3	0.47	1.42	800 342-5734
SEI Intl Tr-Intl Fixed Income	Intl Bond	0.2	2.03	1.91	5	5	0.84	1	800 342-5734
SG Cowen Income + Growth A	Income	-0.9	7.46	12.21	4	3	0.75	1.33	800 221-5616
SG Cowen Large Cap Value Fund A	Growth	-4.2					0.75	0.59	800 221-5616
SG Cowen Large Cap Value Fund B	Growth	-4.8					0.75	0.96	800 221-5616
SG Cowen Large Cap Value Fund I	Growth	-3.2					0.75	0.47	800 221-5616
SG Cowen Opportunity Fund A	Small Co	28.4	7.8	11.91	4	4	0.9	0.82	800 221-5616
SIFE Trust Fund Class B	Financial	-19	1.63		4	4	1	2.25	800 231-0356
SIFE Trust Fund Class C	Financial	-18.9	1.61		4	4	1	2.25	800 231-0356
SIFE Trust Fund Class I	Financial	-18.2	2.68	13.91	4	4	1.25	1.25	800 231-0356
SIFE Trust Fund Class II	Financial	-18.2	3.14		5	4	1	1.5	800 231-0356
SM&R Balanced Fund A	Balanced	10.9					0.75	1.46	
SM&R Balanced Fund B	Balanced	10					0.75	1.96	
SM&R Balanced Fund C	Balanced	8.9					0.75	2.24	
SM&R Balanced Fund T	Balanced	11.5	12.38	13.44	3	1	0.75	1.25	
SM&R Equity Income Fund A	Income	-9.3					0	1.47	
SM&R Equity Income Fund B	Income	-9.4					0.25	1.96	
SM&R Equity Income Fund C	Income	-9					0.25	2.22	
SM&R Equity Income T	Income	-7.9	7.45	12.39	3	2	0.75	1.05	
SM&R Growth Fund A	Growth	8.4					0	1.47	
SM&R Growth Fund B	Growth	9.3					0.25	1.96	
SM&R Growth Fund C	Growth	14.8					0.25	2.22	
SM&R Growth Fund T	Growth	10.7	16.06	17.86	3	3	0.75	0.86	
SMALLCAP World Fund	Global	44.5	20.32	20.22	3	4	0.67	1.09	800 421-9900
SSgA Active International	Foreign	16.1	5.93	8.11	4	3	0.75	1	800 997-7327
SSgA Emerging Markets	Foreign	15.3	-0.48	5.6	4	4	0.75	1.25	800 997-7327
SSgA Growth & Income	Growth/Inc	10.9	24	25.06	2	3	0.84	1.01	800 997-7327
SSgA Intnl Growth Oppty Fund	Foreign	34.7					0.75	1.1	800 997-7327
SSgA Life Solutions Balance	Balanced	11.1					0	0.27	800 997-7327
SSgA Life Solutions Growth	Growth	13.6					0	0.38	800 997-7327

Stock Fund Name	Objective	Annualized Return for			Rank		Max Load	Expense Ratio	Toll-Free Telephone
		1 Year	3 Years	5 Years	Overall	Risk			
SSgA Life Solutions Inc & Growth	Income	8.5					0	0.45	800 997-7327
SSgA Matrix Equity Fund	Growth	6	16.24	20.05	3	3	0.75	0.91	800 997-7327
SSgA S&P 500 Index	Growth	7.1	19.46	23.36	2	3	0.1	0.17	800 997-7327
SSgA SmallCap Fund	Small Co	18.3	4.28	15.05	4	3	0.75	1.07	800 997-7327
SSgA Special Equity	Small Co	71					0.75	1.1	800 997-7327
SSgA Tuckerman Active REIT	Real Est	11.3					0.65	1	800 997-7327
STI Classic Balanced Flex	Balanced	2.3	10.9	13.13	3	1	0.94	2.02	800 428-6970
STI Classic Balanced Inv	Balanced	3.2	11.75	14	3	1	0.94	1.27	800 428-6970
STI Classic Balanced Tr	Balanced	3.5	12.12	14.33	3	1	0.94	0.96	800 428-6970
STI Classic Capital Apprec Flex	Growth	4	16.37	20.26	2	3	1.14	2.29	800 428-6970
STI Classic Capital Apprec Inv	Growth	4.5	16.92	20.86	2	3	1.14	1.81	800 428-6970
STI Classic Capital Apprec Tr	Growth	5.2	17.65	21.61	2	3	1.14	1.16	800 428-6970
STI Classic FL Tax Exempt Flex	Muni State	3.2	3.81	4.63	3	3	0.65	1.37	800 428-6970
STI Classic FL Tax Exempt Inv	Muni State	3.8	4.29	5.13	2	3	0.65	0.86	800 428-6970
STI Classic FL Tax Exempt Tr	Muni State	3.9	4.47	5.3	2	3	0.65	0.67	800 428-6970
STI Classic Growth and Inc Flex	Growth/Inc	0	12.66	15.22	3	2	0.75	1.83	800 428-6970
STI Classic Growth and Inc Inv	Growth/Inc	0.7	13.46	18.09	3	2	0.75	1.08	800 428-6970
STI Classic Growth and Inc Tr	Growth/Inc	0.9	13.49	18.1	3	2	0.75	1.13	800 428-6970
STI Classic Intl Eq Flex	Foreign	9.3	5.89		4	3	1.25	2.52	800 428-6970
STI Classic Intl Eq Index Flex	Foreign	15.6	14.9	13.4	3	3	0.9	2.12	800 428-6970
STI Classic Intl Eq Index Inv	Foreign	16.5	15.44	14.02	3	3	0.9	1.46	800 428-6970
STI Classic Intl Eq Index Tr	Foreign	17	16.16	14.61	3	3	0.9	1.07	800 428-6970
STI Classic Intl Eq Inv	Foreign	10.1	6.66		4	3	1.25	1.83	800 428-6970
STI Classic Intl Eq Tr	Foreign	10.5	7.09		4	3	1.25	1.47	800 428-6970
STI Classic Life Vision Agg Gr Tr	Growth	5.1	7.77		4	2	0.25	0.27	800 428-6970
STI Classic Life Vision Gr & Inc Tr	Growth/Inc	4.6	4.74		4	2	0.25	0.27	800 428-6970
STI Classic Life Vision Mod Gr Tr	Balanced	3.3	6.04		3	1	0.25	0.25	800 428-6970
STI Classic Mid-Cap Equity Flex	Agg Growth	18.3	13.64	14.8	3	3	1.14	2.22	800 428-6970
STI Classic Mid-Cap Equity Inv	Agg Growth	19.1	14.35	15.57	3	3	1.14	1.62	800 428-6970
STI Classic Mid-Cap Equity Tr	Agg Growth	19.7	14.86	16.04	3	3	1.14	1.16	800 428-6970
STI Classic Small Cap Growth Flex	Small Co	29.6					1.14	2.25	800 428-6970
STI Classic Small Cap Growth Inv	Small Co						1.14		800 428-6970
STI Classic Small Cap Growth Tr	Small Co	30.9					1.14	1.19	800 428-6970
STI Classic Small Cap Val Eq Flex	Small Co	-6	-3.03		5	3	1.14	2.27	800 428-6970
STI Classic Small Cap Val Eq Tr	Small Co	-5	-2.01		4	3	1.14	1.21	800 428-6970
STI Classic Tax Sens Gr Stk Flex	Growth	5.6					1.14	2.25	800 428-6970
STI Classic Tax Sens Gr Stk Tr	Growth	6.6					1.14	1.19	800 428-6970
STI Classic Value Income Flex	Income	-20.8	2.26	10.77	3	3	0.8	2.02	800 428-6970
STI Classic Value Income Inv	Income	-20.2	3.01	11.58	4	3	0.8	1.27	800 428-6970
STI Classic Value Income Tr	Income	-19.9	3.39	11.99	3	3	0.8	0.92	800 428-6970
Salomon Brothers Asia Growth A	Pacific	22.8	-0.76		4	5	0.8	1.23	800 725-6666
Salomon Brothers Asia Growth B	Pacific	21.9	-1.53		4	5	0.8	1.98	800 725-6666
Salomon Brothers Asia Growth C	Pacific	21.8	-0.69		4	5	0.8	1.98	800 725-6666
Salomon Brothers Asia Growth O	Pacific	23	0.37		4	5	0.8	0.98	800 725-6666
Salomon Brothers Balanced A	Income	-0.6	7.63		3	1	0.55	0.94	800 725-6666
Salomon Brothers Balanced B	Income	-1.3	6.67		3	1	0.55	1.69	800 725-6666
Salomon Brothers Balanced C	Income	-1.4	6.69		3	1	0.55	1.69	800 725-6666
Salomon Brothers Balanced O	Income	-0.7	7.43		3	1	0.55	0.69	800 725-6666
Salomon Brothers Capital A	Growth	26.9	25.5		1	3	0.8	1.23	800 725-6666
Salomon Brothers Capital B	Growth	26.1	25.18		1	3	0.8	1.98	800 725-6666
Salomon Brothers Capital C	Growth	26.1	25.06		1	3	0.8	1.98	800 725-6666
Salomon Brothers Capital O	Growth	27.1	25.7	28.36	1	3	0.8	2.02	800 725-6666
Salomon Brothers Investors Value A	Growth/Inc	5.6	15.42	21.54	2	3	0.52	0.88	800 725-6666
Salomon Brothers Investors Value B	Growth/Inc	4.8	14.55	19.94	3	3	0.52	1.62	800 725-6666
Salomon Brothers Investors Value C	Growth/Inc	4.8	14.54	18.51	3	3	0.52	1.62	800 725-6666
Salomon Brothers Investors Value O	Growth/Inc	5.8	14.15	21.96	2	2	0.52	0.63	800 725-6666
Salomon Brothers Opportunity	Growth	6.6	8.7	15.67	3	2	1	1.13	800 725-6666
Sand Hill Portfolio Manager Fund	Flexible	12.9	12.28	14.38	3	1	1	1.89	800 527-9500

Stock Fund Name	Objective	Annualized Return for			Rank		Max Load	Expense Ratio	Toll-Free Telephone
		1 Year	3 Years	5 Years	Overall	Risk			
Santa Barbara Bender Growth Fund A	Growth	142.4					1.6	1.82	
Santa Barbara Fds-Bender Growth C	Growth	137.4	61.17		1	5	1.6	4.23	
Santa Barbara Fds-Bender Growth Y	Growth	139.2	62.66		1	5	1.6	3.49	
Schroder All Asia Fund	Pacific	17.1					0.9	1.94	800 464-3108
Schroder Emerging Markets Adv	Foreign	4.8	-5.92		5	4	0.89	1.62	800 464-3108
Schroder Emerging Markets Inv	Foreign	14.4					0.81	1.69	800 464-3108
Schroder Emerging Markets Inv	Foreign	4.7	-5.83	1.42	5	4	0.89	1.37	800 464-3108
Schroder Intl Equity Inv	Foreign	25.7	11.14	13.17	3	2	0.67	0.98	800 464-3108
Schroder Intl Small Companies Inv	Foreign	54.4	29.81		1	4	0.75	1.5	800 464-3108
Schroder Large Cap Equity Inv	Growth	-3.1	14.57	18.48	3	3	0.75		800 464-3108
Schroder Micro Cap Fund I	Small Co	148.6					0.6	2	800 464-3108
Schroder MidCap Value	Growth	10.7					0.94	1.35	800 464-3108
Schroder Small Cap Value Inv	Small Co	13.8	7.31	15.33	4	3	0.94	1.46	800 464-3108
Schroder US Diversified Growth	Growth	14.8	19.76	21.64	2	3	0.75	1.5	800 464-3108
Schroder US Smaller Company Adv	Small Co						0.75	1.54	800 464-3108
Schroder US Smaller Company Inv	Small Co	27.1	10.53	19.16	3	3	0.75	1.35	800 464-3108
Schwab 1000 Index Fund Inv	Growth/Inc	8.3	19.55	23.02	3	3	0.23	0.46	800 435-4000
Schwab Analytics Fund	Growth	13.4	23.23		2	3	0.54	0.75	800 435-4000
Schwab International Index Inv	Foreign	20.4	11.48	13.08	3	3	0.41	0.57	800 435-4000
Schwab MarketManager Bal Port	Balanced	16.6	14.03		3	1	0.54	0.5	800 435-4000
Schwab MarketManager Gr Port	Growth	20.8	16.9		2	2	0.54	0.5	800 435-4000
Schwab MarketManager Intl Port	Foreign	46.7	21.11		1	3	0.54	0.5	800 435-4000
Schwab MarketTrack Bal Port	AssetAlloc	9.9	11.8		3	3	0.54	0.54	800 435-4000
Schwab MarketTrack Conserv Port	AssetAlloc	7.9	9.61		3	1	0.54	0.54	800 435-4000
Schwab MarketTrack Gr Port	AssetAlloc	11.7	13.8		3	3	0.54	0.56	800 435-4000
Schwab S&P 500 Fund - Select	Growth/Inc	7.1	19.38		3	3	0.17	0.19	800 435-4000
Schwab S&P 500 Fund Inv	Growth/Inc	6.9	19.21		2	3	0.17	0.34	800 435-4000
Schwab Small Cap Index Inv	Small Co	19.5	12.03	15.12	4	3	0.3	0.48	800 435-4000
Schwartz Value Fund	Small Co	-6.4	-0.68	6.36	4	2	1.5	1.98	800 543-0407
Scudder 21st Century Growth	Growth	66.4	36.54		3	5	1	1.75	800 225-2470
Scudder Balanced Fund	Balanced	8.5	14.03	15.58	3	2	0.69	1.29	800 225-2470
Scudder Classic Growth Fund	Growth	24.4	22.37		2	3	0.69	1.53	800 225-2470
Scudder Development Fund	Small Co	28.3	19.08	16.77	3	4	0.97	1.52	800 225-2470
Scudder Dividend & Growth	Growth	9.2					0.75	0.75	800 225-2470
Scudder Emerging Markets Growth	Foreign	10.6	-5.26		5	4	1.25	2.25	800 225-2470
Scudder Emerging Markets Inc	Intl Bond	17	-3.09	9.52	3	5	1	1.79	800 225-2470
Scudder Global Bond	Intl Bond	0.1	2.83	3.06	5	4	0.75	1.08	800 225-2470
Scudder Global Discovery Fund	Global	54.4	26.57	23.8	2	4	1.1	1.67	800 225-2470
Scudder Global Fund	Global	11.4	11.12	14.86	3	2	1.1	1.36	800 225-2470
Scudder Gold Fund	Prec Metal	-4.9	-16.31	-7.96	5	5	1	2.04	800 225-2470
Scudder Greater Europe Growth	European	30	22.96	23.92	2	3	1.1	1.43	800 225-2470
Scudder Growth & Income	Growth/Inc	-4.4	7.68	15.54	3	2	0.45	0.8	800 225-2470
Scudder Health Care Fund	Health	63.6					0.84	1.75	800 225-2470
Scudder International Bond	Intl Bond	-1.1	0.97	1.28	5	5	0.81	1.5	800 225-2470
Scudder International Fund	Foreign	29.9	17.42	17.55	3	3	0.8	1.62	800 225-2470
Scudder International Growth & Inc	Growth/Inc	12.5	7.02		4	2	1	1.75	800 225-2470
Scudder Japan Fund	Pacific	56.4	24.09	17.41	3	4	0.77	1	800 225-2470
Scudder Large Company Growth	Growth	28.5	26.77	26.71	1	3	0.69	1.17	800 225-2470
Scudder Large Company Value	Growth	-10	7.77	15.23	4	3	0.6	0.89	800 225-2470
Scudder Latin America Fund	Foreign	14.3	-1.28	11.51	4	5	1.1	2.04	800 225-2470
Scudder Micro Cap Fund	Small Co	-0.1	2.2		5	2	0.75	1.53	800 225-2470
Scudder Pacific Opportunities	Pacific	14.6	-6.14	-1.83	5	5	1.1	2.35	800 225-2470
Scudder Pathway Balanced Port	Balanced	10.3	9.27		3	1	0.1	0	800 225-2470
Scudder Pathway Conservative Port	Income	2.6	5.14		3	1	0	0	800 225-2470
Scudder Pathway Growth Port	Growth	21.2	14.62		1	2	0		800 225-2470
Scudder S&P 500 Index Fund	Growth/Inc	6.8					0.08	0.4	800 225-2470
Scudder Select 1000 Growth Fd	Growth	24.9					0.69		800 225-2470
Scudder Select 500 Fund	Growth/Inc	9.2					0.69		800 225-2470

373

Stock Fund Name	Objective	Annualized Return for			Rank		Max Load	Expense Ratio	Toll-Free Telephone
		1 Year	3 Years	5 Years	Overall	Risk			
Scudder Small Company Value Fund	Small Co	-19.1	-3.25		4	2	0.75	1.32	800 225-2470
Scudder Tax Managed Growth	Growth	-5.2					0.2	1.25	800 225-2470
Scudder Tax Managed Small Company	Small Co	-11.3					0.36	1.5	800 225-2470
Scudder Technology Fund	Technology	124.1					0.84	1.75	800 225-2470
Scudder Value Fund	Growth	-4.4	8.98	16.03	3	3	0.69	1.42	800 621-1048
Security Capital Euro Real Est I	Real Est	-4.5					0.84	1.44	888 732-8748
Security Capital US Real Estate	Real Est	9.3	7.88		4	2	0.59	1.19	888 732-8748
Security Enhanced Index A	Growth	7.7					0.75	1.35	800 888-2461
Security Enhanced Index B	Growth	7.1					0.75	2.14	800 888-2461
Security Enhanced Index C	Growth	6.9					0.75	1.94	800 888-2461
Security Equity Fund A	Growth	2.2	14.86	20.23	3	2	1.02	1.02	800 888-2461
Security Equity Fund B	Growth	1.2	13.66	19.12	3	2	1.02	2.02	800 888-2461
Security Equity Fund C	Growth	-2.5					1.02	2.02	800 888-2461
Security Equity Fund-Global A	Global	52.6	24.05	22.48	2	3	2	2	800 888-2461
Security Equity Fund-Global B	Global	51.5	22.93	21.31	2	3	2	3	800 888-2461
Security Equity Global C	Global	51					2	3	800 888-2461
Security Equity Small Company C	Small Co	94.4					1	1.46	800 888-2461
Security Equity Total Return C	Growth/Inc	3.3					1	2.93	800 888-2461
Security Growth & Income C	Growth/Inc	-21					1.21	2.22	800 888-2461
Security Growth and Income A	Growth/Inc	-20.3	1.78	9.51	5	3	1.21	1.21	800 888-2461
Security Growth and Income B	Growth/Inc	-21.1	0.66	7.61	4	3	1.21	2.22	800 888-2461
Security International Fund A	Foreign	23.9					1.1	2.47	800 888-2461
Security International Fund B	Foreign	23					1.1	3.25	800 888-2461
Security International Fund C	Foreign	23.4					1.1	2.83	800 888-2461
Security Mid Cap Value Fund A	Growth	12.6	22.27		2	3	1	1.33	800 888-2461
Security Mid Cap Value Fund B	Growth	11.4	21		3	3	1	2.39	800 888-2461
Security Mid Cap Value Fund C	Growth	11.3					1	2.27	800 888-2461
Security Select 25 Fund A	Growth	11.7					0.75	1.47	800 888-2461
Security Select 25 Fund B	Growth	10.8					0.75	2.25	800 888-2461
Security Select 25 Fund C	Growth	10.9					0.75	1.97	800 888-2461
Security Small Company A	Small Co	96.1					1	0.73	800 888-2461
Security Small Company B	Small Co	94					1	2.41	800 888-2461
Security Social Awareness A	Growth	8.2	19.43		3	3	1	1.41	800 888-2461
Security Social Awareness B	Growth	6.8	18.08		3	3	1	2.56	800 888-2461
Security Social Awareness C	Growth	6.7					1	2.25	800 888-2461
Security Total Return A	Growth/Inc	4.1	2.06	4.77	5	2	1	2	800 888-2461
Security Total Return B	Growth/Inc	3	1.69	4.38	5	2	1	2.93	800 888-2461
Security Ultra C	Agg Growth	54.1					1.22	0	800 888-2461
Security Ultra Fund A	Agg Growth	55.8	33.22	25.96	2	4	1.22	1.12	800 888-2461
Security Ultra Fund B	Agg Growth	54.5	31.38	24.4	2	4	1.22	2.22	800 888-2461
Segall Bryant Gr & Income A	Growth	13					0.75		877 829-8413
Selected American Shares	Growth/Inc	10.5	19.4	24.81	2	3	0.58	0.92	800 279-0279
Selected Special Shares	Small Co	14.9	20.48	19.49	3	3	0.68	1.26	800 279-0279
Seligman Capital Fund A	Agg Growth	80.2	37.33	31.59	1	4	0.69	1.02	800 221-2783
Seligman Capital Fund B	Agg Growth	78.8	36.23		2	4	0.69	1.8	800 221-2783
Seligman Capital Fund C	Agg Growth	78.7					0.69		800 221-2783
Seligman Capital Fund D	Agg Growth	78.8	36.25	30.58	2	4	0.69	1.8	800 221-2783
Seligman Common Stock Fund A	Growth/Inc	-4.7	8.34	13.63	3	2	0.65	1.12	800 221-2783
Seligman Common Stock Fund B	Growth/Inc	-5.2	7.58		4	2	0.65	1.87	800 221-2783
Seligman Common Stock Fund C	Growth/Inc	-6.3					0.65		800 221-2783
Seligman Common Stock Fund D	Growth/Inc	-5.2	7.62	12.81	3	2	0.65	1.87	800 221-2783
Seligman Communications & Inform C	Technology	55.3					0.86		800 221-2783
Seligman Communications/Info A	Technology	56.6	37.7	26.44	2	4	0.86	1.38	800 221-2783
Seligman Communications/Info B	Technology	55.3	36.62		2	4	0.86	2.18	800 221-2783
Seligman Communications/Info D	Technology	55.3	36.63	25.47	2	4	0.86	2.18	800 221-2783
Seligman Emerging Markets Fund C	Foreign	7.8					1.25		800 221-2783
Seligman Frontier Fund A	Small Co	26.5	7.87	11.66	4	4	0.93	1.62	800 221-2783
Seligman Frontier Fund B	Small Co	25.5	7.05		4	4	0.93	2.31	800 221-2783

Stock Fund Name	Objective	Annualized Return for			Rank		Max Load	Expense Ratio	Toll-Free Telephone
		1 Year	3 Years	5 Years	Overall	Risk			
Seligman Frontier Fund C	Small Co	25.5					0.93		800 221-2783
Seligman Frontier Fund D	Small Co	25.5	7.04	10.82	4	4	0.93	2.31	800 221-2783
Seligman Global Growth Fund C	Global	25.5					1		800 221-2783
Seligman Global Smaller Companies C	Global	24.1					1		800 221-2783
Seligman Global Technology Fund C	Technology	78.6					1		800 221-2783
Seligman Growth Fund A	Growth	31.4	26.96	26.19	1	3	0.69	1.15	800 221-2783
Seligman Growth Fund B	Growth	30.5	26.02		1	3	0.69	1.9	800 221-2783
Seligman Growth Fund C	Growth	30.7					0.69		800 221-2783
Seligman Growth Fund D	Growth	30.7	26.07	25.14	1	3	0.69	1.9	800 221-2783
Seligman Hend Emrg Mkts Gr A	Foreign	8.8	-5.52		4	5	1.25	2.58	800 221-2783
Seligman Hend Emrg Mkts Gr B	Foreign	8	-6.23		4	5	1.25	3.33	800 221-2783
Seligman Hend Emrg Mkts Gr D	Foreign	7.8	-6.23		4	5	1.25	3.33	800 221-2783
Seligman Hend Glb Gr Opp A	Global	26.4	19.53		2	3	1	1.68	800 221-2783
Seligman Hend Glb Gr Opp B	Global	25.4	18.64		2	3	1	2.43	800 221-2783
Seligman Hend Glb Gr Opp D	Global	25.5	18.67		2	3	1	2.43	800 221-2783
Seligman Hend Glb Small Co A	Global	24.9	7.57	12.94	4	3	1	1.7	800 221-2783
Seligman Hend Glb Small Co B	Global	24	6.75		4	3	1	2.45	800 221-2783
Seligman Hend Glb Small Co D	Global	24.1	6.79	11.93	4	3	1	2.45	800 221-2783
Seligman Hend Glbl Tech A	Technology	79.9	42.57	31.76	1	4	1	1.59	800 221-2783
Seligman Hend Glbl Tech B	Technology	78.5	41.48		1	4	1	2.39	800 221-2783
Seligman Hend Glbl Tech D	Technology	78.6	41.43	30.59	2	4	1	2.39	800 221-2783
Seligman Hend Intl Fund A	Foreign	-10.1	-0.26	6.14	5	3	1	1.87	800 221-2783
Seligman Hend Intl Fund B	Foreign	-10.7	-1.07		4	3	1	2.58	800 221-2783
Seligman Hend Intl Fund D	Foreign	-10.7	-1.07	5.33	5	3	1	2.58	800 221-2783
Seligman Income C	Flexible	-1.9					0.59		800 221-2783
Seligman Income Fund A	Flexible	-1.2	4.31	6.92	3	1	0.59	1.14	800 221-2783
Seligman Income Fund B	Flexible	-2	3.49		3	1	0.59	1.88	800 221-2783
Seligman Income Fund D	Flexible	-1.9	3.52	6.1	4	1	0.59	1.88	800 221-2783
Seligman International Growth C	Foreign	-10.7					1		800 221-2783
Seligman Large Cap Value C	Growth	-15.8					0.8	2.27	800 221-2783
Seligman Large-Cap Value A	Growth	-15.1	6.01		5	3	0.8	1.44	800 221-2783
Seligman Large-Cap Value B	Growth	-15.8	5.21		5	3	0.8	2.2	800 221-2783
Seligman Large-Cap Value D	Growth	-15.8	5.24		5	3	0.8	2.2	800 221-2783
Seligman Muni Series-FL A	Muni State	2	4.34	5.14	3	4	0.5	1.02	800 221-2783
Seligman Muni Series-FL D	Muni State	1.4	3.6	4.36	5	4	0.5	1.77	800 221-2783
Seligman Muni Series-SC A	Muni State	1.4	3.79	5.09	3	4	0.5	0.82	800 221-2783
Seligman Muni Series-SC D	Muni State	0.5	2.85	4.16	5	4	0.5	1.72	800 221-2783
Seligman Municipal Series FL C	Muni State	1.4					0.5		800 221-2783
Seligman Municipal Series SC C	Muni State	4					0.5		800 221-2783
Seligman Small Cap Value C	Small Co	-11.1					1	2.89	800 221-2783
Seligman Small-Cap Value A	Small Co	-10.5	-1.87		5	3	1	1.85	800 221-2783
Seligman Small-Cap Value B	Small Co	-11.1	-2.6		5	3	1	2.6	800 221-2783
Seligman Small-Cap Value D	Small Co	-11.1	-2.6		5	3	1	2.6	800 221-2783
Sentinel Balanced A	Balanced	-1.1	7.49	11.32	3	1	0.6	1.1	800 282-3863
Sentinel Balanced B	Balanced	-1.9	6.66		3	1	0.6	1.12	800 282-3863
Sentinel Balanced Fund C	Balanced	-2.3					0.6	1.87	800 282-3863
Sentinel Balanced Fund D	Balanced	-2.4					0.6		800 282-3863
Sentinel Common Stock A	Growth/Inc	-3.7	8.93	15.99	3	2	0.55	1	800 282-3863
Sentinel Common Stock B	Growth/Inc	-4.5	8.04		3	2	0.55	1.85	800 282-3863
Sentinel Common Stock Fund C	Growth/Inc	-4.5					0.55	1.95	800 282-3863
Sentinel Mid Cap Growth Fund B	Growth	50.2					0.6	2.54	800 282-3863
Sentinel Small Company Fd A	Small Co	28.8	17.43	18.32	2	3	0.6	1.3	800 282-3863
Sentinel Small Company Fd B	Small Co	27.7	16.3		3	3	0.6	2.29	800 282-3863
Sentinel World A	Foreign	17.1	10.91	13.65	3	2	0.6	1.23	800 282-3863
Sentinel World B	Foreign	16.1	9.87		3	2	0.6	2.18	800 282-3863
Sentinel World Fund C	Foreign	15.8					0.6	2.35	800 282-3863
Sentry Fund	Growth	-9.3	4.99	11.86	4	3	0.8	0.45	800 533-7827
Sequoia Fund	Growth	-15.4	8.23	18.37	4	4	1	1	800 686-6884

Stock Fund Name	Objective	Annualized Return for			Rank		Max Load	Expense Ratio	Toll-Free Telephone
		1 Year	3 Years	5 Years	Overall	Risk			
Sextant Growth Fund	Growth	22.2	24.23	21.04	3	4	0.38	0.53	800 728-8762
Sextant International Fund	Foreign	45	17.11		3	4	0.76	0.46	800 728-8762
Shadow Stock Fund	Small Co	9.8	10.14	14.1	3	2	1	1.1	800 422-2766
Shelby Fund	Growth	49.3	27.27	22.06	3	4	1	1.12	800 774-3529
Simms Global Equity A	Global	33.8					1	2.22	877 438-7467
Simms Global Equity Y	Global	35					1	1.47	877 438-7467
Simms International Equity A	Foreign	47.9					1	2.37	877 438-7467
Simms International Equity Y	Foreign	48.5					1	1.62	877 438-7467
Simms US Equity A	Growth	20					0.75	2.06	877 438-7467
Simms US Equity Y	Growth	21.2					0.75	1.31	877 438-7467
Sit Balanced Fund	Balanced	17.9	17.55	18.43	2	2	1	1	800 332-5580
Sit Developing Mkts Growth Fund	Foreign	35	1.14	7.5	4	4	2	2	800 332-5580
Sit International Growth Fund	Foreign	33.4	14.43	14.08	3	3	1.5	1.5	800 332-5580
Sit Large Cap Growth	Growth/Inc	27.7	25.77	26.79	1	3	1	1	800 332-5580
Sit Mid Cap Growth Fund	Growth	72.9	31.24	28.65	2	4	1	1	800 332-5580
Sit Small Cap Growth Fund	Small Co	126.2	40.04	32.31	3	5	1.5	1.5	800 332-5580
Skyline-Special Equities-I	Small Co	-8.1	-1.32	10.38	4	3	1.5	1.47	800 458-5222
SmBarney Agg Growth A	Agg Growth	65.2	44.03	32.4	1	4	0.8		800 451-2010
SmBarney Agg Growth B	Agg Growth	63.8	42.88	31.3	1	4	0.8	2	800 451-2010
SmBarney Agg Growth L	Agg Growth	63.9	42.94	31.39	1	4	0.8	1.89	800 451-2010
SmBarney Concert All Soc Aware A	Balanced	3.1	16.02	16.22	3	2	0.75	1.15	800 451-2010
SmBarney Concert All Soc Aware B	Balanced	2.3	15.11	15.33	3	2	0.75	1.92	800 451-2010
SmBarney Concert All Soc Aware L	Balanced	2.3	16.42	15.98	3	2	0.75	1.89	800 451-2010
SmBarney Concert Inv Gr & Inc A	Growth/Inc	1.1	12.44	17.01	2	3	0.65	1.05	800 221-3627
SmBarney Concert Inv Gr & Inc B	Growth/Inc	0.4	11.74	16.25	3	3	0.65	1.8	800 221-3627
SmBarney Concert Inv Gr & Inc I	Growth/Inc	1.4	12.65	17.48	3	3	0.65	0.83	800 221-3627
SmBarney Concert Inv Growth A	Growth	23.4	24.12	23.64	1	3	0.65	1	800 221-3627
SmBarney Concert Inv Growth B	Growth	22.5	23.27	22.82	1	3	0.65	1.75	800 221-3627
SmBarney Concert Inv Growth I	Growth	23.8	24.42	24.33	1	3	0.65	1.25	800 221-3627
SmBarney Concert Inv Intl Eq 1	Foreign	88.4	36.33		2	4	1	1.77	800 221-3627
SmBarney Concert Inv Intl Eq A	Foreign	87.7	35.77	27.61	2	4	1	2.16	800 221-3627
SmBarney Concert Inv Intl Eq B	Foreign	86.3	34.73	26.6	3	4	1	2.91	800 221-3627
SmBarney Concert Inv Small Cap A	Small Co	17.3	16.83	18.7	3	4	0.65	1.47	800 221-3627
SmBarney Concert Inv Small Cap B	Small Co	16.4	15.95	17.8	3	4	0.65	2.22	800 221-3627
SmBarney Concert Peachtree Gr A	Growth	13.6	17.82	16.83	3	3	1	1.5	800 451-2010
SmBarney Concert Peachtree Gr B	Growth	12.2	17.03	16.18	3	3	1	2.27	800 451-2010
SmBarney Concert Peachtree Gr L	Growth	11.8	16.67	14.86	3	3	1	2.14	800 451-2010
SmBarney Contrarian A	Growth						0.84	1.3	800 451-2010
SmBarney Contrarian B	Growth						0.84	2.06	800 451-2010
SmBarney Contrarian L	Growth						0.84	2.06	800 451-2010
SmBarney Inc-Balanced A	Balanced	7.4	14.24	12.42	3	1	0.65	1.08	800 451-2010
SmBarney Inc-Balanced B	Balanced	6.9	13.66	11.89	3	1	0.65	1.56	800 451-2010
SmBarney Inc-Balanced O	Balanced	6.8	13.69	11.9	3	1	0.65	1.5	800 451-2010
SmBarney Inc-Prem Tot Rtrn A	Flexible	8.7	9.45	14.48	3	1	0.75	1.15	800 451-2010
SmBarney Inc-Prem Tot Rtrn B	Flexible	8.2	8.9	14.02	3	1	0.75	1.62	800 451-2010
SmBarney Inc-Prem Tot Rtrn O	Flexible	8.2	8.95	13.79	3	1	0.75	1.62	800 451-2010
SmBarney Intl Equity A	Foreign	22.2	10.27	10.79	4	4	0.84	1.28	800 451-2010
SmBarney Intl Equity B	Foreign	21.2	9.38	10.54	4	4	0.84	2.08	800 451-2010
SmBarney Intl Equity L	Foreign	21.2	9.38	10.11	4	4	0.84	2.08	800 451-2010
SmBarney Intl Equity Y	Foreign	22.7	10.56	11.27	4	4	0.84	0.92	800 451-2010
SmBarney Large Cap Val A	Income	-10	6.55	13.89	3	2	0.56	0.91	800 451-2010
SmBarney Large Cap Val B	Income	-10.7	5.7	12.99	4	2	0.57	1.67	800 451-2010
SmBarney Large Cap Val L	Income	-10.7	5.74	13.01	4	2	0.57	1.66	800 451-2010
SmBarney Muni Bond-FL A	Muni State	1.6	3.99	5.45	3	3	0.5	0.72	800 451-2010
SmBarney Muni Bond-FL B	Muni State	1.1	3.45	4.88	4	3	0.5	1.23	800 451-2010
SmBarney Muni Bond-FL L	Muni State	1	3.4	4.81	4	4	0.5	1.31	800 451-2010
SmBarney Natural Resources A	Energy/Res	-9	-5.21	1.05	5	4	0.75	1.87	800 451-2010
SmBarney Natural Resources B	Energy/Res	-9.4	-5.75	0.43	5	4	0.75	2.52	800 451-2010

Stock Fund Name	Objective	Annualized Return for			Rank		Max Load	Expense Ratio	Toll-Free Telephone
		1 Year	3 Years	5 Years	Overall	Risk			
SmBarney Natural Resources L	Energy/Res	-9.3	-5.68	0.34	5	4	0.75	2.43	800 451-2010
SmBarney Telecom-Income	Utilities	-9.4	24.37	23.19	3	3	0.75	0.89	800 451-2010
SmBarney World-Emerging Mkts A	Foreign	16.2	-11.37	-1.74	4	5	0.1	2.87	800 451-2010
SmBarney World-Emerging Mkts B	Foreign	15.4	-12.04	-2.48	4	5	0.1	3.62	800 451-2010
SmBarney World-Emerging Mkts L	Foreign	15.4	-12.07	-2.49	4	5	0.1	3.79	800 451-2010
SmBarney World-European A	European	36.6	16.59	17.83	2	3	0.84	1.51	800 451-2010
SmBarney World-European B	European	35.4	15.76	15.37	3	3	0.84	2.33	800 451-2010
SmBarney World-European L	European	35.4	15.61	15.35	3	3	0.84	2.31	800 451-2010
SmBarney World-Global Gov Bd A	Intl Bond	3.4	4.75	6.45	2	3	0.75	1.19	800 451-2010
SmBarney World-Global Gov Bd B	Intl Bond	2.7	4.17	5.79	4	3	0.75	1.76	800 451-2010
SmBarney World-Global Gov Bd L	Intl Bond	2.8	4.28	5.96	4	3	0.75	1.65	800 451-2010
SmBarney World-Global Gov Bd Y	Intl Bond	3.8	4.94	6.65	2	3	0.75	0.82	800 451-2010
SmBarney World-Pacific A	Pacific	11.9	-5.79	-0.98	5	4	0.84	2.54	800 451-2010
SmBarney World-Pacific B	Pacific	11	-6.57	-1.75	5	4	0.84	3.52	800 451-2010
SmBarney World-Pacific L	Pacific	11.1	-6.55	-1.78	5	4	0.84	3.41	800 451-2010
Smith Breeden Equity Market Plus	Growth/Inc	4.9	17.57	23.05	3	3	0.69	0.88	800 221-3138
Sound Shore Fund	Growth	-7.2	5.83	15.69	4	3	0.75	0.97	800 551-1980
SouthTrust Core Equity Fund	Growth/Inc	-2.4	10.37	17.14	3	3	0.75	1.01	800 843-8618
Spirit of America Investment Fund A	Real Est	-3.4						0.96	800 452-4892
Spirit of America Investment Fund B	Real Est	-4						0.96	800 452-4892
Standish Ayer & Wood Sm Cap T S Eq	Small Co	82.3	40.8		3	5	0.59	0.5	800 221-4795
Standish Ayer & Wood Tax Sens Eqty	Growth	0.6	10.64		4	3	0.5	0.5	800 221-4795
Standish Fd-Global Fixed Inc	Intl Bond	2.3	5.38	8.66	2	3	0.4	0.54	800 221-4795
Standish Fd-International Eq	Foreign	15.9	9.01	9.92	4	3	0.8	1	800 221-4795
Standish Fd-International Fixed	Intl Bond	3.5	6.58	10.07	1	3	0.4	0.52	800 221-4795
Standish Fd-Small Cap Equity	Small Co	71.1	30.31	26.86	3	5	0.59	0.73	800 221-4795
Standish Fd-Small Cap Equity II	Small Co	82.4	46.09		2	5	0.8	1	800 221-4795
State Street Res. Mid Cap Gr B1	Agg Growth	37.2					0.75		800 562-0032
State Street Res. Strg Gr In B1	Balanced	10.1					0.72		800 562-0032
State Street Research Alpha A	Income	-9.9	4.8	12.48	4	3	0.65	1.25	800 562-0032
State Street Research Alpha B	Income	-10.6	4.11	11.65	3	3	0.65	1.96	800 562-0032
State Street Research Alpha B1	Income	-10.6					0.65	1.86	800 562-0032
State Street Research Alpha C	Income	-10.6	4.12	11.67	3	3	0.65	1.96	800 562-0032
State Street Research Alpha S	Income	-9.6	5.16	12.78	4	3	0.65	0.96	800 562-0032
State Street Research Argo Fund A	Growth/Inc	-13.7	6.48	14.65	4	3	0.65	1.26	800 562-0032
State Street Research Argo Fund B	Growth/Inc	-14.3	5.7	13.8	4	3	0.65	2	800 562-0032
State Street Research Argo Fund B1	Growth/Inc	-14.3					0.65	2	800 562-0032
State Street Research Argo Fund C	Growth/Inc	-14.3	5.74	13.83	4	3	0.65	2	800 562-0032
State Street Research Argo Fund S	Growth/Inc	-13.4	6.74	14.93	4	3	0.65	1.01	800 562-0032
State Street Research Athletes A	Growth	20.3					0.65	1.25	800 562-0032
State Street Research Athletes B	Growth	19.6					0.65	2	800 562-0032
State Street Research Athletes B1	Growth	19.5					0.65	2	800 562-0032
State Street Research Athletes C	Growth	19.4					0.65	2	800 562-0032
State Street Research Athletes S	Growth	20.6					0.65	1	800 562-0032
State Street Research Aurora A	Small Co	35.8	16.44	27.89	2	3	0.84	1.2	800 562-0032
State Street Research Aurora B	Small Co	34.8	15.57	26.93	3	3	0.84	2.29	800 562-0032
State Street Research Aurora B1	Small Co	34.8					0.84	2.33	800 562-0032
State Street Research Aurora C	Small Co	34.8	15.55	26.92	3	3	0.84	2.29	800 562-0032
State Street Research Aurora S	Small Co	36.6	16.82	28.29	2	3	0.84	1.3	800 562-0032
State Street Research Emg Gro A	Small Co	38.5	18.85	21.11	3	5	0.75	1.35	800 562-0032
State Street Research Emg Gro B	Small Co	37.4	17.96	20.21	3	5	0.75	2.14	800 562-0032
State Street Research Emg Gro B1	Small Co	37.5					0.75	2.14	800 562-0032
State Street Research Emg Gro C	Small Co	37.5	18.01	20.24	3	5	0.75	2.14	800 562-0032
State Street Research Emg Gro S	Small Co	38.7	19.18	21.41	3	5	0.75	1.13	800 562-0032
State Street Research Galileo A	Growth	14.2					0.65	1.27	800 562-0032
State Street Research Galileo B	Growth	13.4					0.65	2.02	800 562-0032
State Street Research Galileo B1	Growth	13.4					0.65	2.02	800 562-0032
State Street Research Galileo C	Growth	13.3					0.65	2.02	800 562-0032

Stock Fund Name	Objective	Annualized Return for			Rank		Max Load	Expense Ratio	Toll-Free Telephone
		1 Year	3 Years	5 Years	Overall	Risk			
State Street Research Galileo S	Growth	14.5					0.65	1.02	800 562-0032
State Street Research Glb Res A	Energy/Res	38.2	-3.68	11.24	4	5	0.75	1.59	800 562-0032
State Street Research Glb Res B	Energy/Res	37	-4.42	10.4	4	5	0.75	2.33	800 562-0032
State Street Research Glb Res B1	Energy/Res	37.1					0.75	2.18	800 562-0032
State Street Research Glb Res C	Energy/Res	37.3	-4.41	10.38	4	5	0.75	2.33	800 562-0032
State Street Research Glb Res S	Energy/Res	38.5	-3.45	11.51	4	5	0.75	1.34	800 562-0032
State Street Research Growth A	Growth/Inc	33.3	24.16	19.36	2	3	0.47	1.04	800 562-0032
State Street Research Growth B	Growth/Inc	32.4	23.26	18.47	2	3	0.47	1.79	800 562-0032
State Street Research Growth B1	Growth/Inc	32.4					0.47	1.79	800 562-0032
State Street Research Growth C	Growth/Inc	32.5	23.3	18.5	2	3	0.47	1.79	800 562-0032
State Street Research Intl Eq A	Foreign	54	19.21	14	2	3	0.94	1.93	800 562-0032
State Street Research Intl Eq B	Foreign	52.8	18.38	13.16	2	3	0.94	2.68	800 562-0032
State Street Research Intl Eq B1	Foreign	52.9					0.94	2.68	800 562-0032
State Street Research Intl Eq C	Foreign	52.8	18.35	13.14	2	3	0.94	2.68	800 562-0032
State Street Research Intl Eq S	Foreign	54.4	19.55	14.29	2	3	0.94	1.68	800 562-0032
State Street Research Invest Tr A	Growth	13.8	20.61	23.46	2	3	0.47	0.88	800 562-0032
State Street Research Invest Tr B	Growth	13.4	19.9	22.66	2	3	0.47	1.62	800 562-0032
State Street Research Invest Tr B1	Growth	13					0.47	1.62	800 562-0032
State Street Research Invest Tr C	Growth	13	19.72	22.53	2	3	0.47	1.62	800 562-0032
State Street Research Invest Tr S	Growth	14.1	20.92	23.78	2	3	0.47	0.68	800 562-0032
State Street Research Legacy A	Growth	8					0.65	1.19	800 562-0032
State Street Research Legacy B	Growth	7.5					0.65	1.94	800 562-0032
State Street Research Legacy B1	Growth	7.2					0.65	1.87	800 562-0032
State Street Research Legacy C	Growth	7.2					0.65	1.94	800 562-0032
State Street Research Legacy S	Growth	8.9					0.65	0.94	800 562-0032
State Street Research Mid Cap Gr A	Agg Growth	38.1	20.04	15.36	3	4	0.71	1.41	800 562-0032
State Street Research Mid Cap Gr B	Agg Growth	37	19.09	14.45	3	4	0.75	2.16	800 562-0032
State Street Research Mid Cap Gr C	Agg Growth	37.1	19.12	14.47	3	4	0.75	2.16	800 562-0032
State Street Research Mid Cap Gr S	Agg Growth	38.4	20.34	15.64	3	4	0.75	1.16	800 562-0032
State Street Research Str Inc + S	AssetAlloc	4.6	7.42	9.11	3	1	0.59	0.9	800 562-0032
State Street Research Strat Agg S	AssetAlloc	14.2	13.44	15.78	3	2	0.59	1.1	800 562-0032
State Street Research Strg Gr In A	Balanced	10.8	10.81	13.85	2	1	0.72	1.05	800 562-0032
State Street Research Strg Gr In B	Balanced	10	10	13.01	3	1	0.72	2.02	800 562-0032
State Street Research Strg Gr In C	Balanced	10	9.99	13.02	3	1	0.72	2.02	800 562-0032
State Street Research Strg Gr In S	Balanced	11.2	11.12	14.15	3	1	0.72	1.03	800 562-0032
State Street Rsch Exchange Fund	Growth/Inc	1.5	16.76	22.88	3	2	0.5	0.55	800 562-0032
SteinRoe Balanced Fund	Balanced	8	10.85	13.95	3	1	0.62	1.04	800 338-2550
SteinRoe Capital Opportunities	Agg Growth	45.7	16.65	19.27	3	4	0.75	1.18	800 338-2550
SteinRoe Discipline Stock	Growth	1.4	4.78	11.15	4	3	0.83	1.22	800 338-2550
SteinRoe Growth & Income	Growth/Inc	-2.9	11.75	17.65	3	3	0.75	1.06	800 338-2550
SteinRoe Growth Stock Fund	Growth	31.2	27.71	28.48	1	3	0.72	0.94	800 338-2550
SteinRoe International Fund	Foreign	-0.3	0.73	5.73	5	3	1	1.5	800 338-2550
SteinRoe Young Investor Fund	Growth	16.4	20.29	25.48	2	3	0.78	1.48	800 338-2550
Stellar Fund A	Flexible	12	8.97	11.28	3	1	0.94	1.55	800 677-3863
Stellar Fund Y	Flexible	12.3	9.21	11.52	3	1	0.94	1.3	800 677-3863
StockJungle.com Cmnty Intelligence	Growth						1		800 945-4957
StockJungle.com Mkt Leaders Growth	Growth						1		800 945-4957
StockJungle.com Pure Play Internet	Technology						1		800 945-4957
Stonebridge Growth Fund	Growth/Inc	1	6.69	12.74	2	2	0.64	1.5	800 639-3935
Strategist Balanced Fund	Balanced	-4.2	7.17		3	1	0.53	1	800 328-8300
Strategist Emerging Markets Fund	Foreign	14.4	-2.58		4	4	1.07	2.2	800 328-8300
Strategist Equity Fund	Growth/Inc	7.4	13.89		3	3	0.47	1.25	800 328-8300
Strategist Equity Income Fund	Income	-17.2	4.05		3	3	0.53	1.23	800 328-8300
Strategist Growth Fund	Growth	27.5	24.52		1	4	0.6	1.03	800 328-8300
Strategist Growth Trends Fund	Growth	20.8	20.36		1	3	0.56	0.94	800 328-8300
Strategist Special Growth Fund	Agg Growth	5.7	16.39		3	3	0.65	1.38	800 328-8300
Strategist World Growth Fund	Foreign	18.3	16.94		3	3	0.78	1.75	800 328-8300
Stratton Growth Fund	Growth/Inc	-9.8	5.58	13.17	4	3	0.75	1.09	800 578-8261

Stock Fund Name	Objective	Annualized Return for			Rank		Max Load	Expense Ratio	Toll-Free Telephone
		1 Year	3 Years	5 Years	Overall	Risk			
Stratton Monthly Dividend Reit Shs	Real Est	0	1.15	5.87	4	2	0.63	1.09	800 578-8261
Stratton Small-Cap Value Fund	Small Co	-5	2.35	11.35	5	2	0.71	1.36	800 578-8261
Strong American Utilities Fund	Utilities	0	14.13	16.24	3	2	0.5	1	800 368-1030
Strong Asia Pacific Fund	Pacific	5.8	0.16	2.46	4	4	1	2	800 368-1030
Strong Blue Chip 100 Fund	Growth	29.3	31.61		1	3	0.5	1.19	800 368-1030
Strong Discovery Fund	Agg Growth	23.5	10.19	10.3	4	3	0.75	1.3	800 368-1030
Strong Dow 30 Value	Growth	-2.6					0.8	1.39	800 368-1030
Strong Enterprise Fund	Small Co	94.8					0.75	1.6	800 368-1030
Strong Equity Income	Income	4.8	15.49		3	2	0.55	1.1	800 368-1030
Strong Foreign Major Markets	Global	17.7					1	2	800 368-1030
Strong Growth 20 Fund	Growth	88.7	54.4		1	4	0.75	1.39	800 368-1030
Strong Growth Fund	Growth	63.8	37.78	32.28	2	4	0.75	1.19	800 368-1030
Strong Growth and Income	Growth/Inc	17.6	25.27		1	3	0.55	1.1	800 368-1030
Strong Index 500 Fund	Growth/Inc	6.7	19.17		3	3	0.05	0.9	800 368-1030
Strong International Stock	Foreign	55.6	7.67	10.13	4	4	1	1.8	800 368-1030
Strong Large Cap Growth Fund	Growth/Inc	39.4	32.96	27.44	1	4	0.55	1	800 368-1030
Strong Life Stage Ser Aggress Port	Agg Growth	27.1					0	0	800 368-1030
Strong Life Stage Ser Conserv Port	Income	15.5					0	0	800 368-1030
Strong Life Stage Ser Moderate Port	Growth	21.4					0	0	800 368-1030
Strong Limited Resources	Energy/Res	15.5					0.75	2	800 368-1030
Strong Mid Cap Disciplined	Agg Growth	15.8					0.75	2	800 368-1030
Strong Mid Cap Growth Fund	Growth	66.1	39.68		2	4	0.75	1.69	800 368-1030
Strong Opportunity Fund	Growth	18	22.2	21.32	1	3	0.75	1.19	800 368-1030
Strong Overseas Fund	Foreign	55.6					1	2	800 368-1030
Strong Schafer Balanced	Balanced	-8.5					1	2	800 368-1030
Strong Schafer Value Fund	Growth	-11.1	-4.86	6.48	5	3	1	1.6	800 368-1030
Strong Small Cap Value	Small Co	29.7					0.75	1.8	800 368-1030
Strong Strategic Growth Fund	Growth	8.1					0.75	2	800 368-1030
Strong U.S. Emerging Growth	Agg Growth	105.2					0.75	2	800 368-1030
Strong Value Fund	Growth	-1.3	10.06		3	2	1	1.39	800 368-1030
Style Select Aggressive Gr A	Agg Growth	53	39.25		2	4	1	1.78	800 858-8850
Style Select Aggressive Gr B	Agg Growth	52	38.29		2	4	1	2.43	800 858-8850
Style Select Aggressive Gr II	Agg Growth	51.9	38.27		2	4	1	2.41	800 858-8850
Style Select Focus A	Growth	35.3					0.84	1.44	800 858-8850
Style Select Focus B	Growth	34.3					0.84	2.1	800 858-8850
Style Select Focus II	Growth	34.3					0.84	2.1	800 858-8850
Style Select Focused Gr & Inc A	Growth	37.6					1	1.54	800 858-8850
Style Select Focused Gr & Inc B	Growth	36.6					1	2.37	800 858-8850
Style Select Focused Gr & Inc II	Growth	36.7					1	2.35	800 858-8850
Style Select Intl Equity A	Foreign	22.7	7.03		4	3	1.1	2.02	800 858-8850
Style Select Intl Equity B	Foreign	21.9	6.34		4	3	1.1	2.68	800 858-8850
Style Select Intl Equity II	Foreign	21.9	6.34		4	3	1.1	2.68	800 858-8850
Style Select Large Cap Growth B	Growth	23.6					1	2.43	800 858-8850
Style Select Large Cap Growth II	Growth	23.6					1	2.43	800 858-8850
Style Select Large Cap Value A	Growth	0.2					1	1.78	800 858-8850
Style Select Large Cap Value B	Growth	-0.6					1	2.43	800 858-8850
Style Select Large Cap Value II	Growth	-0.5					1	2.43	800 858-8850
Style Select Mid Cap Growth A	Growth	32.5	26.6		2	4	1	1.76	800 858-8850
Style Select Mid Cap Growth B	Growth	31.6	25.78		2	4	1	2.43	800 858-8850
Style Select Mid Cap Growth II	Growth	31.6	25.86		1	4	1	2.43	800 858-8850
Style Select Small Cap Value A	Small Co	2.9					1	1.78	800 858-8850
Style Select Small Cap Value B	Small Co	2.2					1	2.43	800 858-8850
Style Select Small Cap Value II	Small Co	2.3					1	2.43	800 858-8850
Style Select Value A	Growth	-0.8	7.43		5	3	1	1.77	800 858-8850
Style Select Value B	Growth	-1.4	6.77		5	3	1	1.78	800 858-8850
Style Select Value II	Growth	-1.4	6.77		4	3	1	2.43	800 858-8850
SunAmerica Bal Assets A	Balanced	11.7	18.27	17.83	3	2	0.75	1.44	800 858-8850
SunAmerica Bal Assets B	Balanced	11	17.51	17.1	3	2	0.75	2.06	800 858-8850

379

Stock Fund Name	Objective	Annualized Return for			Rank		Max Load	Expense Ratio	Toll-Free Telephone
		1 Year	3 Years	5 Years	Overall	Risk			
SunAmerica Balanced Assets Fund II	Balanced	10.9					0.75	2.04	800 858-8850
SunAmerica Blue Chip Growth A	Growth	26.6	27.39	25.64	1	3	0.75	2.18	800 858-8850
SunAmerica Blue Chip Growth B	Growth	25.8	26.56	24.83	1	3	0.75	2.2	800 858-8850
SunAmerica Blue Chip Growth Fund II	Growth	25.6					0.75	2.16	800 858-8850
SunAmerica Dogs of Wall Street A	Agg Growth	-25					0.34	0.94	800 858-8850
SunAmerica Dogs of Wall Street B	Agg Growth	-25.4					0.34	1.6	800 858-8850
SunAmerica Dogs of Wall Street II	Agg Growth	-25.4					0.34	1.6	800 858-8850
SunAmerica Growth & Income A	Growth	17.8	21.83	26.45	2	3	0.75	1.43	800 858-8850
SunAmerica Growth & Income B	Growth	17.1	21.08	24.75	2	3	0.75	2.14	800 858-8850
SunAmerica Growth & Income II	Growth	17					0.75	2.14	800 858-8850
SunAmerica Growth Opportunities A	Growth	96.2	46.81	33.44	2	5	0.75	1.58	800 858-8850
SunAmerica Growth Opportunities B	Growth	94.8	45.74	32.47	2	5	0.75	2.33	800 858-8850
SunAmerica Growth Opportunities II	Growth	94.6					0.75	2.35	800 858-8850
SunAmerica Tax Managed B	Growth	1.8					0.84		800 858-8850
SunAmerica Tax Managed II	Growth	1.9					0.84		800 858-8850
TIAA-CREF Growth & Income	Growth/Inc	10.1					0.42	0.46	
TIAA-CREF Growth Equity	Growth	26.6					0.45	0.47	
TIAA-CREF International Equity	Foreign	38.3					0.48	0.5	
TIAA-CREF Managed Allocation	AssetAlloc	15.5					0.48	0	
TIP Target Select Equity	Growth	99.6					1.05	1.3	800 224-6312
Target-International Equity	Foreign	12.9	10.46	13.75	4	2	0.69	0.93	800 225-1852
Target-Large Cap Growth Portf	Growth	53.2	41.31	33.21	1	4	0.69	0.67	800 225-1852
Target-Large Cap Value Portfolio	Growth	-19.6	2.64	11.18	4	3	0.59	0.69	800 225-1852
Target-Small Cap Growth Portf	Small Co	39.1	18.1	19.4	3	4	0.59	0.8	800 225-1852
Target-Small Cap Value Portf	Small Co	2.6	4.39	11.89	4	3	0.59	0.84	800 225-1852
Templeton Capital Accumulator	Growth	11.5	11.11	15.18	4	3	0.75	1.12	800 237-0738
Templeton Developing Markets A	Foreign	-6.3	-7.82	2.56	5	4	1.25	2.02	800 237-0738
Templeton Developing Markets Adv	Foreign	-6	-7.55		5	5	1.25	1.84	800 237-0738
Templeton Developing Markets B	Foreign	-7.2					1.25	2.87	800 237-0738
Templeton Developing Markets C	Foreign	-7	-8.45	1.83	5	5	1.25	2.83	800 237-0738
Templeton Foreign A	Foreign	7.6	6.41	10.5	5	3	1.98	1.12	800 237-0738
Templeton Foreign Adv	Foreign	3.3	1.42		4	3	1.98	0.86	800 237-0738
Templeton Foreign B	Foreign	6.9					1.98	1.86	800 237-0738
Templeton Foreign C	Foreign	6.9	5.65	9.69	5	3	1.98	1.87	800 237-0738
Templeton Foreign Smaller Co A	Foreign	14	5.46	10.22	3	2	1	1.62	800 237-0738
Templeton Foreign Smaller Co Adv	Foreign	14.2	5.66		3	2	1	1.4	800 237-0738
Templeton Foreign Smaller Co B	Foreign	12					1	2.37	800 237-0738
Templeton Global Bond A	Intl Bond	0.4	0.73	4.28	5	4	0.48	1.19	800 237-0738
Templeton Global Opportunities A	Global	18.7	8.24	13.43	4	3	0.8	1.41	800 237-0738
Templeton Global Opportunities B	Global	13.1					0.8	2.18	800 237-0738
Templeton Global Opportunities C	Global	17.9	7.11	11.45	4	3	0.8	2.16	800 237-0738
Templeton Global Smaller Co Gr A	Global	6.9	-1.29	6.53	5	2	0.75	1.38	800 237-0738
Templeton Global Smaller Co Gr Adv	Global	-0.8	-5.97		5	3	0.75	1.12	800 237-0738
Templeton Global Smaller Co Gr B	Global	-1.6					0.75	2.22	800 237-0738
Templeton Global Smaller Co Gr C	Global	6.3	-2.05	5	5	2	0.75	2.12	800 237-0738
Templeton Growth A	Global	6.4	7.89	13.08	3	3	0.6	1.12	800 237-0738
Templeton Growth Adv	Global	6.7	2.84		4	3	0.6	0.86	800 237-0738
Templeton Growth B	Global	5.7					0.6	1.93	800 237-0738
Templeton Growth C	Global	5.6	7.09	9.71	5	3	0.6	1.87	800 237-0738
Templeton Inst-Emerging Markets	Foreign	-4.8	-7.13	2.22	5	5	1.25	1.89	800 237-0738
Templeton International A	European	3.6	8.56	11.16	4	2	0.19	1.85	800 237-0738
Templeton International Adv	European	3.5	8.17		4	2	0.5	1.5	800 237-0738
Templeton International C	European	3	7.93	10.44	3	2	0.19	2.5	800 237-0738
Templeton Latin America A	Foreign	16.8	-5.59	3.73	4	5	1.03	2.35	800 237-0738
Templeton Latin America Adv	Foreign	17.1	-5.35		4	5	1	2	800 237-0738
Templeton Latin America C	Foreign	15.9	-6.2	3.07	4	5	1.03	3	800 237-0738
Templeton Pacific Growth A	Pacific	-6.3	-12.32	-4.29	5	4	0.5	2.02	800 237-0738
Templeton Pacific Growth Adv	Pacific	-6	-11.76		5	4	0.5	1.82	800 237-0738

Stock Fund Name	Objective	Annualized Return for			Rank		Max Load	Expense Ratio	Toll-Free Telephone
		1 Year	3 Years	5 Years	Overall	Risk			
Templeton World A	Global	7.2	10.04	15.26	4	3	0.6	1.04	800 237-0738
Templeton World B	Global	6.3					0.6	2.43	800 237-0738
Templeton World C	Global	6.4	9.2	11.55	4	3	0.6	1.82	800 237-0738
Texas Capital-Value & Growth	Growth/Inc	-18.4	-4.33		5	4	1	1.71	888 839-7424
The Internet Emerging Growth Fund	Technology						1.25		888 386-3999
The Internet Global Growth Fund	Technology						1.25		888 386-3999
The Internet Infrastructure Fund	Technology						1.25		888 386-3999
The Internet New Paradigm Fund	Technology						1.25		888 386-3999
The Medical Fund	Health						1.25		888 386-3999
The Nevis Fund 3101	Growth	112.2					1.5	1.5	
The Wisdom Fund	Growth	0.4					0.5		800 639-7768
Third Avenue Real Estate Value Fund	Real Est	6.6					0.9	1.89	800 443-1021
Third Avenue Sm Cap Value Fund	Small Co	11.2	5.33		5	3	0.9	1.28	800 443-1021
Third Avenue Value Fund	Growth	9.6	8.72	14.95	3	3	0.9	1.09	800 443-1021
Thomas White American Enterprise	Growth	-7					1	1.35	800 811-0535
Thomas White American Opportunities	Growth	-0.6					1	1.35	800 811-0535
Thomas White International	Foreign	14.2	12.2	14.33	3	2	1	1.39	800 811-0535
Thompson and Plumb Balanced	Balanced	12.7	15.23	17.5	2	2	0.84	1.25	800 499-0079
Thornburg Global Value A	Global	42.4					0.88	0.16	800 847-0200
Thornburg Interm Muni-FL A	Muni State	2.9	3.93	4.73	2	2	0.5	1.08	800 847-0200
Thornburg Value Fund A	Growth	25.3	28.71		1	3	0.88		800 847-0200
Thornburg Value Fund C	Growth	24.5	27.92		1	3	0.88	2.25	800 847-0200
Timothy Plan Large/Mid-Cap Value A	Growth	-4.4					0.84		800 846-7526
Timothy Plan Large/Mid-Cap Value B	Growth	-6					0.84		800 846-7526
Timothy Plan Large/Mid-Cap Value C	Growth	-5.5					0.84		800 846-7526
Timothy Plan Small Cap Value A	Growth	21.3	5.66	8.64	4	3	0.84	2.45	800 846-7526
Timothy Plan Small Cap Value B	Growth	20.1	4.62		4	3	0.84	3.12	800 846-7526
Timothy Plan Small-Cap Value C	Growth	17.5					0.84		800 846-7526
Titan Financial Services Fund	Financial	-3.6	10.8		4	4	1	2.06	888 448-4826
Tocqueville Fund A	Flexible	-7.8	6.2	13.28	4	3	0.75	1.36	800 697-3863
Tocqueville Gold Fund	Prec Metal	2.5					1	1.97	800 697-3863
Tocqueville Intl Value Fund	Global	-11	-7.35	1.27	5	4	1	1.82	800 697-3863
Tocqueville Small Cap Val Fund	Small Co	48.6	21.06	21.51	3	4	0.75	1.58	800 697-3863
Torray Fund	Growth/Inc	-4.9	14.45	22.1	3	3	1	1.08	800 443-3036
Touchstone Emerging Growth A	Small Co	52.9	28.36	23.87	2	4	0.8	1.5	800 638-8194
Touchstone Emerging Growth C	Small Co	51.9	27.34	22.86	2	4	0.8	2.25	800 638-8194
Touchstone Intl Equity Fund A	Foreign	29.6	17.15	16.46	3	3	0.94	2.35	800 638-8194
Touchstone Intl Equity Fund C	Foreign	28.3	16.17	15.52	3	3	0.94	2.35	800 638-8194
Transamerica Premier Aggressive Gr	Agg Growth	38.3					0.84	1.38	800 892-7587
Transamerica Premier Small Co	Small Co	72.1					0.84		800 892-7587
Trent Equity Fund	Growth	0	18.72	18.01	3	4	1.14	2	800 282-2340
Turner Micro Cap Growth Fund	Small Co	156.8					1	1.25	800 224-6312
Turner Mid Cap Growth Fund	Growth	80.5	57.94		1	4	0.75	1.08	800 224-6312
Turner Small Cap Growth Fund	Small Co	66	35.35	34.79	3	5	0.55	1.25	800 224-6312
Turner Technology Fund	Technology						1.1		800 224-6312
Turner Top 20 Fund	Growth						1.1		800 224-6312
Tweedy Browne American Value	Growth	-9.4	8.33	15.98	3	2	1.25	1.37	800 432-4789
Tweedy Browne Global Value	Global	7.4	15.36	18.64	1	2	1.25	1.38	800 432-4789
U.S. Global Leaders Growth	Growth	2.8	17.41		3	3	1	1.3	800 282-2340
UAM Acadian Emerging Mkts Inst	Foreign	10.6	-5.31	0.66	5	4	1	1.5	877 826-5465
UAM Analytic Defensive Equity	Growth/Inc	0.3	4.45	9.71	5	4	0.59	1.11	877 826-5465
UAM Analytic Enhanced Equity	Growth	1.5	1.41	11.05	5	4	0.59	1.1	877 826-5465
UAM C&B Balanced Portfolio	Balanced	-4.2	5.26	10.3	3	1	0.63	1	877 826-5465
UAM C&B Equity	Growth	-6.8	6.46	14.5	4	3	0.63	0.86	877 826-5465
UAM C&B Equity for Taxable Invstr	Growth	1.1	8.83		4	3	0.63	1	877 826-5465
UAM CAMBIAR Opportunity	Growth	12.2					1	1.31	877 826-5465
UAM Clipper Focus Portfolio	Growth	-6.6					1	1.39	877 826-5465
UAM DSI Balanced Portfolio	Balanced	-11.6					0.65	1.06	877 826-5465

381

| Stock Fund Name | Objective | Annualized Return for | | | Rank | | Max Load | Expense Ratio | Toll-Free Telephone |
		1 Year	3 Years	5 Years	Overall	Risk			
UAM DSI Discipline Value Instl	Growth	-21.9	0.02	10.18	5	3	0.75	1.13	877 826-5465
UAM DSI Small Cap Value Portfolio	Small Co	32.6					0.84	1.73	877 826-5465
UAM FMA Small Company B	Small Co	8.4					0.75	1.42	877 826-5465
UAM FMA Small Company Inst	Small Co	8.8	5.88	14.05	3	2	0.75	1.03	877 826-5465
UAM FPA Crescent Fd	Financial	-16	0.13	8.91	4	1	1	1.41	877 826-5465
UAM Heitman Real Estate Adv	Real Est	3.6	1.71	10.35	3	2	0.75	1.72	877 826-5465
UAM Heitman Real Estate Inst	Real Est	4.1	2.21	11.9	3	2	0.75	1.21	877 826-5465
UAM ICM Small Company Inst	Small Co	-0.2	6.85	13.21	3	2	0.69	0.83	877 826-5465
UAM II Chicago Mgmt Val Contr	Growth	-17.6	6.91	10.86	4	3	0.63	0.98	877 826-5465
UAM Jacobs International Octagon	Foreign	26	6.08		4	3	1	1.54	877 826-5465
UAM MJI International Equity Inst	Foreign	17.8	10.34	11.38	4	3	0.75	1.5	877 826-5465
UAM MJI International Equity Port B	Foreign	18.3	9.48		2	3	0.75	1.75	877 826-5465
UAM McKee Intl Equity Portf	Foreign	17.5	11.27	13.63	4	3	0.69	1.02	877 826-5465
UAM McKee Small Cap Equity	Small Co	-8.8					1	0.98	877 826-5465
UAM Mckee Domestic Equity	Growth	-1.1	8.24	13.88	5	3	0.65	1.09	877 826-5465
UAM NWQ Special Equity Portfolio A	Small Co	-5					0.84	1.18	877 826-5465
UAM NWQ Special Equity Portfolio B	Small Co	-5.7					0.84	1.59	877 826-5465
UAM Pell Rudman Mid-Cap Growth Port	Small Co	40.7					1	1.3	877 826-5465
UAM Rice Hall James Small Cap	Small Co	22.5	12.22	18.3	4	4	0.75	1.28	877 826-5465
UAM Rice Hall James Small/Mid Cap	Small Co	21.3	17.2		3	3	0.8	1.25	877 826-5465
UAM Sirach Growth Inst	Growth	17.8	21.49	23.09	2	3	0.65	0.96	877 826-5465
UAM Sirach Special Equity Inst	Small Co	64.8	32.06	26.18	3	4	0.69	0.93	877 826-5465
UAM Sirach Strategic Bal Inst	Balanced	11.8	14.98	15.66	3	2	0.65	1.01	877 826-5465
UAM Sterling Partners Bal Inst	Balanced	-9.3	4.43	9.92	3	1	0.75	1.11	877 826-5465
UAM Sterling Partners Eq Inst	Growth	-16.1	4.08		3	3	0.75	0.2	877 826-5465
UAM Sterling Partners Sm Cap Inst	Small Co	4.7	7.09		4	3	1	1.25	877 826-5465
UAM TJ Core Equity Portfolio Svc	Growth	-7.8	14.27		3	2	0.75	1.25	877 826-5465
UAM TS&W Equity Portfolio Inst	Growth	-4.6	8.05	14.47	3	2	0.75	1.04	877 826-5465
UAM TS&W International Eq Inst	Foreign	39	16.03	14.87	3	3	1	1.37	877 826-5465
UBS US Large Cap Equity Fund	Growth/Inc	-23.6					0.69	1.81	800 448-2430
UBS US Large Cap Growth Fund	Growth	18.1					0.69	1.57	800 448-2430
UBS US Small Cap Growth Fund	Small Co	77.5					1	1.91	800 448-2430
UMB Scout Balanced Fund	Balanced	-4.4	2.13		3	1	0.84	0.86	800 996-2862
UMB Scout Regional Fund	Flexible	-8.6	2.85	7.71	5	2	0.84	0.89	800 996-2862
UMB Scout Stock Fund	Growth/Inc	2.7	10.53	11.86	3	2	0.84	0.86	800 996-2862
UMB Scout Stock Select Fund	Growth/Inc	-4.5					0.84	0.84	800 996-2862
UMB Scout WorldWide Fund	Foreign	19.4	16.76	18.21	2	2	0.84	0.85	800 996-2862
US All American Equity	Growth/Inc	2.7	16.03	21.02	3	2	1	1	800 873-8637
US China Region Opportunity	Pacific	9.5	-10.29	-1.02	5	5	1.21	3.18	800 873-8637
US Global Invs Regent Eastern Euro	European	2.6	-3.9		5	4	1.25	4.34	800 873-8637
US Global Resources Fund	Energy/Res	-3.2	-13.35	-0.98	5	4	1	4.33	800 873-8637
US Gold Shares	Prec Metal	-14.6	-31.8	-31.59	5	5	0.75	5.82	800 873-8637
US Income Fund	Income	-1.2	9.23	11.92	3	2	0.75	2.56	800 873-8637
US Mega Trend Fund	Flexible	13.3	9	13.04	3	3	1	2.16	800 873-8637
US Real Estate Fund	Real Est	-4.6	-3.96	6.59	4	2	0.75	3.95	800 873-8637
US World Gold Fund	Prec Metal	-17.5	-25.8	-15.28	5	5	1	2.47	800 873-8637
USAA Aggressive Growth Fund	Agg Growth	65.1	37.47	31.62	3	5	0.5	0.64	800 382-8722
USAA Asset Strategy-Balanced	Balanced	7.9	11.45		3	1	0.75	1.25	800 382-8722
USAA Asset Strategy-Growth	Growth	13.9	12.21		4	2	0.75	1.28	800 382-8722
USAA Asset Strategy-Income	Income	5.2	8.34		3	1	0.5	0.96	800 382-8722
USAA Cornerstone Strategy Fund	Flexible	5.9	6.5	11.26	3	1	0.75	1.05	800 382-8722
USAA Emerging Markets	Foreign	1.4	-6.82	1.09	5	4	1	1.27	800 382-8722
USAA First Start Growth Fund	Growth	10.5					0.75	1.64	800 382-8722
USAA Gold Fund	Prec Metal	-6.8	-11.58	-10.43	5	5	0.75	1.53	800 382-8722
USAA Growth & Income Fund	Growth/Inc	-0.2	10.07	16.76	3	3	0.59	0.89	800 382-8722
USAA Growth & Tax Strategy	Balanced	6	10.34	12.4	3	1	0.5	0.7	800 382-8722
USAA Growth Fund	Growth	13.9	15.58	18.05	3	3	0.75	0.96	800 382-8722
USAA Income Fund	Flexible	4.2	6.07	6.5	3	1	0.23	0.38	800 382-8722

Stock Fund Name	Objective	Annualized Return for			Rank		Max Load	Expense Ratio	Toll-Free Telephone
		1 Year	3 Years	5 Years	Overall	Risk			
USAA Income Stock Fund	Income	-7.1	9.07	13.31	3	2	0.28	0.65	800 382-8722
USAA International Fund	Foreign	20.5	8	12.91	4	3	0.75	1.14	800 382-8722
USAA S&P 500 Index	Growth/Inc	6.9	19.44		2	3	0.1	0.17	800 382-8722
USAA Science & Technology Fund	Technology	39.5					0.75	1.33	800 382-8722
USAA Small Cap Stock Fund	Small Co						0.75		800 382-8722
USAA Tax Exempt-FL	Muni State	-0.1	3.69	5.44	3	4	0.39	0.46	800 382-8722
USAA World Growth Fund	Global	21	13.2	16.25	3	3	0.75	1.19	800 382-8722
UltraEurope ProFund Investor Class	European	17.4					0.9	2	888 776-3637
UltraEurope ProFund Service Class	European	16.6					0.9	3.2	888 776-3637
Undiscovered Mgrs All Cap Val C	Growth	-8.3					0.73		888 242-3514
Undiscovered Mgrs All Cap Val Inst	Growth	-7.3					0.73	0.98	888 242-3514
Undiscovered Mgrs Behavior Gr C	Growth	46.4					0.94		888 242-3514
Undiscovered Mgrs Behavior Gr Inst	Growth	47.8					0.94	1.3	888 242-3514
Undiscovered Mgrs Behavior Gr Inv	Growth	47	32.46				0.94	1.3	888 242-3514
Undiscovered Mgrs Behavior L/S I	Growth	3.8					1.55	2	888 242-3514
Undiscovered Mgrs Behavior Val I	Growth	19.7					1.05	1.39	888 242-3514
Undiscovered Mgrs Core Eq C	Growth						0.73		888 242-3514
Undiscovered Mgrs Core Eq Inst	Growth	-9.7					0.73	0.98	888 242-3514
Undiscovered Mgrs Core Eq Inv	Growth	-10					0.73	0.98	888 242-3514
Undiscovered Mgrs Hidden Value	Growth	-5.2					0.94	1.3	888 242-3514
Undiscovered Mgrs Hidden Value Inv	Growth	-5.4					0.94	1.3	888 242-3514
Undiscovered Mgrs Intl Equity C	Foreign						0.94		888 242-3514
Undiscovered Mgrs Intl Equity Instl	Foreign	39.6					1	1.44	888 242-3514
Undiscovered Mgrs Intl Small Cap Eq	Foreign	70.8					1	1.6	888 242-3514
Undiscovered Mgrs REIT Fund C	Real Est						1.05		888 242-3514
Undiscovered Mgrs REIT Fund Inv	Real Est	8.1					1.05	1.75	888 242-3514
Undiscovered Mgrs REIT I	Real Est	8.5					1.05	1.39	888 242-3514
Undiscovered Mgrs Sm Cap Val C	Small Co	4					1.05		888 242-3514
Undiscovered Mgrs Sm Cap Val Inv	Small Co	4.5					1.05	1.39	888 242-3514
Undiscovered Mgrs SmCap Value Inst	Small Co	5					1.05	1.39	888 242-3514
Undiscovered Mgrs Spec SmCap Val	Small Co	2.2					1.64	1.66	888 242-3514
Unified Asset Allocation Fund	Balanced	6.6	6.77		4	1	0.75	1.26	800 408-4682
Unified Select 2000 Index Fund	Small Co						0.34		800 408-4682
Unified Select 30 Index Fund	Growth						0.34		800 408-4682
Unified Select 500 Index Fund	Growth	5					0.34		800 408-4682
Unified Select Internet Fund	Technology	24.8					0.34		800 408-4682
Unified Starwood Strategic Fund	Growth	29	23.22		3	4	1.25	2.58	800 408-4682
United Association S&P 500 Index I	Growth						0.01		888 766-8043
United Association S&P 500 Index II	Growth						0.01		888 766-8043
Unity Fund A	Growth/Inc	-21.7					0.84	2.1	877 542-3863
Universal Capital Growth	Growth	5.9	21.01	20.9	3	3	1	2	800 537-3446
Valley Forge Fund	Growth	-8	0.48	3.98	4	1	1	1.3	800 548-1942
Value Line Asset Allocation	AssetAlloc	15.1	19.9	22.76	2	3	0.65	1.04	800 223-0818
Value Line Fund	Growth/Inc	11.6	18.11	20.66	3	3	0.67	0.76	800 223-0818
Value Line Income & Growth Fund	Income	18.4	21.14	20.65	2	3	0.68	0.82	800 223-0818
Value Line Leveraged Growth	Agg Growth	18.1	27.54	25.92	2	3	0.75	0.81	800 223-0818
Value Line Multinational Co.	Growth	22.6	22.14		2	3	0.75	1.53	800 223-0818
Value Line Special Situations	Growth	50.2	38.82	28.87	2	4	0.75	0.92	800 223-0818
Van Eck Asia Dynasty A	Pacific	4.1	6.48	5.44	4	5	0.75	2.81	800 826-2333
Van Eck Asia Dynasty B	Pacific	3.3	5.5	4.64	4	5	0.75	3.72	800 826-2333
Van Eck Global Hard Assets A	Other	3.6	-5.02	7.99	4	3	1	2	800 826-2333
Van Eck Global Leaders A	Balanced	22.4	15.85	15.53	2	2	0.75	2	800 826-2333
Van Eck Global Leaders B	Balanced	21.7	15.29	14.84	2	2	0.75	2.5	800 826-2333
Van Eck Intl Investors Gold A	Prec Metal	-16.7	-19.46	-16.83	5	5	0.75	2.08	800 826-2333
Van Eck Natural Resources Fd A	Prec Metal	-13.3	-20.57	-15.36	5	5	0.75	2.5	800 826-2333
Van Eck/Chubb Growth & Income A	Growth/Inc	12.5	10.43	16.4	3	3	0.2	1.32	800 826-2333
Van Eck/Chubb Total Return Fund A	Growth/Inc	13.8	10.5	14.48	3	2	0.2	1.32	800 826-2333
Van Kampen Agg Gr A	Agg Growth	78.8	55.2		1	5	0.75	1.25	800 421-5666

Stock Fund Name	Objective	Annualized Return for			Rank		Max Load	Expense Ratio	Toll-Free Telephone
		1 Year	3 Years	5 Years	Overall	Risk			
Van Kampen Agg Gr B	Agg Growth	77.4	54.07		1	5	0.75	2.33	800 421-5666
Van Kampen Agg Gr C	Agg Growth	77.4	54.12		1	5	0.75	2.33	800 421-5666
Van Kampen Amer Value A	Small Co	4.6	16.36	19.3	3	3	0.84	1.44	800 421-5666
Van Kampen Amer Value B	Small Co	3.8	15.48		3	3	0.84	2.24	800 421-5666
Van Kampen Amer Value C	Small Co	3.8	15.5	18.41	3	3	0.84	2.24	800 421-5666
Van Kampen Asian Growth A	Pacific	13.5	-7.7	-4.06	4	5	1	1.91	800 421-5666
Van Kampen Asian Growth B	Pacific	12.8	-8.35	-4.71	4	5	1	2.7	800 421-5666
Van Kampen Asian Growth C	Pacific	12.8	-8.41	-4.79	5	5	1	2.7	800 421-5666
Van Kampen Comstock A	Growth/Inc	-4.5	13.45	17.86	3	3	0.5	0.89	800 421-5666
Van Kampen Comstock B	Growth/Inc	-5.2	12.6	16.94	3	3	0.5	1.66	800 421-5666
Van Kampen Comstock C	Growth/Inc	-5.2	12.56	16.92	3	3	0.5	1.65	800 421-5666
Van Kampen Emerg Gr A	Agg Growth	87	50.27	39	1	5	0.44	0.84	800 421-5666
Van Kampen Emerg Gr B	Agg Growth	85.6	49.11	37.92	1	5	0.44	1.73	800 421-5666
Van Kampen Emerg Gr C	Agg Growth	85.7	49.12	37.94	1	5	0.44	1.73	800 421-5666
Van Kampen Emerg Mkt A	Foreign	35.4	3.26	7.37	4	5	1.25	2.33	800 421-5666
Van Kampen Emerg Mkt B	Foreign	34.3	2.51		4	5	1.25	3.08	800 421-5666
Van Kampen Emerg Mkt C	Foreign	34.4	2.56	6.32	4	5	1.25	3.08	800 421-5666
Van Kampen Enterprise A	Growth	26.1	22.5	23.98	1	3	0.46	0.91	800 421-5666
Van Kampen Enterprise B	Growth	25.2	21.57	22.99	1	3	0.46	1.68	800 421-5666
Van Kampen Enterprise C	Growth	25.2	21.58	23.01	1	3	0.46	1.67	800 421-5666
Van Kampen Equity Growth A	Growth	27.3					0.8	1.5	800 421-5666
Van Kampen Equity Growth B	Growth	26.3					0.8	2.25	800 421-5666
Van Kampen Equity Growth C	Growth	26.3					0.8	2.25	800 421-5666
Van Kampen Equity Inc A	Income	11.1	14.44	17.58	2	1	0.36	0.81	800 421-5666
Van Kampen Equity Inc B	Income	10	13.54	16.62	2	1	0.36	1.56	800 421-5666
Van Kampen Equity Inc C	Income	10.1	13.59	16.65	2	1	0.36	1.56	800 421-5666
Van Kampen European Equity Fund A	European	13.2					1	1.69	800 421-5666
Van Kampen European Equity Fund B	European	12.4					1	2.45	800 421-5666
Van Kampen European Equity Fund C	European	12.4					1	2.45	800 421-5666
Van Kampen Exchange	Growth	36.7	25.11	26.41	2	3	0.5	0.73	800 421-5666
Van Kampen FL Ins T/F A	Muni State	1.7	3.96	5.34	2	4	0.5	0.4	800 421-5666
Van Kampen FL Ins T/F B	Muni State	0.9	3.16	4.56	4	4	0.5	1.16	800 421-5666
Van Kampen FL Ins T/F C	Muni State	0.9	3.18	4.59	4	4	0.5	1.15	800 421-5666
Van Kampen Focus Eq A	Agg Growth	25.3	27.23		1	3	0.9	1.5	800 421-5666
Van Kampen Focus Eq B	Agg Growth	24.4	26.28		1	3	0.9	2.33	800 421-5666
Van Kampen Focus Eq C	Agg Growth	24.4	26.29		1	3	0.9	2.25	800 421-5666
Van Kampen Gl Mg Ast A	Balanced						1	4.16	800 421-5666
Van Kampen Gl Mg Ast B	Balanced						1	5.08	800 421-5666
Van Kampen Gl Mg Ast C	Balanced						1	5.16	800 421-5666
Van Kampen Glb Govt A	Intl Bond						0.75	1.56	800 421-5666
Van Kampen Glb Govt B	Intl Bond						0.75	2.29	800 421-5666
Van Kampen Glb Govt C	Intl Bond						0.75	2.29	800 421-5666
Van Kampen Global Eq Alloc A	Global	12.8	12.42	16.38	3	2	1	1.69	800 421-5666
Van Kampen Global Eq Alloc B	Global	12	11.57		3	2	1	2.45	800 421-5666
Van Kampen Global Eq Alloc C	Global	12	11.61		3	2	1	2.45	800 421-5666
Van Kampen Global Equity A	Global	3.2					1	1.64	800 421-5666
Van Kampen Global Equity B	Global	2.2					1	2.39	800 421-5666
Van Kampen Global Equity C	Global	2.2					1	2.39	800 421-5666
Van Kampen Global Fixed A	Intl Bond						0.75	1.46	800 421-5666
Van Kampen Global Fixed B	Intl Bond						0.75	2.22	800 421-5666
Van Kampen Global Fixed C	Intl Bond						0.75	2.22	800 421-5666
Van Kampen Gr & Inc A	Growth/Inc	7.3	14.58	18.63	2	2	0.5	0.88	800 421-5666
Van Kampen Gr & Inc B	Growth/Inc	6.5	13.67	17.69	2	2	0.5	1.65	800 421-5666
Van Kampen Gr & Inc C	Growth/Inc	6.4	13.64	17.67	2	2	0.5	1.65	800 421-5666
Van Kampen Intl Magnum A	Foreign	14.6	9.72		4	2	0.8	1.64	800 421-5666
Van Kampen Intl Magnum B	Foreign	13.8	4.77		5	2	0.8	2.39	800 421-5666
Van Kampen Intl Magnum C	Foreign	13.8	4.79		4	2	0.8	2.39	800 421-5666
Van Kampen Latin America A	Foreign	23.3	1.62	18.13	3	5	1.25	2.22	800 421-5666

Stock Fund Name	Objective	Annualized Return for			Rank		Max Load	Expense Ratio	Toll-Free Telephone
		1 Year	3 Years	5 Years	Overall	Risk			
Van Kampen Latin America B	Foreign	22.3	0.99		4	5	1.25	2.95	800 421-5666
Van Kampen Latin America C	Foreign	22.3	0.92	17.28	3	5	1.25	2.95	800 421-5666
Van Kampen Mid Cap Growth Fund A	Growth						0.75		800 421-5666
Van Kampen Mid Cap Growth Fund B	Growth						0.75		800 421-5666
Van Kampen Mid Cap Growth Fund C	Growth						0.75		800 421-5666
Van Kampen Pace A	Growth	4	15.36	19.19	3	3	0.42	0.81	800 421-5666
Van Kampen Pace B	Growth	3.2	14.48	18.26	2	3	0.42	1.61	800 421-5666
Van Kampen Pace C	Growth	3.1	14.48	18.31	3	3	0.42	1.61	800 421-5666
Van Kampen Re Est Secs A	Real Est	2	3.32	12.49	3	2	1	1.81	800 421-5666
Van Kampen Re Est Secs B	Real Est	1.6	2.67	11.73	3	2	1	2.6	800 421-5666
Van Kampen Re Est Secs C	Real Est	1.4	2.6	11.67	3	2	1	2.6	800 421-5666
Van Kampen Tax Mnged Gl Franchise A	Global	19.8					1	1.8	800 421-5666
Van Kampen Tax Mnged Gl Franchise B	Global	19.1					1	2.54	800 421-5666
Van Kampen Tax Mnged Gl Franchise C	Global	18.9					1	2.54	800 421-5666
Van Kampen Technology A	Technology						0.9		800 421-5666
Van Kampen Technology B	Technology						0.9		800 421-5666
Van Kampen Technology Fund C	Technology						0.9		800 421-5666
Van Kampen Util Fund A	Utilities	21.6	21.39	19.39	1	2	0.65	1.23	800 421-5666
Van Kampen Util Fund B	Utilities	20.6	20.49	18.5	2	2	0.65	1.98	800 421-5666
Van Kampen Util Fund C	Utilities	20.7	20.47	18.65	2	2	0.65	1.98	800 421-5666
Van Kampen Value Fund A	Growth	-16.6					0.8	1.44	800 421-5666
Van Kampen Value Fund B	Growth	-17.2					0.8	2.2	800 421-5666
Van Kampen Value Fund C	Growth	-17.2					0.8	2.2	800 421-5666
Van Kampen Wrldwde High Inc A	Intl Bond	11.4	0.8	9.98	3	5	0.75	1.44	800 421-5666
Van Kampen Wrldwde High Inc B	Intl Bond	10.6	0.03		3	5	0.75	2.2	800 421-5666
Van Kampen Wrldwde High Inc C	Intl Bond	10.6	0	8.93	3	5	0.75	2.2	800 421-5666
Van Wagoner Emerging Growth Fund	Agg Growth	124.3	63.84		2	5	1.25	1.88	800 228-2121
Van Wagoner Micro-Cap Fund	Small Co	111.5	55.07		3	5	1.5	1.94	800 228-2121
Van Wagoner Mid-Cap Fund	Agg Growth	70.8	40.9		3	5	1	1.89	800 228-2121
Van Wagoner Post-Venture	Agg Growth	83	64.43		3	5	1.5	1.94	800 228-2121
Van Wagoner Technology Fund	Technology	86.6					1.25	1.94	800 228-2121
Vanguard 500 Index Fund	Growth/Inc	7.3	19.67	23.76	2	3	0.14	0.17	800 662-7447
Vanguard Aggressive Growth	Agg Growth	11.3	6.35		4	3	0.41	0.44	800 662-7447
Vanguard Asset Allocation	AssetAlloc	6.5	15.75	18.29	2	1	0.46	0.48	800 662-7447
Vanguard Capital Opportunity	Growth	98.4	43.9		1	4	0.88	0.93	800 662-7447
Vanguard Emerging Mkts Stock Idx	Foreign	10.8	-3.75	3.07	5	4	0.32	0.57	800 662-7447
Vanguard Equity Income	Income	-9.3	9.44	16.01	3	2	0.39	0.4	800 662-7447
Vanguard Europe Stock Index Fund	European	15.8	16.53	18.8	2	3		0.14	800 662-7447
Vanguard Explorer Fund	Small Co	43.1	20.86	19.08	3	4	0.7	0.7	800 662-7447
Vanguard FL Insured Tax-Free	Muni State	3.6	4.81	5.96	2	4	0.16	0.17	800 662-7447
Vanguard Global Asset Alloc Fund	AssetAlloc	9	10.19		3	1	0.53	0.56	800 662-7447
Vanguard Global Equity Fund	Global	8.4	9.49		4	2	0.65	0.68	800 662-7447
Vanguard Growth & Income Fund	Growth/Inc	8.7	20.33	23.76	1	3	0.34	0.36	800 662-7447
Vanguard Growth Index Fund	Growth	19	27.18	29.3	1	3	0.19	0.22	800 662-7447
Vanguard Index Tr Sm-Cap Idx Fd	Small Co	15.5	11.56	15.49	4	4	0.2	0.25	800 662-7447
Vanguard Index Tr Tot St Mkt Fd	Growth/Inc	9.9	19.08	22.29	3	3	0.17	0.2	800 662-7447
Vanguard Index-Balanced Ptfl	Balanced	8	13.95	15.89	3	1	0.17	0.2	800 662-7447
Vanguard Institutional Index Fd	Growth/Inc	7.4	19.8	23.91	2	3	0.07	0.05	800 662-7447
Vanguard Intl Growth Fund	Foreign	24.9	10.63	14.31	3	3	0.5	0.52	800 662-7447
Vanguard Intl Value Fund	Foreign	9.3	7.38	10.21	4	3	0.42	0.58	800 662-7447
Vanguard Life Strategy-Consv Gr	Income	7	10.97	12.42	3	1	0.28	0	800 662-7447
Vanguard Life Strategy-Growth	Growth	9.7	15.49	17.77	2	2	0.28	0	800 662-7447
Vanguard Life Strategy-Income	Income	5.5	9.1	10.01	2	1	0.28	0	800 662-7447
Vanguard Life Strategy-Mod Gr	Growth/Inc	8.3	13.46	15.27	3	1	0	0	800 662-7447
Vanguard Morgan Growth Fund	Growth	21.1	24.38	25.13	1	3	0.4	0.41	800 662-7447
Vanguard Pacific Stock Index Fund	Pacific	22.2	1.52	2.5	5	4	0.32	0.38	800 662-7447
Vanguard Preferred Stock	Income	-6.6	2.34	5.33	3	1	0.33	0.35	800 662-7447
Vanguard PrimeCap Fund	Growth	39.5	32.57	29.26	1	3	0.47	0.51	800 662-7447

385

Stock Fund Name	Objective	Annualized Return for			Rank		Max Load	Expense Ratio	Toll-Free Telephone
		1 Year	3 Years	5 Years	Overall	Risk			
Vanguard Selected Value Fund	Growth	-8.5	-3.65		5	4	0.68	0.63	800 662-7447
Vanguard Specialized-Energy	Energy/Res	16	7.37	14.48	3	4	0.35	0.47	800 662-7447
Vanguard Specialized-Gold	Prec Metal	-5.8	-10.73	-9.03	5	5	0.68	0.77	800 662-7447
Vanguard Specialized-Health	Health	35.3	28.34	31.13	1	2	0.27	0.42	800 662-7447
Vanguard Specialized-REIT Index	Real Est	3.6	0.93		4	2	0.22	0.32	800 662-7447
Vanguard Specialized-Utilities	Utilities	-1.8	13.1	13.49	3	2	0.34	0.4	800 662-7447
Vanguard Star Fund	Balanced	3.1	10.91	14.32	3	1	0	0	800 662-7447
Vanguard Tax Managed-Balanced	Balanced	12.1	14.32	14.76	3	1	0.14	0.2	800 662-7447
Vanguard Tax Managed-Cap Apprec	Growth	18.9	24.32	24.82	1	3	0.16	0.19	800 662-7447
Vanguard Tax Managed-Gr & Inc	Growth/Inc	7.4	19.71	23.82	2	3	0.14	0.19	800 662-7447
Vanguard Tax-Managed International	Global						0.14		800 662-7447
Vanguard Tax-Managed Small-Cap	Small Co	15.6					0.17	0.19	800 662-7447
Vanguard Tax-Managed Small-Cap Inst	Small Co	15.8					0.17	0.1	800 662-7447
Vanguard Total Intl Stock Index	Foreign	17	8.5		4	3	0.34	0.34	800 662-7447
Vanguard U.S. Growth Fund	Growth	20.5	24.58	26.82	2	3	0.36	0.39	800 662-7447
Vanguard Value Index Fund	Growth	-5.2	11.32	17.59	3	3	0.16	0.22	800 662-7447
Vanguard Wellesley Income	Flexible	-1.8	7.33	9.82	3	1	0.23	0.32	800 662-7447
Vanguard Wellington Fund	Balanced	-4.1	8.11	13.31	3	1	0.28	0.29	800 662-7447
Vanguard Windsor-I	Growth/Inc	-5.9	5.73	13.09	4	3	0.26	0.3	800 662-7447
Vanguard Windsor-II	Growth/Inc	-15.7	7.34	15.91	3	3	0.34	0.36	800 662-7447
Victory Balanced Fund G	Balanced						0.8		800 539-3863
Victory Growth Fund G	Growth						0.75		800 539-3863
Victory LifeChoice Conserv Inv	Balanced	17.1	10.97		3	1	0.2	1.45	800 539-3863
Victory LifeChoice Growth Inv	Growth	9	9.54		3	2	0.2	1.05	800 539-3863
Victory LifeChoice Moderate Inv	Growth	10.6	9.58		3	1	0.2	0.72	800 539-3863
Victory Portf-Balanced A	Balanced	1.5	10.95	13.81	3	1	0.8	1.27	800 539-3863
Victory Portf-Intl Growth A	Foreign	22	11.58	10.05	3	3	1.1	1.75	800 539-3863
Victory Portf-Lakefront Fund	Growth	-3.3	11.19		4	3	1	0.5	800 539-3863
Victory Portf-Real Estate Inv Fd	Real Est	10.4	5.11		3	2	0.8	1.12	800 539-3863
Victory Portf-Special Value A	Growth	2.9	1.99	8.37	4	3	0.8	1.42	800 539-3863
Victory Portf-Stock Index Fund	Growth	6.7	18.88	22.4	2	3	0.59	0.57	800 539-3863
Victory Portf-Value Fund	Growth/Inc	-1.9	15.35	19.99	3	3	1	1.39	800 539-3863
Victory Real Estate Investment G	Real Est						0.8		800 539-3863
Victory Special Value Fund G	Growth						0.8		800 539-3863
Victory Stock Index Fund G	Growth						0.59		800 539-3863
Victory Value Fund G	Growth/Inc						0.75		800 539-3863
Villere Balanced Fund	Balanced						0.75		
Vintage Aggressive Gr	Agg Growth	20.7	20.06		2	3	0.94		800 438-6375
Vintage Balanced	Balanced	7.6	14.46	15.76	2	1	0.75	1.22	800 438-6375
Vintage Equity Fund S	Growth	11.1	18.78	22.89	2	3	0.75	1.36	800 438-6375
Vision Large-Cap Value	Growth	-10.5					0.69	0.95	800 836-2211
Vision Mid Cap Stock Fund	Growth	9.1	9.6	15.31	4	4	0.84	1.34	800 836-2211
Volumetric Fund	Growth	-7.1	4.6	9.28	4	2	1.89	1.9	800 541-3863
Vontobel Eastern European Eq Fd	European	7.5	-19.97		5	5	1.25	3.37	800 527-9500
Vontobel Greater European Bond Fund	Intl Bond	-4.1					1.19	1.97	800 527-9500
Vontobel International Equity	Foreign	23.7	13.62	16.67	3	3	0.9	1.28	800 527-9500
Vontobel US Equity Fund	Foreign	11.1					1.25	2.06	800 527-9500
Vontobel US Value Fund	Growth/Inc	-18.4	3.57	12.49	3	3	0.85	1.62	800 527-9500
WM Bond & Stock Fd A	Balanced	-2.5	6.74	11.73	3	2	0.58	1.05	800 222-5852
WM Bond & Stock Fd B	Balanced	-3.3	5.85	10.77	4	2	0.58	1.85	800 222-5852
WM FL Ins Municipal A	Muni State	0.2	3.77	5.44	3	3	0.5	0.93	800 222-5852
WM FL Ins Municipal B	Muni State	-0.5	2.98	4.64	4	3	0.5	1.67	800 222-5852
WM Growth & Income Fd A	Growth/Inc	5	15.01	20.4	3	3	0.53	1	800 222-5852
WM Growth & Income Fd B	Growth/Inc	4.1	14.12	19.37	3	3	0.53	1.76	800 222-5852
WM Growth Fd A	Growth	44	45.79	33.95	1	4	0.84	1.27	800 222-5852
WM Growth Fd B	Growth	42.8	44.72	32.94	1	4	0.84	2.04	800 222-5852
WM Growth Fund of the Northwest A	Growth	36.4	29.78	28.93	2	4	0.63	1.04	800 222-5852
WM Growth Fund of the Northwest B	Growth	35.2	28.67	27.81	2	4	0.63	2.04	800 222-5852

Stock Fund Name	Objective	Annualized Return for			Rank		Max Load	Expense Ratio	Toll-Free Telephone
		1 Year	3 Years	5 Years	Overall	Risk			
WM International Gr A	Foreign	33.9	8.99	11.09	4	3	1	1.86	800 222-5852
WM International Gr B	Foreign	32.9	8.08	10.21	4	3	1	2.95	800 222-5852
WM Small Cap Stock Fund A	Small Co	81	30.79	24.53	3	5	0.84	1.78	800 222-5852
WM Small Cap Stock Fund B	Small Co	79.4	29.69	23.54	3	5	0.84	2.72	800 222-5852
WPG Growth & Income	Growth/Inc	18.2	18.89	23.66	2	3	0.75	1.03	800 223-3332
WPG International	Foreign	9.5	8.17	9.21	5	2	0.5	2.47	800 223-3332
WPG Quantitative Equity	Growth/Inc	2	15.81	19.33	3	3	0.75	1.11	800 223-3332
WPG Tudor Fund	Agg Growth	53.1	14.25	17.28	3	4	0.9	1.37	800 223-3332
WST Growth Fd Inst	Growth/Inc	2.3					0.75	1.75	800 525-3863
WST Growth Fd Inv	Growth/Inc	1.8					0.75	2.25	800 525-3863
WWW Internet Fund	Technology	63.5	59.02		3	5	2.5	2.43	888 999-8331
Wachovia Balanced Fund A	Balanced	13.8	14.72	16.33	2	1	0.54	1.01	800 994-4414
Wachovia Balanced Fund B	Balanced	13	13.89		2	1	0.54	1.76	800 994-4414
Wachovia Balanced Fund Y	Balanced	14.1	15		2	1	0.54	0.76	800 994-4414
Wachovia Emerging Mkts A	Foreign	16.7	-2.4	3.5	5	4	1	1.6	800 994-4414
Wachovia Emerging Mkts Y	Foreign	17.2	-2.12		4	4	1	1.43	800 994-4414
Wachovia Equity Fund A	Growth	18.8	20.3	22.21	1	3	0.69	1.09	800 994-4414
Wachovia Equity Fund B	Growth	17.8	19.4		1	3	0.69	1.85	800 994-4414
Wachovia Equity Fund Y	Growth	19.1	20.59		1	3	0.69	0.84	800 994-4414
Wachovia Equity Index A	Growth	6.4	18.74	22.96	2	3	0.25	0.68	800 994-4414
Wachovia Equity Index Y	Growth	6.7	19.06		3	3	0.26	0.42	800 994-4414
Wachovia Growth and Income A	Growth/Inc	11.1	18.94	23.67	2	3	0.69	1.09	800 994-4414
Wachovia Personal Equity A	Growth/Inc						0.75	1.14	800 994-4414
Wachovia Personal Equity Y	Growth/Inc						0.75	0.9	800 994-4414
Wachovia Quantitative Equity A	Growth	11.6	19.07	22.89	2	3	0.69	1.11	800 994-4414
Wachovia Quantitative Equity B	Growth	10.8	18.21		2	3	0.69	1.86	800 994-4414
Wachovia Quantitative Equity Y	Growth	11.8	19.36		1	3	0.69	0.85	800 994-4414
Wachovia SC Municipal Bond A	Muni State	2.3	3.73	4.91	3	3	0.26	0.82	800 994-4414
Wachovia SC Municipal Bond Y	Muni State	2.5	3.97		1	3	0.75	0.57	800 994-4414
Wachovia Special Values A	Small Co	0.7	6.44	16.33	3	2	0.79	1.21	800 994-4414
Wachovia Special Values Y	Small Co	0.9	6.69		3	2	0.57	0.96	800 994-4414
Waddell & Reed Adv Accumulative A	Growth	20.3	20.99	22.06	1	2	0.44	0.97	800 366-5465
Waddell & Reed Adv Accumulative B	Growth						0.44		800 366-5465
Waddell & Reed Adv Accumulative C	Growth						0.44		800 366-5465
Waddell & Reed Adv Accumulative Y	Growth	20.8	21.26	22.27	1	2	0.56	0.73	800 366-5465
Walden Social Balanced Fund	Growth/Inc						0.75		
Walden Social Equity Fund	Growth						0.75		
Walden/BBT Domestic Social Equity	Growth						0.5		
Walden/BBT Intl Social Index Fund	Global						0.5		
Wall Street Fund	Growth	71.3	35.44	27.19	3	5	0.75	1.8	800-443-4693
Warburg Pincus Bal Portf Adv	Balanced	5	10.56		3	1	0.42	0.61	800 927-2874
Warburg Pincus Bal Portf Com	Balanced	5.9	11.12	14.18	3	1	0.42	1.6	800 927-2874
Warburg Pincus Cap App Adv	Growth	40.1	30.59	29.53	1	3	0.69	1.47	800 927-2874
Warburg Pincus Core Equity I	Growth	15.4	20.7	23.91	2	3	0.75	0.98	800 927-2874
Warburg Pincus Emerg Gr Adv	Small Co	39.1	19.82	19.84	3	4	0.9	1.67	800 927-2874
Warburg Pincus Emerg Gr Com	Small Co	39.7	20.36	20.38	3	4	0.9	1.21	800 927-2874
Warburg Pincus Emerg Mkts Adv	Foreign	25.8	-8.01	1.74	4	5	1.25	1.9	800 927-2874
Warburg Pincus Emerg Mkts Com	Foreign	26	-6.99	2.37	4	5	0.53	1.64	800 927-2874
Warburg Pincus European Equity Com	European	31.6					1	1.45	800 927-2874
Warburg Pincus European Equity Inst	European	32.1					1	1.15	800 927-2874
Warburg Pincus Focus Fund Cmn	Growth	26.4					0.71	1.25	800 927-2874
Warburg Pincus Focus Fund Inst	Growth	-6					0.71	0.98	800 927-2874
Warburg Pincus Gbl Fixed Inc Adv	Intl Bond	3.1	2.54		3	3	0.5	1.44	800 927-2874
Warburg Pincus Gbl Fixed Inc Com	Intl Bond	5.7	3.85	6.81	3	3	0.5	0.94	800 927-2874
Warburg Pincus Gbl Post-Ven Adv	Global	85.4	48.61		1	4	0.4	1.57	800 927-2874
Warburg Pincus Gbl Post-Ven Com	Global	85.8	49.03		1	4	0.4	1.65	800 927-2874
Warburg Pincus Global Hlth Sci Com	Health	35	24.48		3	4	1	1.59	800 927-2874
Warburg Pincus Global Telecom Cmn	Technology	77.9	66.37		1	5	1	1.64	800 927-2874

Stock Fund Name	Objective	Annualized Return for			Rank		Max Load	Expense Ratio	Toll-Free Telephone
		1 Year	3 Years	5 Years	Overall	Risk			
Warburg Pincus Instl Emerging Mkts	Foreign	33.3	-2.7		4	5	1	1.25	800 927-2874
Warburg Pincus Instl Intl Equity	Foreign	34.5	9.22	13.21	4	3	0.8	0.95	800 927-2874
Warburg Pincus Instl Japan Growth	Pacific	27.8					1.1	1.26	800 927-2874
Warburg Pincus Instl Post Venture	Growth	64.9					1.1	1.25	800 927-2874
Warburg Pincus Instl Small Co Value	Growth	-6.6					0.9	0.98	800 927-2874
Warburg Pincus Instl Value	Growth	-9.5	10.09		4	3	0.75	0.75	800 927-2874
Warburg Pincus Intl Equity Adv	Foreign	28.3	6.1	11.03	4	3	1	1.92	800 927-2874
Warburg Pincus Intl Equity Com	Foreign	28.9	6.6	11.54	4	3	1	1.41	800 927-2874
Warburg Pincus Intl Growth Inst	Foreign	26.6	16.13	15.69	3	3	0.8	1.19	800 927-2874
Warburg Pincus Intl Small Company	Foreign	62.3					1.1	1.56	800 927-2874
Warburg Pincus Japan Growth Adv	Pacific	17.9	20.59		2	5	0.8	2.04	800 927-2874
Warburg Pincus Japan Growth Com	Pacific	18.5	22.06		3	5	0.8	1.76	800 927-2874
Warburg Pincus Japan Small Co Adv	Pacific	21.9	27.04	18.16	3	5	1.25	1.94	800 927-2874
Warburg Pincus Japan Small Co Com	Pacific	22.2	26.84	18.42	3	5	1.25	1.94	800 927-2874
Warburg Pincus Long/Sht Mkt Ntrl	Growth	7.7					1.5	2.25	800 927-2874
Warburg Pincus Major Foreign Mkts	Foreign	39.6	17.08		3	3	1	0.95	800 927-2874
Warburg Pincus Small Co Gr Inst	Small Co	65.3	24.92		3	5	0.9	1.9	800 927-2874
Warburg Pincus Small Co Gr Trust	Small Co	62.2	23.76		3	5	0.9	1.13	800 927-2874
Warburg Pincus Small Co Val Adv	Small Co	2.8	-2.06		5	3	1	2	800 927-2874
Warburg Pincus Small Co Val Com	Small Co	3.2	-1.53		5	3	1.25	1.75	800 927-2874
Warburg Pincus Small Company Growth	Small Co	82.7	34.92		3	5	1	1.39	800 927-2874
Warburg Pincus Tr Emerging Markets	Foreign	24.2					0.81	1.39	800 927-2874
Warburg Pincus Tr Growth & Income	Growth/Inc	-10.1					0.75	1	800 927-2874
Warburg Pincus Tr Intl Equity	Foreign	31	7.83		4	3	1	1.32	800 927-2874
Warburg Pincus Tr Post Venture Cap	Growth	52.3	26.08		3	4	1.25	1.39	800 927-2874
Warburg Pincus Value Fund Adv	Growth/Inc	-11.2	8.56	9.5	4	3	0.75	1.64	800 927-2874
Warburg Pincus Value Fund Com	Growth/Inc	-10.6	9.08	9.99	4	3	0.75	1.13	800 927-2874
Wasatch Core Growth Fund	Growth	18.3	13.19	17.29	3	3	1	1.43	800 551-1700
Wasatch Micro Cap Fund	Small Co	55.7	31.38	32.1	1	4	2	2.45	800 551-1700
Wasatch Micro-Cap Value Fund	Small Co	35.3					1.5	1.94	800 551-1700
Wasatch Small Cap Growth	Small Co	44.8	22.94	19.17	3	4	1	1.46	800 551-1700
Wasatch Ultra Growth	Agg Growth	35.6	18.13	14.89	4	4	1.25	1.8	800 551-1700
Washington Mutual Investors Fund	Growth/Inc	-11.3	9.46	17.3	3	3	0.34	0.6	800 421-9900
Waterhouse Dow 30 Fund	Growth	-2.7					0.2		800 457-6516
Wayne Hummer Growth Fund	Growth	19.1	20.34	20.33	2	3	0.8	0.96	800 621-4477
Wealthbuilder Growth Balanced	Balanced	6.6					0.34	1.25	800 338-1348
Wealthbuilder Growth Portfolio	Growth	11.2					0.34	1.25	800 338-1348
Wealthbuilder Growth and Income	Growth/Inc	12.5					0.34	1.25	800 338-1348
Wells Fargo Agg Bal Equity I	Balanced	10.1					0.5	1	800 222-8222
Wells Fargo Asset Allocation A	AssetAlloc	7.2	16.91	16.44	2	2	0.8	0.94	800 222-8222
Wells Fargo Disciplined Growth I	Growth	13.5					0.5	1.25	800 222-8222
Wells Fargo Diversified Equity A	Growth	10	17.16	20.4	2	2	0.85	1.01	800 222-8222
Wells Fargo Diversified Equity B	Growth	9.2	16.27		3	2	0.85	1.75	800 222-8222
Wells Fargo Diversified Equity C	Growth	9.2					0.85	1.75	800 222-8222
Wells Fargo Diversified Equity I	Growth	10	17.16	20.39	2	2	0.85	1	800 222-8222
Wells Fargo Diversified Sm Cap I	Small Co	13.8					0.25	1.19	800 222-8222
Wells Fargo Diversified Small Cap A	Small Co	13.6					0	1.39	800 222-8222
Wells Fargo Diversified Small Cap B	Small Co	12.8						1.98	800 222-8222
Wells Fargo Equity Income A	Growth/Inc	-9	10.25	16.82	2	2	0.75	0.84	800 222-8222
Wells Fargo Equity Income B	Growth/Inc	-9.7	9.39		3	2	0.75	1.6	800 222-8222
Wells Fargo Equity Income Fund C	Growth/Inc	-9.8					0.75	1.6	800 222-8222
Wells Fargo Equity Income I	Growth/Inc	-9	10.29	16.9	2	2	0.75	0.84	800 222-8222
Wells Fargo Equity Index A	Growth/Inc	6.4	18.67	22.65	2	3	0.5	0.7	800 222-8222
Wells Fargo Equity Value A	Growth	-9.6	3.47	12.64	4	3	0.75	1.17	800 222-8222
Wells Fargo Equity Value B	Growth	-10	2.83	7.79	5	3	0.75	1.83	800 222-8222
Wells Fargo Equity Value I	Growth	-9.6	3.56		5	3	0.75	1.06	800 222-8222
Wells Fargo Growth A	Growth	9.2	18.06	20.07	3	3	0.75	1.12	800 222-8222
Wells Fargo Growth B	Growth/Inc	8.4	17.24	19.32	3	3	0.75	1.79	800 222-8222

388

Stock Fund Name	Objective	Annualized Return for			Rank		Max Load	Expense Ratio	Toll-Free Telephone
		1 Year	3 Years	5 Years	Overall	Risk			
Wells Fargo Growth Balanced Fund C	Balanced	8.6					0.25	1.67	800 222-8222
Wells Fargo Growth Balanced I	Balanced	9.6	15.69	16.8	2	1	0.83	0.93	800 222-8222
Wells Fargo Growth Equity A	Growth	21.5	17.44	19.11	2	3	1.07	1.46	800 222-8222
Wells Fargo Growth Equity B	Growth	20.6	16.57		2	3	1.07	2	800 222-8222
Wells Fargo Growth Equity I	Growth	21.8	17.51	18.65	2	3	1.07	1.25	800 222-8222
Wells Fargo Index Allocation A	AssetAlloc	6.7	18.48	20.2	2	3	0.8	1.27	800 222-8222
Wells Fargo Index I	Growth/Inc	7.1	19.3	23.06	2	3	0.14	0.25	800 222-8222
Wells Fargo International A	Foreign	27	11.25	12.84	3	2	0.38	1.5	800 222-8222
Wells Fargo International B	Foreign	26.3	10.5	12.02	3	2	0.38	2.25	800 222-8222
Wells Fargo International Equity A	Foreign	35.1					1	1.75	800 222-8222
Wells Fargo International Equity B	Foreign	34.2					1	2.39	800 222-8222
Wells Fargo International I	Foreign	27.1	11.29	12.85	3	2	0.38	1.5	800 222-8222
Wells Fargo LifePath 2010 A	AssetAlloc	6.5	10.59	12.3	3	1	0.55	1.25	800 222-8222
Wells Fargo LifePath 2010 B	AssetAlloc	6	10.03		3	1	0.55	1.76	800 222-8222
Wells Fargo LifePath 2020 A	AssetAlloc	7.6	13.52	15.46	3	1	0.55	1.25	800 222-8222
Wells Fargo LifePath 2020 B	AssetAlloc	7.1	12.97		3	1	0.55	1.76	800 222-8222
Wells Fargo LifePath 2030 A	AssetAlloc	9	15.63	17.89	2	2	0.55	1.22	800 222-8222
Wells Fargo LifePath 2030 B	AssetAlloc	8.6	15.05		3	2	0.55	1.75	800 222-8222
Wells Fargo LifePath 2040 A	AssetAlloc	10	17.47	20.34	3	3	0.55	1.3	800 222-8222
Wells Fargo LifePath 2040 B	AssetAlloc	9.5	16.88		2	3	0.55	1.75	800 222-8222
Wells Fargo LifePath Opportunity A	AssetAlloc	5.4	7.23	7.84	3	1	0.55	1.25	800 222-8222
Wells Fargo Moderate Balanced I	Balanced	8	12.16	12.15	3	1	0.53	0.88	800 222-8222
Wells Fargo Sm Cap Opportunities A	Small Co	27.3	10.8		3	3	0.59	1.25	800 222-8222
Wells Fargo Sm Cap Opportunities B	Small Co	26.4	9.96		3	3	0.59	2.06	800 222-8222
Wells Fargo Sm Cap Opportunities I	Small Co	27.4	10.84		3	3	0.59	1.25	800 222-8222
Wells Fargo Small Cap Growth A	Small Co	84.8	31.47	31.57	3	5	0.59	1.36	800 222-8222
Wells Fargo Small Cap Growth B	Small Co	83.7	30.57	31.04	3	5	0.59	2.08	800 222-8222
Wells Fargo Small Cap Growth I	Small Co	85.7	32.15	31.99	3	5	0.59	0.76	800 222-8222
Wells Fargo Small Cap Value Fund	Small Co	16.8					0.5	1.3	800 222-8222
Wells Fargo Small Co Growth I	Small Co	26.9	11.22	16.29	4	4	0.9	1.25	800 222-8222
Westcore Blue Chip	Growth/Inc	-4.8	9.78	16.96	3	3	0.65	1.14	800 392-2673
Westcore Growth and Income	Growth/Inc	39.5	21.82	23.38	2	3	0.65	1.14	800 392-2673
Westcore MIDCO Growth	Agg Growth	42.7	23.02	21.48	3	4	0.65	1.14	800 392-2673
Westcore Mid-Cap Opportunity Fund	Growth	27.3					1.25	1.25	800 392-2673
Westcore Small-Cap Opportunity	Small Co	-0.6	0.88	10.96	4	3	1	1.3	800 392-2673
White Oak Growth Stock	Growth	61.1	41.75	39.72	1	4	0.73	1	888 462-5386
Whitehall Growth Fund	Growth	51.6	34.95	31.56	1	3	0.5	1.06	800 994-2533
Whitehall Growth and Income	Growth/Inc	29.4	20.44	18.42	2	1	0.5	1.1	800 994-2533
Willamette Small Cap Growth fund	Small Co	74.2					1.19		800 713-4276
Willamette Value Fund	Growth/Inc	-17.6					1	3.5	800 713-4276
William Blair Emrg Mkts Growth N	Foreign	17.9					1.39	2.25	800 742-7272
William Blair Funds-Intl Grwth	Foreign	58.5	27.95	23.73	2	4	1.1	1.35	800 742-7272
William Blair Mutual-Val Discvry	Small Co	13.1	12.76		4	3	1.14	1.45	800 742-7272
Wilmington Large Cap Core	Growth	8.6	19.68	20.76	2	2	0.69	0.8	800 254-3948
Wilmington Large Cap Growth Equity	Growth	33.3	25.32	25.83	2	4	0.55	0.75	800 336-9970
Wilshire Targ-Large Co Growth Inst	Growth	22.2	27.68		1	3	0.25	0.61	888 200-6796
Wilshire Targ-Large Co Growth Inv	Growth	21.8	27.38	29.16	1	3	0.25	0.84	888 200-6796
Wilshire Targ-Large Co Val Inst	Growth	-16	4.76		4	3	0.25	0.73	888 200-6796
Wilshire Targ-Large Co Val Inv	Growth	-16.2	4.55	12.52	4	3	0.25	0.73	888 200-6796
Wilshire Targ-Small Co Growth Inst	Small Co	17	6.66		4	4	0.25	1.29	888 200-6796
Wilshire Targ-Small Co Growth Inv	Small Co	16.6	6.45	10.26	4	4	0.25	1.45	888 200-6796
Wilshire Targ-Small Co Val Inst	Small Co	-16	-3.02		5	2	0.25	0.79	888 200-6796
Wilshire Targ-Small Co Val Inv	Small Co	-16.2	-3.19	5.53	5	2	0.25	1.02	888 200-6796
Wilshire Target 5000 Index Instl	Growth	8.9					0		888 200-6796
Wilshire Target 5000 Index Inv	Growth	8.8					0	0.53	888 200-6796
Wireless Fund	Technology						1.94		800-590-0898
Wright EquiFund-Hong Kong	Pacific	30.2	-5.61	3.32	4	5	0.75	2.41	800 232-0013
Wright EquiFund-Japan	Pacific	37.3	9.41	6.23	4	4	0.75	2.14	800 232-0013

Stock Fund Name	Objective	Annualized Return for			Rank		Max Load	Expense Ratio	Toll-Free Telephone
		1 Year	3 Years	5 Years	Overall	Risk			
Wright EquiFund-Mexico	Foreign	-4.6	-0.1	8.34	5	5	0.75	2.14	800 232-0013
Wright EquiFund-Netherlands	European	-2.8	4.18	12.13	4	3	0.75	1.72	800 232-0013
Wright Intl Blue Chip Equity	Foreign	27.1	8.96	11.2	3	3	0.77	1.48	800 232-0013
Wright Major Blue Chip Equity	Growth/Inc	5.2	17.16	20.76	3	3	0.45	1.05	800 232-0013
Wright Selected Blue Chip Eq	Growth/Inc	6	8.86	14.91	3	3	1	1.15	800 232-0013
Yacktman Focused Fund	Growth	-24.2	-8.29		5	3	1	0.92	800 457-6033
Yacktman Fund	Growth	-18.1	-5.58	6.2	5	3	0.65	0.7	800 457-6033

BOND FUNDS

Bond Fund Name	Objective	Annualized Return for			Rank		Max Load	Expense Ratio	Toll-Free Telephone
		1 Year	3 Years	5 Years	Overall	Risk			
1st Source Monogram Income	Corp-Inv	3.30	4.48		3.00	2.00	1.10	.92	800 554-3862
59 Wall Street Inflation Index Sec	Government	8.30	5.71	5.07	3.00	2.00	.25	.65	800 625-5759
59 Wall Street T/F Sh-Int Fix/Inc	Muni Natl	2.50	3.37	3.58	2.00	1.00	.25	.81	800 625-5759
AAL Bond Fund A	Corp-Inv	3.20	4.57	4.90	3.00	3.00	.46	.93	800 553-6319
AAL Bond Fund B	Corp-Inv	2.10	3.60		4.00	3.00	.46	1.89	800 553-6319
AAL Bond Fund I	Corp-Inv	3.70					.46	.54	800 553-6319
AAL High Yield Bond A	Corp-HY	-5.10	-.37		5.00	5.00	.56	1.00	800 553-6319
AAL High Yield Bond B	Corp-HY	-5.70	-1.13		5.00	5.00	.56	1.70	800 553-6319
AAL High Yield Bond Fund I	Corp-HY	-4.60					.56	.76	800 553-6319
AAL Municipal Bond Fund A	Muni Natl	.40	3.73	5.27	4.00	4.00	.45	.81	800 553-6319
AAL Municipal Bond Fund B	Muni Natl	-.30	2.91		4.00	4.00	.45	1.63	800 553-6319
AAL Municipal Bond Fund I	Muni Natl	.90					.45	.51	800 553-6319
AARP Bond Fund for Income	Corp-Inv	2.80	4.41		3.00	3.00	0.00	.98	800 253-2277
AARP GNMA & US Treasury Fund	Govt-Mtg	4.70	5.19	5.63	2.00	2.00	.40	.61	800 253-2277
AARP High Quality Bond Sh-Term Bd	Corp-Inv	3.90	5.09	5.41	2.00	2.00	.47	.90	800 253-2277
AARP Insured Tax Free General	Muni Natl	3.60	4.20	5.29	3.00	3.00	.47	.64	800 253-2277
ABN AMRO Fixed Income Inv	Corp-Inv	2.50	4.27	5.03	4.00	3.00	.50	1.18	800 443-4725
ABN AMRO Fixed Income Tr	Corp-Inv	3.10	4.69	5.40	3.00	3.00	.50	.68	800 443-4725
ABN AMRO Intl Fixed Inv	Intl Bond	-2.30	-.79	-.13	4.00	5.00	.80	1.97	800 443-4725
ABN AMRO Intl Fixed Tr	Intl Bond	-1.80	-.41	.21	5.00	5.00	.80	1.47	800 443-4725
ABN AMRO Tax-Free Fixed Inv	Muni Natl	2.50	4.07	4.98	2.00	3.00	.59	1.36	800 443-4725
ABN AMRO Tax-Free Fixed Tr	Muni Natl	3.00	4.54	5.37	1.00	3.00	.59	.85	800 443-4725
AFBA Five Star High Yield Fund	Corp-HY	.30	1.36		5.00	5.00	1.08	1.08	800 243-9865
AHA Full Mat Fixed Income	Corp-Inv	5.00	6.06	6.17	2.00	3.00	0.00	.16	800 445-1341
AHA Limited Mat Fixed Income	Corp-Inv	4.90	5.62	5.71	1.00	1.00	0.00	.11	800 445-1341
AIM Global Income Fund A	Intl Bond	-2.30	1.72	5.01	4.00	4.00	.08	1.25	800 347-4246
AIM Global Income Fund B	Intl Bond	-2.80	1.23	4.50	4.00	4.00	0.00	1.75	800 347-4246
AIM Global Income Fund C	Intl Bond	-2.70					.69	1.75	800 347-4246
AIM High Income Muni A	Muni Natl	-7.00					.10	.28	800 347-4246
AIM High Income Muni B	Muni Natl	-7.60					.10	1.04	800 347-4246
AIM High Income Muni C	Muni Natl	-7.50					.10	1.04	800 347-4246
AIM High Yield Fund A	Corp-HY	-6.70	-.88	4.46	4.00	5.00	.50	.85	800 347-4246
AIM High Yield Fund B	Corp-HY	-7.40	-1.63	3.69	4.00	5.00	.50	1.62	800 347-4246
AIM High Yield Fund C	Corp-HY	-7.40					.50	1.62	800 347-4246
AIM High Yield II A	Corp-HY	3.20					.46	1.00	800 347-4246
AIM Income Fund A	Dvsfd Bond	-2.40	2.70	5.78	3.00	4.00	.45	.90	800 347-4246
AIM Income Fund B	Dvsfd Bond	-3.20	1.93	4.96	3.00	4.00	.46	1.65	800 347-4246
AIM Income Fund C	Dvsfd Bond	-3.00					.46	1.65	800 347-4246
AIM Interm Govt Fund A	Government	3.60	4.99	5.29	3.00	2.00	.47	.93	800 347-4246
AIM Interm Govt Fund B	Government	2.80	4.20	4.50	4.00	2.00	.47	1.68	800 347-4246
AIM Interm Govt Fund C	Government	2.80					.47	1.68	800 347-4246
AIM Ltd Maturity Treas Ret A	Government	4.30	4.92	5.14	3.00	1.00	.20	.54	800 347-4246
AIM Municipal Bond Fund A	Muni Natl	1.30	3.41	4.47	3.00	2.00	.46	.81	800 347-4246
AIM Municipal Bond Fund B	Muni Natl	.50	2.67	3.66	3.00	2.00	.46	1.57	800 347-4246
AIM Municipal Bond Fund C	Muni Natl	.50					.46	1.57	800 347-4246
AIM Strategic Income A	Intl Bond	-1.70	-1.36	5.94	4.00	5.00	.72	1.35	800 347-4246
AIM Strategic Income B	Intl Bond	-2.30	-1.98	5.24	4.00	5.00	.72	2.00	800 347-4246
AIM Strategic Income C	Intl Bond	-2.30					.72	2.00	800 347-4246
AIM Tax-Exempt Bond Fd of CT	Muni State	2.10	3.62	4.50	3.00	2.00	.34	.98	800 347-4246
AIM Tax-Free Intermediate	Muni Natl	3.20	4.15	4.65	1.00	2.00	.58	.46	800 347-4246
AMF Adjustable Rate Mortgage	Govt-Mtg	5.20	5.24	5.72	1.00	1.00	.45	.48	800 527-3713
AMF Intermediate Mortgage Secs	Govt-Mtg	4.30	5.34	5.53	2.00	2.00	.34	.48	800 527-3713
AMF Short-USG Securities Fund	Government	4.30	5.09	5.16	2.00	1.00	.25	.50	800 527-3713
AMF USG Mortgage Securities	Govt-Mtg	4.80	5.62	6.02	1.00	2.00	.25	.57	800 527-3713
API Trust Treasuries Trust	Government	4.70					.40	.86	800 544-6060
ASAF Federated High Yield Bond A	Corp-HY	-1.70					.69	1.50	800 752-6342

391

Bond Fund Name	Objective	Annualized Return for			Rank		Max Load	Expense Ratio	Toll-Free Telephone
		1 Year	3 Years	5 Years	Overall	Risk			
ASAF Federated High Yield Bond B	Corp-HY	-2.20					.69	2.00	800 752-6342
ASAF Federated High Yield Bond C	Corp-HY	-2.20					.69	2.00	800 752-6342
ASAF Federated High Yield Bond X	Corp-HY	-2.20					.69	2.00	800 752-6342
ASAF Total Return Bond A	Dvsfd Bond	5.40					.65	1.39	800 752-6342
ASAF Total Return Bond B	Dvsfd Bond	4.90					.65	1.89	800 752-6342
ASAF Total Return Bond C	Dvsfd Bond	4.90					.65	1.89	800 752-6342
ASAF Total Return Bond X	Dvsfd Bond	4.90					.65	1.89	800 752-6342
AXP Bond Fund A	Dvsfd Bond	1.60	4.15	5.83	3.00	3.00	.48	.82	800 328-8300
AXP CA Tax Exempt Fund A	Muni CA	2.30	3.82	5.01	3.00	3.00	.46	.79	800 328-8300
AXP Extra Income A	Corp-HY	-2.50	1.42	6.26	3.00	5.00	.56	.91	800 328-8300
AXP Federal Income A	Government	1.40	4.21	5.21	2.00	2.00	.50	.88	800 328-8300
AXP Global Bond A	Intl Bond	-.30	1.67	3.66	5.00	5.00	.75	1.19	800 328-8300
AXP High Yield Tax Exempt A	Muni Natl	1.30	4.00	5.15	2.00	3.00	.44	.70	800 328-8300
AXP Insured Tax Exempt A	Muni Natl	2.20	3.76	4.90	3.00	3.00	.45	.75	800 328-8300
AXP MA Tax Exempt Fund A	Muni State	0.00	3.23	4.69	3.00	3.00	.46	.81	800 328-8300
AXP MI Tax Exempt Fund A	Muni State	-.20	3.10	4.53	3.00	3.00	.46	.82	800 328-8300
AXP MN Tax Exempt Fund A	Muni State	.60	3.66	5.01	3.00	3.00	.52	.78	800 328-8300
AXP NY Tax Exempt Fund A	Muni NY	.90	3.68	4.73	3.00	3.00	1.00	.81	800 328-8300
AXP OH Tax Exempt Fund A	Muni State	.90	3.64	4.82	3.00	3.00	.46	.88	800 328-8300
AXP Selective Fund A	Corp-Inv	3.10	5.05	5.59	3.00	3.00	.51	.89	800 328-8300
AXP Tax Exempt Bond Fund A	Muni Natl	1.00	3.64	5.21	4.00	3.00	.45	.73	800 328-8300
Accessor Fd-Interm Fixed Income	Corp-Inv	2.60	4.38	4.95	4.00	3.00	.51	.86	800 759-3504
Accessor Fd-Mortgage Securities	Govt-Mtg	4.80	5.59	6.16	1.00	2.00	.58	1.02	800 759-3504
Accessor Fd-Short Interm Fixed	Corp-Inv	3.60	4.65	4.81	3.00	1.00	.51	.81	800 759-3504
Achievement ID Muni Bond Retail B	Muni State	1.60					.17	1.75	800 472-0577
Achievement Idaho Muni Bond Inst	Muni State	2.40	3.85	4.83	3.00	3.00	.17	.75	800 472-0577
Achievement Idaho Muni Bond Ret	Muni State	2.20	3.62	4.60	3.00	3.00	.17	1.00	800 472-0577
Achievement Interm Bond Inst	Corp-Inv	3.50	4.90	4.96	4.00	3.00	.34	.75	800 472-0577
Achievement Interm Bond Ret	Corp-Inv	3.20	4.59	4.70	4.00	2.00	.34	1.00	800 472-0577
Achievement Muni Bond Fund Retail B	Muni Natl	-.40					.29	1.75	800 472-0577
Achievement Municipal Bond Inst	Muni Natl	.50	3.87		2.00	3.00	.29	.75	800 472-0577
Achievement Municipal Bond Ret	Muni Natl	.20	3.64		2.00	3.00	.29	1.00	800 472-0577
Achievement Short Term Bond Inst	Corp-Inv	4.70	5.09	5.16	2.00	1.00	.36	.75	800 472-0577
Achievement Short Term Bond Ret	Corp-Inv	4.40	4.79	4.91	2.00	1.00	.29	1.00	800 472-0577
Activa Intermediate Bond Fund	Dvsfd Bond						.34		800 346-2670
Advantus Bond Fund A	Corp-Inv	2.80	3.97	4.96	4.00	3.00	.69	1.14	800 665-6005
Advantus Bond Fund B	Corp-Inv	2.10	3.28	4.18	5.00	3.00	.69	1.89	800 665-6005
Advantus Bond Fund C	Corp-Inv	2.00	3.18	4.11	5.00	3.00	.69	1.89	800 665-6005
Advantus Mortgage Securities A	Govt-Mtg	5.30	6.21	6.45	1.00	2.00	.57	.94	800 665-6005
Advantus Mortgage Securities B	Govt-Mtg	4.40	5.48	5.72	2.00	2.00	.57	1.69	800 665-6005
Advantus Mortgage Securities C	Govt-Mtg	4.40	5.42	5.62	2.00	2.00	.57	1.69	800 665-6005
Aetna Bond Fund A	Corp-Inv	3.30	4.75	5.08	3.00	3.00	.26	1.00	800 238-6263
Aetna Bond Fund B	Corp-Inv	2.40					.26	1.75	800 238-6263
Aetna Bond Fund C	Corp-Inv	2.50					.26	1.75	800 238-6263
Aetna Bond Fund I	Corp-Inv	3.50	5.04	5.54	3.00	3.00	.26	.75	800 238-6263
Aetna Government Fund A	Government	4.30	5.51	5.16	3.00	2.00	.50	.94	800 238-6263
Aetna Government Fund B	Government	3.60					.50	1.69	800 238-6263
Aetna Government Fund C	Government	3.60					.50	1.69	800 238-6263
Aetna Government Fund I	Government	4.60	5.80	5.65	3.00	2.00	.50	.69	800 238-6263
Aetna High Yield A	Corp-HY	3.10					.45	1.19	800 238-6263
Aetna High Yield B	Corp-HY	2.40					.45	1.94	800 238-6263
Aetna High Yield C	Corp-HY	2.30					.45	1.94	800 238-6263
Aetna High Yield I	Corp-HY	3.50					.45	.94	800 238-6263
Aetna Index Plus Bond A	Corp-Inv	4.50					.10	.84	800 238-6263
Aetna Index Plus Bond B	Corp-Inv	3.60					.10	1.60	800 238-6263
Aetna Index Plus Bond C	Corp-Inv	3.70					.10	1.35	800 238-6263
Aetna Index Plus Bond I	Corp-Inv	4.60					.10	.59	800 238-6263
Alabama Tax Free Bond	Muni State	3.30	3.74	4.35	3.00	2.00	.23	.65	800 543-8721

Bond Fund Name	Objective	Annualized Return for			Rank		Max Load	Expense Ratio	Toll-Free Telephone
		1 Year	3 Years	5 Years	Overall	Risk			
Alleghany/Chicago Trust Bond Fd	Corp-Inv	3.90	5.57	5.99	3.00	2.00	.55	.80	800 992-8151
Alleghany/Chicago Trust Muni Bd Fd	Muni Natl	3.00	4.50	4.58	2.00	2.00	.59	.10	800 992-8151
Alliance Bond-Corporate Bond A	Corp-Inv	4.10	2.75	7.24	3.00	5.00	.55	1.11	800 221-5672
Alliance Bond-Corporate Bond B	Corp-Inv	3.40	2.04	6.51	3.00	5.00	.55	1.82	800 221-5672
Alliance Bond-Corporate Bond C	Corp-Inv	3.30	2.01	6.47	3.00	5.00	.55	1.81	800 221-5672
Alliance Bond-US Govt A	Government	4.40	5.33	4.78	4.00	3.00	.56	1.08	800 221-5672
Alliance Bond-US Govt B	Government	3.60	4.62	4.06	4.00	3.00	.56	1.87	800 221-5672
Alliance Bond-US Govt C	Government	3.60	4.62	4.10	4.00	3.00	.56	1.87	800 221-5672
Alliance Global Dollar Govt A	Intl Bond	29.80	2.29	14.14	3.00	5.00	.75	1.59	800 221-5672
Alliance Global Dollar Govt B	Intl Bond	28.60	1.52	13.27	3.00	5.00	.75	2.27	800 221-5672
Alliance Global Dollar Govt C	Intl Bond	28.60	1.57	13.32	3.00	5.00	.75	2.27	800 221-5672
Alliance Global Strategic Inc A	Intl Bond	7.40	6.26		2.00	5.00	.75	1.62	800 221-5672
Alliance Global Strategic Inc Adv	Intl Bond	7.70					.75	1.33	800 221-5672
Alliance Global Strategic Inc B	Intl Bond	6.70	5.54		3.00	5.00	.75	2.33	800 221-5672
Alliance Global Strategic Inc C	Intl Bond	6.70	5.53		3.00	5.00	.75	2.33	800 221-5672
Alliance High Yield Fund A	Corp-HY	-5.30	2.22		5.00	5.00	.75	1.37	800 221-5672
Alliance High Yield Fund Adv	Corp-HY	-4.60	2.30		5.00	5.00	.75	1.10	800 221-5672
Alliance High Yield Fund B	Corp-HY	-5.90	1.55		5.00	5.00	.75	2.10	800 221-5672
Alliance High Yield Fund C	Corp-HY	-5.90	1.55		5.00	5.00	.75	2.08	800 221-5672
Alliance Limited Mat Govt A	Govt-Mtg	2.70	4.05	4.46	4.00	2.00	.65	2.75	800 221-5672
Alliance Limited Mat Govt B	Govt-Mtg	1.90	3.33	3.70	4.00	2.00	.65	3.47	800 221-5672
Alliance Limited Mat Govt C	Govt-Mtg	1.90	3.34	3.71	4.00	2.00	.65	3.47	800 221-5672
Alliance Mortgage Securities A	Govt-Mtg	5.00	4.99	5.63	2.00	2.00	.53	1.70	800 221-5672
Alliance Mortgage Securities B	Govt-Mtg	4.20	4.20	4.81	3.00	2.00	.53	2.43	800 221-5672
Alliance Mortgage Securities C	Govt-Mtg	4.30	4.24	4.84	3.00	2.00	.53	2.41	800 221-5672
Alliance Multi-Market Strategy A	Intl Bond	2.00	4.39	7.93	2.00	1.00	.59	1.34	800 221-5672
Alliance Multi-Market Strategy B	Intl Bond	1.30	2.33	6.30	3.00	2.00	.59	2.04	800 221-5672
Alliance Multi-Market Strategy C	Intl Bond	1.20	3.54	7.12	3.00	2.00	.59	2.04	800 221-5672
Alliance Muni Income II-AZ A	Muni State	2.10	4.92	6.25	1.00	3.00	.62	.78	800 221-5672
Alliance Muni Income II-AZ B	Muni State	1.40	4.20	5.54	1.00	3.00	.62	1.47	800 221-5672
Alliance Muni Income II-AZ C	Muni State	1.40	4.20	5.52	1.00	3.00	.62	1.47	800 221-5672
Alliance Muni Income II-FL A	Muni State	.60	4.16	6.01	3.00	3.00	.62	.72	800 221-5672
Alliance Muni Income II-FL B	Muni State	-.10	3.43	5.25	3.00	3.00	.62	1.42	800 221-5672
Alliance Muni Income II-FL C	Muni State	-.10	3.41	5.27	3.00	3.00	.62	1.42	800 221-5672
Alliance Muni Income II-MA A	Muni State	.80	4.69	6.84	2.00	4.00	.62	.71	800 221-5672
Alliance Muni Income II-MA B	Muni State	.10	3.92	6.08	2.00	4.00	.63	1.41	800 221-5672
Alliance Muni Income II-MA C	Muni State	.10	3.95	6.08	2.00	4.00	.62	1.75	800 221-5672
Alliance Muni Income II-MI A	Muni State	2.90	5.51	6.80	3.00	4.00	.62	.95	800 221-5672
Alliance Muni Income II-MI B	Muni State	2.30	4.56	5.93	3.00	4.00	.63	1.65	800 221-5672
Alliance Muni Income II-MI C	Muni State	2.30	4.56	5.93	3.00	4.00	.62	1.65	800 221-5672
Alliance Muni Income II-MN A	Muni State	2.60	4.70	5.91	2.00	3.00	.62	.75	800 221-5672
Alliance Muni Income II-MN B	Muni State	1.90	3.95	5.14	3.00	3.00	.62	1.45	800 221-5672
Alliance Muni Income II-MN C	Muni State	1.80	3.96	5.12	3.00	3.00	.62	1.44	800 221-5672
Alliance Muni Income II-NJ A	Muni State	.30	4.41	5.88	3.00	4.00	.62	.81	800 221-5672
Alliance Muni Income II-NJ B	Muni State	-.50	3.72	5.12	3.00	4.00	.62	1.53	800 221-5672
Alliance Muni Income II-NJ C	Muni State	-.50	3.71	5.12	3.00	4.00	.62	1.52	800 221-5672
Alliance Muni Income II-OH A	Muni State	-.20	4.08	5.82	3.00	3.00	.62	.75	800 221-5672
Alliance Muni Income II-OH B	Muni State	-.80	3.35	5.06	2.00	3.00	.62	1.45	800 221-5672
Alliance Muni Income II-OH C	Muni State	-.80	3.39	5.08	3.00	3.00	.62	1.44	800 221-5672
Alliance Muni Income II-PA A	Muni State	.10	4.10	6.02	3.00	3.00	.62	.94	800 221-5672
Alliance Muni Income II-PA B	Muni State	-.50	3.41	5.29	2.00	3.00	.62	1.65	800 221-5672
Alliance Muni Income II-PA C	Muni State	-.60	3.37	5.26	2.00	3.00	.62	1.64	800 221-5672
Alliance Muni Income II-VA A	Muni State	1.80	5.46	6.99	1.00	3.00	.62	.67	800 221-5672
Alliance Muni Income II-VA B	Muni State	1.10	4.75	6.26	3.00	3.00	.62	1.37	800 221-5672
Alliance Muni Income II-VA C	Muni State	1.20	4.75	6.26	3.00	3.00	.62	1.37	800 221-5672
Alliance Muni Income-CA A	Muni CA	1.30	4.92	6.48	3.00	3.00	.62	.69	800 221-5672
Alliance Muni Income-CA B	Muni CA	.50	4.18	5.73	3.00	3.00	.62	1.39	800 221-5672
Alliance Muni Income-CA C	Muni CA	.50	4.18	5.73	3.00	3.00	.62	1.39	800 221-5672

Bond Fund Name	Objective	Annualized Return for			Rank		Max Load	Expense Ratio	Toll-Free Telephone
		1 Year	3 Years	5 Years	Overall	Risk			
Alliance Muni Income-Insd CA A	Muni CA	1.80	4.16	5.71	3.00	4.00	.55	.69	800 221-5672
Alliance Muni Income-Insd CA B	Muni CA	1.10	3.40	4.95	4.00	4.00	.55	1.73	800 221-5672
Alliance Muni Income-Insd CA C	Muni CA	1.10	3.39	4.94	4.00	4.00	.55	1.72	800 221-5672
Alliance Muni Income-Insd Natl A	Muni Natl	-.60	3.23	5.24	4.00	4.00	.60	.98	800 221-5672
Alliance Muni Income-Insd Natl B	Muni Natl	-1.30	2.52	4.54	5.00	4.00	.60	1.68	800 221-5672
Alliance Muni Income-Insd Natl C	Muni Natl	-1.30	2.52	4.51	5.00	4.00	.60	1.69	800 221-5672
Alliance Muni Income-NY A	Muni NY	1.30	4.27	5.86	3.00	3.00	.62	.60	800 221-5672
Alliance Muni Income-NY B	Muni NY	.50	3.52	5.12	3.00	3.00	.62	1.32	800 221-5672
Alliance Muni Income-NY C	Muni NY	.50	3.52	5.12	3.00	3.00	.62	1.31	800 221-5672
Alliance Muni Income-National A	Muni Natl	-1.50	3.09	5.25	3.00	3.00	.62	.64	800 221-5672
Alliance Muni Income-National B	Muni Natl	-2.20	2.40	4.54	4.00	3.00	.62	1.35	800 221-5672
Alliance Muni Income-National C	Muni Natl	-2.20	2.38	4.54	4.00	3.00	.62	1.34	800 221-5672
Alliance North American Govt A	Intl Bond	12.40	9.34	15.49	2.00	5.00	.72	2.06	800 221-5672
Alliance North American Govt B	Intl Bond	11.60	8.60	14.59	2.00	5.00	.72	2.75	800 221-5672
Alliance North American Govt C	Intl Bond	11.60	8.60	14.59	2.00	5.00	.72	2.75	800 221-5672
Alliance Short-Term US Govt A	Government	4.00	3.95	4.34	2.00	1.00	.55	1.39	800 221-5672
Alliance Short-Term US Govt B	Government	3.20	3.27	3.62	2.00	1.00	.55	2.10	800 221-5672
Alliance Short-Term US Govt C	Government	3.10	3.20	3.58	2.00	1.00	.55	2.10	800 221-5672
AmSouth Government Income Trust	Government	4.50	5.43	5.79	1.00	2.00	.65	.59	800 451-8382
AmSouth Limited Term Bond Fd B	Corp-Inv	8.40					.65	1.83	800 852-0045
AmSouth-Bond Fund A	Corp-Inv	4.00	5.83	5.68	3.00	3.00	.65	.81	800 451-8382
AmSouth-Bond Fund Trust	Corp-Inv	4.30	5.97	5.76	3.00	3.00	.65	.70	800 451-8382
AmSouth-FL T/F Bond Fd A	Muni State	3.30	3.74	4.19	3.00	3.00	.65	.58	800 451-8382
AmSouth-FL T/F Bond Fd Trust	Muni State	3.40	3.87	4.27	3.00	3.00	.65	.48	800 451-8382
AmSouth-Govt Income Fd A	Government	4.30	5.63	5.92	1.00	2.00	.65	.69	800 451-8382
AmSouth-Limited Term Bd A	Corp-Inv	8.90	6.37	6.02	4.00	4.00	.65	1.22	800 451-8382
AmSouth-Limited Term Trust	Corp-Inv	9.10					.65	.97	800 852-0045
AmSouth-Ltd Term TN T/F A	Muni State	2.10	2.84		3.00	2.00	.65	1.06	800 852-0045
AmSouth-Ltd Term TN T/F B	Muni State	1.20					.65	1.90	800 852-0045
AmSouth-Ltd US Gov A	Government	3.70	4.76		1.00	1.00	.65	.93	800 852-0045
AmSouth-Ltd US Gov B	Government	2.80					.65	1.79	800 852-0045
AmSouth-Ltd US Gov Tr	Government	3.60	4.70		3.00	1.00	.65	.93	800 852-0045
AmSouth-Muni Bond Trust	Muni Natl	3.10	3.63	4.08	3.00	2.00	.40	.60	800 451-8382
AmSouth-TN T/F A	Muni State	2.10	3.17	3.64	3.00	3.00	.65	1.25	800 852-0045
AmSouth-TN T/F B	Muni State	1.40					.65	1.84	800 852-0045
AmSouth-TN T/F Tr	Muni State	2.20					.65	1.00	800 852-0045
Amer Independence Intmed Bond Instl	Corp-Inv	3.40	4.73		3.00	2.00	.40	.77	888 266-8787
Amer Independence KS T-Ex Bd Instl	Muni State	1.70	3.53	4.39	3.00	3.00	.29	.46	888 266-8787
Amer Independence ST Bond Instl	Corp-Inv	4.50	4.97		1.00	1.00	.40	.65	888 266-8787
American AAdvant Interm Bd Inst	Corp-Inv	3.30					.25	.56	800 967-9009
American AAdvant Short Tm Inst	Corp-Inv	4.60	4.91	5.08	2.00	1.00	.25	.63	800 967-9009
American AAdvant Short Tm Mileage	Corp-Inv	4.40	4.73	4.94	2.00	1.00	.25	.84	800 967-9009
American AAdvant Short Tm PlanAhd	Corp-Inv	4.30	4.64	4.93	2.00	1.00	.25	.84	800 967-9009
American AAdvantage Intmed Bd Mlge	Corp-Inv	2.40					.25	.86	800 967-9009
American AAdvantage Intmed Bd Pl Ah	Corp-Inv	2.40					.25	.84	800 967-9009
American Century AZ Int Muni Inv	Muni State	3.90	4.39	4.89	2.00	2.00	.50	.51	800 345-2021
American Century Bond Adv	Corp-Inv	2.30					.69	1.05	800 345-2021
American Century Bond Inv	Corp-Inv	2.60	4.12	4.86	4.00	3.00	.69	.80	800 345-2021
American Century CA H/Y Muni Inv	Muni CA	2.00	4.78	6.47	3.00	3.00	.90	.54	800 345-2021
American Century CA Ins T/F Inv	Muni CA	3.00	4.42	5.75	3.00	4.00	.51	.51	800 345-2021
American Century CA Int-Term T/F	Muni CA	4.40	4.38	5.18	2.00`	2.00	.51	.51	800 345-2021
American Century CA Lg Term T/F	Muni CA	2.60	3.81	5.57	3.00	4.00	.51	.51	800 345-2021
American Century CA Ltd Term T/F	Muni CA	4.00	4.03	4.29	2.00	1.00	.51	.51	800 345-2021
American Century FL Interm Muni	Muni State	4.10	4.72	5.22	1.00	2.00	.51	.51	800 345-2021
American Century GNMA Adv	Govt-Mtg	4.70					.58	.83	800 345-2021
American Century GNMA Inv	Govt-Mtg	4.90	5.37	6.09	1.00	2.00	.58	.58	800 345-2021
American Century High-Yield Inv	Corp-HY	-.40					.65	.90	800 345-2021
American Century Ifl-Adj Treas Inv	Government	6.40	4.45		3.00	2.00	.51	.48	800 345-2021

Bond Fund Name	Objective	Annualized Return for			Rank		Max Load	Expense Ratio	Toll-Free Telephone
		1 Year	3 Years	5 Years	Overall	Risk			
American Century Inter T/F Inv	Muni Natl	4.10	4.39	5.07	2.00	2.00	.52	.51	800 345-2021
American Century Inter Term Bd Adv	Corp-Inv	3.10					.75	1.00	800 345-2021
American Century Inter Term Bd Inv	Corp-Inv	3.30	4.81	5.28	3.00	3.00	.75	.75	800 345-2021
American Century Inter Trm Tre Adv	Government	4.40					.51	.76	800 345-2021
American Century Inter Trm Tre Inv	Government	4.70	5.53	5.60	3.00	3.00	.51	.51	800 345-2021
American Century Intl Bond Adv	Intl Bond	-8.80					.83	1.11	800 345-2021
American Century Intl Bond Inv	Intl Bond	-2.60	1.05	2.60	5.00	5.00	.83	.85	800 345-2021
American Century Lg Term T/F Inv	Muni Natl	2.20	3.99	5.34	3.00	4.00	.52	.51	800 345-2021
American Century LgTerm Treas Adv	Government	6.30					.51	.76	800 345-2021
American Century LgTerm Treas Inv	Government	6.50	8.05	6.97	3.00	5.00	.51	.51	800 345-2021
American Century Ltd Term Tax-Free	Muni Natl	3.90	3.78	4.12	2.00	1.00	.52	.51	800 345-2021
American Century Ltd Trm Bd Adv	Corp-Inv	3.40					.69	.94	800 345-2021
American Century Ltd Trm Bd Inv	Corp-Inv	3.70	4.80	5.21	2.00	1.00	.69	.69	800 345-2021
American Century Prem Mgd Bd	Corp-Inv	3.70	5.26	5.65	3.00	3.00	.10	.45	800 345-2021
American Century Sh-Term Govt Adv	Government	4.60					.58	.83	800 345-2021
American Century Sh-Term Govt Inv	Government	4.70	4.64	4.90	2.00	1.00	.58	.58	800 345-2021
American Century Sh-Term Treas Adv	Government	4.30					.51	.76	800 345-2021
American Century Sh-Term Treas Inv	Government	4.50	4.93	5.04	2.00	1.00	.51	.51	800 345-2021
American Century Tgt Mat.-2000 Inv	Government	4.80	5.94	5.58	2.00	1.00	.58	.58	800 345-2021
American Century Tgt Mat.-2005 Inv	Government	3.70	6.84	6.20	3.00	5.00	.58	.58	800 345-2021
American Century Tgt Mat.-2010 Inv	Government	4.30	8.18	7.18	4.00	5.00	.58	.58	800 345-2021
American Century Tgt Mat.-2015 Inv	Government	5.80	9.85	8.41	4.00	5.00	.58	.58	800 345-2021
American Century Tgt Mat.-2020 Inv	Government	6.70	11.21	9.22	4.00	5.00	.58	.58	800 345-2021
American Fds-Tax Exempt of CA	Muni CA	3.00	4.54	5.59	1.00	3.00	.38	.34	800 421-9900
American Fds-Tax Exempt of MD	Muni State	1.60	4.02	5.13	1.00	2.00	.41	.40	800 421-9900
American Fds-Tax Exempt of VA	Muni State	2.20	3.93	4.86	1.00	2.00	.40	.39	800 421-9900
American High-Income Muni Bond	Muni Natl	.40	3.77	5.86	2.00	2.00	.10	.78	800 421-9900
American High-Income Trust	Corp-HY	1.80	4.81	8.37	3.00	5.00	.46	.40	800 421-9900
American Performance Bond Fund	Corp-Inv	3.80	5.88	5.79	2.00	3.00	.34	.97	800 762-7085
American Performance Interm Bond	Corp-Inv	4.30	5.45	5.49	2.00	2.00	.34	.96	800 762-7085
American Performance Interm T/F	Muni Natl	3.10	3.93	4.60	2.00	3.00	.34	.75	800 762-7085
Anchor International Bond Trust	Intl Bond	.70	-.84	-3.20	4.00	5.00	.75	1.23	
Aon Government Securities Fund	Government	2.60	5.72		3.00	4.00	.45	.22	800 266-3637
Aquila Churchill T/F Fd of KY A	Muni State	2.10	3.97	4.91	2.00	2.00	.40	.71	800 228-4227
Aquila Churchill T/F Fd of KY C	Muni State	1.20	3.10		3.00	2.00	.40	1.57	800 228-4227
Aquila Churchill T/F Fd of KY Y	Muni State	2.30	4.10		2.00	2.00	.40	.56	800 228-4227
Aquila Hawaiian Tax Free Trust A	Muni State	1.70	3.67	4.73	2.00	3.00	.14	.73	800 228-4227
Aquila Hawaiian Tax Free Trust C	Muni State	.80	2.83		3.00	3.00	.14	1.53	800 228-4227
Aquila Hawaiian Tax Free Trust Y	Muni State	1.80	3.92		1.00	3.00	.14	.54	800 228-4227
Aquila Narragansett Ins T/F Inc A	Muni Natl	2.60	4.05	5.35	1.00	3.00	.50	.39	800 228-4227
Aquila Narragansett Ins T/F Inc C	Muni Natl	1.70	3.08		3.00	3.00	.50	1.35	800 228-4227
Aquila Narragansett Ins T/F Inc Y	Muni Natl	2.70	4.30		1.00	3.00	.50	.33	800 228-4227
Aquila Tax-Free Fd For Utah A	Muni State	.50	3.30	4.94	4.00	4.00	.50	.45	800 228-4227
Aquila Tax-Free Fd For Utah C	Muni State	-.20	2.31		4.00	4.00	.50	1.44	800 228-4227
Aquila Tax-Free Fd For Utah Y	Muni State	.80	3.35		4.00	4.00	.50	.42	800 228-4227
Aquila Tax-Free Fd of Colorado A	Muni State	3.20	3.85	4.65	3.00	2.00	.50	.75	800 228-4227
Aquila Tax-Free Fd of Colorado C	Muni State	2.30	2.84		3.00	2.00	.50	1.69	800 228-4227
Aquila Tax-Free Fd of Colorado Y	Muni State	3.30	3.83		2.00	2.00	.50	.69	800 228-4227
Aquila Tax-Free Tr of Arizona A	Muni State	2.20	4.02	4.97	1.00	2.00	.40	.70	800 228-4227
Aquila Tax-Free Tr of Arizona C	Muni State	1.30	3.10		3.00	2.00	.40	1.56	800 228-4227
Aquila Tax-Free Tr of Arizona Y	Muni State	2.40	4.36		1.00	2.00	.40	.56	800 228-4227
Aquila Tax-Free Tr of Oregon A	Muni State	2.60	3.88	4.74	2.00	2.00	.40	.70	800 228-4227
Aquila Tax-Free Tr of Oregon C	Muni State	1.70	3.00		1.00	2.00	.40	1.56	800 228-4227
Aquila Tax-Free Tr of Oregon Y	Muni State	2.70	3.90		1.00	2.00	.40	.56	800 228-4227
Aquinas Fixed Income Fund	Corp-Inv	3.20	4.63	5.03	3.00	2.00	.59	1.00	800 423-6369
Arbor Golden Oak Interm Income A	Corp-Inv	3.10	4.31	4.47	5.00	3.00	.65	1.05	800 545-6331
Arbor Golden Oak Interm Income I	Corp-Inv	3.50	4.57	4.75	4.00	3.00	.50	.80	800 545-6331
Arbor Golden Oak MI Tax-Free A	Muni State	2.70	3.55		2.00	2.00	.50	1.06	800 545-6331

Bond Fund Name	Objective	Annualized Return for			Rank		Max Load	Expense Ratio	Toll-Free Telephone
		1 Year	3 Years	5 Years	Overall	Risk			
Arbor Golden Oak MI Tax-Free I	Muni State	2.90	3.46		2.00	2.00	.50	.81	800 545-6331
Ariel Premier Bond Inst	Corp-Inv	3.20	5.11		2.00	2.00	.45	.45	800 292-7435
Ark Fds-Income Portfolio A	Corp-Inv	3.00	4.52	5.02	4.00	3.00	.50	.94	888 427-5386
Ark Fds-Income Portfolio B	Corp-Inv	2.30					.51	1.69	888 427-5386
Ark Fds-Income Portfolio Inst	Corp-Inv	3.10	4.66	5.23	4.00	3.00	.50	.78	888 427-5386
Ark Fds-Intermed Fixed Inc Inst	Corp-Inv	3.00	4.68		2.00	2.00	.59	.77	888 427-5386
Ark Fds-MD Tax Free Inst	Muni State	1.60	3.54		3.00	3.00	.50	.76	888 427-5386
Ark Fds-MD Tax Free Retail A	Muni State	1.30	3.34		2.00	3.00	.45	.93	888 427-5386
Ark Fds-PA Tax Free Inst	Muni State	.80	2.77		4.00	3.00	.50	.92	888 427-5386
Ark Fds-PA Tax Free Retail A	Muni State	.60	2.61		4.00	3.00	.40	1.10	888 427-5386
Ark Fds-Short Term Treas Inst	Government	4.30	4.93		2.00	1.00	.34	.63	888 427-5386
Ark Fds-Short Term Treas Retail A	Government	4.00	4.71		2.00	1.00	.34	.81	888 427-5386
Ark Fds-US Govt Bond Retail A	Corp-Inv	2.10					.66	1.12	888 427-5386
Ark Short-Term Bond Instl	Corp-Inv	3.20					.34	.96	888 427-5386
Ark US Government Bond Instl	Corp-Inv	1.90					.66	.93	888 427-5386
Armada Bond Fund A	Corp-Inv	5.00	5.19	5.46	4.00	3.00	.69	1.18	800 622-3863
Armada Bond Fund Inst	Corp-Inv	4.50	5.19	5.65	3.00	3.00	.69	.93	800 622-3863
Armada Enhanced Income B	Dvsfd Bond						.45		800 622-3863
Armada Enhanced Income C	Dvsfd Bond						.45		800 622-3863
Armada GNMA B	Govt-Mtg						.55		800 622-3863
Armada GNMA C	Govt-Mtg						.55		800 622-3863
Armada GNMA Sec A	Govt-Mtg	4.70	5.06		1.00	2.00	.55	1.03	800 622-3863
Armada GNMA Sec Inst	Govt-Mtg	4.90	5.43	6.11	1.00	2.00	.55	.78	800 622-3863
Armada Intermediate Bond B	Corp-Inv	2.40					.55	1.57	800 622-3863
Armada Intermediate Bond C	Corp-Inv						.55		800 622-3863
Armada National Tax-Exempt A	Muni Natl	3.40					.55	.46	800 622-3863
Armada National Tax-Exempt B	Muni Natl	2.40					.55	1.16	800 622-3863
Armada National Tax-Exempt C	Muni Natl						.55		800 622-3863
Armada National Tax-Exempt Instl	Muni Natl	3.30					.55	.35	800 622-3863
Armada OH Tax Exempt A	Muni State	3.20	3.92	4.72	3.00	2.00	.55	.38	800 622-3863
Armada OH Tax Exempt C	Muni State						.55		800 622-3863
Armada OH Tax Exempt Inst	Muni State	3.20	4.00	4.76	2.00	2.00	.55	.28	800 622-3863
Armada PA Municipal A	Muni State	3.10	3.71		2.00	2.00	.55	.57	800 622-3863
Armada PA Municipal C	Muni State						.55		800 622-3863
Armada PA Municipal Inst	Muni State	3.10	3.95	4.48	2.00	2.00	.55	.47	800 622-3863
Armada Total Return Advanced B	Corp-Inv						.55		800 622-3863
Armada Total Return Advanced C	Corp-Inv						.55		800 622-3863
Atlas California Municipal Bond A	Muni CA	1.70	3.79	4.83	3.00	3.00	.55	.83	800 933-2852
Atlas California Municipal Bond B	Muni CA	1.30	3.03	4.19	4.00	3.00	.55	1.42	800 933-2852
Atlas National Municipal Bond A	Muni Natl	.50	3.19	4.54	3.00	3.00	.08	.95	800 933-2852
Atlas National Municipal Bond B	Muni Natl	.30	2.84	4.01	5.00	3.00	.08	1.46	800 933-2852
Atlas Strategic Income Fund A	Dvsfd Bond	3.60	4.13		3.00	4.00	.44	1.05	800 933-2852
Atlas Strategic Income Fund B	Dvsfd Bond	3.00	3.45		3.00	4.00	.44	1.80	800 933-2852
Atlas US Govt & Mortgage Sec A	Govt-Mtg	3.20	4.53	5.40	3.00	2.00	.55	1.02	800 933-2852
Atlas US Govt & Mortgage Sec B	Govt-Mtg	3.10	4.25	5.02	3.00	2.00	.55	1.51	800 933-2852
BB&K International Bond Fund	Intl Bond	0.00	2.80	4.64	5.00	4.00	.75	1.32	800 882-8383
BB&T Interm US Govt Bd Inv	Government	3.70	5.51	5.16	3.00	3.00	.50	1.09	800 228-1872
BB&T Interm US Govt Bd Tr	Government	4.00	5.77	5.41	3.00	3.00	.50	.83	800 228-1872
BB&T Intermediate Corp Bond Fund A	Corp-Inv						.59		800 228-1872
BB&T Intermediate Corp Bond Fund B	Corp-Inv						.59		800 228-1872
BB&T Intermediate Corp Bond Trust	Corp-Inv						.59		800 228-1872
BB&T NC Interm Tax Free Inv	Muni State	3.00	3.29	3.86	3.00	2.00	.50	.96	800 228-1872
BB&T NC Interm Tax Free Tr	Muni State	3.10	3.35	3.96	3.00	2.00	.50	.81	800 228-1872
BB&T SC Interm Tax Free A	Muni State	2.80					.50	.95	800 228-1872
BB&T SC Interm Tax Free Tr	Muni State	2.90					.50	.81	800 228-1872
BB&T Sh-Interm USG Inc Inv	Government	3.60	4.74	4.71	3.00	1.00	.50	1.04	800 228-1872
BB&T Sh-Interm USG Inc Tr	Government	3.90	4.97	4.95	3.00	1.00	.50	.79	800 228-1872
BB&T VA Intermediate Tax Free Inv A	Muni State	3.80					.50	1.51	800 228-1872

Bond Fund Name	Objective	Annualized Return for			Rank		Max Load	Expense Ratio	Toll-Free Telephone
		1 Year	3 Years	5 Years	Overall	Risk			
BB&T VA Intermediate Tax Free Tr	Muni State	2.80					.50	.98	800 228-1872
BJB Global Income A	Intl Bond	.90	3.54	3.90	5.00	3.00	.65	1.32	800 435-4659
BNY Hamilton Interm Inv Grade Inst	Corp-Inv	2.40	4.29		3.00	3.00	.69	.80	800-426-9363
BNY Hamilton Interm Inv Grade Inv	Corp-Inv	2.60	4.29		3.00	3.00	.69	1.08	800-426-9363
BNY Hamilton Interm NY T/E Inst	Muni NY	2.60	3.22		2.00	2.00	.69	.84	800-426-9363
BNY Hamilton Interm NY T/E Inv	Muni NY	2.40	3.23	3.87	3.00	2.00	.69	1.09	800-426-9363
BNY Hamilton Interm T/E Inst	Muni Natl	2.70	2.98		3.00	2.00	.69	.80	800-426-9363
BNY Hamilton Interm T/E Inv	Muni Natl	2.40	2.27		3.00	2.00	.69	1.04	800-426-9363
BNY Hamilton Intermediate Gov Inst	Government	3.10	4.54		3.00	2.00	.69	.84	800-426-9363
BNY Hamilton Intermediate Gov Inv	Government	2.70	4.43	4.74	4.00	2.00	.69	1.09	800-426-9363
BT Investment-Interm Tax-Free	Muni Natl	3.10	3.91	4.57	3.00	3.00	.40	.84	800 730-1313
Babson Bond-L Portfolio	Corp-Inv	3.50	5.16	5.43	3.00	3.00	.94	.96	800 422-2766
Babson Bond-S Portfolio	Corp-Inv	3.50	5.15	5.51	3.00	2.00	.94	.67	800 422-2766
Babson Tax Free Inc L Portf	Muni Natl	2.10	3.79	4.84	2.00	3.00	.94	1.03	800 422-2766
Babson Tax Free Inc S Portf	Muni Natl	2.40	2.97	3.66	3.00	1.00	.94	1.01	800 422-2766
Barclays Gbl Inv Bd Index Fund	Corp-Inv	4.00	5.70	5.66	3.00	3.00	.08	.23	888 204-3956
Battery Park High Yield A	Corp-HY	3.10	4.29		3.00	5.00	.65	1.25	888 254-2874
Battery Park High Yield Y	Corp-HY	3.40	4.59		3.00	5.00	.65	1.00	888 254-2874
Bear Stearns Emerg Mkts Debt A	Intl Bond	19.10	5.31	16.39	3.00	5.00	1.14	1.75	800 766-4111
Bear Stearns Emerg Mkts Debt C	Intl Bond	18.40	4.67		3.00	5.00	1.14	2.39	800 766-4111
Bear Stearns H/Y Total Return A	Corp-HY	-4.70					.59	1.00	800 766-4111
Bear Stearns H/Y Total Return B	Corp-HY	-5.30					.59	1.64	800 766-4111
Bear Stearns H/Y Total Return C	Corp-HY	-5.30					.59	1.64	800 766-4111
Bear Stearns Income Portfolio A	Corp-Inv	2.70	3.91	5.51	4.00	3.00	.45	.80	800 766-4111
Bear Stearns Income Portfolio C	Corp-Inv	2.10	3.31	4.12	5.00	3.00	.45	1.44	800 766-4111
Bear Stearns Income Portfolio Y	Corp-Inv	3.00	3.87	4.35	3.00	3.00	.45	.45	800 766-4111
Bernstein CA Muni	Muni CA	3.60	4.12	4.79	2.00	2.00	.50	.64	
Bernstein Diversified Municipal	Muni Natl	3.20	3.98	4.65	2.00	2.00	.50	.61	
Bernstein Govt Short Duration	Government	4.30	4.65	4.82	3.00	1.00	.50	.68	
Bernstein Interm Duration	Government	3.00	4.62	5.25	3.00	2.00	.47	.58	
Bernstein New York Muni	Muni NY	3.40	4.00	4.61	2.00	2.00	.50	.64	
Bernstein Short Duration Plus	Government	4.50	4.83	5.23	2.00	1.00	.50	.64	
Bishop Street HI Muni Bond A	Muni State	3.30	4.40	5.33	1.00	3.00	.34	.40	800 262-9565
Bishop Street HI Muni Retail A	Muni State	3.00					.34	.66	800 262-9565
Bishop Street High Grade Inc Inst	Corp-Inv	4.10	4.86		3.00	3.00	.55	.80	800 262-9565
Bishop Street High Grade Inc Ret A	Corp-Inv	3.30					.55	1.05	800 262-9565
BlackRock Core Bond Blackrock Cl	Corp-Inv	5.00	6.00		2.00	3.00	.50	.40	800 388-8734
BlackRock DE Tax Free Income Instl	Muni State	3.10					.40	.68	800 388-8734
BlackRock DE Tax Free Income Inv A	Muni State	2.60					.40	1.14	800 388-8734
BlackRock DE Tax Free Income Inv B	Muni State	1.80					.40	1.85	800 388-8734
BlackRock DE Tax Free Income Inv C	Muni State	1.80					.40	1.85	800 388-8734
BlackRock DE Tax Free Income Svc	Muni State	2.80					.40	.67	800 388-8734
BlackRock GNMA Fund Instl	Govt-Mtg	5.30					.34	.59	800 388-8734
BlackRock GNMA Fund Inv A	Govt-Mtg	4.80					.34	1.07	800 388-8734
BlackRock GNMA Fund Inv B	Govt-Mtg	4.10					.34	1.82	800 388-8734
BlackRock GNMA Fund Inv C	Govt-Mtg	3.90					.34	1.82	800 388-8734
BlackRock GNMA Fund Svc	Govt-Mtg	5.00					.34	.90	800 388-8734
BlackRock Intmed Term Bond Blkrck	Government	4.60					.50	.45	800 388-8734
BlackRock Intmed Term Bond Inv B	Government	3.10					.50	1.75	800 388-8734
BlackRock KY Tax Free Income Instl	Muni State	2.10					.40	.68	800 388-8734
BlackRock KY Tax Free Income Inv A	Muni State	1.70					.40	1.13	800 388-8734
BlackRock KY Tax Free Income Inv B	Muni State	.90					.40	1.78	800 388-8734
BlackRock KY Tax Free Income Inv C	Muni State	.70					.40	1.57	800 388-8734
BlackRock KY Tax Free Income Svc	Muni State	14.90					.40	1.00	800 388-8734
BlackRock Low Duration Blkrck Cl	Corp-Inv	5.20	5.81		1.00	1.00	.50	.40	800 388-8734
BlackRock Managed Income Inv B	Corp-Inv	3.00					.50	1.86	800 388-8734
BlackRock-Core Bond Inst	Corp-Inv	4.80	5.81	6.13	2.00	3.00	.50	.55	800 388-8734
BlackRock-Core Bond Inv A	Corp-Inv	4.20	5.29		2.00	3.00	.50	1.02	800 388-8734

Bond Fund Name	Objective	Annualized Return for			Rank		Max Load	Expense Ratio	Toll-Free Telephone
		1 Year	3 Years	5 Years	Overall	Risk			
BlackRock-Core Bond Inv B	Corp-Inv	3.40	4.53		3.00	3.00	.50	1.75	800 388-8734
BlackRock-Core Bond Inv C	Corp-Inv	3.40	4.53		3.00	3.00	.50	1.75	800 388-8734
BlackRock-Core Bond Svc	Corp-Inv	4.50	5.46		2.00	3.00	.50	.84	800 388-8734
BlackRock-Govt Inc Inv A	Government	4.40	5.52	5.92	2.00	3.00	.29	1.07	800 388-8734
BlackRock-Govt Inc Inv B	Government	3.70	4.74	5.14	3.00	3.00	.29	1.82	800 388-8734
BlackRock-Govt Inc Inv C	Government	3.70	4.74		3.00	3.00	.29	1.82	800 388-8734
BlackRock-Interm Bd Inst	Government	4.40	5.58	5.84	2.00	2.00	.50	.59	800 388-8734
BlackRock-Interm Bd Inv A	Government	3.80	4.84	5.14	3.00	2.00	.50	1.07	800 388-8734
BlackRock-Interm Bd Svc	Government	4.10	4.90	5.24	3.00	2.00	.50	.90	800 388-8734
BlackRock-Interm Govt Inst	Government	4.60	5.54	5.68	2.00	2.00	.50	.59	800 388-8734
BlackRock-Interm Govt Inv A	Government	4.20	5.09	5.22	3.00	2.00	.50	1.07	800 388-8734
BlackRock-Interm Govt Inv B	Government	3.40	4.27		3.00	2.00	.50	1.82	800 388-8734
BlackRock-Interm Govt Inv C	Government	3.40	4.26		3.00	2.00	.50	1.82	800 388-8734
BlackRock-Interm Govt Svc	Government	4.30	5.23	5.36	3.00	2.00	.50	.90	800 388-8734
BlackRock-Intl Bond Inst	Intl Bond	4.70	7.42		2.00	2.00	.55	1.03	800 388-8734
BlackRock-Intl Bond Inv A	Intl Bond	4.30	6.93		2.00	2.00	.55	1.50	800 388-8734
BlackRock-Intl Bond Inv B	Intl Bond	3.50	6.14		3.00	2.00	.55	2.24	800 388-8734
BlackRock-Intl Bond Inv C	Intl Bond	3.50	6.15		2.00	2.00	.55	2.24	800 388-8734
BlackRock-Intl Bond Svc	Intl Bond	4.30	7.03	8.47	2.00	2.00	.55	1.33	800 388-8734
BlackRock-Low Duration Inst	Corp-Inv	5.10	5.68	5.73	1.00	1.00	.50	.55	800 388-8734
BlackRock-Low Duration Inv A	Corp-Inv	4.70	5.19		1.00	1.00	.50	1.01	800 388-8734
BlackRock-Low Duration Inv B	Corp-Inv	3.50	4.28		2.00	1.00	.50	1.67	800 388-8734
BlackRock-Low Duration Inv C	Corp-Inv	3.90	4.41		2.00	1.00	.50	1.69	800 388-8734
BlackRock-Low Duration Svc	Corp-Inv	4.80	5.34		1.00	1.00	.50	.84	800 388-8734
BlackRock-Mgd Income Inst	Corp-Inv	4.30	5.49	5.87	1.00	3.00	.50	.65	800 388-8734
BlackRock-Mgd Income Inv A	Corp-Inv	3.90	5.03	5.31	3.00	3.00	.50	1.11	800 388-8734
BlackRock-Mgd Income Svc	Corp-Inv	4.00	5.17	5.57	2.00	3.00	.50	.94	800 388-8734
BlackRock-NJ Tax Free Inv A	Muni State	2.20	3.86		3.00	3.00	.50	1.10	800 388-8734
BlackRock-NJ Tax Free Inv B	Muni State	1.40	3.05		4.00	3.00	.50	1.75	800 388-8734
BlackRock-NJ Tax Free Svc	Muni State	2.40	4.01	4.88	2.00	3.00	.50	.90	800 388-8734
BlackRock-OH Tax Free Inst	Muni State	2.90	4.36	5.52	1.00	3.00	.50	.59	800 388-8734
BlackRock-OH Tax Free Inv A	Muni State	2.50	3.89	5.05	3.00	3.00	.50	1.10	800 388-8734
BlackRock-OH Tax Free Inv B	Muni State	1.80	3.13	4.28	4.00	3.00	.50	1.75	800 388-8734
BlackRock-OH Tax Free Svc	Muni State	2.60	4.05	5.21	2.00	3.00	.50	.90	800 388-8734
BlackRock-PA Tax Free Inst	Muni State	2.50	4.51	6.46	1.00	3.00	.50	.59	800 388-8734
BlackRock-PA Tax Free Inv A	Muni State	2.10	4.05	5.22	1.00	3.00	.50	1.08	800 388-8734
BlackRock-PA Tax Free Inv B	Muni State	.80	3.33	4.48	4.00	3.00	.50	1.75	800 388-8734
BlackRock-PA Tax Free Svc	Muni State	2.20	4.20	5.36	1.00	3.00	.50	.90	800 388-8734
BlackRock-Tax Free Inc Inst	Muni Natl	1.10	4.18	5.61	3.00	3.00	.50	.59	800 388-8734
BlackRock-Tax Free Inc Inv A	Muni Natl	.60	3.68	6.00	3.00	3.00	.50	1.09	800 388-8734
BlackRock-Tax Free Inc Inv B	Muni Natl	-.10	2.89		5.00	3.00	.50	1.75	800 388-8734
BlackRock-Tax Free Inc Inv C	Muni Natl	-.10	2.89		5.00	3.00	.50	1.75	800 388-8734
BlackRock-Tax Free Inc Svc	Muni Natl	.80	3.85	5.30	3.00	3.00	.50	.90	800 388-8734
Bond Fund of America (The)	Corp-Inv	3.40	4.82	6.43	1.00	3.00	.32	.34	800 421-9900
Boston 1784 Funds-CT Tax-Ex Inc A	Muni State	2.90	4.35	5.23	1.00	3.00	.73	.80	800 252-1784
Boston 1784 Funds-FL Tax-Ex Inc	Muni State	2.50	4.62		1.00	3.00	.59	.80	800 252-1784
Boston 1784 Funds-Income Fund A	Corp-Inv	6.00	5.27	5.49	4.00	4.00	.64	.80	800 252-1784
Boston 1784 Funds-MA T/E Inc A	Muni State	3.00	4.37	5.15	1.00	3.00	.73	.80	800 252-1784
Boston 1784 Funds-RI T/E Inc A	Muni State	7.30	5.62	6.15	3.00	4.00	.73	.80	800 252-1784
Boston 1784 Funds-S/T Inc A	Government	2.80	4.60	5.07	2.00	1.00	.50	.64	800 252-1784
Boston 1784 Funds-T/E Med Term A	Muni Natl	3.00	4.47	5.41	2.00	3.00	.73	.80	800 252-1784
Boston 1784 Funds-USG Med Term A	Government	9.70	6.95	6.24	3.00	4.00	.73	.80	800 252-1784
Bremer Bond Fund	Dvsfd Bond	2.40	4.12		2.00	2.00	.69	.88	800 595-5552
Brinson Fund-Global Bond I	Intl Bond	-.30	1.81	4.85	5.00	4.00	.90	.90	800 448-2430
Brinson Fund-U.S. Bond Fund I	Corp-Inv	3.70	5.71		2.00	3.00	.50	.59	800 448-2430
Brinson Global Bond	Intl Bond	-.80	1.32	4.35	5.00	5.00	.90	1.38	800 448-2430
Brinson Global Bond Fund N	Intl Bond	-.60	1.52		5.00	4.00	.90	1.14	800 448-2430
Brinson High Yield Fund I	Corp-HY	-2.60					.59	.69	800 448-2430

398

Bond Fund Name	Objective	Annualized Return for			Rank		Max Load	Expense Ratio	Toll-Free Telephone
		1 Year	3 Years	5 Years	Overall	Risk			
Brinson High Yield Fund N	Corp-HY	-2.70					.59	.94	800 448-2430
Brinson U.S. Bond Fund	Corp-Inv	3.40	5.07		3.00	3.00	.50	1.07	800 448-2430
Brinson US Bond Fund N	Corp-Inv	2.50	5.12		3.00	3.00	.50	.84	800 448-2430
Brundage Story&Rose Sh-Interm	Corp-Inv	2.90	4.90	5.32	3.00	2.00	.08	1.14	800 320-2212
Buffalo High Yield Fund	Corp-HY	-.50	1.53	7.00	3.00	5.00	1.00	.05	800 492-8332
CG Cap Mkt Fds-Interm Fixed Inc	Corp-Inv	3.90	4.81	5.21	3.00	2.00	.59	.73	800 544-7835
CG Cap Mkt Fds-Intl Fixed Invt	Intl Bond	-.20	2.40	3.83	5.00	5.00	.50	.92	800 544-7835
CG Cap Mkt Fds-Long Term Bond	Corp-Inv	4.00	5.74	5.83	4.00	5.00	.46	.80	800 544-7835
CG Cap Mkt Fds-Mortgage Backed	Govt-Mtg	4.60	5.45	5.96	1.00	2.00	.55	.80	800 544-7835
CG Cap Mkt Fds-Municipal Bd Invt	Muni Natl	2.10	3.59	4.84	4.00	4.00	.47	.80	800 544-7835
CGM American Tax Free Fund	Muni Natl	1.10	3.56	5.02	3.00	4.00	.59	1.72	800 345-4048
CGM Fixed Income	Corp-HY	4.80	3.41	7.15	4.00	5.00	.65	.84	800 345-4048
CNI Charter CA Tax Exempt Bond I	Muni CA						.27		888 889-0799
CNI Charter Corporate Bond I	Corp-Inv						.40		888 889-0799
CNI Charter High Yield Bond I	Corp-HY						.75		888 889-0799
CNI High Yield Bond A	Corp-HY						.75		888 889-0799
CUFUND Adjustable Rate Mortgage	Govt-Mtg	5.00	5.20	5.57	1.00	1.00	.32	.39	800 538-9683
CUFUND Short Term Maturity	Government	5.10	5.48	5.62	1.00	1.00	.32	.39	800 538-9683
California Invest Tr-CA Ins T/F	Muni CA	4.10	4.45	5.05	2.00	2.00	.50	.55	800 225-8778
California Invest Tr-CA Tax Free	Muni CA	3.80	4.62	5.71	2.00	4.00	.60	.60	800 225-8778
California Invest Tr-US Govt	Government	4.00	6.12	5.94	4.00	4.00	.65	.65	800 225-8778
Calvert Income Portfolio A	Corp-Inv	4.60	9.44	8.09	1.00	4.00	.69	1.41	800 368-2745
Calvert Natl Interm Muni A	Muni Natl	3.80	3.86	4.78	2.00	3.00	.69	.93	800 368-2745
Calvert Social Inv Bond Port B	Corp-Inv	1.80					.55	2.50	800 368-2745
Calvert Social-Bond A	Corp-Inv	3.10	5.22	5.50	2.00	4.00	.55	1.12	800 368-2745
Calvert Tax Free Reserve-Long A	Muni Natl	2.00	3.53	4.62	4.00	4.00	.60	.88	800 368-2745
Calvert Tax Free Reserve-Ltd A	Muni Natl	2.70	3.63	3.83	2.00	1.00	.60	.70	800 368-2745
Calvert Tax Free Reserve-VT A	Muni State	1.20	3.07	4.44	3.00	3.00	.60	.79	800 368-2745
Canandaigua Bond Fund	Muni Natl	3.40	5.24	5.32	2.00	3.00	.50	.34	
Capital World Bond Fund	Intl Bond	-.20	1.69	3.58	5.00	4.00	.64	.54	800 421-9900
Capstone Govt Income Fund	Government	3.00	3.66	3.87	4.00	2.00	.40	1.71	800 262-6631
Chase Income Fund Prem	Corp-Inv	2.70	5.12	5.41	2.00	3.00	.50	.75	888 524-2730
Chase Income Inv	Corp-Inv	2.50					.50	1.00	888 524-2730
Chase Intermediate Term Bond Inv	Corp-Inv	3.40					.50	1.00	888 524-2730
Chase Intermediate Term Bond Prem	Corp-Inv	3.70	4.90	4.81	3.00	2.00	.50	.75	888 524-2730
Chase Sh-Interm Term USG Sec Inv	Government	3.50					.50	1.00	888 524-2730
Chase Sh-Interm Term USG Sec Prem	Government	3.70	4.84	4.73	3.00	2.00	.50	.75	888 524-2730
Chase US Govt Secs Premier Fund	Government	4.30	6.21	5.73	3.00	4.00	.50	.75	888 524-2730
Chase US Govt Securities Inv	Government	4.00					.50	1.00	888 524-2730
Chase Vista Bond A	Corp-Inv	3.00	5.01		2.00	3.00	.29	1.43	800 348-4782
Chase Vista Bond B	Corp-Inv	2.20	4.21		4.00	3.00	.29	1.93	800 348-4782
Chase Vista Bond I	Corp-Inv	3.40	5.34	5.70	3.00	3.00	.29	1.17	800 348-4782
Chase Vista CA Interm T/F Inc A	Muni CA	4.80	4.82	5.50	1.00	3.00	.29	1.44	800 348-4782
Chase Vista NY Tax Free Income A	Muni NY	1.10	3.66	4.88	3.00	3.00	.29	1.18	800 348-4782
Chase Vista NY Tax Free Income B	Muni NY	.30	2.81	4.05	5.00	3.00	.29	1.68	800 348-4782
Chase Vista Select Bond Fund	Dvsfd Bond	3.00	4.91		2.00	3.00	.29	.02	800 348-4782
Chase Vista Select Intmed Bond	Dvsfd Bond	3.20	4.68		3.00	2.00	.29	.04	800 348-4782
Chase Vista Select Intmed Tax Free	Muni Natl	3.80	4.59		1.00	2.00	.29	.51	800 348-4782
Chase Vista Select NJ Tax Free	Muni State	3.40	4.24		2.00	2.00	.29	.66	800 348-4782
Chase Vista Select NY Tax Free	Muni NY	3.70	4.51		1.00	3.00	.29	.53	800 348-4782
Chase Vista Select Short Term Bond	Corp-Inv	3.80	4.84		1.00	1.00	.25	.08	800 348-4782
Chase Vista Select Tax Free Fund	Muni Natl	2.00	4.23		1.00	3.00	.29	.46	800 348-4782
Chase Vista Short Term Bond Fund A	Corp-Inv	3.80	4.38		2.00	1.00	.25	1.36	800 348-4782
Chase Vista Short Term Bond Fund I	Corp-Inv	4.20	4.76	5.24	2.00	1.00	.25	1.01	800 348-4782
Chase Vista Strategic Income A	Dvsfd Bond	4.60					.50	5.25	800 348-4782
Chase Vista Strategic Income B	Dvsfd Bond	4.60					.50	5.76	800 348-4782
Chase Vista Strategic Income C	Dvsfd Bond	4.40					.50	5.73	800 348-4782
Chase Vista Strategic Income I	Dvsfd Bond	4.60					.50	5.07	800 348-4782

Bond Fund Name	Objective	Annualized Return for			Rank		Max Load	Expense Ratio	Toll-Free Telephone
		1 Year	3 Years	5 Years	Overall	Risk			
Chase Vista Tax Free Income A	Muni Natl	1.70	3.94	5.25	3.00	3.00	.29	1.34	800 348-4782
Chase Vista Tax Free Income B	Muni Natl	.80	3.09	4.36	5.00	3.00	.29	1.84	800 348-4782
Chase Vista US Government Sec A	Government	4.00	5.09		3.00	3.00	.29	1.68	800 348-4782
Chase Vista US Government Sec I	Government	4.10	5.28	5.26	3.00	3.00	.29	.98	800 348-4782
Chase Vista US Treasury Income A	Government	4.70	5.51	5.18	4.00	3.00	.23	1.33	800 348-4782
Chase Vista US Treasury Income B	Government	3.70	4.66	4.37	5.00	3.00	.29	1.83	800 348-4782
CitiFunds Intermediate Income A	Corp-Inv	2.60	4.51	4.70	4.00	3.00	.25	.90	800 721-1899
CitiFunds Intermediate Income B	Corp-Inv	1.10					.25	1.39	800 721-1899
CitiFunds NY Tax Free Income A	Muni NY	2.70	4.35	5.46	2.00	4.00	.75	.80	800 721-1899
CitiFunds NY Tax Free Income B	Muni NY	1.80					.75	1.30	800 721-1899
CitiFunds Sh-Term US Gov Inc	Government	4.50	4.93	4.85	3.00	1.00	.34	.80	800 721-1899
Citizens Income	Corp-Inv	3.30	4.79	5.86	2.00	3.00	.65	1.48	800 223-7010
Clover Fixed Income Fund	Corp-Inv	5.10	5.73	6.07	3.00	3.00	.45	.75	800 224-6312
Colorado Bond Shares Tax-Exempt A	Muni State	5.50	6.27	7.24	1.00	1.00	.50	.73	800 572-0069
Columbia Fixed Income Secs	Corp-Inv	3.80	5.12	5.71	3.00	3.00	.50	.66	800 547-1707
Columbia High Yield Fund	Corp-HY	2.90	5.53	7.90	2.00	4.00	.59	.93	800 547-1707
Columbia Municipal Bond Fund	Muni Natl	2.40	3.93	4.89	2.00	3.00	.50	.58	800 547-1707
Columbia National Municipal Bond	Muni Natl	2.60					.50	.65	800 547-1707
Columbia Short Term Bond Fund	Dvsfd Bond	4.90					.25	.25	800 547-1707
Columbia US Govt Securities	Government	3.70	4.60	4.84	3.00	1.00	.50	.89	800 547-1707
Commerce Bond Inst	Corp-Inv	3.20	5.27	5.49	3.00	3.00	.50	.81	800 995-6365
Commerce MO Tax Free Fd	Muni State	3.10	4.01	4.44	2.00	2.00	.50	.65	800 995-6365
Commerce National Tax Free Fd	Muni Natl	3.30	3.91	4.44	2.00	2.00	.50	.69	800 995-6365
Commerce Short Term Govt Bd Fd	Govt-Mtg	4.40	5.37	5.35	2.00	1.00	.50	.68	800 995-6365
Comstock Partners Strategy A	Intl Bond	-11.70	-13.97	-8.98	5.00	5.00	.59	1.75	800 645-6561
Comstock Partners Strategy C	Intl Bond	-11.80	-14.54		5.00	5.00	.59	2.47	800 645-6561
Comstock Partners Strategy O	Intl Bond	-11.40	-13.72	-8.73	5.00	5.00	.59	1.48	800 645-6561
Conseco Fd Grp-Fixed Inc Fund A	Corp-Inv	4.40	4.89		2.00	2.00	.45	1.25	800 986-3384
Conseco Fd Grp-Fixed Inc Fund B	Corp-Inv	4.00					.45	1.60	800 986-3384
Conseco Fd Grp-Fixed Inc Fund C	Corp-Inv	4.10					.45	1.60	800 986-3384
Conseco Fd Grp-Fixed Inc Fund Y	Corp-Inv	5.10	5.71		1.00	2.00	.45	.59	800 986-3384
Conseco Fd Grp-High Yield Fund A	Corp-HY	.60					.69	1.39	800 986-3384
Conseco Fd Grp-High Yield Fund B	Corp-HY	0.00					.69	1.89	800 986-3384
Conseco Fd Grp-High Yield Fund C	Corp-HY	.10					.69	1.89	800 986-3384
Conseco Fd Grp-High Yield Fund Y	Corp-HY	1.00					.69	.90	800 986-3384
Corner Stone New York Muni	Muni NY	-15.40	-7.09	-5.05	5.00	5.00	.48	4.07	800 421-4120
Corner Stone US Govt Strat Inc	Government	-.30	-1.53	2.63	4.00	4.00	.75	4.09	800 421-4120
Countrywide Interm Govt Inc A	Government	2.90	4.49	4.62	3.00	2.00	.48	.98	800 638-8194
Countrywide T/F Tr-Interm A	Muni Natl	3.20	3.60	4.29	3.00	2.00	.50	.98	800 638-8194
Countrywide T/F Tr-Interm C	Muni Natl	2.30	2.83	3.58	3.00	2.00	.50	1.73	800 638-8194
Countrywide T/F Tr-Ohio Insd A	Muni State	2.10	3.61	4.60	2.00	3.00	.50	.75	800 638-8194
Countrywide T/F Tr-Ohio Insd C	Muni State	1.30	2.85	3.90	3.00	3.00	.50	1.50	800 638-8194
Croft-Leominster Income	Corp-Inv	-2.40	2.50	5.64	4.00	5.00	.79	1.78	800 551-0990
DFA Five-Year Government	Government	4.70	5.29	5.04	2.00	1.00	.20	.28	
DFA Global Fixed Income Fund	Intl Bond	4.20	6.21	8.15	1.00	1.00	.25	.39	
DFA Intermediate Govt Fx Inc	Government	3.40	5.48	5.47	3.00	4.00	.14	.23	
DFA One-Yr Fixed Income	Corp-Inv	5.20	5.43	5.58	1.00	1.00	.05	.20	
DFA Two-Year Global Fixed Inc Port	Intl Bond	3.50	5.04		1.00	1.00	.05	.28	
DLJ Winthrop Fixed Income A	Corp-Inv	3.10	4.74	4.79	3.00	2.00	.63	1.00	800 225-8011
DLJ Winthrop Fixed Income B	Corp-Inv	2.20	4.05		4.00	2.00	.63	1.69	800 225-8011
DLJ Winthrop Municipal Trust A	Muni Natl	2.40	3.62	4.42	3.00	2.00	.63	1.00	800 225-8011
DLJ Winthrop Municipal Trust B	Muni Natl	1.60	3.14		3.00	2.00	.63	1.69	800 225-8011
Davis Government Bond A	Govt-Mtg	1.50	3.38	4.14	5.00	2.00	.50	1.37	800 279-0279
Davis Government Bond B	Govt-Mtg	.80	2.60	3.32	5.00	2.00	.50	2.12	800 279-0279
Davis Government Bond Fund C	Govt-Mtg	.30					.50	2.12	800 279-0279
Davis Government Bond Fund Y	Govt-Mtg	1.40					.50	1.12	800 279-0279
Delaware American Govt Bond A	Govt-Mtg	3.80	4.61	4.97	4.00	3.00	.63	1.22	800 523-4640
Delaware American Govt Bond B	Govt-Mtg	3.00	3.88	4.25	4.00	3.00	.63	1.92	800 523-4640

400

Bond Fund Name	Objective	Annualized Return for			Rank		Max Load	Expense Ratio	Toll-Free Telephone
		1 Year	3 Years	5 Years	Overall	Risk			
Delaware American Govt Bond C	Govt-Mtg	3.00	3.89		4.00	3.00	.63	1.92	800 523-4640
Delaware American Govt Bond I	Govt-Mtg	4.10	4.82	5.20	3.00	3.00	.63	.93	800 523-4640
Delaware Corporate Bond A	Corp-Inv	1.60					.50	.80	800 523-4640
Delaware Corporate Bond B	Corp-Inv	.80					.50	1.55	800 523-4640
Delaware Corporate Bond C	Corp-Inv	.80					.50	1.55	800 523-4640
Delaware Delchester Fund A	Corp-HY	-11.30	-2.38	3.22	4.00	5.00	.60	1.10	800 523-4640
Delaware Delchester Fund B	Corp-HY	-11.50	-2.87	2.61	5.00	5.00	.60	1.85	800 523-4640
Delaware Delchester Fund C	Corp-HY	-11.30	-2.80		5.00	5.00	.60	1.85	800 523-4640
Delaware Delchester Fund I	Corp-HY	-11.10	-2.03	3.54	4.00	5.00	.60	.84	800 523-4640
Delaware Extended Duration Bd A	Dvsfd Bond	-.20					.04	.80	800 523-4640
Delaware Extended Duration Bd B	Dvsfd Bond	-.90					.04	1.55	800 523-4640
Delaware Extended Duration Bd C	Dvsfd Bond	-.90					.04	1.55	800 523-4640
Delaware Global Bond A	Intl Bond	-3.50	.93	5.00	5.00	5.00	.75	1.30	800 523-4640
Delaware Global Bond B	Intl Bond	-4.20	.23	4.26	5.00	5.00	.75	2.00	800 523-4640
Delaware Global Bond C	Intl Bond	-4.20	.23		4.00	5.00	.75	2.00	800 523-4640
Delaware Global Bond I	Intl Bond	-3.30	1.24	5.30	5.00	5.00	.75	1.00	800 523-4640
Delaware High Yld Opport A	Corp-HY	3.00	4.96		3.00	4.00	.65	1.27	800 523-4640
Delaware High Yld Opport B	Corp-HY	2.30					.65	1.96	800 523-4640
Delaware High Yld Opport C	Corp-HY	2.30					.65	1.96	800 523-4640
Delaware Ltd Term Govt A	Govt-Mtg	4.20	4.52	4.63	3.00	1.00	.50	1.00	800 523-4640
Delaware Ltd Term Govt B	Govt-Mtg	2.70	3.43	3.62	4.00	1.00	.50	1.85	800 523-4640
Delaware Ltd Term Govt C	Govt-Mtg	2.70	3.47		4.00	1.00	.50	1.85	800 523-4640
Delaware Ltd Term Govt I	Govt-Mtg	3.80	4.49	4.67	3.00	1.00	.50	.84	800 523-4640
Delaware MN HY Muni Bd A	Muni State	-4.00	3.07		3.00	4.00	.55	.55	800 523-4640
Delaware MN Insured A	Muni State	1.50	3.95	4.93	2.00	3.00	.50	.91	800 523-4640
Delaware MN Insured C	Muni State	.80	3.20	4.16	4.00	3.00	.50	1.65	800 523-4640
Delaware Natl High Yld Muni A	Muni Natl	-2.20	3.46	5.53	3.00	2.00	.55	1.00	800 523-4640
Delaware Natl High Yld Muni B	Muni Natl	-2.80	2.66		3.00	3.00	.55	1.75	800 523-4640
Delaware Natl High Yld Muni C	Muni Natl	-2.90	2.69		3.00	3.00	.55	1.75	800 523-4640
Delaware Pooled Tr-Glbl Fxd Income	Intl Bond	-3.30	-.48	1.00	5.00	5.00	.45	.59	800 523-4640
Delaware Pooled Tr-High Yield Bond	Corp-HY	-.20	3.50		3.00	5.00	.25	.57	800 523-4640
Delaware Strategic Income A	Corp-Inv	-2.10	.79		4.00	4.00	.65	1.00	800 523-4640
Delaware Strategic Income B	Corp-Inv	-2.90	.04		5.00	4.00	.65	1.75	800 523-4640
Delaware Strategic Income C	Corp-Inv	-3.60	-.19		5.00	4.00	.65	1.75	800 523-4640
Delaware Strategic Income I	Corp-Inv	-2.60	.81		4.00	4.00	.65	.75	800 523-4640
Delaware TF Arizona A	Muni State	-1.10	3.37	5.61	3.00	4.00	.55	.54	800 523-4640
Delaware TF Arizona B	Muni State	-1.70	2.64	4.86	4.00	4.00	.55	1.29	800 523-4640
Delaware TF Arizona C	Muni State	-1.80	2.62	4.85	4.00	4.00	.55	1.87	800 523-4640
Delaware TF Arizona Ins A	Muni State	1.70	3.91	5.19	2.00	3.00	.55	.84	800 523-4640
Delaware TF Arizona Ins C	Muni State	.90	3.16	4.37	4.00	3.00	.55	1.60	800 523-4640
Delaware TF CA Insured A	Muni CA	2.10	4.42	5.61	3.00	4.00	.55	.96	800 523-4640
Delaware TF CA Insured B	Muni CA	1.40	3.66	4.98	3.00	4.00	.55	1.71	800 523-4640
Delaware TF California A	Muni CA	-1.90	3.80	5.53	4.00	4.00	.55	.25	800 523-4640
Delaware TF California B	Muni CA	-2.70	3.03		4.00	4.00	.55	1.00	800 523-4640
Delaware TF California C	Muni CA	-2.60	3.06	4.71	4.00	4.00	.55	1.00	800 523-4640
Delaware TF Colorado A	Muni State	-.60	3.66	5.25	4.00	4.00	.55	.84	800 523-4640
Delaware TF Colorado C	Muni State	-1.30	2.93	4.44	4.00	4.00	.55	1.60	800 523-4640
Delaware TF Florida A	Muni State	-.20	3.81	5.45	3.00	3.00	.55	.57	800 523-4640
Delaware TF Florida B	Muni State	-.90	3.02		4.00	3.00	.55	1.33	800 523-4640
Delaware TF Florida C	Muni State	-.90	2.97	4.66	4.00	3.00	.55	1.33	800 523-4640
Delaware TF Florida Ins A	Muni State	1.50	4.30	5.45	2.00	3.00	.50	.81	800 523-4640
Delaware TF Florida Ins B	Muni State	.80	3.56	4.77	3.00	3.00	.50	1.57	800 523-4640
Delaware TF Idaho A	Muni State	-1.00	3.24	4.85	4.00	3.00	.55	1.00	800 523-4640
Delaware TF Idaho B	Muni State	-1.80	2.61	4.39	4.00	3.00	.55	1.75	800 523-4640
Delaware TF Idaho C	Muni State	-1.80	2.48	4.21	4.00	3.00	.55	1.75	800 523-4640
Delaware TF Iowa A	Muni State	1.60	3.96	5.31	2.00	3.00	.55	.91	800 523-4640
Delaware TF Kansas A	Muni State	.60	4.24	5.41	3.00	3.00	.55	.94	800 523-4640
Delaware TF MN Inter A	Muni State	.20	2.70	3.58	3.00	2.00	.50	.75	800 523-4640

Bond Fund Name	Objective	Annualized Return for			Rank		Max Load	Expense Ratio	Toll-Free Telephone
		1 Year	3 Years	5 Years	Overall	Risk			
Delaware TF MN Inter C	Muni State	-.60	1.89	2.79	4.00	2.00	.50	1.60	800 523-4640
Delaware TF MO Ins A	Muni State	1.60	3.86	5.16	2.00	3.00	.50	.94	800 523-4640
Delaware TF MO Ins B	Muni State	.90	3.15	4.48	3.00	3.00	.50	1.69	800 523-4640
Delaware TF Minnesota A	Muni State	-.10	3.53	4.88	3.00	3.00	.50	.91	800 523-4640
Delaware TF Minnesota C	Muni State	-.80	2.81	4.13	4.00	3.00	.50	1.65	800 523-4640
Delaware TF ND A	Muni State	.50	3.80	5.26	2.00	3.00	.55	1.00	800 523-4640
Delaware TF ND B	Muni State	-.20	3.05	4.61	3.00	3.00	.55	1.75	800 523-4640
Delaware TF New Mexico A	Muni State	.30	3.76	5.27	3.00	3.00	.55	1.00	800 523-4640
Delaware TF New Mexico B	Muni State	-.40	3.00	5.02	4.00	3.00	.55	1.75	800 523-4640
Delaware TF New York A	Muni NY	.40	2.68	3.48	5.00	3.00	.55	.84	800 523-4640
Delaware TF New York B	Muni NY	-.40	1.94	2.64	5.00	3.00	.55	1.60	800 523-4640
Delaware TF New York C	Muni NY	-.30	1.92	2.59	5.00	3.00	.55	1.60	800 523-4640
Delaware TF Oregon Ins A	Muni State	1.30	3.89	5.12	3.00	4.00	.50	.76	800 523-4640
Delaware TF Oregon Ins B	Muni State	.60	3.20	4.47	4.00	4.00	.50	1.51	800 523-4640
Delaware TF Wisconsin A	Muni State	.70	3.49	4.80	3.00	3.00	.48	1.00	800 523-4640
Delaware Tax Fr USA Interm A	Muni Natl	2.50	3.94	4.78	2.00	2.00	.55	.69	800 523-4640
Delaware Tax Fr USA Interm B	Muni Natl	1.60	3.09	3.91	3.00	2.00	.55	1.55	800 523-4640
Delaware Tax Fr USA Interm C	Muni Natl	1.60	3.07		3.00	2.00	.55	1.55	800 523-4640
Delaware Tax Free Insd A	Muni Natl	1.40	3.29	4.29	3.00	3.00	.58	1.00	800 523-4640
Delaware Tax Free Insd B	Muni Natl	.60	2.50	3.53	5.00	3.00	.58	1.80	800 523-4640
Delaware Tax Free Insd C	Muni Natl	.60	2.47		5.00	3.00	.58	1.80	800 523-4640
Delaware Tax Free USA A	Muni Natl	.80	2.75	3.59	5.00	3.00	.55	1.03	800 523-4640
Delaware Tax Free USA B	Muni Natl	0.00	1.94	2.78	5.00	4.00	.55	1.83	800 523-4640
Delaware Tax Free USA C	Muni Natl	0.00	1.94		5.00	4.00	.55	1.83	800 523-4640
Delaware Tax Free-NJ A	Muni State	0.00					.55	.50	800 523-4640
Delaware Tax Free-NJ B	Muni State	-.80					.55	1.25	800 523-4640
Delaware Tax Free-NJ C	Muni State	-.80					.55	1.25	800 523-4640
Delaware Tax Free-OH A	Muni State	-3.20					.55	.50	800 523-4640
Delaware Tax Free-OH B	Muni State	-3.90					.55	1.25	800 523-4640
Delaware Tax Free-OH C	Muni State	-3.90					.55	1.25	800 523-4640
Delaware Tax Free-PA A	Muni State	-.50	2.83	4.09	5.00	3.00	.57	.94	800 523-4640
Delaware Tax Free-PA B	Muni State	-1.30	1.71	3.08	5.00	3.00	.57	1.75	800 523-4640
Delaware Tax Free-PA C	Muni State	-1.30	2.60		5.00	3.00	.57	1.75	800 523-4640
Delaware US Govt Sec A	Government	4.10	5.12	5.21	3.00	3.00	.55	1.10	800 523-4640
Delaware US Govt Sec B	Government	3.30	4.36	4.64	4.00	3.00	.55	1.85	800 523-4640
Deutsche High Yield Bond Instl	Corp-HY	8.80					.50	.71	800 550-6426
Deutsche High Yield Bond Svc	Corp-HY	8.60					.50	1.01	800 550-6426
Deutsche PreservationPlus Inc	Dvsfd Bond	6.00					.69	5.08	800 368-4031
Deutsche PreservationPlus Instl	Dvsfd Bond	5.20					.34	.40	800 368-4031
Deutsche PreservationPlus Instl Svc	Dvsfd Bond	5.20					.34	.55	800 368-4031
Deutsche PreservationPlus Inv	Dvsfd Bond	4.90					.34	5.16	800 368-4031
Deutsche Short Term Muni Bond Svc	Muni Natl	3.10					.40	.80	800 550-6426
Deutsche US Bond Index Premier	Dvsfd Bond	4.50	5.96		2.00	3.00	.14	.14	800 368-4031
Dodge & Cox Income Fund	Corp-Inv	4.00	5.84	6.12	2.00	3.00	.45	.46	800 621-3979
Dreyfus A Bonds Plus	Corp-Inv	5.90	4.42	5.01	3.00	3.00	.65	.96	800 645-6561
Dreyfus Basic GNMA Fd	Govt-Mtg	5.90	5.74	6.35	1.00	3.00	.59	.65	800 645-6561
Dreyfus Basic Interm Muni Bd	Muni Natl	2.60	4.31	5.34	1.00	3.00	.59	.45	800 645-6561
Dreyfus Basic Municipal Bond Fd	Muni Natl	.90	4.15	5.91	3.00	4.00	.59	.45	800 645-6561
Dreyfus Bond Market Index Basic	Corp-Inv	4.10	5.89	5.85	2.00	3.00	.14	.14	800 645-6561
Dreyfus Bond Market Index Inv	Corp-Inv	3.90	5.66	5.57	3.00	3.00	.14	.40	800 645-6561
Dreyfus CA Intermediate Muni	Muni CA	3.40	4.23	4.85	2.00	2.00	.59	.80	800 645-6561
Dreyfus CA Tax Exempt Bond	Muni CA	2.80	4.27	4.93	3.00	4.00	.59	.71	800 645-6561
Dreyfus CT Intermediate Muni	Muni State	3.00	3.86	4.63	2.00	2.00	.59	.80	800 645-6561
Dreyfus Core Bond	Dvsfd Bond	8.90	7.10	7.71	1.00	4.00	.59	1.04	800 645-6561
Dreyfus Disciplined Int Bd Inv	Corp-Inv	3.40	5.02		3.00	3.00	.55	.80	800 645-6561
Dreyfus Disciplined Int Bd Rest	Corp-Inv	3.70	5.28		3.00	3.00	.55	.55	800 645-6561
Dreyfus FL Intermediate Muni	Muni State	2.60	3.43	4.20	3.00	2.00	.59	.81	800 645-6561
Dreyfus Founders Government Sec F	Government	1.90	4.64	4.51	4.00	3.00	.65	1.31	800 525-2440

402

Bond Fund Name	Objective	Annualized Return for			Rank		Max Load	Expense Ratio	Toll-Free Telephone
		1 Year	3 Years	5 Years	Overall	Risk			
Dreyfus GNMA Fund	Govt-Mtg	4.40	5.09	5.62	3.00	2.00	.59	.93	800 645-6561
Dreyfus General CA Muni Bond	Muni CA	.90	3.57	4.74	4.00	4.00	.59	.77	800 645-6561
Dreyfus General Municipal Bond	Muni Natl	.30	2.99	4.28	4.00	3.00	.55	.85	800 645-6561
Dreyfus General NY Muni Bond	Muni NY	1.30	4.12	5.16	3.00	4.00	.59	.90	800 645-6561
Dreyfus Global Bond	Intl Bond	2.30	3.93	4.56	4.00	4.00	.69	1.34	800 645-6561
Dreyfus High Yield Securities	Corp-HY	5.20	4.36		3.00	5.00	.65	1.10	800 645-6561
Dreyfus Inst Sh-Term Treas Inst	Government	4.60	5.42	5.49	2.00	1.00	.20	.20	800 645-6561
Dreyfus Inst Sh-Term Treas Inv	Government	4.40	5.16	5.24	2.00	1.00	.20	.20	800 645-6561
Dreyfus Insured Muni Bond	Muni Natl	2.00	3.96	4.59	3.00	4.00	.59	.84	800 645-6561
Dreyfus Interm Term Income	Corp-Inv	8.50	9.31		1.00	4.00	.75	.52	800 645-6561
Dreyfus Intermediate Muni Bd	Muni Natl	2.50	3.88	4.63	2.00	2.00	.59	.75	800 645-6561
Dreyfus MA Intermediate Muni Bd	Muni State	3.30	4.08	4.63	2.00	2.00	.59	.80	800 645-6561
Dreyfus MA Tax Exempt Bond	Muni State	1.40	4.03	5.11	3.00	3.00	.59	.81	800 645-6561
Dreyfus Municipal Bond	Muni Natl	-.60	2.84	4.17	4.00	3.00	.59	.72	800 645-6561
Dreyfus NJ Intermediate Muni Bd	Muni State	2.80	3.83	4.48	3.00	2.00	.59	.80	800 645-6561
Dreyfus NJ Municipal Bond	Muni State	1.30	3.75	4.70	3.00	3.00	.59	.90	800 645-6561
Dreyfus NY Tax Exempt Bond	Muni NY	2.00	4.21	5.06	2.00	3.00	.59	.75	800 645-6561
Dreyfus NY Tax Exempt Intermed	Muni NY	3.10	4.08	4.92	2.00	3.00	.59	.80	800 645-6561
Dreyfus PA Intermediate Muni	Muni State	2.90	4.00	4.97	2.00	3.00	.59	.80	800 645-6561
Dreyfus Premier CA Muni A	Muni CA	.10	2.98	4.53	5.00	4.00	.55	.96	888 338-8084
Dreyfus Premier CA Muni B	Muni CA	-.50	2.42	3.91	5.00	4.00	.55	1.47	888 338-8084
Dreyfus Premier CA Muni C	Muni CA	-.60	2.24	3.77	5.00	4.00	.55	1.71	888 338-8084
Dreyfus Premier CT Muni A	Muni State	.60	3.92	5.08	3.00	3.00	.55	.89	888 338-8084
Dreyfus Premier CT Muni B	Muni State	.10	3.39	4.52	3.00	3.00	.55	1.39	888 338-8084
Dreyfus Premier CT Muni C	Muni State	-.20	3.13		4.00	3.00	.55	1.64	888 338-8084
Dreyfus Premier FL Muni A	Muni State	.10	2.65	3.72	4.00	3.00	.55	.92	888 338-8084
Dreyfus Premier FL Muni B	Muni State	-.40	2.18	3.23	5.00	3.00	.55	1.41	888 338-8084
Dreyfus Premier FL Muni C	Muni State	-.70	1.86		5.00	3.00	.55	1.75	888 338-8084
Dreyfus Premier GA Muni A	Muni State	1.80	3.39	4.65	4.00	4.00	.55	.98	888 338-8084
Dreyfus Premier GA Muni B	Muni State	1.30	2.88	4.19	5.00	4.00	.55	1.48	888 338-8084
Dreyfus Premier GA Muni C	Muni State	1.00	2.42		5.00	4.00	.55	1.98	888 338-8084
Dreyfus Premier GNMA A	Govt-Mtg	4.30	5.56	5.90	2.00	2.00	.55	1.04	888 338-8084
Dreyfus Premier GNMA B	Govt-Mtg	3.70	5.02	5.36	3.00	2.00	.55	1.56	888 338-8084
Dreyfus Premier GNMA C	Govt-Mtg	3.40	4.71		3.00	2.00	.55	1.84	888 338-8084
Dreyfus Premier Lmtd MA Muni A	Muni State	3.20	3.71	4.69	3.00	2.00	.50	.75	888 338-8084
Dreyfus Premier Lmtd MA Muni B	Muni State	2.70	3.19	4.06	3.00	2.00	.50	1.25	888 338-8084
Dreyfus Premier Lmtd MA Muni C	Muni State	2.60	3.30	4.08	3.00	2.00	.50	1.25	888 338-8084
Dreyfus Premier Lmtd MA Muni R	Muni State	3.40	3.93	4.75	2.00	2.00	.50	1.25	888 338-8084
Dreyfus Premier Lmtd Muni A	Muni Natl	3.70	3.97	4.78	2.00	2.00	.50	.79	888 338-8084
Dreyfus Premier Lmtd Muni A	Muni Natl	3.20	3.44	4.30	3.00	2.00	.50	1.28	888 338-8084
Dreyfus Premier Lmtd Muni C	Muni Natl	3.20	3.54	4.37	3.00	2.00	.50	1.26	888 338-8084
Dreyfus Premier Lmtd Muni R	Muni Natl	4.00	4.22	5.06	2.00	2.00	.50	.54	888 338-8084
Dreyfus Premier Lmtd Term Hi Inc A	Corp-HY	.40	2.26		3.00	4.00	.69	.94	888 338-8084
Dreyfus Premier Lmtd Term Hi Inc B	Corp-HY	-.10	1.77		5.00	4.00	.69	.14	888 338-8084
Dreyfus Premier Lmtd Term Hi Inc C	Corp-HY	-.20	1.55		5.00	4.00	.69	1.69	888 338-8084
Dreyfus Premier Lmtd Term Hi Inc R	Corp-HY	.80	2.54		4.00	4.00	.69	.69	888 338-8084
Dreyfus Premier Lmtd Term Inc A	Corp-Inv	3.60	4.79	5.08	3.00	3.00	.59	.84	888 338-8084
Dreyfus Premier Lmtd Term Inc B	Corp-Inv	3.10	4.36	4.61	4.00	3.00	.59	1.35	888 338-8084
Dreyfus Premier Lmtd Term Inc C	Corp-Inv	3.10	4.00	4.30	4.00	3.00	.59	1.35	888 338-8084
Dreyfus Premier Lmtd Term Inc R	Corp-Inv	3.80	5.03	5.33	3.00	3.00	.59	.59	888 338-8084
Dreyfus Premier MA Muni A	Muni State	1.00	3.69	4.75	3.00	3.00	.55	.93	888 338-8084
Dreyfus Premier MA Muni B	Muni State	.60	3.18	4.22	4.00	3.00	.55	1.42	888 338-8084
Dreyfus Premier MA Muni C	Muni State	.20	2.92		3.00	3.00	.55	1.69	888 338-8084
Dreyfus Premier MD Muni A	Muni State	-.10	3.52	4.90	3.00	3.00	.55	.90	888 338-8084
Dreyfus Premier MD Muni B	Muni State	-.60	2.99	4.37	4.00	3.00	.55	1.41	888 338-8084
Dreyfus Premier MD Muni C	Muni State	-.90	2.56		3.00	3.00	.55	1.65	888 338-8084
Dreyfus Premier MI Muni A	Muni State	1.50	3.73	5.04	2.00	3.00	.55	.92	888 338-8084
Dreyfus Premier MI Muni B	Muni State	1.00	3.23	4.51	4.00	3.00	.55	1.41	888 338-8084

403

Bond Fund Name	Objective	Annualized Return for			Rank		Max Load	Expense Ratio	Toll-Free Telephone
		1 Year	3 Years	5 Years	Overall	Risk			
Dreyfus Premier MI Muni C	Muni State	.70	2.93		5.00	3.00	.55	1.66	888 338-8084
Dreyfus Premier MN Muni A	Muni State	1.40	3.35	4.45	3.00	3.00	.55	.91	888 338-8084
Dreyfus Premier MN Muni B	Muni State	.80	2.81	3.90	4.00	2.00	.55	1.42	888 338-8084
Dreyfus Premier MN Muni C	Muni State	.60	2.50		4.00	2.00	.55	1.73	888 338-8084
Dreyfus Premier Managed Inc A	Dvsfd Bond	2.00	3.71	4.87	4.00	3.00	.69	.94	888 338-8084
Dreyfus Premier Managed Inc B	Dvsfd Bond	1.20	2.94	4.11	5.00	3.00	.69	1.69	888 338-8084
Dreyfus Premier Managed Inc C	Dvsfd Bond	1.20	2.93	4.09	5.00	3.00	.69	1.69	888 338-8084
Dreyfus Premier Managed Inc R	Dvsfd Bond	2.20	3.94	5.12	3.00	3.00	.69	.69	888 338-8084
Dreyfus Premier Muni Bond A	Muni Natl	-1.30	2.36	4.22	4.00	3.00	.55	.91	888 338-8084
Dreyfus Premier Muni Bond B	Muni Natl	-1.80	1.87	3.70	5.00	3.00	.55	1.41	888 338-8084
Dreyfus Premier Muni Bond C	Muni Natl	-2.10	1.61		5.00	3.00	.55	1.66	888 338-8084
Dreyfus Premier NC Muni A	Muni State	.80	3.78	5.28	3.00	3.00	.55	.93	888 338-8084
Dreyfus Premier NC Muni B	Muni State	.40	3.26	4.75	3.00	3.00	.55	1.43	888 338-8084
Dreyfus Premier NC Muni C	Muni State	.20	2.99		4.00	3.00	.55	1.62	888 338-8084
Dreyfus Premier NJ Muni A	Muni State	-.90	2.92	3.92	5.00	4.00	.55	1.08	888 338-8084
Dreyfus Premier NJ Muni B	Muni State	-1.40	2.44	3.45	5.00	4.00	.55	1.58	888 338-8084
Dreyfus Premier NJ Muni C	Muni State	-1.60	2.38		5.00	4.00	.55	1.87	888 338-8084
Dreyfus Premier NY Muni A	Muni NY	1.00	3.93	5.17	3.00	4.00	.55	.92	888 338-8084
Dreyfus Premier NY Muni B	Muni NY	.40	3.35	4.61	4.00	4.00	.55	1.42	888 338-8084
Dreyfus Premier NY Muni C	Muni NY	.30	3.15		4.00	4.00	.55	1.65	888 338-8084
Dreyfus Premier OH Muni A	Muni State	1.50	3.62	4.94	2.00	3.00	.55	.91	888 338-8084
Dreyfus Premier OH Muni B	Muni State	.90	3.08	4.40	3.00	3.00	.55	1.41	888 338-8084
Dreyfus Premier OH Muni C	Muni State	.70	2.77		3.00	3.00	.55	1.65	888 338-8084
Dreyfus Premier PA Muni A	Muni State	.90	3.84	5.25	3.00	3.00	.55	.92	888 338-8084
Dreyfus Premier PA Muni B	Muni State	.40	3.28	4.70	4.00	3.00	.55	1.42	888 338-8084
Dreyfus Premier PA Muni C	Muni State	.10	3.11		4.00	3.00	.55	1.68	888 338-8084
Dreyfus Premier TX Muni A	Muni State	.50	3.55	5.33	3.00	4.00	.55	.84	888 338-8084
Dreyfus Premier TX Muni B	Muni State	0.00	3.04	4.81	4.00	4.00	.55	1.35	888 338-8084
Dreyfus Premier TX Muni C	Muni State	-.20	2.78		4.00	4.00	.55	1.60	888 338-8084
Dreyfus Premier VA Muni A	Muni State	-.10	3.63	5.18	3.00	3.00	.55	.92	888 338-8084
Dreyfus Premier VA Muni B	Muni State	-.60	3.09	4.64	4.00	3.00	.55	1.42	888 338-8084
Dreyfus Premier VA Muni C	Muni State	-.80	2.83		4.00	3.00	.55	1.65	888 338-8084
Dreyfus Sh-Interm Govt	Government	4.70	5.35	5.24	3.00	2.00	.50	.71	800 645-6561
Dreyfus Sh-Interm Tax Exempt	Muni Natl	3.00	3.79	4.11	2.00	1.00	.50	.72	800 645-6561
Dreyfus Short-Term High Yield	Corp-HY	-4.50	.49		5.00	4.00	.65	1.08	800 645-6561
Dreyfus Short-Term Income Fund	Corp-Inv	6.70	6.13	6.52	1.00	2.00	.50	.80	800 645-6561
Dreyfus UST Interm Term	Government	4.40	4.93	4.90	4.00	4.00	.80	.80	800 645-6561
Dreyfus UST Long Term	Government	3.50	6.51	5.76	3.00	5.00	.40	.80	800 645-6561
Dreyfus UST Sh-Term Fund	Government	4.30	4.88	4.98	3.00	1.00	.69	.80	800 645-6561
Dupree Interm Government Bond	Government	3.80	5.11	5.49	3.00	3.00	.20	.48	800 866-0614
Dupree KY Tax Free Income	Muni State	1.80	3.99	5.09	2.00	2.00	.50	.60	800 866-0614
Dupree KY Tax Free Short-to-Med	Muni State	1.90	3.20	3.71	2.00	1.00	.50	.71	800 866-0614
Dupree NC Tax Free Income	Muni State	1.10	4.51		1.00	3.00	.50	.45	800 866-0614
Dupree NC Tax Free Sh-to-Med	Muni State	2.50	3.34		2.00	1.00	.50	.44	800 866-0614
Dupree TN Tax-Free Income	Muni State	4.70	5.72	6.55	2.00	4.00	.50	.47	800 866-0614
Dupree TN Tax-Free Sh-to-Med	Muni State	2.50	3.48	3.98	2.00	1.00	.50	.56	800 866-0614
Eaton Vance AL Muni A	Muni State	.20	2.87	4.59	5.00	4.00	.35	.81	800 225-6265
Eaton Vance AL Muni B	Muni State	-.50	2.18	3.98	5.00	3.00	.35	1.55	800 225-6265
Eaton Vance AR Muni A	Muni State	1.30	3.74	4.90	3.00	3.00	.29	.78	800 225-6265
Eaton Vance AR Muni B	Muni State	.50	2.95	4.21	4.00	3.00	.29	1.56	800 225-6265
Eaton Vance AZ Muni A	Muni State	.10	3.48	4.97	4.00	4.00	.38	.76	800 225-6265
Eaton Vance AZ Muni B	Muni State	-.80	2.66	4.30	5.00	4.00	.38	1.55	800 225-6265
Eaton Vance CA Ltd Mat Muni A	Muni CA	1.90	3.24	3.92	4.00	3.00	.46	.94	800 225-6265
Eaton Vance CA Ltd Mat Muni B	Muni CA	1.20	2.50	3.36	5.00	3.00	.46	1.62	800 225-6265
Eaton Vance CA Muni A	Muni CA	-.40	3.57	5.60	4.00	4.00	.47	.75	800 225-6265
Eaton Vance CA Muni B	Muni CA	-.30	3.12	4.83	4.00	4.00	.47	1.19	800 225-6265
Eaton Vance CO Muni A	Muni State	-.40	3.08	5.00	4.00	4.00	.23	.58	800 225-6265
Eaton Vance CO Muni B	Muni State	-1.20	2.35	4.37	5.00	4.00	.23	1.41	800 225-6265

404

Bond Fund Name	Objective	Annualized Return for			Rank		Max Load	Expense Ratio	Toll-Free Telephone
		1 Year	3 Years	5 Years	Overall	Risk			
Eaton Vance CT Muni A	Muni State	.60	3.90	5.27	3.00	3.00	.40	.72	800 225-6265
Eaton Vance CT Muni B	Muni State	-.20	3.06	4.50	3.00	3.00	.40	1.54	800 225-6265
Eaton Vance FL Ins Muni A	Muni State	1.30	3.84	5.03	4.00	4.00	.45	.66	800 225-6265
Eaton Vance FL Ins Muni B	Muni State	.60	3.04	4.30	5.00	4.00	.45	1.43	800 225-6265
Eaton Vance FL Ltd Mat Muni B	Muni State	.70	2.24	2.85	4.00	2.00	.46	1.62	800 225-6265
Eaton Vance FL Ltd Mat Muni C	Muni State	.70	2.21	2.79	4.00	2.00	.46	1.65	800 225-6265
Eaton Vance FL Muni A	Muni State	-.30	3.47	4.83	4.00	4.00	.45	.72	800 225-6265
Eaton Vance FL Muni B	Muni State	-1.00	2.71	4.01	5.00	4.00	.45	1.56	800 225-6265
Eaton Vance GA Muni A	Muni State	.50	2.93	4.55	4.00	4.00	.35	.81	800 225-6265
Eaton Vance GA Muni B	Muni State	-.30	2.21	3.88	5.00	4.00	.35	1.56	800 225-6265
Eaton Vance Govt Obligatn A	Govt-Mtg	4.10	4.44	5.13	3.00	2.00	.75	1.23	800 225-6265
Eaton Vance Govt Obligatn B	Govt-Mtg	3.30	3.63	4.37	4.00	2.00	.75	1.98	800 225-6265
Eaton Vance Govt Obligatn C	Govt-Mtg	3.10	3.56	4.21	3.00	2.00	.75	1.98	800 225-6265
Eaton Vance HI Muni A	Muni State	-.40	2.89	4.37	5.00	4.00	.16	.46	800 225-6265
Eaton Vance HI Muni B	Muni State	-1.20	2.31	4.02	5.00	4.00	.17	1.17	800 225-6265
Eaton Vance High Income B	Corp-HY	3.00	6.71	8.99	2.00	5.00	.60	1.75	800 225-6265
Eaton Vance Inc Fd of Boston A	Corp-HY	6.60	8.65	10.46	1.00	5.00	.62	1.00	800 225-6265
Eaton Vance Instl Sht Term Treasury	Government	5.00					.34	.59	800 225-6265
Eaton Vance KS Muni A	Muni State	1.10	3.38	4.78	4.00	4.00	.17	.47	800 225-6265
Eaton Vance KS Muni B	Muni State	.50	2.70	4.24	5.00	4.00	.16	1.27	800 225-6265
Eaton Vance KY Muni A	Muni State	-1.10	3.14	4.79	3.00	3.00	.39	.81	800 225-6265
Eaton Vance KY Muni B	Muni State	-1.70	2.44	4.15	5.00	3.00	.39	1.55	800 225-6265
Eaton Vance LA Muni A	Muni State	-.20	2.83	4.57	4.00	4.00	.22	.78	800 225-6265
Eaton Vance LA Muni B	Muni State	-1.20	2.07	3.86	5.00	4.00	.22	1.54	800 225-6265
Eaton Vance MA Ltd Mat Muni B	Muni State	.20	2.10	3.04	4.00	2.00	.50	1.69	800 225-6265
Eaton Vance MA Muni A	Muni State	-.40	3.56	5.05	4.00	4.00	.44	.68	800 225-6265
Eaton Vance MA Muni B	Muni State	-1.20	2.67	4.22	5.00	4.00	.44	1.59	800 225-6265
Eaton Vance MD Muni A	Muni State	-.10	2.44	4.49	4.00	3.00	.38	.82	800 225-6265
Eaton Vance MD Muni B	Muni State	-1.00	1.67	3.82	4.00	3.00	.38	1.57	800 225-6265
Eaton Vance MI Muni A	Muni State	0.00	2.95	4.57	5.00	4.00	.16	.79	800 225-6265
Eaton Vance MI Muni B	Muni State	-.90	2.33	4.03	5.00	4.00	.16	1.57	800 225-6265
Eaton Vance MN Muni A	Muni State	-.30	3.36	4.66	4.00	4.00	.33	.70	800 225-6265
Eaton Vance MN Muni B	Muni State	-1.10	2.55	3.97	5.00	4.00	.33	1.53	800 225-6265
Eaton Vance MO Muni A	Muni State	-.20	3.43	4.99	4.00	4.00	.34	.81	800 225-6265
Eaton Vance MO Muni B	Muni State	-1.10	2.59	4.27	5.00	4.00	.34	1.58	800 225-6265
Eaton Vance MS Muni A	Muni State	.90	3.51	5.11	3.00	3.00	.16	.83	800 225-6265
Eaton Vance MS Muni B	Muni State	.10	2.82	4.54	4.00	3.00	.16	1.62	800 225-6265
Eaton Vance Municipal Bond A	Muni Natl	-1.50					.47	.67	800 225-6265
Eaton Vance Municipal Bond B	Muni Natl	-2.10					.47	1.40	800 225-6265
Eaton Vance Municipal Bond I	Muni Natl	-1.20	3.73	5.66	4.00	4.00	.47	.67	800 225-6265
Eaton Vance NC Muni A	Muni State	.50	3.52	4.83	4.00	4.00	.40	.75	800 225-6265
Eaton Vance NC Muni B	Muni State	0.00	2.80	4.17	5.00	4.00	.40	1.56	800 225-6265
Eaton Vance NJ Ltd Mat Muni B	Muni State	1.20	2.39	3.30	3.00	2.00	.50	1.71	800 225-6265
Eaton Vance NJ Muni A	Muni State	-.60	3.38	4.95	4.00	4.00	.45	.71	800 225-6265
Eaton Vance NJ Muni B	Muni State	-1.40	2.57	4.07	5.00	4.00	.45	1.56	800 225-6265
Eaton Vance NY Ltd Mat Muni B	Muni NY	1.40	3.10	3.69	3.00	3.00	.45	1.67	800 225-6265
Eaton Vance NY Muni A	Muni NY	1.80	4.20	5.58	3.00	4.00	.45	.72	800 225-6265
Eaton Vance NY Muni B	Muni NY	1.00	3.35	4.74	4.00	4.00	.45	1.57	800 225-6265
Eaton Vance Nat Ltd Mat Muni B	Muni Natl	-.90	2.65	3.44	4.00	2.00	.47	1.71	800 225-6265
Eaton Vance Nat Ltd Mat Muni C	Muni Natl	-1.00	2.43	3.19	4.00	2.00	.47	1.80	800 225-6265
Eaton Vance National Muni A	Muni Natl	-1.30	3.33	5.47	3.00	4.00	.41	.69	800 225-6265
Eaton Vance National Muni B	Muni Natl	-1.90	2.62	4.76	5.00	4.00	.41	1.52	800 225-6265
Eaton Vance OH Ltd Mat Muni B	Muni State	-.20	2.02	3.24	3.00	2.00	.46	1.75	800 225-6265
Eaton Vance OH Muni A	Muni State	-1.10	3.23	4.79	4.00	3.00	.44	.77	800 225-6265
Eaton Vance OH Muni B	Muni State	-1.90	2.37	4.02	4.00	3.00	.44	1.61	800 225-6265
Eaton Vance OR Muni A	Muni State	.60	3.99	4.71	3.00	3.00	.38	.83	800 225-6265
Eaton Vance OR Muni B	Muni State	-.20	3.18	4.05	4.00	3.00	.38	1.61	800 225-6265
Eaton Vance PA Ltd Mat Muni B	Muni State	.10	2.47	3.30	4.00	3.00	.46	1.68	800 225-6265

Bond Fund Name	Objective	Annualized Return for			Rank		Max Load	Expense Ratio	Toll-Free Telephone
		1 Year	3 Years	5 Years	Overall	Risk			
Eaton Vance PA Ltd Mat Muni C	Muni State	.20	2.41	3.24	4.00	3.00	.46	1.70	800 225-6265
Eaton Vance PA Muni A	Muni State	-.80	2.40	4.56	4.00	3.00	.45	.70	800 225-6265
Eaton Vance PA Muni B	Muni State	-1.60	1.58	3.67	5.00	3.00	.45	1.54	800 225-6265
Eaton Vance RI Muni A	Muni State	.60	3.43	4.96	4.00	4.00	.25	.71	800 225-6265
Eaton Vance RI Muni B	Muni State	-.20	2.71	4.50	5.00	4.00	.25	1.53	800 225-6265
Eaton Vance SC Muni A	Muni State	.40	2.92	4.55	4.00	4.00	.28	.80	800 225-6265
Eaton Vance SC Muni B	Muni State	-.60	2.12	3.92	5.00	3.00	.28	1.54	800 225-6265
Eaton Vance Strategic Inc A	Intl Bond	4.80					.56	1.04	800 225-6265
Eaton Vance Strategic Inc B	Intl Bond	4.10	4.12	8.75	2.00	4.00	.56	1.94	800 225-6265
Eaton Vance Strategic Inc C	Intl Bond	4.00	4.08	8.22	2.00	4.00	.56	2.02	800 225-6265
Eaton Vance TN Muni A	Muni State	1.10	3.88	5.39	2.00	3.00	.28	.76	800 225-6265
Eaton Vance TN Muni B	Muni State	.30	3.08	4.67	4.00	3.00	.28	1.58	800 225-6265
Eaton Vance TX Muni A	Muni State	.20	3.65	5.13	3.00	4.00	.16	.71	800 225-6265
Eaton Vance TX Muni B	Muni State	-.60	2.87	4.55	4.00	3.00	.16	1.51	800 225-6265
Eaton Vance VA Muni A	Muni State	.40	3.54	4.87	3.00	3.00	.40	.81	800 225-6265
Eaton Vance VA Muni B	Muni State	-.50	2.70	4.17	5.00	3.00	.40	1.56	800 225-6265
Eaton Vance WV Muni A	Muni State	.40	3.52	5.05	3.00	4.00	.20	.76	800 225-6265
Eaton Vance WV Muni B	Muni State	-.30	2.69	4.33	5.00	4.00	.20	1.59	800 225-6265
Eclipse Ultra Short Term Income	Government	5.40	5.60	5.79	1.00	1.00	.40	.11	800 872-2710
Elfun Income Fund	Corp-Inv	4.10	5.62	6.15	2.00	2.00	.07	.22	800 242-0134
Elfun Tax Exempt Income	Muni Natl	2.90	4.65	5.60	1.00	3.00	.05	.10	800 242-0134
Endowments Bond Portfolio	Corp-Inv	3.90	4.99	5.86	1.00	3.00	.50	.75	800 421-9900
Enterprise-Government Sec A	Govt-Mtg	3.90	5.15	6.14	2.00	2.00	.59	1.30	800 432-4320
Enterprise-Government Sec B	Govt-Mtg	3.40	4.75	5.64	3.00	2.00	.59	1.85	800 432-4320
Enterprise-Government Sec C	Govt-Mtg	3.30	2.10		4.00	2.00	.59	1.85	800 432-4320
Enterprise-High Yield Bond A	Corp-HY	.70	3.99	7.18	3.00	5.00	.59	1.30	800 432-4320
Enterprise-High Yield Bond B	Corp-HY	.20	3.45	6.62	3.00	5.00	.59	1.85	800 432-4320
Enterprise-High Yield Bond C	Corp-HY	.20	.13		4.00	5.00	.59	1.85	800 432-4320
Enterprise-Tax Exempt Income A	Muni Natl	2.40	3.65	4.50	2.00	2.00	.50	1.10	800 432-4320
Enterprise-Tax Exempt Income B	Muni Natl	1.90	3.13	3.97	3.00	3.00	.50	1.64	800 432-4320
EquiTrust High Grade Bond Trad	Corp-Inv	1.50	4.08	4.94	4.00	2.00	.40	1.65	800 247-4170
EquiTrust High Yield Bond Trad	Corp-HY	.20	3.74	6.10	2.00	2.00	.55	1.93	800 247-4170
Eureka Investor Grade Bond Fund A	Dvsfd Bond	3.50					.50	1.12	800 300-8893
Eureka Investor Grade Bond Fund Tr	Dvsfd Bond	3.80					.50	.88	800 300-8893
Evergreen Cap Presv & Inc A	Govt-Mtg	4.70	4.86	5.53	2.00	1.00	.59	.84	800 343-2898
Evergreen Cap Presv & Inc B	Govt-Mtg	3.90	4.06	4.75	3.00	1.00	.59	1.64	800 343-2898
Evergreen Cap Presv & Inc C	Govt-Mtg	3.90	4.10	4.77	3.00	1.00	.59	1.64	800 343-2898
Evergreen Connecticut Muni Bond A	Muni State	2.30					.50	.83	800 343-2898
Evergreen Connecticut Muni Bond B	Muni State	1.50					.50	1.58	800 343-2898
Evergreen Connecticut Muni Bond Y	Muni State	2.60					.50	.57	800 343-2898
Evergreen Diversified Bond A	Dvsfd Bond	1.90					.56	1.22	800 343-2898
Evergreen Diversified Bond B	Dvsfd Bond	1.20	3.76	5.13	4.00	4.00	.56	1.96	800 343-2898
Evergreen Diversified Bond C	Dvsfd Bond	1.30					.56	1.97	800 343-2898
Evergreen Diversified Bond Y	Dvsfd Bond	2.30					.56	.98	800 343-2898
Evergreen FL High Income Muni A	Muni State	-2.50	3.33	5.31	2.00	2.00	.59	.86	800 343-2898
Evergreen FL High Income Muni B	Muni State	-3.10	2.60		3.00	2.00	.59	1.62	800 343-2898
Evergreen FL High Income Muni C	Muni State	-3.10					.59	1.61	800 343-2898
Evergreen FL High Income Muni Y	Muni State	-2.30	3.60		2.00	2.00	.59	.61	800 343-2898
Evergreen FL Muni Bond A	Muni State	.70	3.67	4.97	3.00	3.00	.50	.33	800 343-2898
Evergreen FL Muni Bond B	Muni State	-.20	2.78	4.05	4.00	3.00	.50	1.25	800 343-2898
Evergreen FL Muni Bond C	Muni State	-.20					.50	1.25	800 343-2898
Evergreen FL Muni Bond Y	Muni State	.80	3.80	5.08	3.00	3.00	.50	.25	800 343-2898
Evergreen GA Muni Bond A	Muni State	1.60	4.39	5.56	3.00	3.00	.50	.50	800 343-2898
Evergreen GA Muni Bond B	Muni State	.80	3.63	4.78	3.00	3.00	.50	1.25	800 343-2898
Evergreen GA Muni Bond Y	Muni State	1.80	4.67	5.86	1.00	3.00	.50	.25	800 343-2898
Evergreen High Grade MUNI A	Muni Natl	1.00	3.44	4.75	4.00	4.00	.50	.94	800 343-2898
Evergreen High Grade MUNI B	Muni Natl	.20	2.67	3.97	5.00	4.00	.50	1.69	800 343-2898
Evergreen High Grade MUNI Y	Muni Natl	1.30	3.70	5.02	3.00	4.00	.50	.69	800 343-2898

406

Bond Fund Name	Objective	Annualized Return for			Rank		Max Load	Expense Ratio	Toll-Free Telephone
		1 Year	3 Years	5 Years	Overall	Risk			
Evergreen High Grade Municipal C	Muni Natl	.30					.50	1.65	800 343-2898
Evergreen High Income A	Corp-HY	-1.00					.69	1.11	800 343-2898
Evergreen High Income C	Corp-HY	-1.60					.69	1.58	800 343-2898
Evergreen High Income Fund B	Corp-HY						.69		800 343-2898
Evergreen High Income Fund Y	Corp-HY						.69		800 343-2898
Evergreen High Yield Bond A	Corp-HY	.40					.54	1.20	800 343-2898
Evergreen High Yield Bond B	Corp-HY	-.30	2.84	5.10	3.00	5.00	.54	1.94	800 343-2898
Evergreen High Yield Bond C	Corp-HY	-.20					.54	1.93	800 343-2898
Evergreen High Yield Bond Y	Corp-HY	.60					.54	.91	800 343-2898
Evergreen Interm Bd A	Corp-Inv	2.70	4.19	5.12	4.00	3.00	.59	1.10	800 343-2898
Evergreen Interm Bd B	Corp-Inv	1.90	3.34	4.32	5.00	3.00	.59	1.85	800 343-2898
Evergreen Interm Bd C	Corp-Inv	1.90	3.37	4.32	5.00	3.00	.59	1.85	800 343-2898
Evergreen Interm Bd Y	Corp-Inv	2.90					.59	.84	800 343-2898
Evergreen MD Muni Bd A	Muni State	1.50	3.35	3.87	3.00	3.00	.50	.78	800 343-2898
Evergreen MD Muni Bd B	Muni State	.80					.50	1.53	800 343-2898
Evergreen MD Muni Bd Y	Muni State	1.80	3.60	4.07	3.00	3.00	.50	.54	800 343-2898
Evergreen MD Municipal C	Muni State	.80					.50	1.53	800 343-2898
Evergreen MUNI B	Muni Natl	-1.40	1.95	3.65	5.00	4.00	.41	1.60	800 343-2898
Evergreen Municipal Bond Y	Muni Natl	-.50					.41	.52	800 343-2898
Evergreen NC Muni Bond A	Muni State	.40	4.00	5.16	3.00	3.00	.50	.45	800 343-2898
Evergreen NC Muni Bond B	Muni State	-.40	3.24	4.38	4.00	3.00	.50	1.19	800 343-2898
Evergreen NC Muni Bond Y	Muni State	.60	4.24	5.37	3.00	3.00	.50	.20	800 343-2898
Evergreen NJ MUNI A	Muni State	1.90	3.90	4.89	3.00	3.00	0.00	.50	800 343-2898
Evergreen NJ MUNI B	Muni State	1.00	2.97		4.00	3.00	0.00	1.40	800 343-2898
Evergreen NJ MUNI Y	Muni State	2.00	4.00		3.00	3.00	.50	.40	800 343-2898
Evergreen PA MUNI A	Muni State	1.40	3.68	4.94	3.00	3.00	.53	.81	800 343-2898
Evergreen PA MUNI B	Muni State	1.10	3.12	4.30	4.00	3.00	.53	.41	800 343-2898
Evergreen PA MUNI C	Muni State	1.00	3.09	4.28	4.00	3.00	.53	1.58	800 343-2898
Evergreen PA MUNI Y	Muni State	1.70					.53	.56	800 343-2898
Evergreen Quality Income A	Government	2.00	3.41	4.31	4.00	4.00	.46	1.05	800 343-2898
Evergreen Quality Income C	Government	1.30	2.88	3.82	4.00	4.00	.46	1.55	800 343-2898
Evergreen SC Muni Bond A	Muni State	2.10	3.93	5.45	2.00	3.00	.50	.69	800 343-2898
Evergreen SC Muni Bond B	Muni State	1.30	2.93	4.59	3.00	3.00	.50	1.44	800 343-2898
Evergreen SC Muni Bond Y	Muni State	2.40	4.17	5.70	2.00	3.00	.50	.45	800 343-2898
Evergreen Select Adj Rate I	Govt-Mtg	5.50	5.44	5.99	1.00	1.00	.29	.29	800 343-2898
Evergreen Select Adj Rate IS	Govt-Mtg	5.40	5.35	6.01	1.00	1.00	.29	.55	800 343-2898
Evergreen Select Core Bond I	Dvsfd Bond	4.30	5.01	5.89	3.00	4.00	.40	.41	800 343-2898
Evergreen Select Core Bond IS	Dvsfd Bond	4.10					.40	.67	800 343-2898
Evergreen Select Fixed Inc I	Dvsfd Bond	4.90					.40	.48	800 343-2898
Evergreen Select Fixed Inc IS	Dvsfd Bond	5.30					.40	.73	800 343-2898
Evergreen Select Income Plus I	Dvsfd Bond	3.30					.40	.48	800 343-2898
Evergreen Select Income Plus IS	Dvsfd Bond	3.10					.40	.73	800 343-2898
Evergreen Select Interm MUNI I	Muni Natl	.30					.50	.57	800 343-2898
Evergreen Select Interm MUNI IS	Muni Natl	0.00					.50	.82	800 343-2898
Evergreen Select Interntl Bond I	Intl Bond	-2.80	1.98	4.01	5.00	4.00	.59	.67	800 343-2898
Evergreen Select Interntl Bond IS	Intl Bond	-1.70	2.23	4.04	5.00	4.00	.50	.92	800 343-2898
Evergreen Select Limited Duration S	Dvsfd Bond	4.50					.29	.55	800 343-2898
Evergreen Select Ltd Duration I	Dvsfd Bond	4.60					.20	.29	800 343-2898
Evergreen Select Total Return I	Dvsfd Bond	2.60					.40	.47	800 343-2898
Evergreen Select Total Return S	Dvsfd Bond	2.40					.40	.73	800 343-2898
Evergreen Sh-Intermed Muni A	Muni Natl	2.40	3.47	3.71	3.00	1.00	.50	.75	800 343-2898
Evergreen Sh-Intermed Muni B	Muni Natl	1.50	2.53	2.81	2.00	1.00	.50	1.64	800 343-2898
Evergreen Sh-Intermed Muni Y	Muni Natl	2.50	3.55	3.80	3.00	1.00	.50	.65	800 343-2898
Evergreen Short Duration Inc A	Corp-Inv	3.40	4.68	5.05	3.00	2.00	.50	.81	800 343-2898
Evergreen Short Duration Inc B	Corp-Inv	2.30	3.70	4.09	4.00	2.00	.50	1.71	800 343-2898
Evergreen Short Duration Inc C	Corp-Inv	2.30	3.70	4.07	4.00	2.00	.50	.71	800 343-2898
Evergreen Short Duration Inc Y	Corp-Inv	3.50	4.79	5.16	3.00	2.00	.50	.71	800 343-2898
Evergreen Strategic Inc A	Dvsfd Bond	.50	3.19	5.67	3.00	4.00	.47	1.02	800 343-2898

Bond Fund Name	Objective	Annualized Return for			Rank		Max Load	Expense Ratio	Toll-Free Telephone
		1 Year	3 Years	5 Years	Overall	Risk			
Evergreen Strategic Inc B	Dvsfd Bond	-.40	2.31	4.79	3.00	4.00	.47	1.76	800 343-2898
Evergreen Strategic Inc C	Dvsfd Bond	-.40	2.49	4.90	3.00	4.00	.47	1.77	800 343-2898
Evergreen Strategic Inc Y	Dvsfd Bond	1.10	3.77		2.00	4.00	.47	.75	800 343-2898
Evergreen US Govt A	Government	4.30	5.31	5.48	3.00	2.00	.50	.94	800 343-2898
Evergreen US Govt B	Government	3.50	4.53	4.69	4.00	2.00	.50	1.70	800 343-2898
Evergreen US Govt C	Government	3.50	4.53	4.70	4.00	2.00	.50	1.69	800 343-2898
Evergreen US Govt Y	Government	4.50	5.56	5.74	2.00	2.00	.50	.70	800 343-2898
Evergreen VA Muni Bond A	Muni State	2.00	4.44	5.51	1.00	3.00	.50	.48	800 343-2898
Evergreen VA Muni Bond B	Muni State	1.30	3.67	4.73	3.00	3.00	0.00	1.23	800 343-2898
Evergreen VA Muni Bond Y	Muni State	2.30	4.71	5.77	1.00	3.00	.50	.25	800 343-2898
Excelsior CA Tax Exempt Income	Muni CA	2.90	3.83		2.00	2.00	.38	1.08	800 446-1012
Excelsior Income	Dvsfd Bond	4.40	5.57	5.46	2.00	3.00	.65	.50	800 446-1012
Excelsior Intermed Trm Mgd Inc	Muni Natl	3.70	5.28	5.35	1.00	3.00	.32	.67	800 446-1012
Excelsior Managed Income	Corp-Inv	4.00	5.65	5.48	3.00	3.00	.58	1.03	800 446-1012
Excelsior Sh Term Tax Ex Secs	Muni Natl	3.20	3.66	3.90	2.00	1.00	.29	.57	800 446-1012
Excelsior Short Term Government	Government	4.00	4.79	4.95	2.00	1.00	.29	.67	800 446-1012
Excelsior TXE Long-Term	Muni Natl	.40	3.12	5.22	4.00	4.00	.50	.76	800 446-1012
Excelsior TXE NY Intermediate	Muni NY	3.40	3.88	4.58	3.00	3.00	.47	.78	800 446-1012
Excelsior Tax Exempt Intermed	Muni Natl	3.00	3.92	4.83	2.00	2.00	.29	.57	800 446-1012
Excelsior Total Return Bd	Corp-Inv	4.90	5.70	5.94	3.00	3.00	.65	.50	800 446-1012
Executive Investors Insured TE Fund	Muni Natl	4.90	5.91	7.58	1.00	4.00	.29	.80	800 423-4026
Expedition Invst Grde Bd Inst-Svc	Government	3.50	4.76	4.62	4.00	2.00	0.00	1.12	800 992-2085
Expedition Invst Grde Bond Inst	Government	3.70	4.90		3.00	2.00	.75	.89	800 992-2085
FFTW US Short-Term Fixed	Corp-Inv	5.60	5.12	5.23	1.00	1.00	.29	.25	800 762-4848
FFTW Worldwide Fixed Income	Intl Bond	1.70	4.12	4.42	4.00	4.00	.45	.59	800 762-4848
FFTW Worldwide-Hedged	Intl Bond	4.20	7.55	8.78	1.00	3.00	.25	.45	800 762-4848
FPA New Income Inc	Corp-Inv	2.20	4.68	5.95	2.00	2.00	.50	.59	800 982-4372
FRIC Institutional Fixed Inc I Fd E	Corp-Inv	4.10					.25		
FRIC Institutional Fxd Inc III Fd E	Corp-Inv	3.50					.50		
FRIC Russell Diversified Bond Fd C	Corp-Inv	2.90					.40	1.57	
FRIC Russell Diversified Bond Fd E	Corp-Inv	3.80	5.53		2.00	3.00	.40	.81	
FRIC Russell Multistrategy Bond C	Corp-Inv	2.50					.59	1.81	
FRIC Russell Multistrategy Bond S	Corp-Inv	3.40	5.06	6.17	2.00	2.00	.59	.81	
FRIC Russell Short Term Bond Fund C	Corp-Inv	3.70					.45	1.94	
FRIC Russell Short Term Bond Fund E	Corp-Inv	4.50					.45	1.35	
FRIC Russell Tax Exempt Bond C	Muni Natl	2.20					.29		
FRIC Russell Tax Exempt Bond E	Muni Natl	2.90					.29		
Federated ARMs Fund Instl	Govt-Mtg	4.60	4.75	5.51	1.00	1.00	.40	.55	800 245-5051
Federated ARMs Fund Instl-Svc	Govt-Mtg	4.30	4.50	5.26	2.00	1.00	.59	.80	800 245-5051
Federated Adj Rate US Govt F	Govt-Mtg	4.00	4.25	4.97	2.00	1.00	.59	1.02	800 245-5051
Federated Bond Fund A	Dvsfd Bond	.80	3.75	5.61	3.00	3.00	.75	1.05	800 245-5051
Federated Bond Fund B	Dvsfd Bond	-.10	2.96	4.81	4.00	3.00	.75	1.85	800 245-5051
Federated Bond Fund C	Dvsfd Bond	0.00	3.00	4.83	3.00	4.00	.75	1.85	800 245-5051
Federated Bond Fund F	Dvsfd Bond	.80	3.78	5.61	3.00	3.00	.75	1.08	800 245-5051
Federated Fund for US Govt Sec A	Govt-Mtg	4.90	5.14	5.66	2.00	2.00	.56	.95	800 245-5051
Federated Fund for US Govt Sec B	Govt-Mtg	4.10	4.28	4.80	3.00	2.00	.56	1.72	800 245-5051
Federated Fund for US Govt Sec C	Govt-Mtg	4.10	4.29	4.81	3.00	2.00	.54	1.72	800 245-5051
Federated GNMA Trust Instl	Govt-Mtg	5.30	5.55	6.14	1.00	2.00	.40	.63	800 245-5051
Federated GNMA Trust Instl-Svc	Govt-Mtg	5.10	5.37	5.93	2.00	2.00	.40	.79	800 245-5051
Federated Govt Inc Securities A	Govt-Mtg	4.10	5.52		2.00	3.00	.75	.97	800 245-5051
Federated Govt Inc Securities B	Govt-Mtg	3.30	4.67		3.00	3.00	.75	1.72	800 245-5051
Federated Govt Inc Securities C	Govt-Mtg	3.30	4.73		3.00	3.00	.75	1.72	800 245-5051
Federated Govt Inc Securities F	Govt-Mtg	4.00	5.46	5.69	3.00	3.00	.75	.97	800 245-5051
Federated High Income Bond A	Corp-HY	-2.40	3.05	7.15	2.00	5.00	.75	1.18	800 245-5051
Federated High Income Bond B	Corp-HY	-3.20	2.25		4.00	5.00	.75	1.93	800 245-5051
Federated High Income Bond C	Corp-HY	-3.30	2.24	6.31	3.00	5.00	.75	1.93	800 245-5051
Federated High Yield Trust	Corp-HY	-2.70	2.69	6.83	3.00	5.00	.75	.88	800 245-5051
Federated Income Trust Instl	Govt-Mtg	4.60	5.49	6.05	1.00	2.00	.40	.56	800 245-5051

Bond Fund Name	Objective	Annualized Return for			Rank		Max Load	Expense Ratio	Toll-Free Telephone
		1 Year	3 Years	5 Years	Overall	Risk			
Federated Income Trust Instl-Svc	Govt-Mtg	4.40	5.27	5.82	1.00	2.00	.40	.79	800 245-5051
Federated Interm Income Instl	Corp-Inv	3.60	5.06	5.64	3.00	3.00	.50	.55	800 245-5051
Federated Interm Muni Trust Instl	Muni Natl	1.70	3.26	4.13	3.00	2.00	.35	.56	800 245-5051
Federated International Income A	Intl Bond	-6.40	-1.35	1.70	4.00	5.00	.70	1.42	800 245-5051
Federated International Income B	Intl Bond	-7.00	-2.04	-1.95	4.00	5.00	.70	2.14	800 245-5051
Federated International Income C	Intl Bond	-7.10	-2.06	.95	4.00	5.00	.70	2.14	800 245-5051
Federated Intl High Income A	Intl Bond	9.80	1.28		4.00	5.00	.84	.92	800 245-5051
Federated Intl High Income B	Intl Bond	8.90	.51		4.00	5.00	.84	1.66	800 245-5051
Federated Intl High Income C	Intl Bond	8.90	.51		4.00	5.00	.84	1.66	800 245-5051
Federated Limited Duration Fund	Dvsfd Bond	4.30	5.41		1.00	1.00	.40	.65	800 245-5051
Federated Limited Duration Instl	Dvsfd Bond	4.60	5.71		1.00	1.00	.40	.34	800 245-5051
Federated Limited Term Fd A	Corp-Inv	3.10	4.40	5.08	2.00	1.00	.40	1.10	800 245-5051
Federated Limited Term Fd F	Corp-Inv	3.20	4.48		2.00	1.00	.40	1.00	800 245-5051
Federated MI Interm Muni Tr	Muni State	2.90	3.96	4.69	2.00	2.00	.40	.50	800 245-5051
Federated Muni Opportunities A	Muni Natl	-2.50	2.29		4.00	3.00	.59	1.06	800 245-5051
Federated Muni Opportunities B	Muni Natl	-3.30	1.48		5.00	3.00	.59	1.82	800 245-5051
Federated Muni Opportunities C	Muni Natl	-3.30	1.48		5.00	3.00	.59	1.81	800 245-5051
Federated Muni Opportunities F	Muni Natl	-2.50	2.29	3.64	4.00	3.00	.59	1.06	800 245-5051
Federated Muni Securities Fd A	Muni Natl	1.10	2.95	3.46	4.00	4.00	.59	.86	800 245-5051
Federated Muni Securities Fd B	Muni Natl	.40	2.09		4.00	4.00	.59	1.76	800 245-5051
Federated Muni Securities Fd C	Muni Natl	.30	2.07	2.60	5.00	4.00	.59	1.75	800 245-5051
Federated NC Muni Inc A	Muni State	2.50	3.69	4.73	3.00	3.00	.40		800 245-5051
Federated NY Muni Income Fd FS	Muni NY	.30	3.78	5.39	3.00	3.00	.40	.69	800 245-5051
Federated OH Muni Income Fd F	Muni State	.50	3.59	4.87	3.00	3.00	.40	.90	800 245-5051
Federated PA Muni Income Fund A	Muni State	-.10	3.13	5.08	2.00	3.00	.40	.75	800 245-5051
Federated Sh Term Inc Instl	Corp-Inv	5.70	5.52	5.81	2.00	1.00	.36	.56	800 245-5051
Federated Sh Term Inc Instl-Svc	Corp-Inv	5.50	5.27	5.56	2.00	1.00	.36	.81	800 245-5051
Federated Sh Term Muni Instl	Muni Natl	2.60	3.56	3.81	2.00	1.00	.40	.46	800 245-5051
Federated Sh Term Muni Instl-Svc	Muni Natl	2.40	3.31	3.56	2.00	1.00	.40	.71	800 245-5051
Federated Strategic Income Fund A	Dvsfd Bond	2.70	3.21	6.80	3.00	4.00	.47	1.14	800 245-5051
Federated Strategic Income Fund B	Dvsfd Bond	1.90	2.43		3.00	5.00	.47	1.89	800 245-5051
Federated Strategic Income Fund C	Dvsfd Bond	1.90	2.41	5.99	2.00	4.00	.47	1.89	800 245-5051
Federated Strategic Income Fund F	Dvsfd Bond	2.80	3.22	6.75	3.00	5.00	.47	1.14	800 245-5051
Federated Total Ret Bd Instl	Corp-Inv	4.50	6.11		1.00	3.00	.40	.34	800 245-5051
Federated Total Ret Bd Instl-Svc	Corp-Inv	4.20	5.81		2.00	3.00	.40	.65	800 245-5051
Federated US Gov 1-3yr Instl	Government	4.40	4.97	5.16	2.00	1.00	.40	.54	800 245-5051
Federated US Gov 1-3yr Instl-Svc	Government	4.10	4.70	4.90	3.00	1.00	.40	.79	800 245-5051
Federated US Gov 2-5yr Instl	Government	3.70	5.10	5.19	4.00	2.00	.40	.55	800 245-5051
Federated US Gov 2-5yr Instl-Svc	Government	3.50	4.85	4.96	4.00	2.00	.40	.80	800 245-5051
Federated US Gov 5-10yr Instl	Government	4.10	6.02		3.00	4.00	.50	.29	800 245-5051
Federated US Gov 5-10yr Instl-Svc	Government	3.80	5.76		3.00	4.00	.50	.59	800 245-5051
Federated US Gov Bond Fund	Government	5.60	6.61	6.07	3.00	5.00	.59	.84	800 245-5051
Federated Ultra-Short Bond	Dvsfd Bond	4.80					.40	.45	800 245-5051
Fidelity Adv Emerging Markets Inc C	Intl Bond	23.40					.68	2.24	800 522-7297
Fidelity Adv Emerging Mkts Inc A	Intl Bond	24.40	5.93		3.00	5.00	.68	1.39	800 522-7297
Fidelity Adv Emerging Mkts Inc B	Intl Bond	23.50	5.42	16.28	3.00	5.00	.68	2.10	800 522-7297
Fidelity Adv Emerging Mkts Inc I	Intl Bond	24.60	6.03		3.00	5.00	.68	1.15	800 522-7297
Fidelity Adv Emerging Mkts Inc T	Intl Bond	24.30	5.86	16.89	3.00	5.00	.68	1.40	800 522-7297
Fidelity Adv Govt Investment A	Government	4.60	5.62		3.00	3.00	.45	.89	800 522-7297
Fidelity Adv Govt Investment B	Government	3.60	4.77	4.71	4.00	3.00	.45	1.60	800 522-7297
Fidelity Adv Govt Investment C	Government	3.60					.45	1.69	800 522-7297
Fidelity Adv Govt Investment I	Government	4.70	5.62		3.00	3.00	.45	.68	800 522-7297
Fidelity Adv Govt Investment T	Government	4.40	5.40	5.37	3.00	3.00	.45	.96	800 522-7297
Fidelity Adv High Income A	Corp-HY						.57		800 522-7297
Fidelity Adv High Income B	Corp-HY						.57		800 522-7297
Fidelity Adv High Income C	Corp-HY						.57		800 522-7297
Fidelity Adv High Income Instl	Corp-HY						.57		800 522-7297
Fidelity Adv High Income T	Corp-HY						.57		800 522-7297

409

Bond Fund Name	Objective	Annualized Return for			Rank		Max Load	Expense Ratio	Toll-Free Telephone
		1 Year	3 Years	5 Years	Overall	Risk			
Fidelity Adv High Yield Fund A	Corp-HY	-2.80	4.12		3.00	5.00	.59	.95	800 522-7297
Fidelity Adv High Yield Fund B	Corp-HY	-3.70	3.43	7.08	3.00	5.00	.59	1.70	800 522-7297
Fidelity Adv High Yield Fund C	Corp-HY	-3.70					.59	1.80	800 522-7297
Fidelity Adv High Yield Fund I	Corp-HY	-2.80	4.31		3.00	5.00	.59	.81	800 522-7297
Fidelity Adv High Yield Fund T	Corp-HY	-2.90	4.08	7.80	3.00	5.00	.59	1.05	800 522-7297
Fidelity Adv Interm Bond A	Corp-Inv	3.80	5.01		3.00	2.00	.45	.89	800 522-7297
Fidelity Adv Interm Bond B	Corp-Inv	2.90	4.23	4.38	4.00	2.00	.45	1.62	800 522-7297
Fidelity Adv Interm Bond C	Corp-Inv	3.30					.45	1.73	800 522-7297
Fidelity Adv Interm Bond I	Corp-Inv	4.00	5.18	5.36	3.00	2.00	.52	.67	800 522-7297
Fidelity Adv Interm Bond T	Corp-Inv	3.60	4.89	5.07	3.00	2.00	.45	.97	800 522-7297
Fidelity Adv Mortgage Secs A	Govt-Mtg	4.90	5.15		1.00	2.00	.45	.90	800 522-7297
Fidelity Adv Mortgage Secs B	Govt-Mtg	4.20	4.42		2.00	2.00	.45	1.64	800 522-7297
Fidelity Adv Mortgage Secs I	Govt-Mtg	5.10	5.29		1.00	2.00	.45	.75	800 522-7297
Fidelity Adv Mortgage Secs T	Govt-Mtg	4.80	5.09		1.00	2.00	.45	1.00	800 522-7297
Fidelity Adv Muni Income A	Muni Natl	3.20	4.66		1.00	3.00	.40	.71	800 522-7297
Fidelity Adv Muni Income B	Muni Natl	2.40	3.95	4.69	2.00	3.00	.40	1.45	800 522-7297
Fidelity Adv Muni Income I	Muni Natl	3.30	4.75		1.00	3.00	.40	.58	800 522-7297
Fidelity Adv Muni Income T	Muni Natl	3.10	4.65	5.40	1.00	3.00	.38	.81	800 522-7297
Fidelity Adv Municipal Income C	Muni Natl	2.30					.40	1.57	800 522-7297
Fidelity Adv Short Fixed-Income C	Corp-Inv	3.70					.40	1.73	800 522-7297
Fidelity Adv Short-Fixed Income A	Corp-Inv	4.60	5.16		1.00	1.00	.45	.82	800 522-7297
Fidelity Adv Short-Fixed Income I	Corp-Inv	4.70	5.25		2.00	1.00	.45	.68	800 522-7297
Fidelity Adv Short-Fixed Income T	Corp-Inv	4.50	5.11	5.31	2.00	1.00	.44	.81	800 522-7297
Fidelity Adv Strategic Income A	Corp-Inv	5.30	4.96		3.00	5.00	.57	1.08	800 522-7297
Fidelity Adv Strategic Income B	Corp-Inv	4.60	4.28	7.26	3.00	5.00	.57	1.79	800 522-7297
Fidelity Adv Strategic Income C	Corp-Inv	4.40					.57	1.91	800 522-7297
Fidelity Adv Strategic Income I	Corp-Inv	5.50	5.10		2.00	5.00	.57	.93	800 522-7297
Fidelity Adv Strategic Income T	Corp-Inv	5.30	4.92	7.92	2.00	5.00	.57	1.13	800 522-7297
Fidelity Capital & Income	Corp-HY	-.20	8.60	9.61	3.00	5.00	.57	.81	800 544-8888
Fidelity Freedom Income Fund	Corp-HY	8.50	9.25		1.00	3.00	.10	.07	800 544-8888
Fidelity GNMA Fund	Govt-Mtg	5.50	5.54	6.13	1.00	2.00	.44	.64	800 544-8888
Fidelity Government Income Fund	Government	4.60	5.69	5.54	3.00	3.00	.42	.67	800 544-8888
Fidelity High Income	Corp-HY	-4.60	4.97	8.65	3.00	5.00	.80	.80	800 544-8888
Fidelity Inst Short-Interm Govt I	Government	4.70	5.41	5.65	2.00	1.00	.28	.44	800 544-8888
Fidelity Intermediate Bond	Corp-Inv	4.30	5.43	5.51	2.00	2.00	.44	.65	800 544-8888
Fidelity Intermediate Government	Government	4.40	5.40	5.70	2.00	2.00	.65	.53	800 544-8888
Fidelity International Bond	Intl Bond	3.30	2.19	1.88	4.00	5.00	.69	.65	800 544-8888
Fidelity Invt Grade Bond	Corp-Inv	4.30	5.50	5.74	2.00	3.00	.44	.69	800 544-8888
Fidelity Mortgage Securities	Govt-Mtg	5.10	5.60	6.43	1.00	2.00	.42	.70	800 544-8888
Fidelity New Markets Income	Intl Bond	25.20	5.99	17.54	3.00	5.00	.68	1.08	800 544-8888
Fidelity Short-Term Bond	Corp-Inv	4.80	5.30	5.41	1.00	1.00	.44	.65	800 544-8888
Fidelity Spartan AZ Muni Income	Muni State	3.40	4.23	4.96	2.00	3.00	.55	.54	800 544-6666
Fidelity Spartan CA Muni Inc	Muni CA	3.50	5.02	6.26	1.00	3.00	.39	.48	800 544-6666
Fidelity Spartan CT Muni Income	Muni State	3.40	4.57	5.52	1.00	3.00	.55	.51	800 544-6666
Fidelity Spartan FL Muni Income	Muni State	3.00	4.33	5.49	1.00	3.00	.55	.54	800 544-6666
Fidelity Spartan Govt Income	Government	4.80	5.98	5.89	3.00	3.00	.59	.51	800 544-6666
Fidelity Spartan Intermd Muni Inc	Muni Natl	3.30	4.42	5.38	1.00	2.00	.35	.46	800 544-6666
Fidelity Spartan Invest Grade Bd	Corp-Inv	4.30	5.90	6.02	2.00	3.00	.65	.44	800 544-6666
Fidelity Spartan MA Muni Inc	Muni State	2.90	4.44	5.57	1.00	3.00	.40	.48	800 544-6666
Fidelity Spartan MD Muni Income	Muni State	3.30	4.48	5.48	1.00	3.00	.65	.48	800 544-6666
Fidelity Spartan MI Muni Inc	Muni State	2.80	4.22	5.29	1.00	3.00	.39	.53	800 544-6666
Fidelity Spartan MN Muni Inc	Muni State	2.70	4.12	5.11	1.00	3.00	.40	.51	800 544-6666
Fidelity Spartan Municipal Inc	Muni Natl	3.40	4.63	5.86	1.00	3.00	.40	.48	800 544-6666
Fidelity Spartan NJ Muni Income	Muni State	4.00	4.64	5.40	1.00	3.00	.39	.55	800 544-6666
Fidelity Spartan NY Muni Inc	Muni NY	3.40	4.66	5.77	2.00	4.00	1.00	.50	800 544-6666
Fidelity Spartan OH Muni Inc	Muni State	3.00	4.30	5.30	1.00	3.00	.39	.52	800 544-6666
Fidelity Spartan PA Muni Inc	Muni State	3.00	4.34	5.34	1.00	3.00	.55	.52	800 544-6666
Fidelity Spartan Sh-Interm Muni	Muni Natl	3.40	3.91	4.30	2.00	1.00	.55	.55	800 544-6666

Bond Fund Name	Objective	Annualized Return for			Rank		Max Load	Expense Ratio	Toll-Free Telephone
		1 Year	3 Years	5 Years	Overall	Risk			
Fidelity Target Timeline 2001	Corp-Inv	4.50	6.20		1.00	2.00	.44	.34	800 544-8888
Fidelity Target Timeline 2003	Corp-Inv	3.60	6.08		2.00	3.00	.44	.34	800 544-8888
Fidelity US Bond Index	Corp-Inv	4.30	5.99	6.14	2.00	3.00	.32	.30	800 544-8888
Fifth Third Bond Fd for Inc A	Corp-Inv	3.10	4.66		3.00	2.00	.55	.96	888 799-5353
Fifth Third Bond Fd for Inc C	Corp-Inv	29.40	12.42		5.00	5.00	.55	1.54	888 799-5353
Fifth Third Bond Fd for Inc I	Corp-Inv	3.50					.55	.75	888 799-5353
Fifth Third Municipal Bond A	Muni Natl	1.40	3.01		3.00	3.00	.55	.81	888 799-5353
Fifth Third Municipal Bond I	Muni Natl	1.70					.55	.75	888 799-5353
Fifth Third Ohio Tax Free C	Muni State	1.60	2.66		3.00	3.00	.55	1.55	888 799-5353
Fifth Third Ohio Tax Free I	Muni State	2.30					.55	.81	888 799-5353
Fifth Third Quality Bond A	Corp-Inv	3.20	4.78	4.81	3.00	3.00	.55	.92	888 799-5353
Fifth Third Quality Bond C	Corp-Inv	2.20	3.99		4.00	3.00	.55	1.42	888 799-5353
Fifth Third Quality Bond I	Corp-Inv	3.50					.55	.75	888 799-5353
Fifth Third US Govt Secs A	Government	3.40	4.77	4.73	3.00	2.00	.55	.94	888 799-5353
Fifth Third US Govt Secs C	Government	2.50	3.96		4.00	2.00	.55	1.39	888 799-5353
Fifth Third US Govt Secs I	Government	3.70					.55	.75	888 799-5353
First American Arizona TF A	Muni CA						.69		800 637-2548
First American Arizona TF C	Muni CA						.69		800 637-2548
First American Arizona TF Y	Muni CA						.69		800 637-2548
First American California TF A	Muni CA						.69		800 637-2548
First American California TF C	Muni CA						.69		800 637-2548
First American California TF Y	Muni CA						.69		800 637-2548
First American Colorado TF A	Muni State						.69		800 637-2548
First American Colorado TF C	Muni State						.69		800 637-2548
First American Colorado TF Y	Muni State						.69		800 637-2548
First American Corp Bond A	Corp-Inv						.69		800 637-2548
First American Corp Bond B	Corp-Inv						.69		800 637-2548
First American Corp Bond C	Corp-Inv						.69		800 637-2548
First American Corp Bond Y	Corp-Inv						.69		800 637-2548
First American Fixed Income C	Corp-Inv	3.10					.69	1.35	800 637-2548
First American MN Tax Free Fund C	Muni State	.80					.69	1.35	800 637-2548
First American MN Tax Free Fund Y	Muni State	2.00					.69	.69	800 637-2548
First American OR Intmed Tax-Free A	Muni State	3.00					.69	.69	800 637-2548
First American Strategic Income A	Dvsfd Bond	3.70					.69	1.14	800 637-2548
First American Strategic Income B	Dvsfd Bond	3.40					.69	1.89	800 637-2548
First American Strategic Income C	Dvsfd Bond	3.60					.69	1.55	800 637-2548
First American Strategic Income Y	Dvsfd Bond	4.50					.69	.90	800 637-2548
First American Tax Free Fund C	Muni Natl	0.00					.50	1.35	800 637-2548
First American Tax Free Fund Y	Muni Natl	.70					.50	.80	800 637-2548
First American-CA Interm T/F A	Muni CA	4.20					.69	.69	800 637-2548
First American-CA Interm T/F Y	Muni CA	4.30					.69	.69	800 637-2548
First American-CO Interm T/F A	Muni State	2.70	3.68	4.47	3.00	2.00	.39	.69	800 637-2548
First American-CO Interm T/F Y	Muni State	2.60	3.58	4.41	3.00	2.00	.39	.69	800 637-2548
First American-Fixed Income A	Corp-Inv	3.70	5.18	5.26	3.00	3.00	.69	.94	800 637-2548
First American-Fixed Income B	Corp-Inv	2.90	4.44	4.49	4.00	3.00	.69	1.69	800 637-2548
First American-Fixed Income Y	Corp-Inv	3.90	5.48	5.54	3.00	3.00	.69	.69	800 637-2548
First American-Interm Income A	Corp-Inv	3.60	5.08	5.32	3.00	2.00	.46	.84	800 637-2548
First American-Interm Income Y	Corp-Inv	3.70	5.08	5.32	3.00	2.00	.51	.69	800 637-2548
First American-Interm Tax Free A	Muni Natl	3.00	3.75	4.51	3.00	2.00	.50	.69	800 637-2548
First American-Interm Tax Free Y	Muni Natl	3.10	3.81	4.53	3.00	2.00	.50	.69	800 637-2548
First American-Limited Term A	Corp-Inv	4.90	5.17	5.44	1.00	1.00	.69	.59	800 637-2548
First American-Limited Term Y	Corp-Inv	5.00	5.20	5.45	1.00	1.00	.69	.59	800 637-2548
First American-MN Int T/F Fund A	Muni State	2.90	3.75	4.48	3.00	2.00	.41	.69	800 637-2548
First American-MN Int T/F Fund Y	Muni State	2.90	3.70	4.52	3.00	2.00	.50	.69	800 637-2548
First American-MN Tax Free A	Muni State	1.70	4.05	5.20	1.00	3.00	.50	.94	800 637-2548
First American-OR Interm T/F Y	Muni State	3.00					.69	.69	800 637-2548
First American-Tax Free A	Muni Natl	.50	3.44	4.94	3.00	3.00	.50	1.05	800 637-2548
First Fds-Bond Portfolio I	Corp-Inv	3.30	5.38	5.58	3.00	3.00	.50	.47	800 442-1941

Bond Fund Name	Objective	Annualized Return for			Rank		Max Load	Expense Ratio	Toll-Free Telephone
		1 Year	3 Years	5 Years	Overall	Risk			
First Fds-Bond Portfolio II	Corp-Inv	3.00	5.11		3.00	3.00	.50	.81	800 442-1941
First Fds-Bond Portfolio III	Corp-Inv	2.70	4.37	4.51	4.00	3.00	.50	1.55	800 442-1941
First Fds-Tennessee Tax Free I	Muni State	2.80	4.46		1.00	2.00	.14	.35	800 442-1941
First Fds-Tennessee Tax Free II	Muni State	2.70	4.41		1.00	2.00	.14	.44	800 442-1941
First Fds-Tennessee Tax Free III	Muni State	2.30	4.05		2.00	2.00	.14	.75	800 442-1941
First Funds Intmed Bond Fund I	Dvsfd Bond	3.90					.50	.35	800 442-1941
First Funds Intmed Bond Fund II	Dvsfd Bond	3.60					.50	.68	800 442-1941
First Funds Intmed Bond Fund III	Dvsfd Bond	3.10					.50	1.21	800 442-1941
First Hawaii-Interm Muni Fund	Muni State	2.10	3.21	3.79	3.00	1.00	.50	.89	888-200-4134
First Hawaii-Muni Bond	Muni State	1.00	3.30	4.31	3.00	2.00	.50	.89	888-200-4134
First Inv Fund for Income A	Corp-HY	-1.10	4.02	7.67	3.00	4.00	.73	1.30	800 423-4026
First Inv Government A	Govt-Mtg	4.40	5.00	5.38	3.00	2.00	1.00	1.19	800 423-4026
First Inv Insd NY Tax Free A	Muni NY	2.80	3.85	4.61	3.00	3.00	.75	1.06	800 423-4026
First Inv Insured Tax Ex A	Muni Natl	2.80	3.89	4.83	3.00	3.00	.75	1.11	800 423-4026
First Inv Multi Ins T/F-CA A	Muni CA	4.80	5.25	6.14	2.00	4.00	.75	.80	800 423-4026
First Inv Multi Ins T/F-MA A	Muni State	2.80	4.07	5.10	2.00	3.00	.75	.80	800 423-4026
First Inv Multi Ins T/F-MI A	Muni State	3.10	4.43	5.27	2.00	3.00	.75	.85	800 423-4026
First Inv Multi Ins T/F-MN A	Muni State	3.50	4.66	5.37	1.00	2.00	.75	.50	800 423-4026
First Inv Multi Ins T/F-NJ A	Muni State	3.30	4.23	5.11	2.00	3.00	.75	.93	800 423-4026
First Inv Multi Ins T/F-OH A	Muni State	3.40	4.39	5.52	1.00	3.00	.75	.80	800 423-4026
First Investors CO Ins Tax Free A	Muni State	3.40	4.89	5.97	1.00	3.00	.75	.46	800 423-4026
First Investors CT Ins Tax Free A	Muni State	3.20	4.51	5.40	1.00	3.00	.75	.80	800 423-4026
First Investors FL Ins Tax Free A	Muni State	3.00	4.18	5.37	2.00	3.00	.75	.80	800 423-4026
First Investors GA Ins Tax Free A	Muni State	3.90	4.98	6.03	2.00	4.00	.29	.46	800 423-4026
First Investors Investment Grade A	Corp-Inv	1.90	4.61	5.05	3.00	3.00	.75	1.10	800 423-4026
First Investors MD Ins Tax Free A	Muni State	3.40	4.83	5.73	1.00	3.00	.75	.50	800 423-4026
First Investors MO Ins Tax Free A	Muni State	3.70	4.97	5.97	1.00	3.00	.75	.47	800 423-4026
First Investors NC Ins Tax Free A	Muni State	3.30	5.05	6.11	1.00	3.00	.75	.44	800 423-4026
First Investors OR Ins Tax Free A	Muni State	3.90	4.91	5.85	1.00	3.00	.75	.50	800 423-4026
First Investors PA Ins Tax Free A	Muni State	2.90	4.33	5.39	1.00	3.00	.75	.83	800 423-4026
First Investors US Govt Plus I	Government	3.20	5.83	5.00	4.00	4.00	.29	1.28	800 423-4026
First Investors VA Ins Tax Free A	Muni State	3.20	4.48	5.38	1.00	3.00	.75	.80	800 423-4026
First Omaha Fixed Income Fund	Corp-Inv	1.40	4.42	4.69	4.00	4.00	.55	1.05	800 662-4203
First Omaha Sh-Inter Fixed Inc	Corp-Inv	3.00	4.33	4.63	4.00	2.00	.50	1.12	800 662-4203
Firstar Bond IMMDEX Inst	Corp-Inv	5.00	6.10	6.19	2.00	3.00	.29	.46	800 982-8909
Firstar Bond IMMDEX Ret A	Corp-Inv	4.70	5.83	5.92	2.00	3.00	.29	.70	800 982-8909
Firstar Bond IMMDEX Retail B	Corp-Inv	3.40					.29	1.53	800 982-8909
Firstar Interm Bond Mkt Inst	Corp-Inv	4.70	5.57	5.75	2.00	2.00	.50	.55	800 982-8909
Firstar Interm Bond Mkt Ret	Corp-Inv	4.40	5.31	5.51	2.00	2.00	.50	.80	800 982-8909
Firstar Intmed Bond Mkt Retail B	Corp-Inv	2.30					.50	1.61	800 982-8909
Firstar Short Term Bond Mkt Inst	Corp-Inv	4.90	5.47	5.65	1.00	1.00	.59	.55	800 982-8909
Firstar Short Term Bond Mkt Ret A	Corp-Inv	4.70	5.21	5.41	2.00	1.00	.59	.80	800 982-8909
Firstar Short-Term Bond Mkt Ret B	Corp-Inv	3.50					.59	1.61	800 982-8909
Firstar Stellar Strategic Income B	Dvsfd Bond	.30	.59	3.02	4.00	4.00	.94	1.26	800 677-3863
Firstar Stellar US Govt Income A	Government	3.30	4.78	4.93	4.00	3.00	.59	.91	800 677-3863
Firstar Tax Exmpt Intmed Bond Ret B	Muni Natl	1.60					.50		800 982-8909
Firstar Tax-Exempt Inter Bd Inst	Muni Natl	2.70	3.78	4.27	2.00	1.00	.50	.60	800 982-8909
Firstar Tax-Exempt Inter Bd Ret A	Muni Natl	2.40	3.52	4.02	3.00	1.00	.50	.85	800 982-8909
Flag Investors Mgd Muni Fd A	Muni Natl	2.60	4.04	5.02	3.00	4.00	.40	.90	800 767-3524
Flag Investors Sh-Int Term Inc A	Corp-Inv	4.10	5.00	5.48	3.00	2.00	.11	.69	800 767-3524
Flag Investors Sht Intmed Inc Instl	Corp-Inv	4.40	5.28		2.00	2.00	.11	.45	800 767-3524
Flag Investors Tot Return UST A	Government	5.60	6.66	5.89	3.00	4.00	.27	1.18	800 767-3524
Flex Fund-U.S. Government Bond	Government	4.00	6.46	5.22	3.00	4.00	.40	1.00	800 325-3539
Fortis Advantage-High Yield A	Corp-HY	-.60	1.69	4.69	3.00	4.00	.71	1.15	800 800-2000
Fortis Advantage-High Yield B	Corp-HY	-1.30	1.00	4.02	4.00	4.00	.71	1.81	800 800-2000
Fortis Advantage-High Yield C	Corp-HY	-1.30	1.01	4.00	4.00	4.00	.71	1.81	800 800-2000
Fortis Advantage-High Yield H	Corp-HY	-1.30	1.05	4.03	4.00	4.00	.71	1.81	800 800-2000
Fortis Strategic Income Fund A	Corp-Inv	2.80					.80	1.10	800 800-2000

Bond Fund Name	Objective	Annualized Return for			Rank		Max Load	Expense Ratio	Toll-Free Telephone
		1 Year	3 Years	5 Years	Overall	Risk			
Fortis Strategic Income Fund B	Corp-Inv	2.00					.80	1.85	800 800-2000
Fortis Strategic Income Fund C	Corp-Inv	2.00					.80	1.85	800 800-2000
Fortis Strategic Income Fund H	Corp-Inv	1.90					.80	1.85	800 800-2000
Fortis Tax-Free MN A	Muni State	1.80	3.53	4.38	3.00	3.00	.71	1.10	800 800-2000
Fortis Tax-Free MN B	Muni State	1.10	2.78	3.60	3.00	3.00	.71	1.86	800 800-2000
Fortis Tax-Free MN C	Muni State	1.10	2.78	3.61	3.00	3.00	.71	1.86	800 800-2000
Fortis Tax-Free MN E	Muni State	2.10	3.79	4.63	2.00	3.00	.71	.85	800 800-2000
Fortis Tax-Free MN H	Muni State	1.20	2.26	3.28	3.00	3.00	.71	1.86	800 800-2000
Fortis Tax-Free National A	Muni Natl	2.20	3.51	4.67	3.00	3.00	.77	1.18	800 800-2000
Fortis Tax-Free National B	Muni Natl	1.30	2.72	3.87	4.00	3.00	.77	1.93	800 800-2000
Fortis Tax-Free National C	Muni Natl	1.30	2.69	3.82	4.00	3.00	.77	1.93	800 800-2000
Fortis Tax-Free National E	Muni Natl	2.30	3.73	4.89	3.00	3.00	.77	.93	800 800-2000
Fortis Tax-Free National H	Muni Natl	1.30	2.66	3.81	4.00	3.00	.77	1.93	800 800-2000
Fortis US Govt Securities A	Government	3.30	4.95	5.29	3.00	3.00	.70	1.03	800 800-2000
Fortis US Govt Securities B	Government	2.60	4.16	4.49	4.00	3.00	.70	1.78	800 800-2000
Fortis US Govt Securities C	Government	2.70	4.20	4.52	4.00	3.00	.70	1.78	800 800-2000
Fortis US Govt Securities E	Government	3.60	5.17	5.53	3.00	3.00	.70	.78	800 800-2000
Fortis US Govt Securities H	Government	2.60	4.16	4.50	4.00	3.00	.70	1.78	800 800-2000
Forum Investors Bond	Corp-Inv	.10	3.65	5.37	2.00	3.00	.40	.69	800 943-6786
Forum Investors High Grade Bond	Corp-Inv	3.10					1.00	.69	800 943-6786
Forum Maine Municipal Bond	Muni State	3.20	4.12	4.85	2.00	2.00	.40	.59	800 943-6786
Forum New Hampshire Bond	Muni State	2.90	4.25	4.83	2.00	2.00	.40	.59	800 943-6786
Forum Taxsaver Bond	Muni Natl	2.20	3.58	4.68	2.00	2.00	.40	.71	800 943-6786
Franklin AGE High Income A	Corp-HY	-2.50	2.19	6.37	4.00	5.00	.46	.71	800 342-5236
Franklin AGE High Income Adv	Corp-HY	-2.40	2.30		5.00	5.00	.46	.58	800 342-5236
Franklin AGE High Income B	Corp-HY	-3.00					.46	1.23	800 342-5236
Franklin AGE High Income C	Corp-HY	-3.00	1.85	5.89	4.00	5.00	.46	1.23	800 342-5236
Franklin AZ Ins Tax-Free Inc A	Muni State	.80	3.81	5.40	3.00	4.00	.63	.36	800 342-5236
Franklin Adjustable US Govt Sec A	Govt-Mtg	4.90	4.72	5.57	2.00	1.00	.50	.95	800 342-5236
Franklin Alabama Tax-Free Inc A	Muni State	.70	3.08	4.68	3.00	3.00	.56	.70	800 342-5236
Franklin Alabama Tax-Free Inc C	Muni State	0.00	2.53	4.15	4.00	3.00	.56	1.27	800 342-5236
Franklin Arizona Tax-Free Inc A	Muni State	.70	3.47	4.69	3.00	3.00	.47	.63	800 342-5236
Franklin Arizona Tax-Free Inc C	Muni State	.10	2.91	4.16	4.00	3.00	.47	1.18	800 342-5236
Franklin CT Tax-Free Inc A	Muni State	-.60	3.13	4.66	3.00	3.00	.56	.71	800 342-5236
Franklin CT Tax-Free Inc C	Muni State	-1.10	2.54	4.08	5.00	3.00	.56	1.28	800 342-5236
Franklin California H/Y Muni A	Muni CA	-1.90	3.76	5.75	3.00	4.00	.16	.44	800 342-5236
Franklin California H/Y Muni C	Muni CA	-2.40	3.26		3.00	4.00	.16	.98	800 342-5236
Franklin California Ins Tax-Free A	Muni CA	2.20	4.39	5.35	2.00	3.00	.46	.59	800 342-5236
Franklin California Ins Tax-Free C	Muni CA	1.60	3.83	4.81	3.00	3.00	.46	1.15	800 342-5236
Franklin California Inter Tax-Free	Muni CA	3.90	4.73	5.93	1.00	2.00	.61	.59	800 342-5236
Franklin California Tx-Fr Inc A	Muni CA	1.40	4.13	5.28	3.00	3.00	.45	.56	800 342-5236
Franklin California Tx-Fr Inc B	Muni CA	.80					.45	1.13	800 342-5236
Franklin California Tx-Fr Inc C	Muni CA	.80	3.56	4.70	2.00	3.00	.45	1.13	800 342-5236
Franklin Colorado Tax-Free Inc A	Muni State	.80	3.61	4.99	3.00	3.00	.56	.69	800 342-5236
Franklin Colorado Tax-Free Inc C	Muni State	.20	3.04	4.46	4.00	3.00	.56	1.26	800 342-5236
Franklin FL Ins Tax-Free Inc A	Muni State	1.40	4.39	5.57	3.00	4.00	.63	.41	800 342-5236
Franklin Federal Interm Tax-Free A	Muni Natl	1.10	3.71	4.88	3.00	2.00	.63	.75	800 342-5236
Franklin Federal Tax-Free Inc A	Muni Natl	1.50	4.12	5.33	1.00	2.00	.46	.59	800 342-5236
Franklin Federal Tax-Free Inc B	Muni Natl	1.00					.46	1.16	800 342-5236
Franklin Federal Tax-Free Inc C	Muni Natl	1.00	3.49	4.71	3.00	2.00	.46	1.16	800 342-5236
Franklin Florida Tax-Free Inc A	Muni State	1.30	3.94	4.94	3.00	3.00	.46	.60	800 342-5236
Franklin Florida Tax-Free Inc C	Muni State	.70	3.38	4.38	4.00	3.00	.46	1.16	800 342-5236
Franklin Georgia Tax-Free Inc A	Muni State	1.40	3.65	4.76	3.00	3.00	.58	.76	800 342-5236
Franklin Georgia Tax-Free Inc C	Muni State	.80	2.99	4.15	4.00	3.00	.58	1.31	800 342-5236
Franklin Global Government Inc A	Intl Bond	2.40	2.97	5.65	5.00	5.00	.59	1.10	800 342-5236
Franklin Global Government Inc Adv	Intl Bond	2.60	3.10		5.00	5.00	.59	.97	800 342-5236
Franklin Global Government Inc C	Intl Bond	1.90	2.47	5.11	5.00	5.00	.59	1.62	800 342-5236
Franklin High Yield Tax-Free Inc A	Muni Natl	-1.20	3.33	5.21	3.00	3.00	.46	.61	800 342-5236

Bond Fund Name	Objective	Annualized Return for			Rank		Max Load	Expense Ratio	Toll-Free Telephone
		1 Year	3 Years	5 Years	Overall	Risk			
Franklin High Yield Tax-Free Inc B	Muni Natl	-1.70					.46	1.17	800 342-5236
Franklin High Yield Tax-Free Inc C	Muni Natl	-1.70	2.80	4.68	3.00	3.00	.46	1.17	800 342-5236
Franklin Insured Tax-Free Inc A	Muni Natl	1.70	4.00	4.88	2.00	3.00	.46	.61	800 342-5236
Franklin Insured Tax-Free Inc C	Muni Natl	1.20	3.48	4.37	3.00	3.00	.46	1.17	800 342-5236
Franklin Kentucky Tax-Free Inc A	Muni State	.30	3.74	5.27	3.00	3.00	.63	.41	800 342-5236
Franklin Louisiana Tax-Free Inc A	Muni State	.90	3.66	5.00	3.00	3.00	.60	.75	800 342-5236
Franklin Louisiana Tax-Free Inc C	Muni State	.40	3.10	4.47	4.00	3.00	.60	1.31	800 342-5236
Franklin MA Ins Tax-Free A	Muni State	1.60	3.92	4.89	3.00	3.00	1.00	1.23	800 342-5236
Franklin MA Ins Tax-Free C	Muni State	1.00	3.34	4.33	4.00	3.00	1.00	1.23	800 342-5236
Franklin MI Ins Tax-Free Inc A	Muni State	2.30	4.56	5.24	1.00	3.00	.46	.63	800 342-5236
Franklin MI Ins Tax-Free Inc C	Muni State	1.70	3.96	4.67	2.00	3.00	.46	1.18	800 342-5236
Franklin MN Ins Tax-Free Inc A	Muni State	1.30	3.61	4.49	3.00	3.00	.50	.67	800 342-5236
Franklin MN Ins Tax-Free Inc C	Muni State	.70	3.02	3.93	4.00	3.00	.50	1.22	800 342-5236
Franklin Maryland Tax-Free Inc A	Muni State	1.00	3.81	5.12	3.00	3.00	.56	.73	800 342-5236
Franklin Maryland Tax-Free Inc C	Muni State	.50	3.36	4.53	4.00	3.00	.56	1.29	800 342-5236
Franklin Missouri Tax-Free Inc A	Muni State	.80	3.68	5.02	3.00	3.00	.55	.69	800 342-5236
Franklin Missouri Tax-Free Inc C	Muni State	.30	3.12	4.45	4.00	3.00	.50	1.25	800 342-5236
Franklin NC Tax-Free Inc A	Muni State	1.00	3.69	4.91	3.00	3.00	.55	.69	800 342-5236
Franklin NC Tax-Free Inc C	Muni State	.50	3.17	4.39	4.00	3.00	.55	1.25	800 342-5236
Franklin NY Ins Tax-Free Inc A	Muni NY	1.50	4.11	5.22	1.00	3.00	.55	.71	800 342-5236
Franklin NY Ins Tax-Free Inc C	Muni NY	1.10	3.46	4.66	3.00	3.00	.55	1.26	800 342-5236
Franklin NY Interm Tax-Free A	Muni NY	3.30	4.66	5.58	1.00	3.00	.63	.45	800 342-5236
Franklin New Jersey Tax-Free Inc A	Muni State	1.40	4.08	5.07	2.00	3.00	.48	.65	800 342-5236
Franklin New Jersey Tax-Free Inc C	Muni State	.90	3.51	4.53	3.00	3.00	.48	1.20	800 342-5236
Franklin New York Tax-Free Inc A	Muni NY	2.30	4.83	5.60	1.00	3.00	.46	.58	800 342-5236
Franklin New York Tax-Free Inc B	Muni NY	1.70					.46		800 342-5236
Franklin New York Tax-Free Inc C	Muni NY	1.70	4.23	5.00	1.00	3.00	.46	1.15	800 342-5236
Franklin Ohio Ins Tax-Free Inc A	Muni State	1.90	4.13	5.06	1.00	3.00	1.00	1.20	800 342-5236
Franklin Ohio Ins Tax-Free Inc C	Muni State	1.30	3.59	4.56	3.00	3.00	1.00	1.20	800 342-5236
Franklin Oregon Tax-Free Inc A	Muni State	1.40	3.67	4.82	3.00	3.00	.52	.67	800 342-5236
Franklin Oregon Tax-Free Inc C	Muni State	.80	3.10	4.85	3.00	3.00	.52	1.22	800 342-5236
Franklin PA Tax-Free Inc A	Muni State	.90	3.73	4.92	3.00	3.00	.48	.65	800 342-5236
Franklin PA Tax-Free Inc C	Muni State	.40	3.20	4.39	4.00	3.00	.48	1.20	800 342-5236
Franklin PR Tax-Free Inc A	Muni State	1.40	4.18	5.34	2.00	3.00	.56	.73	800 342-5236
Franklin PR Tax-Free Inc C	Muni State	.80	3.63	4.74	3.00	3.00	.56	1.30	800 342-5236
Franklin Short-Int US Govt Sec A	Government	4.20	4.76	4.91	3.00	1.00	.56	.79	800 342-5236
Franklin Short-Int US Govt Sec Adv	Government	4.00	4.72		2.00	1.00	.56	.68	800 342-5236
Franklin Strategic Income A	Dvsfd Bond	2.00	4.21	8.18	3.00	5.00	.55	.57	800 342-5236
Franklin Strategic Income B	Dvsfd Bond	1.50					.55	.97	800 342-5236
Franklin Strategic Mortgage A	Govt-Mtg	5.10	5.89	6.49	1.00	2.00	.40	.81	800 342-5236
Franklin Templeton Global Currency	Intl Bond	-2.20	-.08	-.50	5.00	4.00	.65	1.12	800 342-5236
Franklin Templeton Hard Curr A	Intl Bond	-1.40	-2.18	-5.04	5.00	5.00	.65	1.11	800 342-5236
Franklin Templeton Hard Curr Adv	Intl Bond	-1.20	-1.96		5.00	5.00	.65	1.06	800 342-5236
Franklin Tennessee Muni Bond A	Muni State	-.50	3.63	5.28	4.00	4.00	.63	.40	800 342-5236
Franklin Texas Tax-Free Inc A	Muni State	-1.00	2.86	4.45	3.00	3.00	.59	.77	800 342-5236
Franklin Texas Tax-Free Inc C	Muni State	-1.40	2.52	4.25	4.00	3.00	.59	1.33	800 342-5236
Franklin US Government Sec A	Govt-Mtg	4.80	5.34	6.10	1.00	2.00	.45	.66	800 342-5236
Franklin US Government Sec Adv	Govt-Mtg	5.10	5.25		1.00	2.00	.45	.56	800 342-5236
Franklin US Government Sec B	Govt-Mtg	5.10					.45	1.22	800 342-5236
Franklin US Government Sec C	Govt-Mtg	4.20	4.74	6.61	1.00	2.00	.45	1.21	800 342-5236
Franklin Virginia Tax-Free Inc A	Muni State	1.30	3.79	4.86	3.00	3.00	.54	.68	800 342-5236
Franklin Virginia Tax-Free Inc C	Muni State	.70	3.26	4.36	4.00	3.00	.54	1.23	800 342-5236
Fremont Bond Fund	Corp-Inv	5.50	6.46	7.18	1.00	3.00	.40	.56	800 548-4539
Fremont CA Intermediate Tx Fr	Muni CA	4.00	4.43	5.15	1.00	2.00	.29	.46	800 548-4539
Frontegra Total Return Bond	Dvsfd Bond	6.80	6.60		1.00	3.00	.50	.50	888 825-2100
GE Fixed Income Fund A	Corp-Inv	3.70	4.80	5.19	3.00	3.00	.34	1.05	800 242-0134
GE Fixed Income Fund B	Corp-Inv	2.70	4.14	4.60	3.00	3.00	.34	1.55	800 242-0134
GE Fixed Income Fund Y	Corp-Inv	3.70	5.14	5.60	2.00	3.00	.34	.55	800 242-0134

414

Bond Fund Name	Objective	Annualized Return for			Rank		Max Load	Expense Ratio	Toll-Free Telephone
		1 Year	3 Years	5 Years	Overall	Risk			
GE Government Secs Fund A	Government	3.90	5.33	5.45	3.00	3.00	.40	1.10	800 242-0134
GE Government Secs Fund B	Government	3.10	4.69	4.74	4.00	3.00	.40	1.60	800 242-0134
GE High Yield A	Corp-HY	1.50					.59	1.19	800 242-0134
GE High Yield B	Corp-HY	.80					.59	1.69	800 242-0134
GE High Yield Y	Corp-HY	1.80					.59	.69	800 242-0134
GE Institutional Income	Corp-Inv	4.50					.34	.30	800 242-0134
GE S&S Long Term Bond	Corp-Inv	4.00	5.58	6.17	2.00	2.00	.05	.08	800 242-0134
GE S&S Short Term Bond	Government	-9.40	.20	2.30	4.00	5.00	.29	.94	800 242-0134
GE Short-Term Government B	Government	3.60	4.35	4.53	3.00	1.00	.29	1.30	800 242-0134
GE Short-Term Government Y	Government	4.60	5.29	5.48	2.00	1.00	.29	.75	800 242-0134
GE Tax Exempt Income Fund A	Muni Natl	2.70	3.23	3.48	3.00	3.00	.34	1.10	800 242-0134
GE Tax Exempt Income Fund B	Muni Natl	2.00	1.70	2.90	4.00	3.00	.34	1.60	800 242-0134
GE Tax Exempt Income Fund Y	Muni Natl	3.00	4.08	4.73	3.00	3.00	.34	.59	800 242-0134
GMO Tr Domestic Bond III	Government	3.70	4.40	5.15	4.00	4.00	.10	.25	
GMO Tr Emerging Country Debt III	Intl Bond	37.00	4.99	23.74	3.00	5.00	.34	.56	
GMO Tr Emerging Country Debt IV	Intl Bond	37.10					.29	.51	
GMO Tr Global Bond III	Intl Bond	3.20	3.47		4.00	5.00	.19	.34	
GMO Tr Inflation Indexed Bd III	Government	6.70	5.20		2.00	2.00	.10	.25	
GMO Tr International Bond III	Intl Bond	3.20	1.75	5.11	4.00	5.00	.25	.40	
GMO Tr US Bond Global Alpha A III	Intl Bond	4.60	2.41		4.00	5.00	.25	.40	
GMO Tr US Bond Global Alpha B III	Intl Bond	3.50					.20	.34	
Gabelli Westwood Interm Bond Ret	Corp-Inv	3.80	4.82	5.63	3.00	3.00	.59	1.06	800 422-3554
Galaxy CT Municipal Bond Inst	Muni State	3.00	4.37	5.32	2.00	3.00	.75	1.06	800 628-0414
Galaxy CT Municipal Bond Ret	Muni State	2.70	4.13	5.09	2.00	3.00	.75	1.27	800 628-0414
Galaxy High Quality Bond B	Government	3.20	4.66		4.00	4.00	.75	1.77	800 628-0414
Galaxy High Quality Bond Inst	Government	4.00	5.41	5.57	3.00	4.00	.75	1.03	800 628-0414
Galaxy High Quality Bond Ret A	Government	3.90	5.26	5.41	3.00	4.00	.75	.98	800 628-0414
Galaxy II-Municipal Bond Inv	Muni Natl	3.10	3.96	4.73	2.00	2.00	.25	.59	800 628-0414
Galaxy II-US Treasury Idx Inv	Government	5.00	6.13	5.85	3.00	3.00	.10	.40	800 628-0414
Galaxy Intermediate Bond Inst	Government	4.60	5.37	5.28	2.00	2.00	.75	.91	800 628-0414
Galaxy Intermediate Bond Ret	Government	4.20	5.06	4.99	3.00	2.00	.75	.96	800 628-0414
Galaxy MA Municipal Bond Ret	Muni State	2.30	3.96	4.93	2.00	3.00	.75	1.18	800 628-0414
Galaxy NY Muni Bond Inst	Muni NY	3.00	4.33	5.23	2.00	4.00	.55	.96	800 628-0414
Galaxy NY Muni Bond Ret	Muni NY	2.70	4.11	5.00	3.00	4.00	.55	1.16	800 628-0414
Galaxy Short Term Bond B	Corp-Inv	3.40	4.05		3.00	1.00	.75	2.02	800 628-0414
Galaxy Short Term Bond Inst	Corp-Inv	4.40	5.01	5.17	2.00	1.00	.75	1.05	800 628-0414
Galaxy Short Term Bond Ret	Corp-Inv	4.00	4.71	4.89	3.00	1.00	.75	1.31	800 628-0414
Galaxy Tax Exempt Bond B	Muni Natl	1.60	3.27		3.00	3.00	.75	1.75	800 628-0414
Galaxy Tax Exempt Bond Inst	Muni Natl	2.40	4.11	5.13	2.00	3.00	.75	.91	800 628-0414
Galaxy Tax Exempt Bond Ret	Muni Natl	2.20	3.88	4.80	2.00	3.00	.75	1.13	800 628-0414
Glenmede Core Fixed-Income Port	Government	4.20	6.07	6.13	2.00	3.00		.55	800 442-8299
Glenmede Intermediate Muni	Muni Natl	3.80	4.49	5.01	2.00	2.00		.17	800 442-8299
Glenmede NJ Muni Fund	Muni State	3.40	3.83	4.71	2.00	2.00		.23	800 442-8299
Goldman S. Adj Rate Govt Inst	Govt-Mtg	4.50	4.80	5.85	1.00	1.00	.40	.48	800 292-4726
Goldman S. Core Fixed Inc A	Corp-Inv	3.30	5.09		3.00	3.00	.40	.93	800 292-4726
Goldman S. Core Fixed Inc B	Corp-Inv	2.70	4.95		3.00	3.00	.40	1.68	800 292-4726
Goldman S. Core Fixed Inc C	Corp-Inv	2.60					.40	1.68	800 292-4726
Goldman S. Global Income A	Intl Bond	3.10	5.28	7.27	2.00	3.00	.90	1.34	800 292-4726
Goldman S. Global Income B	Intl Bond	2.60	4.70		2.00	3.00	.90	1.84	800 292-4726
Goldman S. Global Income C	Intl Bond	2.60					.90	1.84	800 292-4726
Goldman S. Government Income A	Government	3.70	4.63	5.34	3.00	3.00	.54	.97	800 292-4726
Goldman S. Government Income B	Government	3.00	3.87		4.00	3.00	.54	1.72	800 292-4726
Goldman S. Government Income C	Government	3.00					.54	1.72	800 292-4726
Goldman S. Government Income Inst	Government	4.00					.54	.57	800 292-4726
Goldman S. Government Income Svc	Government	4.00					.54	1.08	800 292-4726
Goldman S. High Yield A	Corp-HY	.70					.55	1.15	800 292-4726
Goldman S. High Yield B	Corp-HY	.10					.55	1.90	800 292-4726
Goldman S. High Yield C	Corp-HY	.10					.55	1.90	800 292-4726

Bond Fund Name	Objective	Annualized Return for			Rank		Max Load	Expense Ratio	Toll-Free Telephone
		1 Year	3 Years	5 Years	Overall	Risk			
Goldman S. Municipal Income A	Muni Natl	1.20	3.51	5.29	3.00	4.00	.55	.93	800 292-4726
Goldman S. Municipal Income B	Muni Natl	.40	3.65		4.00	4.00	.55	1.68	800 292-4726
Goldman S. Municipal Income C	Muni Natl	.40					.55	1.68	800 292-4726
Goldman S. Municipal Income Inst	Muni Natl	1.50					.55	.54	800 292-4726
Goldman S. Municipal Income Svc	Muni Natl	1.20					.55	1.04	800 292-4726
Goldman S. Short Dur Gov C	Govt-Mtg	3.20					.50	1.54	800 292-4726
Goldman S. Short Dur Gov Inst	Govt-Mtg	4.10	4.94	5.76	1.00	1.00	.50	.39	800 292-4726
Goldman S. Short Dur T/F C	Government	1.50					.40	1.54	800 292-4726
Goldman S. Short Dur T/F Inst	Muni Natl	2.60	3.68	4.17	1.00	1.00	.40	.39	800 292-4726
Government Street Bond Fund	Corp-Inv	3.60	4.72	5.15	3.00	2.00	.50	.72	800 543-8721
Governor Intermed Term Inc Ret	Corp-Inv	3.20	4.57		3.00	3.00	.29	.56	800 766-3960
Governor Ltd Dur Govt Secs Ret	Government	4.30	4.64		1.00	1.00	.59	.58	800 766-3960
Governor PA Muni Bond Ret	Muni State	2.00	3.24		3.00	2.00	.29	.58	800 766-3960
Govett Global Income Fund A	Intl Bond	-1.80	1.13	.90	5.00	4.00	.75	2.35	800 821-0803
Guardian Investment Quality Bond	Corp-Inv	3.40	5.01	5.37	3.00	2.00	.50	.80	800 221-3253
Guardian Tax-Exempt	Muni Natl	2.70	4.22	5.22	2.00	3.00	.50	.80	800 221-3253
HGK Fixed Income Fund	Dvsfd Bond	2.00	4.17	3.97	4.00	3.00	.25	1.00	877 362-4099
HSBC Fixed Income Fund	Corp-Inv	4.10	5.30	5.25	3.00	2.00	.55	.93	800 662-3343
HSBC NY Tax Free Bond Fund	Muni NY	1.90	3.99	5.24	1.00	3.00	.45	1.00	800 662-3343
Harbor Fund-Bond	Corp-Inv	4.70	6.38	7.18	2.00	3.00	.69	.60	800 422-1050
Harbor Fund-Short Duration	Corp-Inv	5.30	5.43	5.72	1.00	1.00	.40	.29	800 422-1050
Harris Insight Bond Fund A	Corp-Inv	4.10					.35	.84	800 982-8782
Harris Insight Bond Inst	Corp-Inv	4.50	5.63		2.00	3.00	1.00	.59	800 982-8782
Harris Insight Bond N	Corp-Inv	4.20	5.38		3.00	3.00	.80	.84	800 982-8782
Harris Insight Interm Govt Bd Inst	Government	4.90	5.35		1.00	2.00	1.00	.50	800 982-8782
Harris Insight Interm Govt Bd N	Government	4.70	5.09		2.00	2.00	.25	.75	800 982-8782
Harris Insight Intermed T/E Inst	Muni Natl	4.60	4.21		2.00	2.00	.59	.80	800 982-8782
Harris Insight Intermed T/E N	Muni Natl	4.30	3.98		2.00	2.00	.59	1.05	800 982-8782
Harris Insight Intmed Govt Bd A	Government	4.70					.23	.75	800 982-8782
Harris Insight Intmed TE Bond A	Muni Natl	.20					.59		800 982-8782
Harris Insight Short Intmed Bd A	Corp-Inv	3.80					.40		800 982-8782
Harris Insight Short/Int Bd Inst	Corp-Inv	4.60	5.15		2.00	2.00	.34	.59	800 982-8782
Harris Insight Short/Int Bd N	Corp-Inv	4.30	4.88	5.20	3.00	2.00	.69	.84	800 982-8782
Harris Insight Tax Exempt Bd Inst	Muni Natl	3.70	4.23		3.00	3.00	.59	.80	800 982-8782
Harris Insight Tax Exempt Bd N	Muni Natl	3.40	3.99		3.00	4.00	.59	1.05	800 982-8782
Harris Insight Tax Exempt Bnd A	Muni Natl						.59		800 982-8782
Hartford Bond Income Strategy Y	Corp-Inv	4.90	5.74		2.00	3.00	.65	.81	888 843-7824
Hartford Bond Strategy (The) A	Corp-Inv	4.40	5.28		3.00	3.00	.65	1.28	888 843-7824
Hartford Bond Strategy (The) B	Corp-Inv	3.70	4.54		3.00	3.00	.65	1.97	888 843-7824
Hartford Bond Strategy (The) C	Corp-Inv	3.70					.65	1.98	888 843-7824
Hartford High Yield B	Corp-HY	.40					.75	1.39	888 843-7824
Hartford High Yield C	Corp-HY	.40					.75	.93	888 843-7824
Hartford High Yield Fund B	Corp-HY	-.20					.75	2.10	888 843-7824
Hartford High Yield Fund C	Corp-HY	-.10					.75	2.10	888 843-7824
Heartland Government Fund	Government	-.90	3.61	4.62	4.00	3.00	.65	.80	800 432-7856
Heartland High Yield Muni Bd	Muni Natl	-4.20	3.12		2.00	3.00	.59	.94	800 432-7856
Heartland Sh Duration H/Y Muni	Muni Natl	-.40	2.90		3.00	1.00	.40	.73	800 432-7856
Heartland Taxable Sht Dur Muni Bond	Muni Natl	5.80					.59		800 432-7856
Heartland WI Tax Free Fund	Muni State	-.70	3.10	4.79	3.00	2.00	.65	.83	800 432-7856
Heritage Income Tr-High Yld Bd A	Corp-HY	-6.70	-.12	4.31	4.00	4.00	.59	1.18	800 421-4184
Heritage Income Tr-High Yld Bd B	Corp-HY	-7.20					.59	1.69	800 421-4184
Heritage Income Tr-High Yld Bd C	Corp-HY	-7.20	-.63	3.82	4.00	4.00	.59	1.69	800 421-4184
Heritage Income Tr-Intmed Govt A	Government	4.40	5.22	4.97	3.00	2.00	0.00	.92	800 421-4184
Heritage Income Tr-Intmed Govt B	Government	4.10					.59	1.19	800 421-4184
Heritage Income Tr-Intmed Govt C	Government	4.20	4.99	4.71	4.00	2.00	.50	1.19	800 421-4184
Hibernia LA Muni Income	Muni State	2.40	4.23	5.19	1.00	3.00	.36	.66	800 999-0124
Hibernia Total Return Bond Fund	Corp-Inv	3.30	4.68	4.91	4.00	3.00	.69	.95	800 999-0124
Hibernia US Government Income	Government	4.20	5.36	5.49	3.00	2.00	.39	.68	800 999-0124

Bond Fund Name	Objective	Annualized Return for			Rank		Max Load	Expense Ratio	Toll-Free Telephone
		1 Year	3 Years	5 Years	Overall	Risk			
Highmark Bond Fund Fid	Corp-Inv	3.90	5.39	5.55	3.00	3.00	.50	.75	800 433-6884
Highmark Bond Fund Inv	Corp-Inv	3.90	5.41	5.60	3.00	3.00	.50	.75	800 433-6884
Highmark CA Interm TF Bond B	Muni CA						.50		800 433-6884
Highmark CA TF Inter Fid	Muni CA	4.50	4.84	5.58	2.00	2.00	.50	.45	800 433-6884
Highmark CA TF Inter Ret A	Muni CA	4.40	4.71	5.52	2.00	2.00	.50	.45	800 433-6884
Highmark Intermed Bd Fid	Corp-Inv	4.10	5.24	5.20	3.00	2.00	.50	.75	800 433-6884
Highmark Intermed Bd Inv	Corp-Inv	4.10	5.28	5.33	3.00	2.00	.50	.75	800 433-6884
Homestead Funds-Short Term Bond	Corp-Inv	4.80	5.37	5.59	2.00	1.00	.47	.81	800 258-3030
Homestead Funds-Short Term Govt	Government	4.40	4.75	4.92	3.00	1.00	0.00	.90	800 258-3030
Hotchkis & Wiley Low Duration	Corp-Inv	5.40	5.26	6.20	1.00	1.00	.46	.57	800 236-4479
Hotchkis & Wiley Sh-Term Invest	Corp-Inv	4.80	5.48	5.88	1.00	1.00	.40	.47	800 236-4479
Hotchkis & Wiley Total Return Bd	Dvsfd Bond	2.60	5.27	6.64	3.00	3.00	.55	.65	800 236-4479
Huntington Fixed Income Inv	Corp-Inv	2.30	4.50	5.98	4.00	4.00	.50	.97	800 253-0412
Huntington Fixed Income Tr	Corp-Inv	2.60	5.09	5.26	4.00	4.00	.50	.72	800 253-0412
Huntington Int Govt Income Inv	Government	3.70	4.67	4.96	4.00	2.00	.45	.97	800 253-0412
Huntington Int Govt Income Tr	Government	4.00	4.89	5.17	2.00	2.00	.45	.72	800 253-0412
Huntington MI Tax Free Inv	Muni State	2.80	3.66	4.46	3.00	2.00	.55	.95	800 253-0412
Huntington MI Tax Free Tr	Muni State	3.00	3.91	4.66	2.00	2.00	.55	.70	800 253-0412
Huntington Mortgage Secs Inv	Govt-Mtg	3.80	5.14	6.58	2.00	2.00	.29	1.00	800 253-0412
Huntington Mortgage Secs Tr	Govt-Mtg	4.20	5.27	6.74	1.00	2.00	.29	.75	800 253-0412
Huntington OH Tax Free Inv	Muni State	3.00	3.58	3.93	3.00	2.00	.50	1.05	800 253-0412
Huntington OH Tax Free Tr	Muni State	3.30	3.98	4.34	2.00	2.00	.50	.80	800 253-0412
Huntington Short-Interm Income Tr	Corp-Inv	4.00	5.06	5.26	3.00	2.00	.50	.71	800 253-0412
IAA Trust Long-Term Bond Fund	Corp-Inv	4.20	5.79		1.00	3.00	.75	1.09	800 245-2100
IAA Trust Short-Term Govt Bond Fund	Government	4.40	4.78		2.00	1.00	.50	.90	800 245-2100
IAA Trust Tax Exempt Bond	Muni Natl	3.20	4.22	5.14	2.00	3.00	.50	1.07	800 245-2100
IAI Bond Fund	Corp-Inv	.90	3.57	4.93	3.00	3.00	1.07	1.10	800 945-3863
IAI Institutional Bond	Corp-Inv	2.30	4.05	5.03	4.00	3.00	.50	.50	800 945-3863
ICON Fds-S/T Fixed Income	Corp-Inv	3.80	4.61		1.00	1.00	.65	1.27	888 389-ICON
IDEX AEGON Income Plus A	Corp-HY	.80	3.75	5.87	3.00	3.00	.59	1.27	888 233-4339
IDEX AEGON Income Plus B	Corp-HY	.20	3.07		4.00	3.00	.59	1.91	888 233-4339
IDEX AEGON Income Plus C	Corp-HY						.59		888 233-4339
IDEX AEGON Income Plus M	Corp-HY	.20	3.17	5.26	3.00	3.00	.59	1.82	888 233-4339
IDEX JCC Flexible Income A	Corp-HY	3.00	5.68	6.76	1.00	3.00	.90	1.85	888 233-4339
IDEX JCC Flexible Income B	Corp-HY	2.30	4.97		1.00	3.00	.90	2.50	888 233-4339
IDEX JCC Flexible Income C	Corp-HY						.90		888 233-4339
IDEX JCC Flexible Income M	Corp-HY	2.40	5.07	6.15	1.00	3.00	.90	2.39	888 233-4339
ING High Yield Bond A	Corp-HY	4.90					.65	.98	877 463-6464
ING High Yield Bond B	Corp-HY	4.30					.65	1.70	877 463-6464
ING High Yield Bond C	Corp-HY	4.40					.65	1.75	877 463-6464
ING High Yield Bond X	Corp-HY	4.30					.65	1.72	877 463-6464
ING Intermediate Bond A	Dvsfd Bond	5.10					.50	.94	877 463-6464
ING Intermediate Bond B	Dvsfd Bond	4.20					.50	1.62	877 463-6464
ING Intermediate Bond C	Dvsfd Bond	4.30					.50	1.67	877 463-6464
ING Intermediate Bond X	Dvsfd Bond	4.30					.50	1.65	877 463-6464
ING International Bond A	Intl Bond	-3.90					1.00	1.47	877 463-6464
ING International Bond B	Intl Bond	-4.60					1.00	2.12	877 463-6464
ING International Bond C	Intl Bond	-4.60					1.00	2.20	877 463-6464
ING International Bond X	Intl Bond	-4.50					1.00	2.08	877 463-6464
INVESCO High Yield Ret	Corp-HY	1.80	5.71	9.00	2.00	5.00	.40	.47	800 525-8085
INVESCO High-Yield Fund C	Corp-HY						.40		800 525-8085
INVESCO Select Income Fund C	Dvsfd Bond						.50		800 525-8085
INVESCO Select Income Ret	Dvsfd Bond	2.80	5.18	6.37	2.00	3.00	.50	.52	800 525-8085
INVESCO Tax-Free Bond	Muni Natl	2.50	3.52	4.91	3.00	3.00	.55	.91	800 525-8085
INVESCO Tax-Free Bond C	Muni Natl						.55		800 525-8085
INVESCO US Government Securities C	Government						.55		800 525-8085
INVESCO US Govt Securities	Government	4.90	6.39	5.85	3.00	4.00	.55	1.01	800 525-8085
ISI Managed Municipal Fund	Muni Natl	2.60	4.04	5.04	3.00	4.00	.27	.90	800 882-8585

Bond Fund Name	Objective	Annualized Return for			Rank		Max Load	Expense Ratio	Toll-Free Telephone
		1 Year	3 Years	5 Years	Overall	Risk			
ISI North American Govt Bond	Government	6.10	7.11	7.40	2.00	4.00	.40	1.25	800 882-8585
ISI Total Return US Treasury	Government	5.50	6.67	5.90	3.00	4.00	.27	1.19	800 882-8585
Idaho Tax-Exempt Fund	Muni State	2.90	3.80	4.50	2.00	2.00	.46	.40	800 728-8762
Independence One Fixed Income	Corp-Inv	4.10	5.17		3.00	2.00	.75	1.03	800 622-4644
Intermediate Bd Fd Of America	Corp-Inv	4.90	5.22	5.47	3.00	2.00	.38	.35	800 421-9900
Investek Fixed Income	Corp-Inv	3.30	4.90	5.58	2.00	3.00	.45	.90	800 525-3863
Ivy Fund-Bond A	Corp-Inv	-4.40	-.49	3.65	5.00	4.00	.75	1.42	800 456-5111
Ivy Fund-Bond Adv	Corp-Inv	-4.10					.75	1.37	800 456-5111
Ivy Fund-Bond B	Corp-Inv	-5.10	-1.27	2.83	5.00	4.00	.75	2.33	800 456-5111
Ivy Fund-Bond C	Corp-Inv	-5.10	-1.22		5.00	4.00	.75	2.16	800 456-5111
Ivy Intl Strategic Bond A	Intl Bond	-2.00					.75		800 456-5111
Ivy Intl Strategic Bond Advisor	Intl Bond	1.20					.75		800 456-5111
Ivy Intl Strategic Bond B	Intl Bond	-5.60					.75		800 456-5111
Ivy Intl Strategic Bond C	Intl Bond	-5.60					.75		800 456-5111
Ivy Intl Strategic Bond I	Intl Bond	-4.80					.75		800 456-5111
J. Hancock Bond Fund A	Corp-Inv	3.40	5.04	5.85	2.00	3.00	.50	1.07	800 225-5291
J. Hancock Bond Fund B	Corp-Inv	2.60	4.31	5.11	4.00	3.00	.50	1.77	800 225-5291
J. Hancock CA Tax Free A	Muni CA	2.20	4.71	6.23	2.00	3.00	.55	.76	800 225-5291
J. Hancock CA Tax Free B	Muni CA	1.50	3.93	5.43	3.00	3.00	.55	1.51	800 225-5291
J. Hancock High Yield Bond A	Corp-HY	.30	1.74	7.39	2.00	5.00	.59	.97	800 225-5291
J. Hancock High Yield Bond B	Corp-HY	-.40	.95	6.52	4.00	5.00	.54	1.72	800 225-5291
J. Hancock High Yield Bond C	Corp-HY	-.40					.54	1.72	800 225-5291
J. Hancock High Yield T/F A	Muni Natl	-2.10	3.08	4.11	3.00	2.00	.57	1.00	800 225-5291
J. Hancock High Yield T/F B	Muni Natl	-2.80	2.32	3.33	4.00	2.00	.57	1.72	800 225-5291
J. Hancock Interm Govt A	Government	4.40	5.66	5.59	3.00	3.00	.40	1.03	800 225-5291
J. Hancock Interm Govt B	Government	3.70	4.82	4.77	3.00	2.00	.71	1.77	800 225-5291
J. Hancock MA Tax Free Income A	Muni State	1.10	4.21	5.43	3.00	3.00	.50	.70	800 225-5291
J. Hancock MA Tax Free Income B	Muni State	.40	3.48		3.00	3.00	.50	1.40	800 225-5291
J. Hancock NY Tax Free Income A	Muni NY	1.60	4.05	5.33	3.00	3.00	.50	.73	800 225-5291
J. Hancock NY Tax Free Income B	Muni NY	.90	3.36		4.00	3.00	.50	1.43	800 225-5291
J. Hancock Strategic Income A	Dvsfd Bond	3.10	5.77	8.51	2.00	4.00	.42	.89	800 225-5291
J. Hancock Strategic Income B	Dvsfd Bond	2.40	5.09	7.82	2.00	4.00	.46	1.59	800 225-5291
J. Hancock Strategic Income C	Dvsfd Bond	2.40					.42	1.59	800 225-5291
J. Hancock Tax Free Bond A	Muni Natl	1.50	4.03	5.65	3.00	3.00	.53	.85	800 225-5291
J. Hancock Tax Free Bond B	Muni Natl	.70	3.26	4.89	4.00	3.00	.53	1.61	800 225-5291
J.P. Morgan Bond Fund	Corp-Inv	3.50	4.84	5.42	2.00	3.00	.29	.68	800 766-7722
J.P. Morgan CA Bond Fund	Muni CA	4.00	4.33		1.00	2.00	.29	.86	800 766-7722
J.P. Morgan Emerging Mkts Debt	Intl Bond	25.00	3.48		4.00	5.00	.69	2.50	800 766-7722
J.P. Morgan Global Strategic Inc	Intl Bond	3.90					.45	1.57	800 766-7722
J.P. Morgan Instl-Bond Fd	Corp-Inv	5.10	5.50	5.90	1.00	2.00	.29	.50	800 766-7722
J.P. Morgan Instl-Bond Fund Ultra	Corp-Inv	3.80					.29	.35	800 766-7722
J.P. Morgan Instl-CA Bond Fd	Muni CA	4.40	4.57		1.00	2.00	.29	.70	800 766-7722
J.P. Morgan Instl-Glbl Strat Inc	Intl Bond	4.20	3.81		3.00	4.00	.45	.78	800 766-7722
J.P. Morgan Instl-NY Tax Exempt	Muni NY	3.30	4.11	4.91	2.00	2.00	.29	.50	800 766-7722
J.P. Morgan Instl-Sh Term Bd	Corp-Inv	4.30	5.15	5.49	1.00	1.00	.25	.52	800 766-7722
J.P. Morgan Instl-Tax Aware En Inc	Corp-HY	3.70					.25		800 766-7722
J.P. Morgan Instl-Tax Exempt Bd	Muni Natl	3.00	3.97	4.75	2.00	2.00	.29	.53	800 766-7722
J.P. Morgan NY Tax Exempt Bond	Muni NY	3.00	3.93	4.69	2.00	2.00	.29	.73	800 766-7722
J.P. Morgan Short Term Bond Fd	Corp-Inv	4.00	4.90	5.26	1.00	1.00	.25	.81	800 766-7722
J.P. Morgan Tax Exempt Bond Fd	Muni Natl	2.70	3.82	4.59	3.00	2.00	.29	.67	800 766-7722
JP Morgan Tx Aware Enhanced Inc Sel	Corp-HY	2.80					.25		800 766-7722
Janus Fd Inc-Federal Tax Ex	Muni Natl	0.00	3.16	4.91	4.00	4.00	.59	.66	800 525-3713
Janus Fd Inc-Flexible Income	Dvsfd Bond	1.80	5.67	7.24	2.00	3.00	.56	.81	800 525-3713
Janus Fd Inc-High-Yield Bond	Corp-HY	6.10	6.34		2.00	4.00	.75	1.02	800 525-3713
Janus Fd Inc-Short Term Bond	Corp-Inv	5.20	5.22	5.88	1.00	1.00	.65	.63	800 525-3713
John Hancock CA Tax-Free Income C	Muni CA	1.40					.55	1.61	800 225-5291
John Hancock Government Income C	Government	3.30					.63		800 225-5291
John Hancock High Yield Tax-Free C	Muni Natl	-2.80					.57	1.76	800 225-5291

418

Bond Fund Name	Objective	Annualized Return for			Rank		Max Load	Expense Ratio	Toll-Free Telephone
		1 Year	3 Years	5 Years	Overall	Risk			
John Hancock Intermediate Govt C	Government	3.60					.40	1.77	800 225-5291
John Hancock MA Tax-Free Income C	Muni State	.40					.50		800 225-5291
John Hancock NY Tax-Free Income C	Muni NY	.90					.50	1.43	800 225-5291
John Hancock Tax-Free Bond C	Muni Natl	.60					.53	1.70	800 225-5291
JohnsonFamily Intmed Fixed Income	Corp-Inv	2.80					.45	.84	
Kansas Insured Intermediate Fd	Muni State	1.60	2.78	3.86	3.00	1.00	.50	.75	800 276-1262
Kansas Municipal Fund	Muni State	.90	2.72	4.17	3.00	2.00	.29	.94	800 276-1262
Kemper Global Income A	Intl Bond	-.20	1.52	2.65	4.00	4.00	.75	1.71	800 621-1048
Kemper Global Income B	Intl Bond	-1.00	.79	1.91	5.00	4.00	.75	2.35	800 621-1048
Kemper Global Income C	Intl Bond	-1.10	.83	1.99	5.00	4.00	.75	2.20	800 621-1048
Kemper High Yield Fund A	Corp-HY	-2.20	2.41	6.46	2.00	5.00	.52	.10	800 621-1048
Kemper High Yield Fund B	Corp-HY	-3.00	1.60	5.59	4.00	5.00	.52	1.77	800 621-1048
Kemper High Yield Fund C	Corp-HY	-3.10	1.58	5.44	4.00	5.00	.52	1.71	800 621-1048
Kemper High Yield Opportunity A	Corp-HY	-4.70					.65	1.45	800 621-1048
Kemper High Yield Opportunity B	Corp-HY	-5.60					.65	2.27	800 621-1048
Kemper High Yield Opportunity C	Corp-HY	-5.60					.65	2.25	800 621-1048
Kemper Inc & Cap Preservation A	Corp-Inv	2.60	4.21	5.07	4.00	3.00	.54	1.00	800 621-1048
Kemper Inc & Cap Preservation B	Corp-Inv	1.60	3.29	4.09	4.00	3.00	.54	1.86	800 621-1048
Kemper Inc & Cap Preservation C	Corp-Inv	2.30	3.52	4.29	5.00	3.00	.54	1.80	800 621-1048
Kemper Municipal Bond Fund A	Muni Natl	2.40	4.11	5.42	2.00	3.00	.40	.68	800 621-1048
Kemper Municipal Bond Fund B	Muni Natl	1.50	3.26	5.70	3.00	3.00	.40	1.52	800 621-1048
Kemper Municipal Bond Fund C	Muni Natl	1.50	3.24	4.26	3.00	3.00	.40	1.54	800 621-1048
Kemper State Tax Free Inc-CA A	Muni CA	3.50	4.41	5.55	2.00	4.00	.55	.75	800 621-1048
Kemper State Tax Free Inc-CA B	Muni CA	2.70	3.60	4.72	3.00	4.00	.55	1.57	800 621-1048
Kemper State Tax Free Inc-CA C	Muni CA	3.00	3.41	4.46	4.00	4.00	.55	1.58	800 621-1048
Kemper State Tax Free Inc-FL A	Muni State	2.20	3.52	4.89	3.00	3.00	.55	.81	800 621-1048
Kemper State Tax Free Inc-FL B	Muni State	1.60	2.73	4.10	3.00	3.00	.55	1.62	800 621-1048
Kemper State Tax Free Inc-FL C	Muni State	1.50	2.74	4.05	4.00	3.00	.55	1.62	800 621-1048
Kemper State Tax Free Inc-NY A	Muni NY	2.40	3.94	5.16	3.00	4.00	.55	.83	800 621-1048
Kemper State Tax Free Inc-NY B	Muni NY	1.60	3.10	4.17	3.00	3.00	.55	1.64	800 621-1048
Kemper State Tax Free Inc-NY C	Muni NY	1.70	3.09	4.14	4.00	4.00	.55	1.64	800 621-1048
Kemper State Tax Free Inc-OH A	Muni State	1.60	3.72	5.08	2.00	3.00	.55	.86	800 621-1048
Kemper State Tax Free Inc-OH B	Muni State	.70	3.00	4.32	3.00	3.00	.55	1.65	800 621-1048
Kemper State Tax Free Inc-OH C	Muni State	.70	2.95	4.27	4.00	3.00	.55	1.64	800 621-1048
Kemper Strategic Income A	Dvsfd Bond	-.30	2.31	4.98	4.00	5.00	.56	1.07	800 621-1048
Kemper Strategic Income B	Dvsfd Bond	-1.30	1.31	3.98	5.00	5.00	.56	2.08	800 621-1048
Kemper Strategic Income C	Dvsfd Bond	-1.00	1.51	4.05	5.00	4.00	.56	1.87	800 621-1048
Kemper U.S. Govt Securities A	Govt-Mtg	4.30	5.38	5.78	2.00	2.00	.41	.81	800 621-1048
Kemper U.S. Govt Securities B	Govt-Mtg	3.40	4.45	4.84	3.00	2.00	.41	1.71	800 621-1048
Kemper U.S. Mortgage Fund A	Govt-Mtg	3.90	5.20	5.59	2.00	2.00	.50	.96	800 621-1048
Kemper U.S. Mortgage Fund B	Govt-Mtg	2.90	4.23	4.66	3.00	2.00	.50	1.87	800 621-1048
Kemper U.S. Mortgage Fund C	Govt-Mtg	3.20	4.46	4.84	3.00	2.00	.50	1.66	800 621-1048
Kent Fds-Income Inst	Corp-Inv	2.80	5.31	5.64	3.00	4.00	.59	.82	800 633-5368
Kent Fds-Income Inv	Corp-Inv	2.50	5.00	5.01	4.00	4.00	.59	1.08	800 633-5368
Kent Fds-Intermediate Bond Inst	Corp-Inv	3.50	4.79	5.01	3.00	2.00	.55	.76	800 633-5368
Kent Fds-Intermediate Bond Inv	Corp-Inv	3.30	4.60	4.80	3.00	2.00	.55	1.01	800 633-5368
Kent Fds-Intermediate T/F Inst	Muni Natl	3.50	4.06	4.65	2.00	2.00	.50	.72	800 633-5368
Kent Fds-Intermediate T/F Inv	Muni Natl	3.10	3.80	4.39	3.00	2.00	.50	.97	800 633-5368
Kent Fds-MI Muni Ltd Mat Inst	Muni State	3.00	3.67	4.01	2.00	1.00	.45	.69	800 633-5368
Kent Fds-MI Muni Ltd Mat Inv	Muni State	2.80	3.54	3.87	2.00	1.00	.45	.84	800 633-5368
Kent Fds-Short Term Bond Inst	Corp-Inv	4.40	5.07	5.19	3.00	1.00	.50	.75	800 633-5368
Kent Fds-Short Term Bond Inv	Corp-Inv	4.40	4.99	5.05	3.00	1.00	.50	.90	800 633-5368
Kent Fds-Tax Free Income Inst	Muni Natl	3.00	4.12	4.92	2.00	3.00	.55	.81	800 633-5368
Kent Fds-Tax Free Income Inv	Muni Natl	2.80	3.77	4.69	2.00	3.00	.55	1.06	800 633-5368
LKCM Fixed Income Fund	Corp-Inv	3.90					.50	.95	800 688-5526
Lazard Bond Inst	Corp-Inv	2.80	4.14	5.03	3.00	2.00	.50	.73	800 823-6300
Lazard Bond Open	Corp-Inv	2.50	3.86		3.00	2.00	.50	1.12	800 823-6300
Lazard High Yield Port - Instl	Corp-HY	-4.90					.75	1.05	800 823-6300

419

Bond Fund Name	Objective	Annualized Return for			Rank		Max Load	Expense Ratio	Toll-Free Telephone
		1 Year	3 Years	5 Years	Overall	Risk			
Lazard High Yield Port - Open	Corp-HY	-5.10					.75	1.35	800 823-6300
Lazard Intl Fixed Income Inst	Intl Bond	1.70	1.16	.98	5.00	5.00	.75	1.05	800 823-6300
Lazard Intl Fixed Income Open	Intl Bond	1.50	.78		5.00	5.00	.75	1.77	800 823-6300
Lazard Strategic Yield Inst	Corp-HY	2.80	2.49	6.38	3.00	3.00	.75	.90	800 823-6300
Lazard Strategic Yield Open	Corp-HY	2.40	2.08		4.00	3.00	.75	1.25	800 823-6300
Lebenthal NJ Municipal Bond	Muni State	.90	4.28	5.84	3.00	4.00	.25	.69	800 221-5822
Lebenthal NY Muni Bond B	Muni NY	-.20					.23	1.55	800 221-5822
Lebenthal NY Municipal Bond A	Muni NY	.60	4.23	5.59	3.00	3.00	.23	.77	800 221-5822
Lebenthal Taxable Municipal Bond	Muni Natl	4.20	6.37	7.20	3.00	4.00	.25	.80	800 221-5822
Legg Mason Global Income Trust	Intl Bond	1.10	.54	2.79	4.00	5.00	.75	1.87	800 822-5544
Legg Mason High Yield Port Nav	Corp-HY	-12.30					.65	.81	800 822-5544
Legg Mason Invest Grade Inc Nav	Corp-Inv	4.50	4.83		2.00	4.00	.20	.45	800 822-5544
Legg Mason MD Tax-Free Inc Prim	Muni State	2.10	3.83	4.72	2.00	3.00	.26	.69	800 822-5544
Legg Mason PA Tax Free Inc Nav	Muni State	2.20					.26	.45	800 822-5544
Legg Mason PA Tax-Free Inc Prim	Muni State	1.80	4.00	4.84	2.00	3.00	.07	.69	800 822-5544
Legg Mason Tax Free Interm Inc	Muni Natl	3.20	3.73	4.23	2.00	2.00	.55	.69	800 822-5544
Legg Mason Tax Inc-High Yld Prim	Corp-HY	-3.10	3.65	8.13	3.00	5.00	.65	1.30	800 822-5544
Legg Mason Tax Inc-Inv Grd Prim	Corp-Inv	4.00	5.09	5.97	2.00	3.00	.59	1.00	800 822-5544
Legg Mason Tax Inc-USG Int Prim	Government	4.60	4.70	5.10	3.00	2.00	.34	1.00	800 822-5544
Legg Mason US Govt Intmed Term Nav	Government	9.50	6.45	6.41	3.00	3.00	.34	.46	800 822-5544
Lexington GNMA Income Fund	Govt-Mtg	3.50	6.17	6.64	3.00	2.00	.59	1.62	800 526-0056
Lexington Global Inc	Intl Bond	.40	3.32	7.24	3.00	5.00	1.00	1.89	800 526-0056
Liberty Stein Roe High-Yield Muni	Muni Natl	-.80	3.55	5.26	3.00	2.00	.55	.77	800 338-2550
Liberty-Colonial CA Tax Exempt A	Muni CA	3.10	4.63	6.02	3.00	4.00	.80	.89	800 345-6611
Liberty-Colonial CA Tax Exempt B	Muni CA	2.40	3.86	5.15	4.00	4.00	.80	1.63	800 345-6611
Liberty-Colonial CA Tax Exempt C	Muni CA	2.60					.80	1.34	800 345-6611
Liberty-Colonial CT Tax Exempt A	Muni State	2.80	4.49	5.76	1.00	3.00	.20	.78	800 345-6611
Liberty-Colonial CT Tax Exempt B	Muni State	2.00	3.72	4.89	2.00	3.00	.20	1.53	800 345-6611
Liberty-Colonial CT Tax Exempt C	Muni State	2.30					.51	1.22	800 345-6611
Liberty-Colonial FL Tax Exempt A	Muni State	1.60	3.89	5.13	3.00	4.00	.07	.93	800 345-6611
Liberty-Colonial FL Tax Exempt B	Muni State	.80	3.12	4.36	5.00	4.00	.07	1.68	800 345-6611
Liberty-Colonial FL Tax Exempt C	Muni State	1.10					.51	1.38	800 345-6611
Liberty-Colonial Fed Sec A	Government	2.20	4.78	5.01	4.00	4.00	.59	1.12	800 345-6611
Liberty-Colonial Fed Sec B	Government	1.40	4.00	4.23	4.00	4.00	.59	1.87	800 345-6611
Liberty-Colonial Fed Sec C	Government	1.60					.59	1.72	800 345-6611
Liberty-Colonial H/Y Muni A	Muni Natl	-3.60	2.58	4.60	4.00	3.00	.56	1.11	800 345-6611
Liberty-Colonial H/Y Muni B	Muni Natl	-4.30	1.82	3.83	3.00	3.00	.56	1.86	800 345-6611
Liberty-Colonial H/Y Muni C	Muni Natl	-4.10					.56	1.70	800 345-6611
Liberty-Colonial H/Y Secs A	Corp-HY	-1.30	4.09	7.72	3.00	5.00	.59	1.19	800 345-6611
Liberty-Colonial H/Y Secs B	Corp-HY	-2.00	3.31	6.78	3.00	5.00	.59	1.94	800 345-6611
Liberty-Colonial H/Y Secs C	Corp-HY	-1.90	3.46		4.00	5.00	.59	1.80	800 345-6611
Liberty-Colonial Income Fund A	Corp-Inv	1.40	4.77	5.76	2.00	3.00	.50	1.11	800 345-6611
Liberty-Colonial Income Fund B	Corp-Inv	.60	3.79	4.73	3.00	3.00	.50	1.86	800 345-6611
Liberty-Colonial Income Fund C	Corp-Inv	.80					.50	1.70	800 345-6611
Liberty-Colonial Interm T/E Fd A	Muni Natl	3.00	4.34	5.25	2.00	3.00	.55	.80	800 345-6611
Liberty-Colonial Interm T/E Fd B	Muni Natl	2.40	3.67	4.58	3.00	3.00	.55	1.44	800 345-6611
Liberty-Colonial Interm T/E Fd C	Muni Natl	2.80					.55	1.00	800 345-6611
Liberty-Colonial Interm US Govt A	Govt-Mtg	2.90	4.80	5.17	3.00	3.00	.59	1.12	800 345-6611
Liberty-Colonial Interm US Govt B	Govt-Mtg	2.10	3.85	4.29	4.00	3.00	.59	1.87	800 345-6611
Liberty-Colonial Interm US Govt C	Govt-Mtg	2.30					.59	1.72	800 345-6611
Liberty-Colonial MA Tax Exempt A	Muni State	1.90	3.94	5.33	3.00	3.00	.52	.92	800 345-6611
Liberty-Colonial MA Tax Exempt B	Muni State	1.20	3.02	4.46	4.00	3.00	.51	1.66	800 345-6611
Liberty-Colonial MA Tax Exempt C	Muni State	1.50					.51	1.37	800 345-6611
Liberty-Colonial MI Tax Exempt A	Muni State	.80	4.30	5.46	4.00	4.00	.52	1.00	800 345-6611
Liberty-Colonial MI Tax Exempt B	Muni State	0.00	3.38	4.60	5.00	4.00	.40	1.75	800 345-6611
Liberty-Colonial MI Tax Exempt C	Muni State	.30					.51	1.44	800 345-6611
Liberty-Colonial MN Tax Exempt A	Muni State	-1.10	3.41	4.98	4.00	4.00	.38	1.03	800 345-6611
Liberty-Colonial MN Tax Exempt B	Muni State	-1.80	2.50	4.13	5.00	4.00	.38	1.78	800 345-6611

Bond Fund Name	Objective	Annualized Return for			Rank		Max Load	Expense Ratio	Toll-Free Telephone
		1 Year	3 Years	5 Years	Overall	Risk			
Liberty-Colonial MN Tax Exempt C	Muni State	-1.50					.51	1.47	800 345-6611
Liberty-Colonial NC Tax Exempt A	Muni State	1.10	3.91	5.32	2.00	4.00	0.00	1.10	800 345-6611
Liberty-Colonial NC Tax Exempt B	Muni State	.40	3.14	4.56	4.00	4.00	0.00	1.85	800 345-6611
Liberty-Colonial NC Tax Exempt C	Muni State	.70					.51	1.55	800 345-6611
Liberty-Colonial NY Tax Exempt A	Muni NY	2.40	4.51	5.71	3.00	4.00	.59	.79	800 345-6611
Liberty-Colonial NY Tax Exempt B	Muni NY	1.70	3.58	4.84	4.00	4.00	.59	1.54	800 345-6611
Liberty-Colonial NY Tax Exempt C	Muni NY	2.00					.59	1.23	800 345-6611
Liberty-Colonial OH Tax Exempt A	Muni State	1.00	3.74	5.21	3.00	4.00	.46	.94	800 345-6611
Liberty-Colonial OH Tax Exempt B	Muni State	.30	2.84	4.34	5.00	4.00	.46	1.69	800 345-6611
Liberty-Colonial OH Tax Exempt C	Muni State	.60					.51	1.39	800 345-6611
Liberty-Colonial Sh Dur US Govt A	Government	3.90	4.57	5.13	2.00	1.00	.55	.80	800 345-6611
Liberty-Colonial Sh Dur US Govt B	Government	3.20	3.89	4.46	3.00	1.00	.55	1.44	800 345-6611
Liberty-Colonial Sh Dur US Govt C	Government	3.70	4.36	4.93	2.00	1.00	.55	1.00	800 345-6611
Liberty-Colonial Strategic Inc A	Dvsfd Bond	1.20	3.86	6.47	3.00	4.00	.63	1.17	800 345-6611
Liberty-Colonial Strategic Inc B	Dvsfd Bond	.40	3.08	5.79	3.00	4.00	.63	1.92	800 345-6611
Liberty-Colonial Strategic Inc C	Dvsfd Bond	.60	3.25		4.00	4.00	.63	1.78	800 345-6611
Liberty-Colonial Tax Exempt A	Muni Natl	-.30	3.83	4.92	4.00	4.00	.55	.97	800 345-6611
Liberty-Colonial Tax Exempt B	Muni Natl	-1.00	2.91	4.04	5.00	4.00	.55	1.72	800 345-6611
Liberty-Colonial Tax Exempt C	Muni Natl	-.80					.55	1.58	800 345-6611
Liberty-Colonial Tax Exempt Ins A	Muni Natl	2.90	4.44	5.32	3.00	4.00	.56	1.06	800 345-6611
Liberty-Colonial Tax Exempt Ins B	Muni Natl	2.10	3.54	4.46	4.00	4.00	.56	1.81	800 345-6611
Liberty-Colonial Tax Exempt Ins C	Muni Natl	2.40					.56	1.51	800 345-6611
Liberty-Crabbe Huson Contrar Inc A	Corp-Inv	4.20	7.33	7.04	3.00	4.00	.75	.80	800 345-6611
Liberty-Crabbe Huson OR T/E A	Muni State	1.70	3.09	3.96	4.00	4.00	.97	.97	800 345-6611
Limited Term New York Muni Fd A	Muni NY	2.20	4.21	5.03	1.00	2.00	.41	.76	800 525-7048
Limited Term New York Muni Fd B	Muni NY	1.40	3.20		2.00	1.00	.42	1.53	800 525-7048
Limited Term New York Muni Fd C	Muni NY	1.40	3.45		2.00	2.00	.42	1.51	800 525-7048
Lipper High Income Bond Prem	Corp-HY	2.90	5.07		3.00	4.00	.75	1.14	800 547-7379
Lipper High Income Bond Ret	Corp-HY	3.00	4.93		3.00	4.00	.75	1.39	800 547-7379
Lipper High Income Bond Retail	Corp-HY	2.40	4.73		3.00	4.00	.75	1.39	800 547-7379
Loomis Sayles Bond Inst	Corp-Inv	3.70	6.41	9.27	3.00	5.00	.59	.72	800 626-9390
Loomis Sayles Bond Ret	Corp-Inv	3.40	6.13		3.00	5.00	.59	1.00	800 626-9390
Loomis Sayles Global Bond Inst	Intl Bond	-1.90	3.74	9.16	4.00	5.00	.59	.90	800 626-9390
Loomis Sayles Global Bond Ret	Intl Bond	-2.10	3.45		3.00	5.00	.59	1.14	800 626-9390
Loomis Sayles High Yield Inst	Corp-HY	9.00	6.16		3.00	5.00	.59	.75	800 626-9390
Loomis Sayles Interm Mty Bd Inst	Dvsfd Bond	4.60	4.57		2.00	2.00	.40	.55	800 626-9390
Loomis Sayles Interm Mty Bd Ret	Dvsfd Bond	4.40	4.29		1.00	2.00	.40	.80	800 626-9390
Loomis Sayles Invstmnt Gr Bd Inst	Corp-Inv	3.90	6.39		2.00	5.00	.40	.55	800 626-9390
Loomis Sayles Invstmnt Gr Bd Ret	Corp-Inv	3.70	6.15		3.00	5.00	.40	.80	800 626-9390
Loomis Sayles Muni Bond Inst	Muni Natl	2.40	4.19	5.28	2.00	4.00	.40	.56	800 626-9390
Loomis Sayles Sh-Term Bond Inst	Corp-Inv	4.60	5.29	5.48	2.00	2.00	.25	.50	800 626-9390
Loomis Sayles Sh-Term Bond Ret	Corp-Inv	4.30	4.88		1.00	2.00	.25	.55	800 626-9390
Loomis Sayles US Govt Sec Inst	Government	6.30	7.15	6.79	3.00	4.00	.29	.54	800 626-9390
Lord Abbett Bond Debenture A	Corp-HY	3.00	5.01	7.89	1.00	4.00	.46	.88	888 522-2388
Lord Abbett Bond Debenture B	Corp-HY	2.40	4.30		2.00	4.00	.46	1.56	888 522-2388
Lord Abbett Bond Debenture C	Corp-HY	2.50	4.31		3.00	4.00	.46	1.56	888 522-2388
Lord Abbett Bond Debenture P	Corp-HY	4.00					.46	.97	888 522-2388
Lord Abbett Bond Debenture Y	Corp-HY	3.20					.46	.57	888 522-2388
Lord Abbett Global-Income A	Intl Bond	-3.20	.76	2.80	5.00	4.00	.50	1.17	888 522-2388
Lord Abbett Global-Income B	Intl Bond	-3.70	.12		4.00	4.00	.50	1.89	888 522-2388
Lord Abbett Global-Income C	Intl Bond	-3.90	.11		4.00	4.00	.50	1.86	888 522-2388
Lord Abbett Global-Income P	Intl Bond	-3.60					.50	1.28	888 522-2388
Lord Abbett High Yield A	Corp-HY	2.40					.59	.29	888 522-2388
Lord Abbett High Yield B	Corp-HY	1.90					.59	.92	888 522-2388
Lord Abbett High Yield C	Corp-HY	2.00					.59	.92	888 522-2388
Lord Abbett High Yield Y	Corp-HY	3.00					.59		888 522-2388
Lord Abbett Invt Tr-US Govt A	Government	3.60	5.47	5.47	3.00	3.00	.50	1.02	888 522-2388
Lord Abbett Invt Tr-US Govt B	Government	2.80	4.83		3.00	3.00	.50	1.67	888 522-2388

421

Bond Fund Name	Objective	Annualized Return for			Rank		Max Load	Expense Ratio	Toll-Free Telephone
		1 Year	3 Years	5 Years	Overall	Risk			
Lord Abbett Invt Tr-US Govt C	Government	3.20	4.80		3.00	3.00	.50	1.62	888 522-2388
Lord Abbett Tax Free Inc-CA A	Muni CA	1.00	3.66	4.68	4.00	4.00	.50	.88	888 522-2388
Lord Abbett Tax Free Inc-CA C	Muni CA	.40	3.00		5.00	4.00	.50	1.58	888 522-2388
Lord Abbett Tax Free Inc-CT A	Muni State	.10	3.40	4.77	3.00	3.00	.25	.83	888 522-2388
Lord Abbett Tax Free Inc-FL A	Muni State	-.40	2.99	4.05	4.00	3.00	.50	.93	888 522-2388
Lord Abbett Tax Free Inc-FL C	Muni State	-.80	2.34		4.00	3.00	.50	1.58	888 522-2388
Lord Abbett Tax Free Inc-GA A	Muni State	2.80	4.96		2.00	4.00	.50	.20	888 522-2388
Lord Abbett Tax Free Inc-HI A	Muni State	.50	3.46	4.69	4.00	3.00	.50	.93	888 522-2388
Lord Abbett Tax Free Inc-MI A	Muni State	1.90	3.94	5.19	2.00	3.00	.50	.68	888 522-2388
Lord Abbett Tax Free Inc-MN A	Muni State	.60	3.55		3.00	3.00	.50	.22	888 522-2388
Lord Abbett Tax Free Inc-MO A	Muni State	1.20	3.60	4.69	3.00	3.00	.50	.93	888 522-2388
Lord Abbett Tax Free Inc-NJ A	Muni State	1.20	3.74	4.97	3.00	4.00	.50	.88	888 522-2388
Lord Abbett Tax Free Inc-NY A	Muni NY	1.00	3.67	4.63	3.00	3.00	.50	.85	888 522-2388
Lord Abbett Tax Free Inc-NY C	Muni NY	.50	3.02		4.00	3.00	.50	1.58	888 522-2388
Lord Abbett Tax Free Inc-Natl A	Muni Natl	.40	3.87	5.27	3.00	4.00	.50	.88	888 522-2388
Lord Abbett Tax Free Inc-Natl B	Muni Natl	-.20	3.36		4.00	4.00	.50	.71	888 522-2388
Lord Abbett Tax Free Inc-Natl C	Muni Natl	-.30	3.16		3.00	4.00	.50	1.60	888 522-2388
Lord Abbett Tax Free Inc-PA A	Muni State	1.20	4.02	5.12	3.00	3.00	.50	.88	888 522-2388
Lord Abbett Tax Free Inc-TX A	Muni State	-.70	2.97	4.73	4.00	4.00	.50	.92	888 522-2388
Lord Abbett Tax Free Inc-WA A	Muni State	.40	3.70	5.41	3.00	4.00	.50	.66	888 522-2388
Lord Abbett World Bond-Debenture A	Intl Bond	4.90					.75	.33	888 522-2388
Lord Abbett World Bond-Debenture B	Intl Bond	4.20					.75	.68	888 522-2388
Lord Abbett World Bond-Debenture C	Intl Bond	4.10					.75	.68	888 522-2388
Lutheran Brotherhood High Yld A	Corp-HY	.80	3.40	6.98	2.00	5.00	.34	.85	800 328-4552
Lutheran Brotherhood High Yld B	Corp-HY	.10					.34	1.61	800 328-4552
Lutheran Brotherhood High Yld Y	Corp-HY	2.00					.34	.60	800 328-4552
Lutheran Brotherhood Income A	Corp-Inv	3.60	5.00	5.26	3.00	3.00	.58	.81	800 328-4552
Lutheran Brotherhood Income B	Corp-Inv	2.80					.58	1.56	800 328-4552
Lutheran Brotherhood Income Y	Corp-Inv	4.00					.58	.56	800 328-4552
Lutheran Brotherhood Ltd Maturity A	Corp-HY						.29		800 328-4552
Lutheran Brotherhood Ltd Maturity B	Corp-HY						.29		800 328-4552
Lutheran Brotherhood Ltd Maturity Y	Corp-HY	2.40	.80	.47			.29		800 328-4552
Lutheran Brotherhood Muni A	Muni Natl	2.70	4.50	5.51	1.00	3.00	.32	.69	800 328-4552
Lutheran Brotherhood Muni B	Muni Natl	2.00					.32	1.44	800 328-4552
Lutheran Brotherhood Muni Y	Muni Natl	2.90					.32	.45	800 328-4552
MAS Domestic Fix Inc Instl	Corp-Inv	2.90	4.74	5.52	3.00	3.00	.35	.53	800 354-8185
MAS Fixed Income Instl	Corp-Inv	3.90	4.92	6.70	2.00	3.00	.37	.46	800 354-8185
MAS Fixed Income-II Instl	Corp-Inv	3.30	4.94	6.10	2.00	3.00	.37	.46	800 354-8185
MAS Global Fixed Income Instl	Intl Bond	.30	2.62	3.48	5.00	4.00	.37	.53	800 354-8185
MAS High Yield Secs Instl	Corp-HY	2.00	5.36	9.44	3.00	5.00	.38	.47	800 354-8185
MAS Interm Dur Fixed Income Instl	Dvsfd Bond	3.40	4.85	5.85	2.00	2.00	.23	.48	800 354-8185
MAS Intl Fixed Income Instl	Intl Bond	.30	1.87	2.09	5.00	5.00	.37	.52	800 354-8185
MAS Ltd Dur Fixed Income Instl	Corp-Inv	4.90	5.11	5.47	2.00	1.00	.29	.40	800 354-8185
MAS Municipal Instl	Muni Natl	2.60	4.30	6.53	3.00	4.00	.28	.51	800 354-8185
MAS Special Purpose Fix Inc Instl	Corp-HY	3.90	4.91	6.45	2.00	3.00	.37	.47	800 354-8185
MDL Broad Market Fixed Income	Corp-Inv	4.00					.45	.90	877 362-4099
MFS AL Municipal Bond Fund A	Muni State	2.40	4.02	5.19	2.00	3.00	.55	.94	800 343-2829
MFS AR Municipal Bond Fund A	Muni State	2.70	4.13	5.09	1.00	3.00	.55	.77	800 343-2829
MFS Bond Fund A	Corp-Inv	2.30	3.79	5.20	3.00	4.00	.38	.95	800 343-2829
MFS Bond Fund B	Corp-Inv	1.60	3.05	4.45	5.00	4.00	.38	1.65	800 343-2829
MFS Bond Fund C	Corp-Inv	1.50	6.08	4.46	5.00	5.00	.38	1.65	800 343-2829
MFS CA Municipal Bond Fund A	Muni CA	2.30	4.54	5.55	3.00	4.00	.55	1.56	800 343-2829
MFS FL Municipal Bond Fund A	Muni State	2.30	4.08	4.87	3.00	3.00	.55	.68	800 343-2829
MFS GA Municipal Bond Fund A	Muni State	2.30	3.83	4.92	2.00	3.00	.55	.96	800 343-2829
MFS Global Govts Fund A	Intl Bond	.30	1.11	1.84	4.00	4.00	.75	1.37	800 343-2829
MFS Global Govts Fund B	Intl Bond	-.50	.35	1.06	5.00	4.00	.75	2.12	800 343-2829
MFS Global Govts Fund C	Intl Bond	-.40	.38	1.10	4.00	4.00	.75	2.12	800 343-2829
MFS Government Ltd Maturity A	Government	4.40	4.94	5.07	2.00	1.00	.40	.81	800 343-2829

Bond Fund Name	Objective	Annualized Return for			Rank		Max Load	Expense Ratio	Toll-Free Telephone
		1 Year	3 Years	5 Years	Overall	Risk			
MFS Government Mortgage A	Govt-Mtg	5.10	5.01	5.44	3.00	2.00	.45	.93	800 343-2829
MFS Government Mortgage B	Govt-Mtg	4.20	4.25	4.70	3.00	2.00	.45	1.67	800 343-2829
MFS Government Securities A	Government	4.00	5.39	5.41	3.00	3.00	.40	.93	800 343-2829
MFS Government Securities B	Government	3.30	4.75	4.73	4.00	3.00	.40	1.59	800 343-2829
MFS Government Securities C	Government	3.30	4.70		3.00	3.00	.40	1.59	800 343-2829
MFS High Income Fund A	Corp-HY	1.80	4.91	7.92	3.00	5.00	.45	.98	800 343-2829
MFS High Income Fund B	Corp-HY	1.00	4.12	7.10	3.00	5.00	.45	1.68	800 343-2829
MFS High Income Fund C	Corp-HY	1.30	4.23	7.18	3.00	5.00	.45	1.68	800 343-2829
MFS Limited Maturity Fund A	Corp-Inv	4.00	4.34	4.98	2.00	1.00	.40	.83	800 343-2829
MFS Limited Maturity Fund B	Corp-Inv	3.30	3.51	4.08	3.00	1.00	.40	1.61	800 343-2829
MFS Limited Maturity Fund C	Corp-Inv	3.30	3.42	4.06	3.00	1.00	.40	1.68	800 343-2829
MFS MA Municipal Bond Fund A	Muni State	1.30	3.57	4.70	3.00	3.00	.55	1.00	800 343-2829
MFS MD Municipal Bond Fund A	Muni State	2.00	3.90	4.91	3.00	3.00	.55	1.03	800 343-2829
MFS MS Municipal Bond Fund A	Muni State	2.30	4.56	5.68	1.00	3.00	.55	.72	800 343-2829
MFS MS Municipal Bond Fund B	Muni State	1.50	3.74	4.83	3.00	3.00	.55	1.51	800 343-2829
MFS Municipal Bond A	Muni Natl	2.60	3.81	4.80	3.00	4.00	.39	.56	800 343-2829
MFS Municipal Bond B	Muni Natl	1.70	3.02	3.93	4.00	4.00	.39	1.37	800 343-2829
MFS Municipal High Income Fd A	Muni Natl	-.40	3.79	4.62	2.00	3.00	.60	.79	800 343-2829
MFS Municipal High Income Fd B	Muni Natl	-1.20	2.95	3.75	4.00	3.00	.60	1.61	800 343-2829
MFS Municipal Income Fund A	Muni Natl	1.60	4.20	4.97	2.00	3.00	.70	1.08	800 343-2829
MFS Municipal Income Fund B	Muni Natl	.90	3.41	4.16	4.00	3.00	.70	1.83	800 343-2829
MFS Municipal Income Fund C	Muni Natl	.90	3.41	4.20	3.00	3.00	.70	1.81	800 343-2829
MFS Municipal Lmtd Maturity A	Muni Natl	3.00	3.39	3.70	3.00	1.00	.40	.88	800 343-2829
MFS Municipal Lmtd Maturity B	Muni Natl	2.10	2.57	2.89	3.00	1.00	.40	1.65	800 343-2829
MFS Municipal Lmtd Maturity C	Muni Natl	2.20	2.55	2.85	4.00	1.00	.40	1.72	800 343-2829
MFS NC Municipal Bond Fund A	Muni State	1.50	3.65	4.82	3.00	3.00	.45	.97	800 343-2829
MFS NY Municipal Bond Fund A	Muni NY	2.40	4.13	5.22	2.00	4.00	.55	.93	800 343-2829
MFS PA Municipal Bond Fund A	Muni State	2.90	4.70	5.66	1.00	3.00	.55	.45	800 343-2829
MFS SC Municipal Bond Fund A	Muni State	1.20	3.44	4.60	3.00	3.00	.45	1.02	800 343-2829
MFS Strategic Income Fund A	Dvsfd Bond	4.60	3.59	6.46	3.00	5.00	1.15	.89	800 343-2829
MFS TN Municipal Bond Fund A	Muni State	1.40	3.76	4.90	3.00	3.00	.55	1.02	800 343-2829
MFS VA Municipal Bond Fund A	Muni State	1.90	3.79	4.64	3.00	3.00	.55	.98	800 343-2829
MFS WV Municipal Bond Fund A	Muni State	1.30	3.42	4.55	3.00	3.00	.55	1.02	800 343-2829
MMA Praxis Intermediate Income B	Corp-Inv	2.00	4.19	4.49	4.00	3.00	.33	1.12	800 977-2947
MSD & T Intermediate Tax Exempt Fd	Muni Natl	3.10					.22	.76	
MSD & T National Tax Exempt Bond Fd	Muni Natl	3.60					.22	.73	
MSD & T Total Return Bond Fund	Muni Natl	4.80					.22	.61	
MSDW CA-Tax Free Inc A	Muni CA	2.40					.53	.78	800 869-6397
MSDW CA-Tax Free Inc B	Muni CA	2.40	3.78	4.72	3.00	3.00	.53	.97	800 869-6397
MSDW CA-Tax Free Inc C	Muni CA	2.00					.53	1.33	800 869-6397
MSDW CA-Tax Free Inc D	Muni CA	2.70					.53	.57	800 869-6397
MSDW Diversified Inc A	Dvsfd Bond	-2.20					.40	.68	800 869-6397
MSDW Diversified Inc B	Dvsfd Bond	-2.70	.82	3.39	5.00	2.00	.40	1.37	800 869-6397
MSDW Diversified Inc C	Dvsfd Bond	-2.70					.40	1.37	800 869-6397
MSDW Diversified Inc D	Dvsfd Bond	-1.50					.40	.53	800 869-6397
MSDW Federal Sec Tr A	Government	3.60					.55	.86	800 869-6397
MSDW Federal Sec Tr B	Government	2.80	4.84	4.92	4.00	4.00	.55	1.54	800 869-6397
MSDW Federal Sec Tr C	Government	2.70					.55	1.54	800 869-6397
MSDW Federal Sec Tr D	Government	3.80					.55	.68	800 869-6397
MSDW Hawaii Municipal Tr	Muni State	.80	3.61	4.78	3.00	4.00	0.00	.48	800 869-6397
MSDW High Yield A	Corp-HY	-5.90					.50	.68	800 869-6397
MSDW High Yield B	Corp-HY	-6.40					.50	1.23	800 869-6397
MSDW High Yield C	Corp-HY	-6.70					.50	1.34	800 869-6397
MSDW High Yield D	Corp-HY	-5.70	.14	5.07	2.00	5.00	.50	.48	800 869-6397
MSDW Inst Muni Bond A	Muni Natl						.29	.46	800 548-7786
MSDW Inst-Emg Mkt Debt A	Intl Bond	24.10	-3.56	12.76	3.00	5.00	1.00	1.46	800 548-7786
MSDW Inst-Emg Mkt Debt B	Intl Bond	23.40	-3.75		3.00	5.00	1.00	1.71	800 548-7786
MSDW Inst-Fixed Inc A	Corp-Inv	3.90	4.83	5.72	2.00	3.00	.23	.46	800 548-7786

Bond Fund Name	Objective	Annualized Return for			Rank		Max Load	Expense Ratio	Toll-Free Telephone
		1 Year	3 Years	5 Years	Overall	Risk			
MSDW Inst-Fixed Inc B	Corp-Inv	4.00	4.76		3.00	3.00	.23	.60	800 548-7786
MSDW Inst-Global Fixed A	Intl Bond	-.30	2.57	3.79	5.00	4.00	.13	.50	800 548-7786
MSDW Inst-Global Fixed B	Intl Bond	-.40	2.38		5.00	4.00	.13	.65	800 548-7786
MSDW Inst-High Yield A	Corp-HY	1.30	5.41	9.33	2.00	5.00	.37	.61	800 548-7786
MSDW Inst-High Yield B	Corp-HY	1.10	4.92		3.00	5.00	.37	.86	800 548-7786
MSDW Int Income Sec A	Corp-Inv	.50					.59	.97	800 869-6397
MSDW Int Income Sec B	Corp-Inv	-.30	3.03	3.80	5.00	3.00	.59	1.72	800 869-6397
MSDW Int Income Sec C	Corp-Inv	-.20					.59	1.72	800 869-6397
MSDW Int Income Sec D	Corp-Inv	.60					.59	.88	800 869-6397
MSDW Limited Term Muni Tr	Muni Natl	3.00	3.63	4.46	3.00	2.00	.50	.85	800 869-6397
MSDW Multi State-AZ	Muni State	2.20	3.66	4.78	2.00	3.00	.34	.65	800 869-6397
MSDW Multi State-CA	Muni CA	2.30	4.27	5.72	2.00	3.00	.34	.60	800 869-6397
MSDW Multi State-FL	Muni State	2.50	4.14	5.15	1.00	3.00	.34	.61	800 869-6397
MSDW Multi State-MA	Muni State	1.80	3.91	5.14	1.00	3.00	.07	.81	800 869-6397
MSDW Multi State-MI	Muni State	1.50	3.86	5.22	1.00	3.00	.10	.80	800 869-6397
MSDW Multi State-MN	Muni State	.10	2.71	4.37	3.00	2.00	0.00	1.03	800 869-6397
MSDW Multi State-NJ	Muni State	1.40	4.01	5.15	1.00	3.00	.34	.68	800 869-6397
MSDW Multi State-NY	Muni NY	1.70	4.16	5.50	2.00	3.00	.01	.89	800 869-6397
MSDW Multi State-OH	Muni State	2.00	3.91	5.23	1.00	3.00	.08	.76	800 869-6397
MSDW Multi State-PA	Muni State	1.60	3.69	4.96	3.00	3.00	.34	.63	800 869-6397
MSDW NY-Tax Free Inc A	Muni NY	1.00					.55	.88	800 869-6397
MSDW NY-Tax Free Inc B	Muni NY	.60	3.28	4.41	5.00	3.00	.55	1.46	800 869-6397
MSDW NY-Tax Free Inc C	Muni NY	.70					.55	1.46	800 869-6397
MSDW NY-Tax Free Inc D	Muni NY	1.20					.55	.71	800 869-6397
MSDW North American Gov Inc Tr	Intl Bond	3.40	5.49	6.08	3.00	2.00	.65	1.79	800 869-6397
MSDW Sel Muni Reinvest	Muni Natl	1.80	3.52	4.72	4.00	3.00	.50	.93	800 869-6397
MSDW Sh-Term US Treasury	Government	3.70	4.83	4.85	3.00	1.00	.34	.80	800 869-6397
MSDW Short Term Bond	Corp-Inv	4.40	5.31	5.55	1.00	1.00	.23	.30	800 869-6397
MSDW Tax-Exempt Sec A	Muni Natl	2.40					.42	.64	800 869-6397
MSDW Tax-Exempt Sec B	Muni Natl	2.00					.42	1.10	800 869-6397
MSDW Tax-Exempt Sec C	Muni Natl	1.80					.42	1.19	800 869-6397
MSDW Tax-Exempt Sec D	Muni Natl	2.60	4.41	5.45	1.00	3.00	.42	.50	800 869-6397
MSDW US Govt Secs A	Govt-Mtg	4.70					.50	.69	800 869-6397
MSDW US Govt Secs B	Govt-Mtg	4.60	5.31	5.55	2.00	2.00	.50	1.29	800 869-6397
MSDW US Govt Secs C	Govt-Mtg	4.00					.50	1.29	800 869-6397
MSDW US Govt Secs D	Govt-Mtg	4.90					.50	.54	800 869-6397
MSDW World Wide Inc A	Intl Bond	-2.50					.75	1.43	800 869-6397
MSDW World Wide Inc B	Intl Bond	-3.10	.74	3.99	5.00	4.00	.75	2.06	800 869-6397
MSDW World Wide Inc C	Intl Bond	-3.10					.75	2.06	800 869-6397
MSDW World Wide Inc D	Intl Bond	-2.30					.75	1.20	800 869-6397
Magna Intermediate Govt Bond	Government	2.30	3.91	4.49	5.00	3.00	.40	.81	800 219-4182
MainStay Bond Inst Fd	Corp-Inv	3.20	4.77	5.27	3.00	3.00	.20	.75	800 624-6782
MainStay CA Tax Free A	Muni CA	.30	2.71	4.31	5.00	4.00	.40	1.23	800 624-6782
MainStay CA Tax Free B	Muni CA	0.00	2.48	3.90	5.00	4.00	.50	1.48	800 624-6782
MainStay CA Tax Free C	Muni CA	0.00					.47	1.48	800 624-6782
MainStay Global High Yield A	Intl Bond	18.60					.50	1.69	800 624-6782
MainStay Global High Yield B	Intl Bond	17.60					.50	2.45	800 624-6782
MainStay Global High Yield C	Intl Bond	17.40					.50	2.45	800 624-6782
MainStay Government Fund A	Government	4.10	5.47	5.17	3.00	3.00	.59	1.12	800 624-6782
MainStay Government Fund B	Government	3.20	4.68	4.57	4.00	3.00	.59	1.87	800 624-6782
MainStay Government Fund C	Government	3.20					.59	1.87	800 624-6782
MainStay High Yield Corp Bond A	Corp-HY	12.60	9.03	11.51	2.00	5.00	.56	1.00	800 624-6782
MainStay High Yield Corp Bond B	Corp-HY	3.90	5.69	9.24	3.00	5.00	.56	1.75	800 624-6782
MainStay High Yield Corp Bond C	Corp-HY	3.90					.56	1.75	800 624-6782
MainStay Indexed Bond Inst Fd	Corp-Inv	4.20	5.31	5.51	3.00	3.00	.10	.50	800 624-6782
MainStay Intl Bond A	Intl Bond	-2.00	.21	3.79	5.00	5.00	.40	1.47	800 624-6782
MainStay Intl Bond C	Intl Bond	-2.80					.40	2.22	800 624-6782
MainStay NY Tax Free A	Muni NY	1.60	3.55	4.87	3.00	4.00	.50	1.23	800 624-6782

Bond Fund Name	Objective	Annualized Return for			Rank		Max Load	Expense Ratio	Toll-Free Telephone
		1 Year	3 Years	5 Years	Overall	Risk			
MainStay NY Tax Free B	Muni NY	1.50	3.26	4.46	4.00	4.00	.50	1.48	800 624-6782
MainStay NY Tax Free C	Muni NY	1.50					.33	1.48	800 624-6782
MainStay Sh-Term Bond Inst Fd	Corp-Inv	4.30	4.94	5.24	2.00	1.00	.14	.59	800 624-6782
MainStay Strategic Income A	Dvsfd Bond	2.50	3.23		4.00	4.00	.56	1.42	800 624-6782
MainStay Strategic Income B	Dvsfd Bond	1.70	2.47		5.00	4.00	.56	2.18	800 624-6782
MainStay Strategic Income C	Dvsfd Bond	1.70					.59	2.18	800 624-6782
MainStay Tax Free Bond Fund A	Muni Natl	.50	2.78	4.34	4.00	4.00	.59	1.02	800 624-6782
MainStay Tax Free Bond Fund B	Muni Natl	.10	2.51	4.08	4.00	4.00	.59	1.27	800 624-6782
MainStay Tax Free Bond Fund C	Muni Natl	.10					.59	1.27	800 624-6782
Managers Bond Fund	Corp-Inv	4.10	6.08	7.26	3.00	5.00	.62	1.28	800 835-3879
Managers Global Bond Fund	Intl Bond	-3.40	1.98	2.02	5.00	5.00	.69	1.58	800 835-3879
Managers Sh-Interm Bond	Corp-Inv	3.20	4.32	5.12	3.00	1.00	.50	1.32	800 835-3879
Marshall Government Income A	Government	3.40					.75	1.09	800 236-8560
Marshall Government Income Y	Government	3.50	5.04	5.57	3.00	2.00	.75	.85	800 236-8560
Marshall Intermediate Bond A	Corp-Inv	4.30					.59	.93	800 236-8560
Marshall Intermediate Bond Y	Corp-Inv	4.50	5.16	5.34	2.00	2.00	.59	.70	800 236-8560
Marshall Intermediate Tax Free	Muni Natl	3.00	3.85	4.41	3.00	2.00	.17	.93	800 236-8560
Marshall Short-Term Income	Corp-Inv	3.90	4.80	5.24	2.00	1.00	.59	.51	800 236-8560
Mason Street Fds-High Yield Bd A	Corp-HY	-1.50	1.49		5.00	5.00	.75	1.30	888 627-6678
Mason Street Fds-High Yield Bd B	Corp-HY	-2.20	.77		5.00	5.00	.75	1.94	888 627-6678
Mason Street Fds-Muni Bond A	Muni Natl	3.40	5.12		1.00	3.00	.29	.84	888 627-6678
Mason Street Fds-Muni Bond B	Muni Natl	2.70	4.33		1.00	3.00	.29	1.50	888 627-6678
Mason Street Fds-Select Bond A	Dvsfd Bond	4.20	5.58		3.00	3.00	.29	.84	888 627-6678
Mason Street Fds-Select Bond B	Dvsfd Bond	4.50	4.58		3.00	3.00	.29	1.50	888 627-6678
MassMutual Inst-Core Bond S	Dvsfd Bond	4.30	5.62	5.82	3.00	3.00	.45	.55	
MassMutual Inst-Prime Fund S	Corp-Inv	5.80	5.43	5.40	1.00	1.00	.45	.51	
MassMutual Inst-Short-Term Bd S	Dvsfd Bond	4.70	5.50	5.44	2.00	1.00	.45	.54	
McM Fixed Income Fund	Dvsfd Bond	3.50	5.30	5.55	3.00	3.00	.34	.50	800 788-9485
McM Intermediate Fixed Income Fund	Dvsfd Bond	3.50	5.13	5.34	3.00	2.00	.34	.50	800 788-9485
Members Bond Fd A	Corp-Inv	3.80					.50	2.25	800 877-6089
Members Bond Fd B	Corp-Inv	3.10					.50	3.00	800 877-6089
Members High Income Fd A	Corp-HY	2.10					.55	2.22	800 877-6089
Members High Income Fd B	Corp-HY	1.50					.55	2.97	800 877-6089
Memorial Corporate Bond Instl	Corp-Inv	2.60					.34	.64	888 263-5593
Memorial Corporate Bond Trust	Corp-Inv						.34		888 263-5593
Memorial Government Bond Instl	Government	3.70					.34	.68	888 263-5593
Memorial Government Bond Trust	Government						.34		888 263-5593
Mercantile-Bond Index Inst	Government	3.70	5.54		3.00	3.00	.29	.81	800 452-2724
Mercantile-Bond Index Inv	Government	3.70	5.46		2.00	3.00	.29	.81	800 452-2724
Mercantile-Bond Index Tr	Government	4.00	5.78		2.00	3.00	.29	.52	800 452-2724
Mercantile-Govt/Corp Bond B	Dvsfd Bond	2.80	4.54	3.87	4.00	3.00	.45	1.65	800 452-2724
Mercantile-Govt/Corp Bond Inst	Dvsfd Bond	3.40	5.22	4.47	3.00	3.00	.45	.95	800 452-2724
Mercantile-Govt/Corp Bond Inv	Dvsfd Bond	3.40	5.22	4.45	3.00	3.00	.45	.95	800 452-2724
Mercantile-Govt/Corp Bond Tr	Dvsfd Bond	3.70	4.98	4.39	3.00	3.00	.45	.66	800 452-2724
Mercantile-Interm Corp Bond Inst	Corp-Inv	1.70	4.63		3.00	3.00	.55	1.08	800 452-2724
Mercantile-Interm Corp Bond Inv	Corp-Inv	1.70	4.56		3.00	3.00	.55	1.08	800 452-2724
Mercantile-Interm Corp Bond Tr	Corp-Inv	2.00	4.89		3.00	3.00	.55	.78	800 452-2724
Mercantile-MO T/Exempt Bond Inv A	Muni State	1.40	3.52	4.62	2.00	3.00	.45	.85	800 452-2724
Mercantile-MO T/Exempt Bond Inv B	Muni State	.60	2.70	3.72	3.00	3.00	.45	1.65	800 452-2724
Mercantile-MO T/Exempt Bond Tr	Muni State	1.50	3.68	4.73	2.00	3.00	.45	.66	800 452-2724
Mercantile-National Municipal B	Muni Natl	1.30	3.31		4.00	4.00	.55	1.75	800 452-2724
Mercantile-National Municipal Inv	Muni Natl	2.40	4.04		3.00	4.00	.55	.94	800 452-2724
Mercantile-National Municipal Tr	Muni Natl	2.30	4.32		3.00	4.00	.55	.75	800 452-2724
Mercantile-Short Interm Muni Inv	Muni Natl	2.40	3.17		3.00	2.00	.55	1.00	800 452-2724
Mercantile-Short Interm Muni Tr	Muni Natl	2.40	3.31		3.00	2.00	.55	.76	800 452-2724
Mercantile-U.S. Govt B	Government	3.10	3.88	4.03	3.00	1.00	.45	1.66	800 452-2724
Mercantile-U.S. Govt Inst	Government	3.70	4.49	4.68	3.00	2.00	.45	.95	800 452-2724
Mercantile-U.S. Govt Inv	Government	3.70	4.51	4.65	3.00	1.00	.45	.96	800 452-2724

425

Bond Fund Name	Objective	Annualized Return for			Rank		Max Load	Expense Ratio	Toll-Free Telephone
		1 Year	3 Years	5 Years	Overall	Risk			
Mercantile-U.S. Govt Tr	Government	4.00	4.83	5.02	3.00	1.00	.45	.66	800 452-2724
Merrill Lynch AZ Muni A	Muni State	1.90	3.93	4.94	3.00	3.00	.50	.93	800 637-3863
Merrill Lynch AZ Muni B	Muni State	1.40	3.41	4.41	3.00	3.00	.50	1.43	800 637-3863
Merrill Lynch Adj Rate Sec B	Govt-Mtg	4.20	4.20	4.92	2.00	1.00	.50	1.69	800 637-3863
Merrill Lynch Adj Rate Sec D	Govt-Mtg	4.70	4.74	5.45	1.00	1.00	.50	1.16	800 637-3863
Merrill Lynch CA Insd Muni A	Muni CA	2.20	4.03	5.75	3.00	4.00	.55	.90	800 637-3863
Merrill Lynch CA Insd Muni B	Muni CA	1.70	3.51	5.23	4.00	4.00	.55	1.40	800 637-3863
Merrill Lynch CA Muni A	Muni CA	1.90	3.90	5.27	3.00	4.00	.55	.65	800 637-3863
Merrill Lynch CA Muni B	Muni CA	1.40	3.37	4.76	4.00	4.00	.55	1.14	800 637-3863
Merrill Lynch Corp Bd-Hi Inc A	Corp-HY	-.90	1.64	5.84	3.00	5.00	.40	.48	800 637-3863
Merrill Lynch Corp Bd-Hi Inc B	Corp-HY	-1.80	.83	5.01	3.00	5.00	.40	1.25	800 637-3863
Merrill Lynch Corp Bd-Hi Inc C	Corp-HY	-1.70	.83	4.96	3.00	5.00	.40	1.31	800 637-3863
Merrill Lynch Corp Bd-Hi Inc D	Corp-HY	-1.30	1.34	5.52	3.00	5.00	.40	.73	800 637-3863
Merrill Lynch Corp Bd-Interm A	Corp-Inv	2.60	4.69	5.21	3.00	3.00	.35	.67	800 637-3863
Merrill Lynch Corp Bd-Interm B	Corp-Inv	2.10	4.15	4.67	4.00	3.00	.35	1.17	800 637-3863
Merrill Lynch Corp Bd-Invst Grd A	Corp-Inv	1.90	4.28	4.90	4.00	3.00	.35	.57	800 637-3863
Merrill Lynch Corp Bd-Invst Grd B	Corp-Inv	1.10	3.48	4.10	5.00	3.00	.35	1.34	800 637-3863
Merrill Lynch FL Muni A	Muni State	.40	3.39	4.74	3.00	3.00	.55	.68	800 637-3863
Merrill Lynch FL Muni B	Muni State	-.10	2.86	4.21	4.00	3.00	.55	1.19	800 637-3863
Merrill Lynch Global Bond A	Intl Bond	-1.70	2.16	2.85	5.00	4.00	.59	1.02	800 637-3863
Merrill Lynch Global Bond B	Intl Bond	-2.60	1.37	2.05	5.00	4.00	.59	1.80	800 637-3863
Merrill Lynch Global Bond C	Intl Bond	-2.50	1.32	1.99	5.00	4.00	.59	1.85	800 637-3863
Merrill Lynch Global Bond D	Intl Bond	-2.00	1.90	2.59	5.00	4.00	.59	1.27	800 637-3863
Merrill Lynch Interm Govt Bond D	Government	3.40	5.13	4.82	4.00	3.00	.40	.82	800 637-3863
Merrill Lynch MA Muni A	Muni State	.20	2.71	4.46	4.00	4.00	.55	.94	800 637-3863
Merrill Lynch MA Muni B	Muni State	-.30	2.21	3.94	5.00	4.00	.55	1.45	800 637-3863
Merrill Lynch MI Muni B	Muni State	-.40	2.03	3.72	5.00	4.00	.55	1.43	800 637-3863
Merrill Lynch MN Muni A	Muni State	2.50	4.25	5.02	1.00	2.00	.55	1.02	800 637-3863
Merrill Lynch MN Muni B	Muni State	2.00	3.72	4.49	3.00	2.00	.55	1.53	800 637-3863
Merrill Lynch Muni Insd A	Muni Natl	1.30	3.56	4.77	4.00	4.00	.35	.41	800 637-3863
Merrill Lynch Muni Insd B	Muni Natl	.60	2.83	3.98	5.00	4.00	.35	1.17	800 637-3863
Merrill Lynch Muni Insd C	Muni Natl	.60	2.73	3.93	5.00	4.00	.35	1.22	800 637-3863
Merrill Lynch Muni Insd D	Muni Natl	1.00	3.31	4.51	4.00	4.00	.35	.67	800 637-3863
Merrill Lynch Muni Interm-Trm A	Muni Natl	3.80	4.45	5.08	3.00	3.00	.55	.79	800 637-3863
Merrill Lynch Muni Interm-Trm B	Muni Natl	3.60	4.14	4.76	3.00	3.00	.55	1.10	800 637-3863
Merrill Lynch Muni Ltd Mat A	Muni Natl	3.30	3.62	3.81	2.00	1.00	.33	.42	800 637-3863
Merrill Lynch Muni Ltd Mat B	Muni Natl	3.00	3.25	3.45	2.00	1.00	.33	.78	800 637-3863
Merrill Lynch Muni Natl A	Muni Natl	.60	3.34	5.14	2.00	4.00	.47	.55	800 637-3863
Merrill Lynch Muni Natl B	Muni Natl	0.00	2.59	4.35	4.00	4.00	.47	1.31	800 637-3863
Merrill Lynch Muni Natl C	Muni Natl	-.10	2.54	4.29	4.00	4.00	.47	1.36	800 637-3863
Merrill Lynch Muni Natl D	Muni Natl	.50	3.08	4.88	4.00	4.00	.47	.81	800 637-3863
Merrill Lynch NC Muni B	Muni State	1.10	3.23	4.41	4.00	3.00	.55	1.45	800 637-3863
Merrill Lynch NJ Muni A	Muni State	-1.00	2.94	4.26	5.00	4.00	.55	.75	800 637-3863
Merrill Lynch NJ Muni B	Muni State	-1.50	2.41	3.73	5.00	4.00	.55	1.26	800 637-3863
Merrill Lynch NY Muni A	Muni NY	0.00	3.15	4.66	4.00	4.00	.55	1.20	800 637-3863
Merrill Lynch NY Muni B	Muni NY	-.50	2.68	4.16	5.00	4.00	.55	.69	800 637-3863
Merrill Lynch Ohio Muni A	Muni State	.40	3.22	4.79	2.00	3.00	.55	.92	800 637-3863
Merrill Lynch Ohio Muni B	Muni State	-.10	2.70	4.26	5.00	3.00	.55	1.42	800 637-3863
Merrill Lynch PA Muni A	Muni State	1.20	3.77	4.96	3.00	3.00	.55	.80	800 637-3863
Merrill Lynch PA Muni B	Muni State	.60	3.24	4.43	3.00	3.00	.55	1.31	800 637-3863
Merrill Lynch Short-Trm Global B	Intl Bond	5.20	4.46	4.56	2.00	1.00	.55	1.64	800 637-3863
Merrill Lynch Short-Trm Global D	Intl Bond	5.70	5.02	5.12	2.00	1.00	.55	1.10	800 637-3863
Merrill Lynch TX Muni A	Muni State	.50	2.52	3.99	5.00	4.00	.55	.97	800 637-3863
Merrill Lynch TX Muni B	Muni State	0.00	2.02	3.47	5.00	4.00	.55	1.48	800 637-3863
Merrill Lynch World Income A	Intl Bond	10.00	-3.19	1.90	3.00	5.00	.59	.94	800 637-3863
Merrill Lynch World Income B	Intl Bond	9.00	-3.99	1.12	4.00	5.00	.59	1.72	800 637-3863
Merriman Flexible Bond	Corp-Inv	2.10	2.97	4.58	5.00	3.00	1.00	1.50	800 423-4893
Metropolitan West Low Dur Bd Fd	Dvsfd Bond	4.90	6.48		1.00	1.00	.47	.69	

426

Bond Fund Name	Objective	Annualized Return for			Rank		Max Load	Expense Ratio	Toll-Free Telephone
		1 Year	3 Years	5 Years	Overall	Risk			
Metropolitan West Tot Ret Bd Fd	Dvsfd Bond	3.80	7.24		1.00	2.00	.55	.96	
Monetta Trust-Interm Bond Fund	Corp-Inv	3.40	5.36	5.88	2.00	3.00	.34	.56	800 666-3882
Monterey PIA Global Bond	Intl Bond	.50	2.11		5.00	4.00	.40	.48	800 628-9403
Monterey PIA Income	Government	2.60	4.58	5.08	4.00	3.00	.40	1.10	800 628-9403
Monterey PIA Short-Term Govt	Government	5.30	5.24	5.84	1.00	1.00	.20	.29	800 628-9403
Montgomery CA T/F Short-Interm R	Muni CA	3.70	4.37	5.20	2.00	2.00	.50	.68	800 572-3863
Montgomery Sh Dur Govt Bond R	Government	4.60	5.64	5.91	2.00	1.00	.50	1.35	800 572-3863
Montgomery Tot Return Bond R	Dvsfd Bond	5.30	6.37		1.00	3.00	.50	1.15	800 572-3863
Morgan Grenfell EmergMkt Debt Fd	Intl Bond	30.20	-1.67	10.07	3.00	5.00	1.00	1.34	800 730-1313
Morgan Grenfell Fixed Income I	Corp-Inv	4.10	5.78	6.41	2.00	3.00	.40	.56	800 730-1313
Morgan Grenfell Fixed Income Svc	Corp-Inv	3.90					.40	.82	800 730-1313
Morgan Grenfell Global Fixed	Intl Bond	2.20	2.52	3.02	5.00	5.00	.50	1.03	800 550-6426
Morgan Grenfell Intl Fx Inc A	Intl Bond	.60	1.83	2.67	5.00	5.00	.50	.55	800 550-6426
Morgan Grenfell Muni Bond Fd I	Muni Natl	2.40	4.19	5.42	1.00	2.00	.40	.55	800 550-6426
Morgan Grenfell Muni Bond Svc	Muni Natl	2.20					.40	.80	800 550-6426
Morgan Grenfell Sh Term Fix Inc	Corp-Inv	6.00	5.99	6.08	1.00	1.00	.40	.55	800 550-6426
Morgan Grenfell Sh Term Muni Fd I	Muni Natl	3.60	4.29	5.13	1.00	1.00	.40	.55	800 550-6426
Mosaic Government Fd	Government	3.00	4.88	4.36	4.00	3.00	.62	1.12	888 670-3600
Mosaic Intermediate Income Fd	Dvsfd Bond	2.20	2.98	5.16	4.00	3.00	.63	1.12	888 670-3600
Mosaic Tax Free National Fd	Muni Natl	2.40	3.58	4.54	3.00	3.00	.62	1.06	888 670-3600
Mosaic Tax Free Tr-AZ	Muni State	1.30	3.15	4.29	3.00	3.00	.63	1.11	888 670-3600
Mosaic Tax Free Tr-MD	Muni State	.90	2.93	3.97	4.00	3.00	.63	1.12	888 670-3600
Mosaic Tax Free Tr-MO	Muni State	1.30	3.32	4.35	3.00	3.00	.63	1.09	888 670-3600
Mosaic Tax Free Tr-VA	Muni State	1.00	3.25	4.59	4.00	3.00	.63	1.01	888 670-3600
Munder All Season Conservative Y	Corp-Inv	4.70	3.62		4.00	5.00	.34	.40	800 438-5789
Munder Bond A	Corp-Inv	2.50	4.80	5.10	4.00	3.00	.50	.96	800 438-5789
Munder Bond B	Corp-Inv	1.80	4.05		5.00	3.00	.50	1.71	800 438-5789
Munder Bond C	Corp-Inv	1.70	4.08		3.00	3.00	.50	1.71	800 438-5789
Munder Bond K	Corp-Inv	2.50	4.83	5.13	4.00	3.00	.50	.96	800 438-5789
Munder Bond Y	Corp-Inv	2.80	5.13	5.37	4.00	3.00	.50	.71	800 438-5789
Munder Intermediate Bond A	Corp-Inv	3.70	4.79	4.92	3.00	2.00	.50	.94	800 438-5789
Munder Intermediate Bond B	Corp-Inv	3.00	3.99	4.15	4.00	2.00	.50	1.69	800 438-5789
Munder Intermediate Bond C	Corp-Inv	3.40	4.02		4.00	2.00	.50	1.69	800 438-5789
Munder Intermediate Bond K	Corp-Inv	3.80	4.76	4.92	3.00	2.00	.50	.94	800 438-5789
Munder Intermediate Bond Y	Corp-Inv	4.10	5.02	5.18	3.00	2.00	.50	.69	800 438-5789
Munder International Bond B	Intl Bond	-.40	.97		5.00	5.00	.50	1.88	800 438-5789
Munder International Bond C	Intl Bond	-3.30					.50	1.88	800 438-5789
Munder International Bond Fund A	Intl Bond	.30					.50	1.13	800 438-5789
Munder International Bond K	Intl Bond	.20	1.60		5.00	5.00	.50	1.13	800 438-5789
Munder International Bond Y	Intl Bond	.60	1.95		5.00	5.00	.50	.89	800 438-5789
Munder MI Tax-Free Bond A	Muni State	2.60	4.07	5.05	3.00	4.00	.50	1.00	800 438-5789
Munder MI Tax-Free Bond B	Muni State	1.80	3.40	4.34	4.00	4.00	.50	1.75	800 438-5789
Munder MI Tax-Free Bond C	Muni State	1.80	3.41		3.00	4.00	.50	1.75	800 438-5789
Munder MI Tax-Free Bond K	Muni State	2.50	4.11	5.08	3.00	4.00	.50	1.00	800 438-5789
Munder MI Tax-Free Bond Y	Muni State	2.90	4.37	5.36	3.00	4.00	.50	.75	800 438-5789
Munder Tax Free Bond A	Muni Natl	2.80	4.01		3.00	4.00	.50	.97	800 438-5789
Munder Tax Free Bond B	Muni Natl	1.90	3.11	4.00	4.00	4.00	.50	1.72	800 438-5789
Munder Tax Free Bond K	Muni Natl	2.70	3.94	4.79	3.00	4.00	.50	.97	800 438-5789
Munder Tax Free Bond Y	Muni Natl	3.00	4.20	5.05	3.00	4.00	.50	.72	800 438-5789
Munder Tax-Free Bond Fund C	Muni Natl	2.30					.50	1.72	800 438-5789
Munder Tax-Free Short Int Bond A	Muni Natl	2.70	3.45	3.83	3.00	2.00	.50	.95	800 438-5789
Munder Tax-Free Short Int Bond B	Muni Natl	1.80	2.66		2.00	2.00	.50	1.70	800 438-5789
Munder Tax-Free Short Int Bond K	Muni Natl	2.70	3.45	3.80	3.00	2.00	.50	.95	800 438-5789
Munder Tax-Free Short Int Bond Y	Muni Natl	3.00	3.71	4.07	3.00	2.00	.50	.70	800 438-5789
Munder US Government Income A	Government	3.80	5.17	5.44	3.00	3.00	.50	.95	800 438-5789
Munder US Government Income B	Government	3.00	4.35		4.00	3.00	.50	1.70	800 438-5789
Munder US Government Income C	Government	2.90	4.29		4.00	3.00	.50	1.70	800 438-5789
Munder US Government Income K	Government	3.70	5.13	5.42	3.00	3.00	.50	.95	800 438-5789

Bond Fund Name	Objective	Annualized Return for			Rank		Max Load	Expense Ratio	Toll-Free Telephone
		1 Year	3 Years	5 Years	Overall	Risk			
Munder US Government Income Y	Government	4.00	5.39	5.68	3.00	3.00	.50	.70	800 438-5789
ND Tax-Free Fund B	Muni State	.10	1.87	4.08	3.00	2.00	.59	1.30	800 276-1262
Nations CA Muni Bond Fund Inv B	Muni CA	.50					.50	1.65	
Nations CA Muni Bond Fund Pr A	Muni CA	2.20					.50		
Nations CA Muni Bond Inv A	Muni CA	2.60	4.49	5.39	2.00	3.00	.50	.91	800 321-7854
Nations FL Interm Muni Inv A	Muni State	2.60	3.75	4.50	3.00	2.00	.40	.69	800 321-7854
Nations FL Interm Muni Inv B	Muni State	2.00	3.16	4.03	3.00	2.00	.40	1.30	800 321-7854
Nations FL Interm Muni Inv C	Muni State	2.10	3.19	4.04	3.00	2.00	.40	1.36	800 321-7854
Nations FL Interm Muni Pr A	Muni State	2.90	4.01	4.74	2.00	2.00	.40	.50	800 321-7854
Nations FL Muni Bond Inv A	Muni State	3.10	4.21	5.25	2.00	3.00	.40	.80	800 321-7854
Nations FL Muni Bond Inv B	Muni State	2.40	3.39	4.52	3.00	3.00	.40	1.44	800 321-7854
Nations FL Muni Bond Inv C	Muni State	2.30	3.38	4.60	3.00	3.00	.40	1.53	800 321-7854
Nations FL Muni Bond Pr A	Muni State	3.40	4.28	5.38	1.00	3.00	.40	.59	800 321-7854
Nations GA Interm Muni Inv A	Muni State	2.60	3.78	4.51	3.00	2.00	.40	.69	800 321-7854
Nations GA Interm Muni Inv B	Muni State	2.00	3.18	4.03	3.00	2.00	.40	1.30	800 321-7854
Nations GA Interm Muni Inv C	Muni State	1.80	3.07	3.96	3.00	2.00	.40	1.31	800 321-7854
Nations GA Interm Muni Pr A	Muni State	2.90	3.86	4.64	3.00	2.00	.40	.50	800 321-7854
Nations GA Muni Bond Inv A	Muni State	1.30	3.85	5.13	2.00	3.00	.50	.80	800 321-7854
Nations GA Muni Bond Inv B	Muni State	.60	3.18	4.54	4.00	3.00	.50	1.44	800 321-7854
Nations GA Muni Bond Inv C	Muni State	.80	3.20	4.63	4.00	3.00	.50	1.48	800 321-7854
Nations GA Muni Bond Pr A	Muni State	1.50	4.06	5.39	1.00	3.00	.50	.59	800 321-7854
Nations Government Secs Inv A	Government	3.70	4.96	4.78	3.00	3.00	.50	.97	800 321-7854
Nations Government Secs Inv B	Government	3.00	4.33	4.23	4.00	3.00	.50	1.58	800 321-7854
Nations Government Secs Inv C	Government	2.90	4.22	4.21	4.00	3.00	.50	1.59	800 321-7854
Nations Government Secs Pr A	Government	3.90	5.24	5.05	3.00	3.00	.50	.72	800 321-7854
Nations Interm Muni Inv A	Muni Natl	2.30	3.59	4.57	3.00	2.00	.40	.69	800 321-7854
Nations Interm Muni Inv B	Muni Natl	1.50	2.93	4.06	3.00	2.00	.40	1.30	800 321-7854
Nations Interm Muni Inv C	Muni Natl	1.60	2.99	4.07	3.00	2.00	.40	1.20	800 321-7854
Nations Interm Muni Pr A	Muni Natl	2.50	3.77	4.75	2.00	2.00	.40	.50	800 321-7854
Nations Investment Grade Bd Pr A	Dvsfd Bond	3.80	5.00	5.11	3.00	3.00	.40	.68	800 321-7854
Nations Investment Grade Bond Fd A	Dvsfd Bond	3.50	4.78	4.97	4.00	3.00	.50	.88	800 321-7854
Nations Investment Grade Bond Fd B	Dvsfd Bond	2.60	4.08	4.31	5.00	3.00	.50	1.47	800 321-7854
Nations Investment Grade Bond Fd C	Dvsfd Bond	2.50	4.10	4.44	5.00	3.00	.50	1.39	800 321-7854
Nations MD Interm Muni Inv A	Muni State	2.60	3.67	4.30	3.00	2.00	.40	.69	800 321-7854
Nations MD Interm Muni Inv B	Muni State	1.90	3.02	3.79	3.00	2.00	.40	1.30	800 321-7854
Nations MD Interm Muni Inv C	Muni State	1.80	2.99	3.76	3.00	2.00	.40	1.32	800 321-7854
Nations MD Interm Muni Pr A	Muni State	2.80	3.88	4.49	3.00	2.00	.40	.50	800 321-7854
Nations MD Muni Bond Inv A	Muni State	2.60	4.04	5.13	2.00	3.00	.50	.80	800 321-7854
Nations MD Muni Bond Inv B	Muni State	1.90	3.36	4.48	3.00	3.00	.50	1.44	800 321-7854
Nations MD Muni Bond Inv C	Muni State	1.90	3.42	4.61	3.00	3.00	.50	1.46	800 321-7854
Nations MD Muni Bond Pr A	Muni State	2.90	4.38	5.41	1.00	3.00	.50	.59	800 321-7854
Nations Muni Income Fd Inv A	Muni Natl	.90	3.68	5.29	3.00	3.00	.50	.80	800 321-7854
Nations Muni Income Fd Inv B	Muni Natl	.10	2.97	4.63	4.00	3.00	.50	1.44	800 321-7854
Nations Muni Income Fd Inv C	Muni Natl	.10	3.02	4.74	4.00	3.00	.50	1.36	800 321-7854
Nations Muni Income Fd Pr A	Muni Natl	1.10	3.88	5.50	3.00	3.00	.50	.59	800 321-7854
Nations NC Interm Muni Inv A	Muni State	2.50	3.65	4.46	3.00	2.00	.40	.69	800 321-7854
Nations NC Interm Muni Inv B	Muni State	1.80	2.99	3.94	3.00	2.00	.40	1.30	800 321-7854
Nations NC Interm Muni Inv C	Muni State	1.70	2.94	3.92	3.00	2.00	.40	1.31	800 321-7854
Nations NC Interm Muni Pr A	Muni State	2.80	3.86	4.67	2.00	2.00	.40	.50	800 321-7854
Nations NC Muni Bond Inv A	Muni State	1.70	3.96	5.10	1.00	3.00	.50	.80	800 321-7854
Nations NC Muni Bond Inv B	Muni State	1.10	3.30	4.47	4.00	3.00	.50	1.44	800 321-7854
Nations NC Muni Bond Inv C	Muni State	1.00	3.28	4.54	5.00	3.00	.50	1.46	800 321-7854
Nations NC Muni Bond Pr A	Muni State	2.10	4.22	5.34	1.00	3.00	.50	.59	800 321-7854
Nations SC Intermed Muni Inv A	Muni State	2.60	3.71	4.52	3.00	2.00	.40	.69	800 321-7854
Nations SC Intermed Muni Inv B	Muni State	1.80	3.03	3.98	3.00	2.00	.40	1.30	800 321-7854
Nations SC Intermed Muni Inv C	Muni State	1.90	3.03	3.98	3.00	2.00	.40	1.32	800 321-7854
Nations SC Intermed Muni Pr A	Muni State	2.80	3.90	4.71	1.00	2.00	.40	.50	800 321-7854
Nations SC Muni Bond Inv A	Muni State	2.20	3.77	5.09	2.00	3.00	.50	.80	800 321-7854

Bond Fund Name	Objective	Annualized Return for			Rank		Max Load	Expense Ratio	Toll-Free Telephone
		1 Year	3 Years	5 Years	Overall	Risk			
Nations SC Muni Bond Inv B	Muni State	1.50	3.07	4.45	4.00	3.00	.50	1.43	800 321-7854
Nations SC Muni Bond Inv C	Muni State	1.50	3.07	4.51	4.00	3.00	.50	1.43	800 321-7854
Nations SC Muni Bond Pr A	Muni State	2.50	3.99	5.30	1.00	3.00	.50	.59	800 321-7854
Nations Sh-Interm Govt Inv A	Government	3.80	4.56	4.69	3.00	2.00	.29	.78	800 321-7854
Nations Sh-Interm Govt Inv B	Government	3.10	3.89	4.13	3.00	2.00	.29	1.37	800 321-7854
Nations Sh-Interm Govt Inv C	Government	3.10	3.90	4.17	3.00	2.00	.29	1.34	800 321-7854
Nations Sh-Interm Govt Pr A	Government	4.00	4.76	4.89	3.00	2.00	.29	.57	800 321-7854
Nations Sh-Term Inc Inv A	Corp-Inv	4.10	4.96	5.24	3.00	1.00	.29	.69	800 321-7854
Nations Sh-Term Inc Inv B	Corp-Inv	3.40	4.63	4.97	3.00	1.00	.29	.84	800 321-7854
Nations Sh-Term Inc Inv C	Corp-Inv	3.10	4.32	4.79	3.00	1.00	.29	1.01	800 321-7854
Nations Sh-Term Inc Pr A	Corp-Inv	4.10	5.09	5.50	3.00	1.00	.29	.50	800 321-7854
Nations Sh-Term Muni Inc Inv A	Muni Natl	3.50	3.95	4.11	2.00	1.00	.29	.59	800 321-7854
Nations Sh-Term Muni Inc Inv B	Muni Natl	3.00	3.68	3.89	2.00	1.00	.29	.75	800 321-7854
Nations Sh-Term Muni Inc Inv C	Muni Natl	2.70	3.52	3.79	2.00	1.00	.29	.82	800 321-7854
Nations Sh-Term Muni Inc Pr A	Muni Natl	3.70	4.17	4.33	2.00	1.00	.29	.40	800 321-7854
Nations Strategic Inc Fd Inv A	Dvsfd Bond	.20	3.47	4.40	3.00	3.00	.40	.94	800 321-7854
Nations Strategic Inc Fd Inv B	Dvsfd Bond	-.60	2.85	3.82	5.00	3.00	.40	1.55	800 321-7854
Nations Strategic Inc Fd Inv C	Dvsfd Bond	-.50	2.81	3.87	5.00	3.00	.40	1.56	800 321-7854
Nations Strategic Income Fund Pr A	Dvsfd Bond	.40	3.74	4.66	4.00	3.00	.40	.69	800 321-7854
Nations TN Interm Muni Inv A	Muni State	1.80	3.42	4.33	3.00	2.00	.40	.69	800 321-7854
Nations TN Interm Muni Inv B	Muni State	1.20	2.80	3.83	3.00	2.00	.40	1.30	800 321-7854
Nations TN Interm Muni Inv C	Muni State	.70	2.62	3.75	3.00	2.00	.40	1.11	800 321-7854
Nations TN Interm Muni Pr A	Muni State	2.20	3.68	4.57	3.00	2.00	.40	.50	800 321-7854
Nations TN Muni Bond Inv A	Muni State	1.80	3.80	5.20	2.00	3.00	.50	.80	800 321-7854
Nations TN Muni Bond Inv B	Muni State	1.10	3.13	5.27	4.00	3.00	.50	1.44	800 321-7854
Nations TN Muni Bond Inv C	Muni State	1.00	3.09	4.63	4.00	3.00	.50	1.45	800 321-7854
Nations TN Muni Bond Pr A	Muni State	2.00	4.03	5.43	2.00	3.00	.50	.59	800 321-7854
Nations TX Interm Muni Inv A	Muni State	2.80	3.70	4.47	3.00	2.00	.40	.69	800 321-7854
Nations TX Interm Muni Inv B	Muni State	2.00	3.03	3.94	3.00	2.00	.40	1.30	800 321-7854
Nations TX Interm Muni Inv C	Muni State	2.00	3.00	3.93	3.00	2.00	.40	1.33	800 321-7854
Nations TX Interm Muni Pr A	Muni State	3.00	3.92	4.68	2.00	2.00	.40	.50	800 321-7854
Nations TX Muni Bond Inv A	Muni State	2.50	4.29	5.41	2.00	3.00	.50	.80	800 321-7854
Nations TX Muni Bond Inv B	Muni State	1.70	3.60	4.76	3.00	3.00	.50	1.44	800 321-7854
Nations TX Muni Bond Inv C	Muni State	1.70	3.47	4.76	3.00	3.00	.50	1.45	800 321-7854
Nations TX Muni Bond Pr A	Muni State	2.70	4.50	5.65	1.00	3.00	.50	.59	800 321-7854
Nations US Govt Bond Inv A	Government	2.50	4.17	4.66	4.00	3.00	.50	.83	800 321-7854
Nations US Govt Bond Inv B	Government	1.50	3.45	3.89	5.00	3.00	.50	1.43	800 321-7854
Nations US Govt Bond Inv C	Government	1.20	3.29		4.00	3.00	.50	1.34	800 321-7854
Nations US Govt Bond Pr A	Government	1.60	5.26	5.40	4.00	4.00	.50	.58	800 321-7854
Nations VA Interm Muni Inv A	Muni State	2.80	3.75	4.31	3.00	2.00	.40	.69	800 321-7854
Nations VA Interm Muni Inv B	Muni State	2.10	3.09	3.87	3.00	2.00	.40	1.30	800 321-7854
Nations VA Interm Muni Inv C	Muni State	1.40	2.84	3.71	3.00	2.00	.40	1.34	800 321-7854
Nations VA Interm Muni Pr A	Muni State	3.10	3.96	4.60	2.00	2.00	.40	.50	800 321-7854
Nations VA Muni Bond Inv A	Muni State	1.70	4.04	5.34	1.00	3.00	.50	.80	800 321-7854
Nations VA Muni Bond Inv B	Muni State	1.10	3.37	4.70	3.00	3.00	.50	1.44	800 321-7854
Nations VA Muni Bond Inv C	Muni State	1.00	3.36	4.78	3.00	3.00	.50	1.44	800 321-7854
Nations VA Muni Bond Pr A	Muni State	2.10	4.29	5.57	1.00	3.00	.50	.59	800 321-7854
Nationwide Bond A	Corp-Inv	2.10					.50	1.05	800 848-0920
Nationwide Bond B	Corp-Inv	1.50					.50	1.64	800 848-0920
Nationwide Bond D	Corp-Inv	2.20	4.88	5.37	3.00	3.00	.50	.79	800 848-0920
Nationwide Inter US Govt Bond A	Government	4.10					.50	1.03	800 848-0920
Nationwide Inter US Govt Bond B	Government	3.00					.50	1.62	800 848-0920
Nationwide Inter US Govt Bond D	Government	4.20	5.46	5.64	3.00	3.00	.50	.78	800 848-0920
Nationwide L/T US Govt Bond A	Government	4.20					.50	1.04	800 848-0920
Nationwide L/T US Govt Bond B	Government	3.70					.50	1.63	800 848-0920
Nationwide Long-Term US Govt D	Government	4.00	5.67	5.80	3.00	4.00	.50	.79	800 848-0920
Nationwide Tax-Free Inc A	Muni Natl	1.60					.50	.95	800 848-0920
Nationwide Tax-Free Inc B	Muni Natl	.90					.50	1.56	800 848-0920

Bond Fund Name	Objective	Annualized Return for			Rank		Max Load	Expense Ratio	Toll-Free Telephone
		1 Year	3 Years	5 Years	Overall	Risk			
Nationwide Tax-Free Inc D	Muni Natl	1.80	3.89	5.01	2.00	3.00	.50	.69	800 848-0920
Neuberger Berman High Yld Bond Fd	Corp-HY	-13.10					.65	1.00	800 877-9700
Neuberger Berman Ltd Mat Bd Fd	Corp-Inv	3.00	3.98	4.79	3.00	1.00	.52	.30	800 877-9700
Neuberger Berman Ltd Mat Bd Tr	Corp-Inv	2.40	3.62	4.55	3.00	1.00	.81	.81	800 877-9700
Neuberger Berman Muni Sec	Muni Natl	3.20	4.10	4.70	2.00	2.00	.52	.66	800 877-9700
Nicholas Income Fund	Corp-HY	-5.80	1.14	5.51	4.00	5.00	.35	.50	800 227-5987
Nicholas-Applegate High Qual Bd I	Corp-Inv	3.70	5.76		1.00	3.00	.45	.42	800 551-8043
Nicholas-Applegate High Yld Bond I	Corp-HY	6.10	8.89		1.00	5.00	.59	1.09	800 551-8043
Nicholas-Applegate Sh Intm F/Inc I	Corp-Inv	5.00	5.52		1.00	1.00	.29	.34	800 551-8043
North American Core Bond A	Corp-Inv	1.60	4.25	4.93	4.00	3.00	.59	1.25	800 872-8037
North American Core Bond B	Corp-Inv	1.10	3.59	4.29	5.00	3.00	.59	1.89	800 872-8037
North American Core Bond C	Corp-Inv	1.10	3.66	4.34	5.00	3.00	.59	1.89	800 872-8037
North American Natl Muni Bond A	Muni Natl	1.40	3.41	5.07	3.00	3.00	.60	1.00	800 872-8037
North American Natl Muni Bond B	Muni Natl	.60	2.56	4.21	4.00	3.00	.60	1.85	800 872-8037
North American Natl Muni Bond C	Muni Natl	.60	2.56	4.21	4.00	3.00	.60	1.85	800 872-8037
North American Strategic Inc A	Dvsfd Bond	2.30	2.67	6.92	2.00	4.00	.75	1.50	800 872-8037
North American Strategic Inc B	Dvsfd Bond	1.50	2.03	6.42	3.00	4.00	.75	2.14	800 872-8037
North American Strategic Inc C	Dvsfd Bond	1.50	2.17	6.35	3.00	4.00	.75	2.14	800 872-8037
North American USG Secs A	Govt-Mtg	2.70	4.53	4.85	3.00	2.00	.59	1.25	800 872-8037
North American USG Secs B	Govt-Mtg	2.00	3.81	4.08	4.00	2.00	.59	1.89	800 872-8037
North American USG Secs C	Govt-Mtg	2.00	3.81	4.19	4.00	2.00	.59	1.89	800 872-8037
Northeast Investors Trust	Corp-HY	-2.60	2.64	7.99	4.00	5.00	.66	.60	800 225-6704
Northern CA Tax-Exempt Fund	Muni CA	3.30	4.67		3.00	4.00	.69	1.16	800 595-9111
Northern FL Interm Tax Exempt Bond	Muni State	3.00	4.02		2.00	2.00	.69	.84	800 595-9111
Northern Fixed Income Fund	Corp-Inv	3.20	4.93	5.49	3.00	3.00	.75	1.08	800 595-9111
Northern High Yield Fixed Income	Corp-HY	1.10					.75	.17	800 595-9111
Northern High Yield Municipal Fund	Corp-HY	-3.60					.69	.84	800 595-9111
Northern Instl Bond A	Corp-Inv	3.30	5.63	6.30	3.00	3.00	.59	.35	800 595-9111
Northern Instl Bond C	Corp-Inv	3.00	5.41		3.00	3.00	.25	.59	800 595-9111
Northern Instl Bond D	Corp-Inv	1.90	4.97	5.72	3.00	3.00	.25	.75	800 595-9111
Northern Instl Int'l Bond A	Intl Bond	-.60	.95	2.10	5.00	5.00	.90	.95	800 595-9111
Northern Instl Intl Bond Fund D	Intl Bond	-2.90	-.70		4.00	5.00	.69	1.35	800 595-9111
Northern Instl Short Interm Bond A	Corp-Inv	2.80	5.25	5.47	3.00	1.00	.59	.35	800 595-9111
Northern Instl Short Interm Bond D	Corp-Inv	1.80	4.70	4.97	3.00	1.00	.25	.75	800 595-9111
Northern Instl US Govt Sec A	Government	4.40	5.36	5.48	2.00	1.00	.59	.35	800 595-9111
Northern Instl US Govt Sec C	Government	-1.00	3.11		4.00	1.00	.25	.59	800 595-9111
Northern Instl US Govt Sec D	Government	3.50	4.80	4.96	3.00	1.00	.25	.75	800 595-9111
Northern Instl US Treasury Index A	Government	5.10	6.31	6.05	3.00	3.00	.40	.26	800 595-9111
Northern Instl US Treasury Index D	Government	4.20	5.76	5.54	3.00	3.00	.14	.65	800 595-9111
Northern Intermediate Tax Exempt	Muni Natl	2.70	3.51	4.03	3.00	2.00	.69	1.06	800 595-9111
Northern Tax Exempt Fund	Muni Natl	2.20	4.00	5.09	3.00	4.00	.69	1.08	800 595-9111
Northern US Government Fund	Government	3.70	5.11	5.14	3.00	2.00	.75	1.07	800 595-9111
Nuveen CA Insd Muni Bond Fund A	Muni CA	2.00	3.85	5.17	2.00	3.00	.54	.93	800 621-7227
Nuveen CA Insd Muni Bond Fund C	Muni CA	1.50	3.29	4.60	3.00	3.00	.54	1.47	800 621-7227
Nuveen CA Insd Muni Bond Fund R	Muni CA	2.20	4.03	5.41	2.00	3.00	.54	.73	800 621-7227
Nuveen CA Muni Bond Fund A	Muni CA	1.80	4.08	5.47	2.00	3.00	.54	.90	800 621-7227
Nuveen CA Muni Bond Fund C	Muni CA	1.20	3.52	4.84	3.00	3.00	.54	1.44	800 621-7227
Nuveen CA Muni Bond Fund R	Muni CA	1.80	4.25	5.70	2.00	3.00	.54	.70	800 621-7227
Nuveen High Yield Fund A	Muni Natl	5.40					.59		800 621-7227
Nuveen High Yield Fund B	Muni Natl	.20					.59		800 621-7227
Nuveen High Yield Fund C	Muni Natl	.50					.59		800 621-7227
Nuveen High Yield Fund R	Muni Natl	1.30					.59		800 621-7227
Nuveen Income Fund A	Government	7.50					.59	1.05	800 621-7227
Nuveen Income Fund B	Government	1.60					.59	1.80	800 621-7227
Nuveen Income Fund C	Government	1.90					.59	1.80	800 621-7227
Nuveen Income Fund R	Government	2.70					.59	.80	800 621-7227
Nuveen Insured Municipal Bond A	Muni Natl	1.70	4.01	5.13	1.00	3.00	.47	.81	800 621-7227
Nuveen Insured Municipal Bond C	Muni Natl	1.20	3.47	4.63	3.00	3.00	.47	1.36	800 621-7227

430

Bond Fund Name	Objective	Annualized Return for			Rank		Max Load	Expense Ratio	Toll-Free Telephone
		1 Year	3 Years	5 Years	Overall	Risk			
Nuveen Insured Municipal Bond R	Muni Natl	1.80	4.19	5.37	1.00	3.00	.47	.61	800 621-7227
Nuveen MA Insured Muni Bond A	Muni State	1.80	3.57	4.46	3.00	2.00	.55	1.01	800 621-7227
Nuveen MA Insured Muni Bond C	Muni State	1.30	2.99	3.83	3.00	2.00	.55	1.56	800 621-7227
Nuveen MA Insured Muni Bond R	Muni State	1.90	3.72	4.67	2.00	2.00	.55	.81	800 621-7227
Nuveen MA Muni Bond Fund A	Muni State	1.00	3.36	4.57	3.00	2.00	.55	1.02	800 621-7227
Nuveen MA Muni Bond Fund C	Muni State	.60	2.86	3.95	4.00	2.00	.55	1.57	800 621-7227
Nuveen MA Muni Bond Fund R	Muni State	1.20	3.56	4.77	2.00	2.00	.55	.81	800 621-7227
Nuveen MD Muni Bond Fund A	Muni State	0.00	3.06	4.25	4.00	3.00	.55	.94	800 621-7227
Nuveen MD Muni Bond Fund C	Muni State	-.50	2.53	3.61	5.00	3.00	.55	1.50	800 621-7227
Nuveen MD Muni Bond Fund R	Muni State	.10	3.24	4.44	3.00	3.00	.55	.75	800 621-7227
Nuveen Municipal Bond A	Muni Natl	1.80	4.10	5.30	1.00	3.00	.45	.77	800 621-7227
Nuveen Municipal Bond C	Muni Natl	1.10	3.42	4.58	3.00	3.00	.45	1.32	800 621-7227
Nuveen Municipal Bond R	Muni Natl	1.80	4.28	5.42	1.00	3.00	.45	.56	800 621-7227
Nuveen NY Insured Muni Bond A	Muni NY	2.20	3.88	4.85	2.00	3.00	.54	.92	800 621-7227
Nuveen NY Insured Muni Bond C	Muni NY	1.60	3.34	4.20	3.00	3.00	.54	1.46	800 621-7227
Nuveen NY Insured Muni Bond R	Muni NY	2.30	4.07	5.04	2.00	3.00	.54	.71	800 621-7227
Nuveen-Flagship AZ Muni Bond A	Muni State	1.00	3.63	5.18	3.00	4.00	.55	.83	800 621-7227
Nuveen-Flagship AZ Muni Bond C	Muni State	.40	3.07	4.51	5.00	4.00	.55	1.38	800 621-7227
Nuveen-Flagship AZ Muni Bond R	Muni State	1.10	3.74	4.98	3.00	4.00	.55	.63	800 621-7227
Nuveen-Flagship All Amer Muni A	Muni Natl	-.90	3.41	5.29	3.00	3.00	.48	.81	800 621-7227
Nuveen-Flagship All Amer Muni C	Muni Natl	-1.40	2.73	4.63	3.00	3.00	.48	1.36	800 621-7227
Nuveen-Flagship CO Muni Bond A	Muni State	-2.00	3.02	5.07	4.00	4.00	.55	.95	800 621-7227
Nuveen-Flagship CO Muni Bond B	Muni State	-2.60	2.26		5.00	4.00	.55	1.67	800 621-7227
Nuveen-Flagship CO Muni Bond C	Muni State	-2.40	2.47		5.00	4.00	.55	1.48	800 621-7227
Nuveen-Flagship CO Muni Bond R	Muni State	-1.90	3.17		5.00	4.00	.55	.75	800 621-7227
Nuveen-Flagship FL Muni Bond A	Muni State	1.10	3.70	4.76	2.00	3.00	.54	.83	800 621-7227
Nuveen-Flagship FL Muni Bond C	Muni State	.50	3.11	4.71	3.00	3.00	.54	1.38	800 621-7227
Nuveen-Flagship FL Muni Bond R	Muni State	1.10	3.83	4.98	1.00	3.00	.54	.64	800 621-7227
Nuveen-Flagship GA Muni Bond A	Muni State	.10	3.60	5.25	3.00	4.00	.55	.73	800 621-7227
Nuveen-Flagship GA Muni Bond C	Muni State	-.50	3.05	4.70	4.00	4.00	.55	1.29	800 621-7227
Nuveen-Flagship Interm Muni A	Muni Natl	1.60	3.76	5.20	2.00	3.00	.50	.97	800 621-7227
Nuveen-Flagship KS Muni Bond A	Muni State	-.20	3.38	4.94	4.00	4.00	.55	.75	800 621-7227
Nuveen-Flagship KY Muni Bond A	Muni State	.10	3.36	4.78	3.00	3.00	.55	.81	800 621-7227
Nuveen-Flagship KY Muni Bond C	Muni State	-.40	2.81	4.21	4.00	3.00	.55	1.37	800 621-7227
Nuveen-Flagship LA Muni Bond A	Muni State	-.60	3.33	5.27	4.00	4.00	.55	.75	800 621-7227
Nuveen-Flagship LA Muni Bond C	Muni State	-1.10	2.76	4.69	4.00	4.00	.55	1.29	800 621-7227
Nuveen-Flagship LtdTerm Muni A	Muni Natl	2.00	3.62	4.32	3.00	2.00	.42	.77	800 621-7227
Nuveen-Flagship MI Muni Bond A	Muni State	0.00	3.26	4.78	3.00	3.00	.55	.83	800 621-7227
Nuveen-Flagship MI Muni Bond C	Muni State	-.50	2.71	4.22	5.00	3.00	.55	1.38	800 621-7227
Nuveen-Flagship MO Muni Bond A	Muni State	0.00	3.49	4.89	3.00	3.00	.55	.85	800 621-7227
Nuveen-Flagship MO Muni Bond C	Muni State	-.60	2.91	4.35	4.00	3.00	.55	1.40	800 621-7227
Nuveen-Flagship NC Muni Bond A	Muni State	.40	3.26	4.65	3.00	3.00	.55	.73	800 621-7227
Nuveen-Flagship NC Muni Bond C	Muni State	-.30	2.69	4.06	5.00	4.00	.55	1.23	800 621-7227
Nuveen-Flagship NM Muni Bond A	Muni State	-.30	3.58	5.09	3.00	3.00	.55	.90	800 621-7227
Nuveen-Flagship OH Muni Bond A	Muni State	.30	3.52	4.67	3.00	3.00	.55	.84	800 621-7227
Nuveen-Flagship OH Muni Bond C	Muni State	-.10	2.99	4.17	4.00	3.00	.55	1.39	800 621-7227
Nuveen-Flagship OH Muni Bond R	Muni State	.40	3.53	4.76	3.00	3.00	.55	.65	800 621-7227
Nuveen-Flagship PA Muni Bond A	Muni State	-1.50	2.98	4.65	4.00	3.00	.55	.68	800 621-7227
Nuveen-Flagship PA Muni Bond C	Muni State	-2.00	2.36	4.06	4.00	3.00	.55	1.23	800 621-7227
Nuveen-Flagship PA Muni Bond R	Muni State	-1.50	3.07	4.96	3.00	3.00	.55	.48	800 621-7227
Nuveen-Flagship TN Muni Bond A	Muni State	.40	3.23	4.62	3.00	3.00	.54	.83	800 621-7227
Nuveen-Flagship TN Muni Bond C	Muni State	-.10	2.68	4.03	5.00	3.00	.54	1.38	800 621-7227
Nuveen-Flagship VA Muni Bond A	Muni State	.90	3.88	5.15	3.00	3.00	.55	.85	800 621-7227
Nuveen-Flagship VA Muni Bond C	Muni State	.40	3.30	4.67	3.00	3.00	.55	1.40	800 621-7227
Nuveen-Flagship VA Muni Bond R	Muni State	.90	4.06	5.45	2.00	3.00	.55	.66	800 621-7227
Nuveen-Flagship WI Muni Bond A	Muni State	-.10	3.61	4.77	4.00	4.00	.55	.68	800 621-7227
Nvest Bond Income Fund A	Corp-Inv	3.80	5.63	6.51	2.00	4.00	.42	.97	800 225-5478
Nvest Bond Income Fund B	Corp-Inv	3.10	4.85	5.72	3.00	4.00	.42	1.72	800 225-5478

| Bond Fund Name | Objective | Annualized Return for | | | Rank | | Max Load | Expense Ratio | Toll-Free Telephone |
		1 Year	3 Years	5 Years	Overall	Risk			
Nvest Bond Income Fund C	Corp-Inv	3.10	4.84	5.71	3.00	4.00	.42	1.72	800 225-5478
Nvest Bond Income Fund Y	Corp-Inv	4.20	5.92	6.79	2.00	4.00	.42	.72	800 225-5478
Nvest Govt Securities A	Government	2.80	4.78	4.89	4.00	4.00	.65	1.36	800 225-5478
Nvest Govt Securities B	Government	2.10	4.04	4.15	5.00	4.00	.65	2.10	800 225-5478
Nvest Govt Securities Y	Government	3.20	5.10	5.17	3.00	4.00	.65	1.11	800 225-5478
Nvest High Income Fund A	Corp-HY	-3.40	2.13	6.27	3.00	5.00	.69	1.31	800 225-5478
Nvest High Income Fund B	Corp-HY	-4.20	1.37	5.52	4.00	5.00	.69	2.06	800 225-5478
Nvest High Income Fund C	Corp-HY	-4.10					.69	2.06	800 225-5478
Nvest Interm CA Tax Free A	Muni CA	2.30	3.79	5.35	2.00	2.00	.52	.84	800 225-5478
Nvest Interm CA Tax Free B	Muni CA	1.40	2.98	4.57	3.00	2.00	.52	1.60	800 225-5478
Nvest Ltd Term US Govt A	Government	3.50	4.38	4.66	3.00	2.00	.64	1.34	800 225-5478
Nvest Ltd Term US Govt B	Government	2.80	3.71	3.97	4.00	2.00	.64	1.98	800 225-5478
Nvest Ltd Term US Govt C	Government	2.80	3.71	3.97	4.00	2.00	.64	1.98	800 225-5478
Nvest Ltd Term US Govt Y	Government	3.90	4.80	5.03	3.00	2.00	.64	.98	800 225-5478
Nvest MA Tax Free Income A	Muni State	.60	3.27	4.81	3.00	3.00	.57	1.00	800 225-5478
Nvest MA Tax Free Income B	Muni State	-.10	2.58	4.11	5.00	3.00	.57	1.64	800 225-5478
Nvest Municipal Income A	Muni Natl	.70	3.65	4.97	3.00	2.00	.44	.93	800 225-5478
Nvest Municipal Income B	Muni Natl	-.10	2.88	4.23	4.00	2.00	.44	1.67	800 225-5478
Nvest S/T Corp Income A	Govt-Mtg	3.30	3.66	4.58	3.00	1.00	.53	.69	800 225-5478
Nvest S/T Corp Income B	Govt-Mtg	2.60	2.88	3.83	4.00	1.00	.54	1.44	800 225-5478
Nvest Strategic Income A	Dvsfd Bond	4.30	4.96	9.08	3.00	5.00	.65	1.22	800 225-5478
Nvest Strategic Income B	Dvsfd Bond	3.40	4.14	8.25	3.00	5.00	.65	1.97	800 225-5478
Nvest Strategic Income C	Dvsfd Bond	3.50	4.15	8.23	3.00	5.00	.65	1.97	800 225-5478
OVB Government Securities A	Government	3.70	5.52	5.61	3.00	3.00	.75	.85	800 545-6331
OVB Government Securities B	Government	3.40	5.23	5.36	3.00	3.00	.75	1.08	800 545-6331
OVB WV Tax-Exempt Income A	Muni State	1.90	3.88	5.00	1.00	3.00	.45	.75	800 545-6331
OVB WV Tax-Exempt Income B	Muni State	1.70	3.66	4.76	2.00	3.00	.45	1.00	800 545-6331
Ocean State Tax-Exempt Fund	Muni State	2.40	3.59	4.74	2.00	2.00	.59	.98	800 992-2207
One Group Short-Term Muni Bond A	Muni Natl	2.50					.34	.85	800 480-4111
One Group Short-Term Muni Bond B	Muni Natl	2.10					.34	1.55	800 480-4111
One Group Short-Term Muni Bond I	Muni Natl	2.90					.34	.61	800 480-4111
One Group-AZ Municipal Bond A	Muni State	2.40	3.10		3.00	2.00	.45	.85	800 480-4111
One Group-AZ Municipal Bond B	Muni State	1.60	1.78		3.00	2.00	.45	1.50	800 480-4111
One Group-AZ Municipal Bond I	Muni State	2.70	3.70		2.00	3.00	.45	.60	800 480-4111
One Group-Bond A	Corp-Inv	3.70	5.64	6.58	3.00	3.00	.59	.85	800 480-4111
One Group-Bond B	Corp-Inv	3.00	4.87		2.00	3.00	.59	1.57	800 480-4111
One Group-Bond C	Corp-Inv	3.40					.59	1.46	800 480-4111
One Group-Bond I	Corp-Inv	3.90	5.87	6.64	2.00	3.00	.59	.64	800 480-4111
One Group-Government Bond A	Government	4.20	5.41	5.51	3.00	3.00	.45	.86	800 480-4111
One Group-Government Bond B	Government	3.40	4.73	4.84	3.00	3.00	.45	1.52	800 480-4111
One Group-Government Bond C	Government	3.40					.45	1.52	800 480-4111
One Group-Government Bond I	Government	4.30	5.62	5.75	2.00	3.00	.45	.61	800 480-4111
One Group-High Yield Bond A	Corp-HY	-1.00					.75	1.12	800 480-4111
One Group-High Yield Bond B	Corp-HY	-1.40					.75	1.77	800 480-4111
One Group-High Yield Bond C	Corp-HY	-1.70					.75	1.76	800 480-4111
One Group-High Yield Bond I	Corp-HY	-.70					.75	.89	800 480-4111
One Group-Inc Bond Fund A	Corp-Inv	3.80	5.17	5.38	3.00	3.00	.59	.86	800 480-4111
One Group-Inc Bond Fund B	Corp-Inv	3.10	4.44	5.31	3.00	3.00	.59	1.52	800 480-4111
One Group-Inc Bond Fund I	Corp-Inv	4.20	5.46	5.67	2.00	3.00	.59	.61	800 480-4111
One Group-Interm Tax Free A	Muni Natl	2.00	3.62	4.69	3.00	2.00	.39	.83	800 480-4111
One Group-Interm Tax Free B	Muni Natl	1.50	2.99	4.04	3.00	2.00	.39	1.48	800 480-4111
One Group-Interm Tax Free I	Muni Natl	2.20	3.57	4.76	2.00	3.00	.39	.58	800 480-4111
One Group-Intermediate Bond A	Corp-Inv	3.90	5.26	6.19	2.00	2.00	.59	.83	800 480-4111
One Group-Intermediate Bond B	Corp-Inv	3.20	4.52		3.00	2.00	.59	1.50	800 480-4111
One Group-Intermediate Bond C	Corp-Inv	3.40					.59	1.50	800 480-4111
One Group-Intermediate Bond I	Corp-Inv	4.10	5.51	6.42	1.00	2.00	.59	.61	800 480-4111
One Group-KY Municipal A	Muni State	2.50	3.68	4.63	2.00	2.00	.40	.85	800 480-4111
One Group-KY Municipal B	Muni State	1.90	3.02	4.00	3.00	2.00	.40	1.51	800 480-4111

| Bond Fund Name | Objective | Annualized Return for | | | Rank | | Max Load | Expense Ratio | Toll-Free Telephone |
		1 Year	3 Years	5 Years	Overall	Risk			
One Group-KY Municipal I	Muni State	2.80	3.97	4.97	2.00	2.00	.40	.60	800 480-4111
One Group-LA Muni Bond A	Muni State	2.50	3.50	4.53	2.00	2.00	.40	.85	800 480-4111
One Group-LA Muni Bond B	Muni State	1.90	2.87	3.81	3.00	2.00	.40	1.51	800 480-4111
One Group-LA Muni Bond I	Muni State	2.80	3.70	4.61	2.00	2.00	.40	.60	800 480-4111
One Group-MI Muni Bond A	Muni State	.90	3.61	4.84	3.00	3.00	.40	.88	800 480-4111
One Group-MI Muni Bond B	Muni State	.50	2.97		5.00	4.00	.40	1.59	800 480-4111
One Group-MI Muni Bond I	Muni State	1.30	3.86	5.04	3.00	3.00	.40	.66	800 480-4111
One Group-Muni Income A	Muni Natl	.10	3.38	4.53	3.00	2.00	.40	.81	800 480-4111
One Group-Muni Income B	Muni Natl	-.60	2.81	3.92	3.00	2.00	.40	1.46	800 480-4111
One Group-Muni Income C	Muni Natl	-.60					.40	1.46	800 480-4111
One Group-Muni Income I	Muni Natl	.30	3.77	4.85	2.00	2.00	.40	.56	800 480-4111
One Group-OH Municipal A	Muni State	1.90	3.58	4.70	3.00	2.00	.40	.81	800 480-4111
One Group-OH Municipal B	Muni State	1.20	2.76	3.86	3.00	2.00	.40	1.45	800 480-4111
One Group-OH Municipal I	Muni State	2.20	3.70	4.79	2.00	2.00	.40	.56	800 480-4111
One Group-Short Term Bond A	Government	4.60	5.08	5.29	2.00	1.00	.59	.78	800 480-4111
One Group-Short Term Bond B	Government	4.00	4.66	4.80	3.00	1.00	.59	1.13	800 480-4111
One Group-Short Term Bond I	Government	4.80	5.36	5.59	1.00	1.00	.59	.53	800 480-4111
One Group-Tax Free Bond A	Muni Natl	2.40	3.99	4.68	2.00	3.00	.45	.86	800 480-4111
One Group-Tax Free Bond B	Muni Natl	1.80	3.29	4.15	3.00	3.00	.45	1.57	800 480-4111
One Group-Tax Free Bond I	Muni Natl	2.60	4.27	5.19	2.00	3.00	.45	.63	800 480-4111
One Group-Treasury & Agency A	Government	4.30	5.20		3.00	2.00	.20	.59	800 480-4111
One Group-Treasury & Agency B	Government	3.60	4.60		3.00	2.00	.20	1.10	800 480-4111
One Group-Treasury & Agency I	Government	4.40	5.28		2.00	2.00	.20	.35	800 480-4111
One Group-Ultra Sh Term Bond A	Corp-Inv	5.40	5.17	5.58	1.00	1.00	.29	.56	800 480-4111
One Group-Ultra Sh Term Bond B	Corp-Inv	4.90	4.73	5.01	2.00	1.00	.29	1.03	800 480-4111
One Group-Ultra Sh Term Bond I	Corp-Inv	5.70	5.44	5.81	1.00	1.00	.29	.32	800 480-4111
One Group-WV Municipal Bond A	Muni State	2.60	3.62		2.00	3.00	.40	.84	800 480-4111
One Group-WV Municipal Bond B	Muni State	1.80	3.03		3.00	3.00	.40	1.50	800 480-4111
One Group-WV Municipal Bond I	Muni State	2.80	3.77		2.00	2.00	.40	.60	800 480-4111
Oppenheimer Bond Fund A	Corp-Inv	1.80	3.94	5.08	3.00	3.00	.73	1.26	800 525-7048
Oppenheimer Bond Fund B	Corp-Inv	1.20	3.15	4.28	3.00	3.00	.73	2.00	800 525-7048
Oppenheimer Bond Fund C	Corp-Inv	1.10	3.14		4.00	3.00	.73	2.00	800 525-7048
Oppenheimer Bond Fund Y	Corp-Inv	2.10					.73	.82	800 525-7048
Oppenheimer CA Municipal Fund A	Muni CA	-.60	3.26	5.01	4.00	4.00	.55	.91	800 525-7048
Oppenheimer CA Municipal Fund B	Muni CA	-1.50	2.44	4.22	5.00	4.00	.55	1.66	800 525-7048
Oppenheimer CA Municipal Fund C	Muni CA	-1.50	2.45	3.56	5.00	4.00	.55	1.66	800 525-7048
Oppenheimer Champion Income Fd A	Corp-HY	1.90	4.73	7.77	3.00	5.00	.60	1.09	800 525-7048
Oppenheimer Champion Income Fd B	Corp-HY	1.00	3.89		3.00	5.00	.60	1.84	800 525-7048
Oppenheimer Champion Income Fd C	Corp-HY	1.00	3.91	6.90	3.00	5.00	.60	1.84	800 525-7048
Oppenheimer FL Municipal Fund A	Muni State	-.30	3.22	4.75	3.00	3.00	.59	.94	800 525-7048
Oppenheimer FL Municipal Fund B	Muni State	-1.10	2.43	3.98	5.00	3.00	.59	1.69	800 525-7048
Oppenheimer FL Municipal Fund C	Muni State	-1.10	2.41		5.00	3.00	.59	1.69	800 525-7048
Oppenheimer High Yield Fund A	Corp-HY	.70	3.95	7.37	3.00	5.00	.59	.98	800 525-7048
Oppenheimer High Yield Fund B	Corp-HY	-.10	3.13	6.50	3.00	5.00	.59	1.78	800 525-7048
Oppenheimer High Yield Fund C	Corp-HY	-.10	3.12		3.00	5.00	.59	1.78	800 525-7048
Oppenheimer High Yield Fund Y	Corp-HY	.90					.59	.76	800 525-7048
Oppenheimer Insured Muni Fd A	Muni Natl	-.70	2.99	4.76	4.00	4.00	.45	.90	800 525-7048
Oppenheimer Insured Muni Fd B	Muni Natl	-1.40	2.23	3.97	5.00	4.00	.45	1.65	800 525-7048
Oppenheimer Insured Muni Fd C	Muni Natl	-1.40	2.24		5.00	4.00	.45	1.65	800 525-7048
Oppenheimer Intermd Muni Fd A	Muni Natl	-.10	3.37	4.83	3.00	3.00	.47	.91	800 525-7048
Oppenheimer Intermd Muni Fd B	Muni Natl	-.80	2.59		4.00	3.00	.47	1.66	800 525-7048
Oppenheimer Intermd Muni Fd C	Muni Natl	-.80	2.59	4.04	4.00	3.00	.47	1.66	800 525-7048
Oppenheimer Intl Bond Fund A	Intl Bond	10.70	2.64	7.79	3.00	5.00	.75	1.28	800 525-7048
Oppenheimer Intl Bond Fund B	Intl Bond	9.70	1.81	7.10	3.00	5.00	.75	2.04	800 525-7048
Oppenheimer Intl Bond Fund C	Intl Bond	9.70	1.85	7.12	3.00	5.00	.75	2.04	800 525-7048
Oppenheimer Limited Term Govt Fd A	Government	4.20	5.24	5.71	2.00	1.00	.41	.85	800 525-7048
Oppenheimer Limited Term Govt Fd B	Government	3.40	4.45	4.93	3.00	1.00	.41	1.62	800 525-7048
Oppenheimer Limited Term Govt Fd C	Government	3.40	4.42	4.89	3.00	1.00	.41	1.61	800 525-7048

Bond Fund Name	Objective	Annualized Return for			Rank		Max Load	Expense Ratio	Toll-Free Telephone
		1 Year	3 Years	5 Years	Overall	Risk			
Oppenheimer Limited Term Govt Fd Y	Government	4.50					.41	.41	800 525-7048
Oppenheimer Main St CA Muni Fd A	Muni CA	.30	3.91	5.49	4.00	4.00	.55	.52	800 525-7048
Oppenheimer Main St CA Muni Fd B	Muni CA	-.60	2.87	4.46	4.00	4.00	.55	1.52	800 525-7048
Oppenheimer Municipal Bond Fd A	Muni Natl	-2.10	2.82	4.80	4.00	4.00	.52	.86	800 525-7048
Oppenheimer Municipal Bond Fd B	Muni Natl	-2.90	2.04	3.99	3.00	4.00	.52	1.64	800 525-7048
Oppenheimer Municipal Bond Fd C	Muni Natl	-2.90	2.04		5.00	4.00	.52	1.64	800 525-7048
Oppenheimer NJ Municipal Fund A	Muni State	-3.90	2.07	3.97	5.00	4.00	.59	.63	800 525-7048
Oppenheimer NJ Municipal Fund B	Muni State	-4.60	1.34	3.19	5.00	4.00	.59	1.37	800 525-7048
Oppenheimer NJ Municipal Fund C	Muni State	-4.60	1.33		5.00	4.00	.59	1.85	800 525-7048
Oppenheimer NY Municipal Fund A	Muni NY	.10	3.44	4.96	3.00	3.00	.52	.88	800 525-7048
Oppenheimer NY Municipal Fund B	Muni NY	-.70	2.65	4.15	5.00	3.00	.52	1.64	800 525-7048
Oppenheimer NY Municipal Fund C	Muni NY	-.70	2.65		5.00	3.00	.52	1.64	800 525-7048
Oppenheimer PA Municipal Fund A	Muni State	-3.70	1.88	3.93	4.00	3.00	.59	.90	800 525-7048
Oppenheimer PA Municipal Fund B	Muni State	-4.30	1.15	3.14	5.00	3.00	.59	1.64	800 525-7048
Oppenheimer PA Municipal Fund C	Muni State	-4.40	1.12		5.00	3.00	.59	1.64	800 525-7048
Oppenheimer Strat Income Fd A	Dvsfd Bond	5.50	4.12	7.23	2.00	4.00	.52	.93	800 525-7048
Oppenheimer Strat Income Fd B	Dvsfd Bond	4.40	3.33	6.42	3.00	4.00	.52	1.68	800 525-7048
Oppenheimer Strat Income Fd C	Dvsfd Bond	4.70	3.43	6.41	3.00	4.00	.52	1.68	800 525-7048
Oppenheimer Strat Income Fd Y	Dvsfd Bond	5.90					.52	.57	800 525-7048
Oppenheimer US Govt Trust Fund A	Government	4.60	5.15	5.87	2.00	2.00	.57	1.03	800 525-7048
Oppenheimer US Govt Trust Fund B	Government	4.00	4.36		4.00	2.00	.57	1.78	800 525-7048
Oppenheimer US Govt Trust Fund C	Government	3.80	4.32	5.05	4.00	2.00	.57	1.79	800 525-7048
Oppenheimer US Govt Trust Fund Y	Government	5.00					.57	.79	800 525-7048
Oppenheimer World Bond Fund B	Intl Bond	8.20					.75	2.64	800 525-7048
Oppenheimer World Bond Fund C	Intl Bond	8.10					.75	2.64	800 525-7048
PDP Inst'l Managed Bond Port. X	Corp-Inv	4.80	3.96	6.27	3.00	4.00	.45	.55	800 243-4361
PDP Inst'l Managed Bond Port. Y	Corp-Inv	4.60	3.70	6.02	3.00	4.00	.45	.80	800 243-4361
PIMCO Emerging Markets Bond A	Intl Bond	22.60					.84	1.25	800 426-0107
PIMCO Emerging Markets Bond Admin	Intl Bond	22.80					.84	1.10	800 426-0107
PIMCO Emerging Markets Bond B	Intl Bond	21.70					.84	2.00	800 426-0107
PIMCO Emerging Markets Bond C	Intl Bond	21.80					.84	2.00	800 426-0107
PIMCO Emerging Markets Bond Inst	Intl Bond	23.10					.84	.84	800 426-0107
PIMCO Foreign Bond Fund A	Intl Bond	4.80	6.28		1.00	3.00	.50	.94	800 426-0107
PIMCO Foreign Bond Fund Admin	Intl Bond	5.00	6.53		1.00	3.00	.50	.75	800 426-0107
PIMCO Foreign Bond Fund B	Intl Bond	4.00	5.50		2.00	3.00	.50	1.69	800 426-0107
PIMCO Foreign Bond Fund C	Intl Bond	4.00	5.53		2.00	3.00	.50	1.69	800 426-0107
PIMCO Foreign Bond Fund D	Intl Bond	4.80					.50	.94	800 426-0107
PIMCO Foreign Bond Fund Inst	Intl Bond	5.30	6.79	11.32	1.00	3.00	.50	.50	800 426-0107
PIMCO Global Bond Fund Admin	Intl Bond	2.20	2.34		5.00	5.00	.55	.80	800 426-0107
PIMCO Global Bond Fund II A	Intl Bond	4.20	5.02		3.00	3.00	.25	.94	800 426-0107
PIMCO Global Bond Fund II B	Intl Bond	3.40	4.23		3.00	3.00	.25	1.69	800 426-0107
PIMCO Global Bond Fund II C	Intl Bond	3.40	4.21		3.00	3.00	.25	1.69	800 426-0107
PIMCO Global Bond Fund Inst	Intl Bond	2.40	2.54	4.78	5.00	4.00	.55	.55	800 426-0107
PIMCO Global Bond II Fund Instl	Intl Bond	4.60					.25	.55	800 426-0107
PIMCO High Yield Fund A	Corp-HY	.80	4.68		3.00	4.00	.25	.90	800 426-0107
PIMCO High Yield Fund Admin	Corp-HY	.90	4.83	8.02	1.00	4.00	.25	.75	800 426-0107
PIMCO High Yield Fund B	Corp-HY	0.00	3.88		3.00	4.00	.25	1.64	800 426-0107
PIMCO High Yield Fund C	Corp-HY	0.00	3.89		3.00	4.00	.25	1.64	800 426-0107
PIMCO High Yield Fund D	Corp-HY	.80					.25	.90	800 426-0107
PIMCO High Yield Fund Inst	Corp-HY	1.20	5.07	8.29	1.00	4.00	.25	.50	800 426-0107
PIMCO Long Term US Govt A	Government	5.50	7.81		3.00	5.00	.25	1.34	800 426-0107
PIMCO Long Term US Govt Admin	Government	5.70					.25	1.14	800 426-0107
PIMCO Long Term US Govt B	Government	4.70	7.00		4.00	5.00	.25	2.12	800 426-0107
PIMCO Long Term US Govt C	Government	4.70	6.98		4.00	5.00	.25	2.16	800 426-0107
PIMCO Long Term US Govt Inst	Government	5.90	8.22	7.71	3.00	5.00	.25	.89	800 426-0107
PIMCO Low Duration Fund A	Dvsfd Bond	4.60	5.39		1.00	1.00	.25	.90	800 426-0107
PIMCO Low Duration Fund Admin	Dvsfd Bond	4.80	5.61	6.32	1.00	1.00	.25	.68	800 426-0107
PIMCO Low Duration Fund B	Dvsfd Bond	3.80	4.62		1.00	1.00	.25	1.64	800 426-0107

434

| Bond Fund Name | Objective | Annualized Return for | | | Rank | | Max Load | Expense Ratio | Toll-Free Telephone |
		1 Year	3 Years	5 Years	Overall	Risk			
PIMCO Low Duration Fund C	Dvsfd Bond	4.10	4.87		1.00	1.00	.25	1.39	800 426-0107
PIMCO Low Duration Fund D	Dvsfd Bond	4.70					.25	.75	800 426-0107
PIMCO Low Duration Fund II Inst	Dvsfd Bond	5.10	5.51	5.98	1.00	1.00	.25	.56	800 426-0107
PIMCO Low Duration Fund III Inst	Dvsfd Bond	4.60	5.42		1.00	1.00	.25	.50	800 426-0107
PIMCO Low Duration Fund Inst	Dvsfd Bond	5.10	5.88	6.58	1.00	1.00	.42	.42	800 426-0107
PIMCO Low Duration II Admin	Dvsfd Bond	4.30					.25	.84	800 426-0107
PIMCO Low Duration III Admin	Dvsfd Bond	4.40					.25	.75	800 426-0107
PIMCO Low Duration Mortgage Inst	Govt-Mtg	5.30					.25	2.37	800 426-0107
PIMCO Moderate Duration Inst	Dvsfd Bond	4.70	5.74		2.00	2.00	.25	.45	800 426-0107
PIMCO Municipal Bond A	Muni Natl	1.60					.25	.85	800 426-0107
PIMCO Municipal Bond B	Muni Natl	.80					.25	.85	800 426-0107
PIMCO Municipal Bond C	Muni Natl	1.10					.25	1.35	800 426-0107
PIMCO Municipal Bond D	Muni Natl	1.50					.25	.84	800 426-0107
PIMCO Municipal Bond Fund Admin	Muni Natl	1.60					.25	.75	800 426-0107
PIMCO Municipal Bond Fund I	Muni Natl	1.90					.25	.50	800 426-0107
PIMCO PAP Emerging Markets Inst	Intl Bond	39.10					.40		800 426-0107
PIMCO Real Return Bond C	Corp-Inv	7.50	6.00		2.00	2.00	.25	1.42	800 426-0107
PIMCO Real Return Bond D	Corp-Inv	8.00					.25	.92	800 426-0107
PIMCO Real Return Bond Instl	Corp-Inv	8.50	6.95		1.00	2.00	.25	.52	800 426-0107
PIMCO Real Return Fund A	Corp-Inv	8.00	6.48		2.00	2.00	.25	.92	800 426-0107
PIMCO Real Return Fund B	Corp-Inv	7.20	5.73		1.00	2.00	.25	1.67	800 426-0107
PIMCO Short Term Fund A	Corp-Inv	5.50	5.43		1.00	1.00	.45	.84	800 426-0107
PIMCO Short Term Fund Admin	Corp-Inv	5.60	5.55		1.00	1.00	.45	.69	800 426-0107
PIMCO Short Term Fund B	Corp-Inv	4.70	4.59		1.00	1.00	.45	1.60	800 426-0107
PIMCO Short Term Fund C	Corp-Inv	5.20	5.06		1.00	1.00	.45	1.14	800 426-0107
PIMCO Short Term Fund D	Corp-Inv	5.60					.45	.75	800 426-0107
PIMCO Short Term Fund Inst	Corp-Inv	5.90	5.80	6.49	1.00	1.00	.45	.45	800 426-0107
PIMCO Total Return Fund A	Corp-Inv	4.50	6.13		1.00	3.00	.25	.90	800 426-0107
PIMCO Total Return Fund Admin	Corp-Inv	4.70	6.39	7.11	2.00	3.00	.25	.68	800 426-0107
PIMCO Total Return Fund B	Corp-Inv	3.70	5.36		2.00	3.00	.25	1.64	800 426-0107
PIMCO Total Return Fund C	Corp-Inv	3.70	5.36		2.00	3.00	.25	1.64	800 426-0107
PIMCO Total Return Fund D	Corp-Inv	4.10					.25	.75	800 426-0107
PIMCO Total Return Fund II Admin	Corp-Inv	4.40	6.01	6.46	2.00	3.00	.25	.75	800 426-0107
PIMCO Total Return Fund II Inst	Corp-Inv	4.70	6.28	6.76	2.00	3.00	.25	.50	800 426-0107
PIMCO Total Return Fund III Inst	Corp-Inv	3.00	6.08	6.85	2.00	3.00	.25	.50	800 426-0107
PIMCO Total Return Fund Inst	Corp-Inv	5.00	6.66	7.36	1.00	3.00	.25	.42	800 426-0107
PIMCO Total Return III Admin	Corp-Inv	2.80	5.82		3.00	3.00	.25	.75	800 426-0107
PIMCO Total Return Mortgage D	Govt-Mtg	5.20					.25	.90	800 426-0107
PIMCO Total Return Mortgage Inst	Govt-Mtg	5.60					.25	.50	800 426-0107
Pacific Advisors Govt Secs	Government	7.40	9.48	6.91	3.00	5.00	.65	.75	800 282-6693
Pacific Advisors Govt Securities C	Government	6.50					.65	1.02	800 282-6693
Pacific Capital Divers Fixed I	Dvsfd Bond	3.00	4.83	4.65	4.00	4.00	.59	.72	800 424-2295
Pacific Capital Divers Fixed Ret	Dvsfd Bond	2.70	5.08	4.74	4.00	4.00	.59	.97	800 424-2295
Pacific Capital Sh-Int Treas A	Government	3.60	4.99	5.20	3.00	2.00	.50	.67	800 424-2295
Pacific Capital Sh-Int Treas I	Government	3.40	4.78	4.57	4.00	2.00	.50	.93	800 424-2295
Pacific Capital T/F Secs B	Muni Natl	1.60					.59	1.69	800 424-2295
Pacific Capital T/F Secs I	Muni Natl	2.50	4.29	5.21	1.00	3.00	.59	.70	800 424-2295
Pacific Capital T/F Sh-Interm I	Muni Natl	2.80	3.24	3.70	3.00	2.00	.50	.72	800 424-2295
Pacific Capital T/F Sh-Interm Ret	Muni Natl	2.50	2.86	3.25	3.00	1.00	.59	.97	800 424-2295
Pacific Capital UST Secs I	Government	4.80	6.01	5.15	3.00	3.00	.59	.76	800 424-2295
Pacific Capital UST Secs Ret	Government	4.60	5.87	4.97	3.00	3.00	.59	1.01	800 424-2295
Pacific Captl Diversified Fxd Inc B	Dvsfd Bond	2.30	4.14	4.08	5.00	4.00	.59	1.71	800 424-2295
PaineWebber CA Tax-Free Inc A	Muni CA	2.30	4.34	6.94	3.00	4.00	.50	.76	800 647-1568
PaineWebber CA Tax-Free Inc B	Muni CA	1.60	3.53	4.40	5.00	4.00	.50	1.59	800 647-1568
PaineWebber CA Tax-Free Inc C	Muni CA	1.80	3.77	4.63	4.00	4.00	.50	1.33	800 647-1568
PaineWebber CA Tax-Free Inc Y	Muni CA	2.70					.50	.55	800 647-1568
PaineWebber Global Income A	Intl Bond	1.10	3.41	4.82	5.00	3.00	.73	1.14	800 647-1568
PaineWebber Global Income B	Intl Bond	-.10	2.42	3.91	5.00	3.00	.73	2.04	800 647-1568

Bond Fund Name	Objective	Annualized Return for			Rank		Max Load	Expense Ratio	Toll-Free Telephone
		1 Year	3 Years	5 Years	Overall	Risk			
PaineWebber Global Income C	Intl Bond	.60	2.90	4.33	5.00	3.00	.73	1.64	800 647-1568
PaineWebber Global Income Y	Intl Bond	1.00	3.56	4.76	4.00	3.00	.73	.81	800 647-1568
PaineWebber High Income A	Corp-HY	-14.90	-3.77	2.77	4.00	5.00	.50	.92	800 647-1568
PaineWebber High Income B	Corp-HY	-15.60	-4.46	2.07	4.00	5.00	.50	1.67	800 647-1568
PaineWebber High Income C	Corp-HY	-15.30	-4.19	2.21	4.00	5.00	.50	1.41	800 647-1568
PaineWebber High Income Y	Corp-HY	-15.20					.50	.66	800 647-1568
PaineWebber Inv Grade Income A	Corp-Inv	1.70	4.02	5.45	2.00	4.00	.50	.93	800 647-1568
PaineWebber Inv Grade Income B	Corp-Inv	.90	3.13	4.65	3.00	4.00	.50	1.68	800 647-1568
PaineWebber Inv Grade Income C	Corp-Inv	1.20	3.37	4.86	4.00	4.00	.50	1.42	800 647-1568
PaineWebber Inv Grade Income Y	Corp-Inv	1.80					.50	.66	800 647-1568
PaineWebber Low Dur US Gov Inc A	Government	3.80	4.83	5.56	2.00	1.00	.50	.95	800 647-1568
PaineWebber Low Dur US Gov Inc B	Government	2.90	3.71	4.54	4.00	1.00	.50	1.77	800 647-1568
PaineWebber Low Dur US Gov Inc C	Government	3.10	3.91	4.74	3.00	1.00	.50	1.60	800 647-1568
PaineWebber Muni High Income A	Muni Natl	-3.10	2.88	4.93	3.00	3.00	.59	1.12	800 647-1568
PaineWebber Muni High Income B	Muni Natl	-3.80	2.22	4.23	3.00	3.00	.59	1.87	800 647-1568
PaineWebber Muni High Income C	Muni Natl	-3.60	2.54	4.56	2.00	3.00	.59	1.62	800 647-1568
PaineWebber Muni High Income Y	Muni Natl	-2.90					.59	.86	800 647-1568
PaineWebber NY Tax-Free Inc A	Muni NY	1.60	4.05	5.20	3.00	4.00	.59	1.02	800 647-1568
PaineWebber NY Tax-Free Inc B	Muni NY	.80	3.29	4.44	4.00	4.00	.59	1.77	800 647-1568
PaineWebber NY Tax-Free Inc C	Muni NY	1.10	3.55	4.68	3.00	4.00	.59	1.52	800 647-1568
PaineWebber Natl Tax-Free Inc A	Muni Natl	1.40	3.86	4.76	3.00	3.00	.50	.93	800 647-1568
PaineWebber Natl Tax-Free Inc B	Muni Natl	.50	3.04	3.94	4.00	3.00	.50	1.71	800 647-1568
PaineWebber Natl Tax-Free Inc C	Muni Natl	.80	3.35	4.23	3.00	3.00	.50	1.46	800 647-1568
PaineWebber PACE Global Fixed Inc	Intl Bond	-1.90	2.84		5.00	5.00	.59	.94	800 647-1568
PaineWebber PACE Govt Fixed Inc	Government	5.00	5.73		1.00	2.00	.50	.86	800 647-1568
PaineWebber PACE Interm Fixed Inc	Corp-Inv	4.00	5.02		3.00	2.00	.40	.80	800 647-1568
PaineWebber PACE Muni Fixed Inc	Muni Natl	1.50	3.54		2.00	2.00	.40	.84	800 647-1568
PaineWebber PACE Strat Fixed Inc	Corp-Inv	3.80	5.38		3.00	4.00	.50	.88	800 647-1568
PaineWebber Strategic Income B	Dvsfd Bond	-2.30	1.27	4.99	4.00	4.00	.67	2.08	800 647-1568
PaineWebber Strategic Income C	Dvsfd Bond	-2.10	1.55	5.28	2.00	4.00	.75	1.82	800 647-1568
PaineWebber Strategic Income Y	Dvsfd Bond	-1.30					.75	1.06	800 647-1568
PaineWebber US Govt Income A	Govt-Mtg	3.60	5.01	4.88	3.00	3.00	.50	1.03	800 647-1568
PaineWebber US Govt Income B	Govt-Mtg	2.70	4.16	4.08	4.00	3.00	.50	1.85	800 647-1568
PaineWebber US Govt Income C	Govt-Mtg	3.00	4.47	4.37	4.00	3.00	.50	1.55	800 647-1568
Parnassus Income Fd-CA Tax Fr	Muni CA	4.60	4.95	6.14	1.00	3.00	.50	.67	800 999-3505
Parnassus Income Fd-Fixed Inc	Corp-Inv	.70	3.73	4.84	4.00	3.00	.50	.78	800 999-3505
Pauze US Govt Total Return Bond A	Government	-.50	2.66	3.29	5.00	5.00	.59	1.39	800 327-7170
Payden & Rygel CA Muni Income Fd R	Muni CA	3.50					.32	.50	800 572-9336
Payden & Rygel Emrg Mkt Bond Fd R	Intl Bond	17.10					.45	.80	800 572-9336
Payden & Rygel Global Fixed Inc R	Intl Bond	4.70	6.98	7.25	1.00	3.00	.33	.50	800 572-9336
Payden & Rygel Global Short Bond R	Intl Bond	4.40	5.40		1.00	1.00	.29	.50	800 572-9336
Payden & Rygel High Income R	Corp-HY	.30					.34	.58	800 572-9336
Payden & Rygel Inv Quality Bd R	Corp-Inv	2.20	4.78	5.27	3.00	3.00	.28	.50	800 572-9336
Payden & Rygel Limited Maturity R	Corp-Inv	5.40	5.42	5.44	1.00	1.00	.28	.35	800 572-9336
Payden & Rygel Short Bond R	Corp-Inv	5.00	5.15	5.21	2.00	1.00	.28	.50	800 572-9336
Payden & Rygel Short Dur T/E R	Muni Natl	3.40	3.61	3.79	2.00	1.00	.32	.50	800 572-9336
Payden & Rygel Tax Exempt Bd R	Muni Natl	3.20	4.04	4.89	3.00	2.00	.32	.50	800 572-9336
Payden & Rygel Total Return R	Dvsfd Bond	1.30	4.87		3.00	3.00	.28	.50	800 572-9336
Payden & Rygel US Government R	Government	4.50	5.58	5.52	2.00	2.00	.28	.40	800 572-9336
Penn Capital Strategic HY Bond	Corp-HY	-.50					.68	.68	800 224-6312
Performance Fds-Intrm Govt Cons	Government	3.00	4.51	4.67	4.00	3.00	.50	1.10	800 737-3676
Performance Fds-Intrm Govt Inst	Government	3.40	4.77	4.94	4.00	3.00	.50	.83	800 737-3676
Performance Fds-Short Govt Cons	Government	4.60	4.94	4.99	3.00	1.00	.40	.93	800 737-3676
Performance Fds-Short Govt Inst	Government	4.80	5.20	5.25	3.00	1.00	.40	.68	800 737-3676
Performance Intmed Term Govt B	Government	2.50					.50	1.84	800 737-3676
Permanent Portfolio Treasury	Government	4.20	4.05	4.16	2.00	1.00	.75	.97	800 531-5142
Permanent Portfolio Versatile Bd	Corp-Inv	4.40	4.43	4.69	2.00	1.00	.75	1.00	800 531-5142
Phoenix-Duff & Phelps Core Bd A	Government	2.50	4.09	4.49	4.00	3.00	.45	1.03	800 243-4361

436

Bond Fund Name	Objective	Annualized Return for			Rank		Max Load	Expense Ratio	Toll-Free Telephone
		1 Year	3 Years	5 Years	Overall	Risk			
Phoenix-Duff & Phelps Core Bd B	Government	1.80	3.33	3.72	5.00	3.00	.45	1.78	800 243-4361
Phoenix-Goodwin California T/E A	Muni CA	2.40	3.99	5.05	3.00	4.00	.45	1.00	800 243-4361
Phoenix-Goodwin California T/E B	Muni CA	1.80	3.23	4.27	4.00	4.00	.45	1.75	800 243-4361
Phoenix-Goodwin Emerging Mkts A	Intl Bond	21.70	-1.20		3.00	5.00	.75	1.57	800 243-4361
Phoenix-Goodwin Emerging Mkts B	Intl Bond	20.80	-1.95		3.00	5.00	.75	2.31	800 243-4361
Phoenix-Goodwin High Yield A	Corp-HY	3.50	2.11	7.44	3.00	5.00	.66	1.13	800 243-4361
Phoenix-Goodwin High Yield B	Corp-HY	2.60	1.35	6.64	3.00	5.00	.66	1.88	800 243-4361
Phoenix-Goodwin Multi-Sec F/I A	Dvsfd Bond	4.50	1.24	6.00	3.00	5.00	.55	1.13	800 243-4361
Phoenix-Goodwin Multi-Sec F/I B	Dvsfd Bond	3.80	.46	5.20	3.00	5.00	.55	1.88	800 243-4361
Phoenix-Goodwin Multi-Sec F/I C	Dvsfd Bond	3.70					.69	1.89	800 243-4361
Phoenix-Goodwin Multi-Sector ST A	Corp-Inv	4.40	3.93	6.75	2.00	4.00	.55	1.00	800 243-4361
Phoenix-Goodwin Multi-Sector ST B	Corp-Inv	3.90	3.34	6.17	3.00	4.00	.55	1.50	800 243-4361
Phoenix-Goodwin Tax Exempt A	Muni Natl	1.70	2.93	4.21	3.00	3.00	.45	1.02	800 243-4361
Phoenix-Goodwin Tax Exempt B	Muni Natl	.90	2.18	3.44	4.00	3.00	.45	1.77	800 243-4361
Phoenix-Seneca Bond A	Dvsfd Bond	3.50					.50	2.45	800 243-4361
Phoenix-Seneca Bond B	Dvsfd Bond	2.60					.50	3.20	800 243-4361
Phoenix-Seneca Bond C	Dvsfd Bond	2.70					.50	3.20	800 243-4361
Phoenix-Seneca Bond X	Dvsfd Bond	3.70	6.60		2.00	3.00	.50	1.07	800 243-4361
Phoenix-Zweig Government Fund B	Government	1.50	4.29		3.00	4.00	.59	2.00	800 243-4361
Phoenix-Zweig Series Tr-Gov Secs A	Government	2.10	4.99	4.49	4.00	4.00	.59	1.30	800 243-4361
Phoenix-Zweig Series Tr-Gov Secs C	Government	1.70	4.53	4.01	5.00	4.00	.59	1.75	800 243-4361
Pilgrim Government Securities Inc A	Govt-Mtg	2.80	4.02	4.53	4.00	2.00	.50	1.39	800 992-0180
Pilgrim Government Securities Inc B	Govt-Mtg	2.20	3.19		4.00	2.00	.50	2.14	800 992-0180
Pilgrim Government Securities Inc M	Govt-Mtg	2.30	3.47		4.00	2.00	.50	1.89	800 992-0180
Pilgrim Government Securities T	Government	42.80	15.50	11.95	4.00	5.00	.65	1.55	800 992-0180
Pilgrim High Total Return A	Corp-HY	-15.80	-5.57	2.44	5.00	5.00	.68	1.30	800 992-0180
Pilgrim High Total Return B	Corp-HY	-16.40	-6.27	1.86	5.00	5.00	.68	2.02	800 992-0180
Pilgrim High Total Return C	Corp-HY	-17.00	-6.51	1.53	5.00	5.00	.68	2.02	800 992-0180
Pilgrim High Yield A	Corp-HY	-5.20	0.00	5.70	4.00	5.00	.59	1.00	800 992-0180
Pilgrim High Yield B	Corp-HY	-5.90	-.67		4.00	5.00	.59	1.75	800 992-0180
Pilgrim High Yield M	Corp-HY	-5.70	-.45		4.00	5.00	.59	1.50	800 992-0180
Pilgrim High Yld Fd II A	Corp-HY	3.50					.59	1.10	800 992-0180
Pilgrim High Yld Fd II B	Corp-HY	3.60					.59	1.75	800 992-0180
Pilgrim High Yld Fd II C	Corp-HY	2.90					.59	1.75	800 992-0180
Pilgrim High Yld Fd II Q	Corp-HY	3.50					.59	.90	800 992-0180
Pilgrim Strategic Income A	Government	3.50	5.80	5.41	2.00	3.00	.40	.90	800 992-0180
Pilgrim Strategic Income B	Government	3.00	5.34	5.05	3.00	3.00	.40	1.29	800 992-0180
Pilgrim Strategic Income C	Government	3.00	5.33	5.00	3.00	3.00	.40	1.29	800 992-0180
Pilgrim Strategic Income Q	Government	3.50	5.82	3.85	2.00	3.00	.40	.70	800 992-0180
Pillar Fixed Income A	Corp-Inv	3.10	4.55	4.79	4.00	2.00	.47	1.05	800 932-7782
Pillar Fixed Income B	Corp-Inv	2.10	3.75		4.00	2.00	.47	1.80	800 932-7782
Pillar Fixed Income I	Corp-Inv	3.20	4.75	5.08	2.00	2.00	.47	.80	800 932-7782
Pillar High Yield Bond A	Corp-HY	-3.00					.85	1.50	800 932-7782
Pillar High Yield Bond B	Corp-HY	-3.70					.85	2.25	800 932-7782
Pillar High Yield Bond I	Corp-HY	-2.80					.85	1.25	800 932-7782
Pillar Intermediate Govt A	Government	2.60	3.99	4.42	4.00	2.00	.59	1.05	800 932-7782
Pillar Intermediate Govt I	Government	3.00	4.24	4.69	4.00	2.00	.59	.80	800 932-7782
Pillar NJ Municipal Secs A	Muni State	2.30	3.15	4.01	3.00	2.00	.47	1.05	800 932-7782
Pillar NJ Municipal Secs I	Muni State	2.60	3.44	4.34	3.00	2.00	.46	.80	800 932-7782
Pillar PA Municipal Secs A	Muni State	-.50	1.98	3.21	5.00	4.00	.47	1.05	800 932-7782
Pillar PA Municipal Secs I	Muni State	-.20	2.30	3.56	4.00	4.00	.11	.80	800 932-7782
Pioneer America Income Trust A	Government	4.70	5.15	5.26	3.00	3.00	.35	1.02	800 225-6292
Pioneer America Income Trust B	Government	3.80	4.38	4.56	4.00	3.00	.35	1.79	800 225-6292
Pioneer America Income Trust C	Government	4.00	4.65		3.00	3.00	.35	1.71	800 225-6292
Pioneer Bond Fund A	Corp-Inv	1.30	4.20	4.73	4.00	3.00	.50	1.04	800 225-6292
Pioneer Bond Fund B	Corp-Inv	.40	3.33	3.86	5.00	3.00	.50	1.86	800 225-6292
Pioneer Bond Fund C	Corp-Inv	.40	3.14		5.00	3.00	.50	1.86	800 225-6292
Pioneer High Yield A	Corp-HY	27.50					.90	1.89	800 443-1021

Bond Fund Name	Objective	Annualized Return for			Rank		Max Load	Expense Ratio	Toll-Free Telephone
		1 Year	3 Years	5 Years	Overall	Risk			
Pioneer Limited Maturity Bond A	Government	3.20	4.23	4.68	3.00	1.00	.50	.84	800 225-6292
Pioneer Limited Maturity Bond B	Government	2.00	3.19	3.78	4.00	1.00	.50	1.70	800 225-6292
Pioneer Tax Free Income Fund A	Muni Natl	1.90	3.87	4.96	2.00	3.00	.47	.92	800 225-6292
Pioneer Tax Free Income Fund B	Muni Natl	1.20	3.17	4.21	4.00	3.00	.47	1.68	800 225-6292
Pioneer Tax Free Income Fund C	Muni Natl	1.10	3.13		3.00	3.00	.47	1.63	800 225-6292
Preferred Fixed Income Fund	Corp-Inv	3.70	4.56	5.23	2.00	2.00	.50	.94	800 662-2465
Preferred Short-Term Government	Government	4.50	4.48	4.83	2.00	1.00	.34	.70	800 662-2465
Price (T. Rowe) CA Tax Free	Muni CA	2.70	4.59	5.88	2.00	3.00	.41	.57	800 638-5660
Price (T. Rowe) Corporate Income	Corp-Inv	2.40	4.17		4.00	4.00	.47	.80	800 638-5660
Price (T. Rowe) Emerging Mkts Bd	Intl Bond	23.00	1.53	13.20	3.00	5.00	.77	1.25	800 638-5660
Price (T. Rowe) FL Ins Intrm T/F	Muni State	3.40	3.91	4.58	3.00	2.00	.36	.59	800 638-5660
Price (T. Rowe) GA Tax Free	Muni State	2.20	4.31	5.61	1.00	3.00	.41	.65	800 638-5660
Price (T. Rowe) GNMA Fund	Govt-Mtg	4.70	5.45	5.88	2.00	2.00	.46	.70	800 638-5660
Price (T. Rowe) Global Bond	Intl Bond	.50	1.65	3.28	5.00	5.00	.67	1.00	800 638-5660
Price (T. Rowe) High Yield	Corp-HY	1.40	5.36	7.97	2.00	4.00	.61	.81	800 638-5660
Price (T. Rowe) Internatl Bond	Intl Bond	-1.40	.57	1.84	5.00	5.00	.67	.91	800 638-5660
Price (T. Rowe) MD Sh-Term T/F	Muni State	3.20	3.59	3.77	2.00	1.00	.41	.61	800 638-5660
Price (T. Rowe) MD Tax Free	Muni State	2.50	4.22	5.29	1.00	3.00	.41	.51	800 638-5660
Price (T. Rowe) NJ Tax Free	Muni State	1.40	4.04	5.19	3.00	3.00	.41	.65	800 638-5660
Price (T. Rowe) NY Tax Free	Muni NY	2.00	4.28	5.44	3.00	4.00	.41	.58	800 638-5660
Price (T. Rowe) New Income	Corp-Inv	3.60	4.44	5.01	4.00	3.00	.46	.71	800 638-5660
Price (T. Rowe) Short Term Bond	Corp-Inv	4.10	4.91	5.14	2.00	1.00	.45	.72	800 638-5660
Price (T. Rowe) Short-Term USG	Government	4.40	4.93	5.22	3.00	1.00	.47	.69	800 638-5660
Price (T. Rowe) Spectrum Inc	Dvsfd Bond	2.10	5.23	7.10	3.00	4.00	.45	0.00	800 638-5660
Price (T. Rowe) Summit GNMA	Govt-Mtg	4.70	5.60	6.05	2.00	3.00	.59	.59	800 638-5660
Price (T. Rowe) Summit Ltd Bond	Dvsfd Bond	3.90	5.10	5.27	3.00	2.00	.45	.55	800 638-5660
Price (T. Rowe) Summit Muni Inc	Muni Natl	1.60	4.55	6.05	2.00	4.00	.50	.50	800 638-5660
Price (T. Rowe) Summit Muni Intrm	Muni Natl	2.90	4.23	5.12	2.00	2.00	.50	.50	800 638-5660
Price (T. Rowe) T/F High Yld	Muni Natl	-1.30	3.15	5.00	3.00	3.00	.61	.70	800 638-5660
Price (T. Rowe) T/F Income	Muni Natl	2.10	4.18	5.34	2.00	3.00	.46	.55	800 638-5660
Price (T. Rowe) T/F Insd Interm	Muni Natl	3.40	4.10	4.76	2.00	2.00	.38	.65	800 638-5660
Price (T. Rowe) T/F Sh-Interm	Muni Natl	3.50	3.87	4.19	2.00	1.00	.41	.53	800 638-5660
Price (T. Rowe) US Treas Interm	Government	4.00	5.51	5.33	3.00	4.00	.63	.61	800 638-5660
Price (T. Rowe) US Treas Long	Government	5.60	7.79	6.65	3.00	5.00	.36	.66	800 638-5660
Price (T. Rowe) VA Short-Term Bond	Muni State	3.20	3.62	3.75	2.00	1.00	.41	.61	800 638-5660
Price (T. Rowe) VA Tax Free	Muni State	2.60	4.34	5.57	1.00	3.00	.41	.56	800 638-5660
Primary US Government Fund	Government	2.50	4.14	4.65	4.00	1.00	.65	1.00	800 443-6544
Principal Bond Fund A	Corp-Inv	.40	3.96	4.83	4.00	4.00	.47	1.02	800 247-4123
Principal Bond Fund B	Corp-Inv	-.30	3.23	4.09	5.00	4.00	.47	1.77	800 247-4123
Principal Bond Fund C	Corp-Inv	-.70					.47		800 247-4123
Principal Government Secs Income C	Govt-Mtg	3.70					.45		800 247-4123
Principal Govt Securities Income A	Govt-Mtg	4.80	5.63	6.08	2.00	3.00	.45	.84	800 247-4123
Principal Govt Securities Income B	Govt-Mtg	3.80	4.91	5.32	3.00	3.00	.45	1.55	800 247-4123
Principal Govt Securities Income R	Govt-Mtg	4.20	5.01		2.00	3.00	.45	1.50	800 247-4123
Principal High Yield Fund A	Corp-HY	-1.80	.58	4.76	3.00	4.00	.59	1.38	800 247-4123
Principal High Yield Fund B	Corp-HY	-2.50	-.20	3.82	5.00	4.00	.59	1.96	800 247-4123
Principal High Yield Fund C	Corp-HY	-4.50					.59		800 247-4123
Principal Limited-Term Bond Fund C	Corp-Inv	3.60					.50		800 247-4123
Principal Ltd Term Bond A	Corp-Inv	3.90	4.80		2.00	2.00	.50	1.00	800 247-4123
Principal Ltd Term Bond B	Corp-Inv	3.60	3.43		3.00	1.00	.50	1.35	800 247-4123
Principal Presv-Government	Government	2.90	5.14	5.04	4.00	3.00	.59	1.10	800 826-4600
Principal Presv-Tax Exempt	Muni Natl	-1.50	2.05	3.91	5.00	4.00	.57	1.10	800 826-4600
Principal Presv-WI Tax Exempt	Muni State	-.50	3.15	4.39	3.00	3.00	.50	.80	800 826-4600
Principal Tax Exempt Bond Fund A	Muni Natl	.30	3.38	5.17	3.00	2.00	.46	.80	800 247-4123
Principal Tax Exempt Bond Fund B	Muni Natl	-.10	2.78	4.51	3.00	2.00	.46	1.37	800 247-4123
Principal Tax-Exempt Bond Fund C	Muni Natl	-1.00					.46		800 247-4123
Prudential Diversified Bond A	Dvsfd Bond	2.80	3.14	5.42	3.00	4.00	.50	.75	800 225-1852
Prudential Diversified Bond B	Dvsfd Bond	2.30	2.60	4.91	3.00	4.00	.50	.75	800 225-1852

Bond Fund Name	Objective	Annualized Return for			Rank		Max Load	Expense Ratio	Toll-Free Telephone
		1 Year	3 Years	5 Years	Overall	Risk			
Prudential Diversified Bond C	Dvsfd Bond	2.30	2.59	4.91	3.00	4.00	.50	.75	800 225-1852
Prudential Diversified Bond Z	Dvsfd Bond	3.00	3.34		3.00	4.00	.50	.75	800 225-1852
Prudential Global Tot Ret A	Intl Bond	-.80	2.35	5.88	4.00	4.00	.75	1.28	800 225-1852
Prudential Global Tot Ret B	Intl Bond	-1.20	1.78		5.00	4.00	.75	1.28	800 225-1852
Prudential Global Tot Ret C	Intl Bond	-1.20	1.78		5.00	4.00	.75	1.28	800 225-1852
Prudential Global Tot Ret Z	Intl Bond	-.50	2.55		5.00	4.00	.75	1.28	800 225-1852
Prudential Government Inc A	Government	3.80	5.25	5.34	3.00	3.00	.50	.68	800 225-1852
Prudential Government Inc B	Government	3.20	4.64	4.68	4.00	3.00	.50	.68	800 225-1852
Prudential Govt Sec-Short/Inter A	Government	3.90	4.30	4.87	3.00	2.00	.40	.72	800 225-1852
Prudential Hg Yield Total Ret A	Corp-HY	-1.70					.34	.89	800 225-1852
Prudential Hg Yield Total Ret B	Corp-HY	-2.20					.34	.89	800 225-1852
Prudential Hg Yield Total Ret C	Corp-HY	-2.20					.34	.89	800 225-1852
Prudential Hg Yield Total Ret Z	Corp-HY	-1.50					.34	.89	800 225-1852
Prudential High Yield Fd A	Corp-HY	-1.10	2.70	6.65	3.00	5.00	.41	.53	800 225-1852
Prudential High Yield Fd B	Corp-HY	-1.50	2.16	6.09	4.00	5.00	.40	.53	800 225-1852
Prudential High Yield Fd C	Corp-HY	-1.50	2.16	6.07	4.00	5.00	.41	.53	800 225-1852
Prudential International Bond A	Intl Bond	-.80	1.66	5.56	5.00	4.00	.75	1.55	800 225-1852
Prudential International Bond B	Intl Bond	-1.50	1.06		5.00	4.00	.75	1.55	800 225-1852
Prudential International Bond C	Intl Bond	-1.50	1.06		5.00	4.00	.75	1.55	800 225-1852
Prudential International Bond Z	Intl Bond	-.70	1.87		5.00	4.00	.75	1.55	800 225-1852
Prudential Muni-CA A	Muni CA	3.60	4.48	5.52	2.00	4.00	.50	.68	800 225-1852
Prudential Muni-CA B	Muni CA	3.30	4.14	5.12	3.00	4.00	.50	.68	800 225-1852
Prudential Muni-CA Income A	Muni CA	1.90	4.51	5.90	3.00	4.00	.50	.56	800 225-1852
Prudential Muni-FL A	Muni State	1.90	4.03	5.31	2.00	3.00	.50	.69	800 225-1852
Prudential Muni-FL B	Muni State	1.60	3.69	4.95	3.00	3.00	.50	.69	800 225-1852
Prudential Muni-High Income A	Muni Natl	-1.50	3.29	4.97	2.00	2.00	.50	.51	800 225-1852
Prudential Muni-High Income B	Muni Natl	-1.80	2.96	4.60	3.00	2.00	.50	.51	800 225-1852
Prudential Muni-Insured A	Muni Natl	2.80	4.13	5.07	3.00	4.00	.50	.59	800 225-1852
Prudential Muni-Insured B	Muni Natl	2.60	3.79	4.70	3.00	4.00	.50	.59	800 225-1852
Prudential Muni-MA A	Muni State	.70	3.34	4.67	4.00	3.00	.50	.92	800 225-1852
Prudential Muni-MA B	Muni State	.60	3.05	4.30	5.00	3.00	.50	.92	800 225-1852
Prudential Muni-NC A	Muni State	1.50	3.74	4.92	3.00	3.00	.50	.84	800 225-1852
Prudential Muni-NC B	Muni State	1.10	3.37	4.55	4.00	3.00	.50	.84	800 225-1852
Prudential Muni-NJ A	Muni State	1.70	3.91	4.92	3.00	3.00	.50	.64	800 225-1852
Prudential Muni-NJ B	Muni State	1.40	3.54	4.55	3.00	3.00	.50	.64	800 225-1852
Prudential Muni-NJ C	Muni State	1.20	3.29	4.30	4.00	3.00	.50	.64	800 225-1852
Prudential Muni-NY A	Muni NY	2.10	4.11	5.13	3.00	4.00	.50	.61	800 225-1852
Prudential Muni-NY B	Muni NY	1.90	3.74	4.76	3.00	4.00	.50	.61	800 225-1852
Prudential Muni-OH A	Muni State	1.50	3.60	4.69	3.00	3.00	.50	.73	800 225-1852
Prudential Muni-OH B	Muni State	1.30	3.26	4.29	3.00	3.00	.50	.73	800 225-1852
Prudential Muni-OH C	Muni State	1.00	3.01	4.03	4.00	4.00	.50	.73	800 225-1852
Prudential Muni-PA B	Muni State	.70	2.88	4.38	4.00	3.00	.50	.61	800 225-1852
Prudential National Muni A	Muni Natl	1.40	3.78	4.98	3.00	4.00	.47	.60	800 225-1852
Prudential National Muni B	Muni Natl	1.20	3.47	4.62	4.00	4.00	.47	.60	800 225-1852
Prudential Sh Term Corp Bond Fd A	Corp-Inv	4.10	4.79	5.44	2.00	1.00	.40	.80	800 225-1852
Prudential Sh Term Corp Bond Fd B	Corp-Inv	3.60	4.24	4.83	3.00	1.00	.40	.80	800 225-1852
Prudential Sh Term Corp Bond Fd C	Corp-Inv	3.70	4.25	4.84	4.00	1.00	.40	.80	800 225-1852
Putnam AZ Tax Exempt A	Muni State	1.60	3.53	4.78	2.00	3.00	.50	.69	800 225-1581
Putnam AZ Tax Exempt B	Muni State	1.00	2.91	4.05	4.00	3.00	.50	1.48	800 225-1581
Putnam AZ Tax Exempt M	Muni State	4.80	4.27		3.00	3.00	.50	1.18	800 225-1581
Putnam American Government A	Government	4.20	5.33	5.63	3.00	3.00	.56	.48	800 225-1581
Putnam American Government B	Government	3.30	4.62	4.88	3.00	3.00	.56	.86	800 225-1581
Putnam American Government M	Government	3.90	5.12	5.42	3.00	3.00	.56	.61	800 225-1581
Putnam American Govt Income Fund C	Government						.56		800 225-1581
Putnam CA Tax Exempt Income A	Muni CA	2.50	4.11	5.35	2.00	3.00	.45	.39	800 225-1581
Putnam CA Tax Exempt Income B	Muni CA	1.90	3.43	4.59	3.00	3.00	.45	1.41	800 225-1581
Putnam CA Tax Exempt Income C	Muni CA						.45		800 225-1581
Putnam CA Tax Exempt Income M	Muni CA	2.10	3.73	4.98	3.00	3.00	.45	.54	800 225-1581

439

Bond Fund Name	Objective	Annualized Return for			Rank		Max Load	Expense Ratio	Toll-Free Telephone
		1 Year	3 Years	5 Years	Overall	Risk			
Putnam Diversified Income A	Dvsfd Bond	2.70	2.16	5.05	3.00	4.00	.54	.46	800 225-1581
Putnam Diversified Income B	Dvsfd Bond	2.00	1.39	4.25	4.00	4.00	.54	.83	800 225-1581
Putnam Diversified Income M	Dvsfd Bond	2.40	1.88	4.78	3.00	4.00	.54	.58	800 225-1581
Putnam Diversified Income Y	Dvsfd Bond	3.00	2.41		4.00	4.00	.54	.34	800 225-1581
Putnam FL Tax Exempt Income A	Muni State	1.90	3.69	4.96	2.00	3.00	.50	.97	800 225-1581
Putnam FL Tax Exempt Income B	Muni State	1.00	2.92	4.22	4.00	3.00	.50	1.62	800 225-1581
Putnam FL Tax Exempt Income M	Muni State	1.40	3.33	4.62	3.00	3.00	.50	1.28	800 225-1581
Putnam Global Govt Income A	Intl Bond	.10	-.05	3.24	5.00	5.00	.69	.60	800 225-1581
Putnam Global Govt Income B	Intl Bond	-.60	-.80	2.19	5.00	5.00	.69	.98	800 225-1581
Putnam Global Govt Income M	Intl Bond	-.10	-.98	2.55	5.00	5.00	.69	.73	800 225-1581
Putnam Global Govt Income Trust C	Intl Bond						.69		800 225-1581
Putnam High Yield Advantage A	Corp-HY	-.20	.71	5.10	4.00	5.00	.56	.47	800 225-1581
Putnam High Yield Advantage B	Corp-HY	-.90	0.00	4.33	4.00	5.00	.56	.85	800 225-1581
Putnam High Yield Advantage M	Corp-HY	-.50	.46	4.83	4.00	5.00	.56	.60	800 225-1581
Putnam High Yield Trust A	Corp-HY	.40	1.52	6.09	3.00	5.00	.55	.46	800 225-1581
Putnam High Yield Trust B	Corp-HY	-.30	.82	5.34	4.00	5.00	.55	.82	800 225-1581
Putnam Income Fund A	Corp-Inv	1.90	2.91	4.58	5.00	3.00	.50	.48	800 225-1581
Putnam Income Fund B	Corp-Inv	1.00	2.12	3.76	5.00	3.00	.50	.86	800 225-1581
Putnam Income Fund M	Corp-Inv	1.60	2.68	4.35	5.00	3.00	.50	.61	800 225-1581
Putnam Intermed US Govt Income A	Government	4.20	5.18	5.59	2.00	2.00	.59	.50	800 225-1581
Putnam Intermed US Govt Income B	Government	3.70	4.65	4.95	3.00	2.00	.59	.80	800 225-1581
Putnam Intermed US Govt Income M	Government	4.20	5.09	5.55	2.00	2.00	.59	.57	800 225-1581
Putnam Intmed US Government Inc C	Government						.59		800 225-1581
Putnam MA Tax Exempt Inc II A	Muni State	1.60	3.70	5.27	2.00	3.00	.50	.96	800 225-1581
Putnam MA Tax Exempt Inc II B	Muni State	1.00	3.03	4.40	3.00	3.00	.50	1.62	800 225-1581
Putnam MA Tax Exempt Inc II M	Muni State	1.50	3.43	4.82	3.00	3.00	.50	1.27	800 225-1581
Putnam MI Tax Exempt Inc II A	Muni State	-.20	2.72	4.58	4.00	3.00	.50	1.00	800 225-1581
Putnam MI Tax Exempt Inc II B	Muni State	-.60	2.09	3.86	5.00	3.00	.50	1.64	800 225-1581
Putnam MI Tax Exempt Inc II M	Muni State	-.30	2.43	4.00	3.00	3.00	.50	1.30	800 225-1581
Putnam MN Tax Exempt Inc II A	Muni State	.10	2.87	4.37	4.00	3.00	.50	.92	800 225-1581
Putnam MN Tax Exempt Inc II B	Muni State	-.50	2.26	3.70	5.00	3.00	.50	1.57	800 225-1581
Putnam MN Tax Exempt Inc II M	Muni State	-.20	2.62	3.93	3.00	3.00	.50	1.21	800 225-1581
Putnam Muni Income Fund A	Muni Natl	.40	3.64	5.11	3.00	3.00	.56	.97	800 225-1581
Putnam Muni Income Fund B	Muni Natl	-.10	3.06	4.45	3.00	3.00	.56	1.58	800 225-1581
Putnam Muni Income Fund M	Muni Natl	.20	3.35	4.83	3.00	3.00	.56	1.22	800 225-1581
Putnam Municipal Income C	Muni Natl						.56		800 225-1581
Putnam NJ Tax Exempt Income A	Muni State	1.60	3.41	4.57	3.00	3.00	.50	.98	800 225-1581
Putnam NJ Tax Exempt Income B	Muni State	1.10	2.92	4.24	4.00	3.00	.50	1.63	800 225-1581
Putnam NJ Tax Exempt Income M	Muni State	1.30	3.11	4.52	3.00	3.00	.50	1.29	800 225-1581
Putnam NY Tax Exempt Income A	Muni NY	2.90	3.81	4.96	2.00	3.00	.50	.41	800 225-1581
Putnam NY Tax Exempt Income B	Muni NY	2.20	3.17	4.30	3.00	3.00	.50	.73	800 225-1581
Putnam NY Tax Exempt Income M	Muni NY	2.40	3.20	4.51	3.00	4.00	.50	.56	800 225-1581
Putnam NY Tax Exempt Opport A	Muni NY	1.00	3.35	4.84	3.00	3.00	.50	.48	800 225-1581
Putnam NY Tax Exempt Opport B	Muni NY	.20	2.81	4.31	4.00	3.00	.50	.81	800 225-1581
Putnam NY Tax Exempt Opport M	Muni NY	.70	3.07	4.70	4.00	3.00	.50	.64	800 225-1581
Putnam OH Tax Exempt Inc II A	Muni State	.90	3.16	4.61	3.00	3.00	.50	.91	800 225-1581
Putnam OH Tax Exempt Inc II B	Muni State	.30	2.49	3.93	4.00	3.00	.50	1.56	800 225-1581
Putnam OH Tax Exempt Inc II M	Muni State	.60	2.85	4.02	3.00	3.00	.50	1.20	800 225-1581
Putnam PA Tax Exempt A	Muni State	.30	2.76	4.44	4.00	3.00	.50	.97	800 225-1581
Putnam PA Tax Exempt B	Muni State	-.40	2.10	3.77	5.00	3.00	.50	1.62	800 225-1581
Putnam PA Tax Exempt M	Muni State	.10	2.18		4.00	3.00	.50	1.28	800 225-1581
Putnam Strategic Income A	Dvsfd Bond	2.70	2.04		3.00	4.00	.69	1.31	800 225-1581
Putnam Strategic Income B	Dvsfd Bond	2.00	1.37		4.00	4.00	.69	2.06	800 225-1581
Putnam Strategic Income M	Dvsfd Bond	2.50	1.76		3.00	4.00	.69	1.56	800 225-1581
Putnam Tax Exempt Income A	Muni Natl	1.30	3.52	5.05	3.00	3.00	.47	.40	800 225-1581
Putnam Tax Exempt Income B	Muni Natl	.70	2.85	4.36	4.00	3.00	.47	.40	800 225-1581
Putnam Tax Exempt Income M	Muni Natl	1.00	3.22	4.75	4.00	3.00	.47	.55	800 225-1581
Putnam Tax-Free Inc:Hi-Yield A	Muni Natl	-1.20	3.04	4.52	3.00	2.00	.54	.86	800 225-1581

440

Bond Fund Name	Objective	Annualized Return for 1 Year	3 Years	5 Years	Rank Overall	Risk	Max Load	Expense Ratio	Toll-Free Telephone
Putnam Tax-Free Inc:Hi-Yield B	Muni Natl	-1.70	2.51	4.07	3.00	2.00	.54	1.37	800 225-1581
Putnam Tax-Free Inc:Hi-Yield M	Muni Natl	-1.50	2.77	4.21	3.00	2.00	.54	1.16	800 225-1581
Putnam Tax-Free Inc:Insured A	Muni Natl	2.70	3.47	4.65	3.00	3.00	.57	.93	800 225-1581
Putnam Tax-Free Inc:Insured B	Muni Natl	2.30	3.45	4.58	3.00	3.00	.57	.90	800 225-1581
Putnam Tax-Free Inc:Insured M	Muni Natl	2.40	3.26	4.82	3.00	3.00	.57	1.23	800 225-1581
Putnam US Government Income Trust C	Govt-Mtg						.42		
Putnam US Govt Income Tr A	Govt-Mtg	4.50	5.28	5.87	2.00	2.00	.42	.42	800 225-1581
Putnam US Govt Income Tr B	Govt-Mtg	3.70	4.45	5.05	3.00	2.00	.42	.80	800 225-1581
Putnam US Govt Income Tr M	Govt-Mtg	4.30	5.00	5.58	3.00	2.00	.42	.55	800 225-1581
Quaker Fixed Income	Corp-Inv	1.60	4.44		3.00	3.00	.45	1.40	800-220-8888
RSI Retirement Active Manage Bond	Govt-Mtg	2.40	5.47	5.63	3.00	4.00	.34	.78	800 772-3615
RSI Retirement Intermediate Bond	Corp-Inv	3.60	4.90	5.17	3.00	2.00	.38	1.13	800 772-3615
RSI Retirement Short Term Invest	Corp-Inv	5.00	4.81	4.83	2.00	1.00	.25	.80	800 772-3615
Rainier Interm Fixed Inc Portfolio	Corp-Inv	4.00	5.45	5.25	3.00	2.00	.45	1.04	800 248-6314
Regions Fixed Income Fd A	Corp-Inv	3.60	4.84	5.09	3.00	2.00	.75	.96	800 433-2829
Regions Fixed Income Fd B	Corp-Inv	3.40	4.74	5.05	3.00	2.00	.75	1.21	800 433-2829
Regions Ltd Mat Govt A	Government	4.20					.69	1.02	800 433-2829
Regions Ltd Mat Govt B	Government	4.00	4.56	4.69	3.00	1.00	.69	1.27	800 433-2829
Republic Bond Fund A	Corp-Inv	2.70	4.14		3.00	3.00	.55		800 782-8183
Republic NY Tax Free Bond A	Muni NY	1.50	3.85	4.89	3.00	3.00	.25	.77	800 782-8183
Reynolds Govt Bond Fund	Corp-Inv	4.10	4.63	4.72	2.00	1.00	.75	.90	800 773-9665
Riggs Bond R	Dvsfd Bond						.75		800 934-3883
Riggs Interm Tax-Free Bond R	Muni Natl						.75		800 934-3883
Riggs Long Term Tax-Free Bond R	Muni Natl						.75		800 934-3883
Riggs US Government Securities Y	Corp-Inv						.75		800 934-3883
Riggs US Govt Securities R	Corp-Inv	4.30	5.74	5.42	3.00	3.00	.34	1.58	800 934-3883
Riverfront US Government Inc A	Government	4.20	4.60	4.83	3.00	2.00	.40	1.10	800 424-2295
Riverfront US Government Inc B	Government	3.00	3.67	3.90	4.00	2.00	.40	1.89	800 424-2295
Rochester Fund Municipals A	Muni NY	-.10	3.87	5.43	3.00	4.00	.46	.71	800 525-7048
Rochester Fund Municipals B	Muni NY	-1.00	3.00		3.00	4.00	.46	1.57	800 525-7048
Rochester Fund Municipals C	Muni NY	-.90	3.02		3.00	4.00	.46	1.55	800 525-7048
Roulston Government Securities	Government	3.10	4.85	4.92	4.00	3.00	.25	2.14	800 332-6459
Rushmore MD Tax Free	Muni State	1.20	3.73	4.59	2.00	2.00	.62	.93	800 343-3355
Rushmore US Government Bond	Government	5.30	7.18	6.17	4.00	5.00	.50	.80	800 343-3355
Rushmore VA Tax Free	Muni State	.70	3.39	4.52	3.00	3.00	.62	.93	800 343-3355
Rydex Series-Juno Fund	Government	.60	-.36	.50	4.00	5.00	.90	1.56	800 820-0888
Rydex Series-US Government Bd	Government	2.30	5.74	4.26	4.00	5.00	.50	.95	800 820-0888
SAFECO Advisor High Yield Bond A	Corp-HY	.50	4.11		3.00	5.00	.65	1.23	800 624-5711
SAFECO Advisor High Yield Bond B	Corp-HY	-.10	3.37		3.00	5.00	.65	2.06	800 624-5711
SAFECO Advisor I-T Treas Bond A	Government	3.20	5.24		2.00	3.00	.55	1.31	800 624-5711
SAFECO Advisor I-T Treas Bond B	Government	2.50	4.50		3.00	3.00	.55	2.06	800 624-5711
SAFECO Advisor Managed Bond A	Dvsfd Bond	3.70	4.33		4.00	4.00	.50	1.37	800 624-5711
SAFECO Advisor Managed Bond B	Dvsfd Bond	2.80	3.43		5.00	4.00	.50	2.12	800 624-5711
SAFECO CA Tax Free Inc A	Muni CA	.40	3.60		4.00	5.00	.50	.96	800 624-5711
SAFECO CA Tax Free Inc B	Muni CA	-.30	2.91		4.00	5.00	.50	1.69	800 624-5711
SAFECO CA Tax Free Inc Fd	Muni CA	.70	3.98	5.71	4.00	5.00	.50	.68	800 624-5711
SAFECO GNMA Fund	Govt-Mtg	3.70	4.99	5.95	1.00	2.00	.55	.95	800 624-5711
SAFECO High-Yield Bond Fd	Corp-HY	.70	4.29	6.91	3.00	5.00	.65	1.00	800 624-5711
SAFECO Insured Municipal Bond	Muni Natl	1.00	3.77	5.48	4.00	4.00	.50	.86	800 624-5711
SAFECO Interm-Term Municipal Bd	Muni Natl	2.80	3.88	4.67	3.00	2.00	.50	.81	800 624-5711
SAFECO Interm-Term US Treas Fd	Government	3.50	5.57	5.20	4.00	3.00	.55	.94	800 624-5711
SAFECO Managed Bond Fd	Dvsfd Bond	1.00	3.43	3.87	4.00	4.00	.50	.94	800 624-5711
SAFECO Municipal Bond A	Muni Natl	.70	3.94		3.00	4.00	.61	.86	800 624-5711
SAFECO Municipal Bond B	Muni Natl	-.10	3.07		5.00	4.00	.61	1.59	800 624-5711
SAFECO Municipal Bond Fd	Muni Natl	1.00	4.22	5.61	3.00	4.00	.61	.54	800 624-5711
SEI Asset Alloc-Dvrs Consv Inc A	Dvsfd Bond	6.00	9.90		2.00	4.00	.10	.11	800 342-5734
SEI Asset Alloc-Dvrs Consv Inc D	Dvsfd Bond	4.90	7.85		2.00	5.00	.10	1.12	800 342-5734
SEI California Municipal-29 A	Muni CA	4.40					.55	.90	800 342-5734

Bond Fund Name	Objective	Annualized Return for			Rank		Max Load	Expense Ratio	Toll-Free Telephone
		1 Year	3 Years	5 Years	Overall	Risk			
SEI Daily Inc Tr-GNMA Bond A	Govt-Mtg	5.30	5.61	6.14	1.00	2.00	.40	.59	800 342-5734
SEI Daily Inc Tr-Int Dur Gov Bd A	Government	4.60	5.70	5.72	3.00	2.00	.10	.50	800 342-5734
SEI Daily Inc Tr-Sh Dur Gov Bd A	Government	5.00	5.55	5.69	2.00	1.00	.10	.45	800 342-5734
SEI Daily Inc Tr-Sh Dur Gov Bd B	Government	4.60	5.08	5.27	2.00	1.00	.10	.75	800 342-5734
SEI Index Fds-Bond Index	Corp-Inv	4.30	5.84	5.91	2.00	3.00	.32	.38	800 342-5734
SEI Instl Managed Tr-Core Fixed A	Corp-Inv	4.80	5.83	6.06	2.00	3.00	.51	.59	800 342-5734
SEI Instl Managed Tr-High Yld Bd A	Corp-HY	-1.70	3.66	7.77	3.00	4.00	.65	.84	800 342-5734
SEI Intl Tr-Intl Fixed Income	Intl Bond	.20	2.03	1.91	5.00	5.00	.84	1.00	800 342-5734
SEI Massachuttes Municipals-18 A	Muni State	2.70					.55	.59	800 342-5734
SEI New Jersey Municipal-27 A	Muni State	3.00					.55	.59	800 342-5734
SEI New York Municipal-28 A	Muni NY	3.50					.55	.92	800 342-5734
SEI Tax-Exempt PA Municipal A	Muni State	2.90					1.50	.59	800 342-5734
SEI Tax-Exempt Tr-Interm Muni A	Muni Natl	3.40	4.28	5.02	2.00	2.00	.55	.59	800 342-5734
SEI Tax-Exempt Tr-PA Muni A	Muni State	3.40	4.28	5.09	1.00	2.00	.40	.47	800 342-5734
SG Cowen Government Securities A	Government	4.20	5.15	5.40	4.00	5.00	.59	.20	800 221-5616
SG Cowen Intermediate Fixed Inc A	Corp-Inv	1.70	4.65	5.09	4.00	3.00	0.00	.32	800 221-5616
SM&R Government Bond Fund A	Government	2.70					.50	1.26	
SM&R Government Bond Fund B	Government	2.30					.50	1.82	
SM&R Government Bond Fund C	Government	2.00					.50	2.12	
SM&R Government Bond Fund T	Government	3.70	4.93	5.27	3.00	2.00	.50	1.02	
SM&R Tax Free Fund A	Muni Natl	2.30					.50	1.46	
SM&R Tax Free Fund B	Muni Natl	1.90					.50	2.10	
SM&R Tax Free Fund C	Muni Natl	2.30					.50	2.37	
SM&R Tax-Free Fund T	Muni Natl	2.70	4.41	5.51	1.00	3.00	.50	.70	
SSgA Bond Market Fund	Corp-Inv	3.80	5.33		2.00	3.00	.29	.50	800 997-7327
SSgA High Yield Bond	Corp-HY	5.90					.29	.65	800 997-7327
SSgA Intermediate Fund	Government	3.90	5.12	5.38	3.00	2.00	.80	.59	800 997-7327
SSgA Yield Plus Fund	Corp-Inv	5.20	5.03	5.31	2.00	1.00	.25	.41	800 997-7327
STI Classic FL Tax Exempt Flex	Muni State	3.20	3.81	4.63	3.00	3.00	.65	1.37	800 428-6970
STI Classic FL Tax Exempt Inv	Muni State	3.80	4.29	5.13	2.00	3.00	.65	.86	800 428-6970
STI Classic FL Tax Exempt Tr	Muni State	3.90	4.47	5.30	2.00	3.00	.65	.67	800 428-6970
STI Classic GA Tax Exempt Flex	Muni State	2.50	3.29	4.10	3.00	3.00	.65	1.37	800 428-6970
STI Classic GA Tax Exempt Inv	Muni State	2.90	3.75	4.57	3.00	3.00	.65	.86	800 428-6970
STI Classic GA Tax Exempt Tr	Muni State	3.10	4.00	4.81	3.00	3.00	.65	.67	800 428-6970
STI Classic High Income Flex	Dvsfd Bond	10.20	6.57	5.90	5.00	5.00	.80	1.90	800 261-3863
STI Classic Inv Grade Bond Flex	Corp-Inv	-.10	3.75	4.15	4.00	4.00	.73	1.65	800 428-6970
STI Classic Inv Grade Bond Inv	Corp-Inv	.30	4.27	4.69	3.00	4.00	.73	1.16	800 428-6970
STI Classic Inv Grade Bond Tr	Corp-Inv	.80	4.68	5.10	3.00	4.00	.73	.77	800 428-6970
STI Classic Inv Grade T/E Flex	Muni Natl	3.70	4.23	5.08	2.00	2.00	.73	1.64	800 428-6970
STI Classic Inv Grade T/E Inv	Muni Natl	4.30	4.82	5.58	1.00	2.00	.73	1.69	800 428-6970
STI Classic Inv Grade T/E Tr	Muni Natl	4.80	5.23	6.00	1.00	2.00	.73	.77	800 428-6970
STI Classic Ltd-Trm Fed Mtg Flex	Govt-Mtg	2.80	4.27	4.64	4.00	1.00	.65	1.27	800 428-6970
STI Classic Ltd-Trm Fed Mtg Inv	Govt-Mtg	3.20	4.60	4.94	4.00	1.00	.65	.92	800 428-6970
STI Classic Ltd-Trm Fed Mtg Tr	Govt-Mtg	3.60	4.89	5.22	3.00	1.00	.65	.67	800 428-6970
STI Classic MD Municipal Bond Flex	Muni State	.50	3.27		4.00	3.00	.65	1.59	800 428-6970
STI Classic MD Municipal Bond Tr	Muni State	1.40	4.11		2.00	3.00	.65	.69	800 428-6970
STI Classic Sh-Term Bond Flex	Corp-Inv	3.40	4.36	4.61	4.00	1.00	.65	1.21	800 428-6970
STI Classic Sh-Term Bond Inv	Corp-Inv	3.80	4.73	4.92	3.00	1.00	.65	.86	800 428-6970
STI Classic Sh-Term Bond Tr	Corp-Inv	4.00	4.91	5.11	3.00	1.00	.65	.67	800 428-6970
STI Classic Sh-Term Treas Flex	Government	3.90	4.55	4.61	3.00	1.00	.65	1.07	800 428-6970
STI Classic Sh-Term Treas Inv	Government	4.00	4.75	4.91	2.00	1.00	.65	.81	800 428-6970
STI Classic Sh-Term Treas Tr	Government	4.30	4.91	5.06	2.00	1.00	.65	.67	800 428-6970
STI Classic US Govt Secs Flex	Government	3.40	4.74	4.66	3.00	3.00	.73	1.67	800 428-6970
STI Classic US Govt Secs Inv	Government	3.90	5.21	5.16	3.00	3.00	.73	1.16	800 428-6970
STI Classic US Govt Secs Tr	Government	4.40	5.68	5.58	3.00	3.00	.73	.77	800 428-6970
STI Classic VA Interm Muni Inv	Muni State	2.10	3.54	4.33	3.00	2.00	.50	.79	800 428-6970
STI Classic VA Interm Muni Tr	Muni State	2.10	3.51	4.32	3.00	2.00	.50	.83	800 428-6970
STI Classic VA Muni Bond Flex	Muni State	-.30	2.78	3.62	5.00	3.00	.65	1.64	800 428-6970

Bond Fund Name	Objective	Annualized Return for			Rank		Max Load	Expense Ratio	Toll-Free Telephone
		1 Year	3 Years	5 Years	Overall	Risk			
STI Classic VA Muni Bond Tr	Muni State	.60	3.67	4.50	3.00	3.00	.65	.76	800 428-6970
Salomon Brothers High Yld Bd A	Corp-HY	2.30	1.36	8.54	3.00	5.00	.75	1.31	800 725-6666
Salomon Brothers High Yld Bd B	Corp-HY	1.70	.60	7.71	3.00	5.00	.75	2.04	800 725-6666
Salomon Brothers High Yld Bd C	Corp-HY	2.00	.70	7.77	3.00	5.00	.75	1.85	800 725-6666
Salomon Brothers High Yld Bd O	Corp-HY	2.70	1.56	8.75	3.00	5.00	.75	1.06	800 725-6666
Salomon Brothers Natl Interm A	Muni Natl	3.40	4.02	4.57	2.00	2.00	.50	.75	800 725-6666
Salomon Brothers Natl Interm B	Muni Natl	2.60	3.25	3.74	3.00	2.00	.50	1.50	800 725-6666
Salomon Brothers Natl Interm C	Muni Natl	2.80	3.31	3.81	3.00	2.00	.50	1.29	800 725-6666
Salomon Brothers Natl Interm O	Muni Natl	3.60	4.29	4.82	1.00	2.00	.50	.50	800 725-6666
Salomon Brothers Strategic Bd A	Dvsfd Bond	6.00	4.12	7.73	2.00	4.00	.75	1.23	800 725-6666
Salomon Brothers Strategic Bd B	Dvsfd Bond	5.20	3.31	6.65	3.00	4.00	.75	1.98	800 725-6666
Salomon Brothers Strategic Bd C	Dvsfd Bond	5.50	3.47	6.72	3.00	4.00	.75	1.79	800 725-6666
Salomon Brothers Strategic Bd O	Dvsfd Bond	6.20	4.36	7.73	2.00	4.00	.75	.98	800 725-6666
Salomon Brothers US Government A	Government	5.50	5.81	5.69	1.00	2.00	.59	.84	800 725-6666
Salomon Brothers US Government B	Government	4.80	5.00	4.89	2.00	2.00	.59	1.60	800 725-6666
Salomon Brothers US Government C	Government	5.10	5.10	5.11	2.00	2.00	.59	1.38	800 725-6666
Salomon Brothers US Government O	Government	6.00	6.12	5.96	1.00	2.00	.59	.59	800 725-6666
Schroder Investment Grade Inc Inv	Corp-Inv	3.60	4.78	4.82	4.00	3.00	.50	.76	800 464-3108
Schroder Sh-Term Investment	Corp-Inv						.40	1.03	800 464-3108
Schwab CA Long-Term T/F	Muni CA	1.40	4.25	5.72	3.00	4.00	.29	.48	800 435-4000
Schwab CA Sh-Interm Tax Free	Muni CA	3.70	3.87	4.45	2.00	1.00	.29	.48	800 435-4000
Schwab Long-Term Tax Free Bond	Muni Natl	.70	3.43	4.94	4.00	4.00	.04	.48	800 435-4000
Schwab Short-Interm Tax Free	Muni Natl	3.20	3.65	4.08	3.00	1.00	.48	.48	800 435-4000
Schwab Short-Term Bd Mkt Index	Government	4.80	5.27	5.37	3.00	1.00	.30	.81	800 435-4000
Schwab Total Bd Market Index	Government	4.50	5.59	5.83	2.00	3.00	.29	.34	800 435-4000
Scudder CA Tax Free Bond Fund	Muni CA	3.70	4.82	5.90	2.00	4.00	.50	.76	800 225-2470
Scudder Corporate Bond	Corp-Inv	3.20					0.00	2.06	800 225-2470
Scudder Emerging Markets Inc	Intl Bond	17.00	-3.09	9.52	3.00	5.00	1.00	1.79	800 225-2470
Scudder GNMA Fund	Govt-Mtg	4.40	5.17	5.78	2.00	2.00	.63	.40	800 225-2470
Scudder Global Bond	Intl Bond	.10	2.83	3.06	5.00	4.00	.75	1.08	800 225-2470
Scudder High Yield Bond Fund	Corp-HY	-2.30	4.08		2.00	5.00	0.00	.75	800 225-2470
Scudder Income Fund	Corp-Inv	3.10	4.33	5.27	3.00	3.00	.38	.94	800 225-2470
Scudder International Bond	Intl Bond	-1.10	.97	1.28	5.00	5.00	.81	1.50	800 225-2470
Scudder Limited Term Tax Free	Muni Natl	3.10	3.67	4.16	2.00	1.00	.59	.75	800 225-2470
Scudder MA Ltd Term Tax Free	Muni State	2.50	3.43	3.96	2.00	1.00	.59	.75	800 225-2470
Scudder MA Tax Free Fund	Muni State	3.20	4.36	5.48	1.00	3.00	.59	.72	800 225-2470
Scudder Managed Muni Bond	Muni Natl	3.70	4.61	5.80	1.00	3.00	.51	.64	800 225-2470
Scudder Medium-Term Tax Free	Muni Natl	3.20	4.03	4.86	2.00	2.00	.56	.71	800 225-2470
Scudder NY Tax Free Fund	Muni NY	3.20	4.33	5.40	3.00	4.00	.63	.81	800 225-2470
Scudder OH Tax Free Fund	Muni State	2.80	4.15	5.43	1.00	3.00	.59	.61	800 225-2470
Scudder Short-Term Tax Free	Corp-Inv	2.90	3.73	4.49	2.00	1.00	.53	.84	800 225-2470
Security Diversified Income A	Govt-Mtg	2.30	4.81	5.37	3.00	3.00	.50	.80	800 888-2461
Security Diversified Income B	Govt-Mtg	1.20	3.68	4.19	5.00	3.00	.50	1.82	800 888-2461
Security Municipal Bond A	Muni Natl	3.20	4.09	4.89	3.00	3.00	.50	1.02	800 888-2461
Security Municipal Bond B	Muni Natl	2.50	3.16	3.78	3.00	3.00	.50	1.78	800 888-2461
Selected US Govt Income	Government	.40	3.03	3.88	4.00	2.00	.50	1.50	800 279-0279
Seligman High Yield Bond A	Corp-HY	-2.70	2.43	7.06	3.00	5.00	.58	1.07	800 221-2783
Seligman High Yield Bond B	Corp-HY	-3.60	1.64		4.00	5.00	.58	1.82	800 221-2783
Seligman High Yield Bond D	Corp-HY	-3.40	1.70	6.25	4.00	5.00	.58	1.85	800 221-2783
Seligman High-Yield Bond C	Corp-HY	-3.40					.58	1.82	800 221-2783
Seligman Muni Series Tr CA HY C	Muni CA	1.00					.50		800 221-2783
Seligman Muni Series Tr CA Qual C	Muni CA	1.30					.50		800 221-2783
Seligman Muni Series-CA H/Y A	Muni CA	2.10	4.18	5.34	3.00	4.00	.50	.85	800 221-2783
Seligman Muni Series-CA H/Y D	Muni CA	1.00	3.18	4.38	5.00	4.00	.50	1.76	800 221-2783
Seligman Muni Series-CA Qlty A	Muni CA	2.40	4.14	5.51	3.00	4.00	.50	.81	800 221-2783
Seligman Muni Series-CA Qlty D	Muni CA	1.30	3.20	4.52	5.00	4.00	.50	1.70	800 221-2783
Seligman Muni Series-CO A	Muni State	.40	3.32	4.25	4.00	3.00	.50	.90	800 221-2783
Seligman Muni Series-CO D	Muni State	-.50	2.34	3.26	5.00	3.00	.50	1.80	800 221-2783

Bond Fund Name	Objective	Annualized Return for			Rank		Max Load	Expense Ratio	Toll-Free Telephone
		1 Year	3 Years	5 Years	Overall	Risk			
Seligman Muni Series-FL A	Muni State	2.00	4.34	5.14	3.00	4.00	.50	1.02	800 221-2783
Seligman Muni Series-FL D	Muni State	1.40	3.60	4.36	5.00	4.00	.50	1.77	800 221-2783
Seligman Muni Series-GA A	Muni State	1.50	3.96	5.23	3.00	4.00	.29	.89	800 221-2783
Seligman Muni Series-GA D	Muni State	.50	3.04	4.34	5.00	4.00	.35	1.79	800 221-2783
Seligman Muni Series-LA A	Muni State	1.40	3.66	5.08	3.00	3.00	.50	.86	800 221-2783
Seligman Muni Series-LA D	Muni State	.50	2.73	4.15	4.00	3.00	.50	1.78	800 221-2783
Seligman Muni Series-MA A	Muni State	.20	3.50	4.76	4.00	4.00	.50	.82	800 221-2783
Seligman Muni Series-MA D	Muni State	-.70	2.57	3.84	5.00	4.00	.50	1.72	800 221-2783
Seligman Muni Series-MD A	Muni State	1.50	4.04	5.04	2.00	3.00	.50	.89	800 221-2783
Seligman Muni Series-MD D	Muni State	.70	3.09	4.10	4.00	3.00	.50	1.79	800 221-2783
Seligman Muni Series-MI A	Muni State	2.50	4.26	5.30	2.00	3.00	.50	.81	800 221-2783
Seligman Muni Series-MI D	Muni State	1.60	3.29	4.34	3.00	3.00	.50	1.70	800 221-2783
Seligman Muni Series-MN A	Muni State	1.30	3.63	4.16	3.00	3.00	.50	.83	800 221-2783
Seligman Muni Series-MN D	Muni State	.40	2.69	3.25	4.00	3.00	.50	1.73	800 221-2783
Seligman Muni Series-MO A	Muni State	1.50	3.72	4.89	4.00	4.00	.50	.90	800 221-2783
Seligman Muni Series-MO D	Muni State	.60	2.79	3.95	4.00	4.00	.50	1.80	800 221-2783
Seligman Muni Series-NC A	Muni State	1.00	3.68	4.93	3.00	3.00	.50	1.08	800 221-2783
Seligman Muni Series-NC D	Muni State	.10	2.90	4.13	5.00	3.00	.11	1.83	800 221-2783
Seligman Muni Series-NJ A	Muni State	.50	3.77	4.70	4.00	4.00	.50	1.07	800 221-2783
Seligman Muni Series-NJ D	Muni State	-.40	2.94	3.91	5.00	4.00	.50	1.82	800 221-2783
Seligman Muni Series-NY A	Muni NY	1.80	4.51	5.65	3.00	4.00	.50	.81	800 221-2783
Seligman Muni Series-NY D	Muni NY	.70	3.52	4.67	4.00	4.00	.50	1.71	800 221-2783
Seligman Muni Series-Natl A	Muni Natl	.30	3.87	5.28	3.00	4.00	.50	.82	800 221-2783
Seligman Muni Series-Natl D	Muni Natl	-.50	2.95	4.30	5.00	4.00	.50	1.72	800 221-2783
Seligman Muni Series-OH A	Muni State	1.40	3.98	4.87	3.00	3.00	.50	.81	800 221-2783
Seligman Muni Series-OH D	Muni State	.50	3.05	3.99	5.00	3.00	.50	1.70	800 221-2783
Seligman Muni Series-OR A	Muni State	1.70	4.25	5.06	3.00	3.00	.50	.88	800 221-2783
Seligman Muni Series-OR D	Muni State	.80	3.27	4.10	4.00	3.00	.50	1.78	800 221-2783
Seligman Muni Series-PA A	Muni State	1.10	3.89	5.03	3.00	4.00	.50	1.22	800 221-2783
Seligman Muni Series-PA D	Muni State	.30	3.13	4.50	5.00	4.00	.50	1.97	800 221-2783
Seligman Muni Series-SC A	Muni State	1.40	3.79	5.09	3.00	4.00	.50	.82	800 221-2783
Seligman Muni Series-SC D	Muni State	.50	2.85	4.16	5.00	4.00	.50	1.72	800 221-2783
Seligman Municipal Series CO C	Muni State	-.50					.50		800 221-2783
Seligman Municipal Series FL C	Muni State	1.40					.50		800 221-2783
Seligman Municipal Series GA C	Muni State	.50					.50		800 221-2783
Seligman Municipal Series LA C	Muni State	.50					.50		800 221-2783
Seligman Municipal Series MA C	Muni State	-.70					.50		800 221-2783
Seligman Municipal Series MD C	Muni State	.70					.50		800 221-2783
Seligman Municipal Series MI C	Muni State	1.70					.50		800 221-2783
Seligman Municipal Series MN C	Muni State	.40					.50		800 221-2783
Seligman Municipal Series MO C	Muni State	.60					.50		800 221-2783
Seligman Municipal Series NC C	Muni State	.10					.50		800 221-2783
Seligman Municipal Series NY C	Muni NY	.70					.50		800 221-2783
Seligman Municipal Series Natl C	Muni Natl	-.50					.50		800 221-2783
Seligman Municipal Series OH C	Muni State	.50					.50		800 221-2783
Seligman Municipal Series OR C	Muni State	.80					.50		800 221-2783
Seligman Municipal Series SC C	Muni State	4.00					.50		800 221-2783
Seligman NJ Municipal Fund C	Muni State	-.40					.50		800 221-2783
Seligman PA Municipal Fund C	Muni State	.30					.50		800 221-2783
Seligman US Government Securities C	Government	3.10					.50	2.39	800 221-2783
Seligman US Govt Securities A	Government	3.70	4.92	4.74	4.00	3.00	.50	1.17	800 221-2783
Seligman US Govt Securities B	Government	3.10	4.19		4.00	3.00	.50	1.92	800 221-2783
Seligman US Govt Securities D	Government	3.10	4.18	3.88	4.00	3.00	.50	2.00	800 221-2783
Sentinel Bond A	Corp-Inv	2.10	4.10	4.66	4.00	4.00	.53	.70	800 282-3863
Sentinel Bond B	Corp-Inv	1.20	3.23		5.00	4.00	.53	1.61	800 282-3863
Sentinel Government Securities	Government	4.80	5.53	5.45	3.00	3.00	.53	.85	800 282-3863
Sentinel High Yield Bond A	Corp-HY	1.40	4.24		3.00	5.00	.75	1.27	800 282-3863
Sentinel High Yield Bond B	Corp-HY	1.00	3.90		3.00	5.00	.75	1.61	800 282-3863

Bond Fund Name	Objective	Annualized Return for			Rank		Max Load	Expense Ratio	Toll-Free Telephone
		1 Year	3 Years	5 Years	Overall	Risk			
Sentinel NY Tax Free Fund	Muni NY	2.40	4.64	5.47	3.00	4.00	.53	.94	800 282-3863
Sentinel PA Tax Free Income	Muni State	1.30	3.49	4.70	4.00	3.00	.55	.69	800 282-3863
Sentinel Short Maturity Govt	Govt-Mtg	5.00	5.25	5.48	1.00	1.00	.53	.76	800 282-3863
Sentinel Tax Free Income A	Muni Natl	2.10	4.05	5.00	3.00	3.00	.53	.71	800 282-3863
Sit Bond Fund	Dvsfd Bond	2.40	4.66	5.50	3.00	2.00	.80	.80	800 332-5580
Sit MN Tax Free Income	Muni State	-1.10	3.29	4.75	3.00	2.00	.80	.80	800 332-5580
Sit Tax Free Income Fund	Muni Natl	-.60	3.54	5.15	3.00	3.00	.79	.70	800 332-5580
Sit US Government Fund	Government	4.60	5.41	5.86	2.00	1.00	.80	.80	800 332-5580
SmBarney AZ Municipals A	Muni State	.80	3.64	5.00	3.00	3.00	.50	.88	800 451-2010
SmBarney AZ Municipals B	Muni State	.30	4.27	5.17	4.00	4.00	.50	1.41	800 451-2010
SmBarney Adj Rate Govt A	Govt-Mtg	4.40	4.66	5.08	2.00	1.00	.59	1.80	800 451-2010
SmBarney Adj Rate Govt B	Govt-Mtg	4.40	4.61	5.04	2.00	1.00	.59	4.54	800 451-2010
SmBarney CA Municipals A	Muni CA	1.90	4.31	6.04	3.00	4.00	.48	.70	800 451-2010
SmBarney CA Municipals B	Muni CA	1.40	3.79	5.49	4.00	4.00	.48	1.19	800 451-2010
SmBarney Concert Inv Govt A	Government	2.70	3.47	3.75	4.00	3.00	.59	1.46	800 221-3627
SmBarney Concert Inv Govt B	Government	2.00	2.87	3.09	5.00	3.00	.59	2.10	800 221-3627
SmBarney Concert Inv Govt I	Government	2.70	3.64	4.36	4.00	3.00	.59	.96	800 221-3627
SmBarney Concert Inv Muni I	Muni Natl	1.30	3.73	5.08	2.00	3.00	.59	1.00	800 221-3627
SmBarney Inc-Div Strat Inc A	Dvsfd Bond	2.80	4.12	6.42	2.00	2.00	.65	6.37	800 451-2010
SmBarney Inc-Div Strat Inc B	Dvsfd Bond	2.10	3.61	5.90	2.00	2.00	.65	5.87	800 451-2010
SmBarney Inc-Div Strat Inc L	Dvsfd Bond	2.30	3.75	6.02	2.00	2.00	.65	6.00	800 451-2010
SmBarney Inc-Div Strat Inc Y	Dvsfd Bond	3.00	4.44		1.00	2.00	.65	6.75	800 451-2010
SmBarney Inc-High Income A	Corp-HY	1.00	2.71	6.83	3.00	5.00	.69	1.05	800 451-2010
SmBarney Inc-High Income B	Corp-HY	.50	2.19	6.30	3.00	5.00	.69	1.55	800 451-2010
SmBarney Inc-High Income L	Corp-HY	.50	2.24	6.37	3.00	5.00	.69	1.47	800 451-2010
SmBarney Inc-High Income Y	Corp-HY	1.30	3.01		2.00	5.00	.69	.71	800 451-2010
SmBarney Inc-Muni High Inc A	Muni Natl	-1.90	2.97	4.65	3.00	3.00	.59	.81	800 451-2010
SmBarney Inc-Muni High Inc B	Muni Natl	-2.40	2.44	4.13	4.00	3.00	.59	1.31	800 451-2010
SmBarney Intrm Mat CA Muni A	Muni CA	3.90	4.26	5.18	2.00	2.00	.50	.88	800 451-2010
SmBarney Intrm Mat CA Muni L	Muni CA	-45.40	-15.67	-6.96	4.00	5.00	.48	1.23	800 451-2010
SmBarney Intrm Mat NY Muni A	Muni NY	3.30	4.13	4.94	2.00	3.00	.50	.76	800 451-2010
SmBarney Inv-Govt Secs A	Government	2.90	4.71	5.08	4.00	4.00	.55	.92	800 451-2010
SmBarney Inv-Govt Secs B	Government	2.50	4.21	4.37	4.00	4.00	.55	1.43	800 451-2010
SmBarney Inv-Invst Grd Bd A	Corp-Inv	.30	5.19	5.75	4.00	5.00	.65	1.02	800 451-2010
SmBarney Inv-Invst Grd Bd B	Corp-Inv	-.20	4.70	5.24	4.00	5.00	.65	1.52	800 451-2010
SmBarney Inv-Invst Grd Bd L	Corp-Inv	-.10	4.75	5.29	4.00	5.00	.65	1.44	800 451-2010
SmBarney MA Municipals A	Muni State	-.70	3.25	4.98	3.00	4.00	.50	.81	800 451-2010
SmBarney MA Municipals B	Muni State	-1.20	2.74	4.44	4.00	4.00	.50	1.32	800 451-2010
SmBarney Managed Govt A	Govt-Mtg	4.30	4.83	5.31	3.00	3.00	.65	5.17	800 451-2010
SmBarney Managed Govt B	Govt-Mtg	3.80	4.29	4.77	4.00	3.00	.65	4.63	800 451-2010
SmBarney Managed Govt L	Govt-Mtg	3.80	4.40	4.75	3.00	3.00	.65	4.75	800 451-2010
SmBarney Managed Munis A	Muni Natl	1.20	3.61	5.17	4.00	4.00	.46	.67	800 451-2010
SmBarney Managed Munis B	Muni Natl	.60	3.06	5.11	4.00	4.00	.46	1.18	800 451-2010
SmBarney Muni Bond-FL A	Muni State	1.60	3.99	5.45	3.00	3.00	.50	.72	800 451-2010
SmBarney Muni Bond-FL B	Muni State	1.10	3.45	4.88	4.00	3.00	.50	1.23	800 451-2010
SmBarney Muni Bond-FL L	Muni State	1.00	3.40	4.81	4.00	4.00	.50	1.31	800 451-2010
SmBarney Muni Bond-GA A	Muni State	1.50	4.05	5.90	3.00	3.00	.45	.64	800 451-2010
SmBarney Muni Bond-Ltd A	Muni Natl	1.20	3.31	4.30	3.00	3.00	.50	.71	800 451-2010
SmBarney Muni Bond-Ltd L	Muni Natl	1.10	3.30	4.19	3.00	3.00	.50	.93	800 451-2010
SmBarney Muni Bond-NY A	Muni NY	1.80	4.20	5.59	3.00	4.00	.50	.69	800 451-2010
SmBarney Muni Bond-NY B	Muni NY	1.20	3.62	5.01	3.00	4.00	.50	1.22	800 451-2010
SmBarney Muni Bond-NY L	Muni NY	1.30	3.60	4.98	3.00	4.00	.50	1.27	800 451-2010
SmBarney Muni Bond-Natl A	Muni Natl	1.30	3.73	5.32	3.00	4.00	.45	.66	800 451-2010
SmBarney Muni Bond-Natl B	Muni Natl	.80	3.37	4.78	4.00	4.00	.45	1.15	800 451-2010
SmBarney Muni Bond-Natl L	Muni Natl	.60	3.31	4.76	4.00	4.00	.45	1.23	800 451-2010
SmBarney Muni Bond-PA A	Muni State	-.50	3.83	5.32	4.00	4.00	.45	.50	800 451-2010
SmBarney Muni Bond-PA L	Muni State	-1.10	3.21	4.81	4.00	4.00	.45	1.07	800 451-2010
SmBarney NJ Municipals A	Muni State	-1.10	2.94	4.53	4.00	3.00	.50	.75	800 451-2010

445

Bond Fund Name	Objective	Annualized Return for			Rank		Max Load	Expense Ratio	Toll-Free Telephone
		1 Year	3 Years	5 Years	Overall	Risk			
SmBarney NJ Municipals B	Muni State	-1.60	2.40	4.00	4.00	3.00	.50	1.28	800 451-2010
SmBarney NJ Municipals L	Muni State	-1.70	2.32	3.50	5.00	3.00	.50	1.32	800 451-2010
SmBarney Sh Term High Grade Bd A	Government	2.70	4.39	4.41	3.00	2.00	.45	.96	800 451-2010
SmBarney US Govt A	Govt-Mtg	4.70	5.22	5.69	2.00	3.00	.45	5.61	800 451-2010
SmBarney US Govt B	Govt-Mtg	4.30	4.72	5.18	3.00	3.00	.45	5.09	800 451-2010
SmBarney US Govt L	Govt-Mtg	4.30	4.58	5.13	3.00	3.00	.45	5.13	800 451-2010
SmBarney World-Global Gov Bd A	Intl Bond	3.40	4.75	6.45	2.00	3.00	.75	1.19	800 451-2010
SmBarney World-Global Gov Bd B	Intl Bond	2.70	4.17	5.79	4.00	3.00	.75	1.76	800 451-2010
SmBarney World-Global Gov Bd L	Intl Bond	2.80	4.28	5.96	4.00	3.00	.75	1.65	800 451-2010
SmBarney World-Global Gov Bd Y	Intl Bond	3.80	4.94	6.65	2.00	3.00	.75	.82	800 451-2010
Smith Breeden Interm Dur USG Ser	Government	3.60	5.07	5.87	1.00	2.00	.69	.88	800 221-3138
Smith Breeden Sh Dur USG Fund	Government	3.90	4.44	5.12	2.00	1.00	.69	.78	800 221-3138
SouthTrust Bond Fund	Corp-Inv	3.30	5.20	5.22	4.00	4.00	.59	.83	800 843-8618
SouthTrust Income Fund	Dvsfd Bond	4.10	5.13		3.00	2.00	.29	.75	800 843-8618
Standish Fd-Controlled Maturity	Corp-Inv	4.40	5.20		1.00	1.00	.34	.29	800 221-4795
Standish Fd-Fixed Income Fund	Corp-Inv	3.10	4.57	6.02	2.00	3.00	.34	.35	800 221-4795
Standish Fd-Fixed Income II	Corp-Inv	1.00	3.51		3.00	3.00	.40	.40	800 221-4795
Standish Fd-Global Fixed Inc	Intl Bond	2.30	5.38	8.66	2.00	3.00	.40	.54	800 221-4795
Standish Fd-Interm Tax Exempt	Muni Natl	3.20	4.17	5.18	2.00	2.00	.40	.63	800 221-4795
Standish Fd-International Fixed	Intl Bond	3.50	6.58	10.07	1.00	3.00	.40	.52	800 221-4795
Standish Fd-MA Interm Tax Exempt	Muni State	2.90	4.05	4.83	2.00	2.00	.40	.65	800 221-4795
Standish Fd-Short Term Asset Res	Corp-Inv	5.50	5.56	5.73	1.00	1.00	.25	.35	800 221-4795
State Street Research Govt Inc A	Government	3.90	5.59	5.75	3.00	3.00	.58	1.03	800 562-0032
State Street Research Govt Inc B	Government	3.10	4.80	4.94	3.00	3.00	.58	1.78	800 562-0032
State Street Research Govt Inc B1	Government	3.10					.58	1.71	800 562-0032
State Street Research Govt Inc C	Government	3.20	4.80	5.21	3.00	3.00	.58	1.78	800 562-0032
State Street Research Govt Inc S	Government	4.10	5.83	6.18	2.00	3.00	.58	.78	800 562-0032
State Street Research High Inc A	Corp-HY	-6.30	1.77	5.96	4.00	5.00	.56	1.06	800 562-0032
State Street Research High Inc B	Corp-HY	-7.00	.97	5.17	4.00	5.00	.56	1.81	800 562-0032
State Street Research High Inc B1	Corp-HY	-7.00					.56	1.73	800 562-0032
State Street Research High Inc C	Corp-HY	-7.00	1.03	5.17	4.00	5.00	.56	1.81	800 562-0032
State Street Research High Inc S	Corp-HY	-5.90	2.05	6.23	4.00	5.00	.56	.81	800 562-0032
State Street Research NY Tx Fr A	Muni NY	.90	3.47	4.84	3.00	4.00	.55	1.11	800 562-0032
State Street Research NY Tx Fr B	Muni NY	.20	2.71	4.06	5.00	4.00	.55	1.86	800 562-0032
State Street Research NY Tx Fr B1	Muni NY	.30					.55	1.86	800 562-0032
State Street Research NY Tx Fr C	Muni NY	.30	2.71	4.06	5.00	4.00	.55	1.86	800 562-0032
State Street Research NY Tx Fr S	Muni NY	1.20	3.73	5.09	3.00	4.00	.55	.85	800 562-0032
State Street Research Strat Inc A	Dvsfd Bond	.10	3.48		4.00	3.00	.75	1.35	800 562-0032
State Street Research Strat Inc B	Dvsfd Bond	-.60	2.72		4.00	3.00	.75	2.10	800 562-0032
State Street Research Strat Inc B1	Dvsfd Bond	-.60					.75	2.10	800 562-0032
State Street Research Strat Inc C	Dvsfd Bond	-.60	2.72		3.00	3.00	.75	2.10	800 562-0032
State Street Research Strat Inc S	Dvsfd Bond	.30	3.70		2.00	3.00	.75	1.10	800 562-0032
State Street Research Tax-Ex A	Muni Natl	.90	3.94	5.25	3.00	3.00	.55	1.08	800 562-0032
State Street Research Tax-Ex B	Muni Natl	.10	3.17	4.50	4.00	3.00	.55	1.83	800 562-0032
State Street Research Tax-Ex B1	Muni Natl	0.00					.55	1.83	800 562-0032
State Street Research Tax-Ex C	Muni Natl	.10	3.18	4.50	4.00	3.00	.55	1.83	800 562-0032
State Street Research Tax-Ex S	Muni Natl	1.10	4.17	5.53	3.00	3.00	.55	.82	800 562-0032
SteinRoe High Yield	Corp-HY	-.80	5.59		3.00	5.00	.46	1.00	800 338-2550
SteinRoe Income Fund	Dvsfd Bond	4.70	4.65	5.94	2.00	3.00	.60	.83	800 338-2550
SteinRoe Intermediate Bd	Corp-Inv	4.40	5.53	6.28	2.00	3.00	.50	.71	800 338-2550
SteinRoe Intermediate Muni	Muni Natl	3.00	3.90	4.81	3.00	2.00	.46	.69	800 338-2550
SteinRoe Managed Munis	Muni Natl	1.70	3.94	5.28	2.00	3.00	.52	.71	800 338-2550
Stellar Insured Tax Free Bond A	Muni Natl	3.10	4.29		2.00	3.00	.50	.79	800 677-3863
Strategist Government Income Fund	Government	-.30	3.85		3.00	2.00	.52	1.09	800 328-8300
Strategist High Yield Fund	Corp-HY	-1.40	1.67		4.00	5.00	.57	1.18	800 328-8300
Strategist Quality Income	Corp-Inv	3.10	4.99		2.00	3.00	.52	1.09	800 328-8300
Strategist Tax Free High Yield	Muni Natl	-.70	3.42		3.00	3.00	.46	.94	800 328-8300
Strategist World Income Fund	Intl Bond	.20	1.95		5.00	5.00	.78	1.35	800 328-8300

Bond Fund Name	Objective	Annualized Return for			Rank		Max Load	Expense Ratio	Toll-Free Telephone
		1 Year	3 Years	5 Years	Overall	Risk			
Strong Advantage Fund	Corp-Inv	5.70	5.44	5.99	1.00	1.00	.34	.69	800 368-1030
Strong Corporate Bond	Corp-Inv	3.90	5.69	7.25	2.00	4.00	.37	.90	800 368-1030
Strong Global High Yield Bond	Intl Bond	2.30					.69	2.00	800 368-1030
Strong Government Securities Inv	Govt-Mtg	4.00	5.54	5.84	2.00	2.00	.34	.80	800 368-1030
Strong High Yield Bond	Corp-HY	4.00	6.67		1.00	5.00	.37	.80	800 368-1030
Strong High-Yield Muni	Muni Natl	-5.50	2.40	4.73	3.00	4.00	.34	.69	800 368-1030
Strong International Bond	Intl Bond	.50	.42	1.35	5.00	5.00	.69	1.69	800 368-1030
Strong Municipal Advantage Fund	Muni Natl	2.90	3.91		2.00	1.00	.59	.50	800 368-1030
Strong Municipal Bond	Muni Natl	-3.80	2.95	4.28	4.00	4.00	.59	.69	800 368-1030
Strong Short-Term Bond Inv	Corp-Inv	4.60	5.10	6.14	1.00	1.00	.37	.80	800 368-1030
Strong Short-Term Global Bond	Intl Bond	5.10	4.94	6.88	1.00	1.00	.62	1.10	800 368-1030
Strong Short-Term HY Bond	Corp-HY	4.20	7.96		1.00	2.00	.37	.80	800 368-1030
Strong Short-Term HY Muni Bond	Muni Natl	.20					.59	.20	800 368-1030
Strong Short-Term Muni Bd	Muni Natl	2.60	4.20	4.85	2.00	1.00	.25	.59	800 368-1030
Summit Emerging Mkts Bond Fund	Intl Bond	8.00					.75	2.18	800 272-3442
Summit High Yield	Corp-HY	.50	1.31	8.49	3.00	5.00	.50	1.70	800 272-3442
SunAmerica Diversified Inc A	Dvsfd Bond	6.70	2.35	6.47	3.00	5.00	.65	1.45	800 858-8850
SunAmerica Diversified Inc B	Dvsfd Bond	5.60	1.72	5.73	3.00	5.00	.65	2.08	800 858-8850
SunAmerica Diversified Income II	Dvsfd Bond	6.50					.65		800 858-8850
SunAmerica Federal Securities A	Govt-Mtg	5.30	6.12	6.49	1.00	2.00	.52	1.40	800 858-8850
SunAmerica Federal Securities B	Govt-Mtg	4.60	5.38	5.67	2.00	2.00	.52	2.06	800 858-8850
SunAmerica Federal Securities II	Govt-Mtg	4.90					.52		800 858-8850
SunAmerica High Income A	Corp-HY	-.40	2.69	6.50	3.00	5.00	.75	1.51	800 858-8850
SunAmerica High Income B	Corp-HY	-1.00	2.02	5.84	3.00	5.00	.75	2.12	800 858-8850
SunAmerica High Income II	Corp-HY	-.90					.75	2.10	800 858-8850
SunAmerica Tax Exempt Insd A	Muni Natl	2.00	3.53	4.71	3.00	3.00	.50	1.23	800 858-8850
SunAmerica Tax Exempt Insd B	Muni Natl	1.50	2.96	4.09	4.00	3.00	.50	1.90	800 858-8850
SunAmerica Tax-Exempt Insured II	Muni Natl	1.70					.50		800 858-8850
SunAmerica US Gov Sec A	Government	3.50	4.49	5.03	3.00	2.00	.73	1.50	800 858-8850
SunAmerica US Gov Sec B	Government	2.90	3.84	4.36	4.00	2.00	.73	2.14	800 858-8850
SunAmerica US Government Secs II	Government	7.20					.73		800 858-8850
TIAA-CREF Bond Plus Fund	Government	4.70					.29	.40	
Target-Intermediate-Term Bond	Corp-Inv	5.30	5.85	6.42	1.00	2.00	.45	.68	800 225-1852
Target-International Bond	Intl Bond	-4.90	-1.00	-.54	5.00	5.00	.50	1.37	800 225-1852
Target-Mortgage Backed Secs	Govt-Mtg	4.50	5.46	6.32	1.00	2.00	.45	.75	800 225-1852
Target-Total Return Bond Portf	Dvsfd Bond	3.30	5.51	6.31	2.00	3.00	.45	.79	800 225-1852
Tax-Exempt Bd Fd of America	Muni Natl	1.90	4.15	5.47	1.00	2.00	.34	.33	800 421-9900
Templeton Global Bond A	Intl Bond	.40	.73	4.28	5.00	4.00	.48	1.19	800 237-0738
Templeton Global Bond Adv	Intl Bond	.60	1.15		5.00	4.00	.48	.94	800 237-0738
Templeton Global Bond C	Intl Bond	-.20	-.16	3.55	5.00	4.00	.48	1.60	800 237-0738
Thompson and Plumb Bond	Corp-Inv	2.70	4.65	4.49	4.00	3.00	.65	.97	800 499-0079
Thornburg Interm Muni-FL A	Muni State	2.90	3.93	4.73	2.00	2.00	.50	1.08	800 847-0200
Thornburg Interm Muni-NM A	Muni State	2.50	3.71	4.41	2.00	1.00	.50	1.01	800 847-0200
Thornburg Interm Muni-Natl A	Muni Natl	1.00	3.16	4.41	3.00	2.00	.50	1.02	800 847-0200
Thornburg Interm Muni-Natl C	Muni Natl	.60	2.77	4.00	3.00	2.00	.50	1.87	800 847-0200
Thornburg Interm Muni-Natl I	Muni Natl	1.20	3.43		2.00	2.00	.50	.78	800 847-0200
Thornburg Ltd Term Income Fd A	Corp-Inv	3.80	4.49	5.79	3.00	2.00	.50	1.17	800 847-0200
Thornburg Ltd Term Income Fd C	Corp-Inv	3.40	4.03	5.37	4.00	2.00	.50	2.22	800 847-0200
Thornburg Ltd Term Income Fd I	Corp-Inv	4.20	4.75		3.00	2.00	.50	1.02	800 847-0200
Thornburg Ltd Term Muni-CA A	Muni CA	3.10	3.86	4.39	2.00	1.00	.50	.98	800 847-0200
Thornburg Ltd Term Muni-CA C	Muni CA	2.80	3.48	3.99	2.00	1.00	.50	1.39	800 847-0200
Thornburg Ltd Term Muni-Natl A	Muni Natl	2.90	3.52	4.12	3.00	1.00	.45	.95	800 847-0200
Thornburg Ltd Term Muni-Natl C	Muni Natl	2.60	3.12	3.68	3.00	1.00	.45	1.37	800 847-0200
Thornburg Ltd Term Muni-Natl I	Muni Natl	3.40	3.89		2.00	1.00	.45	.59	800 847-0200
Thornburg Ltd Term US Govt Fd A	Government	3.80	4.67	5.11	3.00	2.00	.38	.94	800 847-0200
Thornburg Ltd Term US Govt Fd C	Government	3.30	4.25	4.68	4.00	2.00	.38	1.97	800 847-0200
Thornburg Ltd Term US Govt Fd I	Government	4.20	5.06		2.00	2.00	.38	1.13	800 847-0200
Timothy Plan Fixed-Income A	Government	-4.80					.59		800 846-7526

Bond Fund Name	Objective	Annualized Return for			Rank		Max Load	Expense Ratio	Toll-Free Telephone
		1 Year	3 Years	5 Years	Overall	Risk			
Timothy Plan Fixed-Income B	Government	-5.20					.59		800 846-7526
Timothy Plan Fixed-Income C	Government	-4.30					.59		800 846-7526
Touchstone Bond Fund A	Dvsfd Bond	2.70	4.57	5.03	3.00	2.00	.55	.90	800 638-8194
Touchstone Bond Fund C	Dvsfd Bond	1.60	3.43	3.94	4.00	2.00	.55	1.64	800 638-8194
Trust for Credit Uns-Govt Sec	Govt-Mtg	5.40	5.36	5.34	1.00	1.00	.20	.33	
Trust for Credit Uns-Mortgage	Govt-Mtg	5.10	5.55	5.98	1.00	1.00	.20	.28	
Turner Core High Quality Fixed Inc	Corp-Inv						.50		800 224-6312
Turner Sh Dur US Govt-1 Yr Instl	Government	5.40					.25	0.00	800 224-6312
Turner Sh Dur US Govt-3 Yr Instl	Government	4.50					.25	.23	800 224-6312
Turner Short Duration Govt 1yr Adv	Government	5.70					.25	1.29	800 224-6312
Turner Short Duration Govt 3yr	Government	4.90					.25		800 224-6312
U.S. Government Securities Fund	Government	4.30	5.29	5.45	3.00	2.00	.01	.40	800 421-9900
UAM BHM&S Total Return Bd Inst	Corp-Inv	2.90	4.56		4.00	3.00	.34	1.07	877 826-5465
UAM BHM&S Total Return Bd Svc	Corp-Inv	2.40	4.24		4.00	3.00	.34	1.43	877 826-5465
UAM DSI Limited Maturity	Corp-Inv	3.50	3.94	4.74	3.00	1.00	.45	1.00	877 826-5465
UAM II Chicago Mgmt Interm Bd	Corp-Inv	3.70	4.96	4.62	3.00	2.00	.47	.80	877 826-5465
UAM Mckee US Government Inst	Government	2.00	4.00	4.12	5.00	3.00	.45	1.15	877 826-5465
UAM Sirach Bond Fund A	Corp-Inv	3.10					.34	.30	877 826-5465
UAM Sirach Bond Fund B	Corp-Inv	3.40					.34	.16	877 826-5465
UAM TS&W Fixed Inc Portfolio Inst	Corp-Inv	3.00	5.07	5.19	3.00	3.00	.45	.77	877 826-5465
UBS High Yield Fund	Corp-HY	-.30					.59	1.55	800 448-2430
UMB Scout Bond Fund	Corp-Inv	3.40	4.80	4.97	3.00	2.00	.84	.86	800 996-2862
US Near-Term Tax Free	Muni Natl	2.60	3.68	4.11	2.00	1.00	.50	.69	800 873-8637
US Tax-Free Fund	Muni Natl	1.60	3.51	4.73	2.00	3.00	.75	1.44	800 873-8637
USAA GNMA Trust	Govt-Mtg	3.00	4.79	5.57	3.00	3.00	.12	1.00	800 382-8722
USAA High-Yield Opportunities Fund	Corp-HY						.50		800 382-8722
USAA Intermediate-Term Bond Fund	Dvsfd Bond						.50		800 382-8722
USAA Short Term Bond	Corp-HY	5.50	5.56	5.97	1.00	1.00	.23	.50	800 382-8722
USAA Tax Exempt-CA Bond	Muni CA	1.60	4.51	6.13	3.00	4.00	.32	.39	800 382-8722
USAA Tax Exempt-FL	Muni State	-.10	3.69	5.44	3.00	4.00	.39	.46	800 382-8722
USAA Tax Exempt-Intermediate	Muni Natl	2.00	4.32	5.46	1.00	2.00	.28	.35	800 382-8722
USAA Tax Exempt-Long Term	Muni Natl	.10	3.72	5.40	3.00	3.00	.28	.35	800 382-8722
USAA Tax Exempt-NY Bond	Muni NY	1.60	4.42	5.65	3.00	3.00	.42	.57	800 382-8722
USAA Tax Exempt-Short Term	Muni Natl	3.50	4.13	4.61	2.00	1.00	.28	.38	800 382-8722
USAA Tax Exempt-TX	Muni State	-1.80	3.25	5.62	3.00	4.00	.50	.86	800 382-8722
USAA Tax Exempt-VA Bond	Muni State	1.30	4.08	5.44	3.00	3.00	.34	.42	800 382-8722
Value Line Aggressive Inc Tr	Corp-HY	-1.80	2.12	8.32	3.00	5.00	.75	.81	800 223-0818
Value Line NY Tax Exempt	Muni NY	2.30	4.00	5.01	3.00	4.00	.59	.97	800 223-0818
Value Line Tax Exempt Natl Bond	Muni Natl	.90	3.53	4.77	3.00	3.00	.50	.63	800 223-0818
Value Line US Govt Securities	Government	3.60	5.25	5.38	3.00	3.00	.50	.65	800 223-0818
Van Eck/Chubb Govt Securities A	Government	3.80	5.40	5.64	3.00	3.00	.65	1.00	800 826-2333
Van Eck/Chubb Tax-Exempt Fund A	Muni Natl	1.40	3.78	4.81	1.00	3.00	.45	1.00	800 826-2333
Van Kampen CA Ins T/F A	Muni CA	2.30	4.17	5.53	3.00	4.00	.47	1.66	800 421-5666
Van Kampen CA Ins T/F B	Muni CA	1.70	3.42	4.76	4.00	4.00	.47	1.65	800 421-5666
Van Kampen CA Ins T/F C	Muni CA	1.70	3.42	4.76	4.00	4.00	.47	1.64	800 421-5666
Van Kampen Corp Bond A	Corp-Inv	1.90	3.93	5.12	3.00	4.00	.47	1.08	800 421-5666
Van Kampen Corp Bond B	Corp-Inv	1.00	3.08	4.29	4.00	4.00	.47	1.86	800 421-5666
Van Kampen Corp Bond C	Corp-Inv	1.00	3.08	4.27	3.00	4.00	.47	1.86	800 421-5666
Van Kampen FL Ins T/F A	Muni State	1.70	3.96	5.34	2.00	4.00	.50	.40	800 421-5666
Van Kampen FL Ins T/F B	Muni State	.90	3.16	4.56	4.00	4.00	.50	1.16	800 421-5666
Van Kampen FL Ins T/F C	Muni State	.90	3.18	4.59	4.00	4.00	.50	1.15	800 421-5666
Van Kampen Glb Govt A	Intl Bond						.75	1.56	800 421-5666
Van Kampen Glb Govt B	Intl Bond						.75	2.29	800 421-5666
Van Kampen Glb Govt C	Intl Bond						.75	2.29	800 421-5666
Van Kampen Global Fixed A	Intl Bond						.75	1.46	800 421-5666
Van Kampen Global Fixed B	Intl Bond						.75	2.22	800 421-5666
Van Kampen Global Fixed C	Intl Bond						.75	2.22	800 421-5666
Van Kampen Govt Secs A	Government	4.30	5.18	5.20	3.00	3.00	.53	1.02	800 421-5666

448

Bond Fund Name	Objective	Annualized Return for			Rank		Max Load	Expense Ratio	Toll-Free Telephone
		1 Year	3 Years	5 Years	Overall	Risk			
Van Kampen Govt Secs B	Government	3.40	4.42	4.42	4.00	3.00	.53	1.77	800 421-5666
Van Kampen Govt Secs C	Government	3.50	4.44	4.43	4.00	3.00	.53	1.77	800 421-5666
Van Kampen H/Y & Total Return A	Corp-HY	1.20	4.45		3.00	5.00	.75	1.25	800 421-5666
Van Kampen H/Y & Total Return B	Corp-HY	.30	3.45		3.00	5.00	.75	2.00	800 421-5666
Van Kampen H/Y & Total Return C	Corp-HY	.40	3.67		3.00	5.00	.75	2.00	800 421-5666
Van Kampen H/Y Muni A	Muni Natl	-1.10	4.37	5.88	1.00	2.00	.52	.90	800 421-5666
Van Kampen H/Y Muni B	Muni Natl	-1.90	3.57	5.08	1.00	2.00	.52	1.64	800 421-5666
Van Kampen H/Y Muni C	Muni Natl	-1.90	3.59	5.09	1.00	2.00	.52	1.64	800 421-5666
Van Kampen Hi Inc Corp A	Corp-HY	1.90	3.37	7.35	3.00	5.00	.53	1.03	800 421-5666
Van Kampen Hi Inc Corp B	Corp-HY	1.00	2.60	6.52	3.00	5.00	.53	1.80	800 421-5666
Van Kampen Hi Inc Corp C	Corp-HY	1.00	2.61	6.53	3.00	5.00	.53	1.79	800 421-5666
Van Kampen Hi Yield A	Corp-HY	2.80	3.35	6.89	3.00	5.00	.75	1.16	800 421-5666
Van Kampen Hi Yield B	Corp-HY	2.10	2.59	6.10	2.00	5.00	.75	1.92	800 421-5666
Van Kampen Hi Yield C	Corp-HY	2.10	2.55	6.07	2.00	5.00	.75	1.92	800 421-5666
Van Kampen Ins T/F Inc A	Muni Natl	2.10	3.67	4.88	3.00	4.00	.50	.91	800 421-5666
Van Kampen Ins T/F Inc B	Muni Natl	1.30	2.86	4.08	5.00	4.00	.50	1.67	800 421-5666
Van Kampen Ins T/F Inc C	Muni Natl	1.20	3.41	4.40	4.00	4.00	.50	1.67	800 421-5666
Van Kampen Int Muni A	Muni Natl	1.60	4.11	5.02	1.00	2.00	.50	1.09	800 421-5666
Van Kampen Int Muni B	Muni Natl	.90	3.28	4.24	3.00	2.00	.50	1.82	800 421-5666
Van Kampen Int Muni C	Muni Natl	.90	3.32	4.26	3.00	2.00	.50	1.83	800 421-5666
Van Kampen Ltd Govt A	Govt-Mtg	4.10	4.45	4.63	3.00	1.00	.50	1.39	800 421-5666
Van Kampen Ltd Govt B	Govt-Mtg	3.40	3.72	3.91	3.00	1.00	.50	2.16	800 421-5666
Van Kampen Ltd Govt C	Govt-Mtg	3.40	3.75	3.90	3.00	1.00	.50	2.16	800 421-5666
Van Kampen Muni Inc A	Muni Natl	-.80	2.54	4.42	4.00	3.00	.47	.91	800 421-5666
Van Kampen Muni Inc B	Muni Natl	-1.40	1.79	3.64	5.00	3.00	.47	1.66	800 421-5666
Van Kampen NY T/F A	Muni NY	.20	4.42	6.04	3.00	4.00	.59	.35	800 421-5666
Van Kampen NY T/F B	Muni NY	-.40	3.48	5.16	4.00	4.00	.59	1.11	800 421-5666
Van Kampen NY T/F C	Muni NY	-.40	3.47	5.16	4.00	4.00	.59	1.10	800 421-5666
Van Kampen PA T/F A	Muni State	0.00	3.33	4.88	3.00	3.00	.59	1.02	800 421-5666
Van Kampen PA T/F B	Muni State	-.80	2.54	4.09	5.00	3.00	.59	1.78	800 421-5666
Van Kampen PA T/F C	Muni State	-.80	2.52	4.07	5.00	3.00	.59	1.78	800 421-5666
Van Kampen Strat Inc A	Dvsfd Bond	4.20	.75	5.82	3.00	5.00	1.03	1.53	800 421-5666
Van Kampen Strat Inc B	Dvsfd Bond	3.50	0.00	5.02	4.00	5.00	1.03	2.29	800 421-5666
Van Kampen Strat Inc C	Dvsfd Bond	3.50	0.00	5.02	4.00	5.00	1.03	2.27	800 421-5666
Van Kampen T/F Hi Inc A	Muni Natl	-2.00	2.85	4.43	3.00	3.00	.50	.93	800 421-5666
Van Kampen T/F Hi Inc B	Muni Natl	-2.70	2.07	3.63	4.00	3.00	.50	1.69	800 421-5666
Van Kampen T/F Hi Inc C	Muni Natl	-2.70	2.07	3.63	4.00	3.00	.50	1.68	800 421-5666
Van Kampen US Govt A	Govt-Mtg	3.50	4.62	5.29	3.00	2.00	.51	.93	800 421-5666
Van Kampen US Govt B	Govt-Mtg	2.70	3.77	4.44	4.00	2.00	.51	1.75	800 421-5666
Van Kampen US Govt C	Govt-Mtg	2.60	3.72	4.41	4.00	2.00	.51	1.73	800 421-5666
Van Kampen USG Tr Inc A	Government	3.90	4.78	4.94	3.00	2.00	.51	1.16	800 421-5666
Van Kampen USG Tr Inc B	Government	3.10	4.00	4.16	4.00	2.00	.51	1.92	800 421-5666
Van Kampen USG Tr Inc C	Government	3.10	4.00	4.16	4.00	2.00	.51	1.92	800 421-5666
Van Kampen Wrldwde High Inc A	Intl Bond	11.40	.80	9.98	3.00	5.00	.75	1.44	800 421-5666
Van Kampen Wrldwde High Inc B	Intl Bond	10.60	.03		3.00	5.00	.75	2.20	800 421-5666
Van Kampen Wrldwde High Inc C	Intl Bond	10.60	0.00	8.93	3.00	5.00	.75	2.20	800 421-5666
Vanguard Admiral Long Term UST	Government	6.40	7.96	7.05	3.00	5.00	.11	.14	800 662-7447
Vanguard Admiral-Intermed UST	Government	4.60	6.12	5.93	3.00	4.00	.11	.14	800 662-7447
Vanguard Admiral-Short Term UST	Government	4.70	5.40	5.54	2.00	1.00	.11	.14	800 662-7447
Vanguard Bond Index-Intermed Bd	Corp-Inv	3.40	5.62	5.82	3.00	4.00	.16	.20	800 662-7447
Vanguard Bond Index-Long Term Bd	Corp-Inv	4.30	7.03	6.71	3.00	5.00	.14	.20	800 662-7447
Vanguard Bond Index-Short Term	Corp-Inv	4.50	5.61	5.76	2.00	1.00	.16	.20	800 662-7447
Vanguard Bond Index-Total Bd Mkt	Corp-Inv	4.60	5.99	6.19	2.00	3.00	.16	.20	800 662-7447
Vanguard CA Tax Free Insd-IT	Muni CA	5.00	4.96	5.82	1.00	2.00	.14	.17	800 662-7447
Vanguard CA Tax Free Insd-LT	Muni CA	4.30	5.18	6.37	2.00	4.00	.16	.19	800 662-7447
Vanguard FL Insured Tax-Free	Muni State	3.60	4.81	5.96	2.00	4.00	.16	.17	800 662-7447
Vanguard Fixed-GNMA	Govt-Mtg	5.50	5.83	6.52	1.00	2.00	.26	.28	800 662-7447
Vanguard Fixed-High Yield	Corp-HY	2.00	4.98	7.42	2.00	4.00	.26	.28	800 662-7447

Bond Fund Name	Objective	Annualized Return for			Rank		Max Load	Expense Ratio	Toll-Free Telephone
		1 Year	3 Years	5 Years	Overall	Risk			
Vanguard Fixed-Interm Corp	Corp-Inv	3.30	5.05	5.60	3.00	4.00	.23	.26	800 662-7447
Vanguard Fixed-Intermd Treasury	Government	4.40	5.98	5.80	3.00	4.00	.23	.27	800 662-7447
Vanguard Fixed-Long Term Corp	Corp-Inv	1.60	5.27	5.87	4.00	5.00	.27	.29	800 662-7447
Vanguard Fixed-Long Term UST	Government	6.30	7.85	6.96	3.00	5.00	.23	.28	800 662-7447
Vanguard Fixed-Sh Term Corp Fd	Corp-Inv	4.80	5.55	5.82	1.00	1.00	.23	.26	800 662-7447
Vanguard Fixed-Sh Term Federal	Government	4.80	5.37	5.61	2.00	1.00	.23	.27	800 662-7447
Vanguard Fixed-Sh Term Treasury	Government	4.60	5.33	5.46	2.00	1.00	.23	.27	800 662-7447
Vanguard Muni-High Yield	Muni Natl	1.50	4.25	5.56	2.00	3.00	.17	.20	800 662-7447
Vanguard Muni-Insd Long-Term	Muni Natl	3.60	4.70	5.79	2.00	4.00	.17	.20	800 662-7447
Vanguard Muni-Intermediate	Muni Natl	4.10	4.33	5.11	2.00	2.00	.16	.19	800 662-7447
Vanguard Muni-Limited Term	Muni Natl	3.60	3.98	4.24	1.00	1.00	.16	.20	800 662-7447
Vanguard Muni-Long Term	Muni Natl	2.80	4.42	5.80	2.00	4.00	.16	.19	800 662-7447
Vanguard Muni-Short Term	Muni Natl	3.60	3.73	3.82	2.00	1.00	.16	.19	800 662-7447
Vanguard NJ Tax Free Insd LT	Muni State	3.20	4.62	5.47	2.00	3.00	.17	.20	800 662-7447
Vanguard NY Tax-Free Insured	Muni NY	3.10	4.67	5.69	2.00	4.00	.17	.20	800 662-7447
Vanguard OH T/F-Long	Muni State	3.20	4.47	5.54	1.00	3.00	.14	.20	800 662-7447
Vanguard PA Tax Free Insd LT	Muni State	3.30	4.59	5.60	1.00	3.00	.17	.20	800 662-7447
Victory Intermediate Income G	Corp-Inv						.75		800 539-3863
Victory Investment Quality Bond G	Corp-Inv						.75		800 539-3863
Victory NY Tax-Free FUnd G	Muni NY						.55		800 539-3863
Victory National Municipal Bond G	Muni Natl						.55		800 539-3863
Victory Portf-Fund for Income G	Government	4.70	5.61	5.79	2.00	2.00	.25	.89	800 869-5999
Victory Portf-Intermediate Inc	Corp-Inv	3.40	4.77	4.90	4.00	2.00	.75	.98	800 539-3863
Victory Portf-Investment Qual Bd	Corp-Inv	2.90	4.55	4.88	3.00	3.00	.75	1.10	800 539-3863
Victory Portf-Lmtd Term Income	Corp-Inv	4.10	4.59	4.81	3.00	1.00	.50	.93	800 539-3863
Victory Portf-NY Tax Free A	Muni NY	2.50	3.48	4.26	2.00	2.00	.55	.94	800 539-3863
Victory Portf-National Muni A	Muni Natl	4.20	4.91	5.88	1.00	3.00	.55	.79	800 539-3863
Victory Portf-OH Municipal Bond	Muni State	2.60	4.39	5.48	1.00	3.00	.59	.92	800 539-3863
Vintage Income	Corp-Inv	4.10	4.94	4.94	3.00	2.00	.59	1.01	800 438-6375
Vintage Limited Term Bond	Corp-Inv	2.90	4.15	4.31	4.00	2.00	.50	1.05	800 438-6375
Vintage Municipal Bond	Muni Natl	3.10	3.57	4.25	3.00	2.00	.50	.93	800 438-6375
Vision NY Municipal Income Fund	Muni NY	1.40	3.41	4.73	4.00	3.00	.69	1.03	800 836-2211
Vision US Government Securities	Government	4.00	5.03	5.22	3.00	3.00	.69	.91	800 836-2211
Vontobel Greater European Bond Fund	Intl Bond	-4.10					1.19	1.97	800 527-9500
WM CA Ins Interm Muni A	Muni CA	4.30	4.31	5.22	2.00	2.00	.50	.91	800 222-5852
WM CA Ins Interm Muni B	Muni CA	3.50	3.51	4.42	3.00	2.00	.50	1.65	800 222-5852
WM CA Municipal Bond A	Muni CA	1.70	4.31	5.60	3.00	4.00	.36	.88	800 222-5852
WM CA Municipal Bond B	Muni CA	1.00	3.42	4.76	4.00	4.00	.36	1.62	800 222-5852
WM FL Ins Municipal A	Muni State	.20	3.77	5.44	3.00	3.00	.50	.93	800 222-5852
WM FL Ins Municipal B	Muni State	-.50	2.98	4.64	4.00	3.00	.50	1.67	800 222-5852
WM Income Fd A	Corp-Inv	4.70	5.73	6.30	2.00	3.00	.50	1.09	800 222-5852
WM Income Fd B	Corp-Inv	4.10	4.94	5.49	2.00	3.00	.50	1.82	800 222-5852
WM Short Term Income Fund A	Corp-Inv	5.00	5.07	5.28	2.00	1.00	.04	.81	800 222-5852
WM Short Term Income Fund B	Corp-Inv	4.10	4.23	4.46	3.00	1.00	.04	1.59	800 222-5852
WM Tax Exempt Bond A	Muni Natl	1.50	3.49	4.64	4.00	3.00	.47	.89	800 222-5852
WM Tax Exempt Bond B	Muni Natl	.70	2.68	3.87	5.00	3.00	.47	1.64	800 222-5852
WM US Govt Securities A	Govt-Mtg	4.40	5.86	5.82	1.00	2.00	.50	.93	800 222-5852
WM US Govt Securities B	Govt-Mtg	3.50	5.02	4.96	3.00	2.00	.50	1.68	800 222-5852
WPG Core Bond Fund	Government	4.00	5.54	5.55	2.00	3.00	.59	.50	800 223-3332
WPG Intermediate Muni Bond	Muni Natl	3.50	4.34	5.09	2.00	2.00	0.00	.84	800 223-3332
Wachovia Fixed Income Fund A	Corp-Inv	3.90	5.23	5.44	3.00	3.00	.47	.96	800 994-4414
Wachovia Fixed Income Fund B	Corp-Inv	2.70	4.27		4.00	3.00	.50	1.71	800 994-4414
Wachovia Fixed Income Fund Y	Corp-Inv	4.20	5.46		2.00	3.00	.50	.71	800 994-4414
Wachovia GA Municipal Bond Fund A	Muni State	1.80	3.17	1.74	3.00	3.00	.13	1.15	800 994-4414
Wachovia GA Municipal Bond Fund Y	Muni State	2.00	3.51		3.00	3.00	.75	.91	800 994-4414
Wachovia Intermed Fixed Income A	Corp-Inv	3.10	5.25	5.06	3.00	3.00	.47	.88	800 994-4414
Wachovia NC Municipal Bond A	Muni State	2.20	3.41	4.64	3.00	3.00	.30	1.10	800 994-4414
Wachovia NC Municipal Bond Y	Muni State	2.40	3.70		3.00	3.00	.75	.84	800 994-4414

Bond Fund Name	Objective	Annualized Return for			Rank		Max Load	Expense Ratio	Toll-Free Telephone
		1 Year	3 Years	5 Years	Overall	Risk			
Wachovia S/T Fixed Income Fund A	Corp-Inv	4.10	4.83	5.03	3.00	1.00	.32	.88	800 994-4414
Wachovia S/T Fixed Income Fund Y	Corp-Inv	4.30	5.01		2.00	1.00	.63	.63	800 994-4414
Wachovia SC Municipal Bond A	Muni State	2.30	3.73	4.91	3.00	3.00	.26	.82	800 994-4414
Wachovia SC Municipal Bond Y	Muni State	2.50	3.97		1.00	3.00	.75	.57	800 994-4414
Wachovia VA Muni Bond A	Muni State	2.20	3.95	4.66	2.00	3.00	.39	.93	800 994-4414
Warburg Pincus Fixed Income Adv	Corp-Inv	2.80	4.32		3.00	2.00	.36	1.00	800 927-2874
Warburg Pincus Fixed Income Com	Corp-Inv	3.00	4.60	6.02	2.00	2.00	.50	.75	800 927-2874
Warburg Pincus Gbl Fixed Inc Adv	Intl Bond	3.10	2.54		3.00	3.00	.50	1.44	800 927-2874
Warburg Pincus Gbl Fixed Inc Com	Intl Bond	5.70	3.85	6.81	3.00	3.00	.50	.94	800 927-2874
Warburg Pincus High Yield Cmn	Corp-HY	-1.10	2.76		3.00	4.00	.69	.94	800 927-2874
Warburg Pincus High Yield Inst	Corp-HY	3.80	4.63	7.11	3.00	5.00	.69	.68	800 401-2230
Warburg Pincus Interm Mat Com	Government	3.70	5.16	5.44	3.00	2.00	.50	.59	800 927-2874
Warburg Pincus Intmed Mat Govt Adv	Government	2.90					.11	.84	800 927-2874
Warburg Pincus Muni Bond I	Muni Natl	2.70	4.20	4.81	2.00	3.00	.69	.98	800 927-2874
Warburg Pincus NY Int Muni Bd Com	Muni NY	3.60	3.81	4.42	2.00	2.00	.40	.59	800 927-2874
Warburg Pincus Strat Gl Fx Inc I	Intl Bond	-1.40	1.10	3.42	5.00	4.00	.50	.73	800 927-2874
Warburg Pincus Tr II-Fixed Income	Corp-Inv	4.00	5.62		2.00	2.00	.50	.98	800 927-2874
Warburg Pincus US Core Fixed Inc I	Government	2.50	5.11	6.21	1.00	2.00	.37	.44	800 927-2874
Wasatch-Hoisington US Treasury	Government	6.10	8.09	7.29	4.00	5.00	.50	.75	800 551-1700
Wayne Hummer Income Fund	Corp-Inv	3.60	5.04	5.40	3.00	3.00	.50	1.01	800 621-4477
Weitz Series-Fixed Income	Corp-Inv	1.40	4.61	5.26	3.00	2.00	.50	.75	800 232-4161
Wells Fargo AZ Tax-Free A	Muni State	.50	2.86	4.03	5.00	4.00	.50	.72	800 222-8222
Wells Fargo CA Limit Term T/F A	Muni CA	3.70	3.79	4.24	2.00	1.00	.50	.75	800 222-8222
Wells Fargo CA Tax-Free A	Muni CA	3.10	4.74	5.77	2.00	4.00	.50	.75	800 222-8222
Wells Fargo CA Tax-Free B	Muni CA	2.20	3.98	5.08	3.00	4.00	.50	1.44	800 222-8222
Wells Fargo CO Tax-Free A	Muni State	.90	3.76	5.47	3.00	4.00	.35	.59	800 222-8222
Wells Fargo CO Tax-Free B	Muni State	.20	3.02	4.71	4.00	4.00	.35	1.35	800 222-8222
Wells Fargo CO Tax-Free I	Muni State	1.00	3.81	5.50	3.00	4.00	.35	.59	800 222-8222
Wells Fargo Diversifed Bond I	Dvsfd Bond	5.70	6.86	6.08	3.00	4.00	.32	.69	800 222-8222
Wells Fargo Income A	Dvsfd Bond	2.80	5.20	5.15	3.00	4.00	.50	.75	800 222-8222
Wells Fargo Income B	Dvsfd Bond	1.90	4.37	4.38	5.00	4.00	.50	1.50	800 222-8222
Wells Fargo Income Inst	Dvsfd Bond	2.90	5.25	5.20	3.00	4.00	.50	.75	800 222-8222
Wells Fargo Intermediate Gov Inc A	Government	4.20	5.67		2.00	3.00	.33	.68	800 222-8222
Wells Fargo Intermediate Gov Inc B	Government	3.30	4.73		3.00	3.00	.33	1.42	800 222-8222
Wells Fargo Intermediate Gov Inc I	Government	4.20	5.68	5.43	3.00	3.00	.33	.68	800 222-8222
Wells Fargo Limited Term Gov Inc A	Government	3.50	4.79	5.11	3.00	2.00	.45	.95	800 222-8222
Wells Fargo MN Inter T/F Inst	Muni State	2.20					.50	.59	800 222-8222
Wells Fargo MN Tax-Free A	Muni State	0.00	3.55	4.90	3.00	4.00	.50	.59	800 222-8222
Wells Fargo MN Tax-Free B	Muni State	-.80	2.79	4.13	5.00	4.00	.50	1.35	800 222-8222
Wells Fargo MN Tax-Free I	Muni State	0.00	3.57	5.00	3.00	4.00	.50	.59	800 222-8222
Wells Fargo National Tax-Free A	Muni Natl	.40	3.91	5.48	3.00	4.00	.50	.59	800 222-8222
Wells Fargo National Tax-Free B	Muni Natl	-.30	3.14	4.70	4.00	4.00	.50	1.35	800 222-8222
Wells Fargo National Tax-Free I	Muni Natl	.70	3.97	5.54	3.00	4.00	.50	.59	800 222-8222
Wells Fargo OR Tax-Free A	Muni State	-.40	2.91	4.18	5.00	4.00	.50	.67	800 222-8222
Wells Fargo OR Tax-Free B	Muni State	-1.10	2.12	3.23	5.00	4.00	.50	1.51	800 222-8222
Wells Fargo Stable Income A	Corp-Inv	4.90	5.25	5.51	2.00	1.00	.29	.65	800 222-8222
Wells Fargo Stable Income B	Corp-Inv	4.10	4.40		2.00	1.00	.29	1.39	800 222-8222
Wells Fargo Stable Income I	Corp-Inv	5.10	5.31	5.55	1.00	1.00	.29	.65	800 222-8222
Wells Fargo Strategic Income I	Dvsfd Bond	6.70	9.40	9.75	1.00	4.00	.10	.80	800 222-8222
Wells Fargo Variable Rate Gov A	Govt-Mtg	5.20	3.86	4.53	2.00	1.00	.50	.78	800 222-8222
Westcore CO Tax Exempt	Muni State	2.70	3.71	4.51	3.00	3.00	.50	.53	800 392-2673
Westcore Intermediate Bond	Corp-Inv	3.70	4.95	5.40	3.00	2.00	.45	.84	800 392-2673
Westcore Long-Term Bond	Corp-Inv	3.50	5.89	6.23	4.00	5.00	.45	.94	800 392-2673
Western Asset Tr-Core Portf	Corp-Inv	5.10	6.17	6.32	2.00	3.00	.36	.50	800 822-5544
Western Asset Tr-Interm Duration	Corp-Inv	1.80	4.65	5.47	2.00	2.00	.25	.45	800 822-5544
Whitehall Income Fund	Corp-Inv	2.80	5.08	5.07	4.00	3.00	.40	1.09	800 994-2533
William Blair Mutual-Income Fund	Corp-Inv	4.10	5.19	5.40	3.00	2.00	.60	.68	800 742-7272
Wilmington Short/Interm Bond I	Corp-Inv	4.20	5.54	5.60	3.00	2.00	.34	.50	800 254-3948

451

Bond Fund Name	Objective	Annualized Return for			Rank		Max Load	Expense Ratio	Toll-Free Telephone
		1 Year	3 Years	5 Years	Overall	Risk			
Wright Current Income Fd	Govt-Mtg	5.10	5.26	5.83	2.00	2.00	.41	.90	800 232-0013
Wright Total Return Bond Fund	Corp-Inv	3.20	5.27	5.21	3.00	4.00	.40	.90	800 232-0013
Wright US Treasury Fund	Government	4.50	5.89	5.55	3.00	4.00	.39	.93	800 232-0013
Wright US Treasury Near-Term Bond	Government	3.80	4.57	4.81	3.00	1.00	.40	.91	800 232-0013

GLOSSARY OF FUND INVESTMENT TERMS

Adviser.   Organization or person hired by a mutual fund to provide professional management and guidance.

Aggressive Growth Fund.   Mutual fund that seeks high growth by employing aggressive investment strategies. Such funds typically own shares of small, emerging companies that offer the potential for rapid growth.

Alpha.   Excess return provided by an investment that is uncorrelated with the general stock market.

Annual Report.   Yearly summary sent by mutual funds to shareholders, showing which securities are owned and discussing performance over the period under review.

Ask or Offer Price.   Lowest amount a seller is willing to take for shares of a stock or closed-end fund. In the case of no-load funds, it represents the net asset value plus any sales charges.

Asset Allocation.   Act of spreading an investment portfolio across various categories, such as stocks, bonds, and money market funds.

Assets.   Investment holdings owned by a fund.

Automatic Reinvestment.   Shareholder-authorized purchase of additional shares using fund dividends and capital gains distributions.

Average Maturity.   Length of time before a bond issuer must return the holder's principal. Bonds are issued for a variety of maturities, from 30 days to more than 30 years. Bond mutual funds attempt to maintain a portfolio of securities with different maturities. When taken together, the overall fund's average maturity can then be measured.

Balanced Fund.   Mutual fund that invests in a blended portfolio of stocks, bonds, and cash.

Bear Market.   Period of time in which prices on the stock market are generally falling.

Beta.   Coefficient measure of a stock's or mutual fund's relative volatility in relation to the Standard & Poor's 500 Index, which has a beta of 1.

453

Bid Price.   Highest amount a buyer is willing to pay for shares of a stock or mutual fund. Also referred to as the *redemption price*. This is the same as *net asset value,* except for funds with back-end sales loads.

Blue Chip.   Common stock of a nationally known company with a long record of profit growth and dividend payments, and a reputation for quality products and services.

Blue-Sky Laws.   State laws governing the registration and distribution of mutual fund shares. All 50 states and the District of Columbia regulate mutual funds.

Bond.   Any interest-bearing or discounted government or corporate obligation to pay a specified sum of money, usually at regular intervals.

Bond Fund.   Mutual fund that holds bonds of various maturities and safety ratings.

Book Value.   What a company would be worth if all assets were sold (assets minus liability). Also, the price at which an asset is carried on a balance sheet.

Bottom-Up Investing.   Process used to search for individual stocks without regard for overall economic trends.

Broker.   Person who acts as an intermediary between a buyer and seller.

Bull Market.   Period of time in which security prices are generally rising.

Buy-and-Hold Strategy.   Technique that calls for accumulating and keeping shares of a mutual fund for many years, regardless of price swings.

Call.   Option contract giving the holder the right to purchase a specified security at a stated price during a specific time period.

Capital Appreciation.   Increase in the market value of a mutual fund's securities. This is reflected in the increased net asset value of a fund's shares.

Capital Depreciation.   Decline in the value of a given investment, including the net asset value of a fund's shares.

Capital Gains Distribution.   Payment to fund shareholders of profits realized for securities sold at a premium to their original cost. For tax purposes, shares held more than 12 months are treated as long-term capital gains, with a maximum tax rate of 20 percent. However, gains from securities held less than 12 months are taxed as ordinary income by the Internal Revenue Service.

Cash Equivalent.   Investment that can easily be turned into cash. Examples include certificates of deposit and money market funds.

Cash Position.   Percentage of a fund's portfolio invested in cash and cash equivalents, minus current liabilities.

Certificate of Deposit.   Instrument issued by a bank or savings and loan that pays a specific amount of interest for a set time period. If you take your money out before the maturity date, you must pay an early-withdrawal penalty.

Check-Writing Privilege.   Service offered by most discount brokers and large fund families allowing shareholders to write checks against their money market fund holdings. This cash continues to earn interest until a check clears.

Classes of Shares (i.e., Class A, Class B).   Trend among fund organizations to provide multiple purchase options for the same fund. This is a way of disguising sales load in various ways. Class A shares, for example, might require payment of an up-front load. Class B shares, on the other hand, might impose a 12b-1 fee and redemption fee instead.

Closed-End Fund. Investment company that issues a limited number of shares and is traded on a stock exchange. The value of such funds is determined by market supply and demand; shares are not necessarily traded at net asset value.

Commercial Paper. Short-term, unsecured promissory notes issued by corporations to finance immediate credit needs.

Commission. Fee paid by investors to a broker or other sales agent for the purchase of investment products. Also referred to as a *sales load.*

Common Stock. Security representing ownership of a corporation's assets that generally carries voting rights. Common stock dividends, however, are always paid after the company has met its obligations for bonds, debentures, and preferred stock.

Compounding. Earnings on top of earnings.

Contractual Plan. Program for the accumulation of mutual fund shares in which an investor agrees to invest a fixed amount on a regular basis for a specific number of years.

Contrarian. Investor who does the opposite of the majority at any particular time.

Convertible Securities. Securities that can be exchanged for other securities of the issuer under certain conditions; usually, the exchange is from preferred stock or bonds into common stock.

Corporate Bond Fund. Mutual fund that holds bonds of various maturities and safety ratings issued by a private or publicly traded company.

Credit Risk. Possibility that a bond issuer will default on the payment of interest and return of principal. Risk is minimized by investing in bonds issued by large blue-chip corporations or government agencies.

Current Assets. In a mutual fund, cash plus cash equivalents, minus current liabilities.

Current Liabilities. Obligations due within one year or sooner.

Custodian. Person or organization (usually a bank or trust company) that holds the securities and other assets of a mutual fund.

Debenture. Bond secured only by the general credit of a corporation.

Distribution. Dividends paid from net investment income plus realized capital gains.

Diversification. Act of spreading risk by putting assets into several different investment categories (i.e., stocks, bonds, and cash).

Diversified Investment Company. Under the Investment Company Act, a company (or fund) that, with respect to 75 percent of total assets, has not invested more than 5 percent nor holds more than 10 percent of the outstanding voting securities of any one company.

Dividend. Distribution of earnings to shareholders.

Dividend Yield. Cash dividend paid per share each year, divided by the current share price.

Dollar-Cost Averaging. Process of accumulating positions in mutual funds over time by investing a set amount of money on a regular basis. This allows the investor to buy more shares when prices are down and fewer when they are up.

Dow Jones Industrial Average.   Oldest and most widely quoted stock market indicator. It represents the price direction of 30 blue-chip stocks on the New York Stock Exchange. However, it doesn't always give an accurate view of what's happening with the market as a whole, because it completely ignores small-cap and mid-cap stocks.

Earnings.   Net income after all charges, divided by the number of outstanding shares.

Equity Income Fund.   Mutual fund that seeks to produce a high level of income without undue risk by investing primarily in a combination of dividend-paying stocks, corporate bonds, and convertibles.

Exchange Privilege.   Option enabling fund shareholders to shift investments from one fund to another, usually at no cost.

Ex-Dividend Date.   Day on which a mutual fund's declared distributions are deducted from the fund's net asset value and distributed to shareholders.

Expense Ratio.   Percent of assets taken from a fund to cover all operating costs.

Family of Funds.   Group of mutual funds managed and distributed by the same company; each fund typically has its own investment objective.

Fixed-Income Security.   Preferred stock or debt instrument, such as a bond, with a stated percentage or dollar amount of income paid at regular intervals.

401(k) Plan.   Employer-sponsored retirement plan enabling employees to defer taxes on a portion of their salaries by making a contribution. In some cases, employers will match part or all of an employee's contribution.

403(b) Plan.   Employer-sponsored retirement plan enabling employees of universities, public schools, and nonprofit organizations to defer taxes on a portion of their salaries by earmarking it for the retirement plan.

Front-End Load.   Sales fee charged to investors of some funds at the time shares are purchased.

Fund Family.   Group of mutual funds managed and distributed by the same company.

Fund Symbol.   Letter code used to identify a fund on the exchange.

General Government Bond (Short/Intermediate Term).   Mutual fund that seeks to provide current income and stability of principal by investing in a blend of U.S. government-backed securities. The average maturity of bonds in this type of portfolio is usually ten years or less.

Global Stock Fund.   Mutual fund that seeks growth by investing primarily in stocks of companies located around the world, including the United States.

Government Agency Issues.   Debt securities issued by governmental enterprises, federal agencies, and international institutions.

Growth Fund.   Mutual fund that seeks long-term growth without undue risk by investing in the stocks of solid U.S.-based companies.

Growth and Income Fund.   Mutual fund that seeks both growth of capital and current income by investing in dividend-paying stocks with the potential for growth.

Growth Stock.   Stock of a corporation that shows greater-than-average gains in earnings.

Hedge Fund. Mutual fund that hedges its market commitments by holding securities likely to increase in value, while *selling short* other securities likely to decrease. The sole objective is capital appreciation.

High-Yield Bond Fund. Mutual fund that invests in corporate bonds that pay high interest and typically have low credit ratings. Such securities are also known as junk bonds.

Income. Dividends, interest, and/or short-term capital gains paid to a mutual fund's shareholders.

Income Fund. Mutual fund for which the primary objective is to generate current income.

Index Fund. Mutual fund that seeks to match the returns of a particular market index, such as the Standard & Poor's 500 or Russell 2000. These funds essentially allow investors to "buy the market" but not outperform it.

Individual Retirement Account (IRA). Tax-deferred account established to hold funds until retirement.

Inflation. Persistent upward movement in the general price level of goods and services; its effect is to reduce the purchasing power of money.

Institutional Investor. Organization (a mutual fund, bank, or insurance company) that trades a large volume of securities.

Interest Rate Risk. Chance that market rates will rise above the fixed rate of a bond, thus reducing the bond's principal value and total return. (The opposite is also true. If rates fall, the principal value of the bond will rise.) Interest rate risk can be minimized by investing in short-term bond funds.

International Equity Fund. Mutual fund that seeks growth by investing in securities of companies located in developing markets outside of the United States, such as in Japan, New Zealand, Australia, Canada, and Western Europe. International equity funds entail an added degree of risk because of political instability, currency fluctuations, foreign taxes, and differences in financial reporting standards.

Investment Company. Corporation, trust, or partnership that invests pooled shareholder dollars in securities, in line with the organization's objective. Mutual funds, also known as "open-end" investment companies, are the most popular type of investment company.

Investment Company Act of 1940. Federal statute enacted by Congress in 1940, requiring the registration and regulation of investment companies (mutual funds).

Investment Management Company. Organization hired to advise the directors and trustees of a mutual fund in selecting and supervising assets in the fund's portfolio.

Investment Objective. Investors' long-term goal; the reason for placing money in a mutual fund in the first place.

Keogh Plan. Tax-favored retirement program for the self-employed and their employees.

Large-Cap Growth Fund. Mutual fund that invests in established, growing companies with market capitalizations of $5 billion or more.

Large-Cap Value Fund.   Mutual fund that invests in established companies with market capitalizations of $5 billion or more, when their securities are available at what the manager deems to be bargain prices.

Liquidity.   Ability to redeem all or part of mutual fund shares, on any business day, for the closing net asset value.

Load.   Sales commission assessed by some mutual funds to compensate the person who sells them (usually a stockbroker or financial planner). There are two types of loads: (1) front-end loads are taken at the time of the initial purchase; (2) back-end loads are collected when fund shares are redeemed. Loads typically range from 2 to 8 percent.

Long-Term Funds.   Mutual fund designed for capital appreciation over an extended period of time.

Management Fee.   Amount paid by a mutual fund for the services of an investment adviser.

Market Capitalization.   Calculated by multiplying the number of shares outstanding by the per-share price of a stock. Equities can be categorized into several different classes, including micro-cap, small-cap, mid-cap, and large-cap. The general guidelines for these classifications are as follows:

- **Micro-Cap**—stock market capitalizations of $0 to $300 million.
- **Small-Cap**—stock market capitalizations of $300 million to $1 billion.
- **Mid-Cap**—stock market capitalizations of $1 billion to $5 billion.
- **Large-Cap**—stock market capitalizations of $5 billion or more.

Market Order.   Order to buy or sell a security at the best available price.

Mid-Cap Growth Fund.   Mutual fund that invests in growing medium-size companies with market capitalizations generally between $1 billion and $5 billion.

Mid-Cap Value Fund.   Mutual fund that invests in medium-size companies with market capitalizations generally between $1 billion and $5 billion, when securities are available at what the manager deems to be bargain prices.

Money Market Fund.   Highly liquid mutual fund that invests in short-term securities and seeks to maintain a stable net asset value of $1 per share (although this is not guaranteed).

Mortgage-Backed Securities Fund.   Mutual fund that invests in mortgage pass-through instruments, such as those issued by the Government National Mortgage Association (GNMA).

Municipal Fund.   Fund that deals in bonds issued by a state, city, municipality, or revenue district. Municipal bonds, also known as *munis,* are exempt from federal and, in some cases, state and local income taxes.

Mutual Fund.   Investment company that raises money from shareholders and puts it to work in stocks, options, bonds, or money market securities. Offers investors diversification, professional management, liquidity, and convenience.

NASDAQ Composite.   An index (formerly National Association of Securities Dealers Automated Quotation System) weighted by market value and representing domestic companies that are sold over-the-counter.

National Association of Securities Dealers (NASD).   Self-regulatory organization with authority over firms that distribute mutual fund shares and other securities.

Net Asset Value (NAV).   Market worth of one share of a mutual fund. Calculated by adding up the fund's total assets, subtracting any liabilities, and dividing the resulting figure by the number of shares outstanding.

No-Load Fund.   Mutual fund for which shares are bought and sold at the prevailing net asset value, without any sales charges or commissions.

Open-End Fund.   Mutual fund that stands ready to issue and redeem an unlimited number of shares as requested by investors.

Operating Expenses.   Costs paid from a fund's assets, before earnings are distributed to shareholders, to cover overhead and operations.

Over-the-Counter Market.   Universe of securities, both stocks and bonds, not listed on a national or regional exchange (like the New York Stock Exchange or NASDAQ stock market). Over-the-counter transactions are primarily conducted through an informal network or by auction.

Payroll Deduction Plan.   Arrangement that some employers offer employees to accumulate mutual fund shares. Employees authorize their employer to deduct a specified amount from their salaries at stated times, and to transfer the proceeds to a fund.

Pension Plan.   Retirement program based on a defined formula providing employees with benefits paid during the remainder of their lifetime, upon reaching a stated age.

Pension Rollover.   Opportunity to take distributions from a qualified pension or profit-sharing plan and reinvest the proceeds in an individual retirement account (IRA) within 60 days from the date of distribution.

Performance Record.   Statistical record of the returns a fund and/or fund manager has produced over a stated period of time.

Pooling.   Concept behind mutual funds; the assets of various investors with common goals are brought together and invested in a single diversified portfolio.

Portfolio.   Collection of investment securities owned by an individual or institution—perhaps including stocks, bonds, and money market instruments.

Portfolio Manager.   Person responsible for investing a fund's pool of assets in accordance with the provisions set forth in the prospectus.

Portfolio Turnover.   Measure of trading activity in a fund. Shows how frequently a manager buys and sells securities in the portfolio.

Preferred Stock.   Equity instrument that generally carries a fixed dividend that must be satisfied before dividends are paid to holders of common shares.

Price-to-Earnings Ratio.   Price of a stock divided by its earnings per share.

Principal.   Initial amount of money invested in a fund.

Professional Management.   Ability to hire an experienced professional to decide which securities in the fund's portfolio should be bought and sold. A major advantage to mutual fund investing.

Prospectus. Official document describing a mutual fund's investment objectives, policies, services, fees, and past performance history.

Proxy Statement. Information about fund matters, sent to shareholders of record annually for a vote. (Sadly, many fund investors don't even bother to vote. Fund trustees can then get their way on such matters as raising operating expenses and changing investment policies, when these outcomes may not be in the best interest of shareholders.)

Prudent Man Rule. Law governing the investment of trust funds in states that give broad discretion to trustees.

Qualified Plans. Retirement plans that meet the requirements of Sections 401(k), 403(a), or 403(b) of the Internal Revenue Code and/or the Self-Employed Individuals Tax Retirement Act.

Record Date. Date by which shareholder must own shares in a fund in order to receive the announced distribution.

Redemption. Act of selling shares in a mutual fund.

Redemption-In-Kind. Redemption of investment company shares for which payment is made in portfolio securities rather than cash.

Registered Investment Company. Investment company that has filed a registration statement with the Securities and Exchange Commission (SEC) under the requirements of the Investment Company Act of 1940.

Reinvestment. Process of using mutual fund dividends and capital gains distributions to automatically buy additional shares, thus increasing overall holdings.

Return on Investment. Amount of money an investment earns over a given period of time. This figure is often expressed as a percentage.

Risk. Accepted possibility that an investment will fluctuate in value.

Risk/Reward Tradeoff. Principle stating that an investment must offer higher potential returns to compensate for the likelihood of increased volatility. Investors are normally willing to accept higher risk on long-term investments, because the effects of price volatility generally diminish over time. Conversely, they seek lower risk with short-term investments, where accessibility and preservation of principal override the need for maximum return.

Rollover. Shifting of assets from one qualified retirement plan to another without incurring a penalty.

Roth IRA. Tax-deferred account in which contributions are nondeductible, but earnings grow tax-free. Eligibility for the Roth IRA gradually phases out at income levels of $95,000 to $110,000 for individuals, and $150,000 to $160,000 for married couples.

Sales Load. Amount charged for the sale of mutual fund shares by a stockbroker or other financial professional. The cost is usually added to the fund's net asset value.

Sector Fund. Mutual fund that invests in the securities of a single industry or country-specific region.

Securities and Exchange Commission (SEC). Federal agency charged with regulating the registration and distribution of mutual fund shares.

Senior Securities. Notes, bonds, debentures, or preferred stocks that have a claim to assets and earnings that supercedes claims by holders of common stock.

Series Funds. Funds organized with separate portfolios of securities, each with its own unique investment objective.

Shareholder. Investor who owns shares in a mutual fund.

Short Sale. Sale of a security that is borrowed, not owned, in the hope that the price will go down so it can be repurchased at a lower price, therefore generating a profit through the underlying spread.

Short-Term Funds. Mutual funds that invest in securities with the intention of holding them for one year or less (i.e., money market funds).

Small-Cap Growth Fund. Mutual fund that invests in small, fast-growing companies with market capitalizations generally under $1 billion.

Small-Cap Value Fund. Mutual fund that invests in small, growing companies with market capitalizations generally under $1 billion, whose securities are available at what the manager deems to be bargain prices.

Small-Company or Small-Cap Fund. Mutual fund that seeks capital appreciation by investing in the stocks of small, fast-growing companies.

Standard & Poor's Composite Index of 500 Stocks (S&P 500). Index that tracks the performance of 500 widely held common stocks, weighted by market value. It includes mostly blue-chip names and represents some two-thirds of the U.S. stock market's total value.

Statement of Additional Information (SAI). Supplement to a prospectus; contains updated and more complete information about a mutual fund. (Also referred to as "Part B" of the registration statement.)

Stock. Representation of ownership in a corporation. Usually issued in terms of shares.

Systematic Withdrawal Plan. Program in which fund shareholders receive regular automatic distributions from their investments. Shares are redeemed to meet the shareholders' income needs, and payments are sent out monthly, quarterly, or annually, as specified.

Tax-Deferred Income. Dividends, interest, and capital gains received from investments held in qualified retirement plans, such as IRAs, Keoghs, 401(k)s, and 403(b)s. This income is not subject to current taxation. Instead, it is taxed upon withdrawal.

Time Horizon. Length of time money is to be invested in a fund. Time horizon helps to pinpoint the types of investments that should be included in a portfolio mix. The longer the time horizon, the more risk one can afford to take, because of the ability to weather any short-term declines in the market.

Total Return. Measure of a fund's overall performance during a given period of time. Encompasses all aspects affecting return, including dividends, capital gains distributions, and changes in net asset value.

Transfer Agent. Organization or person hired by a mutual fund to prepare and maintain records on shareholders' accounts.

Treasury Bill.   Non-interest-bearing security issued at a discount to its value by the U.S. Treasury. Maturity is one year or less.

Turnover Ratio.   Measure of how frequently a manager buys and sells securities in the portfolio. The higher the number, the more trading that occurs.

12b-1 Fee.   Mutual fund expense used to pay for marketing and distribution costs.

Underwriter.   Organization or person acting as the distributor of a mutual fund's shares to broker/dealers and investors.

U.S. Government Bond.   Bond issued by the U.S. Treasury or other government agency. Considered among the safest investments available, because they are backed by the full faith and credit of the U.S. government.

Value Fund.   Mutual fund with the objective of buying stocks in companies whose shares are considered to be undervalued, as measured by price-to-earnings ratio, book value, or other valuation benchmark.

Variable Annuity.   Investment contract sold by an insurance company. Accumulates capital, often through mutual fund investments, which is later converted to an income stream, often at retirement.

Volatility.   Measure of risk that refers to how a fund's share price moves up or down compared to its underlying index.

Warrant.   Option to buy a specific number of shares of stock at a stated price during a limited time period.

Wash Sale.   Purchase and sale of a security either simultaneously or within a short time period. Wash sales that take place within 30 days of the underlying purchase do not quality for a tax loss deduction under rules set forth by the Internal Revenue Service.

Withdrawal Plan.   Program in which shareholders receive income on principal payments at regular intervals from their mutual fund investments.

Yield.   Measure of the net income (dividends and interest minus expenses) earned by the securities in a fund's portfolio during a specific period of time.

Yield to Maturity.   The rate of return offered on a debt security if held to maturity.

INDEX

Page numbers in italics refer to tables.